MIRCEA ELIADE

Critical Categories in the Study of Religion

Series Editor: Russell T. McCutcheon, Associate Professor, Department of Religious Studies, University of Alabama

Critical Categories in the Study of Religion aims to present the pivotal articles that best represent the most important trends in how scholars have gone about the task of describing, interpreting, and explaining the position of religion in human life. The series focuses on the development of categories and the terminology of scholarship that make possible knowledge about human beliefs, behaviours, and institutions. Each volume in the series is intended as both an introductory survey of the issues that surround the use of various key terms as well as an opportunity for a thorough retooling of the concept under study, making clear to readers that the cognitive categories of scholarship are themselves historical artefacts that change over time.

Published:
Syncretism in Religion
A Reader
Edited by Anita M. Leopold and Jeppe S. Jensen

Ritual and Religious Belief
A Reader
Edited by Graham Harvey

Defining Hinduism
A Reader
Edited by J. E. Llewellyn

Religion and Cognition
A Reader
Edited by D. Jason Slone

Forthcoming:
Myths and Mythologies
A Reader
Edited by Jeppe S. Jensen

Readings in the Theory of Religion
Map, Text, Body
Edited by Scott S. Elliott and Matthew Waggoner

Defining Religion
A Reader
Edited by Tim Murphy

Defining Islam
A Reader
Edited by Andrew Rippin

Religious Experience
A Reader
Edited by Russell T. McCutcheon

Defining Judaism
A Reader
Edited by Martin S. Jaffee

What is Religious Studies?
A Reader in Disciplinary Formation
Edited by Steven J. Sutcliffe

Defining Buddhisms
A Reader
Edited by Karen Derris and Natalie Gummer

MIRCEA ELIADE

A Critical Reader

Edited by

Bryan Rennie

LONDON • OAKVILLE

Published by

Equinox Publishing Ltd.
UK: Equinox Publishing Ltd., Unit 6, The Village, 101 Amies St.,
London SW11 2JW
USA: DBBC, 28 Main Street, Oakville, CT 06779

First published 2006

This selection and introductory material
© Bryan Rennie 2006

British Library Cataloguing-in-Publication Data
A catalogue record for this book is available from the British Library.

| ISBN | 1 904768 93 8 | (hardback) |
| | 1 904768 94 6 | (paperback) |

| ISBN-13 | 9781904768937 | (hardback) |
| | 9781904768944 | (paperback) |

Library of Congress Cataloging-in-Publication Data
Mircea Eliade : a critical reader / edited by Bryan Rennie.
   p. cm. -- (Critical categories in the study of religion)
 Includes bibliographical references and index.
 ISBN 1-904768-93-8 (hb) -- ISBN 1-904768-94-6 (pb)
 1. Eliade, Mircea, 1907- I. Rennie, Bryan S., 1954- II. Series.
 BL43.E4M575 2006
 200.92--dc22

                                          2006003291

Typeset by ISB Typesetting, Sheffield
www.sheffieldtypesetting.com

Printed and bound in Great Britain by Lightning Source UK Ltd, Milton Keynes, and in the USA by Lightning Source Inc., La Vergne, TN

CONTENTS

Contents

Part I

INTRODUCTION

1

GENERAL INTRODUCTION

Bryan Rennie

This is not an attempt to answer the questions raised for the academic study of religion by the work of Eliade and the style of his History of Religions; rather it seeks to serve as a useful introduction for scholars at whatever stage of their studies who wish to consider these questions. All too often such scholars are forced to rely on reading one or two of Eliade's most general works (*The Quest, The Myth of the Eternal Return, The Sacred and the Profane,* or *Patterns in Comparative Religion*) and a single analysis of Eliade (such as my *Reconstructing Eliade*). This can hardly serve to give a reliable impression of a vast and complex life's work and of the difficult theoretical problems that it poses. All too often important texts are located in difficult-to-find journals, and the inexperienced scholar remains unaware of the significance of, say, the Preface to *Shamanism*, or the relevance of Eliade's fictional output. It is in an attempt to improve this situation that these articles have been brought together. They provide a more adequate and accessible foundation upon which scholars might construct their initial understanding of Eliade and begin a more detailed and theoretically nuanced investigation, reducing misconceptions engendered by a limited exposure to the texts.

Mircea Eliade's published work is notoriously vast, and scholarly reaction is not only correspondingly extensive, but extensively varied. It is thus impossible to include everything of importance or to satisfy every reader. I particularly feel the absence of Eliade's observations on religion and art, but decided to omit these as they have been capably edited and presented by Diane Apostolos-Cappadona in *Symbolism, the Sacred, and the Arts.* Also omitted are selections from Eliade's works on *Yoga* and *Shamanism* (although I include the "Foreword" from the latter, 256–62 below). These, like Eliade's *Journals,* are readily available and stand on their own. Certain other worthwhile topics remain absent for a variety of reasons. For instance, the symbolism of the center was the central organizing theme of Carl Olson's *Theology and Philosophy of Eliade*. Eliade's use of the term "archetype" has been capably discussed by Mac Linscott Ricketts in "The Nature and Extent of Eliade's 'Jungianism.' " Eliade's telling use of the idea of "homology," on the other hand, has not yet received the attention it deserves, but this is not the place for it. Suffice it to say that, while the original Greek simply meant agreement or assent, the term had considerable currency in Eliade's day, both among comparative linguists and comparative anatomists. Charles Darwin mentioned that "we find in distinct languages striking homologies due to community of descent" (*Descent of Man*, I, ii, 59). Evolutionary biologists such as Darwin used the term to mean the correspondences between, say, a bat's wing, a dolphin's fin, and the human hand. The implied homologies among religion, language, and anatomy need to be considered elsewhere.

Several notable and admirable recent analyses are also absent since they are otherwise readily available and it is more immediately valuable to cover the earlier ground and to establish the interested scholar's knowledge of the Eliadean texts and the historical development of the various criticisms. The work of Tomoko Masuzawa, Daniel Pals, Sam Gill, and Russell McCutcheon are listed in the bibliography and well-worth consulting. The whole of Mac Linscott Rickett's two-volume *Mircea Eliade: The Romanian Roots* is also an invaluable resource. Where scholars desire to go further with their study of Eliade and related questions a supportive bibliography makes this more easily possible.

Although I have tried my best to avoid other lacunae I am certain that some exist. It is impossible to encapsulate a writer such as Eliade in an anthology but nonetheless every scholar of religion needs to pass through the stages of the study represented by Eliade's syntheses and needs to be introduced to the thought that Eliade expressed, even if Eliade did not originate that thought himself.

Not all of the selections have been chosen for their positive qualities. It cannot be over-emphasized that the scholar should not simply accept any of these texts as the definitive descriptions of a privileged perception. Commentators' interpretations of different Eliadean terms—nostalgia for paradise, cosmic Christianity, *homo religiosus*, archaic humanity, creative hermeneutics, and so on—should always be treated with critical caution. Several of the selections illustrate the abuses to which critical analysis of earlier texts of questionable authority can be put. It should also be said that even in cases where the advancement of the writer's own interests exceeds the writer's critical accuracy, important observations and communication can nonetheless be made. One of the most instructive and valuable lessons of this anthology might well lie in closely observing where commentators have, with great care, attention, and confidence, seriously misinterpreted their subject.

I will take this opportunity, at the beginning of this anthology, to divorce myself from Eliade's use of gender-exclusive language. It would be inappropriate to correct his usage, which was typical of the context in which he wrote. This is not, however, a facsimile edition and I have attempted to render the text into uniform American English. I have also occasionally attempted to correct and to clarify Eliade's sometimes obscure bibliographic references, although I am aware that some problems remain. The reader should be aware that the single word, *Yoga*, is often used as an abbreviation for Eliade's *Yoga, Immortality and Freedom*, just as *The Eternal Return* has become a commonplace abbreviation of his *Cosmos and History: The Myth of the Eternal Return*. Finally, this is an introduction which has to serve for a variety of readers, hence the inclusion of both introductory texts, such as the entry on Hierophany from the *Encyclopedia of Religion*, and more esoteric works from Eliade's early years. It is to be hoped that the whole spectrum of readers will benefit from their inclusion.

2

THE LIFE AND WORK OF MIRCEA ELIADE

Bryan Rennie

Mircea Eliade was born in Bucharest, Romania, on 13 March 1907. He was of the city dwelling, middle class, separated from peasant roots by two generations. His father had changed his own surname from Iremia (Jeremiah) to Eliade in 1899. Mircea attended the Strada Mântuleasa primary school and the Spiru Haret high school where he developed an interest in the natural sciences, particularly entomology and botany, but where he failed courses in Romanian, French, and German. This failure seems to have impelled him to greater effort and he became a voracious reader and began to write imaginative fiction at the age of 12. His first publication, at the age of 14, was a natural science piece concerning a wasp predatory upon the silkworm. That same year, in the same *Journal of Popular Science and Travels* (*Ziarul ştiinţelor populare şi călătoriilor*), he published his first autobiographical fragments, one of which consisted largely of the narration of a peasant legend told by a local guide. His first published work of imaginative fiction, "How I Found the Philosopher's Stone," came later in 1921. By the end of high school his interests had moved from natural science to literature and philosophy and he determined to study philology and philosophy at university.

His autobiographical fiction indicates his modernist, scientific bent, convinced of the importance of both traditional religions and folk traditions but unable to accept mysteries or dogmas surpassing rational explanation. His American biographer, Mac Linscott Ricketts, suggests that "Perhaps Eliade's real 'religion' at this time could be said to have been faith in the unlimited power of the disciplined will ... Although he has denied being influenced at this time by Nietzsche ... Eliade nourished a deep, secret wish to become a kind of 'superman,' to control his own will" (*Romanian Roots*, I, 72). This passion for self-discipline must have been active when Eliade read the five-volume *Geschichte des Altertums* by Edward Meyer, despite his earlier difficulty with German, and again during his seventeenth or eighteenth year when he taught himself both Italian and English so as to read Raffaele Pettazzoni and James George Frazer.

In 1925 Eliade enrolled in the department of philosophy of the University of Bucharest. There he came under the influence of Nae Ionescu (1890–1940), an assistant professor of logic and metaphysics and an active journalist with a keen interest in both science and religion. Ionescu's principal tenets included the "separation of planes." For Ionescu, the theological, metaphysical, and scientific planes were seen as mutually exclusive and irreducible one to another. This may well be the source of Eliade's celebrated "irreducibility of the sacred," although that can also be related to Immanuel Kant's non-reductionistic philosophy of pure reason, practical reason, and aesthetic judgment. Ionescu also emphasized lived-experience (*trăire* in Romanian). As Mac Ricketts points out, Ionescu thought that "philosophy is an act of life, an act of lived-experience (*trăire*)" [97—quoting from Ionescu's published course of lectures, *Metaphysica I*, 12 (Paris: Ion Cuşa, 1978)]. Ricketts continues,

> In everyday Romanian speech *trăire*, the noun, and its verbal cognate are used to refer to life, living, enduring, feeling, experience, etc. *Trăire* is approximately equivalent to the German *Erlebnis*. Nae Ionescu used the word not only for metaphysical cognition, but also for the way one should approach life in general—to "live-experience" it to the fullest. (*Romanian Roots*, I, 105)

The concepts of *trăire* and "authenticity" became the central emphases of a group of students taught by Ionescu in Bucharest in the 20s and 30s, including Eliade. It has been suggested that Ionescu's concept of *trăire* was at least influenced by Wilhelm Dilthey's *Erlebnis*. Ricketts explains:

> For Dilthey, *Erlebnis* was the peculiarly human faculty by which man, as distinct from animals, perceives the universe. It is the posture of the artist before the universe which enables him to feel a oneness with its essence. In order for the historian to grasp the inner meaning and purpose of history, Dilthey said that a preliminary act of sympathy or *Erlebnis* was necessary. The inner states of the human subject being studied by the historian must first be relived or re-experienced before his history can be written. (105)

(For more on "*Trăirism*" see Ricketts, *Romanian Roots*, I, 96–98; 104–108; 286; 428–30; 563; 589–90; 746–48; 776; and 1327 n. 96.)

Eliade's thesis of 1928 examined "Contributions to Renaissance Philosophy" including Marcilio Ficino, Pico della Mirandola, and Giordano Bruno, and, under the influence of Renaissance Humanism, he turned to India to "universalize" the "provincial" philosophy of Western Europe. Having earned his licentiate degree, and a grant from the Maharaja of Kassimbazar to study in India, Eliade sailed east that same year. He studied Sanskrit and philosophy at the University of Calcutta under Surendranath Dasgupta (1885–1952), a Cambridge-educated Bengali, author of the five-volume, *History of Indian Philosophy*. In 1930, however, Eliade was expelled from Dasgupta's home under suspicion of some romantic liaison with Dasgupta's daughter, Maitreyi. He traveled around India, visiting sites of religious interest, participating in the famous Kumbh-Mela festival at Allahabad, and staying at the Svarga ashram at Rishikesh.

Eliade returned to Bucharest in 1932 and the publication of his novel, *Maitreyi*, in 1933 assured his status as a novelist. He was to publish a total of ten novels by 1940. *Maitreyi*, his third, was an apparently realistic account of his liaison with Maitreyi. It even included the actual street address and telephone number of the house in Calcutta. The novel later occasioned a response from Maitreyi Devi herself, in the form of her own novel, *It Does not Die*, refuting Eliade's claim to sexual intimacy.

One factor that has occasioned suspicions about Eliade is this "mythologization" or "fictionalization" of his autobiography; the dividing line between his biography and his fiction is not always easy to draw. This is most clear in relation to Eliade's period in India, but might be true of other portions of his life. The publication in English of both *Maitreyi* and *It Does not Die* in 1994 brought the sometimes confused relationship between his fiction and his biography pointedly to the pubic notice. The particulars of the accounts in each novel differ considerably although both conform to the same historical basis.

The Romanian scholar, Liviu Bordaş, has convincingly demonstrated that Eliade's autobiographical accounts of his stay in India is somewhat "mythologized"—particularly the account of his stay at the Ashram at Rishikesh, implications of esoteric initiation, the account of his forced departure from India after three years in order to satisfy his military service, and his intention to eventually return to a "cave in Himalaya." While the misrepresentation of fact is minor—six months instead of the actual three at the Ashram, an exaggerated "initiation" into Tantric mysteries, determination to perform military duty as opposed to inability to avoid it, and so on—it is enough to cast doubt on other autobiographical details.

Back in Bucharest, Eliade also successfully submitted his analysis of Yoga as his doctoral thesis at the Philosophy department in 1933. First published in French as *Yoga: Essai sur les origines de la mystique Indienne* (Paris, 1936), it was revised and became one of his major works, *Yoga, Immortality, and Freedom* (1958). Also in 1933 he began living with Nina Mareş, a single mother and secretary at the telephone company, and they married in October 1934. As Ionescu's assistant at the University of Bucharest, Eliade lectured on Aristotle's *Metaphysics* and Nicholas of Cusa's *Docta Ignorantia*, among other things. Ionescu continued to be a significant influence on Eliade and on other young

Romanian intellectuals, many of whom participated in an intellectual group called "Criterion," which brought informed debate of significant issues to the Bucharest public. Eliade stated explicitly that "[e]verything the 'young generation' debated during that time—'experience,' 'adventure,' 'Orthodoxy,' 'authenticity,' 'lived experience,'—had its roots in the ideas of Nae Ionescu" (*Rosa Vânturilor*, 431), and "authenticity" and "lived-experience" remained the watchwords of the generation of which Eliade was increasingly seen to be "leader."

Ionescu also influenced some of the Criterion group in their support for the ultra-rightist movement, the Legion of the Archangel Michael, founded by Corneliu Zelea Codreanu in 1927. Between 1936 and 1938 Eliade wrote journalistic articles in support of this group and it has been claimed that he ran for public office with the legionary party. Eliade was a supporter of the Legion of the Archangel Michael (also known as the Iron Guard), and this organization was anti-Semitic, but was Eliade anti-Semitic himself? Saul Bellow's 2000 novel, *Ravelstein*, features a Romanian historian of religions apparently concealing an anti-Semitic past and Bellow was a close friend from Eliade's Chicago years. The same year saw the publication in English of the journal of Eliade's friend of the 1930s, Mihail Sebastian. Sebastian was a Jewish writer who attributed the deterioration of his friendship with Eliade to the latter's politics.

Even with newly available information an entirely unambiguous judgment remains elusive. There is significant doubt that Eliade ever was anti-Semitic. While Bellow's novel may be inspired by reality, it remains fiction, and although Eliade temporarily championed the Legion of the Archangel Michael there is a distinction between an involvement with the politics of the right and anti-Semitism, and a brief period of political activity does not necessarily indicate either a clear or a life-long ideological commitment. Mac Ricketts makes a convincing case that the lapse between Eliade and Sebastian was due to other than political factors (*Former Friends and Forgotten Facts*).

Through the course of the early 1930s Eliade had taken a deliberately "apolitical" stance in the specific sense of withholding allegiance from the increasingly radical popular parties of both left and right. He saw these parties as rootless, foreign, brutal, and uncultured, and he championed tradition, culture, and the intellect in opposition. However, he was increasingly drawn into a nationalist position whose dangers are now all too well known. Although there were suspicions that the Criterion group was crypto-communist and it had at least two Jewish members it also had members whose sympathies were to the right and in 1932 some of these founded a review called *Axa* (*The Axis*) which gave open support to the Legion. Eliade, however, never contributed to that journal. In fact, in 1933, along with some thirty other intellectuals and artists, he signed a protest against the return to barbarism portended by anti-Semitic persecutions in Hitler's Germany. The same year his article "Racism in the Cinema" protested against "Aryan" racist apologetics, and he explicitly rejected the confusion of nationalism and anti-Semitism in an article objecting to the expulsion from Romania of the Jewish scholars Moses Gaster and Lazăr Şăineanu in 1885 and 1901 respectively. In 1934 he wrote (under the pseudonym "Ion Plăeşu") an article, "Against Left and Right," arguing against the totalitarianism of both political extremes and he refused to become directly involved with any political allegiances.

In 1934 Sebastian's autobiographical novel on the contemporary position of Romanian Jewish intellectuals appeared. *De două mii de ani (For Two Thousand Years)* bore a preface by Ionescu, who was editor of the widely circulated review, *Cuvântul*, to which both men had regularly contributed before its prohibition in 1934. This preface was openly anti-Semitic, in theological if not racial terms, but Sebastian retained it out of loyalty. Eliade responded in print, attempting to mediate between his friend and their professor and to reject the latter's anti-Semitism, again on theological grounds. However, while Eliade opposed the most extreme manifestations of anti-Semitism he failed to appreciate the dangers of other anti-Semitic rhetoric.

At the beginning of 1935, Eliade's journalism openly continued to denounce both Nazism and Communism as forms of modern idolatry that dissolve moral distinctions in favor of biological or social criteria. He maintained his "apolitical" stance, arguing that the greatest weapon of any writer is independence vis-à-vis every political group. Yet it is in this period that the beginnings of his slide into political involvement can be seen. Eliade's "apolitical" stance was universally criticized. His appeal for cultural sophistication rather than the popularist barbarism of political mass movements was largely ignored. Even though he was not engaged in Ionescu's political activities, Eliade's friendship with the philosopher and his former affiliation with *Cuvântul* sufficed to establish a connection to the right. At the same time, he was distanced from the somewhat inept and corrupt incumbent "liberal" government, who refused to provide adequate financial support for cultural activity. One of Eliade's perennial themes of the period was the unhappy financial situation of writers in Romania. He was critical of the state duty on writers' royalties, introduced in 1935. He accused both the State and the public of indifference. The refusal of the government to found an institute of Middle Eastern and Oriental Studies made Eliade sharply aware of the contrast between, for example, fascist Italy, which had such an institute, and Romania, which did not.

Eliade's scorn for the left at that time was based mainly upon his belief that the principal superstition of the modern period concerned single, universal explanations which effectively removed human freedom. Among these he counted Hegelian historicism, Freudianism, and Marxism. Unable to sympathize with either the left or the incumbent government, Eliade at first showed no leanings to the right either. In December of 1935, he noted that one "youth leader" described his mission as "the reconciliation of Romania with God." Here Eliade saw a religious appeal which called upon neither class struggle, nor political interests, nor economic instincts, nor biological distinctions. The leader was Corneliu Zelea Codreanu, the founder of the Legion of the Archangel Michael. This was the earliest expression of Eliade's admiration for Codreanu although he did not at that time extol the movement itself. Eliade seems to have seen Codreanu's "religious" appeal as a means of popularizing the type of cultural creation that he had hitherto attributed to the intellectual and writer by appealing to deep traditional roots. Eliade clearly considered creators of culture to be a country's most potent force, the most effective patriots, thanks to whom a nation "conquers eternity." He elaborates, "[n]o matter what happens in Italy now no historical power can remove Italy from her place in eternity. No revolution, no massacre, no catastrophe can wipe out Dante, Michelangelo, Leonardo" ("România în eternitate," *Vremea*, October 13, 1935). This cultural, "religious," and "traditional" appeal of Codreanu attracted his support.

There is disagreement as to whether Eliade actually enrolled in the Legion. No Legionary records remain and possibly none were ever kept. Government archives of the period indicate that the police suspected him of joining sometime in 1935 and belonging to a Legionary cell or "nest" led by Radu Demetrescu Gyr. However, most commentators think it very unlikely that he joined before 1937, and some insist that he belonged to a different nest associated with the journal *Axa*. Thus suspicions remain unproven and no certain evidence of membership has ever been produced. What is certain is that he contributed his written support to the Legion, and thereby supported an openly anti-Semitic movement whose leader proclaimed a Jewish conspiracy, and whose second-in-command, Ion Moța, had translated the anti-Semitic propaganda, *The Protocols of the Elders of Zion*, into Romanian.

Eliade's own writings express no clear anti-Semitism. Only three of his "Legionary" articles mention Jews and it is clear that his rhetoric proceeded from a sentiment of general xenophobia commonly associated with nationalism (see 412–22 below). He continued to denounce elsewhere the intolerant, vulgar anti-Semitism he perceived around him. In June of 1936 he wrote an article in homage to Moses Gaster, who had made a large donation of old books and manuscripts to the Romanian Academy. Thus Eliade opposed anti-Semitism that might reduce Romania's culture, as had Gaster's expulsion, but was ready to accept anti-Semitism which would deny Jews equal status with ethnic Romanians. That he was also prepared to deny such status to ethnic Bulgarians and Hungarians hardly excuses his position, but it does put it into perspective: relations between ethnic and non-ethnic Romanians had been problematic since the founding of the nation in 1881.

Eliade's last supportive article appeared in February 1938, shortly before the Legion was proscribed by the government. Codreanu was arrested in April and clandestinely executed in November. Eliade spent almost four months, from July to November, in an internment camp for suspected Legionary sympathizers, although he neither acknowledged membership in, nor made any declaration of separation from, the Legion. After his release he ceased to express any sympathies for the Iron Guard, and concentrated on his own cultural productivity. He was appointed to the Press Services section of the Romanian Cultural Legation to London in April 1940. This appointment came from the Royalist dictatorship responsible for the execution of Codreanu and the massacre of some 250 Legionaries in 1939. One wonders whether Eliade's appointment was a sign of his distance from the remaining Legionaries or, on the contrary, a sign of the government's deliberate attempt at a rapprochement with them. That they still had considerable political influence became obvious in September 1940, when a "National Legionary State" was declared in Romania. In the legation in London, Eliade boasted of his support for the Legion and his suffering on its behalf, but the National Legionary State lasted only four months and Eliade did not benefit from it. In February 1941, when England broke diplomatic relations with Romania, he was posted to neutral Portugal. During his tenure as a functionary of the Office of Press and Propaganda of a country allied to Nazi Germany and a state enforcing openly anti-Semitic policies, Eliade produced neither anti-Semitic nor pro-Nazi rhetoric. His wife, Nina, died of cancer in Portugal in 1944 and he remained there until the end of the war, after which he moved to Paris.

In Paris, George Dumézil, a scholar of comparative mythology, found Eliade a part-time post at the Sorbonne teaching comparative religion. From this time on, most of Eliade's scholarly work was composed in French. It was in Paris where Eliade met his second wife, Christinel Cotrescu, another Romanian, whom he married in 1950. His second marriage, like his first, remained childless. At the prompting of Joachim Wach, a scholar of religion at the University of Chicago, Eliade was invited to give the 1956 Haskell Lectures there on "Patterns of Initiation" (*Birth and Rebirth*, 1958). On Wach's death in 1958 Eliade was invited to assume the chair of the History of Religions department in Chicago. There he stayed until his own death in 1986, publishing extensively on the History of Religions, keeping his journals, and continuing to write fiction in Romanian. His fiction remained largely unpublished in English although there are some significant exceptions, including the novel he regarded as his *chef d'oeuvre*, *The Forbidden Forest* (*Noaptea de Sânziene*). Since his early novels and short stories in Romania, Eliade had written in a style which utilized a dialectic of realism and fantasy, comparable to "magic realism." His most common technique was to write in a realistic manner but gradually to introduce fantastic elements until the world of the commonplace transforms into some mythic realm. Some of his work, however, is more directly fantastic. "Un Om Mare" ("A Great Man"), for example, has its protagonist grow to enormous size. Another, *Mistress Christina* (*Domnişoara Christina*), is a vampire story. Other novels are apparently realistic, as is his *Forbidden Forest*. One, *Nuntă în cer* ("Marriage in Heaven"), was translated into Italian and won the

Elba-Brignetti prize for the best foreign language novel in Italian in 1983. His *Maitreyi* was made into a French language film starring Hugh Grant.

At the University of Chicago Eliade launched the journals *History of Religions* and *The Journal of Religion*; he was a member of the committee on social thought; and he was editor-in-chief of the first edition of Macmillan's *Encyclopedia of Religion*. Through these activities, as well as his continued publication in the history of religions, the publication of his *Autobiography* and *Journals*, and his tuition of a generation of successful scholars of religion, he was, from the early 1960s through the mid 1970s, the most influential single figure in establishing the History of Religions as an academic discipline in the United States.

Despite this focus on the history of religions Eliade maintained a philosophical agenda, although he never explicitly systematized his position. In *Cosmos and History: The Myth of the Eternal Return* (1954), a book he considered subtitling *Introduction to a Philosophy of History*, Eliade differentiated between religious and non-religious humanity by applying Henri Bergson's distinction between perceptions of time (*Essai sur les données immédiates de la conscience*, 1889). Eliade contended that the perception of time as a homogenous, linear, and unrepeatable medium is a peculiarity of "modern," non-religious humanity. "Archaic" or religious humanity (*homo religiosus*), in comparison, apprehends time as heterogenous, divided between linear, profane time and cyclical and reactualizable, sacred time, called by Eliade, *illud tempus*. Myths and rituals give repeated access to this sacred time ("the eternal return") and thus protect religious humanity against the "terror of history," a form of existential anxiety in which the absolute "givenness" of historical time causes helplessness. Eliade tended to undermine this distinction, however, insisting that non-religious humanity in any pure sense is non-existent and that religiousness, understood in this way, is ubiquitous. Myth and *illud tempus*, the temporal continuum of mythic event, still exist, although concealed, in the world of "non-religious" humanity and there is no "solution of continuity between the archaic mind and scientific ideologies of the nineteenth century" (*Quest*, 41 n. 2). Eliade set himself against "the historicistic position, in all its varieties and shapes—from Nietzsche's 'destiny' to Heidegger's 'temporality' " (*The Eternal Return*, 152). That is, he regarded the attempt to restrict "real" time exclusively to historical time as an unacceptable reduction and he considered, for example, the atheistic existentialism of Jean-Paul Sartre to be arid and hopeless.

Eliade defined religion in terms of humanity's relation to the "sacred," and the precise nature of his concept of the sacred has also been the subject of contention. Some see it as corresponding to a conventional concept of deity, or to Rudolf Otto's *ganz andere* ("wholly other")—an ontologically independent reality. Others have detected a closer resemblance to Emile Durkheim's social sacred. Eliade does identify the sacred and the real, yet he states repeatedly that "the sacred is a structure of human consciousness" (*Quest*, i; *A History of Religious Ideas*, vol. I, xiii, and see below, 58). This would seem to support an interpretation in which both the sacred and the real are human projections and it is reminiscent of Kant's identification of reality as a category of the understanding. Thus the sacred can be identified as simultaneously a structure of consciousness and the source of significance, meaning, power and Being. Its manifestations can be seen as appearances of the holy, of power, or of Being (hierophanies, kratophanies, or ontophanies), just as, for Kant, space and time are irreducibly perceived as external continua, although they are identified as the *a priori* postulates of the understanding. It is surely no coincidence that the title of Eliade's major work, *Yoga, Immortality, and Freedom*, echoes the ideas of pure reason that for Kant become the postulates of practical reason: God, Immortality, and Freedom.

Eliade's identification of the sacred and the real places individual human apprehensions of the sacred and the real on an initially equal level, rather than assuming any particular apprehension to have a privileged access to the real. Adopting this attitude, Eliadean History of Religions does not presume exhaustive knowledge of what "the real" actually is. This is consonant with more recent critical theory and epistemology and encourages openness to alternative belief systems. Insofar as mythical entities and events have a real effect on the existential situation of believers they are regarded as real/sacred entities and events.

The philosophical influences on Eliade from Kant through Otto and others are yet to be traced with real precision. Eliade's *The Sacred and the Profane*, first published in German as *Das Heilige und das Profane* (Hamburg, 1957), was explicitly written in response to Otto's *Das Heilige* (Breslau, 1918; *The Idea of the Holy*, London, 1926), but Eliade goes beyond Otto in describing the dialectic of the sacred and the profane. He insists that believers are prepared by their lived experience and religious background to experience hierophany, that is, the apprehension of the real/sacred in the historically apparent/profane. It is an indispensable element of Eliade's analysis that any historical entity *could* be apprehended as such a hierophany with appropriate preparation and that all hierophany *must* be mediated by means of historical realities. His conclusion is that all things reveal, but at the same time conceal, the nature of Being.

In Eliade's quest to recover the meanings of hierophanies for those who apprehend them he attempts to analyze and understand religious data by applying concepts from the German hermeneutical tradition going back to Schleiermacher and Dilthey and continued by Wach and Gerardus van der Leeuw. Eliade agrees with them that religious data are intelligible because, as human expressions, they are in accord with our own lived experience. Although he is most often identified as a phenomenologist of religion he frequently insisted that he was a phenomenologist only insofar as he sought to discover the *meanings* of religious data. His hermeneutical phenomenology is most evident in his morphological approach in *Patterns in Comparative Religion* (1958), where he groups religious phenomena ahistorically by structural themes such as water symbolism or the symbolism of the center. Later, he attempted to complement that methodology with the chronological organization of his *History of Religious Ideas* (1976–83). However, in considering Eliade's sources and influences, it should be borne in mind that he considered, to give just one example, the first-/second-century Indian Buddhist, Nagarjuna, to have produced "one of the most original ontological creations known to the history of thought" (*History of Religious Ideas*, vol. II, 225). That is to say that Eliade's openness to the influence of Asian philosophy should not be ignored, nor should his roots in Eastern Orthodox Christianity. It may well be Eliade's greatest contribution to the contemporary understanding of religions that he combines all of these influences in a pluralistic philosophy of religion that manages to take all religious traditions seriously as authentic expressions of lived existential situations.

Since his death in 1986 Eliade's status has been problematic and his value debated in the West. However, most of his books remain in print and continue to sell strongly to popular readers and to academic readers elsewhere in the world. Despite the defense of his work mounted by some writers, criticism of his thought has been consistent and influential. It is worthy of note that, despite condemnations of his political past, this material has so far revealed no evidence of egregious wrong-doing. Nevertheless, the case has important implications for scholars' reflexive understanding in the study of religions, emphasizing as it does the need for meticulous self-awareness of possible complicity with institutional power structures.

It is clear that Eliade's unquestionable influence requires careful scholarly investigation. Due to his position as an internationally successful synthesizer of studies of religion, his case has become emblematic of several key issues: the role played by the "great man" figure in academic disciplines; the "insider/outsider" question in the study of religion; historiography and the interpretation of historical evidence in relation to ideology; and the interpenetration of lived experience, political activity, and theoretical categories. Scholars need to understand clearly how scholars' specifically academic production is affected by other activities.

Unclear in the Eliadean corpus is his personal theological position. Although early articles make clear his somewhat surprisingly credulous stance in respect of claims regarding supernatural phenomena and his later theoretical work makes plain his understanding of the sacred as the real, *par excellence*, he has also expressed a modern skepticism concerning a historically incredible God (Ricketts, *Romanian Roots*, 123 and Girardot, "Smiles and Whispers," 152). In a body of writing as extensive as Eliade's, it is unrealistic to expect consistency, but such inconsistencies perpetuate the debate over his theological position.

Some have seen a latent theological agenda in his work, where others have read a strictly phenomenological description of human behaviors. So the question remains, what did Eliade himself believe, and does his personal belief add to or detract from his value as a scholar of religion?

Other closely connected questions arising from Eliade's work concern historicism and the potential ubiquity of religion. It has been one of the most repeated criticisms of Eliade that he is "anti-historical," "ahistorical," or perhaps "ahistoricist." That is, his "morphology" ignores the historical context of religious realities, grouping and analyzing by superficial similarities, and also that he grants effective agency to "sacred" categories which lack historical autonomy. Eliade's position, most clearly stated in *The Myth of the Eternal Return*, is that the modern evaluation of historical realities as the only source of significance, meaning, truth, and power, is itself an ascription of a religious nature, brought about by developments in the history of religions. Thus even modern historicists who limit all effective causality to historical realities can be classed as religious in this way and such religiousness is ubiquitous. All human beings are religious according to the preface to *The Quest*, and the sacred is a ubiquitous category of human consciousness. This, however, is another of Eliade's contentious claims. Scholarly consensus is lacking with respect to this question, too. Is it accurate to describe all of humanity as religious? Is it at all helpful to define religion so as to remove entirely the possibility of truly "non-religious" people? Is it at all meaningful to recognize the agency of "ahistorical entities"? Here the central question of reductionism appears. Eliade takes religion and religiousness to be irreducible realities. That is, they cannot be explained or defined without remainder in entirely non-religious terms. Religion is thus a reality *sui generis*—of its own unique natural sort. These, too, remain undecided issues in the study of religion.

The initial approach and institutional training of scholars of religion will never be disconnected from their answers to any of these questions. Those who prefer to conceive the study of religion as an enterprise more closely allied to the social sciences than to the humanities will tend to avoid dependence upon empirically unavailable and thus "non-historical" concepts and categories, and will be more ready to recognize a religious/non-religious dichotomy determined along lines of dependence upon or independence from such concepts and categories. Those who prefer to conceive of the study of religion as a humanistic discipline more closely allied to a philosophical anthropology will be more open to the consideration of religious concepts and categories as the effective products of human culture whose "historical reality" may thus be constrained but is nonetheless factual. In this context the English-language distinction between the humanities and the sciences is less helpful than the Germanic distinction between *Geisteswissenschaft* and *Naturwissenschaft*. Eliade's History of Religions clearly belongs to the former—on that one point at least consensus can be reached.

Whatever is finally deemed to be the value of the Eliadean *oeuvre*, the clarification of the questions raised in its consideration can only serve to further clarify our understanding of religion and the processes involved in its study.

3

INTRODUCTION TO *THE SACRED AND THE PROFANE*

Mircea Eliade

Editor's Introduction

The introduction from Eliade's mature work, *The Sacred and the Profane* (1959), serves as a useful introduction to his position and his methodology. In opposition to the Nietzschean refusal of the apparent/real distinction and a rejection of any non-empirical real (as in *Twilight of the Idols*), Eliade agrees with Rudolf Otto in accepting as a fact that the sacred/real is other than the phenomenally apparent but impinges on subjective awareness with some criterion of distinction. This occurs in and through the profane objects of ordinary perception which are apprehended as revelatory of the true nature of the noumenal. The possibility of a wholly profane cosmos with no authentic experience of such revelation and thus no "sacred" Eliade sees as "a recent discovery in the history of the human spirit." The analysis of the more prevalent state in which the experience of the sacred does occur is his primary concern.

෩ ෪

The extraordinary interest aroused all over the world by Rudolf Otto's *Das Heilige* [*The Idea of the Holy*], published in 1917, still persists. Its success was certainly due to the author's new and original point of view. Instead of studying the *ideas* of God and religion, Otto undertook to analyze the modalities of *the religious experience*. Gifted with great psychological subtlety, and thoroughly prepared by his twofold training as theologian and historian of religions, he succeeded in determining the content and specific characteristics of religious experience. Passing over the rational and speculative side of religion, he concentrated chiefly on its irrational aspect. For Otto had read Luther and had understood what the "living God" meant to a believer. It was not the God of the philosophers—of Erasmus, for example; it was not an idea, an abstract notion, a mere moral allegory. It was a terrible *power*, manifested in the divine wrath.

In *Das Heilige* Otto sets himself to discover the characteristics of this frightening and irrational experience. He finds the *feeling of terror* before the sacred, before the awe-inspiring mystery (*mysterium tremendum*), the majesty (*majestas*) that emanates an overwhelming superiority of power; he finds *religious fear* before the fascinating mystery (*mysterium fascinans*) in which perfect fullness of being flowers. Otto characterizes all these experiences as numinous (from Latin *numen*, god), for they are induced by the revelation of an aspect of divine power. The numinous presents itself as something "wholly other" (*ganz andere*), something basically and totally different. It is like nothing human or cosmic; confronted with it, man senses his profound nothingness, feels that he is only a creature, or, in the words in which Abraham addressed the Lord, is "but dust and ashes" (Genesis 18:27).

The sacred always manifests itself as a reality of a wholly different order from "natural" realities. It is true that language naïvely expresses the *tremendum*, or the *majestas*, or the *mysterium fascinans* by terms borrowed from the world of nature or from man's secular mental life. But we know that this analogical terminology is due precisely to human inability to express the *ganz andere*; all that goes beyond man's natural experience, language is reduced to suggesting by terms taken from that experience.

After forty years, Otto's analyses have not lost their value; readers of this book will profit by reading and reflecting on them. But in the following pages we adopt a different perspective. We propose to present the phenomenon of the sacred in all its complexity, and not only in so far as it is *irrational*. What will concern us is not the relation between the rational and nonrational elements of religion but the *sacred in its entirety*. The first possible definition of the sacred is that it is *the opposite to profane*. The aim of the following pages is to illustrate and define this opposition between sacred and profane.

When the Sacred Manifests Itself

Man becomes aware of the sacred because it manifests itself, shows itself, as something wholly different from the profane. To designate the *act of manifestation* of the sacred, we have proposed the term *hierophany*. It is a fitting term, because it does not imply anything further; it expresses no more than is implicit in its etymological content, i.e., that *something sacred shows itself* to us (*Patterns*, 7). It could be said that the history of religion—from the most primitive to the most highly developed—is constituted by a great number of hierophanies, by manifestations of sacred realities. From the most elementary hierophany—e.g. manifestation of the sacred in some ordinary object, a stone or a tree—to the supreme hierophany (which, for a Christian, is the incarnation of God in Jesus Christ) there is no solution of continuity. In each case we are confronted by the same mysterious act—the manifestation of something of a wholly different order, a reality that does not belong to our world, in objects that are an integral part of our natural "profane" world.

The modern Occidental experiences a certain uneasiness before many manifestations of the sacred. He finds it difficult to accept the fact that, for many human beings, the sacred can be manifested in stones or trees, for example. But as we shall soon see, what is involved is not a veneration of the stone in itself, a cult of the tree in itself. The sacred tree, the sacred stone are not adored as stone or tree; they are worshiped precisely because they are *hierophanies*, because they show something that is no longer stone or tree but the *sacred*, the *ganz andere*.

It is impossible to overemphasize the paradox represented by every hierophany, even the most elementary. By manifesting the sacred, any object becomes *something else*, yet it continues to remain *itself*, for it continues to participate in its surrounding cosmic milieu. A *sacred* stone remains *a stone*; apparently (or more precisely from the profane point of view), nothing distinguishes it from all other stones. But for those to whom a stone reveals itself as sacred, its immediate reality is transmuted into a supernatural reality. In other words, for those who have a religious experience all nature is capable of revealing itself as cosmic sacrality. The cosmos in its entirety can become a hierophany.

The man of the archaic societies tends to live as much as possible in the sacred or in close proximity to consecrated objects. The tendency is perfectly understandable, because, for primitives as for the man of all premodern societies, the *sacred* is equivalent to a *power*, and, in the last analysis, to *reality*. The sacred is saturated with being. Sacred power means reality and at the same time enduringness and efficacy. The polarity sacred-profane is often expressed as an opposition between *real* and *unreal* or pseudoreal. (Naturally, we must not expect to find the archaic languages in possession of this philosophical terminology, *real-unreal*, etc.; but we find the *thing*.) Thus it is easy to understand that religious man deeply desires *to be*, to participate in *reality*, to be saturated with power.

Our chief concern in the following pages will be to elucidate this subject to show in what ways religious man attempts to remain as long as possible in a sacred universe, and hence what his total experience of life proves to be in comparison with the experience of the man without religious feeling, of the man who lives, or wishes to live, in a desacralized world. It should be said at once that the *completely* profane world, the wholly desacralized cosmos, is a recent discovery in the history of the human spirit. It does not devolve upon us to show by what historical processes and as the result of what changes in spiritual attitudes and behavior modern man has desacralized his world and assumed a profane existence. For our purpose it is enough to observe that desacralization pervades the entire experience of the nonreligious man of modern societies and that, in consequence, he finds it increasingly difficult to rediscover the existential dimensions of religious man in the archaic societies.

Two Modes of Being in the World

The abyss that divides the two modalities of experience—sacred and profane—will be apparent when we come to describe sacred space and the ritual building of the human habitation, or the varieties of the religious experience of time, or the relations of religious man to nature and the world of tools, or the consecration of human life itself, the sacrality with which man's vital functions (food, sex, work and so on) can be charged. Simply calling to mind what the city or the house, nature, tools, or work have become for modern and nonreligious man will show with the utmost vividness all that distinguishes such a man from a man belonging to any archaic society, or even from a peasant of Christian Europe. For modern consciousness, a physiological act—eating, sex, and so on—is in sum only an organic phenomenon, however much it may still be encumbered by tabus (imposing, for example, particular rules for "eating properly" or forbidding some sexual behavior disapproved by social morality). But for the primitive, such an act is never simply physiological; it is, or can become, a sacrament, that is, a communion with the sacred.

The reader will very soon realize that *sacred* and *profane* are two modes of being in the world, two existential situations assumed by man in the course of his history. These modes of being in the world are not of concern only to the history of religions or to sociology; they are not the object only of historical, sociological, or ethnological study. In the last analysis, the *sacred* and *profane* modes of being depend upon the different positions that man has conquered in the cosmos; hence they are of concern both to the philosopher and to anyone seeking to discover the possible dimensions of human existence.

It is for this reason that, though he is a historian of religions, the author of this book proposes not to confine himself only to the perspective of his particular science. The man of the traditional societies is admittedly a *homo religiosus*, but his behavior forms part of the general behavior of mankind and hence is of concern to philosophical anthropology, to phenomenology, to psychology.

The better to bring out the specific characteristics of life in a world capable of becoming sacred, I shall not hesitate to cite examples from many religions belonging to different periods and cultures. Nothing can take the place of the example, the concrete fact. It would be useless to discuss the structure of sacred space without showing, by particular examples, how such a space is constructed and why it becomes qualitatively different from the profane space by which it is surrounded. I shall select such examples from among the Mesopotamians, the Indians, the Chinese, the Kwakiutl and other primitive peoples. From the historico-cultural point of view, such a juxtaposition of religious data pertaining to peoples so far removed in time and space is not without some danger. For there is always the risk of falling back into the errors of the nineteenth century and, particularly, of believing with Tylor or Frazer that the reaction of the human mind to natural phenomena is uniform. But the progress accomplished in cultural ethnology and in the history of religions has shown that this is not always true, that man's reactions to nature are often conditioned by his culture and hence, finally, by history.

But the important thing for our purpose is to bring out the specific characteristics of the religious experience, rather than to show its numerous variations and the differences caused by history. It is somewhat as if, in order to obtain a better grasp of the poetic phenomenon, we should have recourse to a mass of heterogeneous examples, and, side by side with Homer and Dante, quote Hindu, Chinese, and Mexican poems; that is, should take into consideration not only poetics possessing a historical common denominator (Homer, Virgil, Dante) but also creations that are dependent upon other aesthetics. From the point of view of literary history, such juxtapositions are to be viewed with suspicion; but they are valid if our object is to describe the poetic phenomenon as such, if we propose to show the essential difference between poetic language and the utilitarian language of everyday life.

The Sacred and History

Our primary concern is to present the specific dimensions of religious experience, to bring out the differences between it and profane experience of the world. I shall not dwell on the variations that religious experience of the world has undergone in the course of time. It is obvious, for example, that the symbolisms and cults of Mother Earth, of human and agricultural fertility, of the sacrality of woman, and the like, could not develop and constitute a complex religious system except through the discovery of agriculture; it is equally obvious that a pre-agricultural society, devoted to hunting, could not feel the sacrality of Mother Earth in the same way or with the same intensity. Hence there are differences in religious experience explained by differences in economy, culture, and social organization—in short, by history. Nevertheless, between the nomadic hunters and the sedentary cultivators there is a similarity in behavior that seems to us infinitely more important than their differences: *both live in a sacralized cosmos*, both share in a cosmic sacrality manifested equally in the animal world and in the vegetable world. We need only compare their existential situations with that of a man of the modern societies, *living in a desacralized cosmos*, and we shall immediately be aware of all that separates him from them. At the same time we realize the validity of comparisons between religious facts pertaining to different cultures; all these facts arise from a single type of behavior, that of *homo religiosus*.

Part II

ELIADE'S UNDERSTANDING OF RELIGION

Early Understanding

4

FOLKLORE AS AN INSTRUMENT OF KNOWLEDGE

Mircea Eliade

Translated by Mac Linscott Ricketts

Editor's Introduction

Eliade's perhaps surprisingly credulous position in respect of "parapsychological" phenomena can be seen as an early step in his undertaking to analyze "the sacred" as it has been apprehended and reported by human agents. Eliade's publications in this volume span fifty years from this article until his death and it would be unreasonable to expect perfect consistency and to ignore development and change. That said, Eliade's later position seems to have been broadly formed by this, his thirtieth year. The article re-affirms the position stated in "Magie şi metapsihică" (*Cuvântul*, June 17, 1927) written before Eliade visited India. Both show his early tendency to a methodological openness, "to take all religious traditions seriously as authentic expressions of lived existential situations." His later position, shown in the introduction to *The Sacred and the Profane*, obviously developed under the influence of this attitude. The later Eliade, however, cannot be entirely judged by the belief of the 20 and 30-year-old in, for example, the existence of a distinct "primitive mentality" and of human "mental evolution"—as is clear from "Notes on the Symbolism of the Arrow" (below, 141–52). However, the younger Eliade's critique of "historicism" may go a great way to explaining his later antipathy to historicist positions in *The Myth of the Eternal Return* (1949). The question of the respective influences of his Eastern Orthodox background and his "Indian Experience" of 1928–32 have been much debated. I direct the reader to the writings of Sergiu Al-George, Douglas Allen, and Mac Ricketts in the bibliography, and to the articles by Ansgar Paus and A. F. C. Webster in this volume. Suffice it to say that by 1937 these various influences had done their work. This article first appeared as "Folklorul ca instrument de cunoaştere," in *Revista Fundaţilor Regale,* IV, 4 (April 19, 1937): 137–52. It is here translated from the Romanian by Mac Linscott Ricketts and published with the kind permission of Professor Ricketts and the Eliade Literary Estate.

ℰ ℭ

I n this article we propose to answer a precise question: *in what way and to what extent can ethnographic and folkloric documents serve as instruments for gaining knowledge?* We must explain from the outset that we are not concerned here with the problems and methods of the philosophy of culture. Naturally, any ethnographic document and any folkloric creation can serve, within the framework of the philosophy of culture, as a means for gaining knowledge of a *style* or the decipherment of a *symbol.* Instruments of work and methods of philosophy are today, especially, much appreciated, by the European and Romanian publics alike. It suffices to recall Lucien Blaga's *Trilogia Culturii* in order to realize to what beautiful results such studies can lead. Along with syntheses of the type of Blaga's, other works of equal importance can be mentioned, which, starting also from ethnographic and folkloric documents, or based on certain important texts (the Vedas, etc.) and on Classical and archaic Asian architectural monuments, try to demonstrate the existence of a single spiritual tradition, a primordial vision of the world. Opposing any organistic or historicistic conceptions of the philosophy of culture, these authors endeavor to establish the *unity of traditions* and symbols which lie at the base of ancient Oriental, Amerindian, and Occidental civilizations, and even of "ethnographic" cultures. Let us mention, among these latter authors, René Guénon, Julius Evola (both "dilettantes"), Ananda Coomaraswamy (a specialist in Indian art and iconography), Walter Andrae (Assyriologist and archeologist; cf. in particular *Die Ionische Säule*, Berlin, 1933), Paul Mus (orientalist and archeologist), Alfred Jeremias (Assyriologist, specialist in Sumerian problems), etc. We must emphasize, in connection with these authors, that they do not in the least exclude the "peculiarity" of cultures; they assert, however, that the same *meanings* and the same *symbols* explain each of them in part. It is, in a sense, a restoration of an intellectualistic position toward problems of culture and history: a position which seeks general and uniform laws for the explanation of all spiritual forms of human life, in all times and places. The authors of whom we speak, however, refuse the uniform criteria of explanation of certain modern sociological schools. They refuse, in general, to start from "facts," moving from

26

lower to higher, so to speak, being content to seek the meaning of a symbol, a form of life, or a ritual in their conformity with certain traditional canons.

But whether they are claimed by the philosophy of culture, or whether they solicit the attention of researchers like those mentioned above, ethnographic and folkloric materials, we must acknowledge, reward the labor with which they were gathered only through such efforts at understanding. The work which thousands of savants have expended in the past hundred years would be a disappointing expense of passion and intelligence if through it we could not penetrate into certain zones of knowledge not reached by other instruments of investigation. So far as we are concerned, we appreciate equally the results of the philosophy of culture and of "ecumenical" studies—especially those of Ananda Coomaraswamy and Carl Hentze—founded on archeological, folkloric, and ethnographic documents. We believe, however, that folkloric materials can serve also another sort of knowledge than that afforded by the philosophy of culture, namely, this: we believe that problems directly connected with man, with the structure and limits of his knowledge, can be studied almost to their final resolution, starting from folkloric and ethnographic data. In other words, we do not hesitate to accord to these manifestations of the "popular soul" or to the so-called "primitive mentality" the value of facts which constitute the human experience in general.[1]

It is well known, especially as a result of discussions of the theory of Sir James Frazer, in what so-called *contagious magic* consists. We are not interested here in the validity of Frazer's *theory* about magic and the differences that exist between magic and religion. The reader who wishes to follow this theoretical controversy will find elements in R. R. Marett (*The Threshold of Religion*, 2nd ed., 29, 38, 73, 190), Lowie (*Primitive Religion*, 136–50), Schmidt (*Der Ursprung der Gottesidee*, 1st ed., 510–14). What interest us are the ethnographic and folkloric documents collected and grouped in Frazer's grandiose work, *The Golden Bough*. We refer to this collection because it is accessible to all, capable of being consulted in a popular edition (*Le Rameau d'or*, 1924), as well as in the scholarly edition (the first volume from *The Magic Art*, which exists also in a French version, published by Guethner).

Frazer calls *contagious magic* that group of primitive and folk beliefs which entails the idea of a "sympathetic" bond between a man and anything with which he is in direct contact. "The most familiar example of contagious magic is the sympathy that is supposed to exist between a man and anything detached from his body, such as his fingernails or his hair, so that any one who has gotten control of the hair or nails of a man, no matter how far away he may be, can exert his will over that person from whom they were cut" (*Le Rameau d'or*, 36; *The Magic Art*, vol. I, 175). This belief is universal, and Frazer cites an impressive number of testimonies collected from "primitives" and peoples of Antiquity, from cultured Asia and Christianized Europe. Everything—organic or inorganic—that was once in direct contact with the body of a person, still retains, for a long time after it has been separated from him, a "fluid," magical, "sympathetic" connection with that body. Teeth, the placenta, the umbilical cord, the blood that flowed from a wound, the weapon that wounded him, the clothing worn, objects held in the hand, footprints—all these remain for a very long time in a mysterious connection with the one who had them. The magical virtue of the objects preserved in an invisible connection with the human body is, undoubtedly, very much a nuisance for the "primitive." Because a sorcerer, or even an enemy superficially initiated into the secrets of magic, can at any time provoke the illness or death of a man, working directly upon an insignificant object which once had been in contact with him. For example, if a wizard burns the nail clippings of a man, that man dies. In the Wotjobaluk tribe, a sorcerer brings a rug close to the fire, and the owner of the rug immediately falls ill. In an island of the New Hebrides group, a man who wishes to kill another procures an undergarment worn by that man and burns it slowly in a fire. In Prussia, it is said if you cannot catch a thief, the best thing you can do is to search for some object lost by him (preferably, an item of clothing) and beat it well; the thief will immediately become ill.

Savants and historians who have concerned themselves with such primitive and popular beliefs have asserted, with one accord, that we are confronted here with a case of false logic. The primitive, pre-rational mind applies erroneously the laws of causality—they say. The conception of a "fluid," magical connection which links the man to that with which he was once in touch, is born from an imperfect knowledge of the laws of reality; it is, thus, a superstition, a false generalization, which finds no justification in experience.

We believe that this subject of the concept of contagious magic can be attacked also from another point of view. First of all, we must ask if such a "fluid" connection between man and objects touched by him is perfectly refuted by human experience, studying this human experience in its broadest extent, and not only on the normal planes. As a matter of fact, we know that this "fluid" link is substantiated also today, in the case of subjects belonging to European and American cultures, and has been examined seriously by Dufay, Azam, Phaneg, Pagenstecher, Prof. Charles Richet, and others. Buchanan, who was the first to study the parapsychic phenomenon, dubbed it with the detestable name of *psychometria*, which quite rightly revolts Charles Richet. The French professor prefers to use the term *cryptesthesia pragmatica* for the faculty of certain people to "see" persons, objects, or even whole episodes while touching something carried for a long time in contact with the human body (Richet, *Traité de Métapsychique*, 2nd ed., 222–31). A few examples will help us to understand better what *cryptesthesia pragmatica* or *psychometria* means.

Monsieur Dufay cited the case of Maria B. ... While Maria was under hypnosis, he showed her an object that once belonged to a murderer. Straightway she described the murderer...

Madame Piper, on several occasions, by touching a lock of hair, or some object having belonged to such-and-such a person, gave precise details about that person...

Miss Edith Hawthorne has given good examples of *cryptesthesia pragmatica*. Mr. Samuel Jones sent her a fossil found by a miner in a coal seam. Now the father of this miner had been killed in an accident in this mine twenty years earlier. Miss Hawthorne said that she had a terrible vision, a man prostrate on the floor, lifeless, ghastly, blood coming from his nose and mouth. Other interesting but vague information was derived from numerous objects sent by Mr. Jones to Miss Hawthorne. (228)

Similar happenings, of a sufficient preciseness, have been collected by Dr. Osty. In an article of ours, published ten years ago ("Magie şi metapsihică," *Cuvântul*, June 17, 1927), we mentioned several observations of the director of the Institute for Psychic Studies in Paris. Dr. Osty asks a slightly ill woman to write a few random lines on a piece of paper, and then he presents the paper to a "subject," Mme. Berly, without indicating anything. The subject portrays as exactly as possible the woman who had written them; she shows her suffering from illness of the liver and the stomach, weak with fever—details which no one knew. It is interesting to note that the lines written had been copied at random from a newspaper, and from the graphological point of view, they did not indicate any sort of weakness. Likewise, it must be stated that all the doctors who had examined the sick woman considered her to be suffering from another disease than what she had in reality, so it is not possible to explain this "guessing" as a telepathic reading by the "subject" of Dr. Osty's thoughts. Finally, a last detail: not one of the doctors has suspected the near death of the patient which the "subject" had specified, and which was fulfilled in a very short time. Dr. Osty also examined a "subject," M. de Fleuière, who recognized the image of the abbot Vianney, who died between 1853 and 1863, from nothing but a small scrap of his vestment. It is unnecessary to add that we are not interested here in the scientific explanation of these phenomena, if they are explained through clairvoyance, hypnosis, or pathology. One thing alone must be underscored: the existence, beyond any doubt, of a human faculty through which certain subjects reestablish the connection between an ordinary person and objects which that one once had with him. This faculty, which we can call whatever we wish, using terms as ugly as we like, has for our research a different significance. Because, once human experience admits within its limits *cryptesthesia pragmatica*, we no longer have the right to reject *a priori* the *reality* of those phenomena and beliefs which lie at the basis of "contagious magic," considering them mere "superstitions," creations of "primitive mentality," etc. Of course, we do not assert that every statement collected by ethnographers or folklorists relative to "contagious magic" is based on a *concrete fact*. We do not know, for example, if the owner of that rug about which we spoke above became ill in the hour when the sorcerer held the rug close to the fire. We know, however, that the "fluid" connection between the rug and its owner *could have existed*, and that a "subject" or a "sorcerer" *could have* established this connection. This fact has an immense importance for our research. Because, if indeed the "fluid" connection between a man and the objects with which he once was in contact is verified by cases of *cryptesthesia pragmatica*, studied by psychologists, then nothing hinders us from presupposing that at the basis of belief in contagious magic there lies, not a *false application of the principle of causality*, but an *experience*. In other words, it seems to us more natural to explain the belief in contagious magic through *cases* of *cryptesthesia pragmatica*, than to explain it through a "false conception." All we know about the "primitive mentality" gives us the right to our thesis: "the less civilized," as they are called, have a spiritual life apparently full of the fantastic, but based on concrete experience. The tendency toward the concrete, the experiential character of the "primitive" soul, is today unanimously accepted by ethnology. The rich mental life of a primitive is amazing. So that, instead of our explaining belief in contagious magic through *false logic*, we explain it through the *reality* of the metapsychic phenomena that gave birth to this belief.

The objection will be raised: cases of *cryptesthesia pragmatica* are rather rare, while belief in contagious magic is universal. To this we reply: cases of *cryptesthesia in the modern world*, and especially the cases *studied*, are rare. Now it is widely recognized today that the mental evolution of man has been accompanied by a radical change in human spiritual experience. New mental faculties have appeared or developed beyond measure, while others have disappeared or have become extremely rare. Cases of *cryptesthesia pragmatica* can be considered—in the modern world—as *monsters*; they have *survived* the radical transformations of the psychic and metapsychic realized by "civilization." In the second place, the universal belief in contagious magic presupposes the existence of "subjects" with psychometric faculties in every tribe where we meet with this belief, or in every village where it survives. This belief has been born as a result of concrete events, and it was accepted everywhere. Just as in modern society everybody *believes* in electricity, even without being capable of controlling it or using it.

The first conclusion that derives from our investigation would be this: *certain primitive and folkloric beliefs have concrete experiences as their basis*. Far from having been *imagined*, they express, confusedly and incoherently, certain *happenings* which human experience accepts within its limits. Let us see if we can carry this reasoning further.

Ethnographic and folkloric collections are full of "miracles," which legendary magicians or heroes are supposed to have performed. It is unnecessary to state that no savant, and no modern man, of a scientific formation accords to these "miracles" the slightest credibility. In general, that considerable body of ethnographic, hagiographic, and folkloric legends is considered as a huge ocean of *superstition*, as proof of the dramatic wanderings of the human mind on the road to truth. All those who have sought to find an explanation for these superstitions, these beliefs in miracles, have endeavored to find their *origin*: the fear of death, belief in spirits, collective hysteria, fraud, illusion, etc. No one in the nineteenth century bothered his brain to make a refutation of these beliefs. The only concern of savants was to explain the way the beliefs had imposed themselves on the human consciousness. Through what trick or what superstition, the men of science and the historians wondered, have peoples come to believe, for example, that the human body can rise up in the air, or that it can remain untouched by hot coals? No one took the pains to demonstrate the impossibility of such phenomena, since everyone was in accord that miracles cannot exist. Moreover, faced with hagiographic documents relating some of the "miracles" of the Saints, historians and psychologists did not even raise the question of the "criticism of the texts" or the "traditions"—but they concerned themselves with only one problem: through what collective psychosis or what fraud was this "superstition" repeated? Those who, in the middle of the last century, studied several "secular miracles," in particular levitation, striving to control their observations and verify them "experimentally," carried out this duty mainly in view of a personal hypothesis. Such was the case, for example, with de Roches, who wrote about levitation in 1897, and whose book, *Recueil de documents relatifs à lévitation*, tries to reconcile spiritualism with certain "electric" theories about the human body.

Legends about the levitation of certain men are very common, and they are met as often in civilized milieux as in "primitive societies." Porphyry and Iamblicus assert that Pythagoras had the power to raise himself high in the air. Damis, disciple of Apolonius of Tyana, writes that he saw with his own eyes "Brahmans rising to two cubits above the ground." In India, this belief is extremely widespread; the Buddha and other "mystics" or "magicians" could fly through the air due to certain occult faculties (cf. our book, *Yoga: Essai sur les origines de la mystique Indienne*, 257, n. 1, etc.). The same tradition is found in China (Wieger, *Histoire des croyances religieuses et des opinions philosophiques en Chine*, 362, etc.), and Islam (Carra de Vaux, *Les penseurs de l'Islam*, vol. IV, 244; Massignon, *Al Hallaj, martyr mystique de l'Islam*, vol. I, 263).

Howitt collected secrets from a Kurnai magician called Mundauin, who claimed that the *mrarts* (spirits) lifted him into the air one day. Another man of the same camp confirmed the tale; one night the magician's wife cried out, "Look, he's flying!" He had also been heard whistling through the air, first on one side then another ... According to North American Indians, sorcerers are thought to possess similar powers ... A French missionary, Father Papetard, abbot of African Missions in Nice, told Dr. Imbert-Gourbeyre that "during his stay in Oregon ... he had, more than once, seen sorcerers raise themselves into the air two or three feet above the ground and walk on the tips of blades of grass." ... In the Congo, associates of the Bouiti secret society say that initiates sometimes remain suspended for more than ten minutes a meter above the ground. For his part, Father Trilles tells of having seen initiates of the *Ngil* brotherhood (of the Fân) raise themselves up by a sort of levitation. (Oliver Leroy, *La léviatation*, Paris, 1928, 24–26, where references to the documents cited above are found)

Identical phenomena, or, if you prefer, identical superstitions, are found in Christian Europe. In particular, the biographies of Catholic saints abound in such testimonies. Of course, starting from the premise that levitation is impossible since it disregards the laws of gravity all the secular scholars who have studied the lives of the saints have ascribed no reality to these testimonies. Here we find a grave contradiction of that which is called the "historicistic spirit of the nineteenth century," ... "Historicism," which is considered a glory of the nineteenth century, bases its understanding of the world on *facts*, on *documents*; the great revolution which the "historicists" declare that they have accomplished in the judgment of reality is the *primacy of the document*. In this primacy of the document is found the justification which critics make of both "abstract history" and "romantic history." They do not believe anything not confirmed by the *document*, and they do not believe the document until it has been subjected to "textual criticism." But there exist a considerable number of "documents" which the historical science of the last century and of our own does not take into account: for instance, the hagiographic documents which refer to the "miracles" of the saints. And it takes no account of them, not because the *authenticity* of these documents is in doubt, not because textual criticism has demonstrated their uncertainty, but simply because they have to do with miracles, with impossible things. Here we see the contradiction of the "historicistic spirit," because an historian, who declares himself the slave of the document, does not have the right to reject a text for *rational*, philosophical reasons; this implies an *a prioristic* theory of the real which cannot prevail over an historicist without his renouncing his point of departure, the *primacy of the document*.

How serious this contradiction of "historicists" can sometimes become is shown by the case of St. Joseph de Copertino (1603–1663). This saint is known especially for his large number of "levitations," made over the course of some thirty-five years (28 March 1628–18 September 1663). In Professor Leroy's book (123–39) several dozen documents are found, including some of the most significant, and which no historian has taken the trouble to reject according to the method of textual criticism. The veracity of a document is assured by the number of witnesses, the responsibility of these witnesses (their psychology, whether they are "partisans" or "opponents," etc.), and other criteria which we cannot analyze here. Now, in the case of St. Joseph de Copertino who lived rather close to our modern era, the documentary material does not suffer any criticism. Hundreds of thousands of people were present, over a period of thirty-five years, at the levitations of the saint. "When he lived with the monks of Pietrarubbis café-bars opened in the vicinity of the monastery to accommodate the curious who flocked there in order to witness Joseph's rapture" (Leroy, 137). The levitation took place in the cities through which Joseph passed, in front of popular crowds as well as the "notables." Pope Urban VIII saw him, as did the great admiral of Castille and Prince John Frederick of Brunswick—who was so overwhelmed by the miracle that he left the Lutheran Church and became a Catholic, then was enrolled as protector in the Franciscan order. "One of the Chambellans, Lutheran like himself, declared that he regretted having witnessed a sight that cast doubt upon his convictions" (Leroy, 135). Those who wish to examine more closely these documents relative to St. Joseph de Copertino's levitations will find the necessary references in Leroy's book. There too are collected several hundred additional testimonies concerning other Catholics, and even "mediums." Leroy, basing himself on research and documents collected from psychologists, proved, beyond any shadow of doubt, the reality of cases of levitation in the "secular" world—although, as he himself observes (287 ff.), the levitation of mystics differs from that of "mediums." For instance, while the bodies of saints seem (apparently, at least) to lose their weight, the body of the medium, although high off the ground, seems to be resting on something, supported by something invisible. While the levitation of mystics lasts, sometimes, for hours, the levitation of mediums lasts only a short time (from a few seconds to several minutes). Also, it is interesting to observe that the levitations of mystics can take place anywhere, in any conditions, spontaneously and without the temperature's being modified. In contrast, the levitations of mediums take place usually in a special room, in a half-light, with a noticeably lowered temperature (295–96). In any event, the documents and arguments of Professor Leroy—who, be it mentioned in passing, is an eminent ethnologist—leads to this conclusion, among others: that the levitations of saints and of mediums are not identical, neither in their physical character nor in their psychological circumstances.

We do not propose to examine here the best-studied cases of "secular" levitations. We refer the reader to Leroy's book and to the *Traité* of Charles Richet (*op. cit.*, 719ff.) for preliminary explanations. We call attention, however, to one detail perhaps less known: the photographs published recently (*Illustrated London News*, June 1936; reproduced in *Time*, June 29, 1936, 62) showing a yogin in South India named Subbayah Pullavar, suspended parallel with the ground at a distance of fifty to sixty centimeters. The photos are taken by an English farmer, in broad daylight, in front of many natives. The yogin's body is rigid, as in a cataleptic state, and two pictures show him from different angles, removing any trace of doubt. Anyone who knows even a little about the doctrines of yogis realizes that Subbayah Pullavar—who stated to the farmer that he has been doing this for twenty years, and that it is a technique which his family has known for centuries—cannot be an ascetic with a very advanced spiritual life, because otherwise he would not be practicing such "miracles" on command and in front of photographic film. Nevertheless, the document exists, and it is added to the other documents, less perfect, previously known.

Figure 1. *The photographs from Time magazine of Subbayah Pullavar, suspended parallel with the ground*

Another "miracle" of which ethnography, hagiography, and folklore speak is the so-called incombustibility of the human body. This phenomenon is known in India (cf. *Yoga*, 253, n. 1), in Persia (Claude Huart, *Les Saints des derviches tourneurs*, vol. I, 56), and among the primitives of Europe. Again, Leroy has assembled the most rich and precise body of material on this phenomenon, in his book *Les hommes salamandres. Sur l'incombustibilité du corps humain*. With the same method, Leroy demonstrates the historicity of numerous "miracles" of Catholic mystics, who were seen by a large number of persons walking through fire. But, since in general this criticism of traditions and texts does not convince, Leroy cites an extraordinary happening which took place a few years ago at Madras, and which was witnessed by an immense number of persons. A yogin announces that he will pass through fire. The Maharajah prepares a trench half a meter deep, three meters wide, and ten meters long, with hot coals and I don't know how many cords of wood. He then invites all the "notables" of the city, the English colony, the Protestant missionaries, and even the Bishop of Madras, together with several Catholic prelates. The coals are so hot in the middle of the tropical day that no one can come closer than three or four meters to the trench. The yogin, barefoot and almost naked, walks across the coals. Then, after sitting down at a corner of the trench in a posture of deep meditation, he invites any of those watching who wish to cross also. At first, several barefoot Indians cross, then a European, then follow the Maharajah with the Bishop of Madras and all the other Europeans, and last of all, the princely brass band, in a body! The Bishop, whose documented letter about the event Leroy publishes, declares that as he approached the hot coals he felt a pleasant coolness, and he walked on the fire as if he were treading on fresh grass. All the witnesses testify that at this time the yogin seemed to be suffering horrible pains, moaning and writhing, as if all the heat of that huge mass of coals were being absorbed by him. At the end of the letters, the Bishop asserts that he does not doubt the "miracle," but he considers it a demonic thing ...

We cease here with our examples. Based on the well-verified cases of levitation and the incombustibility of the human body, we have the right to make the following assertion: *in certain circumstances the human body can escape the laws of gravity and the conditions of organic life*. The *psychology* of these "miracles" does not interest us, if, for example, we have to do with mystical or demonic states, with neuropaths, the "possessed," or saints. We are establishing only the *reality* of these exceptional happenings, and we wonder if the ethnographic beliefs and folkloric legends having to do with levitation and the incombustibility of the human body, far from being the creation of a "primitive mentality," do not have their source in *concrete experiences*. We find it much easier to believe that a "primitive" comes to assert the incombustibility of the body by starting from an *event* which he has witnessed, than to believe that he imagined this thing through who knows what obscure process of the mind.

If our thesis be accepted, two important consequences follow, which could be formulated in this way:

1. At the base of popular beliefs from the "ethnographic phase" as well as that of the folklore of civilized peoples lie *facts*, and not *fantastic creations*.
2. Having verified experientially *some* of these beliefs and superstitions (for example, *cryptesthesia pragmatica*, levitation, and the incombustibility of the human body), we have the right to suspect that at the base of *other* popular beliefs lie *concrete facts*.

Let us examine these consequences more closely. Obviously, when we assert that at the *base* of popular beliefs lie concrete experiences and not fantastic creations, we are not overlooking all those processes of alteration and exaggeration of realities, processes we know are peculiar to "primitive mentality." Folklore has its own laws: the *folkloric presence* fundamentally modifies every concrete fact, according it new meaning and values. Moreover, not all beliefs and legends created around, let us say, levitations, were provoked by a concrete fact, by a real levitation. Some beliefs were diffused from a certain center, and they were embraced by a people because they corresponded to its mental laws, its fantastic horizon. We must take into account, of course, the laws of folkloric creation, the obscure alchemy of primitive mentality. Nevertheless, the *initial fact* is an experience, and we cannot insist enough on this point.

As far as the second consequence of our investigation is concerned, it can have an overwhelming importance. Because, if it is true that ethnography and folklore put documents at our disposal having an experiential source, then we have the right to accord some faith to *all* the beliefs that ethnographers and folklorists collect. If it has been proven experientially that man can have a "fluid contact" with objects he has touched, that he can raise himself into the air, that he can pass unharmed though fire, and if all these "miracles" abound in folklore, then why don't we believe in other folkloric "miracles"? Why don't we believe, for instance, that in certain circumstances man can become invisible? Of course, it is not a matter here of "believing" blindly in all popular legends and superstitions, but of not rejecting them *en bloc* as delusions of the primitive spirit. Once it has been proven that the biological and physical laws can be suspended—in levitation and the incombustibility of the human body—nothing can hinder us from believing that these laws can be suspended in *other* circumstances: for instance, in the case of the disappearance of the human body. The frequency of the experiential verifications of some of the folkloric "miracles" does not play too important a role. A million experiences of levitation are not necessary for us to believe in the suspension of gravity, just as there is no need of a million comets for us to believe in the existence of comets. The frequency and laws of statistics cannot apply when it is a matter of phenomena of an exceptional character.

The problem of death, in our opinion, can be attacked from a new point of view, if we take account of the above facts and conclusions. Above all, it is fitting that we ask to what extent the argument of positivists against the survival of the "soul" can be valid when we have a considerable number of cases (levitation, incombustibility) which prove the *autonomy* of man within the compass of physical and biological laws. Positivists, in general, have denied the possibility of the survival of the soul, based on the laws of organic life (the brain-consciousness relationship, the condition of the cell, etc.). But these laws of life are sometimes suspended, for instance, in the case of flesh that hot coals do not harm. It is true that the circumstances in which incombustibility is realized are *exceptional*, but just as exceptional is the fact of death. The brain-consciousness correlation can be perfectly valid in the human condition, but no one can tell us if this is nullified in the moment of death. ... Of course, it is not a matter of the survival of the soul, which is a metaphysical problem, but only of the conditions of the survival of human consciousness.

Note

1. In the present article we are doing nothing but justifying a method for working. For that reason, we will cite only those facts absolutely necessary to illustrate our theses. The documentary and bibliographical material will find its place in a book of larger proportions, in preparation.

The Elements of Eliade's Understanding

The Sacred

THE STRUCTURE AND MORPHOLOGY OF THE SACRED

Mircea Eliade

Editor's Introduction

The elements of Eliade's understanding of religion are interdependent and interpenetrating, as was obvious from the introduction to *The Sacred and the Profane*, and the reader should be cautious in attempting to formulate an understanding of any one of these elements without attempting to understand them all. The following selection has something to say, not only about the sacred, but also about hierophany, the dialectic of the sacred and the profane, and *illud tempus*. However, an initial consideration of the sacred is rewarding in the attempt to understand all these other interpenetrating elements.

The *Traité d'Histoire des Religions* was published in French in 1949, the same year that saw the publication of Eliade's *Mythe de l'éternel retour*. These followed on the publication of the French revision of his doctoral dissertation on Yoga (*Yoga: Essai sur les origines de la mystique Indienne*) and *Metallurgy, Magic, and Alchemy*, both in 1936. By the late fifties, when the *Traité* was translated into English as *Patterns in Comparative Religion*, his understanding of religion and its associated phenomena was more carefully articulated. Readers must decide for themselves whether Eliade's terms are useful or too broad and vague to be of any real utility. Also raised is the important question, to be dealt with later, of Eliade's attitude to history, but it is clear that Eliade is not "anti-historical" in any simple sense of the term.

Finally the claim that "somewhere, at a given time, each human society chose for itself a certain number of things, animals, plants, gestures and so on, and turned them into hierophanies" is very significant. Hierophanization is taken explicitly to be a human act and not the self-disclosure of some transcendental presence. Also worthy of note is the tendency "to take all religious traditions seriously as authentic expressions of lived existential situations." Eliade insists that the absence in one culture of the specific form of and the hallmarks attributed to "sophisticated" thought in another does not indicate the absence of sophistication.

This excerpt comes from *Patterns in Comparative Religion*, 1–4, 10–23, 26, 29–30 (London: Sheed and Ward, 1958, translated from the French by Willard Trask). All rights reserved. Copyright © 1958 by Sheed and Ward. Reprinted by permission of the University of Nebraska Press and Continuum International Publishers.

ℰ ℛ

The Sacred and the Profane

All the definitions given up until now of the religious phenomenon have one thing in common: each has its own way of showing that the sacred and the religious life are the opposite of the profane and the secular life. But as soon as you start to fix limits to the notion of the sacred you come upon difficulties—difficulties both theoretical and practical. For, before you attempt any definition of the phenomenon of religion, you must know where to look for the evidence, and, first and foremost, for those expressions of religion that can be seen in the "pure state"—that is, those which are "simple" and as close as possible to their origins. Unfortunately, evidence of this sort is nowhere to be found; neither in any society whose history we know, nor among the "primitives," the uncivilized peoples of today. Almost everywhere the religious phenomena we see are complex, suggesting a long historical evolution.

Then, too, assembling one's material presents certain important practical difficulties. Even if one were satisfied with studying only one religion, a lifetime would scarcely be long enough to complete the research, while, if one proposed to compare religions, several lifetimes would not suffice to attain the end in view. Yet it is just such a comparative study that we want, for only thus can we discover both the changing morphology of the sacred, and its historical development. In embarking, therefore, on this study, we must choose a few among the many religions which have been discovered by history, or ethnology, and then only some of their aspects or phases.

This choice, even if confined to the major manifestations, is a delicate matter. If we want to limit and define the sacred, we shall have to have at our disposal a manageable number of expressions of religion. If it starts by being difficult, the diversity of those expressions becomes gradually paralyzing. We are faced with rites, myths, divine forms, sacred and venerated objects, symbols, cosmologies, theologoumena, consecrated men, animals and plants, sacred places, and more. And each category has its own morphology—of a branching and luxuriant richness. We have to deal with a vast and ill-assorted mass of material, with a Melanesian cosmogony myth or Brahman sacrifice having as much right to our consideration as the mystical writings of a St. Teresa or a Nichiren, an Australian totem, a primitive initiation rite, the symbolism of the Borobudur temple, the ceremonial costumes and dances of a Siberian shaman, the sacred stones to be found in so many places, agricultural ceremonies, the myths and rites of the Great Goddesses, the enthroning of an ancient king or the superstitions attaching to precious stones. Each must be considered as a hierophany in as much as it expresses in some way some modality of the sacred and some moment in its history; that is to say, some one of the many kinds of experience of the sacred man has had. Each is valuable for two things it tells us: because it is a hierophany, it reveals some modality of the sacred; because it is a historical incident, it reveals some attitude man has had towards the sacred. For instance, the following Vedic text addressing a dead man: "Crawl to your Mother, Earth! May she save you from the void!" (*Rg Veda* 10.18.10). This text shows the nature of earth worship; the earth is looked upon as the Mother, *Tellus Mater*; but it also shows one given stage in the history of Indian religions, the moment when Mother Earth was valued—at least by one group—as a protectress against the void, a valuation which was to be done away with by the reform of the Upaniṣads and the preaching of Buddha.

To return to where we began, each category of evidence (myths, rites, gods, superstitions, and so on) is really equally important to us if we are to understand the religious phenomenon. And this understanding will always come about in relation to history. Every hierophany we look at is also an historical fact. Every manifestation of the sacred takes place in some historical situation. Even the most personal and transcendent mystical experiences are affected by the age in which they occur. The Jewish prophets owed a debt to the events of history, which justified them and confirmed their message; and also to the religious history of Israel, which made it possible for them to explain what they had experienced. As a historical phenomenon—though not as personal experience—the nihilism and ontologism of some of the Mahayana mystics would not have been possible without the Upaniṣadic speculations, the evolution of Sanskrit and other things. I do not mean that every hierophany and every religious experience whatsoever is a unique and never-to-be-repeated incident in the working of the spirit. The greatest experiences are not only alike in content, but often also alike in their expression. Rudolf Otto discovered some astonishing similarities between the vocabulary and formula of Meister Eckhardt and those of Śaṅkara.

The fact that a hierophany is always a historical event (that is to say, always occurs in some definite situation) does not lessen its universal quality. Some hierophanies have a purely local purpose; others have, or attain, world-wide significance. The Indians, for instance, venerate a certain tree called *aśvattha*; the manifestation of the sacred in that particular plant species has meaning only for them, for only to them is the *aśvattha* anything more than just a tree. Consequently, that hierophany is not only of a certain time (as every hierophany must be), but also of a certain place. However, the Indians also have the symbol of a cosmic tree (*Axis Mundi*), and this mythico-symbolic hierophany is universal, for we find Cosmic Trees everywhere among ancient civilizations. But note that the *aśvattha* is venerated because it embodies the sacred significance of the universe in constant renewal of life; it is venerated, in fact, because it embodies, is part of, or symbolizes the universe as represented by all the Cosmic Trees in all mythologies. But although the *aśvattha* is explained by the same symbolism that we find in the Cosmic Tree, the hierophany which turns a particular plant-form into a sacred tree has a meaning only in the eyes of that particular Indian society.

To give a further example—in this case a hierophany which was left behind by the actual history of the people concerned—the Semites at one time in their history adored the divine couple made up of Ba'al, the god of hurricane and fecundity, and Belit, the goddess of fertility (particularly the fertility of the earth). The Jewish prophets held these cults to be sacrilegious. From their standpoint—from the standpoint, that is, of those Semites who had, as a result of the Mosaic reforms, reached a higher, purer and more complete conception of the Deity—such a criticism was perfectly justified. And yet the old Semitic cult of Ba'al and Belit *was* a hierophany: it showed (though in unhealthy and monstrous forms) the religious value of organic life, the elementary forces of blood, sexuality and fecundity. This revelation maintained its importance, if not for thousands, at least for hundreds of years. As a hierophany it held sway until the time when it was replaced by another, which—completed in the religious experience of an élite—proved itself more satisfying and of greater *perfection*. The "divine form" of Yahweh prevailed over the "divine form" of Ba'al; it manifested a more perfect holiness, it sanctified life without in any way allowing to run wild the elementary forces concentrated in the cult of Ba'al, it revealed a spiritual economy in which man's life and destiny gained a totally new value; at the same time it made possible a richer religious experience, a communion with God at once purer and more complete. This hierophany of Yahweh had the final victory; because it represented a universal modality of the sacred, it was by its very nature open to other cultures; it became, by means of Christianity, of world-wide religious value. It can be seen, then that some hierophanies are, or can in this way become, of universal value and significance, whereas others may remain local or of one period—they are not open to other cultures, and fall eventually into oblivion even in the society which produced them.

ℬℭ

What I propose is by no means always easy. To the Western mind, which almost automatically relates all ideas of the sacred, of religion, and even of magic to certain historical forms of Judaeo-Christian religious life, alien hierophanies must appear largely as aberrations. Even for those disposed to consider certain aspects of exotic—and particularly of Oriental—religions quite sympathetically, it is hard to understand the sacred value attached to stones, say, or the mystique of eroticism. And even if he can see some justification for these queer hierophanies (labeling them "fetishism" or something of the sort), it is quite certain that there are others the modern man will never come to accept, which he cannot see as having the value of a hierophany at all, in which he can discern no modality of the sacred. Walter Otto noted in his *Die Götter Griechenlands* (Bonn, 1928) how difficult it is for a modern to find any religious meaning in "perfect forms," one of the categories of the divine current among the ancient Greeks. The difficulty is even greater when it comes to considering a symbol as a manifestation of the sacred, to thinking of the seasons, the rhythm or the fullness of forms (any and every form) as so many modes of the sacred. In the pages that follow I shall try to show that they were held to be such by primitive cultures. If only we can get away from the prejudices of the lecture-room, can consider such beliefs not simply as pantheism, fetishism, infantilism and so on, but as what they actually meant to those who held them, we shall be better able to understand the past and present meaning of the sacred in primitive cultures; and at the same time our chances of understanding the modes and the history of religion will increase too.

We must get used to the idea of recognizing hierophanies absolutely everywhere, in every area of psychological, economic, spiritual and social life. Indeed, we cannot be sure that there is anything—object, movement, psychological function, being or even game—that has not at some time in human history been somewhere transformed into a hierophany. It is a very different matter to find out *why* that particular thing should have become a hierophany, or should have stopped being one at any given moment. But it is quite certain that anything man has ever handled, felt, come in contact with or loved *can* become a hierophany. We know, for instance, that all the gestures, dances and games children have, and many of their toys, have a religious origin—they were once the gestures and objects of worship. In the same way musical and architectural instruments, means of transport (animals, chariots, boats and so on) started by being sacred objects, sacred activities. It is unlikely that there is any animal or any important species of plant in the world that has *never* had a place in religion. In the same way too, every trade, art, industry and technical skill either began as something holy, or has, over the years, been invested with religious value. This list could be carried on to include man's everyday movements (getting up, walking, running), his various employments (hunting, fishing, agriculture), all his physiological activities (nutrition, sexual life, etc.); perhaps too the essential words of the language, and so on. Obviously it would be wrong to imagine the whole of mankind's having gone through all these stages; to see every society in turn reaching the sacred in all these ways. Such an evolutionist hypothesis might have been conceivable a few generations ago, but is now completely impossible. But somewhere, at a given time, each human society chose for itself a certain number of things, animals, plants, gestures and so on, and turned them into hierophanies; and as this has been going on for tens of thousands of years of religious life, it seems improbable that there remains anything that has not at some time been so transfigured.

The Dialectic of Hierophanies

I mentioned at the beginning of this chapter that all the definitions that have ever been given of the religious phenomenon make the sacred the opposite of the profane. What I have just said—that anything whatever can become at any given moment a hierophany—may seem to contradict all these definitions. If anything whatever may embody separate values, can the sacred–profane dichotomy have any meaning? The contradiction is, in fact, only a surface one, for while it is true that anything at all can become a hierophany, and that in all probability there is nothing that has not, somewhere, some time, been invested with a sacred value, it still remains that no one religion or race has ever been found to contain all these hierophanies in its history. In other words, in every religious framework there have always been profane beings and things beside the sacred. (The same cannot be said of physiological actions, trades, skills, gestures and so on, but I shall come to this distinction later.) Further: while a certain class of things may be found fitting vehicles of the sacred, there always remain some things in the class which are not given this honor.

For instance, in the so-called "worship of stones" not all stones are held to be sacred. We shall always find that *some* stones are venerated because they are a certain shape, or because they are very large, or because they are bound up with some ritual. Note, too, that it is not a question of actually worshiping the stones; the stones are venerated precisely because they are not simply stones but hierophanies, something outside their normal status as things. The dialectic of a hierophany implies a more or less clear choice, a singling-out. A thing becomes sacred in so far as it embodies (that is, reveals) something other than itself. Here we need not be concerned with whether that something other comes from its unusual shape, its efficacy or simply its "power"—or whether it springs from the thing's fitting in with some symbolism or other, or has been given it by some rite of consecration, or acquired by its being placed in some position that is instinct with sacredness (a sacred zone, a sacred time, some "accident"— a thunderbolt, crime, sacrilege or such). What matters is that a hierophany implies a *choice*, a clear-cut separation of this thing which manifests the sacred from everything else around it. There is always something *else,* even when it is some whole sphere that becomes sacred—the sky, for instance, or a certain familiar landscape, or the "fatherland." The thing that becomes sacred is still separated in regard to itself, for it only becomes a hierophany at the moment of stopping to be a mere profane something, at the moment of acquiring a new "dimension" of sacredness.

This dialectic shows itself very clearly at the elementary level of those vivid hierophanies so often mentioned in ethnological writings. Everything unusual, unique, new, perfect or monstrous at once becomes imbued with magico-religious powers and an object of veneration or fear according to the circumstances (for the sacred usually produces this double reaction). Writes A. C. Kruyt,

> When a dog is always lucky in hunting, it is *measa* (ill-starred, a bringer of evil), for too much good luck in hunting makes the Toradja uneasy. The mystic virtue by means of which the animal is enabled to seize his prey must necessarily be fatal to his master; he will soon die, or his rice-crop will fail, or, more often still, there will be an epidemic among his cattle or his pigs. This belief is general throughout Central Celebes. (translated and quoted by Lévy-Bruhl in *Primitives and the Supernatural*, 45–46)

Perfection in any sphere is frightening, and this sacred or magic quality of perfection may provide an explanation for the fear that even the most civilized societies seem to feel when faced with a genius or a saint. Perfection is not of this world. It is something different, it comes from somewhere else.

This same fear, this same scrupulous reserve, applies to everything alien, strange, new—that such astonishing things should be present is the sign of a force that, however much it is to be venerated, may be dangerous. In the Celebes,

> if the fruit of the banana appears, not at the end of the stalk but in the middle, it is *measa* ... People usually say that it entails the death of its owner... When a certain variety of pumpkin bears two fruits upon a single stem (a similar case to a twin birth) it is *measa*. It will cause a death in the family of the man who owns the field in which it is growing. The pumpkin plant must be pulled up, for nobody must eat it. (Kruyt, quoted by Lévy-Bruhl, 191)

As Edwin W. Smith says, "it is especially strange, unusual things, uncommon sights, new-fangled habits, strange foods and ways of doing things that are regarded as manifestations of the hidden powers" (quoted by Lévy-Bruhl, 192). At Tana, in the New Hebrides, all disasters were attributed to the white missionaries who had just come (Lévy-Bruhl, 164). This list could easily be made longer.[1]

The Taboo and the Ambivalence of the Sacred

I will come later to the question of how far such things can be considered hierophanies. They are in any case kratophanies, that is manifestations of power, and are therefore feared and venerated. This ambivalence of the sacred is not only in the psychological order (in that it attracts or repels), but also in the order of values; the sacred is at once "sacred" and "defiled." Commenting on Virgil's phrase *auri sacra fames*, Servius (*On the Aenead.*, iii, 75) remarks quite rightly that *sacer* can mean at the same time accursed and holy. Eustathius (*On the Iliad*, xxiii, 429) notes the same double meaning with *hagios*, which can express at once the notion "pure" and the notion "polluted" (Harrison, 59). And we find this same ambivalence of the sacred appearing in the early Semitic world (Robertson Smith, *The Religion of the Semites*, 446–54) and among the Egyptians (Albright, 321 n. 45).

All the negative valuations of "defilement" (contact with corpses, criminals and so on) result from this ambivalence of hierophanies and kratophanies. It is dangerous to come near any defiled or consecrated object in a profane state—without, that is, the proper ritual preparation. What is called taboo—from a Polynesian word that the ethnologists have taken over—means just that: it is the fact of things, or places, or persons, being cut off, or "forbidden," because contact with them is dangerous. Generally speaking, any object, action or person which either has naturally, or acquires by some shift of ontological level, force of a nature more or less uncertain, is, or becomes, taboo. The study of the nature of taboos and of things, persons or actions that are taboo, is quite a rich one. You can get some idea of this by glancing through Part II of Frazer's *The Golden Bough*: *Taboo and the Perils of the Soul*, or Webster's huge catalogue in his book *Taboo*. Here I will simply quote a few examples from Van Gennep's monograph, *Tabou et totémisme à Madagascar*. The Malagasy word that corresponds to *taboo* is *fady, faly*, which means what is "sacred, forbidden, out of bounds, incestuous, ill-omened" (12)—really, in other words, what is dangerous (23). *Fady* were "the first horses brought on to the island, rabbits brought by the missionaries, all new merchandise, above all, European medicines" (salt, iodine, rum, pepper and so on, 37). Here again, you see, we find the unusual and the new transformed into kratophanies. They are generally mere lightning-flashes, for such taboos are not lasting in their nature; as soon as things are known and handled, fitted into the primitive cosmos, they lose all power to upset the order of things. Another Malagasy term is *loza*, which the dictionaries tell us means: "All that is outside, or runs counter to, the natural order; any public calamity, or unusual misfortune, sin against the natural law, or incest" (36).

Clearly death and sickness are phenomena that also come within the category of the unusual and frightening. Among the Malagasy and elsewhere the sick and the dead are sharply cut off from the rest of the community by "interdicts." It is forbidden to touch a dead man, to look at him, or to mention his name. There is another series of taboos applying to women, to sex, to birth, and to certain special situations: for instance, a soldier may not eat a cock that has died in a battle, nor any animal whatever killed by a *sagaie*; one must not slay any male animal in the house of a man who is armed or at war.[2] In each case the interdict is a provisional one due to a temporary concentration of powers in some person or thing (a woman, a corpse, a sick man), or to someone's being in a dangerous situation (a soldier, huntsman, fisherman, and so on). But there are also permanent taboos: those attaching to a king or a holy man, to a name or to iron, or to certain cosmic regions (the mountain of Ambondrome which none dares approach (194), lakes, rivers, or even whole islands, 195ff.). In this case the taboos are based on the specific mode of being of the person or thing tabooed. A king is an absolute powerhouse of forces simply because he is a king, and one must take certain precautions before approaching him; he must not be directly looked at or touched; nor must he be directly spoken to, and so on. In some areas the ruler must not touch the ground, for he has enough power in him to destroy it completely; he has to be carried, or to walk on carpets all the time. The precautions considered necessary when dealing with saints, priests and medicine men come from the same kind of fear. As for the "tabooing" of certain metals (iron, for instance), or certain places (islands and mountains), there may be various causes—the novelty of the metal, or the fact that it is used for secret work (by sorcerers and smelters, for instance); the majesty or the mystery of certain mountains, or the fact that they cannot be fitted, or have not as yet been fitted, into the local universe, and so on.

However, the elements of the taboo itself are always the same: certain things, or persons, or places belong in some way to a different order of being, and therefore any contact with them will produce an upheaval at the ontological level which might well prove fatal. You will find the fear of such an upheaval—ever present because of this difference in the order of being between what is profane and what is hierophany or kratophany—even in people's approach to consecrated food, or food thought to contain certain magico-religious powers. "Certain food is so holy that it must not be eaten at all, or be eaten in small portions only" (Westermarck, 125). That is why in Morocco people visiting the sanctuaries or celebrating feasts eat only very little of the dishes they are offered. When the wheat is on the threshing-floor one tries to increase its "power" (*baraka*), yet if too much power accumulates it may become harmful. For the same reason, if honey is too rich in *baraka* it is dangerous (126).

This ambivalence, by which the sacred at once attracts and repels, will be more usefully discussed in the second volume of this study.[3] What can be noted now is the self-contradictory attitude displayed by man in regard to all that is sacred (using the word in its widest sense). On the one hand he hopes to secure and strengthen his own reality by the most fruitful contact he can attain with hierophanies and kratophanies; on the other, he fears he may lose it completely if he is totally lifted to a plane of being higher than his natural profane state; he longs to go beyond it and yet cannot wholly leave it. This ambivalence of attitude towards the sacred is found not only where you have negative hierophanies and kratophanies (fear of corpses, of spirits, of anything defiled), but even in the most developed religious forms. Even such theophanies as are revealed by the great Christian mystics repel the vast majority of men as well as attracting them (the repulsion may appear under many forms—hatred, scorn, fear, willful ignorance, or sarcasm).

As I have said, manifestations of the unaccustomed and the extraordinary generally provoke fear and withdrawal. Some particular examples of taboos, and of actions, things and persons tabooed have shown us the workings by which kratophanies of the unusual, the disastrous, the mysterious, and so on, are set apart from the round of ordinary experience. This setting-apart sometimes has positive effects; it does not merely isolate, it elevates. Thus ugliness and deformities, while marking out those who possess them, at the same time make them sacred. So, among the Ojibwa Indians, "many receive the name of witches without making any pretension to the art, merely because they are deformed or ill-looking." All esteemed witches or wizards among these Indians are, as a rule, "remarkably wicked, of a ragged appearance and forbidding countenance." Reade states that in the Congo all dwarfs and albinos are elevated to the priesthood. "There is little doubt that the awe with which this class of men is generally regarded, in consequence of their outward appearance, also accounts for the belief that they are endowed with secret powers" (G. Landtmann, quoted by Nathan Soderblom, 15).

That shamans, sorcerers and medicine men are recruited for preference from among neuropaths and those who are nervously unbalanced is due to this same value set upon the unaccustomed and the extraordinary. Such stigmata indicate a choice; those who have them must simply submit to the divinity or the spirits who have thus singled them out, by becoming priests, shamans, or sorcerers. Obviously natural external qualities of this sort (ugliness, weakness, nervous disorder, etc.) are not the only means by which the choice is made; the religious calling often comes as a result of certain ritual practices to which the candidate submits willingly or otherwise, or of a selection carried out by the fetish-priest (Soderblom, 13f.). But in every case a choice has been made.

Mana

The unknown and the extraordinary are disturbing epiphanies: they indicate the presence of something *other* than the natural; the presence, or at least the call of that something. A particularly cunning animal, anything novel, any monstrosity—all these are as clearly marked out as a man who is exceptionally ugly, neurotic, or shut off from the rest of the community by any sort of distinguishing mark (whether natural, or acquired by means of a ceremony whose object is to mark out the "elect"). Such examples may help us to understand the Melanesian idea of *mana* from which some authors have thought it possible to trace the origins of every religious phenomenon. *Mana* is, for the Melanesians, that mysterious but active power which belongs to certain people, and generally to the souls of the dead and all spirits (Codrington, 118). The tremendous act of creating the cosmos could only be performed by the *mana* of the Divinity; the head of a family also possesses *mana*, the English conquered the Maoris because their *mana* was stronger, the worship of a Christian missionary has a higher *mana* than that of the old rites. Even latrines have a certain *mana* in that they are "receptacles of power"—for human bodies and their excretions have it (Van der Leeuw, "Religion in Essence and Manifestation," 25).

But men and things only possess *mana* because they have received it from higher beings, or, in other words, because and in so far as they have a mystical sharing of life with the sacred. "If a stone is found to have a supernatural power, it is because a spirit has associated itself with it; a dead man's bone has with it *mana*, because the ghost is with the bone; a man may have so close a connection with a spirit or ghost that he has *mana* in himself also, and can so direct it as to effect what he desires" (Codrington, 119ff.) It is a force different in quality from physical forces, and it works arbitrarily. A man is a good fighter not because of his own strength or resources but because of the strength he gets from the *mana* of some dead fighter; this *mana* may lie in the little stone amulet hanging round his neck, in some leaves fastened to his belt, or in some spoken formula. The fact that a man's pigs multiply or his garden thrives is due to his possessing certain stones containing the particular *mana* of pigs and of trees. A boat is fast only if it has *mana*, and the same applies to a net catching fish, or an arrow delivering a mortal wound (Codrington, 120). Everything that *is* supremely, possesses *mana*; everything, in fact, that seems to man effective, dynamic, creative or perfect.

The English anthropologist Marett thought it possible to detect, in this belief in the existence of an impersonal force, a pre-animist phase of religion—in opposition to the theories of Tylor and his school, who held that the first phase of religion could only be animism. I do not want, at the moment, to discuss exactly how far one is right in speaking of any "first phase" of religion; nor do I want to see whether the identification of such a primal phase will prove to be the same thing as finding the "origins" of religion itself. I have only mentioned these few instances of *mana* to illuminate the kratophany-hierophany dialectic at its most elementary level. (And be it clearly understood that "most elementary" does not mean in any sense most primitive psychologically, nor oldest chronologically: the elementary level means a simple and undisguised modality of the sacred made manifest.) The instances I have quoted serve to illustrate the fact that a kratophany or hierophany singles out an object from its fellows in the same way as the unknown, the extraordinary and the new. However, note that in the first place the idea of *mana*, though it is to be found in religions outside the Melanesian area, is not a universal idea, and therefore can hardly be taken to represent the first phase of all religions, and, in the second, that it is not quite correct to see *mana* as an impersonal force.

There are certainly non-Melanesian peoples[4] who believe in the same sort of force, a force that can make things powerful, *real* in the fullest sense. The Sioux call this force *wakan*; it exists everywhere in the universe, but only manifests itself in extraordinary phenomena (such as the sun, the moon, thunder, wind, etc.) and in strong personalities (sorcerers, Christian missionaries, figures of myth and legend, and so on). The Iroquois use the term *orenda* to mean the same idea: a storm possesses *orenda*, the *orenda* of a bird that is hard to bring down is very cunning, a man who is enraged is a prey to his *orenda*, etc. *Oki* to the Hurons, *zemi* to the West Indians, *megbe* to the African pygmies (Bambuti)—all these words mean the same sort of thing as *mana*. But, let me repeat, not everyone possesses *oki, zemi, megbe, orenda* and so on; only divinities, heroes, souls of the dead, or men and things in some way connected with the sacred, such as sorcerers, fetishes, idols and so on. To quote only one of the modern ethnologists who have described these magico-religious phenomena— and in this case our author is dealing with an ancient people whose belief in *mana* has been much controverted—Paul Schebesta writes

> *Megbe* is everywhere, but its power is not shown everywhere with the same intensity, nor in the same manner. Some animals are richly endowed with it; one man may possess more *megbe*, another less. Capable men become eminent simply because of the amount of *megbe* they amass. Sorcerers too have a great deal. It seems to be power bound up with the soul-shadow, destined to disappear with it at death and either transfer itself to someone else, or become changed into the Totem. (64)

Although some scholars have added certain other terms to this list (the Masai's *ngai*, the Malagasy *andriamanitha*, the Dayaks' *petara*, and so on), and there are those who would place a similar interpretation upon the Indian *brahman*, the Iranian *Kvarenah*, the Roman *imperium*, the Nordic *hamingja*—the idea of *mana* is not found everywhere. *Mana* does not appear in all religions, and even where it does appear it is neither the only nor the oldest religious form. "*Mana*, in other words, is by no means universal, and its use, therefore, as a foundation on which to build up a general theory of primitive religion is not only misleading but also fallacious" (Hogbin, 274). Indeed, even among the varying formulae (*mana, wakan, orenda*, etc.) there are, if not glaring differences, certainly nuances not sufficiently observed in the early studies. Paul Radin, for instance, when analyzing the conclusions drawn by Jones, Fletcher and Hewitt from their researches on *wakanda* and *manito* among the Sioux and the Algonquins, remarks that these terms mean "sacred," "strange," "remarkable," "wonderful," "unusual," "powerful"—without conveying the slightest notion of "inherent power."[5]

Marett—and others—thought that *mana* represented an "impersonal force," although Codrington had already drawn attention to the fact that this power, though "itself impersonal, is always connected with some person who directs it … No man has this force of himself; all he does he does with the help of personal beings, spirits of nature or the spirits of his ancestors" (*The Melanesians*, 119, 121). Recent researches (Hocart, Hogbin, Capell) have specified more clearly the nature of these distinctions established by Codrington. "How can it be impersonal, if it is always bound up with personal beings?" asks Hocart. In Guadalcanal and Malaita, for instance, *nanama* is exclusively possessed by the spirits of the dead, though they can use their power to benefit man. "A man may work very hard, but unless he wins the approval of the spirits, and they use their power for his benefit, he will never become wealthy" (Hogbin, 297). "Every endeavor is made to secure the favor of the spirits so that *mana* will always be available. Sacrifices are the commonest method of winning approval, but certain other ceremonies are also supposed to be pleasing" (Hogbin, 264).

Then, too, Radin notes that the Indian makes no opposition between personal and impersonal, or corporal and incorporeal. "What he seems to be interested in is the question of existence, of reality; and everything that is perceived by the senses, thought of, felt and dreamt of, exists. It follows, consequently, that most of the problems connected with the nature of spirit as personal or impersonal do not exist" (Hogbin, 352). We must, it seems, put the problem in ontological terms: what *exists* and what is *real*, what *does not exist*—rather than in the terms of personal or impersonal, and corporal or incorporeal—concepts to which the "primitives" did not attach the same significance as later cultures. Anything possessing *mana* exists on the ontological level and is for that reason efficacious, fecund, fertile. We cannot therefore really talk of *mana* as "impersonal," for such a notion would have no meaning within the mental limits of the primitive. Nowhere do we find *mana* existing of itself, standing apart from things, cosmic events, beings or men. Further still, you will find, on a close analysis, that a thing, a cosmic phenomenon, in fact any being whatever, possesses *mana* thanks either to the intervention of some spirit, or to getting involved in an epiphany of some divine being.

There seems in fact to be no justification for seeing *mana* as an impersonal magic force. To go on from this to seeing a pre-religious phase—dominated solely by magic—must therefore be equally mistaken. Such a theory is invalidated in any case by the fact that not all peoples (particularly the most primitive) have any such belief as that in *mana*; and also by the fact that magic—although it is to be found more or less everywhere—never exists apart from religion. Indeed, magic does not dominate the spiritual life of "primitive" societies everywhere by any means; it is, on the contrary, in the more developed societies that it becomes so prevalent. (As instances I would quote the Kurnai of Australia and the Fuegians, among whom it is very little practiced; and it is far less known among certain Eskimo and Koryak societies than among their Ainu and Samoyed neighbors, who are far above them in cultural and other ways.)

ഇ ൠ

The sacred is always manifested through some thing; the fact that this something (which I have termed "hierophany") may be some object close at hand, or something as large as the world itself, a divine figure, a symbol, a moral law or even an idea, does not matter. The dialectic works in the same way: the sacred expresses itself through something other than itself; it appears in things, myths or symbols, but never wholly or directly. From this point of view, therefore, a sacred stone, an avatar of Viṣṇu, a statue of Jupiter, or an appearance of Yahweh will *all* be held by the believer as at once real and inadequate simply because in every case the sacred manifests itself limited and incarnate. This paradox of incarnation which makes hierophanies possible at all—whether the most elementary or the supreme Incarnation of the Word in Christ—is to be found everywhere in religious history; I shall be returning to this problem elsewhere. However, the attitude which I have labeled idolatrous is based (whether consciously or not hardly matters) on this view of *all* hierophanies as being part of a whole. It would preserve the older hierophanies, by according them value on a different religious level, and the performance of a function there. ...

In fact, this paradoxical coming-together of sacred and profane, being and non-being, absolute and relative, the eternal and the becoming, is what every hierophany, even the most elementary, reveals. ... This coming-together of sacred and profane really produces a kind of breakthrough of the various levels of existence. It is implied in every hierophany whatever, for every hierophany shows, makes manifest, the coexistence of contradictory essences: sacred and profane, spirit and matter, eternal and non-eternal, and so on. That the dialectic of hierophanies, of the manifestation of the sacred in material things, should be an object for even such complex theology as that of the Middle Ages serves to prove that it remains *the* cardinal problem of any religion. One might even say that all hierophanies are simply prefigurations of the miracle of the Incarnation, that every hierophany is an abortive attempt to reveal the mystery of the coming together of God and man. Ockham, for instance, even went so far as to write: "Est articulus fidei quod Deus assumpsit naturam humanam. Non includit contradictionem, Deus assumere naturam assinam. Pari ratione potest assumere lapidum aut lignum." It does not, therefore, seem absurd in the least to study the nature of primitive hierophanies in the light of Christian theology: God is free to manifest himself under any form—even that of stone or wood. Leaving out for a moment the word "God," this may be translated: the sacred may be seen under any sort of form, even the most alien. In fact, what is paradoxical, what is beyond our understanding, is not that the sacred can be manifested in stones or in trees, but that it can be manifested at all, that it can thus become limited and relative.[6]

The Complexity of "Primitive" Religion

The examples I have so far quoted help, I think, to establish certain guiding principles:

(1) The sacred is qualitatively different from the profane, yet it may manifest itself no matter how or where in the profane world because of its power of turning any natural object into a paradox by means of a hierophany (it ceases to be itself, *as* a natural object, though in appearance it remains unchanged);

(2) This dialectic of the sacred belongs to all religions, not only to the supposedly "primitive" forms. It is expressed as much in the worship of stones and trees, as in the theology of Indian avatars, or the supreme mystery of the Incarnation;

(3) Nowhere do you find *only* elementary hierophanies (the kratophanies of the unusual, the extraordinary, the novel, *mana*, etc.), but also traces of religious forms which evolutionist thought would call superior (Supreme Beings, moral laws, mythologies, and so on);

(4) We find everywhere, even apart from these traces of higher religious forms, a system into which the elementary hierophanies fit. The "system" is always greater than they are: it is made up of all the religious *experiences* of the tribe (*mana*, kratophanies of the unusual, etc., totemism, ancestor worship, and much more), but also contains a corpus of traditional *theories* which cannot be reduced to elementary hierophanies: for instance, myths about the origin of the world and the human race, myths explaining present human conditions, the theories underlying various rites, moral notions, and so on. It is important to stress this last point.

Notes

1. Cf. for instance, Lévy-Bruhl, *Primitive Mentality* (London: George Allen and Unwin, 1923), 36, 261–64, 352 sq; H. Webster, *Taboo*, 230ff.
2. Van Gennep, *Tabou et totémisme à Madagascar* (Paris: E. Leroux, 1904), 20ff.; cf. also R. Lehmann, *Die Polynesischen Tabusitten*, Leipzig, 1930, 101ff.; Webster, *Taboo*, 261ff.
3. This may refer to the then projected *History of Religious Ideas*, but Eliade notoriously left many projected volumes uncompleted [ed.].
4. And, besides, *mana is* not a concept of all Melanesians, for it is unknown at Ontong Java (North-East Solomons), at Wogeo (New Guinea) (Hogbin, "Mana," *Man*, 1914, xiv, 268ff.), at Wagawaga, Tubetube, etc. (Capell, "The Word 'Mana," *Oceania*, 1938, vol. ix, 92).
5. "Religion of the North American Indians," *Journal of American Folklore*, 1914, vol. xxvii, 349.
6. One could attempt to vindicate the hierophanies which preceded the miracle of the incarnation in the light of Christian teaching, by showing their importance as a series of prefigurations of that Incarnation. Consequently, far from thinking of pagan religious

ways (fetishes, idols and such) as false and degenerate stages in the religious feeling of mankind fallen in sin, one may see them as desperate attempts to prefigure the mystery of the Incarnation. The whole religious life of mankind—expressed in the dialectic of hierophanies—would, from this standpoint, be simply a waiting for Christ.

6

THE SACRED IN THE SECULAR WORLD

Mircea Eliade

Editor's Introduction

The apprehension of certain profane phenomena as authentically revelatory of a powerful reality that is simultaneously concealed and revealed within them is characteristic of Eliade's understanding of religion. It is further characteristic of his understanding that this key element, the sacred, is not entirely lost to the secular world, but is more profoundly concealed and more subtly revealed. Also characteristic is Eliade's usage of the term "modern man" to mean specifically non-religious people. It is in this article that Eliade gives his most fully ramified explanation of his insistence—repeated in *The Quest* (p. i), in the second volume of his *Journal* (*No Souvenirs*) (p. 1), and in his *History of Religious Ideas* (vol. I, xiii)—that "the sacred is an element in the structure of human consciousness." It is in this article that one also finds a close link between phenomenology, religion, meaning, and exemplary patterns or models. My own analysis of this can be found in the Introduction and chapter 16 of my *Reconstructing Eliade*. "The Sacred in the Secular World" was an editorial summation of lectures and discussions given at the Conference on the Philosophy of Religion at Boston College, Summer, 1968. Edited by Christopher J. Arthur and originally published in *Cultural Hermeneutics* 1 (1973): 101–13. All rights reserved. Copyright © 1973 by D. Reidel Publishing Company, Dordrecht, Holland. Reprinted by permission of Sage Publications, Ltd.

ॐ ॐ

My investigations as a historian and phenomenologist of religion have led me to refer to man previous to our own age as *homo religiosus*. But I want to go farther than that. I am convinced that whatever modern, secularized man might think of himself, he still occupies a sacred dimension.

The fact that this dimension is not immediately obvious in our society should not deter us from attempting to decipher it. How are we to go about this attempt, though? The study of the history of religions has already provided us with the appropriate tools. In the discussion that follows, I will apply the findings and methodology of that study to modern man in order to demonstrate that and how a hermeneutical analysis of secular man reveals the sacred in his way of life.

The Sacred and the Structure of Human Consciousness

If, in the history of religions, the idea of the sacred is related to the idea of being and meaning, the historian of religions—who is also a phenomenologist because of his concern with meaning—will eventually discover something which has not always been evident: that the sacred is an element in the structure of human consciousness, that it is a part of the human mode of being in the world. The expression "being in the world" is not used here in the post-Heideggerian sense of Being-in-the-world, but in the pre-Heideggerian sense. It means that man simply discovers himself in the world, that the structure of his consciousness is such that somewhere in his experience there is something absolutely real and meaningful, something that is a source of value for him. As far as I understand it, the structure of human consciousness is such that man cannot live without looking for being and meaning. If the sacred means being, the real, and the meaningful, as I hold it does, then the sacred is a part of the structure of human consciousness.

When man becomes aware of his specific mode of being in the world, he realizes that he is a mortal being, that he is created. His creation is recounted mythically in a sacred history and he realizes that he is merely the result of what happened. We can take as an example the archaic culture of tropical planters who not only became aware of themselves as mortal beings, but also became aware of their own responsibility *vis-à-vis* the life of the cosmos. They thought that without their work, their ritual, the world of vegetation could not go on. Their awareness of responsibility forced them to repeat some tragic and cruel rituals, such as human sacrifices, cannibalism, and orgies; all of these are religious behavior, though looked on by us as savage and cruel. But they give meaning, and that meaning is not just human meaning. It is religious meaning. And the distinctive religious quality of this meaning is more than just finding what is to be and what is not to be, what is real and what is unreal: The sacred, the religious, carries with it a redemptive power as well. This power comes through the following of an exemplary model for action, through repeating what a god or hero did, through doing something transhuman. The idea of redemption through following an exemplary model is something that I find in the human consciousness.

The primitives found their models, and their insights into being and meaning through myth. Modern man has largely rejected myth, or so he says, and with it the sacred. But he can say that only if he misunderstands the basic nature of myth. To illustrate what I mean: That which is "gospel" for the Christian is myth for the primitive. In order for religion to reveal to man the truth or meaning of life, it is not necessary to use the expressions of myth.—The world of meaning of modern man plays the same function that myth played among the primitives. So long as modern man is interested in discovering the meaning of life, that meaning can serve as a model for human life, and thus is still in the same family as the archaic myth which presented the exemplary model for ritual repetition. The sacred, therefore, remains an element in modern man's structure of consciousness.

The evolutionary view of man is prevalent today, but a historian of religion generally works from a non-evolutionary view of human consciousness. When a man becomes aware of his mode of being, he has something in common both with the so-called primitive and the modern philosopher. We know from letters and publications of anthropologists that what the philosopher calls "angst," anxiety and death, was experienced by the primitives. I mean that *la grande situation humaine* has probably been the same in every era. I consider this a kind of basic universal. Where does meaning come from in manifestations of the religious such as myth and ritual? The meaning is in the mind, as the phenomenologists would say, but it is not a creation of the mind. Before the discovery of agriculture, man did not grasp the religious meaning of vegetation. But with the discovery, man identified his destiny with the destiny of a plant; he translated the meaning of human existence into vegetative terms. As is the case with a plant, I am born from a seed, I will die, I will be buried, and I will come to life again. This meaning is certainly in the mind, yet it could not have developed before the discovery of agriculture. At the same time we cannot say that this religious intentionality of the vegetation is a creation of the mind; it was already there in the fact that vegetative life starts from seeds, goes into flower and then dies and comes again. The intention is there and that intention is grasped by the human spirit, but it is not invented or created by the human mind because the intention is in the agricultural process.

The meaning, then, is given in the intentionality of the structure. The structure of the agricultural is called a fertility religion. It is not a human elaboration, not a human mind consciously putting values there to transform a natural process into a religious process. When man grasped the intention, agriculture became a religious act for him. The intention of vegetation became cultivation, and no longer wildness. Another problem that confronts us is the way in which the social consciousness in modern man reveals itself. A non-religious man today ignores what he considers the sacred but, in the structure of his consciousness, could not be without the ideas of being and the meaningful. He may consider these purely human aspects of the structure of consciousness. What we see today is that man considers himself to have nothing sacred, no god; but still his life has a meaning, because without it he could not live; he would be in chaos. He looks for being and does not immediately call it being, but meaning or goals; he behaves in his existence as if he had a kind of center. He is going somewhere, he is doing something. We do not see anything religious here; we just see man behaving as a human being. But as a historian of religion, I am not certain that there is nothing religious here. There might be a new, religious expression which cannot yet be recognized as such, simply because it is some-thing completely new, just because we speak of the new consciousness in purely humanistic terms, this does not mean that the new consciousness is not a con-tinuation of what being is—meaning, a social being, and so on. I cannot consider exclusively what that man tells me when he consciously says, "I don't believe in God; I believe in history," and so on. For example, I do not think that Jean-Paul Sartre gives all of himself in his philosophy, because I know that Sartre sleeps and dreams and likes music and goes to the theater. And in the theater he gets into a temporal dimension in which he no longer lives his "*moment historique.*" There he lives in quite another dimension. We live in another dimension when we listen to Bach. Another experience of time is given in drama. We spend two hours at a play, and yet the time represented in the play occupies years and years. We also dream. This is the complete man. I cannot cut this complete man off and believe someone immediately when he consciously says that he is not a religious man. I think that unconsciously, this man still behaves as the *homo religiosus*, has some source of value and meaning, some images, is nourished by his unconscious, by the imaginary universe of the poems he reads, of the plays he sees; he still lives in different universes. I cannot limit his universe to that purely self-conscious, rationalistic universe which he pretends to inhabit, since that universe is not human.

Synchronicity

Time is perhaps the most important factor in discovering modern man's rela-tionship to the sacred. I have already said that a historian of religions generally works from a non-evolutionary view of human consciousness and, therefore, from a synchronic rather than a diachronic time schema. To examine this fur-ther, let us consider the ideas of the historicist Benedetto Croce on the theory of historiography, in which he tried to understand how it is possible for modern man to understand something which happened thousands of years ago. He came to the conclusion that understanding a historical event is a historiographical anamnesis, that is to say, the historian becomes a contemporary of the event. He stands alongside Napoleon at Waterloo, and he dares understand the battle only after he has made the anamnesis. Similarly, when he truly understands an Australian ritual, he has taken the Australian myths seriously, and has allowed the Australian culture—however foreign and repugnant it may be to modern man—to enlighten us. Also, after Jacob Burckhardt wrote his book on *The Civilization of the Renaissance*, and that period became meaningful and accessible to the general reader, the readers gained not only information, but also a new meaning for human life. When, through an anamnesis, one realizes that understanding imparts new meaning, the anamnesis becomes creative, because it effects a transformation. It changes his life.

The structure of the sacred in the human consciousness is built on the structure of synchronicity, as opposed to the diachronic structure of radical historicism. Yet we have seen—in what I have said about Sartre, and in the theory of Croce—that even among the historicists there are allowances for a synchronic structure. When I discuss the time structure of the sacred, I am no longer related to temporal differences in a diachronic context; I have the right to jump from the ancient Neolithic Near East to India and Africa in examining the world of the agriculturalist, although it arose at different times in these places. That structure which I am grasping is based on intentionality; it is not the historical present, nor is it a creation of the mind.

The key feature of synchronicity to be found in myth is repetition. In following the admonitions of the myth, which is supposed to present exemplary models for life, e.g. models for fishing or hunting, for working the land, for getting married, etc., one always repeats something which was revealed from the beginning. Why is it so important when it looks so monotonous, so paralyzing to human life, always to be doing what was done before? There is a religious meaning, a religious value to repetition. If man goes again to the mythical event which is being re-actualized, he does not go back in historical time, bur rather he goes out of his profane time to the sacred, mythical time when the gods or the heroes were with him. So the repetition, through ritual, always recaptures the sacred time; through synchronicity, the mythic becomes the actual.

This synchronic structure is especially significant for and helpful to the modern existential consciousness. An illustration of what I mean is found in the remarkable and dangerous fishing expeditions of the Polynesians. When they go out, they pretend that they are repeating what was done at the beginning by their culture hero. They are trying to dehistoricize their situation, pretending that they are not doing now in history, not themselves creating a historical event in historical time. In history we can never anticipate what will happen tomorrow. History is always open to change, so they pretend that they are beyond the reach of its power. They are not starting a new historical event with all its attendant risk, but pretend that they are doing what has already been successfully done and that they will, therefore, come back alive and laden with fish. There-fore, the repetition is not, as it may seem to be, simply monotonous and nega-tive. It helps man to pass through existential crises and live life by restoring to him the dimension of the sacred and the universal and by negating the tension-filled historic now. It is religious, because it redeems man from his own situation.

The Historian of Religion as Phenomenologist

We see here the need for a historian of religions to go beyond mere accumula-tion of data. Rather, he must try to grasp the center of a religious belief, the meaning of it—just as I have been discussing the meaning of mythic time—in order to do justice to the religion itself and also to do justice to ourselves, to enrich ourselves with meanings that are new for us, rather than passing off all myth as superstition. As an illustration, let us consider the following. Despite the many differences and historical developments in Christianity, almost everyone would agree that its center is the notion of the Incarnation, God made man, and man's subsequent redemption. But let us say a Chinese came to Europe to understand Christianity and applied the methods of sociological or anthropo-logical field work in a village in France or Italy. He stays six months, watches the people, sees a church, an occasional procession, and a man called a priest reading from some large book. He will make a scientific description of what the people in that village do, but he may well miss the meaning of Christianity or even of those peasants in that place. This has happened with so many anthro-pological monographs, the work of men who do wonderful field work and description, but miss the meaning of what they describe and give us fragmen-tary information which makes the religion appear to be nothing more than a superstition.

So at some point the historian of religion must become a phenomenologist of religion, because he tries to find meaning. Without hermeneutics, the history of religion is just another history—bare facts, special classifications, and so on. With the problem of hermeneutics—meaning—we see that every manifestation of the sacred—symbol, myth, ritual—tells of something which is absolutely real, something which is meaningful for that culture, tribe, or religion in which the manifestation takes place. Once the historian of religion takes on the search for meaning, he can, following the phenomenological principle of suspension of judgment, assume the structure of synchronicity, and, therefore, as I have said before, bring together the meanings evident in many different cultures and eras.

I consider this kind of history of religion to be a kind of prolegomenon or introduction to a new type of philosophy. I insist on calling it a new type, because I think that when documents and meanings of cultures, tribes or religions are taken seriously and articulated by philosophers, a philosophical anthropology broader than what we have at this moment will be built. The two or three which we have are based on an attempt to understand the Greek, the Hebrew, the Christian, the agnostic or the Muslim; but there is a fantastically large world which is ignored, and I am sure that when this world of meaning is assimilated by philosophers and phenomenologists, new philosophical anthropologies will be created.

I think that for a philosopher nothing can be more suggestive, challenging and fertile than to have dialogue with these previously unassimilated meanings. When Whitehead said that the history of Western philosophy was just a series of footnotes to Plato, he was correct, because for two thousand five hundred years, whatever was beautiful and new in philosophy was, nonetheless, always in dialogue with Plato. Now when we discover the world of meaning which includes not only the philosophies of India, China, and Japan, but also the theologies, the mythologies, and the rituals of the whole archaic world, there will be many new openings to be considered by philosophy, because philosophy is interested in knowing *la situation humaine.* This new philosophy will discover all kinds of human situations which will probably enrich our understanding of the human mind and will probably give us new problems to investigate—problems which have never been investigated before, because Western philosophy has always been in dialogue with Plato.

Religious Creativity and the Historian of Religion

The history of religions is in many ways a history of creative breakthroughs, of man's own creative acts. There is no pattern of predictability in these, no promise of what the future holds other than that the future of religion depends on the continuing creativity of man in this direction. No one contemporary with Mohammed could say that eighty years later, a large part of the Persian Empire and the Mediterranean region would be Muslim, because no one could have predicted Mohammed. Nor did anyone predict Buddha, who changed India. So we cannot say what will happen tomorrow. What we are sure of from history is that if something does happen, it will only be the result of a new creative act; otherwise, we will remain where we are.

We can compare this type of creativity, this type of breakthrough to creativity in any cultural or scientific dimension. Newton and Einstein each made creative breakthroughs in science; Picasso, Shakespeare, and DaVinci did in art. When a great genius makes a breakthrough, he changes the world of values or art. Before the Cubists, before abstract art, no one could see the beauty in something which was not somehow a copy of nature; afterwards, we realized that there are beautiful things outside that realm. The same thing can be applied in the religious realm: Mohammed's appearance was a creative one, as was

Buddha's and many others'. Their creation was not the traditional type of creation *ex nihilo*, but an instance of the human mind giving an answer to a situation which was considered to be without any answer. As nature is always creating new forms, so are the artist and the *homo religiosus*.

In the absence of such a breakthrough, we have the past to turn to, and this, of course, is the function of the historian of religions. Working within the structure of synchronicity, we can introduce the modern age to the creative breakthroughs of past ages. Using the tool of hermeneutics, the historian can discover the meanings of the past, such as the breakthrough to the vegetation cults from the religions of the hunter. Through a hermeneutical anamnesis of what happened at that time in human mind, we find man discovering that his destiny as a human being is homologous with the destiny of a plant, a mystical participation of man and plant. Anthropologists who have not looked for the intentionality of this act have rendered it impotent for our time; but, in order to gain a creative understanding of the past, we must start philologically and historically and then look for the intentionality contained within the data we have.

All of this may seem irrelevant to the idea of a modern creative breakthrough. But each new understanding of a past phenomenon represents a creative breakthrough for the individual achieving it. I return to my statement that the anamnesis is a creative act because it brings about a transformation in the consciousness of the individual undergoing it; like the Polynesian fisherman, he is no longer bound by his own historical situation. But while the hermeneutic can help us to understand creatively both foreign cultures and our own culture, it is not itself the unpredictable breakthrough I referred to earlier. That breakthrough will not come when the hermeneutic has put together all the meanings of culture. It will come as a creative epiphany; some charismatic human being will bring meaning to millions through some new understanding, some new religious form. That will be true religious creativity; in the meantime, we must seek a deeper understanding of what we have already.

Religious Creativity and Language

The kind of charismatic religious creativity that I have been discussing manifests itself through language. Religious creativity implies helping others to see things; it implies the establishment of a repeatable model that can be acted out in the lives of others. If a purely mystical experience is involved, it is buried there; it is not communicated and does not become a model which can be meaningfully imitated; it is a purely ecstatic experience. There are quite a number of these that do not have any influence on the religion or the tribe or the general population. Only language can make the mystical experience into the religiously creative one. Language is the community in the individual. All world history is in me now because I use language. So even if I have a purely individual religion with my own rites and the like, it is still a community expression if it is expressed through language. If one has the call for creative reinvention to serve his own religious needs, he will probably tell others. Language, in short, founds the religious community.

It is difficult to imagine why there is language unless it indicates also that we have something in common. But what we have in common extends beyond any single religious community, time, or place. The history of religions focuses on this all-embracing aspect of language, its ability to bring men together in the universal community. On becoming more and more familiar with the manifestations of the sacred, the historian discovers that together they constitute a language in the sense that they do not tell us fragmentary, autonomous, and independent things about the universe—the transhuman, supernatural universe—they do not tell us something that happened here and something that happened there, but rather they constitute a language unto itself—a language telling us the history of something which did happen, and which happened as an organic complex having well-articulated directions. It is a language that invites us to understand the meaning of the religious world through the manifestations of the sacred, a language that points to something outside this world. New acts of religious creativity continue and enrich this language always in the direction of a deepened understanding of this dimension of human life.

Religious Creativity and the Secularized World

It is this language of religious creativity, linking past eras with the present in the synchronic search for meaning, that establishes a connection with the modern secularized world. One of the characteristics of this modern culture is that man makes himself through history, either in the existential mode following Sartre and Heidegger, or in the Marxist-historicist mode following philosophers like Croce and Ortega y Gasset. Man makes himself through history according to this scheme; there is no model and everything that has happened in history is meaningful because it is done by man. This non-religious man, the man who pretends that he makes himself in history, is still a descendent of the *homo religiosus*. If he says that man is only a historical being, then he must accept also that historically he is a product of his believing forefathers. Although he thinks he has emptied himself of all religious values, he is still related to them historically.

A parable sometimes credited to William Blake is appropriate to mention here. It tells of what happened to Adam and Eve when they were supposed to have run away from Paradise. They did not run away, and we are in fact still in their Paradise, with this difference: We cannot see it any more. We have lost the possibility of grasping Paradise; but it is still around us, and its meaning is still with us.

So it is with the modern man who thinks that he has left the religious world. There are several areas in which the sacred surfaces in our secular culture, and even among the historicists themselves—as I have already pointed out using Sartre as an example. One of these areas is art, even though its religious significance is not always readily realized. Such a case was Picasso's "Guernica," because nothing in it—except possibly the bull, the only clearly religious symbol—was there to tell us that this was a very important religious painting. Tillich and other specialists of culture, however, were able to discover the sacred character of the painting through a hermeneutical analysis. They made a similar analysis of the work of the sculptor Brancuşi, whose work did not seem immediately religious but was just something to which we were not accustomed. It seemed purely artistic and absolutely secular, but it contained a religious meaning. Brancuşi wanted to create, and although he did not realize that this creation was a religious act, what he wanted to say was religious.

To explain this a little further, I will return to the example of "Guernica." The symbols put there, unconsciously or not, the colors, the organization of the painting, all present a world of meanings which is fundamentally religious, telling us about the despair of a man who is destroyed by man, without having a God to ask for help. The religious meaning of it is discerned by a critical hermeneutical analysis. It is a creation of the human mind in the sense that Picasso, depressed by the historical situation, rediscovered a series of symbols and images of religious significance. But this world of meaning is not his creation; "Guernica" is his creation. Its religious meaning is the set of patterns which he put there without being aware of their significance, which gives to us a religious meaning. This is the dividing line of creation and discovery: Picasso has created "Guernica," and in so doing, he has discovered a world of religious meaning previously closed to him.

But not only the hermeneutics of art lead us to an understanding of the religious character of our apparently secular society. A hermeneutics of social reality presents a similar picture. We do not have to wait for a new creativity to understand our time hermeneutically. I have said that a religious creativity must be social in nature, and it is in the social world that we frequently discover the religious intentionalities underlying our secular culture. To use the social reality of death, for example, in its most striking manifestation of the sixties: Why is there a myth of Kennedy? How did that myth get started? Why did that event become a myth in the good sense of that word, giving meaning and a model? It was a religious event. The sacrifice of life became meaningful and creative for millions of Americans; the reality of death had touched them at their roots.

Similarly, the modern commitment to social action and social justice is founded on a religious intentionality. The civil rights movement has been of great value as a religious experience in America, whether or not it is conscious of this. The assassination of Martin Luther King, its outstanding creative figure, concretized a model for many of the black groups, much as Kennedy's death had done five years before.

I am sure that I cannot say that for modern, secular man there is nothing that is sacred; the possibility exists, as I have shown, that it is instead merely hidden, camouflaged, temporarily unrecognizable. I have a feeling we are witnessing the second fall. In the beginning, man could see and understand God; after the first fall, he could only reconstruct using his reason; and now, sacredness is fallen to the unconscious level, outside of man's manageable range. But the unconscious clearly remains an important and creative resource; man cannot live without imagination, without dreams, without discovering the sacred worlds of other men through art and culture. Therefore, I find the sacred still playing an important role in the modern world, even though this is less evident than it has been in the past.

In discussing the sacred, we always return to viewing it as a structure of the human consciousness rather than as a set of historical data. The character of the sacred underlies man's search for being and meaning and, therefore, is not limited to the remote past, nor to the distinct religions of the world. It is limited by the idea of redemption, though: The sacred quest for meaning is always tied in with another world of some sort or other, with the possibility for transformation.

Transformation implies an other, something beyond the realm of the individual himself, and to effect a transformation is to make a discovery. What we refer to as creative acts in a religious sense are precisely individual discoveries of the other dimension. These discoveries were originally couched in myths, but our modern society has its equivalents. They appear in the world of the artist; they appear in the society at large; they appear in the concern for social justice; they appear in the anamnesis. All of them involve a going out of self into a world of a different time, an idealized time, a synchronic scheme that makes the past and the future equally valuable with the present. The sacred always exists *in illo tempore* and, as such, distances itself from the historistic anxiety of the individual locked within the present. Creative acts of a religious nature follow this pattern—they speak in language and are, therefore, bonds of community. Many modern, religiously creative acts draw directly from the reservoir of the unconscious and are, therefore, part of timeless patterns of the workings of the collective human mind in discovering its roots.

In this way, the sacred remains very much a part of the modern, secular way of life. It is an underlying structure of man. It comes from without, and simply takes on new forms in time in defining its own continuing language. The secular historicist has not abolished the sacred but has given it a different orientation; and this orientation can be clearly discerned through a hermeneutical analysis performed with the help of a phenomenological history of religions.

7

Before "the Sacred" became Theological: Rereading the Durkheimian Legacy[*]

William Paden

Editor's Introduction

William Paden's article on Eliade's understanding of the sacred stands as one of the clearest defenses of Eliade's concept of the sacred against the frequently leveled criticism that it is overly theological and based on a simplistic assumption of independent ontology. Paden traces the development of and influences upon the concept of the sacred as Eliade would have inherited it from his academic forebears. Although Eliade regarded Durkheim as one of the "masters of reductionism," he had read extensively in all of the areas that Paden covers and could only have been influenced by them. Neither Paden nor I mean to imply that Eliade's use of the concept of the sacred is identical to Durkheim's. However, this background knowledge is indispensable to the avoidance of overly-simplistic ascriptions of meaning to Eliade's concept. It is worthy of note that Paden's analysis supports Eliade's understanding of the ubiquity of religion by allowing that "the principle of individual rights in a secular society" may be "holy." From *Religion and Reductionism: Essays on Eliade, Segal, and the Challenge of the Social Sciences for the Study of Religion*, edited by Thomas A. Idinopulos and Edward Yonan, 198–210 (Leiden: E. J. Brill, 1994). All rights reserved. Copyright © 1994 by Brill Academic Publishers. Published by permission of Brill Academic Publishers and the author.

§ ৎ

We should also need to know what constitutes these sacred things ....
Here we have a group of phenomena which are irreducible to any other
group of phenomena. (Emile Durkheim "Concerning the Definition of
Religious Phenomena," 88)

Critics have objected that the concept of the sacred as used in Eliadean
phenomenology of religion is too theological and ontological to be
appropriate for modern religious studies.[1] They claim that the expression, "the
sacred," refers either implicitly or explicitly to an *a priori* religious reality—to
an object that is transcendent, mysterious, wholly other, unknowable, and
which therefore is not ultimately an object for analysis. Thus the linchpin
concept that once defined, unified, and inspired the history of religions field—
that to some extent gave it a reason for existing—appears now to divide it into
opposing camps. On the surface, the division seems to have something to do
with those who would imply some religious privilege for "the sacred" and
those who would like to abandon the term and its overtones.

Because much of the current debate about the irreducibility of religion is
epitomized in this question of discourse about the sacred, this essay examines
some of the pre-Eliadean uses of the term among the Durkheimians, exploring
how the question of irreducibility posed itself before "the sacred" became
reified, and then drawing some contemporary conclusions.

For Durkheim, "the sacred" is not synonymous with a transcendental, mysterious, unknowable object of religious experience. It is not a term for mystery,
power, force, or mana. It is not an object at all. It is certainly not divinity, nor is
it something that "manifests" itself. It is most certainly not the Wholly Other.

In fact, Durkheim primarily uses the term as an adjective, as in "sacred
things." Here it is not a term of revelation but an index of a system of behavior
and representation which follows its own rules.[2] Even apart from Durkheim's
sociological explanations, it is an intelligible category of description.

Yet it was not Durkheimian language which was to form the predominant
model of the sacred (or the holy) in modern religious studies. Rather, this was
anticipated through the work of those like the English anthropologist R. R.
Marett[3] and the Scandinavian religionists Nathan Soderblom and Edvard
Lehmann. Whether from the anthropological or theological side, these and
their descendants adopted "mana" as a prototype for "the sacred" or "the
holy," making such expressions synonyms for the supernatural object to which
religious behavior was the response. Thus Soderblom and Lehmann construed
religion as a set of patterned responses to "the holy" and had published works
on this by 1914,[4] before Otto's classic—forming a trajectory that was to become
the mainstream phenomenology of religion movement.

It is this second, object-oriented approach to the sacred that may be called
the theological or supernatural model, and might as well be called the "mana
model." In it the sacred is the name for the transcendent reality to which

religious experience points and to which it responds. This mana model is the one that has come under criticism.

The Durkheimian paradigm, though, sees the sacred not as a religious object but as a category of world classification and ritual behavior. And because Durkheim's *le sacré* belongs in a different theoretic universe than Otto's *das Heilige*, this has ramifications for interpreting Eliadean categories—which are under some debt to the French school—and for interpreting the reductionism issue generally.

Rereading Durkheim on the Sacred

It may be hard for historians of religion to read Durkheim with fresh eyes, without the religionist frames that have pigeon-holed him and dismissed him as a sociological reductionist. While everyone knows his definitions about the polarity of the sacred and the profane, few appear to have systematically analyzed his extended terminology on this or have identified the various linguistic and conceptual matrices in which he refers to *le sacré*. It is ironic that so many historians of religion have ignored the Durkheimian material, since it is precisely the French school that established the irreducibility of the category of the sacred and gave it such systematic elaboration.

To begin, it is important to distinguish two different and alternating discursive contexts in the *Elementary Forms*: the descriptive and the explanatory.[5] In the first, Durkheim is concerned to establish and describe the existence of religious facts or phenomena. Sacredness is such a fact. It is part of the special nature and structure of religious data, representation that is different in kind than other forms of valuations.

But it is at a second, causalistic level that Durkheim tries to *explain* the data of the sacred by exposing its origins in the chemistry of collective power and symbols.

Thus Durkheim's method is to first describe religion, and then explain it; first characterize religious beliefs and practices, and then show their origin; first depict sacredness as a phenomenon, and then account for it in terms of collective consciousness; first point to the nature of religious experience, and then "the reality at the bottom of the experience." While part of Durkheim's initial, formal definition is that religions are group affairs, at that early point in the book this is not yet in itself an explanation, only an ostensibly descriptive characterization. Only later in the argument will Durkheim explain how collective life is the actual source of religion. Likewise, in his first chapter on ritual (in Part III), Durkheim provides a systematic, in many ways phenomenological, account of the logic and dynamics of the sacred-profane relationship, with little mention of sociological concepts until the end of his analysis. The descriptive value of this material on the nature of incompatible worlds easily stands on its own, independent of his concluding attempts to explain asceticism in terms of the subordination of individuality to social ideals or to account for the "contagiousness" of sacredness in terms of the fluidity of collective imagination.

The 1898 treatise on sacrifice by Henri Hubert and Marcel Mauss had already created a prototype for analyzing the structure of a religious phenomenon prior to analyzing it sociologically.[6] The essay focused on the formal structure and processes of the ritual negotiation of sacred and profane realms, and only in the last three paragraphs did it add the suggestion that religious facts should ultimately be seen as social facts. Unlike the condescending approach of Frazerian rationalism, for Hubert and Mauss the realm of the sacred here and in other places becomes a range of material not to be dismissed as primitive but to be impartially respected and systematically investigated. Co-creators with Durkheim of the *Année* approach to the sacred,[7] they wrote in a time which antedated the split between the so-called phenomenology of religion and sociology, and certainly saw themselves as general students of the "science of religious phenomena." If the essay on sacrifice represents the first non-theological, systematic use of the concept of the sacred-profane as a polarity of worlds or symbolic domains,[8] a concept Durkheim later adopted, we should also note that the terms sacred and profane here are not intrinsically sociological and explanatory, but descriptive, structural, and even emic—obviously drawn *from* the grammar and vocabulary of religion (like the term sacrifice) and in turn reflecting its internal behaviors.

Elementary Forms of Durkheim's Concept of the Sacred

There are two facets of Durkheim's terminology to distinguish and consider here. In each, sacredness is understood as an irreducible factor in the description of religious life. In the first and widest usage, sacred objects are those that are separated from ordinary contact. In the second, "sacred and profane" are a reciprocal pair understood to represent the poles of either a separative or transformative process.

Sacred Things

By far the most prevalent use of the term "sacred" in the *Elementary Forms* is not as a noun but as an adjective—most typically in Durkheim's favorite expression, "sacred things," but also in "sacred objects," "sacred beings," or the "sacred character" of a thing. Such phrases constitute the vast majority of all occurrences of the term. These generic expressions underscore the point that the *nature* of the objects that are sacred is completely incidental to the fact *that* they are sacred *to* some group. That certain things are sacred to a culture is an accessible, visible, observation of behavior; the *content* of what is sacred is a

71

different matter and is "infinitely varied in relation to different periods of time and different societies ..." ("Concerning the Definition of Religious Phenomena," 87).

As early as this 1899 essay, Durkheim maintained that logically prior to any concept of gods is "a vast category of sacred things" which are the nuclear facts of religious life and thought (84–87). In his later, formal characterization of religion in the *Elementary Forms*, the first part of the definition still keeps this terminology, namely that a religion is "a unified system of beliefs and practices *relative to sacred things*, that is, things set apart and *forbidden*" (*Elementary Forms*, 62, italics added). This adjectival usage of the term is central and functions to some extent independently of Durkheim's other references to the polar, dichotomous nature of sacred and profane realms.[9] Every society has certain entities marked off with special respect and power, and religious thought and behavior construct themselves around these privileged foci. While not all religions have gods, all have systems of respect for what is sacred (52). The path of the monks in non-theistic Buddhism is holy ("the deliverance from suffering is a holy thing as is the whole of life which is a preparation for it," "Concerning the Definition of Religious Phenomena," 87), so is a humble totemic emblem, and so may be the principle of individual rights in a secular society. The mark of what is sacred is the inviolability that surrounds it and protects its profanization, and it could easily be shown that Durkheim built his concept of sacredness largely out of the notion of taboo.[10]

Here sacredness has no content of its own. It is purely relational. It is what is not to be profaned. As such, the term is metaphysically neutral. There is no ontological referent, nor are there dismissive rationalist insinuations or inflative romantic agendas. The sacred is simply whatever is *deemed* sacred by any group.

Now if sacredness is a value placed *on* objects rather than a power that shines *through* objects because of their intrinsic, extraordinary qualities, then the difference between this aspect of the Durkheimian approach and the theological model here could not be greater. The classical, religionist model was interested in *kinds* of objects that mediate the sacred by virtue of their inherent form or the inherentness of the supernatural in that form. Thus the typical format of phenomenologies of religion is presented as an encyclopedic hierarchy of levels of objects, grouped first according to patterns in nature, e.g. sky, earth, trees, or stones, and then "higher" forms like gods. Places, objects, and times were understood as "expressions" of the holy or the supernatural. In essence, sacred things in this second model are sacred because they are modes or symbols of divinity, or in the older language, forms of "apprehending the Infinite"— and not because they have been "made" inviolable by the projected values of a group.

Even when Durkheim maintains the connection of sacrality and collective, totemic objects, we are in many ways still in the realm of description rather than explanation. When Durkheim says that the totemic symbol is "the very type of sacred thing" and that "it is in connection with it, that things are classified as sacred or profane" (*Elementary Forms*, 140), and when he presents the *churinga* as a prime example of sacredness, he is still analyzing sacredness descriptively as a socioreligious fact rather than causally as a social product (which he will of course go on to do). One does not have to be a sociologist to make the observation that among the kinds of things that humans deem sacred, those that specifically represent collective identity are especially representative.[11] It is an observation about where sacredness is most intensely focused.

Finally, once one has identified the existence of sacred things and the behaviors that go with them, then a basis for comparative differentiation between their contents becomes meaningful. The differences will be definable in terms of the varying cultural or religious ideals embodied in them, and Durkheim was clearly interested in the changing history of such values, just as historians of religion are.

So here is Durkheim's elementary, and one might even say, commonsense, use of the adjective "sacred."

Sacred-Profane as a Polarity

The second Durkheimian vocabulary about sacrality posits the polar, interdependent relationship of sacred and profane states.

Critics have rightly challenged those initial statements of Durkheim's that define sacred and profane as exclusive realms.[12] But the bulk of the *Elementary Forms* shows that there is more to this notorious dichotomy than just a static system of classification. As Steven Lukes points out, the confusion comes partly from Durkheim not having clearly distinguished between the sacred and the profane as 1) classes of *things* or *realms*, and 2) as relationships *to* things (27). Certainly Durkheim's characterization that religious phenomena "always suppose a bipartite division of the whole universe ... into two classes which embrace all that exists, but which radically exclude each other" (*Elementary Forms*, 56), *can* be read to imply that he is speaking of sacred and profane as fixed properties of objects. Yet throughout his book, Durkheim himself subverts his own assertions that religious worlds are forever divided by watertight dualities, showing that the profane state is subject to transformation. The profane can become sacred through rite and religious practice. Objects remain profane *only* as long as they have not been "metamorphosed" by "the religious imagination," and society can "constantly create sacred things out of ordinary ones" (243). Sacred and profane are ultimately relative to shifting situations.

This is worked out in Book Three of the *Elementary Forms* and its first chapter on ritual.[13] Here we find direct development of the concept of sacralization that was analyzed in the Hubert and Mauss essay on sacrifice, where the sacred and profane were described as two worlds that it was the purpose of sacrifice to mediate, and where the devotee's ordinary, profane condition was shown to be transformed in the process. In this section Durkheim shows how the sacred-profane opposition is not just an exclusionary, static distancing but the basis of religious passage or "modification" that takes place by way of the deprofanizing of the participant. The "profane," here, is not an independent force in its own right but whatever is incompatible relative to the sacred.

Durkheim thus begins to stretch the concept of taboo into the larger notion of relative incompatibility. Sacred and profane states cannot coexist *at the same time.* From an understanding of this incongruity, not from sociological analysis, he describes the rationale for the religious phenomena of sacred time and space, abstentions of all kinds, initiations and all systems of asceticism, renunciation, and spiritual discipline. In Durkheim's hands interdiction ceases to represent savage ignorance or negative magic and becomes what could be called a basic system of religious logic. Because of their sacredness, some things—whether foods or secret knowledge—are forbidden to the profane person; but by the same token, some things because of their profaneness are forbidden to persons of sacred character. It works both ways. By construing the "forbidden" to mean "incompatible with" Durkheim has pointed the way to the study of the relativity of purity and impurity within a system, as exemplified in Mary Douglas's *Purity and Danger* (1966).

The act of de-profanizing, which takes innumerable religious forms, is dispassionately spelled out in a way that is descriptively respectful of the nature of traditional religious behaviors. Going well beyond his Australian material, Durkheim clarifies a differentiating process or tension that is at the heart of religious life, and his vocabulary here is unreservedly emic. For example, "A man cannot approach his god intimately while he still bears on him marks of his profane life" (*Elementary Forms,* 346). A system governed by the sacred-profane dynamic

> ... does not confine itself to protecting sacred beings from vulgar contact; it acts upon the worshipper himself and modifies his condition positively. The man who has submitted himself to its prescribed interdictions is not the same afterwards as he was before. Before, he was an ordinary being who, for this reason, had to keep at a distance from the religious forces. Afterwards, he is on more equal footing with them; he has approached the sacred by the very act of leaving the profane; he has purified and sanctified himself by the very act of detaching himself from the base and trivial matters that debased his nature. (348)

So in spite of the language about an absolute conceptual duality, a main purpose of religion, by Durkheim's admission, is actually to *overcome* the dualism through metamorphosis, sanctification, renunciation, or even "the sanctifying power" of suffering that "ennobles the soul" (350–55). Durkheim dwells on general examples of asceticism to illustrate the idea that holiness is the systematic rooting out of attachment to the profane world, as with Buddhist saints whose "sanctity" makes them "equal or superior to the gods."[14]

This is a long way from construing the sacred-profane dichotomy simply as a wooden assertion that all religious people somehow believe the universe to be statically divided or rigidly classified in two and only two parts. Anthropologists have of course found no such thing. Yet sacred life as described by Durkheim is not just a representation, but a costly act of passage.

Analysis and Implications

I am not advocating that the concept of the sacred is the only resource for describing and understanding religion, or that it does not have its own liabilities, but only that the term is not necessarily an ontologically privileged category. The French school created a secular discourse about sacredness, yet because of the subsequent anthropological taboo on talking about this category, the quarry has gone mostly unexploited. The term "sacred" here attempts to demark a range of behavioral phenomena; it is an etic category suffused not with metaphysical but with emic grounding and resonance. Where it does not fit the data, the concept should of course be reshaped. Where Durkheim is empirically challengeable, his inaccuracies do not take away from the point that his intention was to be descriptive.

And yet there is something missing from the discussion so far, for isn't Durkheim the great reductionist?

The Question of Explanatory Reductions

I have deliberately bracketed off what to Durkheim was the most important fact about sacredness: that it is an expression of collective power and should ultimately be explained in sociological terms. This was a legitimate theoretical move that can be argued philosophically,[15] but represents a shift in level of discourse. It does not deny the fact that Durkheim has first, on another level, presented a set of data about sacrality. The famous reducer just happens to have been the one to have given us a phenomenology of the irreducible character of the sacred penultimate to his ultimate act of explanatory reduction.

Now what Durkheim as sociologue took as the *source* and ultimate *content* of *le sacré* is what the religious, theological phenomenologies call "the sacred" or "the holy." Durkheim did not do what Marett was beginning to do across the channel and what the phenomenologists (whether of the history of religions or the theological variety) were about to do, namely use the term "sacred" to refer to the object of religion. After all, the sacred was what Durkheim was trying to *explain*—and hence the reasoning would be circular. The animism and naturism hypotheses could not explain sacredness, but the totemism theory could. Collective force, the totemic principle, is what grounded sacrality. Yet Durkheim did not nominally or semantically identify "the sacred" with this force that he so passionately believed lay behind it. Rather, it is this force, or mana, that gives things their sacred character.[16]

While Durkheim could not resist calling the object of religion "society," neither could the religionists resist calling the object of religion "the sacred," a gloss for the supernatural. Neither the Durkheimians nor the religionists could face the data of sacrality without an act of metaphysical reduction.

By the same token, religious life for both a Durkheim and an Otto had a *sui generis* character. Durkheim used the expression repeatedly, especially where he was speaking of religion as a collective form, but also where he was describing the realm of the sacred as distinguished from the realm of the profane or ordinary. Both interpreters tried to show that the sacred was not just explainable in psychological categories, that it has its own mode of experience. To Durkheim, the unique character of religion obviously derived from the unique power collective authority has over individuals, a power that lifted individuals outside themselves and transported them into another realm than that of their profane existence, giving them a higher, more intensive life.

In addition, we should recall that for the Durkheimians the assertion that religion (or the sacred) is social did not mean that religion (or the sacred) was not real, or that it was not religious. To reduce religion to the social was in fact to ground it in reality, as over against rationalist theories that treated religion as a conceptual illusion and as over against theological theories that made the ultimate character of religious life inaccessible and transcendental. Everything that Durkheim says about the *sui generis* character of social reality[17] can be said about religious worlds, since for the French school religious worlds *are* social expressions. The worlds of collective symbols (such as religious worlds), "once born, obey laws all their own" (*Elementary Forms*, 471).

The battle for explanatory supremacy (e.g. what does sacredness "mean" either in general or in any particular culture?) will obviously go on, and it is unavoidable that one's descriptive references to the sacred will still be governed by principles of selection related either to one's own foundationalist groundings, or, in postmodern terms, one's conversational circles. In many cases the latter will involve pedagogical situations which deal with trying to comprehend cross-cultural materials, and it is here where the analytical, neutral approach to the sacred will probably continue to have some use. In contemporary contexts, questions about the nature of sacredness will most likely have to do with a) accuracy in relation to specific cultural data, b) the possibility of descriptive limitation or distortion due to explanatory (or hermeneutical) weightings, c) the appropriateness or relativity of hermeneutical discourse and reductivity to audience purposes, and d) the historicity of the concept itself.

Some Implications

Without elaborating, certain consequences seem to emerge.

First, there emerges the possibility of a middle, descriptive way that does not require taking the object of religion linguistically or hermeneutically captive by either the theological or sociological reduction. A careful phenomenology of sacredness, geared to understanding and depicting the worlds of religious insiders, could analyze ways that cultures negotiate sacrality and profanity, and do this without implying anything about "the Sacred" as a metaphysical referent. Within a comparative, cross-cultural context, this level of analysis would examine religious systems without assuming them to be either right or wrong, and sacrality and profanity (or purity and impurity) could be explored as variables between and within such systems. Sacredness would not be reduced to a single phenomenology of otherness or taboo, but would be examined for the many ways, subtle or otherwise, that it is constituted in human behavior. For example, it is not only *numen*, forceful to the subject, but *sacer*, set apart by the subject as inviolate.[18] It appears not only as "the extraordinary" but as the integrity and transformation of boundaries, the monitoring of the boundaries of culturally and religiously constituted profaneness.

In such an approach there is the possibility of a metaphysically neutral but theoretic, integral, phenomenology of sacredness that seeks descriptive justice to its various subject-object relationships. Each form of cultural activity (e.g., music, dance, science) has its own way of positing the world, and the sacred-profane dynamic is no exception.

Finally, uncovering the pre-theological and even asociological structures of Durkheim's concept of the sacred will make it easier to detect them in Eliade, and easier to sort out the juxtaposition of neo-Durkheimian and perennialist elements in that author's complex and syncretic discourse. Because of the influence of French social anthropology on Eliade, rereading the one figure to some extent requires rereading the other, and it seems to me that much in Eliade should be understood as continuous with the wider Durkheimian tradition as conveyed in the versions of Mauss and Roger Caillois.[19] While that genealogy or French connection is apparently a task yet to be worked out, I am convinced that until it is done we will make little progress in understanding in any other than a hermeneutically preferentialist way the several linguistic matrices of Eliade's notion of "the sacred," or the context of his often-quoted statements about its irreducibility.

Long before Eliade, after all, it was the Durkheimians who spoke of the heterogeneity of sacred and profane modes of existence, of sacred time and space, and of how the sacred requires "dying to the profane condition." And it was they who labored to establish the way sacrality constructed worlds, worlds created out of the stuff of myth and ritual; and it was they for whom religious phenomena had to be taken as facts at their own irreducible level.

The "sacred" is a term of some value in looking at how religious systems maintain their integrity, deal with profanity, and provide transcendence, and our vocabulary for exegeting the history and structure of religious worlds would probably be diminished without it. Perhaps it is a modest value, and perhaps there is less need now to overrate or overuse it. But in spite of our proclivities toward epistemic imperialism, in spite of our needs for hermeneutical loadings, it is not clear that the word must infiltrate an ontology of either the theological or sociological kind.

Notes

* The first version of this essay was presented at a panel for the History of the Study of Religion group at the annual meeting of the American Academy of Religion in New Orleans, November, 1990, and subsequently was published in *Method and Theory in the Study of Religion* 3.1 (Fall, 1991).

1. For example, Hans H. Penner, *Impasse and Resolution*, ch. 1; and Robert A. Segal, *Religion and the Social Sciences*.

2. Ian Hamnett notes that Durkheim's work anticipated structuralist approaches to "systems of symbols." See his "Durkheim and the Study of Religion," in *Durkheim and Modern Sociology*, ed. Steve Fenton (Cambridge: Cambridge University Press, 1984), 202–19. From a different viewpoint, arguing the need to investigate the "sacred" as a behavioral phenomenon is W. Richard Comstock, "A Behavioral Approach to the Sacred: Category Formation in Religious Studies," in *Journal of the American Academy of Religion* XLIX/4 (December, 1981): 625–43. Comstock rightly maintains that Durkheim's sacred/profane distinction refers more to the regulation of behavior than to a metaphysical dualism.

3. See especially Marett's *The Threshold of Religion,* first published in 1909 (though containing some earlier essays) and then in successive editions; and his *Encyclopedia Britannica* article of 1908 on "Religion-Primitive Religion." In these writings Marett apparently becomes the first major figure outside the French school (whose influence he acknowledges) to refer to "the sacred" as the generic object of religion.

4. Nathan Soderblom, *Gudstrons Uppkomst* (The Origins of Religion) (Stockholm: Sebers, 1914), and also his "Holiness (General and Primitive)," in J. Hastings, ed., *Encyclopedia of Religion and Ethics,* VI (1913), 731–41; and Edvard Lehmann's Swedish language textbook on the "science of religion," *Religionsvetenskagen, I: Inledning till Reliaionsvetenskapen* (Stockholm, 1914).

5. I use this distinction here in a way that is parallel to that of Wayne Proudfoot's, but somewhat broader. Cf. his *Religious Experience* (Berkeley: University of California Press, 1985), 196–98.

6. Henri Hubert and Marcel Mauss, *Sacrifice: Its Nature and Function,* trans. W.D. Halls (Chicago: University of Chicago Press, 1964).

7. The significant contribution of Mauss and Hubert to Durkheim's concept of the sacred is carefully reviewed and assessed in François-A. Isambert, "L'elaboration de la notion de sacré dans "l'École Durkheimienne," *Archives de Sciences Sociales des Religions* 42 (1976): 35–56.

8. It should be noted that W. Robertson Smith had used the phrase in his *The Religion of the Semites,* though not as systematically as the Durkheimians. Smith did develop a terminology about "holiness" as the concept that governs the ways gods and humans relate, and referred to holy (or sacred) places, times, persons, and so on, in a way that anticipated and

no doubt influenced later phenomenological vocabularies (cf. 140ff.). Durkheimian language about the sacred was essentially continuous with Smith's, suggesting again that sacrality presents itself here in a phenomenological, descriptive mode and spirit and not just as a causalistic reduction.

9. I find W. S. F. Pickering's analysis supportive on this point. Pickering sees that the concept of the sacred, taken by itself, has considerable use and validity apart from the difficulties summoned up in the idea of an absolute sacred-profane dichotomy. See his *Durkheim's Sociology of Religion: Themes and Theories* (London: Routledge and Kegan Paul, 1984), 149ff.

10. Durkheim could have chosen from many possible models to build his concept of the sacred, but following Frazer and Smith stuck to the notion of taboo and interdiction. It would be interesting to speculate what the *Elementary Forms* might have become if Durkheim had made bonding or loyalty his models, or had even fully pursued his earlier concept that religiousness is about "obligation." Moreover, when he comes to the phenomenon of collective effervescence as the typical sacred moment, Durkheim seems to really mix his schemas, as nothing could be further from taboo.

11. Recall that Durkheim's teacher, Fustel de Coulanges, had drawn attention to the sacredness of hearth fires, domestic and national altars, and tombs. See his *The Ancient City*, trans. Willard Small (Boston: Lee and Shepard, 1874).

12. See, for example, criticisms of the concept by W. E. H. Stanner in "Reflections on Durkheim and Aboriginal Religion," in *Social Organization: Essays Presented to Raymond Firth*, ed. Maurice Freedman, 217–40 (London: Frank Cass and Co., 1967); and W. S. F. Pickering's summary of the issues in *Durkheim's Sociology of Religion*, chs. 7 and 8.

13. Particularly the first two parts of the chapter, 337–56.

14. Even in earlier writings Durkheim had shown a fascination for the renunciative power of the oriental holy man and had noted the mystical capacity to abandon "the ephemeral multiplicity of things" in order to find a holy reality within through meditation. See "Concerning the Definition of Religious Phenomena," 82–83.

15. This point is consonant with Proudfoot's distinction that *explanatory reductions* are free to differ from the insider's viewpoint, whereas *descriptive reductions* are accountable to being corrected if they skew or omit important facts about religious experience.

16. *Elementary Forms*, 229. In this sense, Durkheim too employed a "mana model," but for him it was not a model for the sacred as much as it was an illustration of the religious force of society.

17. For many references to the *sui generis* character of social facts see Durkheim, *The Rules of Sociological Method*, ed. Steven Lukes, trans. W. D. Halls (New York: The Free Press, 1982).

18. The bipolarity is a distinction which corresponds to what linguists like Emile Benveniste find to be two distinct kinds of words for the sacred in Indo-European languages. The one is the "negative" type, referring to that which is forbidden or consecrated and the other is the "positive" type, referring to that which is filled with divine presence, e.g. *weihen* and *hell*, *sacer* and *sanctus*, *yaozdata* and *spenta*, *hagios* and *hieros*. See *Indo-European Language and Society*, trans. Elizabeth Palmer (London: Faber and Faber, 1973), 445ff.

19. For example, the influence of Roger Caillois's neo-Durkheimian synthesis, *L'Homme et le Sacre* (1939) [English version: *Man and the Sacred*, trans. Meyer Barash (Glencoe, Ill.: The Free Press, 1959)] *is* impressive, and anyone who thinks Eliade's notion of the sacred is closer to Otto than the French social anthropologists should reread it. Eliade's *The Sacred and the Profane* (1956) appears to draw liberally from Caillois's approach. For example, here are points Caillois refers to just in the first thirty-two pages: 1) the sacred is defined simply as the opposite of the profane; 2) Otto's book is mentioned appreciatively but is said not to have gone far enough; 3) the distinction of real-unreal is made; 4) it is announced that

the book will isolate several constants in man's attitude toward the sacred; 5) "religious man" is referred to as a generic phrase; 6) the profane world is compared to the sacred "as nothingness is to being;" 7) the sacred is said to be "always more or less what one cannot approach without dying;" 8) the primordial state of chaos, fluidity, and license prior to creation is described; as are 9) the concept of the establishment of order by the ancestors; 10) periodic regeneration; and 11) "it is not merely the individual's mind that is fascinated by the sacred, but all of his being." Caillois existentializes the Durkheimians, whose work he attempts to summarize. More than them, though, he uses "the sacred" as a noun and as the object of religion, indeed as a force that alternatively preserves and dissolves life, inhibits and transgresses—allowing Caillois to speak loosely of "metaphysics of the sacred" that involves the polarity of stability and variation, matter and energy (136–38).

8

THE ONTOLOGY OF THE SACRED

Bryan Rennie

Editor's Introduction

ဢ ၄

What status *does* Eliade afford to the sacred and how do his assumptions affect the coherence and credibility of his thought? In 1982 Antonio Barbosa da Silva analyzed Eliade's sacred as a phenomenological term and as an ontological term (*Phenomenology as a Philosophical Problem*, 175). I am broadly in agreement with Barbosa da Silva's evaluation of the sacred as a phenomenological term. However, I take issue with his analysis of the sacred as an ontological term. Even as "the cosmos as a whole" and the "Ur-datum of Eliade's creative hermeneutics" one must question to what degree the sacred is given a necessary and independent ontology. As the cosmos as a whole it is undoubtedly true that Eliade regards every minute element of cosmic existence as capable of revealing the sacred, as sacralizable, as potentially and inherently sacred, and thus as "real," simply because it exists. The sacred is disclosed in the manifest realm of historical being, in the existential world of historical time and physical space, which itself is ontological. To this extent it unquestionably partakes of the characteristic of being.

Similarly with the sacred as the ur-datum, the presuppositional given of Eliade's hermeneutics, this notion of the sacred is adjectival rather than substantial. It should be remembered that only after Durkheim's usage of the term as a noun was it commonly employed in this way. In Eliade's use it evidently refers to a mode of experience, "a structure of the human consciousness" (*Quest* i; *No Souvenirs* 1; *History of Religious Ideas*, vol. I, xiii; "The Sacred in the Secular World," above, 67), a *relationship* with the real, rather than the real itself. It is the very fact that the sacred as the real is perceived in so many modes, and that we carry our own inner certainty as to what is and is not "real" that permits, in fact positively encourages, so many varied interpretations of Eliade's thought and generates the almost unavoidable impression that he is describing an autonomous, independent ontology. However, detailed analysis without any prior assumption as to the referent of the sacred reveals that the sacred does not occur in Eliade's writings in any context independently of human perception. It is always presented as occurring in and through the act of its perception. It is always presented as an intentional object, without the question of its pure or proper intentionality actually being raised.

Again, this is by no means to *deny* its autonomy, but in the familiar Kantian structure of the noumenal/phenomenal dichotomy, it insists that the sacred is accessible *only* through its manifestations in historical forms. The function of the historian of religions is presumed to be the study of the historical manifestations of the sacred, which exist exclusively (for the historian of religions *qua* historian of religions) in those historical manifestations. For the committed religious believer the sacred might also be held to exist as an element of immediate experience, but that experience *per se* is the object of mystical theology. The *expression* of that experience as a historical datum is the proper object of the history of religions.

To affirm as a given the independent ontology of the sacred as it is described by any individual, group, or tradition is to step immediately beyond the bounds of the study of religion into the practice of a particular religion. This Eliade does not do. However, the temptation to read Eliade as doing precisely that is enormous because of the language which he employs, identifying the sacred as the real. Yet the fact is that he does not seem to conceive of sacrality independent of the act of its perception, leaving the sacred as a potential of human experience, *possibly* an abstract idea, but one which is nevertheless ubiquitous and unimaginably significant throughout human history.

Barbosa da Silva asks whether a sacred object "*really* possesses some intrinsic properties which constitute a necessary condition for the sacredness of [that object] or not." He concludes that this must be the case as far as Eliade is concerned. He specifically rejects the interpretation that "'sacred' means the same as that there is a religious person [who] ... perceives [some object] as sacred"

(179), on the grounds that the necessary condition for the perception of any object as sacred is that the object possesses some intrinsic property which evokes or causes the numinous experience (180). This leads further into the conviction that Eliade attributes some necessary independence to sacrality as a manifest property of sacred objects. However, both interpretations can be reconciled when it is realized that the only *necessary* inherent property that an object must possess in order to be sacralizable is *existence*, its own objecthood. "All nature is capable of revealing itself as cosmic sacrality" (*The Sacred and the Profane*, 12; above, 19). Further, there is no inherent property which is a *sufficient* condition to evoke numinous experience to any and all religious people. Thus there need be no identifiable "inherent property" (apart from the fundamental one of existence) in the sacred object which could be equated with an ontologically independent sacrality. Thus the rejection of the former interpretation is not necessitated; the fact that an object exists and is perceived as sacred *is* the necessary and sufficient condition for its sacrality in Eliade's terms. The perception of the sacred *qua* the real (and the real *qua* the sacred) is the primary characteristic of *homo religiosus*, humanity in the religious mode.

Of course this does, as Barbosa da Silva recognizes, leave the problem of "how to prove that the numinous experience is not an exclusive product of man's mind. If it is so, and if it has only a purely intended object, it can be regarded as a merely subjective experience" (182). I would suggest that the lack of "proof" of the independent existence of the sacred as the source of numinous experience is firstly itself characteristic of Eliade's self-imposed restriction to the history of religions as eschewing personal theological statements. It is thus evidence that Eliade does not insist on the sacred as a specific autonomous ontological entity, although his methodical openness to that possibility permits the alternative interpretation. Second, this lack of proof is completely consistent with his morphology of religious history in which the sacred can only be manifest in historical actualities. Since it cannot otherwise be manifest, that is it cannot otherwise be experienced, it is not susceptible of proof either logically or empirically. The direct experience of believers is not itself communicable, and their subsequent expressions are always and necessarily historical and conditioned and thus proof of nothing but an experience whose intentionality cannot be established unless it be shared.

Barbosa da Silva has already accepted that "whether it [religious experience of the Divine Being as meta-cosmic reality] has a proper intentional object is a very controversial question into which we cannot go here" (70). He has made precisely the same evasion of the theological problem of the pure or proper intentionality of numinous experience as I insist that Eliade does. Yet he accuses Eliade both of assuming the proper intentionality of the sacred and of failing to provide any proof for this assumption. My point is that Eliade does not provide any proof for this assumption because he does not make it.

Hierophany

9

Hierophany

Mircea Eliade and Lawrence Sullivan

Editor's Introduction

Second only in importance to the concept of the sacred itself in Eliade's understanding of religion is the phenomenal event in which the sacred is apprehended as manifest—the hierophany. Written by Mircea Eliade and Lawrence Sullivan, this explanation of hierophany states directly and with examples what hierophany is taken to be and provides a more nuanced understanding, including the subdivisions of theophany and kratophany. However, also revealed is a potential confusion and source of variation in the interpretation of Eliadean categories. While the language permits the active role of the sacred in its own manifestation ("in making itself manifest, the sacred limits itself"), the fact that it is also said to be "made manifest" permits the interpretation of the sacred as the intentional object of human apprehension. The article also raises the issue of our next element of Eliade's thought: the dialectic of the sacred and the profane and so provides an introduction to that section. It is taken from the first edition of the Macmillan *Encyclopedia of Religion*, vol. VI, 313, edited by Mircea Eliade. All rights reserved. Copyright © 1987 by the Gale Group. Reprinted by permission of the Gale Group.

80 CR

Frorom Greek *hiero-*, "sacred," and *phainein*, "to show," is a term designating the manifestation of the sacred. The term involves no further specification. Herein lies its advantage: it refers to any manifestation of the sacred in whatever object throughout history. Whether the sacred appear in a stone, a tree, or an incarnate human being, a hierophany denotes the same act: a reality of an entirely different order than those of this world becomes manifest in an object that is part of the natural or profane sphere.

The sacred manifests itself as a power or force that is quite different from the forces of nature. A sacred tree, for instance, is not worshiped for being a tree. Neither is a sacred stone adored, in and of itself, for its natural properties as a stone. These objects become the focus of religious veneration because they are hierophanies, revealing something that is no longer botanical or geological, but "wholly other."

Forms of Hierophany

The forms of hierophanies vary from one culture to another. The matter is complicated for, throughout the course of history, cultures have recognized hierophanies everywhere in psychological, economic, spiritual, and social life. There is hardly any object, action, psychological function, species of being, or even entertainment that has not become a hierophany at some time. Whatever humans come in contact with can be transformed into a hierophany. Musical instruments, architectural forms, beasts of burden, and vehicles of transportation have all been sacred objects. In the right circumstances, any material object whatever can become a hierophany.

The appearance of the sacred in a hierophany, however, does not eliminate its profane existence. In every religious context some objects in the class of things that convey the sacred (e.g., stone, trees, human beings) always remain profane. No single culture contains within its history all the possible hierophanies. In other words, a hierophany always implies a singling-out. Not all stones are held to be sacred in a culture; only some are venerated, or one, because their properties make them fitting vehicles of the sacred. A hierophany separates the thing that manifests the sacred from everything else around it, from all that remains profane.

The sacred appears in cosmic form as well as in the imaginative life of human beings. Cosmic hierophanies cover the spectrum of cosmic structures. Supreme gods of the sky, such as Num, the sky divinity of the Samoyeds, or Anu, the Babylonian *shar shame* ("sky king"), reflect or share the sacredness attributed to the sky. So do the sovereign gods of the sky who display their power through storm, thunder, and lightning, such as the Greek god Zeus, his Roman counterpart Jupiter, and Yahveh, the Hebrew supreme being.

The sacredness of the earth is an important source of hierophany. Worship of Pachamama, mother goddess of the earth, is an ancient and widespread phenomenon in the South American Andes. Local soil is a sacred presence in countless cultures around the globe. The earth is often an important character in myths about the earliest times of creation. Such is the role of Papa ("earth") in Maori creation accounts and of Gaia in the Greek myths presented by Hesiod. Frequently the earth, as a hierophany of sacred being, appears as the creative partner of a heavenly being. Such a divine couple, deified sky and earth, figured prominently in the mythologies of Oceania, Micronesia, Africa, and the Americas.

The sun became a powerful manifestation of the sacred in central Mexico (among the Mixtec), in the Peruvian Andes (among the Inca), in ancient Egypt, and elsewhere. Furthermore, important cultural heroes who figure largely in the mythic history of various societies (e.g., among the Maasai of Africa, the Turco-Mongols, and Indo-Europeans) often have essential ties to the sun's powers.

In many cultures, the fertility of animals and plants is presided over by the sacredness of the moon. Above all others, the hierophanies of the moon convey the sacredness of life's rhythms: rainy seasons, ocean tides, sowing times, the menstrual cycle. Among Pygmy groups of central Africa, for instance, the moon, called Pe, is the fecund source of new life. Women celebrate her sacredness with drinking and dancing feasts held at the time of the new moon. Through the metamorphosis it undergoes each month, the moon displays its powers of immortality and its ability to regenerate a form of life that even includes the experience of death. Women and snakes become epiphanies of the moon's sacred power through their periodic loss of life in the form of blood and skin. Menstruation sometimes is perceived not only as a shedding of blood but as a shedding of the "skin" that lines the uterus each month or of the "skin" that envelops the body of a new child if conception occurs that month. Snakes are sometimes thought to shed not only skin but also "blood": snake venom is viewed as a species of blood that is "shed" (that is, transmitted from fang to victim) when a snake bites its prey or when venom is consumed in festival brew.

Human physiology itself can become a manifestation of the sacred. Divine kings and the mystical bodies of shamans, transformed by their contact with sacred realities, can themselves become transparent vehicles of sacred powers. Even the breath, soul, blood, pulse, semen, and body warmth of ordinary human beings can be seen as signs of the presence of supernatural forces. In certain yogic traditions, for example, a woman embodies *prakrti*, the eternal source and limitless creative power of nature. The ritual nakedness of this *yogini* makes possible the revelation of a cosmic mystery.

Ordinary items such as roots, herbs, and foods may also manifest the sacred in one tradition or another, as may manufactured items, such as swords, ropes, and puppets. Techniques and skills themselves, the processes of manufacture, reveal sacred powers. Ironworking, spinning, and weaving are frequently sacred activities, carried on by consecrated persons in holy places and periods.

The cosmogonic myths of tribal peoples, the Brahmanic tradition of South Asia, the mystical writings of Nichiren and Teresa of Avila, the enthronement ceremonies of the king in ancient Babylon, the agricultural festivals of Japan, the ritual costumes of dancing shamans in Siberia, the symbolic fixtures of the Borobudur stupa, and initiation rites in various traditions are all hierophanies. They express some modality of the sacred and some moment in its history. Each one of these hierophanies reveals an aspect of the sacred as well as a historical attitude that humans have taken toward the sacred.

Structure and Dialectic of the Sacred

At the most general level of analysis, there exists a structure common to all hierophanies. Whenever the sacred is manifest, it limits itself. Its appearance forms part of a dialectic that occults other possibilities. By appearing in the concrete form of a rock, plant, or incarnate being, the sacred ceases to be absolute, for the object in which it appears remains a part of the worldly environment. In some respect, each hierophany expresses an incomprehensible paradox arising from the great mystery upon which every hierophany is centered: the very fact that the sacred is made manifest at all.

This characteristic structure of manifestation and limitation is common to all hierophanies. The dialectic of appearance and occultation of the sacred becomes a key to understanding religious experience. Once all hierophanies are understood as equivalent in this fundamental respect, two helpful starting points can be found for the study of religious experience. In the first place, all appearances of the sacred, whether sublime or simple, can be seen in terms of the same dialectic of the sacred. In the second place, the entire religious life of humankind is placed on a common footing. Rich and diverse as it is, the religious history of human life evidences no essential discontinuity. The same paradox underlies every hierophany: in making itself manifest, the sacred limits itself.

Theophany and Kratophany

Although *hierophany* is an inclusive term, one can distinguish different types of hierophany. They depend on the form in which the sacred appears, and the meaning with which the sacred imbues the form. In some instances, a hierophany reveals the presence of a divinity. That is, the hierophany is a theophany, the appearance of a god. Theophanies differ widely from one another in form and meaning, depending upon the nature of the divine form appearing in them. A glance at the gods in the pantheon of South Asian mythology or in Aztec mythology shows that divinities can differ markedly in revealing various divine forms of the sacred, even within the same culture. Needless to say, theophanies from different cultures (e.g., Baal, the storm god of the ancient Semites; Viracocha, the creator god of the Inca; and Amaterasu, the Japanese deity of the sun and ancestress of the imperial line) manifest quite different modalities of the sacred. In the form of divine persons, theophanies reveal the distinct religious values of organic life, cosmic order, or the elementary forces of blood and fertility, as well as of purer and more sublime aspects.

A second type of hierophany may be termed a kratophany, a manifestation of power. Kratophanies preserve the sacred in all its ambivalence, both attracting and repelling with its brute power. The unusual, the new, and the strange frequently function as kratophanies. These things, persons, or places can be dangerous and defiling as well as sacred. Corpses, criminals, and the sick often function as kratophanies. Human beings in powerful or ambivalent circumstances (such as women in menses, soldiers, hunters, kings with absolute power, or executioners) are hedged around with taboos and restrictions. People approach sacred foods with etiquette and manners designed to ward off defilement, sickness, and pollution. The precautions that surround saints, sacrificers, and healers stem from fear of confronting the sacred. Kratophanies emphasize the extent to which the manifestation of the sacred intrudes on the order of things. Kratophanies also bring out the contradictory attitude displayed by human beings in regard to all that is sacred. On the one hand, contact with hierophanies secures, renews, and strengthens one's own reality. On the other hand, total immersion in the sacred (or an improper encounter with it) annihilates one's profane existence, an essential dimension of life.

In any case, a hierophany (whether in the form of a theophany or kratophany) reveals the power, the force, and the holiness of the sacred. Even the forces of nature are revered for their power to sanctify life; that is, to make fertility holy. The forces of nature that appear in divine forms or in certain objects make reproductive life partake of the unbounded power and plenty of the sacred.

Impact on Space and Time

Hierophanies directly affect the situation of human existence, the condition by which humans understand their own nature and grasp their destiny. For example, hierophanies alter the fundamental structures of space and time. Every hierophany transforms the place in which it appears, so that a profane place becomes a sacred precinct. For Aboriginal peoples of Australia, for example, the landscape of their native lands is alive. Its smallest details are charged with the meanings revealed in myth. Because the sacred first appeared in those places (to guarantee a food supply and to teach humans how to feed themselves), they become an inexhaustible source of power and sacrality. Humans can return to these places in each generation, to commune with the power that has revealed itself there. In fact, the Aboriginal peoples express a religious need to remain in direct contact with those sites that are hierophanic. One may say that the hierophany, connected with the transformed place of its appearance, is capable of repeating itself. The conviction is widespread that hierophanies recur in a place where the sacred has once appeared. This explains why human habitations and cities are constructed near sanctuaries. Ceremonies of consecration, ground-breaking, or foundation-laying for temples, shrines, sacred cities, capitals, and even bridges and houses, frequently repeat or echo acts of fundamental hierophanies, such as the creation of the world. At times they even provoke a sign indicating the location of a hierophany (e.g., the release of an animal and the sacrifice of it on the spot where it is later found; or geomancy). These rituals of foundation and construction ensure that the site will perpetuate the presence of a hierophany that first appeared within the bounds of a similarly structured location and event. The precincts for festival and ceremony are frequently consecrated for the occasion in this way. Thus, for example, the Yuin, the Wiradjuri, and the Kamilaroi, Aboriginal groups of Australia, prepare a sacred ground for their initiation ceremonies. The ground represents the camp of Baiame, the supreme being.

Hierophanies also transform time. A hierophany marks a breakthrough from profane to magico-religious time. Just as spaces sacralized by a hierophany may be reconstructed through acts of consecration, so the acts of hierophany are repeated in the sacred calendar of each year. Rituals that repeat the moment of a hierophany recreate the conditions of the world in which the sacred originally appeared, and at that moment when the sacred manifests itself again in the same way, extraordinary power overwhelms the profane succession of time. New Year ceremonies are among the most striking examples of the periodic recreation of the world in a state as fresh, powerful, and promising as it was in the beginning. Any fragment of time (e.g., the phases of the moon, the transitions of the human life cycle, the solstices, the rainy seasons, the breeding cycles of animals, the growth cycles of plants) may at any moment become hierophanic. If it witnesses the occurrence of a kratophany or theophany, the moment itself becomes transfigured or consecrated. It will be remembered and repeated. The rhythms of nature are evaluated for their power as hierophanies; that is, for signs of the power to renew and recommence cosmic life. Furthermore, hierophanic moments of time are not limited to cosmic rhythms of nature or biology. In the Judeo-Christian tradition, for example, human history is transfigured into a theophany. The manifestation of God in time guarantees the religious value of Christian images and symbols such as the cross, the holy mountain of Calvary, and the cosmic tree.

Implications for the Study of Symbolic Life

The transfiguration of so many objects into symbols of something else, some sacred reality, has repercussions for understanding the nature of symbols. The study of hierophanies penetrates the meaning of the symbolic life and uncovers the function of symbolism in general. Humans have an innate sense of the symbolic, and all their activities imply symbolism. In particular, religious acts have a symbolic character. From the instant it becomes religious, every act or object is imbued with a significance that is symbolic, referring to supernatural values and realities.

Symbols relate to the sacred in several ways. Sometimes symbolic forms become sacred because they embody directly the spirit or power of transcendent beings (e.g., stones that are the souls of the dead, or represent a god). In these cases the hierophany is effected by a symbolism directly associated with the actual form (i.e., a form apprehended by religious experience, rather than empirical or rational experience) of stone, water, plant, or sky.

At other times the meaning of a religious form may derive from symbolism that is less clear. Religious objects become hierophanies in a less direct way, through the medium of symbolic existence itself. They acquire a religious quality because of the symbolism that imbues them with religious meaning. That is, they become sacred because of their location within a symbolic system. Their sacrality depends upon a consciousness able to make theoretical connections between symbolic expressions. In such cases, the hierophany is effected by the transformation of concrete forms into a nexus of cosmological principles and powers.

For example, the symbolism that has surrounded the pearl throughout history works to transform it into a "cosmological center" that draws together key religious meanings associated with the moon, women, fertility, and birth. The symbolism of the pearl is quite ancient. Pearls appear in prehistoric graves and have a long history of use in magic and medicine. Careful inspection of myths of pearls in many cultures reveals that water imbues pearls with its germinative force. Pearls were included in ritual offerings to river gods. Some pearls have magical power because they were born of the moon. The pearl is like a fetus, and for this reason women wear pearls to come in contact with the fertile powers of hidden creative processes within shells, in amniotic waters, and in the moon. Pearls have also been used in the cure of illnesses associated with the moon. Placed in tombs, pearls renewed the life of the dead by putting them in contact with the powerful regenerative rhythms of the moon, water, and femininity. Covered in pearls, the dead are plunged once more into the cycle of birth, life, death, and rebirth—the career of living forms intimately bound to the moon. In sum, the pearl becomes a hierophany when humans become aware of the cosmological pattern of water, moon, women, and change.

This kind of sacred symbolism has its origins in theory; specifically, a theory of symbols. What gives the sacred object in question (e.g., a pearl) its rich and full religious meaning is the framework of symbolism surrounding it. This is triggered by an awareness of the wider symbolic universe. This conclusion has importance for understanding the role of human reflection in the origin of certain hierophanies. An object becomes sacred, becomes the locus of a hierophany, when humankind becomes aware of the cosmological pattern of principles (e.g., water, moon, change, the cycle of death and birth) centered in it. The theoretical links make possible the experience of the full range of sacrality. The form draws its full meaning from the symbolism that surrounds it and of which it is a part. In fact, symbols extend the range of hierophanies. Objects not directly the locus of a hierophany may become sacred because of their envelopment in a web or pattern of symbolism.

Two related statements should now be made separately. The first consideration is that hierophanies can become symbols. In this respect, symbols are important because they can sustain or even substitute for hierophanies. However, symbols play an even more startling and creative role in religious life: they carry on the process of hierophanization. In fact, the symbol itself is sometimes a hierophany; that is, it reveals a sacred reality which no other manifestation can uncover. A hierophany in its own right, symbolism affords an unbroken solidarity between humankind (*homo symbolicus*) and the sacred. Extending the dialectic of hierophanies, symbolism transforms objects into something other than what they appear to be in the natural sphere. Through symbolism any worldly item may become a sign of transcendent reality and an embodiment of the sacredness of an entire symbolic system. Indeed, we may say that symbolism itself reflects the human need to extend infinitely the process of hierophanization. Looking upon the remarkable number of forms that have manifested the sacred throughout the broad history of religions, one concludes that symbolic life tends to identify the universe as a whole with hierophany and thereby opens human existence to a significant world.

The Dialectic of the Sacred and the Profane

10

THE DIALECTIC OF THE SACRED

Douglas Allen

Editor's Introduction

The sacred is apprehended as being revealed by elements of the profane or phenomenal world while it is simultaneously concealed by the very profane nature of phenomena. This necessitates some kind of dialectical relation between the two. Eliade spoke of the dialectic in the selection from *Patterns* on "the Structure and Morphology of the Sacred" and so did Eliade and Sullivan in "Hierophany," this volume, 86–93 Douglas Allen here attempts to give the whole concept more clarity. This explanation comes from Allen's book, *Structure and Creativity in Religion: Hermeneutics in Mircea Eliade's Phenomenology and New Directions*, 123–30 (The Hague: Mouton, 1978). All rights reserved. Copyright © 1978 by Mouton de Gruyter. Reprinted by permission of Mouton de Gruyter and the author.

ℰℴ ℭℛ

To recreate the conditions for the intentional mode of religious manifestations, we must carefully explicate the structure of the dialectic of the sacred. We shall divide our analysis into three parts: the separation of the hierophanic object and the sacred-profane distinction; the paradoxical relationship between the sacred and the profane; the evaluation and choice implied in the dialectic.

The Separation and Distinction

According to Eliade, the person who has the religious experience believes that something comes from somewhere else and shows itself to him or her. That which appears from somewhere else is the sacred; that through which it appears is the profane.

> To denote the act of manifestation of the sacred, we propose to use the term *hierophany*. This word is convenient because it requires no additional specification; it means nothing more than is implied by its etymological content—namely, that something sacred is shown to us, manifests itself. One may say that the history of religions—from the most elementary to the most developed—is constituted by a number of important hierophanies, manifestations of sacred realities.[1]

What interests *homo religiosus* are hierophanies. These manifestations of the sacred are never unmediated: the sacred is always revealed through something natural, historical, ordinarily profane. The profane alone has no significance for *homo religiosus*, but only insofar as it reveals the sacred.

The process of sacralization involves the "radical ontological separation" of the thing which reveals the sacred from everything else. We find the singularization of a certain stone because of its size or shape or heavenly origin, because it protects the dead or is the site of a covenant, because it represents a theophany or is an image of the "center." A medicine man has been singularized because he has been chosen by gods or spirits, because of his heredity, because of various physical defects (an infirmity, nervous disorder, etc.), or because of an unusual accident or event (lightning, apparition, dream, etc.).[2]

What is important is that there is always something else, something other; that which is singularized is "chosen" because it manifests the sacred. If a large rock is singled out, it is not simply because of its impressive natural dimensions, but rather because its imposing appearance reveals something transcendent: a permanence, a power, an absolute mode of being, which is different from the precariousness of human existence. If the medicine man is singled out, it is because his unusual accident or event is a "sign" of something transcendent: he is a "specialist of the sacred"; he has the capacity to transcend the human and profane, to have contact with and manipulate the sacred.

It is often difficult for the Historian of Religions to recognize hierophanies. We tend to see natural objects where our ancestors saw hierophanies. Eliade has observed that "to the primitive, nature is never purely 'natural.'" We may understand that the sky would reveal a sense of transcendence or infinity, but it often seems incomprehensible that a simple gesture, a normal physiological activity, or a dreary landscape would manifest the sacred. Yet we must be sensitive to the fact that all phenomena are potentially hierophanic.

We must get used to the idea of recognizing hierophanies everywhere, in every area of psychological, economic, spiritual and social life. Indeed, we cannot be sure that there is *anything*—object, movement, psychological function, being or even game—that has not at some time in human history been somewhere transformed into a hierophany. It is a very different matter to find out *why* that particular thing should have become a hierophany, or should have stopped being one at any given moment. But it is quite certain that anything man has ever handled, felt, come in contact with or loved *can* become a hierophany.[3]

At this point, we may note that Eliade's doctrine of hierophanies challenges the naturalistic interpretations of religious phenomena. Because we tend to see natural objects where *homo religiosus* saw hierophanies, there is the tendency to interpret the dialectic of the sacred as a "natural" mode of manifestation. But to do this would be to fail to grasp the true intentionality of the sacred manifestation.

We must now examine the relationship which exists between the sacred and the profane as disclosed by the dialectic of hierophanies. This dialectical relationship has been the source of much confusion and misinterpretation.

The Paradoxical Relationship

Thomas J. J. Altizer seizes upon the point "that the sacred is the opposite of the profane" as Eliade's "cardinal principle" and the key to interpreting Eliade's phenomenological method. This opposition is taken to mean that the sacred and the profane are mutually exclusive or logically contradictory. From this "cardinal principle," Altizer sees the key to Eliade's approach in terms of a "negative dialectic": "a single moment cannot be sacred and profane at once." An understanding of religious myth, for example, is possible "only through a negation of the language of the profane." The "meaning of the sacred is reached by inverting the reality created by modern man's profane choice." In short, to observe the sacred one must totally negate the profane and vice versa.[4] Unfortunately, this interpretation destroys the dialectical complexity of the religious mode of manifestation and leads to an oversimplification and distortion of Eliade's phenomenological method.[5]

Eliade's religious data reveal that in the process of sacralization the sacred and the profane *coexist in a paradoxical relationship*. This process is the intention of the hierophany, an intention which constitutes the structure and lies at the foundation of the hierophany. A series of illustrations from Eliade will clarify this point.

"One must remember the dialectic of the sacred: any object whatever may paradoxically become a hierophany, a receptacle of the sacred, while still participating in its own cosmic environment." "One need only recall the dialectic of hierophany: an object becomes *sacred* while remaining just the same as it is." The dialectic of the sacred consists of the fact that "the sacred expresses itself through some thing other than itself," that "in every case the sacred manifests itself limited and incarnate." It is "this paradox of incarnation which makes hierophanies possible at all" (*Images and Symbols*, 84, 178; *Patterns*, 26 [above, 54]).

As we have seen, "this paradoxical coming-together of sacred and profane ... is what every hierophany, even the most elementary, reveals ... what is paradoxical, what is beyond our understanding, is not that the sacred can be manifested in stones or in trees, but that it can be manifested at all, that it can thus become limited and relative" (*Patterns*, 29–30 [above, 54]). Thus we observe the paradoxical coexistence revealed by the dialectic of the sacred and the profane. What is paradoxical is that an ordinary, finite, historical thing, while remaining a natural thing, can at the same time manifest something which is not finite, not historical, not natural. What is paradoxical is that something transcendent, wholly other, infinite, transhistorical, limits itself by manifesting itself in some relative, finite, historical thing.

The Evaluation and Choice

Our religious data do not simply reveal a distinction between sacred and profane, as seen in their paradoxical coexistence in every hierophany. The dialectic of hierophanies shows that *homo religiosus* is involved in an "existential crisis": in experiencing a hierophany, he or she is called upon to *evaluate* the two orders of being and to make a *choice*. Charles Long describes this sense of evaluation in the following manner:

> The world of man exists as a limitation or qualification of his environment, and this qualification or limitation is at the same time a criticism. Man's world is an ordered world of meaning, but the organizing principle is interpreted as a revelation which comes from a source outside of his ordinary life. It is this source which is given (revealed) and (it) defines any future possibility of man's existence (*Alpha*, 10–11).

In experiencing the dialectic of hierophany, *homo religiosus* faces an "existential crisis"; indeed, one's very existence is called into question. Because of the dichotomy of sacred and profane, as revealed in their paradoxical coexistence, distinction, differentiation, value, and even meaning are all introduced into one's existence.[6] In short, one dimension of being is seen as more significant, as "wholly other" and "powerful" and "ultimate," as containing a surplus of meaning, as paradigmatic and normative in judging one's existence.

Eliade usually describes the person's choice and evaluation "negatively." The dialectic of hierophanies throws the realm of natural ordinary existence into sharp relief. After the "rupture" of the sacred and the profane, the person evaluates her or his natural existence as a "fall." One feels separated from what is now evaluated as "ultimate" and "real." One longs to transcend the "natural" and "historical" mode of being and to live permanently in the sacred.

The upshot of the above discussion seems to be the following. Through the dialectic of hierophanies, the profane is set off in sharp relief; *homo religiosus* "chooses" the sacred and evaluates his or her "ordinary" mode of existence negatively. At the same time, through this evaluation and choice, the human being is given the possibility for meaningful judgments and creative human action and expression. The "positive" religious value of the "negative" evaluation of the profane, we would submit, is expressed in the intentionality toward meaningful communication with the sacred and toward religious action which now appears as a structure in the consciousness of *homo religiosus*.

At this point, a brief digression may be useful in clarifying one of the main sources of misconceptions in interpreting Eliade's phenomenology: most interpreters do not endeavor to understand Mircea Eliade on his own grounds. We may cite an example from our above discussion: *homo religiosus* evaluates his or her natural existence as a "fall."

Many interpreters have seized upon Eliade's personal doctrine of a "fall" as being a pivotal notion in his thought. It is only because of Eliade's "theological assumptions" that he considers modern secularization to be a "fall" [see above, 67].[7] Eliade is a "romantic" who believes that history is a "fall" and who "insists upon the reality of man's prefallen state."[8]

The problem with these interpretations is that Altizer and Hamilton do not take Eliade seriously enough on his own grounds. They are theologians and criticize Eliade's theological position on a "fall." But Eliade at least purports to be a Historian of Religions; his claim is not that Mircea Eliade is committed to these diverse themes of a "fall" but that *homo religiosus* has entertained such beliefs.

To give but one illustration, Eliade finds that "the paradisiac myths" all speak of a "paradisiac epoch" in which primordial beings enjoyed freedom, immortality, easy communication with the gods, etc. Unfortunately, they lost all of this because of "the fall"—the primordial event which caused the "rupture" of the sacred and the profane. These myths help *homo religiosus* to understand his or her present "fallen" existence and express a "nostalgia" for that "prefallen" Paradise (*Myths, Dreams and Mysteries*, 59ff.). If history is a "fall" for *homo religiosus*, it is because historical existence is seen as separated from and inferior to the "transhistorical" (absolute, eternal, transcendent) realm of the sacred.

Summary

We may now summarize the structure of the process of sacralization which is revealed to us in the dialectic of hierophanies:

1. There is always the separation of the hierophanic object and the distinction between the sacred and the profane. From our earlier analysis, we recall that religion exists where the sacred-profane dichotomy has been made, and the sacred always entails some sense of transcendence.

2. This dichotomy is experienced in terms of a certain dialectical tension: the sacred and the profane coexist in a paradoxical relationship. What is paradoxical is that the sacred, which is transcendent (wholly other, ultimate, infinite, transhistorical), limits itself by incarnating itself in something profane (relative, finite, historical, natural). Or, we may express this paradoxical coexistence as follows: what is profane (finite, natural), while remaining a natural thing, at the same time manifests what is sacred (infinite, transcendent).

3. *Homo religiosus* does not simply distinguish the sacred and the profane, a distinction revealed through their paradoxical coexistence in every hierophany. Implied in the dialectic of the sacred is an evaluation and a choice. The sacred is experienced as powerful, ultimate, absolute, meaningful, paradigmatic, normative. It is in terms of the sacred that religious persons interpret their mode of being in the world and define the future possibilities of their existence.

Notes

1. *Myths, Dreams and Mysteries*, 124. See *Patterns*, 7ff. Of course, we have already presented a partial analysis of the sacred-profane distinction in our discussion of Eliade's view of religion and the sacred.

2. *Patterns*, 216–38; *The Eternal Return*, 4; *Shamanism*, 31–32 and *passim*.

3. *Patterns*, 11, 38. In several contexts, Eliade has asserted that Judaeo-Christianity contributed greatly to the process by which we (modern, secular, Western, scientific) tend to see natural objects where "archaic" religions saw hierophanies. The "cosmic religiosity" of earlier religions was criticized: a rock was "only" a rock and should not be worshiped. "Emptied of every religious value or meaning, nature could become the 'object' *par excellence* of scientific investigation." "The Sacred and the Modern Artist," *Criterion* 4/2 (1965): 23.

4. Thomas J. J. Altizer, *Mircea Eliade and the Dialectic of the Sacred*, 34, 39, 45, 65, and *passim*.

5. After completing this section, I came across a very similar criticism of Altizer's interpretation of Eliade's sacred-profane relationship in Ricketts's "Mircea Eliade and the Death of God," 43–48.

6. Eliade, *Myth and Reality*, 139; and G. Richard Welbon, "Some Remarks on the Work of Mircea Eliade," 479. Langdon Gilkey, *Naming the Whirlwind*, 293: "if the sacred be the

foundation of all of our profane life, then our relation to the sacred will determine the patterns of our behavior in every secular realm. For this reason, every religious symbol or myth entails 'models' for our existence, patterns of sacrality by means of which man comprehends the forms of his human existence and so by which he patterns his life and that of his society."

7. See Hamilton, "*Homo Religiosus* and Historical Faith," 212, 214–16. The following discussion would also apply to Eliade's point that "from the Christian point of view" it could be said that modern nonreligion is equivalent to a new or second "fall." See *Sacred and the Profane*, 213; "Archaic Myth and Historical Man," 35–36.

8. See Altizer, *Mircea Eliade and the Dialectic of the Sacred*, 84, 86, 88, 161; and Altizer, "Mircea Eliade and the Recovery of the Sacred," 282–83. See Eliade, *Images and Symbols*, 173; *Cosmos and History*, 162.

Homo Religiosus

11

HOMO RELIGIOSUS

Gregory Alles

Editor's Introduction

Homo religiosus has already been mentioned in this volume, by Eliade in the "Introduction" to *The Sacred and the Profane*, in "The Sacred in the Secular World," by Douglas Allen in his consideration of "the Dialectic of the Sacred and the Profane," and by Rennie in "The Ontology of the Sacred," which make this an opportune moment to attempt some clarification and precision of this concept. Gregory Alles here introduces us to the distinction between *homo religiosus* and modern humanity and the variety of scholarly applications of the term. Thus it will be appropriate next to consult Eliade's essay on *Homo Religiosus* and *Homo Faber* to seek further clarity on Eliade's own characteristic employment of the term. When Eliade considered "modern" or secular humanity in the preceding selection on "The Sacred in the Secular World," it was in specific opposition to humanity in what he considered our more usual or prevalent religious mode—"*homo religiosus*." The article by Gregory Alles is taken from the first edition of the Macmillan *Encyclopedia of Religion*, vol. VI, 442, edited by Mircea Eliade. All rights reserved. Copyright © 1987 by the Gale Group. Reprinted by permission of the Gale Group.

ဆ ရ

When the Swedish botanist Linnaeus developed his system of biological classification in the eighteenth century, the Enlightenment's ideal of rationality strongly governed views of humanity. As a result, Linnaeus designated the human species *Homo sapiens*. Soon, however, the Romantic movement and the incipient human sciences accentuated other dimensions of humanity than the rational. In time, new terms were coined on the Linnaean model to designate humanity in various distinctive aspects: *homo ludens* (G. F. Creuzer and, later, Johan Huizinga), *homo faber* (Henri Bergson), *homo viator* (Gabriel-Honoré Marcel), and others. Perhaps the nineteenth century's growing awareness of the universality of religion, especially in the realm of the "primitives" (as they were then known), made it inevitable that a phrase would emerge to express that aspect of humanity that the Enlightenment's ideal had so opposed: *homo religiosus*, "the religious human." In some circles the expression has gained wide currency, but its sense has not remained constant. Three general meanings of *homo religiosus* are most important to students of religion.

Homo Religiosus as Religious Leader

In one meaning, *homo religiosus* refers to a particularly religious person within a given (religious) community, that is, to a religious leader. The roots of this usage are much older than the Enlightenment and Linnaeus's *Systema naturae*. In antiquity *religiosus* denoted persons who were scrupulously but not excessively attentive to observances due to gods and men (Festus, 278 and 289 M; Cicero, *De natura deorum*, 2.72). In this sense, Cicero could speak of *homines religiosi* (*Epistulae ad familiars*, 1.7.4). Christianization brought overtones of distinctiveness—*religiosi* became persons of special ecclesiastical standing—and this usage was transferred to the vernaculars, as in the English noun *religious* and expressions such as "religious folk" (*Romance of the Rose*, 6149).

Later, in reaction to the Reformation's universalization of the religious life, Pietist and Puritan movements emphasized a religious distinctiveness whose center was subjective and individual rather than objective and institutional (a personal *Nachfolge Christi*). Friedrich Schleiermacher thought of religion as neither knowing nor doing but as an experiential awareness of one's absolute dependence upon God. He conceived Christ as the unique person in whom this consciousness received ultimate expression, the person whose fully immediate and perfectly open relationship with the Father qualified him to be the mediator of the divine.

In the twentieth century *homo religiosus* as religious leader has inherited both the medieval meaning of *religiosus* and the liberal Protestant tradition initiated by Schleiermacher. According to Max Scheler, who developed a full version of this view, *homo religiosus* is a particular type of human personality:

"the man who has God in his heart and God in his actions, who in his own *spiritual figure* is a transformer of souls and is able in new ways to infuse the word of God into hearts that have softened and yield" (Scheler, 127, original italics).

Scheler distinguished the *homo religiosus* from four other exemplars of value: the artist, the leading spirit of a civilization, the hero, and the genius. These other figures are each exemplary in some aspect or other: the hero in deeds, for example; the genius in works. *Homo religiosus*, however, is exemplary in his entire being, which in its totality calls for unquestioning imitation (*Nachfolge*). Moreover, Scheler distinguished several types of *homo religiosus*. Of these, the most significant is the original *homo religiosus*, for historical religious traditions, the founder. Unique in his own community, the founder is the medium for a positive revelation of the holy. The various derived *homines religiosi*— followers, martyrs, reformers, priests, theologians, and others—are lesser in stature and reflect the absolute claim advanced by the existence and nature of the perfect *homo religiosus*.

Among modern historians of religions, Joachim Wach spoke of *homo religiosus* in this sense. Unlike Scheler, however, Wach was heavily indebted to Max Weber. He saw the distinctive character of the *homo religiosus* not in an intrinsic quality or activity of the personality but in the historical and sociological effect of his personal or official charisma.

Religious Humanity

Today, two other senses of *homo religiosus* have eclipsed the definition of *homo religiosus* as religious leader, at least in Anglo-American scholarly parlance. In both cases the term is employed not in a particularistic sense—the *homo religiosus* or *homines religiosi*—but in a generic sense, *homo* referring not to an individual but, as with Linnaeus, to humanity. In one usage, the term is a general designation for all human beings, referring specifically to religion as one constitutive aspect of humanity distinct from others. This usage assumes a fundamental unity of all humankind that is much more than biological, and its proponents speak more of the human condition than they do of concrete religious phenomena.

The Dutch historian of religions Gerardus van der Leeuw openly set this sort of *homo religiosus* in opposition to Scheler's. For van der Leeuw, the human as such emerges in the existential tension between two poles: on the one hand, a fully united collective identity in which the individual is submerged (that is, a primitive mentality, the realm of mysticism); on the other, a duality of subject and object in which a human being strives to render everything a technical object, in the end even itself. With humanity there emerges at the same time both *conscientia* (conscience and consciousness) and, from existential anxiety, a sense of sin—hence God and religion. While van der Leeuw is not unaware of the existence of atheists and agnostics, in his formulation such persons can never escape their own selves, their own *conscientiae*.

More recently, Wilhelm Dupré has seen religion as both a "universal pattern of human self-realization" and a "constitutive presence … in the emergence of man" (Dupré, 310). Dupré exposits his conception of humanity by using three expressions, *homo existens*, *homo symbolicus*, and *homo religiosus*, each of which necessitates the next. The symbol, not the existential situation of the subject in the world, is the pivot upon which Dupré's conceptions turn. Because religion is for him both the quality that gives intensity to any process of symbolization and the dimension in which symbolization originates, Dupré sees humanity as inevitably religious.

Homo Religiosus and *Homo Modernus*

In a third meaning, as in the second, *homo religiosus* is a generic term, but here it does not extend to the entire species. Instead, it characterizes the mode of human existence prior to the advent of a modern, secular consciousness. Thus, this usage differs from the second in the seriousness with which it takes secularization as an abandonment of religion and in the weight it assigns religious elements within the modern, secularized world. Its adherents are able to conceive religion in terms of concrete phenomena normally considered religious (such as myths and rites), without recourse to subtle redefinitions governed by their views of humanity in general. At the same time, they may still appreciate religion's secular manifestations. Because this view appears above all in the influential writings of Mircea Eliade, it is perhaps the most widely known modern use of *homo religiosus*.

Eliade is struck by the difference between the nature and use of symbols in the ancient classical religions and especially among archaic cultures as opposed to the modern Western intelligentsia. He contrasts two distinct modes of existing in and experiencing the world. His *homo religiosus* is driven by a desire for being; modern man lives under the dominion of becoming. *Homo religiosus* thirsts for being in the guise of the sacred. He attempts to live at the center of the world, close to the gods and in the eternal present of the paradigmatic mythic event that makes profane duration possible. His experience of time and space is characterized by a discontinuity between the sacred and the profane. Modern man, however, experiences no such discontinuity. For him, neither time nor space is capable of distinctive valorization. He is determined indiscriminately by all the events of history and by the concomitant threat of nothingness, which produces his profound anxiety.

The break between the two, however, cannot be complete. Determined by history, modern man is thereby determined by his unrenounceable precursor, *homo religiosus*. For support, Eliade points to religious structures in the modern world, such as mythic images suppressed in the modern unconscious and the religious symbols and functions of modern entertainment. Nonetheless, there is a profound difference between archaic reality and modern relic. For *homo religiosus*, recognized structures determine a whole world and a whole person. For modern man, these unrecognized structures are particular and private, repressed or relegated to peripheral activities.

The influence of Eliade's notion of *homo religiosus* can be gauged by the amount of discussion it has provoked among scholars. Some, especially anthropologists, question Eliade's data and methods and have come to the radical conclusion that Eliade's *homo religiosus* is never encountered in the field (see Saliba 1976 [below, 122–30]).

Others point out hidden biases that have skewed what they see as otherwise careful work. Those concerned with women's issues, for example, may find Eliade's view of the genuine human life basically androcentric: Eliade's *homo religiosus* is actually *vir religiosus* (see Valerie Saiving).

A third tack grants Eliade's universal structures but challenges the inferences that he draws. Some wonder, for example, whether archaic structures and their modern survivals might not simply arise from "the organic and psychological constitution of *Homo sapiens*" (Robert F. Brown, 447). Given human biological unity, they question whether Eliade's differentiation of modern man from *homo religiosus* is relevant.

A final critique questions not Eliade's notion of *homo religiosus* but what it sees as his program of revitalizing religious humanity. For example, Kenneth G. Hamilton, a proponent of the death-of-God theology, finds Eliade's preferences opposed to historical faith. Religious humanity surrenders questioning and particularity for openness and universality, and as a result abandons history and morality.

Homo Religiosus in the Study of Religion

Clearly, scholars give the term *homo religiosus* a variety of distinctive meanings. In addition, they use it with great variation in specificity and frequency. The expositions given here rely on careful and exact discussions, but many scholars also use the expression casually, and the precise meanings they intend are often difficult to determine. Again, some in the field assign *homo religiosus* a prominent place in their thought, but others do quite well without mentioning the term at all.

The formulation of an adequate concept of *homo religiosus* as such is only rarely a primary scholarly goal. As the varied and often incompatible meanings of the term show, scholars are generally driven by deeper and more substantive questions about religion, and they formulate different views on religious matters in which a phrase like *homo religiosus*—a Latin expression that attracts the reader's attention—can perform a range of services. Nonetheless, so long as the study of religion is conceived of as a human study, some students will find *homo religiosus* a convenient and useful expression.

12

HOMO FABER AND HOMO RELIGIOSUS

Mircea Eliade

Editor's Introduction

Despite Gregory Alles' admirable attempt to bring system and clarity to Eliade's application of the term *homo religiosus*, considerable potential confusion remains. The following article by Eliade might bring some degree of further clarity, or at least familiarity, through the instructive example of contrasting *homo religiosus* with *homo faber*. Although twenty years have elapsed since its original publication, the contemporary relevance of this meditation on Apocalyptic is marked. While the technological predictions cited in Eliade's article are inaccurate (as is the forecast of the self-destruction of The Rolling Stones), Eliade's diagnosis of the contradictory trends of technological pessimism and optimism as fundamentally religious seems to have been borne out. While the end of the world via uncontrolled technology is still a live possibility, the redemption of the world via technological success seems to be a fading hope (I speak not of actualities but of human aspirations) and the more overtly religious motif of divine eschatology is an increasing concern, particularly in the United States.

This article expresses one of Eliade's perhaps most extreme and speculative ideas: that "modern man takes upon himself the function of temporal duration; in other words, *he takes on the role of time*." This is closely related to his whole analysis of the strained relations of humanity and history. From *The History of Religions: Retrospect and Prospect*, edited by Joseph Kitagawa, 1–12 (New York: Macmillan, 1985). All rights reserved. Copyright © 1985 by the Gale Group. Reprinted by permission of the Gale Group.

ဆဝ ၓ

It has been remarked that the last few decades have been paradoxically characterized by the coexistence of a tragic, neurotic pessimism and a robust, almost candid optimism. A great number of scientists, sociologists, and economists draw increasing attention to the imminent catastrophes that menace our world, not only our Western type of culture and sociopolitical institutions but mankind in general and even life on our planet. Other authors, less numerous but equally energetic, exalt the great scientific discoveries and the fantastic technological conquests accomplished or begun in recent decades. I shall recall here only a few of the arguments and opinions expressed by representatives of both trends of thought. Although these thinkers approach their subjects from opposing positions, they illustrate different aspects of the same cultural process. They share the conviction that we are witnessing the end of our world and are thus on the threshold of some decisive event—either a total extinction or the beginning of a new creation.

... Solvet saeclum in favilla ...

I begin with a few examples from contemporary arts, selected particularly from poetic and musical compositions and films enthusiastically admired by the younger generation. Rock music, discovered and glorified by American and European youth in the 1960s, began under the sign of political, social, and moral revolution. It is significant that at its apex rock music proclaimed the imminent death of the world.[1] In 1962, Bob Dylan became the spokesman for a youth protest movement with his famous "Blowin' in the Wind" and "A Hard Rain's Gonna Fall." In 1964, the British group The Rolling Stones inaugurated their career by playing the most desperately sad blues. Later these young men took to drugs and eventually seemed to espouse satanism. Their singing was a means to end the world as well as a way to their own destruction. The quartet The Doors, formed in 1967 at Los Angeles under the leadership of Jim Morrison, brought out a number of very popular records, inspired by such taboo themes as patricide. Jim Morrison died of alcoholism in Paris in 1971. Magma, a group of French jazz musicians, was organized in 1970. Their leader, Christian Vander, wanted to depict the impending destruction of the world. One famous cut, "Mekanik Destructiw Kommandöh," describes the end of our planet.

"The creatures of rage," wrote a French critic, "the choirs, the music of iron and ice, the apocalyptic uproar—these creatures of rage come to smash the Earth to powder and sweep away the multitudes. And the unlimited putrid chaos of our world is delivered up to the angels of darkness, who come to punish the insane pride of the earthlings" (Manoeuvre, 213). A similar apocalyptic vision inspired the Blue Oyster Cult, founded in New York in 1971. "We are constructing our music in order that it will be the last programme on the computer at the end of the world ...."

In the last twenty years, a number of films have portrayed the end of the world or the more or less total annihilation of mankind as a result of nuclear war.[2] No less striking is the pessimistic tone of the most recent science-fiction novels. In their essay, "De la science-fiction à la science-affliction," Igor and Grichka Bogdanoff observe that, whereas the science-fiction produced from 1945 until the 1960s was dominated by the specter of atomic war, during the last fifteen years the mortal danger has been ecological: excessive pollution, the population explosion, the destruction of nature, the scarcity of resources, and so on (*La Fin du Monde?* 201–209). In his novel, *Stand on Zanzibar* (1968), John Brunner dramatizes the end of the world, brought on by a demographic explosion impossible to control. In *The Sheep Look Up* (Brunner 1972), the rains contain powerful doses of acids, air is respirable only at certain hours of the day, water is only rarely drinkable, and so on. Such a world is a caricature of our own. The end of the world is not in the future, it has already begun: "under our eyes, our world is wasting and grows rotten" (207).

Of course, these terrors—illustrated in the most popular rock music and in so many films about the future and works of science-fiction—are not without foundation. Leaving aside the apocalyptic consequences of a thermonuclear war, the present ecological situation and the population explosion do constitute extremely serious problems. The planetary pollution, which brought thousands of animal species to the verge of extinction and even "killed" a sea,[3] increases continually. In a recent issue of *The Ecologist: Journal of the Post Industrial Age* (vol. 10, January–February 1980), a desperate appeal is made to world authorities, "A Plan to Save the Tropical Forests." One reads such terrifying sentences as: "The tropical rain forests are the world's richest gene banks, and as they start to disappear so do our options for the future. It is just like walking out along a plank and starting to cut away at the wood behind with a saw." "If a culture sins against the forests," writes Ehrenfried Pfeiffer, "its biological decline is inevitable. ... Sixty million years of evolution is being converted into worthless paper packaging. ..."

I will not quote the famous and radically pessimistic report of the *Club of Rome,* many of whose predictions are controversial. But Carl Amery, in his book, *The End of the Providence* (1972), argues that industrial and demographic explosions condemn our species and the entire biosphere to extinction. According to Amery, the end is only a generation or two ahead of us. A similarly pessimistic vision of the future is eloquently presented by Robert L. Heilbroner in *An Inquiry into the Human Prospect* (New York, 1974):

Our movement into the future will be a descent into the black cave of bare and unrelieved survival, a survival characterized by overcrowding, material wants, rigidly determined systems of life and authoritarian government. ... Doubling the population of the earth's poorer regions every quarter of a century, it threatens, unless checked by mass starvation, to place here forty billion persons (as opposed to the present three-and-a half) in 100 years. Such a growth in population seems to require an almost infinite agricultural and industrial expansion if the most tragic levels of starvation are to be averted (cf. Langdon Gilkey, *Reaping the Whirlwind*, 79–81).

But then, writes Heilbroner, the consequence will be

the depletion of the earth's resources, which seems certain surprisingly soon to demand a slow-down and then a halt to industrial expansion. In league with that, there is as well the danger of overreaching the thermal limit for the atmosphere, which long before the extinction limit is reached in a century-and-a-half (three or four generations) will also require a slow-down and a halt to industrial growth. ... The only alternative to such industrial contraction is in the end death.[4]

The "Anti-Sinistrose"

The French writer Louis Pauwels, founder and director of the monthly *Question de ...,* coined the expression "sinistrose" to designate all forms of despair, pessimism, and nihilistic prophecies regarding the future of our world. A special issue of his magazine, a 320-page volume entitled *La Fin du Monde?*, was devoted to the analysis and refutation of some recent expressions of "sinistrose." Here I will use freely the documentation collected in his volume.

A tout seigneur, tout honneur. When presenting an optimistic interpretation of the future, one must begin by evoking the famous scientist-theologian Pierre Teilhard de Chardin.[5] Between 1920 and 1955, Teilhard wrote many books and essays (published posthumously) on cosmic evolution and cosmic redemption. By cosmic redemption, he meant redemption through Christ, that is to say, the transmutation of cosmic matter through the sacrament of the Mass, evidently achieved by the voyages of men in the galaxies during the next several hundred thousand years.

Such an optimistic view of the future—minus Teilhard's theological hope— is shared by a number of economists and scientists. In an interview a few years ago, Herman Kahn affirmed that a population of six billion with a per capita income of $18,000 is not beyond our possibilities. In his book, *The Next 200 Years* (New York, 1976), Kahn proclaims that the world is moving not toward a period of austerity but into universal prosperity. Thus the great problem of the future will be mankind's adaptation to a life of abundance and leisure. This sort of optimism is rejected by one of the contributors to *La Fin du Monde?*[6]

A more adequate analysis of the available data concerning the population explosion and other catastrophic predictions is Pauwels's article, "L'anti-sinistrose" (*La Fin du Monde?*, 227–44). According to Pauwels's sources, the demographic growth of the Third World will be stabilized by the year 2000 (236); the scarcity of food-stuffs is a myth (236–38). Among the anticatastrophic authors, Pauwels quotes Adrian Berry who, in his book, *The Next Ten Thousand Years* (New York, 1974), makes the case that even in the event of nuclear war progress will be only temporarily restrained, not stopped; in fact, there is no limit to what science and technology may accomplish. Berry announces that man will remodel the entire solar system; he speaks of autonomous floating cities and of "domesticated planets."

In an article published in *Analog* and partially translated in *La Fin du Monde?* (245–54), Arthur Clarke summarized his views on the next 120 years. Very soon, space technology will enable man to set up special installations on Mercury in order to obtain solar energy more easily and more abundantly. Clarke predicted visits to planets by 1980 and their colonization by 2000. Some twenty years later, we will begin interstellar explorations, and by 2030, we will contact extraterrestrial beings. For 2100, Clarke foresees an encounter with extraterrestrial beings, a worldbrain, and human immortality.[7]

Tragically pessimistic or utterly optimistic, both trends of thought proclaim the imminent end of our world. Both predictions—that of an Apocalypse and that of a Golden Age—are founded exclusively upon the spectacular development of science and technology. If, following the pessimistic interpretation, our world is to be destroyed, it will not be destroyed for religious reasons (for example, God, punishing us for our sins) but simply as a result of our technological progress. Likewise, the Golden Age and the conquest of immortality predicted by optimists for the next few hundred years will not be gifts of God but the inevitable consequence of man's scientific genius and technological abilities. Nevertheless, both predictions have a religious structure, in the sense that they partake of religious symbolism. Of course, the representatives of these two opposite trends are not aware of the religious implications of their despair or of their hopes. What is significant is that all of them relate the inevitability and the imminence of our world's end to the fantastic realizations of human workmanship.

Making Things More Rapidly Than Nature

For a historian of religion, this apotheosis of *homo faber* is particularly interesting. It reminds him of a whole world of archaic symbols, myths, and rituals. Science and technology began their uninterrupted progress with the discovery of metallurgy. That is, their progress began when man understood that he could collaborate with nature, and finally come to dominate it, by learning how *to make things more rapidly* than nature. Indeed, we are confronted very early with the idea that ores "grow" in the belly of Mother Earth after the manner of embryos. Metallurgy thus takes on the character of obstetrics. The miner and metalworker intervene in the unfolding of subterranean embryology. They accelerate the rhythm of the growth of ores; they collaborate in the work of nature and assist it in effecting a more rapid gestation process. In a word, man, with his various techniques, gradually takes the place of time. His labors replace the work of time (cf. *The Forge and the Crucible*, 8ff.).

With the help of fire, metalworkers transform the ores, that is, the "embryos," into metals, "adults." The underlying belief here is that given enough time, the ores would have become "pure" metals in the womb of the Earth-Mother. Furthermore, these "pure" metals would themselves become gold if allowed to "grow" undisturbed for a few more thousand years (*The Forge and the Crucible*, 50f.). Such beliefs are well known in many traditional societies and survived in western Europe until the end of the Industrial Revolution. I will quote only one Western alchemist of the seventeenth century, who wrote that

> If there were no exterior obstacles to the execution of her designs, Nature would always complete what she wishes to produce. ... That is why we have to look upon the birth of imperfect metals as we would upon abortions and freaks which come about only because Nature has been, as it were, misdirected; or because she has encountered some resistance or certain obstacles which prevent her from behaving in her accustomed way. ... For, although she wishes to produce only one metal, she finds herself constrained to create several. Gold, and only gold, is the legitimate child of her desires. Gold is her legitimate son because only gold is a production of her efforts.[8]

The "nobility" of gold is thus the fruit in its most mature state. The other metals are "common" because they are "green," "not ripe." In other words, nature's final goal is the completion of the mineral kingdom, its ultimate "maturation." The natural transmutation of metals into gold is inscribed in their destiny, for the tendency of nature is toward perfection.

Mythologies of Gold

Such an extravagant exaltation of gold invites us to pause for a moment. There is a splendid mythology of *homo faber*. Myths, legends, and heroic poetry reflect the first, decisive conquests of the natural world achieved by early man. But gold does not belong to the mythology of *homo faber*. Gold is a creation of *homo religiosus*. It was valorized exclusively for symbolic and religious reasons.

Gold was the first metal utilized by plan, although it could be employed neither as a tool nor as a weapon. In the history of technological innovations—that is to say, the passage from stone technology to bronze industry, then to iron and finally to steel—gold played no role whatsoever. Furthermore, its exploitation is the most difficult of any metal. In order to obtain six to twelve grams of gold, one ton of rock has to be brought from the mines up to the surface. The exploitation of alluvial deposits is certainly less complicated but also considerably less productive: a few centigrams from a cubic meter of sand. Compared with the effort invested in securing a few ounces of pure gold, the travail demanded in the exploitation of oil is infinitely simpler and easier. Nevertheless, from prehistoric times to our epoch, men have laboriously pursued the desperate search for gold. The primordial symbolic value of this metal could not be abolished in spite of the progressive desacralization of nature and of human existence.

The Egyptians who, according to Plutarch and Diodorus, hated iron—which they called "the bones of Seth"—considered the flesh of the gods to be of gold. In other words, the gods were *immortal*. That is why, after the model of the gods, the pharaoh was also assigned flesh of gold. Indeed, as the *Brāhmaṇas* repeatedly proclaim, "Gold is immortality." Consequently, obtaining the elixir that transmutes metals into alchemical gold is tantamount to obtaining immortality. I will not discuss here the origins of alchemy nor its development in China, India, and the Islamic, Hellenistic, and Western cultures. In any case, in Eastern as well as in Western alchemy, the transmutation of metals into gold is equivalent to a miraculously rapid maturation. The Elixir (or the Philosopher's Stone) completes and consummates the work of nature (*The Forge and the Crucible*, 48f., 51f., 160f.). As one of the characters in Ben Jonson's play, *The Alchemist*, asserts, "The lead and other metals would be gold if they had time"; and another character adds, "And that our Art doth further" (Act II, scene ii). That is, the alchemist prolongs the dream and the ideology of the miner and metal worker: to perfect nature by accelerating the temporal rhythm. The difference is that the *aurum alchemicum*—the Elixir—also confers health, perennial youth, and even immortality.

The Origins of Modern Science

By the end of the eighteenth century alchemy was supplanted by the new science of chemistry. But earlier, alchemy knew a short period of fame thanks mainly to Isaac Newton. Although Newton declared that some of his alchemical experiments were successful, he never published his results. However, his innumerable alchemical manuscripts—which were neglected until 1940—have been thoroughly investigated by B. J. Teeter Dobbs in her book, *The Foundations of Newton's Alchemy* (see also *The Forge and the Crucible*, 231f.). According to

Dobbs, Newton probed "the whole vast literature of the older alchemy as it has never been probed before or since" (88). The discovery of the force that held the planets in their orbits did not satisfy Newton completely. He sought in alchemy the structure of the small world to match his cosmological system. But in spite of his intensive experiments from about 1668 to 1696, he failed to find the forces that govern the action of small bodies. When, however, he began to work seriously in 1679–1680 on the dynamics of orbital motion, he applied his alchemical ideas on attraction to the entire cosmos.

As McGuire and Rattansi have shown, Newton was convinced that in earliest times God had imparted the secrets of natural philosophy and of true religion to a select few. This knowledge had been subsequently lost but was later partially recovered. After its recovery, it was incorporated in fables and mythic formulations where it would remain hidden from the vulgar. In modern days, it could be more fully recovered from experience (quoted by Dobbs, 90). For this reason, Newton usually turned to the most esoteric sections of alchemical literature, hoping that the real secrets were hidden there. It is highly significant that the founder of modern mechanical science did not reject the primordial secret revelation, nor did he reject the principle of transmutation as the basis of all alchemies. He wrote in his treatise on *Opticks*: "The changing of Bodies into Light, and Light into Bodies, is very conformable to the course of Nature, which seems delighted with Transmutation" (Dobbs, 23). According to Professor Dobbs, "Newton's alchemical thoughts were so securely established on their basic foundations that he never came to deny their general validity, and in a sense the whole of his career after 1675 may be seen as one long attempt to integrate alchemy and the mechanical philosophy" (230).

When the *Principia* was published, Newton's opponents emphatically declared that his forces were in fact occult qualities. Professor Dobbs admits that his critics were right: "Newton's forces were very much like the hidden sympathies and antipathies found in much of the occult literature of the Renaissance period. But Newton had given forces an ontological status equivalent to that of matter and motion. By so doing, and by quantifying the forces, he enabled the mechanical philosophies to rise above the level of imaginary impact mechanism" (211). In his book, *Force in Newton's Physics,* Richard Westfall came to the conclusion that the *wedding* of the Hermetic alchemical tradition with mechanical philosophy produced modern science as its offspring.[9]

In its spectacular development, "modern science" has ignored or rejected its Hermetic heritage. In effect, the triumph of Newton's mechanics abolished his own scientific idea. Newton and his contemporaries had expected quite another type of scientific revolution. Prolonging and expanding the hopes and objectives of the neoalchemist of the Renaissance—that is, the endeavor to redeem nature—men as different as Paracelsus, John Dee, Comenius, J. Valentin Andreae, Ashmole, Fludd, and Newton saw in alchemy the model for a more ambitious enterprise: the perfection of man through a new method of learning.

In their view, such a method would integrate a supraconfessional Christianity with the Hermetic tradition and the natural sciences, that is, medicine, astronomy, and mechanics. This ambitious synthesis was in fact a new, religious creation, and one specifically Christian. It is comparable to the results of the previous integration of Platonic, Aristotelian, and neo-Platonic metaphysical constructs. The type of learning elaborated in the seventeenth century represented the last holistic enterprise attempted in Christian Europe.

Man, Work, and Time

Although alchemy was supplanted by the new science of chemistry, the alchemist's ideals survived, camouflaged in nineteenth-century ideology. Of course, by that time these ideals were radically secularized, but the triumph of experimental science did not abolish them altogether. On the contrary, the new ideology of the nineteenth century crystallized around the myth of infinite progress. Boosted by the experimental sciences and the progress of industrialization, this ideology took up and carried forward the millenarian dream of the alchemist, radical secularization notwithstanding. The myth of the perfection and redemption of nature survives in camouflaged form in the Promethean program of industrialized societies, whose aim is the transformation of nature, and especially the transmutation of nature into "energy." In the nineteenth century man also succeeds in supplanting time. His desire to accelerate the natural tempo of organic and inorganic beings now begins to be fulfilled. The synthetic products of organic chemistry have demonstrated the possibility of accelerating and even eliminating time. Laboratories and factories prepare substances which nature would have taken thousands and thousands of years to produce. We also know the extent to which the "synthetic preparation of life," even in the modest form of a few cells of protoplasm, was the supreme dream of science, from the second half of the nineteenth century to our own time (cf. *The Forge and the Crucible*, 169f.).

By conquering nature through the physico-chemical sciences, man can become nature's rival without being the slave of time. Henceforth, science and labor are to do the work of time. With what he recognizes as most essential in himself—his applied intelligence and capacity for work—modern man takes upon himself the function of temporal duration; in other words, *he takes on the role of time.* Of course, man had been condemned to work from the very beginning. But in traditional societies, work had a religious, a liturgical, dimension. Now, in modern industrialized societies, work has been radically secularized. For the first time in history, man has assumed the task of "doing better and quicker than nature" without the sacred dimension that in other societies made work bearable. The total secularization of work, of human labor, has tremendous consequences, comparable only to the consequences of the domestication of fire and the discovery of agriculture.

But this is quite another problem. What is of interest here is that scientific and technological progress has made it possible to prolong and periodically to regenerate human life (with such indefinite regeneration corresponding to a secularized expression of immortality) as well as to destroy human collectivities, even the whole of humankind.

Are We Condemned to Immortality?

But are these the only consequences envisaged by the great scientists and technologists of our time? I am thinking not of the personal convictions of famous men but of certain significant interpretations of very recent scientific discoveries. I will cite a single example. It is an important example inasmuch as it introduces us to a number of astronomers, astrophysicists, and mathematicians—and such scholars are more open to religious and theological problems than are their colleagues in various divisions of the humanities.

In 1974, a book published in Paris became a best-seller almost immediately and provoked vivid discussion: *La Gnose de Princeton* by Raymond Ruyer. The author, professor of philosophy at the University of Nancy, is well-known for his many works on epistemology, cybernetics, social psychology, and similar topics.[10] While attending an international conference in London, Ruyer discovered the existence of a group of American "gnostics," most of them astronomers, astrophysicists, mathematicians, and biologists from Princeton, Pasadena, and Mount Wilson. Ruyer does not cite names, but he assures us that the manuscript of *La Gnose de Princeton* was read by some of these scholars: "I'm afraid that perhaps they accepted my project [i.e., to publish the book] above all because they do not take the French public very seriously and they count on the power of inattention and on anti-American snobbery in intellectual circles."

According to Ruyer, the group was formed at Princeton in the late 1960s by some astrophysicists and astronomers fascinated by the riddles of cosmology. For these scientists, materialistic explanations of the origin and nature of the universe are invalidated by the most recent discoveries. *Everything* in the universe possesses, like man, a *consciousness*. (This is why they call themselves "Gnostics.") They do not acknowledge a God, but they proclaim the universality of the Spirit, and they believe in a future "super-mankind." They do not publicize their discoveries. For the moment, they prefer to carry on dialogues and discussion within a "discreet" (not "secret") society. Their number has been increasing, to upwards of a few thousands in 1972–73. Lately, philosophers and theologians have been joining their ranks.

Some critics do not exclude the hypothesis that this "gnostic" organization may be simply a stratagem invented by Ruyer in order to expose the ideas which a scientist-philosopher could hold today concerning the most fundamental problems of cosmology, astrophysics, epistemology, and biology. Every idea presented by Ruyer as belonging to the "Princeton Gnostics" strictly corresponds to the present state of science. But the term "gnostics," whether invented by Ruyer or not, is characteristic. Not only does it indicate the supreme importance conceded by contemporary scientists to human—and universal—consciousness; it also reveals a certain nostalgia for a more "discreet" community of scholars, philosophers, and theologians, a nostalgia that reminds us of the "Hermetic Enlightenment" of the seventeenth century.[11]

Now, if everything in the universe possesses consciousness, death becomes irrelevant, and the old beliefs in immortality—"popular" as well as philosophical—appear inadequate if not self-contradictory. Indeed, one can say that we are *condemned* to be immortal or that our old beliefs are, as such, self-contradictory. But it is not my intention here to discuss the metaphysical consequences of the "Princeton Gnosis." (I use this term because Ruyer's book made it famous.) Ruyer presents and interprets for the nonspecialist reader the theoretical consequences of the most recent state of science. As historian of religions, I am fascinated by the religious "prehistory" of a conclusion such as he portrays, that everything in the universe possesses consciousness; in other words, that everything is aware of its specific quality of life. A historian of religions will recall many similar archaic beliefs and ideas, for example, "animism" (the conviction that everything in the world is alive because it possesses a soul) and certain Indian theologies and metaphysics which posit a universal living matter and a considerable number of states of consciousness and unconsciousness.

I hope that my comments are not misunderstood. I do not situate such archaic beliefs and Oriental ideas on the same theoretical level as the conclusions of certain contemporary scientists. But the recent discovery and interpretation of the universality and perenniality of consciousness may encourage the historians of religions to approach the documents of their discipline with greater sympathy and imagination.

In the last analysis, we discover that the latest activities and conclusions of scientists and technologists—the direct descendents of *homo faber*—reactualize, on different levels and perspectives, the same fears, hopes, and convictions that have dominated *homo religiosus* from the very beginning: the fear of death, and even of the catastrophic destruction of life; the hope of conquering death through a ritually constructed post-existence; and, finally, the certitude that the indestructibility of life and the immortality of the soul are to be accepted as they are, as a series of states of consciousness. Of course, certain *homini religiosi* may add that it depends on every one of us to learn how to reach the highest state of consciousness, namely the awareness of pure Being.

Notes

1. I use the documentation collected by Philippe Manoeuvre, "La rock musique et la fin du monde," in *La Fin du Monde?*, Etudes et Documents présentés par Louis Pauwels, *Question de ...* 16 (January–February 1977), 210–17.

2. For instance: "On the Beach" (USA, 1959); "The World, the Flesh, and the Devil" (USA, 1959); "They Are the Damned" (England, 1961); "The Day the Earth Caught Fire" (England, 1962); "Panic in Year Zero" (USA, 1962); "Doctor Strangelove" (USA, 1964); "The Bed-Sittingroom" (England, 1969); "The Ultimate Warrior" (USA, 1975); "The Apocalypse 2024" (USA, 1975).

3. In the mid-1970s an international conference was devoted to "The Mediterranean, a Dead Sea."

4. Quoted by Gilkey, 81–82. See also the entire section devoted to the analysis of the future, 79–96. For a more balanced account of the risks that menace the world in the next two or three generations, cf. Kenneth E. Boulding, *The Meaning of the Twentieth Century* (New York, 1964); *Daedalus* 96/3 (Summer 1967): "Toward the Year 2000: Work in Progress"; Victor Ferkiss, *Technological Man: The Myth and the Reality* (New York, 1969); and Herman and A. J. Wiener, *The Year 2000* (New York, 1967).

5. Teilhard is not quoted in *La Fin du Monde?* among the representatives of "anti-sinistrose." Pauwels and many of his co-workers identify the source of the belief in the imminent end of the world as the Judeo-Christian apocalyptic. See 6ff., 109ff., 131ff.

6. Cf. Lucien Gerardin, "Techniques-Antichrist, Technologies-Messie" (in *La Fin du Monde?*, 173–85), 181.

7. After this essay was completed, I came across a stimulating article by Edward A. Tiryakian, "La fin d'une illusion et l'illusion de la fin," in *Le Progres en Question*, Actes du IXe Colloque de l'Association Internationale des Sociologues de Langue Francaise: Sociologie du Progres, Menton, May 1975, vol. II (Paris, 1978), 381–403. Among contemporary sociologists, Tiryakian distinguishes two different but dialectically related conceptions of the future: (1) the future as uninterrupted progress from the present situation; and (2) the future as an apocalyptic end of the world. According to the author, the second conception will probably dominate the next phase of Western thought (393).

8. *Bibliothèque des Philosophies chimiques*, by M. J. D. R., new edition (Paris, 1741), Preface, xxvii–xxix, quoted in *The Forge and the Crucible*.

9. Richard S. Westfall, *Force in Newton's Physics: The Science of Dynamics in the Seventeenth Century* (London and New York, 1971), 377–78.

10. Particularly important are *La cybernétique de l'information* (1954), *Paradoxes de la conscience et limites de l'automatisme* (1960), *Les puissances idéologiques* (1972), *Les nourritures psychiques* (1975), and *Les cent prochains siècles* (1977).

11. Cf. Francis Yates, *The Rosicrucian Enlightenment* (Chicago, 1972).

13

HOMO RELIGIOSUS IN THE THOUGHT OF MIRCEA ELIADE

John A. Saliba

Editor's Introduction

After an academic explication of Eliade's *Homo religiosus* and an article illustrating this usage by its application, there still remains much to criticize and perhaps much to misunderstand about Eliade's understanding of humanity in our religious mode. One of the earliest and most effective critiques of Eliade's work came in the 1976 volume by John A. Saliba. Gregory Alles pointed out in his article on *Homo religiosus* that "some, especially anthropologists, question Eliade's data and methods and have come to the radical conclusion that Eliade's *Homo religiosus* is never encountered in the field" and he specifically referred to John Saliba's critique. In order to give the reader a clearer idea of the objections raised to Eliade's classification, it is appropriate here to cite Saliba's work at some length. From Homo Religiosus *in the Works of Mircea Eliade* (Leiden: E. J. Brill, 1976). This excerpt comes from pp. 57–65. All rights reserved. Copyright © 1976 by Brill Academic Publishers. Reprinted by permission of Brill Academic Publishers.

ജ ൚

Principal Themes

There is a basic pattern in Eliade's works which underlies the concept of myth, ritual, time, and symbol. This pattern of closely related ideas is threefold in nature. First, it involves the nature of the sacred and its relationship with the profane. Secondly, it is dominated by the theme of death and resurrection. And finally, it takes the position that man has in the course of history degenerated spiritually.

The sacred is seen as "pre-eminently the real" (*Sacred and Profane*, 28). It is a powerful, efficacious force, the source of all life and energy. The sacred is the "wholly other," the transcendent, a reality which does not belong to our world even though it is manifested in and through it. It is also essentially ambivalent. The sacred attracts and repels at the same time; it is the cause of both life and death; it is both useful and dangerous, accessible and inaccessible.[1] Thus, there is an inherent opposition within the concept of the sacred. The opposition it not only internal but also external, in the sense that the sacred is contrasted to the profane. Eliade accepts Roger Caillois' definition of the sacred as that which is opposite to and totally different from the profane.[2] The two concepts— sacred and profane—are two different levels of reality which are opposed to one other. Primitive man's behavior is "governed by belief in an absolute reality opposed to the profane world of 'unrealities' in the last analysis, the latter does not constitute a 'world,' properly speaking; it is the 'unreal' *par excellence*, the uncreated, the non-existence: the void" (*Eternal Return*, 92). The polarity between the sacred and the profane is both archaic and universal (*Yoga*, 96).

This dualism is reflected in the relationship between myth and history. Myth is sacred history; it relates the origin of man and his cultures by reference to the acts of supernatural beings at the dawn of creation (*Rites and Symbols*, x–xi; *Myth and Reality*, 5, 18–19). History, on the other hand, deals with temporary profane reality. Myth is the real, the meaningful, and the holy; history is the unreal, the meaningless, and the sinful.[3] The fullness of reality present at the beginning contains no trace of history. Myth aims at doing away with history. "The man of archaic cultures tolerates 'history' with difficulty and attempts periodically to abolish it" (*Eternal Return*, 36; cf. 76). There is a tendency, especially in preliterate societies, for historical figures to be transported into the plane of mythology (*Shamanism*, 355, 362; *Eternal Return*, 42–43). For archaic man history coincides with myth (*Patterns*, 396). This anti-historical attitude is evident in religious phenomena, for instance, in shamanism and yoga, in religious beliefs and in messianic creeds.[4] Great historical pressures were endured without despair or suicide because of these mythological structures (*Eternal Return*, 151ff.). Traditional man is saved from the "terror of history" because of the mythological archetypes which are repeated and recreated in the rituals.

There is likewise a great dichotomy between sacred time and profane time. The former is momentary, an eternal presence, the latter has duration, a past as well as a future. Profane time, unlike sacred time, is not renewable. "The time of the event that the ritual commemorates or re-enacts is made *present,* represented, so to speak, however far back it may have been in ordinary reckoning" (*Patterns,* 392; cf. 388ff.; *Sacred and the Profane,* 60–68). There is a great tendency in all societies to bring back this mythical time of the beginnings, a return effected by every rite, including the orgies which take place on New Year festivals (*Patterns,* 394–95, 390). Thus, referring to the Australian Aborigines, Eliade writes:

> This is why the initiation ceremonies are so important in the lives of the aborigines; by performing them, they reintegrate the sacred time of the beginning of things, they commune with the presence of Baiamai and other mythical beings, and finally, they regenerate the world. (*Rites and Symbols,* 6)

This nostalgia for a regeneration of time is universal.

> We thus find in man at every level, the same longing to destroy profane time and live in sacred time. Further, we see the desire and hope of regenerating time as a whole, of being able to live—"humanly," "historically"—in eternity, by transforming successive time into a single eternal moment. (*Patterns,* 407)

Such an attitude toward time is part of primitive ontology. Primitive man maintains that his acts are real only insofar as they repeat the paradigmatic gestures of the past and that only through this repetition can there be an abolition of profane time. This interpretation of archaic man's attitude to time is most forcibly put in *The Eternal Return,* where we read:

> This refusal to preserve the memory of the past, even of the immediate past, seems to us to betoken a particular anthropology. We refer to archaic man's refusal to accept himself as a historical being, his refusal to grant value to memory and hence to the unusual events ... that in fact constitute concrete duration. (85 cf. 35)

The same pattern emerges when Eliade deals with sacred and profane place. The former is significantly the real, the meaningful; the latter is the structureless, the formless and the inconsistent (*Sacred and the Profane,* 20). A consecration of a locality involves a transformation of profane space. Temples and shrines were believed to be copies of primeval archetypes (*Patterns,* 396–72). The center is held to be pre-eminently the zone of the sacred, and themes of a sacred mountain situated in the center of the world are obvious signs of a mythical return to creation (*Eternal Return,* 12ff. and 17ff.). Ritual thus becomes the ideal means for providing both a time and a place for man to transform himself from the profane unreality of everyday existence into the sacred reality of the eternal beginnings. In ritual, time is here and now wiped out.[5]

The passage from the profane to the sacred is experienced by man as a death to ordinary, unreal life and a rebirth or resurrection to the real, divine existence. Eliade sees this attempt on man's part to make this transition especially in initiation rites. During these rites the novice goes through a symbolic representation, like seclusion and circumcision, and a symbolic rebirth to a new life. He becomes a new man by re-living the ancient cosmology.

> Everywhere we have found the symbolism of death as the ground of all spiritual birth—that is of regeneration. In all these contexts death signifies the surpassing of the profane, non-sanctified condition, the condition of the "natural man," ignorant of religion and blind to the spiritual. The mystery of initiation discloses to the neophyte, little by little, the true dimension of existence; by introducing him to the sacred, the mystery obliges him to assume the responsibilities of a man.[6]

The same initiatory pattern is found in secret cults, though here the emphasis lies in the new birth (*Rites and Symbols*, 5, 41–80). Moreover shamanistic experiences cannot be understood unless one sees them as initiation techniques. The shaman re-enacts ritually the symbolic death and resurrection before he is accepted as a religious specialist (*Shamanism*, 45, 53ff., 64, 84). "It is only this initiatory death and rebirth that consecrates a shaman" (76). In his trances he descends into hell and ascends to heaven, thereby re-enacting the symbolic death and resurrection (*Images and Symbols*, 164–66). Yoga also is essentially an ecstatic experience whose structure is initiatory. The yogin begins by forsaking the profane world, dying to his family and his society, and attempts to pass beyond the human condition to achieve a rebirth to another mode of being.[7] Other ceremonies and symbols dramatically portray the same pattern. Thus, for example, New Year ceremonies state the primeval passage from chaos to cosmos and thereby regenerate the whole world. Every ritual of the cosmogony is preceded by a symbolic retrogression to chaos. And death and rebirth are at the very heart of aquatic symbolism;[8] in other words, whenever water is used ritually, it expresses the participants' desire to die and to rise again renewed.

The endeavor to pass from the profane to the sacred, to die in order to be reborn on a higher level of existence, is more apparent in primitive man than in modern man. The latter is seen as spiritually inferior to the former. Primitive man considers himself as constituted ultimately by supernatural beings at the beginning of time. Modern man looks upon himself as constituted by history. Modern man makes himself. He rejects the sacred and the transcendent.

> Modern nonreligious man assumes a new existential situation; he regards himself solely as the subject and agent of history, and he refuses all appeal to transcendence. In other words, he accepts no model for humanity outside the human condition as it can be seen in its various historical situations. Man *makes himself*, and he only makes himself completely in

proportion as he desacralizes himself and the world. The sacred is the prime obstacle to his freedom. He will become himself only when he is totally demysticized.[9]

Modern man still has a terror of history and like primitive man he tries to find an escape from time. Myths still persist in his life. But the answer to his problems is given in secular terms (*Sacred and the Profane*, 204–205). He still has vestiges of the religiousness of early man, but demythologization and desacralization, which have a long history, have now reached alarming proportions.[10] While archaic man looked upon all activities as being sacred, the man of contemporary, Western culture has removed the sacred element from his life and world. Even in symbolism one can detect the loss of the sense of the sacred. This change in man's image of himself was made possible by scientific thought.[11]

Religious Man

Eliade's themes on the sacred and the profane and on religious degeneration are also important because they help define religion and religious man. It is interesting to note that nowhere does Eliade give a precise definition of religion or discuss the problem at any length. He maintains that in order to define religion one must have possession of those pure expressions of it which were present at the very beginning. But the evidence for the origin and early stages of religion is wanting (*Patterns*, 1; *Primitives to Zen*, 498–505). Eliade, therefore, prefers to talk about religious life, religious experience and especially religious man. So much so that even in his book, *The Sacred and the Profane,* which he subtitles, *The Nature of Religion*, the topic discussed is religious man rather than religion. One finds, however, in his writings, a number of statements which bring out what he considers as the constitutive elements of religion. Religion is a revelation of the sacred. It deals with meta-empirical reality (*Myths, Dreams and Mysteries*, 18). It is the "corpus of historical technique and rituals" which provides man with the means of keeping in touch with his mythical past ("Australian Religions, Part II," 211–12). And its function is to awaken and sustain the consciousness of another world ("Structures and Changes," 366). Religion is also a philosophy of life. It offers the paradigmatic solution to every existential crisis. Paradox is woven into the very structure of religion. The divine reality is experienced ambivalently, and religion aims at presenting a synthesis, a *coincidentia oppositorum*.[12]

Religion is not just a social or psychological fact. It cannot, therefore, be explained by social, historical, or psychological functions, for these miss the "irreducible element" in religion, namely, the holy (*Patterns*, xiii). The relation between religion and culture is thus viewed with caution. "Religious forms are non-temporal; they are not necessarily bound to time. We have no proof that religious structures are created by certain types of civilization or by certain historic moments" (*Myths, Dreams and Mysteries*, 178). Religious reality transcends the plane of history, even though different religious experiences can be explained by differences in culture (*Sacred and the Profane*, 17; *Myths, Dreams and Mysteries*, 178). There is an element of unity in all religions, a unity which is of greater moment than the differences (*Sacred and the Profane*, 17, 62–63).

Like myth, ritual, and symbol, religion has also degenerated since ancient times (*Myths, Dreams and Mysteries*, 137). Such degeneration is evident in some traditional societies. The best example of this retrogression, repeated in many of Eliade's works, is the case of the so-called "otiose god." These are divinities which have been pushed to the periphery of religious life where they are frequently ignored. Eliade goes as far as to compare the phenomenon of the otiose god to the death of god theology in Western culture, a movement which started with Nietzsche.[13]

The sacred is also at the center of religious life and experience. Religious life is the experience of the kratophanies, hierophanies and theophanies which affect the whole of man's life. It demands the awareness of the sacred and profane dichotomy and it stirs the depths of man's being (*Patterns*, 126; *Myths, Dreams and Mysteries*, 17). On the level of this genuine experience nature is never purely natural. "For those who have a religious experience all nature is capable of revealing itself as cosmic sacrality. The cosmos in its entirety becomes a hierophany" (*Sacred and the Profane*, 12; cf. *Patterns*, 425). The same experience is one of re-entering the mythical paradise of the beginnings. It is found stronger among shamans, the mystics of primitive societies (*Myths, Dreams and Mysteries*, 44, 64–68; *Shamanism*, 265–66).

For Eliade, faith is the new dimension, acquired through religious experience, and it is found mainly in Judaism and Christianity (*Eternal Return*, 108–109). In a passage which is crucial to the understanding of Eliade's own theology of religions, he thus writes on Abraham's sacrifice:

> Whereas, for the entire Paleo-Semitic world, such a sacrifice, despite its religious function, was only custom, a rite whose meaning was perfectly intelligible, in Abraham's case it is an act of faith. He does not understand why the sacrifice is demanded of him; nevertheless he performs it because it was the Lord who demanded it. By this act, which is apparently absurd, Abraham initiates a new religious experience, faith. All others (the whole Oriental world) continue to move in an economy of the sacred that will be transcended by Abraham and his successors. To employ Kierkegaard's terminology, their sacrifices belonged to the "general"; that is, they were based upon archaic theophanies that were concerned only with the circulation of sacred energy in the cosmos... These were acts whose justification lay in themselves; they entered into a logical and coherent system: what had belonged to God must be returned to him. For Abraham, Isaac

was a *gift* from the Lord and not the product of a direct and material conception. Between God and Abraham yawned an abyss; there was a fundamental break in continuity. Abraham's religious act inaugurates a new religious dimension: God reveals himself as personal, as a "totally distinct" existence that ordains, bestows, demands, without any rational (that is, general and foreseeable) justification, and for which all is possible. This new religious dimension renders "faith" possible in the Judaeo-Christian sense. (*Eternal Return*, 109–10; the same idea is repeated on 159–62)

For Eliade, therefore, faith, as understood in Christian theology, cannot be applied to all religious men. The common factor among all religious men is the desire for being. Since the profane is unreal, religious man tries to live as long as possible near his gods, the sacred supernatural beings, to whom he owes his origin. In other words, he wants to inhabit a sacred universe. This desire "is in fact equivalent to his desire to take up his abode in objective reality, not to let himself be paralyzed by the never-ceasing relativity of purely subjective experience" (*Sacred and the Profane*, 28; cf. 13, 64–65, 87, 91, 96).

Sacred space thus acquires importance in the life of religious man. He expresses the dichotomy between the space that is sacred and the lifeless space of the secular world in his ritual (*Sacred and the Profane*, 20). And he, consequently, always seeks to fix his abode at the center of the world, a center represented by shrines and temples and conceived as an organized cosmos (22, 43–44, 65). Just as religious man alternates his existence between sacred and profane space, so also he lives in two kinds of time. He experiences intervals of time that are sacred. For him profane duration can be periodically stopped (70–71, 104). Through sacred time, as well as through sacred space, religious man re-actualizes the cosmogony and re-enters the time of origins where authentic existence came into being. Religious man thus attempts to live in the continual presence of the sacred past (*Sacred and the Profane*, 81, 88–89; *Myth and Reality*, 92).

Religious man is essentially mythical. He is "above all a man paralyzed by the myth of the eternal return" (*Sacred and the Profane*, 93). His greatest hope is to recreate the mythical events. "The more religious man is, the more paradigmatic models does he possess to guide his attitudes and actions" (96; cf. 106). He, therefore, assumes a humanity that has a transhuman, transcendent model. The mythical gods are the models of his actions, and since the gods are always living and vibrant with life and energy, death becomes but another modality of human existence. Also, by desiring and trying to live with his gods, religious man escapes the unreality of the meaningless change inherent in profane space and time (99–100, 148).

Religious man's view of the universe is unique. For him nature has always a religious value and the supernatural is closely linked with the natural. He is led to the former by reflecting on the latter. In other words, for religious man "the world always presents a supernatural valence" (138; cf. 116–18, 150). The world speaks to religious man of his gods and of their doings. His view of the universe is cosmic. He is completely open to the whole world; that is, he communes with his gods and he shares in the sanctity of the universe. This openness enables him to know himself as he really is, a religious creature sharing in the life of the sacred or divine (1–16, 165–67, 169–70, 172). Such an attitude does not imply that religious man is shirking his responsibility. Rather, his responsibility is "on the cosmic plane in contradistinction to the moral, social, or historical responsibilities that are alone regarded as valid in modern civilizations" (93). Religious man has therefore a completely different attitude to life, to the world, and to men than non-religious man. Religious man is not defined by the historical or cultural context in which he lives. This image of religious man is central in Eliade's thought. He writes:

> Religious man assumes a particular and characteristic mode of existence in the world and, despite the great number of historic-religious forms, this characteristic form is always recognizable. Whatever the historical context in which he is placed, *homo religiosus* always believes that there is an absolute reality, *the sacred*, which transcends this world but manifests itself in this world, thereby sanctifying it and making it real. He further believes that life has a sacred origin and that human existence realizes all of its potentialities in proportion as it is religious—i.e., participates in reality. (202)

For religious men, therefore, it is only the spiritual, non-material world which possesses the fullness of being. The present worldly condition acquires its meaning and value only with reference to the other-worldly dimension. It is the fullness of being, the ultimate reality, for which religious man strives.

Notes

1. *Yoga, Immortality and Freedom*, 152, 284; *Myths, Dreams and Mysteries*, 18; *Sacred and the Profane*, 11; *Patterns*, 13–16, 370–71, 384.
2. *Patterns*, xiv, 12ff., 447, 459; *Sacred and the Profane*, 10; *Yoga, Immortality and Freedom*, 96, 100.
3. *Patterns*, 401; *Eternal Return*, 34–35; *Myth and Reality*, 2.
4. *Yoga, Immortality and Freedom*, 67–68, 223, 339–40; *Eternal Return*, 111.
5. *Eternal Return*, 35; *Sacred and the Profane*, 68; cf. *Patterns*, 32.
6. *Myths, Dreams and Mysteries*, 200; cf. *Rites and Symbols*, 13–14, 29, 34, 91, 135; *Sacred and the Profane*, 191–92, 197ff.
7. *Yoga, Immortality and Freedom*, 5–6, 165, 227, 272–73, 310, 323–24, 362ff.
8. For the New Year ceremonies consult *Eternal Return*, 62ff. See *Rites and Symbols*, xiii, for the rituals of cosmogony and *Patterns*, 196ff. for the symbolism of water.
9. *Sacred and the Profane*, 203; cf. *Rites and Symbols*, xiv; *Eternal Return*, 141–44, 154–62.

10. *Myth and Reality*, 111–13; *Myths, Dreams and Mysteries*, 29, 233ff.; *Sacred and the Profane*, 107–12.
11. *Eternal Return*, 28–29; *Sacred and the Profane*, 13, 50–51; *Images and Symbols*, 147; *Shamanism*, 456.
12. *Two and the One*, 82ff., 122ff., 206–207; *Patterns*, 419ff.; *Sacred and the Profane*, 156, 210; *Myths, Dreams and Mysteries*, 17–18.
13. *Patterns*, 43ff.; *Myths, Dreams and Mysteries*, 134–37; *Myth and Reality*, 93–98; *Sacred and the Profane*, 121–25.

Symbols

14

What the Symbols "Reveal"

Mircea Eliade

Editor's Introduction

Eliade's understanding of religious symbolism is central to his analysis of religious phenomena. The systematic or mutually defining nature of the terms of the study are once again apparent here. In this case Eliade's understanding of the religious symbol determines and is determined by his understanding of the role of the Historian of Religions. Originally, Eliade concentrated on the role of the Historian of Religions first. However, I wish to focus first on the understanding of the symbol and then, in a later section, to return to the related question of History of Religions methodology. Nonetheless, the implications of Eliade's following statements for his understanding of methodology, of the *coincidentia oppositorum*, and of the significance of history, should not be neglected here, even though they will be dealt with in more detail below. The present excerpt is a reworking of a 1959 article, "Methodological Remarks on the Study of Religious Symbolism" in *History of Religions: Problems of Methodology*, edited by Eliade and Joseph Kitagawa (Chicago: Chicago University Press) and it appeared in *The Two and the One*, 201–11 by Mircea Eliade, published by the University of Chicago Press. All rights reserved. English translation copyright © 1965 by Harvill Press. Reprinted by permission of the Random House Group Ltd.

৯৪ ৫৩

The task of the historian of religions remains incomplete if he fails to discover the function of symbolism in general. We know what the theologian, the philosopher, and the psychologist have to say about this problem.[1] Let us now examine the conclusions which the historian of religions reaches when he reflects on his own documents.

The first observation that he is forced to make is that the World "speaks" in symbols, "reveals" itself through them. It is not a question of a utilitarian and objective language. A symbol is not a replica of objective reality. It reveals something deeper and more fundamental. Let us try to elucidate the different aspects, the different depths of this revelation.

(1) Symbols are capable of revealing a modality of the real or a condition of the World which is not evident on the plane of immediate experience. To illustrate the sense in which the symbol expresses a modality of the real inaccessible to human experience, let us take an example: the symbolism of the Waters, which is capable of revealing the pre-formal, the potential, the chaotic. This is not, of course, a matter of rational cognition, but of apprehension by the active consciousness prior to reflection. It is of such apprehensions that the World is made. Later, by elaborating the significances thus understood, the first reflections on the creation of the World will be set in motion; this is the point of departure of all the cosmologies and ontologies from the Vedas to the Pre-Socratics.

As for the capacity of symbols to reveal an inner pattern of the World, we will refer to what we said earlier [below, 246–48] about the principal significances of the Cosmic Tree. The Tree reveals the World as a living totality, periodically regenerating itself and, thanks to this regeneration, continually fertile, rich and inexhaustible. Here, too, it is not a question of considered knowledge, but of an immediate comprehension of the "cipher" of the World. The World "speaks" through the medium of the Cosmic Tree, and its "word" is directly understood. The World is apprehended as Life and for primitive thought. Life is a disguise worn by Being.

A corollary of the preceding observations: religious symbols which touch on the patterns of life reveal a deeper Life, more mysterious than that grasped by everyday experience. They reveal the miraculous, inexplicable side of Life, and at the same time the sacramental dimension of human existence. "Deciphered" in the light of religious symbols, human life itself, reveals a hidden side: it comes from "elsewhere," from very far away; it is "divine" in the sense that it is the work of Gods or supernatural Beings.

(2) This brings us to a second general observation: for primitives, symbols are always religious, since they point either to something real or to a World pattern. Now, at the archaic levels of culture, the real—that is to say the powerful, the significant, the living—is equivalent to the sacred. Moreover, the World is a creation of the Gods or of supernatural Beings: to discover a World pattern amounts to revealing a secret or a "ciphered" meaning of the divine work. It is

for this reason that archaic religious symbols imply an ontology; a pre-systematic ontology, of course, the expression of a judgment both of the World and of human existence: judgment which is not formulated in concepts and which cannot always be translated into concepts.

(3) An essential characteristic of religious symbolism is its *multivalence*, its capacity *to express simultaneously several meanings the unity between which is not evident on the plane of immediate experience*. The symbolism of the Moon, for example, reveals a connatural unity between the lunar rhythms, temporal becoming, the Waters, the growth of plants, women, death and resurrection, the human destiny, the weaver's craft, etc. (*Patterns*, 154ff.). In the final analysis, the symbolism of the Moon reveals a correspondence of a "mystical" order between the various levels of cosmic reality and certain modalities of human existence. Let us observe that this correspondence is not indicated by immediate and spontaneous experience, nor by critical reflection. It is the result of a certain mode of "viewing" the World.

Even if we admit that certain of the Moon's functions have been discovered by careful observation of the lunar phases (their relation with rainfall, for instance, and menstruation), it is difficult to imagine that the symbolism could have been built up in its entirety by an act of reason. It requires quite another order of cognition to reveal, for example, the "lunar destiny" of human existence, the fact that man is "measured" by temporal rhythms which are one with the phases of the Moon, that he is consigned to death but that, like the Moon which reappears in the sky after three days of darkness, he also can begin his existence again, and that, in any case, he nourishes the hope of a life beyond the tomb, more certain or better as a consequence of initiation.

(4) This capacity of religious symbolism to reveal a multitude of structurally united meanings has an important consequence: the symbol is capable of *revealing a perspective in which diverse realities can be fitted together or even integrated into a "system."* In other words, a religious symbol allows man to discover a certain unity of the World and at the same time to become aware of his own destiny as an integral part of the World. In the case of lunar symbolism, it is clear in what sense the different meanings of the symbols form a "system." On different registers (cosmological, anthropological, and "spiritual") the lunar rhythm reveals homologous patterns: always it is a matter of modalities of existence subject to the law of Time and cyclic becoming, that is to say of existences destined for a "Life" which carries, in its very structure, death and rebirth. Thanks to the Moon symbolism, the World no longer appears an arbitrary assembly of heterogeneous and divergent realities. The various cosmic levels are mutually related; they are, in a sense, "bound together" by the same lunar rhythm, just as human life is "woven" by the Moon and predestined by the Spinning Goddesses.

Another example will illustrate even better this capacity of symbols to open up a perspective in which things can be understood as united in a system. The symbolism of Night and Darkness—which can be discerned in cosmogonic myths, in initiatory rites, in iconographies featuring nocturnal or underground creatures—reveals the structural unity between the pre-cosmogonic and pre-natal Darkness, on the one hand, and death, rebirth, and initiation on the other.[2] This renders possible not only the intuition of a certain mode of being, but also the comprehension of the "place" of that mode of being in the constitution of the World and the human condition. The symbolism of cosmic Night enables man to see what existed before him and before the World, to understand how things came into existence, and where things "were" before they were there, before him. Once again, this is no speculation but a direct understanding of the mystery that things had a beginning, and that everything which precedes and concerns this beginning has a supreme value for human existence. Consider the great importance of initiatory rites involving a *regressus ad uterum*, as a result of which man believes himself able to start a new existence. Remember also the innumerable ceremonies intended, periodically, to restore the primordial "Chaos" in order to regenerate the World and human society.

(5) Perhaps the most important function of religious symbolism—especially important because of the role it will play in later philosophical speculations—is its *capacity for expressing paradoxical situations or certain patterns of ultimate reality that can be expressed in no other way*. One example will suffice: the symbolism of the Symplegades[3] as it can be deciphered in numerous myths, legends, and images presenting the paradox of a passage from one mode of existence to another—transfer from this world to another, from Earth to Heaven or Hell, or passage from a profane, purely carnal existence to a spiritual existence, etc. The following are the most frequent images: to pass between two clashing rocks or icebergs, or between two mountains in perpetual movement, or between two jaws, or to penetrate the *vagina dentata* and come out unharmed, or enter a mountain that reveals no opening, etc. One understands the significance of all these images: if the possibility of a "passage" exists, it can only be effectuated "in the spirit"—giving the word all the meanings that it is capable of carrying in archaic societies: a discarnate being, the imaginary world, and the world of ideas. One can pass through a Symplegades in so far as one behaves "as a spirit," that is to say shows imagination and intelligence and so proves oneself capable of detaching oneself from immediate reality (*Rites and Symbols*, 64ff.). No other symbol of the "difficult passage"—not even the celebrated motif of the bridge filed to the sharpness of a sword-edge, or the razor mentioned in the *Katha Upanishad* (III, 14) reveals more clearly than the Symplegades that there is a way of being inaccessible to immediate experience, and that this way of being can only be attained by renouncing a crude belief in the impregnability of matter.

One could make similar observations concerning the capacity of symbols to express the contradictory aspects of ultimate reality. Nicolas Cusanus considered the *coincidentia oppositorum* as the most suitable definition of God's nature.

Now, this symbol had long ago been used to signify not only what we call the "totality" or the "absolute" but paradoxical coexistence in the divinity of the opposite and antagonistic principles. The conjunction of the Serpent (or another symbol of the chthonic and unmanifested darkness) and the Eagle (symbol of the solar and unmanifested light) expresses, in iconography or in myth, the mystery of the totality and the cosmic unity (*Patterns*, 419ff.). To repeat, although the concepts of polarity and the *coincidentia oppositorum* have been used systematically since the beginnings of philosophical speculation, the symbols which have obscurely revealed them have not been the product of critical reflection but the result of an existential tension. Assuming its presence in the World, man found himself facing the "cipher" or "word" of the World and this led him to confront the mystery of the contradictory aspects of a reality or sacrality which he was tempted to consider as single and homogeneous. One of the greatest discoveries of the human spirit was naïvely anticipated on the day when, by certain religious symbols, man guessed that oppositions and antagonisms can be fitted and integrated into a unity. From then onwards the negative and sinister aspects of the Cosmos and the Gods not only found a justification but revealed themselves as an integral part of all reality or sacrality.

(6) Finally, we must stress the *existential value of religious symbolism*, that is to say the fact that a symbol *always points to a reality or a situation concerning human existence*. It is above all this existential dimension that distinguishes and divides symbols from concepts. Symbols preserve contact with the deep sources of life; they express, one might say, "the spiritual as life experience." This is why symbols have a kind of "numinous" aura: they reveal that the *modalities of the spirit are at the same time manifestations of Life*, and that consequently, they *directly concern human existence*. A religious symbol not only reveals a pattern of reality or a dimension of existence, it brings at the same time a *meaning to human existence*. This is why even symbols concerning ultimate reality also afford existential revelations to the man who deciphers their message.

A religious symbol translates a human situation into cosmological terms, and vice versa; to be more precise, it reveals the unity between human existence and the structure of the Cosmos. Man does not feel himself "isolated" in the Cosmos; he is open to a World which, thanks to the symbol, becomes "familiar." On the other hand the cosmological significances of a symbolism allow him to escape from a subjective situation and recognize the objectivity of his personal experiences.

It follows that the *man who understands a symbol not only "opens himself" to the objective world, but at the same time succeeds in emerging from his personal situation and reaching a comprehension of the universal*. This is to be explained by the fact that symbols "explode" immediate reality as well as particular situations. When some tree or other incarnates the World Tree, or when the spade is assimilated to the phallus and agricultural labor to the act of generation, etc., one may say that the immediate reality of these objects or activities "explodes" beneath the irruptive force of a deeper reality. The same thing takes place in an individual situation, for example that of the neophyte shut in the initiatory hut: the symbolism "explodes" this particular situation by revealing it as exemplary, that is to say endlessly repeatable in many different contexts (for the initiatory but is approximated to the mother's womb, and also to the belly of a Monster and to Hell, and the darkness symbolizes, as we have seen, cosmic Night, the pre-formal, the fetal state of the World, etc.). *Thanks to the symbol, the individual experience is "awoken" and transmuted into a spiritual act.* To "live" a symbol and correctly decipher its message implies an opening towards the Spirit and finally access to the universal.

The "History" of Symbols

These few general remarks about religious symbolism would certainly require elaboration and finer definition. Being unable to undertake so vast a labor here, let us be content to add some observations. The first concerns what might be called the "history" of a symbol. We have already alluded to the difficulty that a historian of religions meets when, in order to isolate the structure of a symbol, he has to study and compare documents belonging to different cultures and historical eras. To say that a symbol has a "history" may mean two things: (a) that this symbol was formed at a certain historical moment and consequently could not have existed *before* that moment; (b) that this symbol spread from a precise cultural center and that consequently one must not consider it to have been spontaneously rediscovered in all the other cultures in which it is found.

That there have been many symbols dependant on precise historical situations is beyond doubt. It is clear, for example, that the spade cannot have been assimilated to the phallus or agricultural labor to the sexual act before the discovery of agriculture. Similarly, the symbolic value of the figure 7, and consequently the imagery of the seven-branched Cosmic Tree, did not seize men's minds before the discovery of the seven planets, which led, in Mesopotamia, to the conception of the seven planetary heavens. And very many symbols attached themselves to particular socio-political and local situations, and took form at a precise historical moment: the symbols of royalty and matriarchy, for instance, or systems implying the division of a society into two halves, at the same time antagonistic and complementary, etc.

All this being known, it follows that the second possible meaning of the expression "the history of a symbol" is equally right: symbols connected with agriculture, royalty, etc., were very probably diffused with these other cultural elements and their respective ideologies. But to recognize the historical nature of certain religious symbols does not nullify what we have said above concerning the function of religious symbols in general. On the one hand it is important to make clear that, though numerous, these symbols connected with cultural events are sensibly less frequent than the symbols relative to the cosmic structure or the human condition. The majority of religious symbols *point to the world in its totality or one of its structures* (Night, Water Sky, Stars, seasons, vegetation, temporal rhythms, animal life, etc.), or *refer to situations that play a part in all human existence*, to the fact that man has sex, is mortal, and in quest of what we call today the "ultimate reality." In certain cases, archaic symbols relating to death, sexuality, hope of an existence beyond the tomb, etc., have been modified, even replaced by similar symbols brought by migrations of higher cultures. But these modifications, whilst complicating the work of the historian of religions, do not change the central problem. To attempt a comparison with the work of the psychologist: when a European dreams of maize leaves, the importance is not that maize was not imported into Europe till the sixteenth century, that it belongs therefore to the history of Europe, but the fact that as a dream *symbol* the maize leaf is only one of the innumerable varieties of *green leaf*—and the psychologist takes account of this symbolic value and not the historical diffusion of maize. The historian of religions finds himself in an analogous situation when dealing with archaic symbols that have been modified as a result of recent cultural influences: for example, the World Tree, which in Siberia and Central Asia received a new value when it assimilated the Mesopotamian idea of the seven planetary heavens.

In brief, symbols attached to recent cultural events, though dating from historical times, *became religious symbols because they contributed to the "foundation of a World"* in the sense that they allowed these new Worlds revealed by agriculture, by the domestication of animals, by kingship, to "speak," to reveal themselves to men by revealing at the same time new human situations. In other words, symbols bound to new, recent phases of culture were formed in the same manner as the more archaic symbols, that is to say as a result of existential tensions and total apprehensions of the World. Whatever the history of a religious symbol, its function remains the same. To study the origin and diffusion of a symbol does not excuse the historian of religions from his obligation to understand it, and to restore to it all the meanings that it could have had in the course of history.

The second observation to some degree continues the first, since it concerns the capacity of symbols to become richer in the course of history. We have just seen how, under the influence of Mesopotamian ideas, the Cosmic Tree comes to symbolize the seven planetary heavens by its seven branches. And in Christian theology and folklore, the Cross is conceived as erected at the Center of the World, and acting as substitute for the Cosmic Tree. Salvation by the Cross is a new value attached to a precise historical fact—the agony and death of Jesus—but this new idea continues and perfects the idea of the cosmic *renovatio* symbolized by the World Tree (*Images and Symbols*, 151ff.).

All this could be formulated in another manner: symbols are capable of being understood on various levels, one "above" the other. The symbolism of darkness can be read not only in its cosmological, initiatory, and ritual contexts (Cosmic Night, prenatal darkness, etc.), but also in the mystical experience of the "dark night of the soul" of Saint John of the Cross. The case of the Symplegades symbolism is even clearer. As for symbols expressing the *coincidentia oppositorum*, one knows the role they have played in philosophical and theological speculation. But then one may ask whether these "higher" meanings were not, in some degree, implied in the others, whether they were not, if imperfectly understood, at least anticipated by men living on archaic levels of culture. Whence arises an important problem which, unfortunately, we cannot discuss here: how to decide to what degree the "higher" meanings of a symbol are fully recognized and presumed by such and such an individual belonging to such and such a culture?[4] The difficulty of the problem lies in the fact that the symbol is addressed not only to the waking consciousness, but to the whole psychic life. Consequently, even in a case where, after a rigorous inquiry directed to a certain number of individuals, one succeeds in discovering what they think of a certain symbol belonging to their tradition, one has not the right to conclude that the message of the symbol is confined only to those significances of which these individuals are fully conscious. The depth psychologist has taught us that a symbol delivers its message and fulfils its function even when its meaning escapes the conscious mind.

If we admit this, two important consequences follow:

(1) If, at a certain moment in history, a religious symbol has been able clearly to express a transcendental meaning, one is justified in supposing that at an earlier epoch this meaning might have been obscurely anticipated.

(2) In order to decipher a religious symbol, we must not only take all its contexts into consideration, we must above all consider also the meanings which this symbol possessed in what we call its "maturity." Analyzing, in a previous work, the symbolism of the magic flight, we came to the conclusion that it obscurely reveals ideas of liberty and transcendence, but that it is above all on the levels of spiritual activity that the symbolism of flight and ascension becomes completely intelligible (*Myths, Dreams and Mysteries*, 99ff. esp. 110ff.). This does not mean that we must place all the meanings of this symbolism on the same level, from the flight of shamans to the mystical ascension. But since the "cipher" constituted by this symbolism carries in its composition all the values that man has progressively discovered in the course of centuries, in deciphering it we must take into account the most "general" significance: the sole significance which can relate all the particular significances one to another, the sole significance which permits us to understand how all these last ended by forming a single structure.

Notes

1. We would recall Paul Tillich's statement: "This is the great function of symbols: to point beyond themselves, in the power of that to which they point, to open up levels of reality which otherwise are closed, and to open up levels of the human mind of which we otherwise are not aware" (Paul Tillich, "Theology and Symbolism" in *Religious Symbolism,* ed. F. Ernest Johnson [New York, 1955], 107–16, 109).

2. It must be added that Darkness symbolizes not only the pre-cosmic "chaos" but also "orgy" (social confusion) and "madness" (disintegration of the personality).

3. See Ananda K. Coomaraswamy, *Symplegades*, Homage to George Sarton, ed. M. F. Ashley Montagu (New York, 1947), 463–88. See also Carl Hentze, *Tod, Auferstehung, Weltordnung* (Zurich, 1955), especially 45ff.

4. See Eliade, "Centre du Monde, Temple, Maison" in *Le Symbolisme cosmique des Monuments religieux* (Rome, 1957), 57–82, especially 58ff.

15

NOTES ON THE SYMBOLISM OF THE ARROW

Mircea Eliade

Editor's Introduction

Eliade's analysis of the symbolism of the arrow stands on its own as an example of his understanding of the operations of religious symbolism. However, it also contains some notable indications of Eliade's broader understanding. Here he makes a clear rejection of any notion of a "prelogical mentality" that might distinguish archaic from modern humanity. He also makes the fascinating observation that every new pragmatic discovery, every "conquest of the material world," brings about new symbolic possibilities and a "corresponding impact on human imagination." The discovery of the bow and arrow, "the rapidity, the suddenness, and the invisibility of the arrow," opened the human imagination to the possibility of action-at-a-distance and of the swift, effectively instantaneous, connection between physically separated entities. From *Religions in Antiquity*, edited by Jacob Neusner (Leiden: E. J. Brill, 1968), 463–75. All rights reserved. Copyright © 1968 by Brill Academic Publishers. Published by permission of Brill Academic Publishers.

ॐ ☙ ❧

A fascinating monograph could be written about the symbolism of man's tools, and especially of his oldest weapons. Contrary to what may be called "cosmic symbols"—stars, waters, the seasons, vegetation, etc.—which reveal both the structures of the Universe and the human mode of being in the world, the symbolism of tools and weapons discloses specific existential situations. For some time I have been engaged in analyzing the symbolism of the bow and arrows, as it appears in various myths, rituals, and beliefs. The documentation is vast and bewildering; in this article, however, I shall discuss only certain aspects of the arrow symbolism.

To simplify our research, we may group the data according to the following main categories:

1) Sickness caused by shooting darts and, consequently, magical (shamanistic) cures consisting of pulling these out or firing miniature arrows at demons;
2) Shooting arrows against thunder gods;
3) Arrows as symbols of fertility and luck;
4) Miraculous bows and master archers;
5) The oracular function of arrows;
6) Myths of the chain of arrows and other related themes;
7) Arrows in mystical techniques and mystical imagination.

I shall emphasize in particular the last two motifs, but in order for us to fully appreciate their originality a rapid review of the others is necessary.

I) The magico-medical role of the arrow has been repeatedly and competently studied. Scholars from E. B. Tylor to Lauri Honko[1] have collected and analyzed data concerning the reputed origin of sickness as the shooting of "projectiles" (in many cases, arrows) into the body and the related cure through pulling them out or shooting in the direction of the enemy (the "magical bow," found among the Bushmen, is characteristic of all hunter cultures[2]). This idea is widely diffused[3] and has survived in the higher cultures: the sudden, painful ache is called "fairy dart," "Hexenschuss," "häxskott," etc.[4] In many parts of the world demons or spirits are said to provoke sickness by shooting arrows which the healer extracts either by massage[5] or by pulling them out.[6] In some cases, as among the Munda-speaking Savara (Saora) and several South American tribes, the shaman shoots at the patient with a special bow and arrow.[7] The same ritual is attested in the Atharvaveda: "with a *dārbhyuṣa* of bamboo, which has a bowstring made of black wool (and) with black arrows (*bunda-*) that have bunches of wool tied to their points, (he does) what is directed in the *mantras* ..., i.e. while whispering the *mantra* he shoots after each stanza an arrow at the pustules."[8]

For similar reasons, the ritual bow and arrows are important elements in Siberian and Asiatic shamanism (see *Shamanism*, 174ff.). During the *séance,* the shaman keeps two arrows in his right hand.[9] The Buryat shaman uses an arrow while "recalling the soul."[10] We must also point out that in many areas (Central Asia, North Eurasia) there are myths explaining the origin of such magical arrows: they were made from a fallen branch of the Cosmic Tree (cf. Honko, 132ff.).

All of these ideas and beliefs reflect the demonic and ambivalent nature of the bow and arrows. The shooting of darts was probably man's first "mastery over space." The arrow's deadly flight was viewed as something "unnatural," i.e. as something to be explained by magico-religious agencies. In many parts of the world the darts were symbolically assimilated to thunderbolts. The rapidity, the suddenness, and the invisibility of the arrow could not belong to a "natural" world or an "ordinary" life. The mastery of the mysterious art of shooting darts was homologized to the meteorological prodigies of the Supernatural Beings or to the demons' power of causing illness or death.

I do not wish to imply that prehistoric and "primitive" men were not fully aware of the concrete, objective conditions and presuppositions of archery. Their mind was neither "pre-logical" nor paralyzed by a *participation mystique*. It was a fully human mind. But this also means that every significant act was validated and valorized both on the level of empirical experience and in a Universe of images, symbols, and myths. No conquest of the material world was effected without a corresponding impact on human imagination and behavior. And I am inclined to add that the reflections of the objective conquests upon such imaginary Universes are perhaps even more important for the understanding of man.

II) Shooting darts against thunder clouds represents in fact a particular instance of the previous theme. The ritual is attested among various primitive tribes; it was also known in China, in Central Asia and among some ancient Thracian populations. To give only a few examples: the Thunder god of Yurakare of Bolivia is believed to throw lightning from the top of the mountains. "When Thunder was heard, men threatened to shoot him ... Whenever a storm was about to break, women and children were sent into the huts while men shot arrows and recited incantations against this 'fiery being' who threatened to destroy their houses and plantations."[11] Likewise, during storms the Semai (Sakai) of Malacca shoot poisoned darts at the sky, while their women toss fire brands in the air and make a deafening uproar with bamboo canes.[12]

In Asia it was the custom to shoot arrows toward the cloudy or dark sky against the demons. In China, the shooting was aimed at the "Celestial Wolf" which was considered to be the cause of the eclipses.[13] Herodotus informs us that the Getae (IV, 94), the Calydonians (I, 172) and the Psylli (IV, 173) shot arrows to drive off the demons of the thunderstorms, and analogous practices survive in modern Bulgaria.[14] Most probably the scenes of the Mithraic monuments which show Mithra shooting against rain clouds are to be interpreted in the same way.[15]

III) Also somehow related to the keeping away of evil spirits, but having a primarily positive role—for men, bringing luck in hunting; for women, fertility—are rituals of offering miniature bows and arrows at birth. Such bows and arrows are hung above the cradle. Gustav Rank has abundantly shown the prevalence of this practice among the North Eurasian peoples.[16]

The offering of arrows is a well-documented ritual among most Siberian tribes,[17] in Tibet[18] and in China.[19] Also, when the shaman "recalls the soul" of a patient, an arrow is stuck into a vase filled with the food liked best by that patient.[20]

IV) The theme of the miraculous bow and a master archer is especially popular in the mythologies and folklores of Eastern Europe and Asia. Among the numerous motifs and incidents we need recall only two. The first presents the trial of a hero: he has to bend a giant bow and shoot an arrow through a number of obstacles (shield, trees, etc.). The ritual, surviving as a literary motif in the *Odyssey* (XXI), *Mahabharata, Ramayana* and the *Lalitavistara*, was probably related to the ceremony of royal installation.[21] Gabriel Germain considers it to be of Indo-European origin. But in the *Rig Veda* we have a similar myth whose Austro-Asiatic origin has been substantiated by F. B. J. Kuiper: Indra shoots an arrow that passes through a mountain and kills the boar guarding a treasure (a dish of rice) on the farther side of it. The words for the bow (*drumbhuli*), the arrow (*bunda*), the dish of rice (*odand*) and the name of the boar (*Emusa*) are of Munda origin.[22]

The initiatory character of all these tests is evident: the victorious hero conquers a "treasure," a wife or a kingdom. An analogous theme, surviving primarily in folklore, narrates the spectacular shooting of a fabulous bird or a dragon who defends or steals miraculous (golden) apples, etc.[23] The interest of all these myths and tales consists principally in their insistence upon the *apparent impossibility of attaining the goal*. Only a hero, a king, or a Bodhisattva is capable of emerging victorious from a test that surpasses human possibilities.

As we shall see later on, the theme of the "miraculous shooting of an arrow" can be integrated into the symbolism of the thread and thus can come to convey, in certain cultures, a purely metaphysical meaning. Such is the case, for example, in an episode from the *Sarabhanga Jātaka* (V, 130) "where the Bodhisattva Jotipāla (the 'Keeper of Light'), standing at the centre of a field, attaches a thread to the neck of his arrow and with one shot penetrates all four posts, the arrow passing a second time through the first post and then returning to his hand; thus, indeed, he 'sews' all things to himself by means of a single thread."[24]

V) Shooting darts for oracular purposes is attested among the Tibetans[25] (cf. the so-called *mda'dar* or "divination-arrow," used frequently in the rites of the Bon magicians and Buddhist lamas), among the Ostyak[26] and the Buryat.[27] Martti Rasanen has proven that the ritual was also known by the Turks.[28] The original meaning of the oracular shooting of darts seems to be related to the ideas of conquering, organizing, or "re-creating" a territory, and of "fixing" the destiny of a certain period of time.

VI) The myths and tales narrating the ascent to heaven by means of a chain of arrows have been discussed by Wilhelm Wundt, Raffaele Pettazzoni, and Gutmund Hatt.[29] The story can be summarized as follows: a hero "hurls darts; one embeds itself in the celestial vault, then another embeds itself exactly in the notch of the first, a third in the second, and so on until they form a long chain of arrows upon which the hero mounts as upon a ladder to heaven."[30] This mythological theme is popular in North America (especially in the Western regions) and has also been found in South America, Melanesia, and Australia. It seems to be absent in Africa, Polynesia, and, according to Ehrenreich,[31] also in Asia; but G. Hatt quotes some similar myths from Koryak, Chukchee, and Ainu sources (Hatt, 42). The problem of the distribution and probable routes of diffusion of this myth will not detain us here.[32]

None of the three authors cited above has tried to analyze the causes prompting the hero's ascent on his arrow-chain. The most frequent seem to be the following: a) a Supernatural Being retires to Heaven after the creation of the Earth or the civilization of the tribe; b) a hero climbs to Heaven to bring fire to the Earth; c) or to bring back his wife and children who have either been abducted by a celestial being or have gone of their own accord (the Swan motif); d) the ascent to Heaven occurs as the result of an incestuous love between brother and sister; e) or of a love affair with a brother's wife; f) or in order to prove the full possession of magic powers; g) or to wage war on Heaven; h) or in order to meet the gods.

A few examples will illustrate each of the foregoing motifs:

a) The Indian Coos (Kusun family) have this myth: after completing the creation, the Two Brothers "shoot arrows at the heaven, each of which strikes the staff of the preceding one, and thus is formed a ladder by which the two climb to heaven."[33]

b) Among the natives of Lake Condah, a Primordial Being, in order to bring fire from the sky, ascended to Heaven by means of a lance with a line, thrown and stuck in the vault.[34] Both of these themes, a and b, are related to the well-known myth of the withdrawal of Supernatural Beings at the end of the "primordial" epoch.

c) In a Chukchee myth, the hero goes out in search of his abducted wife, a polar bear. He shoots arrows out into the open sea, and land arises where the arrows fall.[35] In an island of the New Hebrides (Logana), a hero abandoned by his wife and son, who have flown to heaven, shoots a hundred darts in succession; the last touches earth and the hero ascends the chain and recovers the lady with her son.[36]

d) Among an Indian tribe of the Rio Jamunda there is the following myth: a woman "fell in love with her brother and visited him unknown at night. The brother felt suspicion and put marks in her face. In the morning when she saw her image in the water she felt ashamed because she was recognized. She took then her bow and arrows and shot up in the sky, forming a chain of arrows by which she climbed up and became the moon."[37]

e) The motif of climbing to Heaven as a result of a love affair with the brother's wife is attested in myths from New Guinea and Australia. Among the Jabin and Tami of New Guinea, the hero, pursued by his brother, shoots into the sky to form an arrow-chain and then escapes by means of it. In some versions he takes along the brother's wife and all of his house-hold—and they become the Pleiades (Hatt, 44). In the Australian (Narrin-yeri) myth, the hero pursues his brother and his two unfaithful wives; the brother hurls towards heaven a barbed lance with a line attached and mounts it with the two women behind him. Finally all are turned into stars.[38]

f) A Tupi-Guarayú myth tells how the god Tamoi demanded proof of their magical powers from his two sons; they shot arrows upwards, one into the butt of another, and climbed the arrow-chain until they reached the sky. There they became the Sun and the Moon.[39]

g) Franz Boas recorded a myth of the Ntlakyapamug in which the birds declare war on Heaven. "After various unfruitful attempts, the bird Tcitúc succeeds in forming a chain of darts which reaches to earth, and on this climb the birds; then they re-descend; but only a few had touched the earth again when the chain broke, and the others remained in the air."[40] In this example the arrow-chain motif has been adapted into an etiologi-cal myth about the origin of birds.

h) There are also journeys to Heaven undertaken in order to prove shaman-istic powers or to meet the celestial gods. "Kumana shamans claimed to be able to climb to the sky on an arrow chain made by shooting each arrow into the butt of the one previously shot. Upon reaching the sky the shamans were welcomed by Narmakon, the Lord of the sky" (Métraux, 94–95).

In reviewing the foregoing myths once again, one can say that the personages attempting—and succeeding—to climb to Heaven by an arrow-chain are gods and cultural heroes at the close of their creative period; primordial beings who, as a result of breaking a taboo (incestuous love) mount to heaven and become astral bodies; mythical heroes climbing to heaven to bring back fire or to recover their wives; shamans and magicians ascending for mystical reasons. In all of these myths the symbolism of the arrow emphasizes not the "magic of flight" (rapidity, instantaneousness, invisibility, etc.), but the communication obtained through a "paradox": the transformation of an eminently fragile and flying object—the arrow—into a solid chain. The "paradox" illustrated by this plastic *coincidentia oppositorum* belongs to the well-known class of "impossibilities rendered possible": symplegades, razor bridges, passing through rocks or moun-tains, "dying and resurrecting," etc. (Cf. *Birth and Rebirth*, 61ff. and *passim*.) We shall presently see how such "paradoxical" images and symbols came to be integrated in mystical techniques and theologies. For the moment, it is important for us to notice that already at a very archaic level of culture, the "imaginary Universes" which had evolved around the art of archery allowed the human mind to reach a perspective from which the "impossibilities" could be resolved.

One may see in such "paradoxes" the prehistory of some *aporiai* that haunted the beginnings of Greek philosophy (for example, Achilles and the tortoise).

Through the paradoxical transformation of flying arrows into a stable and solid chain, a new means of communication between Earth and Heaven has been obtained, comparable to the Cosmic Tree, the Mountain, the Ladder, and so on. As was already surmised by Pettazzoni and Hatt, the absence of the "chain of arrows" theme in some areas may be accounted for through the substitution of other means of communication: the Sky-Tree, the Mountain, the Sky-rope, the Ladder, etc. We have elsewhere studied the symbolism of the *Axis Mundi*,[41] and we do not need to take up this problem again. We might point out, however, that the chain of arrows motif represents the creation of a hunting culture. In other words, the myth of a primordial communication with Heaven and of its catastrophic interruption was already familiar in an archaic stage of culture. The implicit idea is that, in the beginning, the Sky was fairly close to the Earth, and climbing to Heaven was an easy and "natural" thing. The raising of the sky or the withdrawal of Gods and Cultural Heroes marked the end of the primordial epoch.

VII) In a previous article I have briefly presented some pre-Buddhist (Bon) Tibetan traditions of the mythical rope that originally bound Earth to Heaven. "The first king of Tibet was said to have come down from Heaven by a rope. The first Tibetan kings did not die; they mounted again into Heaven. But since the rope has been cut, only souls can ascend to Heaven; the bodies remain on Earth."[42] Two Tibetan texts give a precise description of the way the Mythical Kings reascended to Heaven by means of a rainbow. According to a *bonpo* chronicle, the first kings "avaient tous a leur sinciput une corde *mu* de lumière, corde lointaine (ou tendue), couleur jaune pale (ou brune). Au moment de leur mort, ils se dissolvaient (comme un arc-en-ciel) a partir de leurs pieds et se fondaient dans la corde *mu* du sinciput. La corde *mu* de lumière, a son tour, se fondait dans le ciel. Une variante très proche, dont nous ne connaissons malheureusement que la version mongole, précise: 'quand venait le moment de transmigrer, ils se dissolvaient vers le haut a partir des pieds et, par le chemin de lumière appelé Corde-de-Sainteté qui sortait de leur tête, ils partaient en devenant un arc-en-ciel dans le ciel.' "[43]

What happened to the kings of mythical times *in concreto* now happens to the "soul" of the human being. Through specific yogic practices, the "soul" (i.e. the conscious principle) is let free at the moment of death by way of *brahmarandhra* (the "hole" at the summit of the skull, i.e. of the sinciput) and it is transferred to a certain heaven. The images used to suggest this "transferal" are primarily that of the flying bird, the shooting star or the shooting arrow. In the biography of Milarepa the soul of the departed master is seen as "a bird which takes off through a open hole of the roof." Finally, the soul is seen penetrating through the "hole in the roof" of Heaven as a shooting arrow (Stein, 190). For the non-initiates, the lama accomplishes the "transfer to Heaven" by opening a hole on the skull (i.e. the sinciput) of the dying one. Now it is significant that this operation is called "shooting an arrow by the Hole of the Roof" or "Opening of the Gate of Heaven": "A la mort d'une personne l'âme s'en va par le trou du sinciput ('trou du Brahma,' Brahmarandhara, Chans-pa; bu-ga). L'opération ('pho-ba) faite pour libérer l'âme en la faisant sortir du corps par ce trou est appelée 'tirer une flèche par l'Ouverture du Toit' (skar-khun mda'-'phans). Cette flèche est lumineuse: on l'imagine comme une étoile filante. S'élancent hors de l'Ouverture du Toit de la tête, elle atteint au loin le Trou de Fumée du Ciel ou elle disparaît. Aussi, ce rite du lancement de la flèche-étoile ou de l'âme par le trou du sinciput s'appelle-t-il encore 'ouverture de la Porte du Ciel' (nam-mkka'sgo 'byed)."[44]

One can see from these examples how the symbolism of the flying arrow rejoins that of ascending to Heaven, i.e. the vast and archaic mythology of the communication between Earth and Heaven.[45] The equivalences between rope, rainbow, light-rope, flying bird, shooting star, and shooting arrow emphasize the essential meaning of all these images and symbols: the possibility of ascending to Heaven. Moreover, one can decipher in the Tibetan traditions the remembrance of a precedent, mythical epoch when the ascension to Heaven was carried out *in concreto*; in other words, the "spiritual condition" of the present man is the result of a primordial "fall." In the beginning the separation between "body" and "spirit" did not exist. It is of consequence to stress this aspect of the archaic symbolism, because it reveals a rather profound nostalgia for human completeness and totality.

This is not the place for us to elaborate on these notes. But we must recall a methodological presupposition which underlies all of these studies; our conviction, namely, that the "documents" collected and studied by ethnologists, archaeologists, and folklorists exercise the same claims within the history of the human mind as do the written texts of the poets, the mystics, the theologians, and philosophers of the Great Traditions. This means that human creativity and, ultimately, the history of human culture is more directly related to what man has dreamt, believed, and thought of his specific mode of being in the world than to the works which he has undertaken in order to promote and validate this mode of being.

If this methodological presupposition is accepted, then the exegesis of an "obsolete" symbolism—let us say, that of the arrow—should play a role in the understanding of archaic man which is comparable to the study of the Greek poets and philosophers in the understanding of Western culture. Such a hermeneutical approach overcomes the gap between the "prehistoric" and "primitive" on the one hand, and men belonging to the high cultures, on the other. There is, of course, a radical difference between the levels of these two types of creations, but the act of spiritual creation is the same. This principle is implicitly accepted when the art historian homologizes the ephemeral beauty of, for example, a nomad's hut or a sand-painting to the corresponding perennial forms in architecture and painting. The "primitive" *oeuvres* have an epiphanic nature: the essential thing is that they *came into being*, even if only for a season or a night. Likewise, the different and innumerable "epiphanies" of a given symbolism in a certain type of culture (hunters, planters, pastoralists, etc.) are to be studied and interpreted in their constantly changing contexts. As a matter of fact, each new epiphany of a given symbolism is to be analyzed with the same accuracy and understanding as, let us say, the symbolism of Christos Cosmokrator, such as it unfolds itself in so many and such different ways from its first expression in Byzantium to the splendor of the Western cathedrals, or the provincial and rural reinterpretations attested in Russia and the Balkans. The creativity of "primitive," traditional, and "popular" spiritualities is accessible to us primarily through such epiphanic *oeuvres*, so hard for us to appreciate with our present historiographical criteria. As is well known, these historiographical criteria were elaborated with an end to collecting, chronologically classifying and interpreting non-ephemeral and mainly written documents. In the study of archaic symbolism, chronology and the temporal dimension in general is of less importance. On the contrary, the "creative variations," the reinterpretations and revalorizations of a given symbolism, merit a greater attention than they have attracted until now. On the horizon of archaic and popular spirituality these "creative variations" play an analogous role to, let us say, the personal reinterpretations of the Greco-Roman models by the European writers from Corneille and Racine to Shakespeare, Goethe and Holderlin. If the history of Western literature from the Renaissance to Goethe is, ultimately, a series of creative reinterpretations of the classical and Biblical heritage, the "history" of "primitive" and traditional cultures is constituted by their selective assimilation and creative revalorizations of the primordial symbolism.[46]

Notes

1. Edward B. Tylor, *Researches into the Early History of Mankind and the Development of Civilization* (London, 1865), 275–77; Lauri Honko, *Krankheitsprojektile. Untersuchung Über eine urtümliche Krankheitserklärung*, FF Communications, 178 (Helsinki, 1959), especially 75ff.
2. H. Baumann and D. Westermann, *Les Peuples et let Civilisations de l'Afrique* (Paris, 1948), 103. The "pointing bone" of the Australians plays the same role.
3. Cf. the map # 4, in Honko, 76.
4. See other examples in Rafael Karsten, *The Religion of the Samek* (Leiden, 1955), 43.
5. As, e.g., in Santa Cruz, Solomon Islands; cf. Codrington, 197.
6. As among the Na-khi; cf. J. F. Rock, *The Na-Khi Naga Cult and Related Ceremonies* (Rome, 1952), II, 489.
7. Cf. Rudolph Rahmann, "Shamanistic and Related Phenomena in Northern and Middle India," *Anthropos* 54 (1959): 681–760, 695; R. Karsten, *The Civilizations of the South American Indians* (London, 1926), 159 (the medicine-man shoots into the ailing limb with a miniature bow).

8. Text translated by F. B. J. Kuiper, "An Austro-Asiatic Myth in the Rigveda," 165, quoted by Rahmann, 741.

9. Cf. *Shamanism*, 227. Carrying in his hand the golden arrow, the proof of his Apollonic origin and mission, the Hyperborean Abaris voyaged through many lands dispelling sickness and pestilence. According to a later legend, Abaris did fly through the air on his arrow, like Musaeus; cf. Erwin Rohde, Karl Meuli and Eric R. Dodds, quoted in *Shamanism*, 388.

10. *Shamanism*, 217, quoting Uno Harva, *Die religiöse Vorstellungen der altaischen Volker*, FF Communications, 125 (1938), 268. A similar ritual is reported among the Tibetans and Sherpa; cf. René de Nebesky-Wojkowitz, *Oracles and Demons of Tibet* (The Hague: Mouton, 1956), 367.

11. A. Métraux, *The Native Tribes of Eastern Bolivia and Western Matto Grosso* (Bureau of American Ethnology, Bulletin 134 (Washington, 1942), 12.

12. G. B. Cerruti, *Nel paese dei veleni e fra i cacciatori di teste*, 3rd ed. (Firenze, 1936), 139, quoted by R. Pettazzoni, *L'onniscienza di Dio* (Torino, 1955), 467; cf. Pettazzoni, *The All-Knowing God* (London: Methuen, 1910), 317.

13. Marcel Granet, *Dancer et légendes de la Chine ancienne* (Paris, 1926), vol. I, 233 n. 1, 390 n. 1; vol. II, 538ff.

14. Gavril I. Kazarov, in *Klio*, XII (1912), 356ff. We shall examine these rituals in a forthcoming article on Zalmoxis. [See Eliade, ed., *Zalmoxis: the Vanishing God*, 52–53.]

15. Cf. F. Saxl, *Mithras* (Berlin, 1931), 76; Geo Widengren, "Stand and Aufgaben der iranischen Religionsgeschichte," *Numen* I (1954): 16–83, 40; II *Numen*, II (1955): 47–134, 95; and *Die Religionen Irans* (Stuttgart: W. Kohlhammer, 1965), 44ff.

16. Gustav Rank, "The Symbolic Bow in the Birth Rites of North Eurasian Peoples," *History of Religions* I.2 (1962): 281–90.

17. Uno Harva, *Die religiösen Vorstellungen der altaischen Volker* (Helsinki: Suomalainen tiedeakatemia, 1938), 235, 269.

18. René de Nebesky-Wojkowitz, *Oracles and Demons of Tibet*, 543. On the erotic value of arrow-offerings in connection with the Tibetan marriage, and also on the ritual role of the arrow in promoting the fertility of the field, see S. Hummel, "Eurasiatische Traditionen in der tibetischen Bon-Religion." (*Opuscula Ethnologica Memoriae Ludovici Biro' Sacra* [Budapest, 1959], 165–212), 170f.; cf. also "Der magische Stein in Tibet" (*International Archiv für Ethnographie* XLIX, 1960, 224–40), 237, n. l.

19. Marcel Granet, *Danses et Légendes de la Chine ancienne* (Paris: F. Alcan, 1926), 234, 380, 448.

20. Åke Ohlmarks, *Studien zur Problem des Schamanismus* (Lund, 1939), 137.

21. Gabriel Germain, *Genèse de l'Odyssie* (Paris, 1954), 11–54. On the Chinese parallels cf. 45ff.

22. F. B. J. Kuiper. "An Austroasiatic Myth in the Rig-Veda," *Mededelingen der Koninklÿke Nederlandse Academie van Wetenschappen*, XIII.7 (1950): 163–82. Cf. Eliade, *Yoga, Immortality and Freedom*, 352.

23. K. von Spiess, "Schuß nach dem Vogel," in *Marksteine der Volkskunst*, Bd. I (Berlin, 1937), 288ff. The Chinese materials have been discussed by E. Erkess, "Chinesishe-amerikanischen Mythenparallclen," *Toung Pao* 24 (1926), 32ff. For the Romanian and Caucasian parallels, cf. Octavian Buhociu, "Thèmes Mythiques Carpato-Caucasiens et des Régions riveraines de la Mer Noire," *Ogam* VIII (1956): 259–78.

24. Ananda Coomaraswamy, "The Iconography of Dürer's 'Knots' and Leonardo's 'Concatenation,' " *The Art Quarterly* (Spring 1944): 109–128 (121). On the symbolism of shooting darts toward each cardinal point, see Marcel Granet, *Dances et Légendes de la Chine ancienne*, 233 n. 2, 234, 380, etc.; R.-A. Stein, *Recherches sur l'Epopée et le Barde au Tibet* (Paris, 1959), 278.

25. Nebesky-Wojkowitz, *Oracles and Demons of Tibet*, 543. On the shooting of arrows at the occasion of the Tibetan New Year (the Tibetan State Oracle) cf. 510.
26. K. F. Karjalainen, *Die Religion der Jugra-Volker*, vol. III (Helsinki, 1927), 568, 596, 597.
27. Georje Nioradze, *Der Schamanismus bei den sibirischen Volker* (Stuttgart, 1925), 95.
28. Martti Rasanen, "Wahrsagung and Verlosung mit Pfeil and Bogen," *Symbolae in Honorem Z. V. Togan* (Istanbul, 1950–55), 273–77, 275ff.
29. Wilhelm Wundt, *Völkerpsychologie: Mythus and Religion* (Leipzig, 1909), vol. II, 218ff.; R. Pettazzoni, "The Chain of Arrows: The Diffusion of a Mythical Motif," *Folk-Lore*, XXXV (1924): 151–65; G. Hatt, *Asiatic Influences in American Folklore* (Copenhagen, 1949): 40–48. Pettazzoni published a more complete version of his article in Italian, in *Saggi di storia delle religions e di mitologia* (Rome, 1946), 63–79; but we shall refer exclusively to the article in *Folk-Lore*.
30. Pettazzoni, "The Chain of Arrows," 156–57.
31. Ehrenreich, "Über die Verbreitung and Wanderung der Mythen bei den Naturvölkern Sudamerikas," *XIV International Amerikanisten-Kongress* (Stuttgart, 1906), 676. Cf. also Stith Thompson, *Tales of the North American Indians* (Cambridge, Mass., 1929), 131f., 333, nn. 202–203, on the distribution of the myth among the North American tribes.
32. Pettazzoni and Hatt insist on diffusion. Boas inclines to accept a polygenesis; cf. "Mythology and Folk-Tales of the North American Indians," *Journal of American Folklore* XXVII (1914): 374–410, 384; Hatt, 48.
33. Pettazzoni, "Chain of Arrows," 158, quoting H. B. Alexander, *The Mythology of All Races*, vol. X (Boston, 1916), 221. A similar myth was known by the Australian Tribes of the Adelaide and Encounter Bay: Monona, a Primordial Being, climbs to heaven by a chain of lances (Pettazzoni, "Chain of Arrows," 162–63). The bow being unknown in Australia, the place of the darts is taken by lances.
34. "The myth continues with an account of how all human beings later on ascended to the sky in the same manner, except one man who became the ancestor of all the earth's now living inhabitants"; Hatt, 46, summarizing R. Brough Smyth, *The Aborigines of Victoria* (London, 1878), 1, 462. On the meaning of this type of Australian myths, cf. "Australian Religions: Part I," *History of Religions*, VI (1966), 129.
35. Hatt, 41–42, after Bogoras, *Chukchee Mythology* (Leiden: E. J. Brill; New York: G. E. Stechert & Co., 1910), 112ff.
36. R. Pettazzoni, "Chain of Arrows," 160, quoting P. J. Bt. Suas, "Mythes et légendes des Nouvelles Hebrides," *Anthropos* VII (1912), 579. The same myth, from another source, was published by Frazer, *Anthologia Anthropologica*, I (London: P. Lund, Humphries, 1939), 221. Cf. also Pettazzoni, "Chain of Arrows," 158, a similar myth of the Quinault Indians.
37. Hatt, 42–43, after Ehrenreich, *Die Mythen and Legenden der Süd-amerikanischen Urvölker* (Berlin, 1905), 37, 49.
38. Pettazzoni, "Chain of Arrows," 162. Subsequently the hero also mounts to heaven by the same means; one can still see his canoe floating in the Milky Way. The same myth was recorded among the Euahlayi, with this difference: the hero forms a continuous chain of javelins; Hatt, 46–47, after K. I. Parker, *More Australian Legendary Tales*, 11. Among the Palikur Indians at Rio Uaca in Brazilian Guiana there is a similar myth: in conflict with his brother-in-law, a hero climbed to the sky by means of an arrow-chain, and there became the constellation of Orion (Hatt, 43, after Curt Nimuendajú).
39. Métraux, *The Native Tribes of Eastern Bolivia and Western Matto Grosso*, 95; cf. Pettazzoni, "Chain of Arrows," 159, quoting other source.
40. Pettazzoni, "Chain of Arrows," 157, summarizing Boas.
41. Cf. Eliade, *The Myth of the Eternal Return*, 12ff.; *Patterns*, 367ff.; *Images and Symbols*, 27ff.; *Shamanism*, 259ff.

42. Eliade, *The Two and the One*, 166, after H. Hoffmann and Mathias Hermanns. Cf. also Siegbert Hummel, "Der Motiv der Nabelschnur in Tibet," *Antaios* IV (1963): 572–80.

43. R. A. Stein, *La civilisation tibétaine* (Paris: Dunod, 1962), 189–90. Cf. for some Australian parallels see Eliade, *The Two and the One*, 184–87.

44. Stein, "Architecture et pensée religieuse en Extreme-Orient," *Arts Asiatiques* IV (1957): 163–86, 184.

45. The same idea is implicit in the symbolic usage of the bow and arrows in the Upanishads. The understanding of Brahman is compared to the exact shooting of an arrow: "Taking as the bow the great weapon of the Upanishad, one should place in it the arrow sharpened by meditation. Drawing it with a mind engaged in the contemplation of That (Brahman), O beloved, know that imperishable Brahman as the target." (*Mundaka Upaniṣad*, II, 2, 3. From *The Principal Upaniṣads*. Translated by Sarvepalli Radhakrishnan. London: G. Allen & Unwin, 1953.)

46. I am grateful to my former student, Miss Nancy Auer, for her care in correcting and stylistically improving this text.

16

NORMATIVE ELEMENTS IN ELIADE'S PHENOMENOLOGICAL UNDERSTANDING OF SYMBOLISM

Robert D. Baird

Editor's Introduction

Of course, Eliade's analysis and understanding of religious symbolism is not without its problems and its critics. Robert Baird's critique of 1970 was one of the earliest and clearest of these, with specific relevance to *homo religiosus* and symbolism. Baird is apparently sympathetic to Claas Jouco Bleeker's claim that the History of Religions is an empirical discipline without any philosophical aspirations. Baird states that for Eliade, "[n]ot only are the hierophanies which he describes hierophanies for those involved, but they are *in fact* hierophanies," and thus a shift has been made "from the apparently descriptive to the normative … an ontology has been posited from the start." However, one must wonder whether this is not necessarily the case with any *phenomenological* analysis. Any phenomenon, *x*, is not only an *x* for those involved but is in fact an *x* (that is, a phenomenal *x*). So no ontology is necessarily posited but the *apprehension* of an ontology by the subject who experiences the *x*. Thus the apprehension of beauty in certain objects—especially if this experience is repeated commonly in a social group—is *in fact* the presence of beauty. It could thus remain descriptive and avoid normativity except the claim that such experiences do indeed occur for certain subjects and are *in fact* apprehended as revealing ontology. Baird's criticism was first published in *The Union Seminary Quarterly Review* 25/4 (1970): 505–16 and included as "Phenomenological Understanding: Mircea Eliade," in Baird's book, *Category Formation and the History of Religion*, 86–91 (The Hague: Mouton, 1971). All rights reserved. Copyright © 1971 by Mouton de Gruyter. Reprinted by permission of Mouton de Gruyter.

Mircea Eliade

℘ ℀

We began our discussion of Eliade's phenomenological method by stating that it was primarily concerned with religious structures. It might be countered that this does not mean that it is uninterested in religious people. For, the only way Eliade proposes to adequately understand religious man is by understanding the structures in which he participates. However, the emphasis is certainly on the structures. Participants or believers need not be aware of the "depth of meaning" which Eliade knows is contained in their symbols, myths, or rites. It is true that Eliade's goal is to understand *homo religiosus*. But *homo religiosus* is not an historical but an archetypal religious man. Historical persons participate in this archetype to varying degrees, even though no one fully embodies it nor does anyone entirely cover it. Hence the statements of religious men about the meanings of their rites or symbols is secondary to the way in which the symbols fit into universal structures. And, individuals are understood in terms of these universal structures and not in terms of their religious individuality.

While no one person is the complete embodiment of *homo religiosus,* archaic man comes closest to this model of authentic existence. Eliade begins by convincing us that we should be prepared to admit that *homo religiosus* has had a tendency to extend hierophanies indefinitely. Almost everything has been a hierophany at one time or another to someone or other. This is particularly true for archaic man. But when it is suggested that modern man is poorer because his cosmos has been desacralized, because the human body or the process of eating is no longer a sacrament, a shift has been effected—a shift that is made possible only because an ontological basis has already been posited. If not before, at least here it is clear that Eliade is not dealing merely with what men have held to be sacred, but with the structures of the sacred. His focal point is not only the subjective, but also the objective and hence ontological. Not only are the hierophanies which he describes hierophanies for those involved, but they are *in fact* hierophanies. One would normally expect further argumentation when a shift is made from the apparently descriptive to the normative. Here, however, an ontology has been posited from the start.

Once one sees "the sacred" or "religion" as an ontological reality and once one operates as though its structures are also ontologically real, having identified these structures one has discovered reality. It then follows that those whose lives are lived in the sacred as completely as possible are the most authentic since they exist closest to reality.

It might be worth pointing out that not all phenomenologists of religion have taken Eliade's step of seeing archaic man as the most authentic.

> Modern man has a clearer view of what is genuinely religious, is more able to distinguish the religious from the secular and makes higher demands as to the quality of religion. (Bleeker, *The Sacred Bridge*, 23)

It is not the lack of an ontological basis that pushes Bleeker in a different direction at this point, but it is because his intuitive identification of religion differs from Eliade's. This might lead one to question the notion that we all know what religion is and can readily identify it, even though we have definitional difficulties.

Eliade maintains that it falls within the realm of the historian of religions to articulate a systematic and theoretical interpretation of the religious facts that he finds as a phenomenologist.

> The second prejudice of certain historians of religions, that you must turn to another "specialist" for a world-wide and systematic interpretation of religious facts, is probably to be explained by the philosophical timidity of a great number of scholars. (*The Two and the One*, 195 [below, 245])

In a footnote, Eliade laments the fact that "general theories" which have dominated the history of religions from its beginnings have been the work of linguists, anthropologists, sociologists, and philosophers (195 [below, 250 n. 7]). These are bold statements when one remembers the concern of other historians of religions to disassociate themselves from the work of theologians and philosophers of religion.[1] To urge the historian of religions to philosophize at this point is to add little new to Eliade's method. An ontology has been implied from the start. What is more surprising is that this prior ontology is seldom if ever recognized as such. The result is that it is assumed that the philosophizing will come at the end of an examination of the given religions, when it would have been logically more appropriate in this method to find it at the beginning. For, if the ontological dimension of Eliade's phenomenological approach to the sacred is not validly supported, the conclusion remains equally unsupported. But Eliade thinks the philosophizing must conclude the study. If one fails to philosophize at this point, "this amounts to saying that the historian of religions hesitates to complete his preparatory work as philologist and historian by an act of comprehension, which of course requires an effort of thought" (195 [below, 245]).

Eliade laments the fact that the discipline of the history of religions has had a rather modest role in influencing modern culture. This is largely because historians of religions have been too cautious. Having remained specialized, they fail to recognize the unlimited possibilities that are open to the history of religions. In attempting to remain scientific, thereby avoiding broad generalizations, historians of religions have paid the price of creativity. Eliade urges the historian of religions to go beyond the mere comprehending of religious facts to the level of philosophizing ("Crisis and Renewal," 7).[2] By this kind of thought the history

155

of religions can help to create cultural values (8). The reason why this does not happen often enough is that the majority of historians of religions defend themselves against the messages contained in the documents they study. Eliade is suggesting more than a spontaneous enlivening of the subconscious of modern man, for if his theoretical structures are real, this would simply happen apart from the philosophizing efforts of historians of religions.

It is true that artificial disciplinary barriers have been erected so that if one wants to wear his label with cultic dignity, whether as "historian of religions," "anthropologist," or "theologian," there are some things that he is well advised not to do. But there is no valid reason why Eliade should be excluded from the possibility of philosophizing, or theologizing for that matter. There are various stages in Eliade's method which are philosophical—at the point of departure as well as at the point of destiny. And at all points at which ontology is assumed such philosophizing becomes essential. A failure to recognize the ontological point of departure and the assumption that he is beginning with the given religions which we can all readily identify without the need of a definition leads Eliade to miss the fact that wherever an ontological stance is introduced, philosophical argumentation is needed. It must be said that if historians of religions are going to engage in a phenomenological approach such as Eliade's, and if they are going to be called upon to develop the theoretical and philosophical implications of their findings, then simply being "most familiar with the religious facts" is insufficient preparation.[3] One who engages in such work also needs ability in philosophical method. Whatever theories or conclusions flow from the work of those who attempt to achieve phenomenological understanding will be acceptable and valid only to the extent to which one's descriptions are accurate *and* to the extent to which (where applicable) his normative stages are adequately supported.

We have found that both the methods of Malinowski and Eliade have involved metaphysical positions and that neither seemed more eager than the other to defend the metaphysical dimensions of their systems with the appropriate philosophical or theological reasoning. With the level of functional understanding, however, we found that it was possible to divest the method of Malinowski's "postulates" and still use the method heuristically. This has been cogently argued by Merton. The question now arises as to whether it would be possible to empty Eliade's phenomenological method of its ontological "postulates" and continue to use it as a level of understanding. In the case of Eliade's phenomenological method, we are forced to answer in the negative. Here, if one eliminates the metaphysical, he eliminates the transhistorical religious structures. And, the elimination of the transhistorical religious structures eliminates the possibility of finding a transhistorical religious meaning in a symbol or myth or rite. Without its implied ontology, this method falls to the ground and becomes at best *a means of classifying data.* But classification itself is little more than a scholarly filing system which enables us to know where to find a given thing at a given time. Hence, without positing ontological structures the phenomenological method does not offer a distinct method of understanding, merely a means of classification.

This being said, it remains to be said that the phenomenological method is a legitimate level of understanding to the extent to which one is convinced of the reality of the transhistorical structures and archetypes. These cannot be supported by merely citing historically derived data. For it is the organization of that data into transhistorical structures which makes the method distinct. And, one has no right to do that until some evidence for the existence of the transhistorical structures has been offered. Empirical evidence cannot be used for this task. One must reason philosophically or theologically. These transhistorical structures are not empirically verifiable because they are not empirically falsifiable. There is no way that an examination of historical data will show that they do not exist. It may lead one to identify them differently from the way that Eliade does. But that does not touch at the heart of the problem, which is whether it is legitimate to interpret some material in the light of other material because there exist transhistorical structures in which both participate. Since there are cryptic as well as apparent hierophanies, it follows that those items which do not explicitly identify their place in a religious structure can be assigned such a place. The weight of this method is that it enables one to "understand" those religious symbols, myths, or rites which do not explicitly tell us their meaning. But, since this is the case, there is no way to verify if such "cryptic" hierophanies actually do fit into the transhistorical structures at the places where the phenomenologist says they do, or whether they fit into any such structures, or finally, whether such structures do indeed exist.

It is difficult to improve on the observation of Willard Oxtoby:

> Analogous in a sense to Gestalt psychology, the eidetic vision constitutes a confident, self-validating sense that the pattern which one has distilled represents the real essentials of the data… There is nothing outside one's intuitive grasp of a pattern which validates that pattern. The phenomenologist is obliged simply to set forth his understanding as a whole, trusting that his reader will enter into it. But there is no procedure stated by which he can compel a second phenomenologist to agree with the adequacy and incontrovertibility of his analysis, unless the second phenomenologist's eidetic vision happens to be the same as the first's. For this reason phenomenological expositions of religion are in fact very personal appreciations of it, akin more to certain forms of literary and aesthetic criticism than to the natural or even the social sciences ("Religionswissenschaft Revisited," 597).

In short, the phenomenological understanding of religion, as exhibited in the work of Eliade, will appear useful to all those who share his ontological stance. Whether this sharing is the result of being convinced by philosophical arguments or because of a favorable emotional response to an organizational principle for an overwhelming mass of data only indicates the degree to which a scholar demands critical evidence for his religious commitments. But the phenomenology of Eliade is a normative level of understanding. It could well have been considered alongside Hendrik Kraemer, Hans Küng, and S. Radhakrishnan. This level is considered separately because of its wide acceptance among historians of religions and in order to clarify the limitations of the phenomenological level of understanding.

Of course, as with all normative understanding, if the norm proves erroneous, one no longer has understanding at all, but rather misunderstanding (Oxtoby, 108). Hence, if the universal religious structures on which Eliade bases his understanding of the religious data should turn out to be non-existent, then this approach would result in misunderstanding as well.

However, if cogent arguments are forthcoming in support of the implied ontology, the phenomenological level stands as a legitimate level of understanding. Heinz Robert Schlette has accused Eliade of comparing before he has adequately understood what he compares.

> In the words of M. Eliade too, precipitate comparisons and identifications are found. For example Eliade who, of course, deals with religions by the methods and from the point of view of ethnology, theory of archetypes, morphology of civilizations, theory of mythology and mysticism, considers he must include Christian baptism (the "historical" element having deliberately been put in parenthesis), in a list with "Polynesian, American, ancient Greek and ancient oriental myths and rites" in order "to throw light on the structure of water hierophanies." (*Towards a Theology of Religions*, 53)

Schlette misunderstands Eliade's method. His method implies that, because of the ontological status of religious structures, one reaches "phenomenological" understanding precisely through placing items together which are not identical but structurally homologous.

Notes

1. Cf. Bleeker, "The Phenomenological Method," *The Sacred Bridge*, 7. "In my opinion the phenomenology of religion is an empirical science without philosophical aspirations."
2. "But in the case of the History of Religions, hermeneutics shows itself to be a more complex operation for it is not only a question of comprehending and interpreting 'the religious facts.' Because of their nature these religious facts constitute a material on which one can think—or even ought to think—and think in a creative manner, just as did Montesquieu, Voltaire, Herder, Hegel when they applied themselves to the task of thinking about human institutions and their history."

3. Eliade urges that if general theories are not produced by historians of religions who are most familiar with the religious facts, then "we shall continue to submit to the audacious and irrelevant interpretations of religious realities made by psychologists, sociologists, or devotees of various reductionist ideologies." If historians of religions do not complete their theoretical work the "autonomous discipline" may die. "In this case we must expect a slow but irrevocable process of decomposition, which will end in the disappearance of the History of Religions as an autonomous discipline" ("Crisis and Renewal," 17).

The *Coincidentia Oppositorum*

17

COINCIDENTIA OPPOSITORUM—
THE MYTHICAL PATTERN

Mircea Eliade

Editor's Introduction

One of Eliade's characteristic themes is the "*coincidentia-oppositorum*," the simultaneous occurrence of apparently opposing elements to form a coherent and empowered whole. The following selection is the earliest prolonged consideration of this symbolic motif (1949). I have earlier suggested that

> this fascination with the *coincidentia oppositorum* develops from an inherent recognition that the profane world in its entirety and in its diversity is itself revelatory of genuine ontology, real being, the sacred. Existence, as it presents itself to us, is itself a coincidence of opposites, it *is* both sacred and profane, both real and unreal. It *is* both a concealment and a revelation of the real … The *coincidentia oppositorum* may be the area where Eliade makes a real ontological assumption. (*Reconstructing Eliade*, 36, 40)

The following two examples of Eliade's explanation of the *coincidentia* and John Valk's analysis will help readers evaluate the accuracy and applicability of these conclusions. This excerpt comes from *Patterns in Comparative Religion*, 419–25 (London: Sheed and Ward, 1958, translated from the French by Willard Trask). All rights reserved. Copyright © by Sheed and Ward. Reprinted by permission of the University of Nebraska Press and Continuum International Publishers.

80 03

[M]any of the] myths [collected in *Patterns*, §158] present us with a two-fold revelation: they express on the one hand the diametrical opposition of two divine figures sprung from one and the same principle and destined, in many versions, to be reconciled at some *illud tempus* of eschatology, and on the other, the *coincidentia oppositorum* in the very nature of the divinity, which shows itself, by turns or even simultaneously, benevolent and terrible, creative and destructive, solar and serpentine, and so on (in other words, actual and potential). In this sense it is true to say that myth reveals more profoundly than any rational experience ever could, the actual structure of the divinity, which transcends all attributes and reconciles all contraries. That this mythical experience is no mere deviation is proved by the fact that it enters into almost all the religious experience of mankind, even within as strict a tradition as the Judaeo-Christian. Yahweh is both kind and wrathful; the God of the Christian mystics and theologians is terrible and gentle at once and it is this *coincidentia oppositorum* which is the starting point for the boldest speculations of such men as the pseudo-Dionysius, Meister Eckhardt, and Nicholas of Cusa.

The *coincidentia oppositorum* is one of the most primitive ways of expressing the paradox of divine reality. We shall be returning to this formula when we come to look at divine "forms," to the peculiar structure revealed by every divine "personality," given of course that the divine personality is not to be simply looked upon as a mere projection of human personality. However, although this conception, in which all contraries are reconciled (or rather, transcended), constitutes what is, in fact, the most basic definition of divinity, and shows how utterly different it is from humanity, the *coincidentia oppositorum* becomes nevertheless an archetypal model for certain types of religious men, or for certain of the forms religious experience takes. The *coincidentia oppositorum* or transcending of all attributes can be achieved by man in all sorts of ways. At the most elementary level of religious life there is the orgy: for it symbolizes a return to the amorphous and the indistinct, to a state in which all attributes disappear and contraries are merged. But exactly the same doctrine can also be discerned in the highest ideas of the eastern sage and ascetic, whose contemplative methods and techniques are aimed at transcending all attributes of every kind. The ascetic, the sage, the Indian or Chinese "mystic" tries to wipe out of his experience and consciousness every sort of "extreme," to attain to a state of perfect indifference and neutrality, to become insensible to pleasure and pain, to become completely self-sufficient. This transcending of extremes through asceticism and contemplation also results in the "coinciding of opposites"; the consciousness of such a man knows no more conflict, and such pairs

163

of opposites as pleasure and pain, desire and repulsion, cold and heat, the agreeable and the disagreeable are expunged from his awareness, while something is taking place within him which parallels the total realization of contraries within the divinity. As we saw earlier (*Patterns*, §57), the oriental mind cannot conceive perfection unless all opposites are present in their fullness. The neophyte begins by identifying all his experience with the rhythms governing the universe (sun and moon), but once this "cosmicization" has been achieved, he turns all his efforts towards *unifying* the sun and moon, towards taking into himself the *cosmos as a whole*; he remakes in himself and for himself the primeval unity which was before the world was made; a unity which signifies not the chaos that existed before any forms were created but the undifferentiated *being* in which all forms are merged.

The Myth of Divine Androgyny

Another example will illustrate more clearly still the efforts made by religious man to imitate the divine archetype revealed in myth. Since all attributes exist together in the divinity, then one must expect to see both sexes more or less clearly expressed together. Divine androgyny is simply a primitive formula for the divine bi-unity; mythological and religious thought, before expressing this concept of divine two-in-oneness in metaphysical terms (*esse* and *non esse*), or theological terms (the revealed and unrevealed), expressed it first in the biological terms of bisexuality. We have already noted on more than one occasion how archaic ontology was expressed in biological terms. But we must not make the mistake of taking the terminology superficially in the concrete, profane ("modern") sense of the words. The word "woman," in myth or ritual, is never just woman: it includes the cosmological principle woman embodies. And the divine androgyny which we find in so many myths and beliefs has its own theoretical, metaphysical significance. The real point of the formula is to express—in biological terms—the coexistence of contraries, of cosmological principles (male and female) within the heart of the divinity.

This is not the place to consider the problem which I discussed in my *Mitul Reintegrarii*. We must simply note that the divinities of cosmic fertility are, for the most part, either hermaphrodites or male one year and female the next (cf. for instance the Estonians' "spirit of the forest"). Most of the vegetation divinities (such as Attis, Adonis, Dionysos) are bisexual, and so are the Great Mothers (like Cybele). The primal god is androgynous in as primitive a religion as the Australian as well as in the most highly developed religions in India and elsewhere (sometimes even Dyaus; Puruṣa, the cosmic giant of the *Rig Veda*, 10.90, etc.). The most important couple in the Indian pantheon, Śiva-Kālī, are sometimes represented as a single being (*ardhanarīśvara*). And Tantric iconography swarms with pictures of the God Śiva closely entwined with Śakti, his own "power," depicted as a feminine divinity (Kālī). And then, too, all of Indian erotic mysticism is expressly aimed at perfecting man by identifying him with a "divine pair," that is, by way of androgyny.

Divine bisexuality is an element found in a great many religions[1] and—a point worth noting—even the most supremely masculine or feminine divinities are androgynous. Under whatever form the divinity manifests itself, he or she is ultimate reality, absolute power, and this reality, this power, will not let itself be limited by any attributes whatsoever (good, evil, male, female, or anything else). Several of the most ancient Egyptian gods were bisexual.[2] Among the Greeks, androgyny was acknowledged even down to the last centuries of Antiquity.[3] Almost all the major gods in Scandinavian mythology always preserved traces of androgyny: Odhin, Loki, Tuisco, Nerthus, and so on.[4] The Iranian god of limitless time, Zervan, whom the Greek historians rightly saw as Chronos, was also androgynous[5] and Zervan gave birth to twin sons, Ormuzd and Ahriman, the god of "good" and the god of "evil," the god of "light" and the god of "darkness." Even the Chinese had a hermaphrodite Supreme Divinity, who was the god of darkness and of light;[6] the symbol is a consistent one, for light and darkness are simply successive aspects of one and the same reality; seen apart the two might seem separate and opposed, but in the sight of the wise man they are not merely "twins" (like Ormuzd and Ahriman), but form a single essence, now manifest, now unmanifest.

Divine couples (like Bel and Belit, and so on) are most usually later fabrications or imperfect formulations of the primeval androgyny that characterizes all divinities. Thus, with the Semites, the goddess Tanit was nicknamed "daughter of Ba'al" and Astarte the "name of Ba'al" (Bertholet, 21). There are innumerable cases of the divinity's being given the title of "father and mother" (Bertholet, 19); worlds, beings, men, all were born of his own substance with no other agency involved. Divine androgyny would include as a logical consequence monogeny or autogeny, and very many myths tell how the divinity drew his existence from himself—a simple and dramatic way of explaining that he is totally self-sufficient. The same myth was to appear again, though based this time on a complex metaphysic, in the neo-Platonic and gnostic speculations of late Antiquity.

The Myth of Human Androgyny

Corresponding to this myth of divine androgyny—which reveals the paradox of divine existence more clearly than any of the other formulae for the *coincidentia oppositorum*—there is a whole series of myths and rituals relating to human androgyny. The divine myth forms the paradigm for man's religious experience. A great many traditions hold that the "primeval man," the ancestor, was a hermaphrodite (Tuisco is the type) and later mythical variants speak of "primeval pairs" (Yama—that is, "twin"—and his sister, Yami, or the Iranian pair Yima and Yimagh, or Mashyagh and Mashyanagh). Several rabbinical commentaries give us to understand that even Adam was sometimes thought of as androgynous. In this case, the "birth" of Eve would have been simply the division of the primeval hermaphrodite into two beings, male and female. "Adam and Eve were made back to back, attached at their shoulders; then God separated them with an axe, or cut them in two. Others have a different picture: the first man, Adam, was a man on his right side, a woman on his left; but God split him into two halves."[7] The bisexuality of the first man is an even more living tradition in the societies we call primitive (for instance in Australia, and Oceania)[8] and was even preserved, and improved upon, in anthropology as advanced as that of Plato (*The Symposium*) and the Gnostics (cf. *Mitul Reintegrarii*, 83ff.).

We have a further proof that the androgyny of the first man must be seen as one of the expressions of perfection and totalization in the fact that the first hermaphrodite was very often thought of as spherical (Australia; Plato): and it is well known that the sphere symbolized perfection and totality from the time of the most ancient cultures (as in China). The myth of a primordial hermaphrodite spherical in form thus links up with the myth of the cosmogonic egg. For instance, in Taoist tradition, "breathing"—which embodied, among other things, the two sexes—merged together and formed an egg, the Great One; from this heaven and earth were later detached. This cosmological schema was clearly the model for the Taoist techniques of mystical physiology.[9]

The myth of the hermaphrodite god and bisexual ancestor (or first man) is the paradigm for a whole series of ceremonies which are directed towards a *periodic returning* to this original condition which is thought to be the perfect expression of humanity. In addition to the circumcision and subincision which are performed on young aboriginals, male and female respectively, with the aim of transforming them into hermaphrodites,[10] I would also mention all the ceremonies of "exchanging costume" which are lesser versions of the same thing.[11] In India, Persia, and other parts of Asia, the ritual of "exchanging clothes" played a major part in agricultural feasts. In some regions of India, the men even wore false bosoms during the feast of the goddess of vegetation who was, herself, also, of course, androgynous.[12]

In short, from time to time man feels the need to return—if only for an instant—to the state of perfect humanity in which the sexes exist side by side as they coexist with all other qualities, and all other attributes, in the Divinity. The man dressed in woman's clothes is not trying to make himself a woman, as a first glance might suggest, but for a moment he is effecting the unity of the sexes, and thus facilitating his total understanding of the cosmos. The need man feels to cancel periodically his differentiated and determined condition so as to return to primeval "totalization" is the same need which spurs him to periodic orgies in which all forms dissolve, to end by recovering that "oneness" that was before the creation. Here again we come upon the need to destroy the past, to expunge "history" and to start a new life in a new Creation. The ritual of "exchanging costumes" is similar in essence to the ceremonial orgy; and, indeed, these disguises were very often the occasion for actual orgies to break loose. However, even the wildest variants on these rituals never succeeded in abolishing their essential significance—of making their participants once more share in the paradisal condition of "primeval man." And all these rituals have as their exemplar model the myth of divine androgyny.

If I wished to give more examples of the paradigmatic function of myths I should only have to go again through the larger part of the material given in the preceding chapters. As we have seen, it is not simply a question of a paradigm for ritual, but for other religious and metaphysical experience as well, for "wisdom," the techniques of mystical physiology and so on. The most fundamental of the myths reveal archetypes which man labors to re-enact, often quite outside religious life properly so called. As a single example: androgyny may be attained not only by the surgical operations that accompany Australian initiation ceremonies, by ritual orgy, by "exchanging costumes" and the rest, but also by means of alchemy (cf. *rebis,* formula of the Philosophers' Stone, also called the "hermetic hermaphrodite"), through marriage (e.g. in the Kabbala), and even, in romantic German ideology, by sexual intercourse (See the references in my book, *Mitul Reintegrarii,* 82ff.) Indeed, we may even talk of the "androgynization" of man through love, for in love each sex attains, conquers the "characteristics" of the opposite sex (as with the grace, submission, and devotion achieved by a man when he is in love, and so on).

Notes

1. Cf. Alfred Bertholet, *Das Geschlecht der Gottheit* (Tübingen, 1934).
2. E. A. Wallis Budge, *From Fetish to God in Ancient Egypt* (London: Oxford University Press, 1934), 7, 9.
3. Cf. for instance Carl Gustav Jung and Carl Kerényi, *Essays on a Science of Mythology: The Myth of the Divine Child and the Mysteries of Eleusis,* trans. R. F. C. Hull (Princeton: Princeton University Press, 1963), 70ff.
4. Cf. e.g. Jan de Vries, *Handbuch der germanischen Religionsgeschichte,* vol. II, 306; and *The Problem of Loki* (Helsinki: Suomalainen Tiedeakatemia, Societas Scientiarum Fennica, 1933), 220ff.
5. Émile Benveniste, *The Persian Religion According to the Chief Greek Texts* (Paris: Guethner, 1929), 113ff.
6. Cf. Carl Hentze, *Frühchinesische Bronzen and Kultdarstellungen* (Antwerp: De Sikkel, 1937), 119.
7. *Bereshit rabbah, I* 1, fol. 6, col. 2; etc.; for further texts, see Alexander Krappe, "The Birth of Eve," in *Occident and Orient: Gaster Anniversary Volume,* ed. Bruno Schindler and Arthur Marmorstein (London, 1936), 312–22.
8. Cf. the works of Winthuis.

9. Cf. H. Maspero, "Les Procédés de nourrir le principe vital dans la religion taoiste ancienne," *Journal Asiatique* (April–June, 1937), 207, n. 1.

10. See the studies of Winthuis, Roheim, etc.

11. Cf. for the Greeks, Martin P. Nilsson, *Griechische Feste* (Leipzig: B. G. Teubner, 1906), 370ff.; at carnival time, Géorge Dumézil, *Le Problème des Centaures* (Paris: Guethner, 1929), 140, 180, etc.; in India, Johann Jakob Meyer, *Trilogie altindische Mächte und Feste der Vegetation* (Zurich-Leipzig: Niehan, 1937), vol. I, 76, 86, etc.; during the spring festivals in Europe, ibid., vol. I, 88ff.; Alfred Crawley and Theodore Besterman, *The Mystic Rose* (New York: Boni and Liveright, 1927), vol. I, 313ff., etc.

12. Meyer, *Trilogie altindische*, vol. I, 182ff.

18

POLARITY AND THE *COINCIDENTIA OPPOSITORUM*

Mircea Eliade

Editor's Introduction

This second description of Eliade's understanding of the *coincidentia oppositorum* from *The Quest: History and Meaning in Religion* comes twenty years after the preceding selection. This not only fleshes out his understanding of the *coincidentia*, it also introduces another of Eliade's characteristic themes—his position on the irreducible nature of the religious phenomenon—as he says, "the irreducibility of the spiritual creation to a preexistent system of values." From *The Quest* by Mircea Eliade, 168–73 (Chicago: University of Chicago Press, 1969). All rights reserved. Copyright © 1969 by the University of Chicago Press. Reprinted by permission of the University of Chicago Press.

ℬℭ

In India the two principles, understood somehow as incarnated in Mitra and Varuṇa, furnished an exemplary model for the explanation of both the world and of the dialectical structure of man's mode of being, for the human condition mysteriously comprises a masculine modality and a feminine one, life and death, bondage and freedom, etc. Indeed, Mitra and Varuṇa are set one against the other as day and night, and even as male and female (*Śatapatha Brāhmaṇa*, II, 4, 4, 9 tells us that "Mitra discharges his seed in Varuṇa"), but they are also opposed as "the one who comprehends" (*abhigantṛ*) and "the one who acts" (*karta*), and as brahman and *kshatra,* i.e., "spiritual power" and "temporal power." Moreover, the dualism elaborated by Sāmkhya, with a passive and placid "self" (*purusha*) as spectator, and an active and productive "Nature" (*prakriti*), has been sometimes understood by the Indians as an illustration of the opposition between Mitra and Varuṇa.[1] And a similar correspondence has been worked out in Vedanta with regard to Brahman and *māyā,* for as the old liturgical texts assert, "Mitra is Brahman," and in the Vedas *māyā* is the characteristic technique of Varuṇa the magician.[2] Moreover, as early as the *Rig Veda* (I, 164, 38), Varuṇa has been identified with the manifest.

Of course, the couple Mitra-Varuṇa was not the original model of all the other polarities, but only the most important expression, on the religious and mythological planes, of this principle in which Indian thought has recognized the fundamental structures of the cosmic totality and of human existence. Indeed, later speculation has distinguished *two* aspects of Brahman: *apara* and *para,* "inferior" and "superior," visible and invisible, manifest and nonmanifest. In other words, it is always the mystery of a polarity, all at once a biunity and a rhythmic alternation, that can be deciphered in the different mythological, religious, and philosophical "illustrations": Mitra and Varuṇa, the visible and invisible aspects of Brahman, Brahman and *māyā, purusha* and *prakriti,* and later on Shiva and Shakti, or *samsāra* and Nirvāṇa.

But some of these polarities tend to annul themselves in a *coincidentia oppositorum,* in a paradoxical unity-totality, the *Urgrund* of which I spoke of a moment ago. That it is not only a question of metaphysical speculations, but also of formulas with the help of which India tried to circumscribe a peculiar mode of existence, is proved by the fact that *coincidentia oppositorum* is implied in *jivan mukta,* the "liberated in life," who continues to exist in the world even though he has attained final deliverance; or the "awakened one" for whom Nirvāṇa and *samsāra* appear to be one and the same thing; or the situation of a tantric yogin able to pass from asceticism to orgy without any modification of behavior (see *Yoga*). Indian spirituality has been obsessed by the "Absolute." Now, however one may conceive the Absolute, it cannot be conceived except as beyond contraries and polarities. This is the reason why India includes the orgy among the means of attaining deliverance, while deliverance is denied to those who continue to follow the ethical rules depending on social institutions. The "Absolute," the ultimate liberation, the freedom, *moksha, mukti,* is not accessible to those who have not surpassed what the texts call the "couples of contraries," i.e., the polarities we have discussed.

This Indian reinterpretation recalls certain rituals of archaic societies which, though related to mythologies of a polar structure, pursue the periodic abolition of the contraries by means of a collective orgy. We have seen that the Dayaks suspend all rules and interdictions during the New Year festival. It will be useless to insist on the differences between the Dayak mythico-ritual scenario and the Indian philosophies and "mystical" techniques aiming at the abolition of contraries; the differences are evident. Nevertheless, in both cases the *summum bonum* is situated beyond polarities. To be sure, for the Dayaks the *summum bonum* is represented by the divine totality, which alone can insure a new creation, a new epiphany of the fullness of life, while for the yogins and other contemplatives the *summum bonum* transcends the cosmos and life, for it represents a new existential dimension, that of the *unconditioned,* of absolute freedom and beatitude, a mode of existence known neither in the cosmos nor among the gods, for it is a human creation and accessible exclusively to men. Even the gods, if they desire to obtain absolute freedom, are obliged to incarnate themselves and to conquer this deliverance by the means discovered and elaborated by men.

But, to come back to the comparison between the Dayaks and the Indians, something must be added: the creativity of a specific ethnic group or of a particular religion does not manifest itself solely in the reinterpretation and the revalorization of an archaic system of polarities, but also in the significance given to the *reunion of contraries.* The Dayak orgiastic ritual and the tantric orgy achieve a sort of *coincidentia oppositorum,* but the significance of the transcending of contraries is not the same in the two cases. In other words, neither the experiences made possible by the discovery of the polarities and by the hope of their integration nor the symbolization that articulates and sometimes anticipates these experiences are susceptible of *exhaustion,* even if, in certain cultures, such experiences and symbolizations seem to have exhausted all their possibilities. It is in a total perspective, encompassing the totality of cultures, that we must judge the fecundity of a symbolism which expresses the structures of cosmic life and concurrently renders intelligible man's mode of existing in the world.

Yang and Yin

I have purposely left for the end the example of China. As in the archaic societies of the Americas and Indonesia, the cosmic polarity, expressed by the symbols *yang* and *yin,* was "lived" through the rites, and it also furnished quite early the model for a universal classification. Besides, as in India, the couple of contraries *yang* and *yin* was developed into a cosmology which, on the one hand, systematized and validated innumerable bodily techniques and spiritual disciplines, and on the other hand inspired rigorous and systematic philosophical speculations. I will not present the morphology of *yang* and *yin* nor will I retrace its history. It suffices to remark that polar symbolism is abundantly attested in the iconography of Shang bronzes (1400–1122 BC, according to the traditional Chinese chronology). Carl Hentze, who has devoted a series of important works to this problem, points out that the polar symbols are disposed in such a way as to emphasize their conjunction; for instance, the owl, or another figure symbolizing the darkness, is provided with "solar eyes," while the emblems of light are marked by a "nocturnal" sign.[3] Hentze interprets the conjunction of polar symbols as illustrating religious ideas of renewal of time and spiritual regeneration. According to Hentze, the symbolism of *yang* and *yin* is present in the most ancient ritual objects, long before the first written texts.[4]

This is also the conclusion of Marcel Granet, though he reached it from other sources and by utilizing a different method. Granet recalls that in *Che King* the word *yin* evokes the idea of cold and cloudy weather, and also of what is internal, whereas the term *yang* suggests the idea of sunshine and warmth (*La Pensée Chinois*, 117). In other words, *yang* and *yin* indicate the concrete and antithetical aspects of the weather (118). In *Kouei tsang*, a lost manual of divination known only from some fragments, it is a question of "a time of light" and "a time of obscurity," anticipating the saying of Tchouang tseu: "a (time of) plenitude, a (time of) decrepitude ... a (time of) refining, a (time of) thickening ... a (time of) life, a (time of) death" (132). Thus, the world represents "a totality of a cyclical order (*tao, pien, tong*) constituted by the conjugation of two alternate and complementary manifestations" (127).

Granet thinks that the idea of alternation seems to have entailed the idea of opposition (128). This is clearly illustrated by the structure of the calendar. "*Yang* and *yin* have been summoned to organize the calendar because their emblems evoked with a particular force the rhythmic conjugation of two concrete antithetic aspects" (131). According to the philosophers, during the winter the *yang*, overcome by *yin*, undergoes below the frozen soil a kind of an annual trial from which it emerges invigorated. "The *yang* escapes from its prison at the beginning of spring; then the ice melts and the sources reawaken" (135). Thus the universe shows itself to be constituted by a series of antithetic forms alternating in a cyclical manner.

Fascinated by the sociologism of Durkheim, Marcel Granet was inclined to deduct the conception and the systematic articulation of cosmic rotation from the ancient formulas of Chinese social life. We do not need to follow him on this path. But it is important to notice the symmetry between the complementary alternation of the activities of the two sexes and the cosmic rhythms governed by the interplay of *yang* and *yin*. And because a feminine nature was recognized in everything that is *yin*, and a masculine nature in everything that is *yang*, the theme of hierogamy—which, according to Granet, dominates the entire Chinese mythology—discloses a cosmic as well as religious dimension. The ritual opposition of the two sexes, carried out, in ancient China, as that of two rival corporations (93), expresses simultaneously the complementary antagonism of two modes of being and the alternation of two cosmic principles, *yang* and *yin*. In the collective feasts of spring and autumn, the two antagonistic choirs, arrayed in lines face to face, challenged each other in verse. "The *yang* calls, the *yin* answers." These two formulas are interchangeable; they signify conjointly the cosmic and social rhythms (141). The antagonistic choirs confront each other as shadow and light. The field where they meet represents the totality of space, just as the group symbolizes the totality of human society and of the realities belonging to natural realm (143). A collective hierogamy ended the festivity. As we have noticed, such ritual orgies are well known in many parts of the world. In this case, too, the polarity, accepted as a fundamental rule of life during the year, is abolished, or transcended, through the union of contraries.

We do not need to recall the elaboration of such categories, which was carried out in the systematic work of the philosophers. We may only add that the comparison of the notion of *tao* with the different primitive formulas of the "third term" as a solution of polarities, constitutes a fascinating theme for the historian of ideas. Hopefully, this work will be undertaken soon.

Final Remarks

To conclude, I would like to return to a point which I consider decisive in any comparative analysis, namely the irreducibility of the spiritual creation to a preexistent system of values. In the mythological and religious universe, every *creation* recreates its own structures, just as every great poet reinvents his language. The different types of bipartition and polarity, duality and alternation, antithetical dyads and *coincidentia oppositorum*, are to be found everywhere in the world and at all stages of culture. But the historian of religions is ultimately interested in finding out what a particular culture, or group of cultures, has done with this immediate datum. A hermeneutics which pursues the comprehension of cultural creations hesitates before the temptations of reducing all the species of dyads and polarities to a single fundamental type reflecting certain unconscious logical activities. For, on the one hand, the dichotomies allow themselves to be classified in multiple categories, and, on the other hand, some typical systems are susceptible of being entrusted with an amazing number of functions and values. There is no question of presenting here a complete and detailed morphology of all the species and varieties of religious dichotomies, dyads, and polarities. As a matter of fact, such a considerable undertaking would go far beyond our subject. But the few documents which we have analyzed, and which have been purposely chosen as the most representative, suffice to illustrate our argument. Roughly, one can distinguish: (1) the groups of cosmic polarities and (2) those polarities related directly to the human condition. Certainly, there is a structural solidarity between the cosmic dichotomies and polarities and those connected with man's specific mode of being. Nevertheless, our preliminary distinction is useful, for it is mainly the polarities of the second type that have opened the way, in certain cultures and certain historical moments, to systematic philosophical speculations. Among the cosmic polarities, one may discern those of spatial structure (right/left, high/low, etc.), of temporal structure (day/night, the seasons, etc.) and finally those expressing the process of cosmic life (life/death, the rhythms of vegetation, etc.). As to the dichotomies and polarities related to the human condition, which somehow serve as a cipher of this condition, they are more numerous and, one could say, more "open." The fundamental pair is that of male/female, but there are also ethnic dichotomies ("we"/the foreigners), mythological dichotomies (the antagonistic Twins), religious dichotomies (sacred/profane, which, as a matter of fact, signifies a total dichotomy, relating concurrently to cosmos, life, and human society; gods/adversaries of gods; etc.), and ethical dichotomies (good/evil, etc.). What strikes one first in this provisory and incomplete classification is the fact that a great number of dichotomies and polarities *imply each other mutually*, as, for example, the cosmic polarities and the sexual or religious dichotomy. Ultimately, they express the modalities of life comprehended in rhythm and rotation. As we have already noticed apropos of Kogi and the Indonesians (and the same can be said about the Chinese), the polar antagonism becomes the "cipher" through which man unveils both the structures of the universe and the significance of his own existence. At this stage one cannot speak of religious or ethical "dualism," since the antagonism does not presuppose "evil" or the "demonic." Rigorously dualistic ideas arise from those pairs of contraries in which the two antagonists do not mutually imply each other. This is evident in some cosmogonic myths of California where Coyote continuously and successfully interferes with God's work of creation. A similar situation is to be found in Mänäbush's mythology: his conflict with the inferior Powers was not predestined, but broke out as a consequence of a fortuitous event (the murder of his brother, the Wolf). It will be interesting to determine precisely in what cultures, and at what epochs, the negative aspects of life, until then accepted as constitutive and unexceptionable moments of the cosmic totality, lost their initial function and began to be interpreted as manifestations of *evil*. For it seems that in the religions dominated by a system of polarities, the *idea of evil* arises slowly and with some difficulty; in certain cases the notion of evil even leaves out of its sphere many negative aspects of life (for example, suffering, disease, cruelty, bad luck, death, etc.). We have seen that among the Kogi the *principle of evil* is accepted as an inevitable and necessary moment in the cosmic totality. Finally, it is important to note that the mediation between the contraries also presents a great variety of solutions. There is opposition, clash, and combat, but in certain cases the conflict is resolved in a union which produces a "third term," while in others the polarities seem to coexist paradoxically in a *coincidentia oppositorum*, or they are transcended, i.e., radically abolished or rendered unreal, incomprehensible, or meaningless. (I refer especially to certain Indian metaphysics and "mystical" techniques.) This variety of solutions to the problems raised by the mediation between the contraries—and we must add also the radically "dualistic" positions, which refuse any mediation—merits a special investigation. For if it is true that any solution found to the crisis provoked by the awareness of polarities implies somehow the beginning of wisdom, the very multiplicity and the extreme variety of such solutions arouse the critical reflection and prepare for the coming of philosophy.

Notes

1. See, for example, *Mahābhārata*, XII, 318, 39, quoted by Dumézil, *Mitra-Varuna*, p. 209.
2. Dumézil, 209.
3. Cf. Carl Hentze, *Bronzegerät, Kultbauten, Religion im ältesten China der Shangzeit* (Anvers, 1951), 192ff. See also our observations in *Critique* 83 (April, 1954): 331ff.
4. Carl Hentze, *Das Haus als Weltort der Seele* (Stuttgart, 1961), 99ff. For a general exposition of the problem of polarity see Hermann Köster, *Symbolik des chinesischen Universismus* (Stuttgart, 1958), 17ff.

19

THE CONCEPT OF THE *COINCIDENTIA OPPOSITORUM* IN THE THOUGHT OF MIRCEA ELIADE

John Valk

Editor's Introduction

As well as shedding some light on Eliade's concept of the *coincidentia* and on its analysis by various commentators, John Valk here also makes plain the relevance of Eliade's *coincidentia* for his understanding of time and history. Valk's analysis of "The Concept of the *Coincidentia Oppositorum* in the Thought of Mircea Eliade" was first published in *Religious Studies* 28 (1992): 31–41. All rights reserved. Copyright © 1992 by Cambridge University Press. Reprinted by permission of Cambridge University Press and the author.

ℰↃ ℭℛ

I. Paradox and the *Coincidentia Oppositorum*

Eliade has become an object of intense study. In his endeavors he sought to uncover the deeper, trans-historical meaning of religious expression. He introduced the term "creative hermeneutics" in his more recent writings, and was most intent on discovering what the religious phenomena "had to say."

Eliade's unique approach, however, is not without its difficulties. Scholars have struggled with his entire corpus. Some wonder whether he does not force his own view of reality and religion, his own terms and concepts, upon the various traditions he analyses. Martin Marty, for example, has concluded that "in order to join together such disparate materials, the Romanian-born scholar has imposed his own beliefs and ideas about religiousness."[1] Douglas Allen stressed that "all of Eliade's evaluations of religious phenomena are not on the same 'level' of analysis nor that all can be subsumed under the classification of 'descriptive analysis' " (*Structure and Creativity*, 204).

Attempts have been made to uncover Eliade's own particular view of reality. Kurt Rudolph believes that Eliade's thought rests upon several elements that are "apparently fundamental components of his worldview": (1) the opposition between the sacred and the profane as the basis of religion; (2) symbolism as the primary means of religious expression; (3) prehistory as the fundamental, decisive epoch in the history of religions; and (4) *homo religiosus* as the allegedly ideal form of humanity ("Eliade and the 'History' of Religions," 108). Ansgar Paus, on the other hand, concludes that the integrating nucleus of Eliade's complex individual method does not come from philosophy nor the science of religion. It emerges, rather, from his own specific theology: Eastern Orthodox Christianity and its rich iconological symbolism (in this volume, 392–410).

Adriana Berger assists us further by pointing to the importance of literature in Eliade's writings. She speaks of his "double approach," where culture and knowledge imply the religious. This "double approach" is really a desire for unity. It is a matter not only of "cosmicizing our knowledge" (of harmonizing death, history, and becoming), but of "reconciling two apparently conflicting aspects, the letters and the sciences, within the *coincidentia oppositorum*" ("Eliade's Double Approach," 9).

Berger alludes to Eliade's use of the concept of the *coincidentia oppositorum*, but it is not developed. However, in Eliade's own words it is "one of the most archaic manners by which the paradox of divine reality expressed itself" (*Oceanografie*, 214–15).

It is not surprising, therefore, that we see such frequent use of this term in Eliade's writings. Myths and rituals "imply the absolute *coincidentia oppositorum*" (*Two and the One*, 115). Symbols express the paradoxical coming together of contradictory essences (*Images and Symbols*, 177). The *jivan-mukti* "constitutes a *coincidentia oppositorum*," which can "uncover the secret dimension of reality" (*Two and the One*, 94–96; see also *Yoga*, 363). The tantrist is capable of achieving the *coincidentia oppositorum* "on all levels of Life and Consciousness" (*Two and the One*, 117–18; see also *Yoga*, 206). And the list goes on. Yet, little attention has been focused by scholars on Eliade's use of this concept. Might his use of the *coincidentia oppositorum* throw more light on the present discussion?

Eliade's use of the two fundamental terms, sacred and profane, indicate clearly that he is a "dialectical thinker." What is not clear is the manner in which we are to understand his use of these terms. Their coming together into a unity of opposites, identified by the concept *coincidentia oppositorum*, reflects, he believes, the way religious people view the structure of reality. This theme, he asserts, emerges in virtually all religious patterns.

His frequent use of and reliance on this concept raises a question. Does Eliade discover the principle of the *coincidentia oppositorum* in greater or lesser degree in every religion because it is close to the structure of his own thought or worldview and the means by which he interprets religious phenomena? An examination of Eliade's works with this question in mind and this concept in the foreground will generate new insights into a scholar who himself has given us tremendous insights into religious phenomena. It will also serve as an additional component to the four mentioned by Rudolph, and expand Ansgar Paus's notion that Eliade's integrating nucleus is the theological. A worldview by nature is religious, which in turn includes philosophical and theological ideas and concepts (knowledge).

(a) The Paradoxical Relationship

For Eliade the relationship between the sacred and profane is not dualistic, but paradoxical. The hierophany reveals this paradoxical coming together, and "makes manifest, the co-existence of contradictory essences" (*Patterns*, 29 [above, 54]). Human reason cannot grasp this conceptually. Language at this point fails us. The abiding presence of absolute reality in something finite, limited, and changing can only be expressed in terms of a paradoxical relationship.

People become aware of the sacred through their own concrete (profane) situation. But the sacred mode is not an additional dimension, nor is it distinct from or unrelated to one's "ordinary" way of being in the world: life "is not merely human, it is *at the same time* cosmic."[2]

The sacred mode of existence is a human existence. It is also a celestial ascent; it "belongs to man as such, not to man as an historical being" (*Shamanism*, xiv [below, 259]). But, the two modes of being—sacred and profane—take place "simultaneously upon two parallel planes; that of the temporal, of change and of illusion, and that of eternity, of substance and of reality" (*Patterns*, 460).[3]

(b) Nature of the Paradoxical Relationship

How are we best to understand Eliade's notion of the paradox? On the one hand, the sacred and profane are mutually exclusive and logically contradictory. Sacred reality contradicts profane reality: eternal and temporal being and non-being, absolute and relative. On the other hand, however, the sacred needs the profane as the medium through which it is revealed and apprehended. The sacred cannot do without the profane, nor can the profane do without the sacred if it is to be fully "opened up." The sacred and profane are also mutually complementary. In the hierophany the sacred and profane occur simultaneously.

There they are both contradictory and complementary. They are *simultaneously* mutually exclusive and logically contradictory, and mutually complementary. This is the essence of the paradox.

Thomas Altizer understands Eliade as emphasizing only one side of the paradox, that the sacred negates the profane (*Eliade and the Dialectic of the Sacred*, 65. See also 34, 39, 46 and passim). Ricketts points out, however, that such a "negative dialectic" misses Eliade's point, and is Altizer's "first fundamental error in interpreting Eliade."[4] Robert Avens interprets Eliade in a similar manner to Altizer. According to him the sacred would obliterate the reality of the profane. These two opposites cannot really co-exist without the one negating or excluding the other.[5]

Both Altizer and Avens emphasize one pole of the paradox at the expense of the other. Allen sees this correctly as destroying the dialectical complexity of the religious mode of manifestation, leading inevitably to an oversimplification and distortion of Eliade's phenomenological method (*Structure and Creativity*, 126 [above, 98]). To understand Eliade more fully it is necessary to retain both sides of the paradox. Here the concept of the *coincidentia oppositorum* comes into play.

(c) Coincidentia Oppositorum: *Heuristic Device*

The *coincidentia oppositorum*, according to Eliade, is reflected in the symbols, theories, and beliefs of many different religious traditions. The fundamental doctrines contained in the myths and legends which reflect this concept have their source in those trained in theology and philosophy. And, "the metaphysical implications of the *coincidentia oppositorum* are clearly understood and accepted [by them]" (*Two and the One*, 82).

Eliade admits that most cultures do not consciously apply the principle of the *coincidentia oppositorum*. Yet, according to him, it is used even if it is not realized. This gives us the initial indication that this principle may be used as a heuristic device by Eliade, enabling him to use a concept which, though often more abstract than intended, is nonetheless applicable to the various, and often quite diverse, religious phenomena. His use of the *coincidentia oppositorum* reveals the two-fold implication of the paradox: simultaneously mutually exclusive and logically contradictory, and mutually complementary. Some examples will suffice.

In Indian spirituality the *jivan-mukti*, the man "liberated while living," "is simultaneously in time and in eternity; his existence is a paradox in the sense that it constitutes a *coincidentia oppositorum* beyond the understanding or the imagination" (*Two and the One*, 95; see also *Yoga*, 363). The religious person can realize the "*coincidentia oppositorum* in his own body and his own spirit," and "uncover the secret dimension of reality" (*Two and the One*, 95–96; see also *Yoga*, 5, 10, 18, 54, 66, 98–100).

In the mythical theme of the androgyne a new type of humanity appears; the fusion of both sexes produces a new unpolarized consciousness. Implied is the idea that perfection, and therefore Being, ultimately consists of a unity-totality; "carrying the *coincidentia oppositorum* to all levels and applying it to all contexts" (*Two and the One*, 108). Myths dealing with primordial totality, and the rituals corresponding to them, may not be the same in every case; nonetheless, they "imply the absolute *coincidentia oppositorum*" (*Two and the One*, 115).[6] All relative existence implies a state of duality, consequently resulting in suffering, illusion, and "slavery." The final goal of the Tantricist is to unite the two contrary principles, *Shiva* and *Shakti,* where "the experience of duality is abolished and the phenomenal world is transcended" (*Two and the One*, 118; see also *Yoga*, 96, 135, 206, 257, 268–72).

In alchemy the Philosopher's Stone is equated with a perfect knowledge of God, while at the same time revealing and making apparent the opposites existing within reality. According to Eliade this is all part and parcel of "the very old symbolism of the *coincidentia oppositorum*, universally widespread and well attested in primitive stages of culture" (*Forge and the Crucible*, 166).

(d) *Significance of the* Coincidentia Oppositorum

Eliade presents a whole class of phenomena in which he discovers the meanings implicit in the concept of the *coincidentia oppositorum*. Its frequent use to describe and illuminate the notion of paradox draws attention to the fact that he discovers an element that is widespread in religious consciousness. At the same time we are drawn to the importance of this concept in his own thinking.

That it is important becomes evident in the way he spots this concept emerging in the Western philosophical tradition. In Heraclitus it first receives philosophical elaboration, and strikes Eliade as most telling. Heraclitus speculated that "God is day and night, winter and summer, war and peace, satiety and hunger— *all opposites, this is the meaning*" (*Two and the One*, 81 n. 1). Eliade sensed that Heraclitus developed a view based on a reconciliation of opposites which, once accepted, made sense of archaic mythologies and Indian spirituality.

Eliade discovered a similar pattern in Meister Eckhart. But it was Nicholas of Cusa who called the union of contraries and the mystery of the totality the *coincidentia oppositorum*. Nicholas was important for Eliade because he was able to ground the infinite distinction between God (the sacred) and all things finite (the profane) metaphysically, precisely in the *coincidentia oppositorum* (*Two and the One*, 80–81, 205–206 [above, 134–36]).

Eliade's basic conceptual pattern is quite similar to the tradition of these theologian-philosophers. His conclusion that the *coincidentia oppositorum* shows up in so many diverse cultures and situations gives indication that this concept may enter strongly into his own thinking. This is borne out in his discussions of symbolism and ritual.

Characteristic of the symbol, according to Eliade, is its ability to express not only the "absolute," but also the paradoxical coming together of contradictory essences. The concepts of polarity and the *coincidentia oppositorum* have wide usage in the history of philosophy. The symbols which revealed these concepts, however, are not products of critical reflection but of an existential tension.

Characteristic of the ritual is its ability to open up the vast wealth of information about the nature of reality which is incomprehensible on any other level of perception, including the rational. Eliade's focus on rituals is not incidental. Here the religious experience is realized in its opposition to, and yet in harmony with, profane experience. This explains his emphasis on the forge and the crucible, and his predilection for rope analogies and tantric yoga. In the latter one can find the same traditional metaphysics, "which refused to define ultimate reality otherwise than as the *coincidentia oppositorum*" (*Yoga*, 272; see also *Two and the One*, 118).

In numerous cases Eliade uses this concept, both implicitly and explicitly, to give a more heightened explanation of the paradox. Guilford Dudley feels that it is only by means of a thorough understanding of the principles of yoga in Indian thought that one is able to understand Eliade's ontology (*Religion on Trial*, 105). Dudley raises an important point. It is not, however, the principles of yoga as such which are crucial to Eliade's thinking. It is the pattern which yoga instantiates that is important to his framework, and it is the *coincidentia oppositorum* as exemplified *in* yoga that sheds light on it. Thus, a thorough understanding of this concept assists greatly in grasping the unity and consistency of Eliade's thought. It is in his interpretation of history, however, that we get a clear glimpse of its implications for his own worldview.

II. Potential of History Versus Nostalgia for Paradise

Eliade asserts that a "self-contradictory attitude" occurs in all religions. On the one hand there is the desire to secure and strengthen one's own reality in the sacred. On the other hand there is the fear that individuality may be lost if one is absorbed completely in the sacred. This becomes for Eliade himself an ambivalence towards history. He recognizes that the profane historical condition is necessary to reveal the sacred. Nonetheless, he concludes that a full experience of the sacred entails abolishing profane existence. His attitude towards history includes both rejection and affirmation.

Cain asserts that this rejecting and affirming of history results from Eliade's own method: the historical-cultural gives way to the "trans-historical intentionality" ("Attitudes Towards History," 14). However, it is not his focus on the trans-historical intentionality itself that reflects the ambivalence; it is the way he interprets this intentionality. That intentionality has been displayed in the history of religions in both positive and negative attitudes towards the unfolding of time and history.

(a) Rejection of History

When Eliade examines the "archetypal lifestyle" of archaic humankind he focuses mainly on the implied rejection of all that is profane, including time and history. To be archetypal was to be anti-historical and nostalgic for Paradise. History, on the other hand, was regarded "in some measure [as] a fall of the sacred, a limitation and a diminution" (*Shamanism*, xix, and *The Eternal Return*, 158 [this volume, 262]).

Allen feels that Eliade is here simply reflecting the view of archaic humankind (*Structure and Creativity*, 129). Cain disagrees. He asserts that Eliade's own worldview is implicit in this interpretation of history (14–16). Eliade's understanding of the Hebrew view of history bears that out.

(b) Hebrew View of History

For the Hebrews the historical event became a theophany; the sacred was revealed *in* history. History became a dimension of the sacred. Each historical event was a further and irreversible revelation of God. Humans were able to advance their knowledge and experience of the sacred through history (*The Eternal Return*, 102–107).

This positive and linear view of history was, however, only momentary for Eliade. He feels that the Hebrews were not entirely successful in transcending the cyclical pattern. They too longed for the end of history, and tolerated it only because it was known that it would one day cease. Their "paradisial state" was at the beginning *and* at the end of the historical period (111).

Eliade's understanding of the Hebrew view again reflects two sides of the paradox. History becomes a means to the sacred, yet it is also to be abolished. It can be distracting; its peace and prosperity often caused the people to turn away from God. That same paradox surfaces in his interpretation of Christianity.

(c) Time and History in Christianity

For Christianity the Kingdom of God was not just a future possibility: it was also attainable at any moment. The coinciding of opposites—the Kingdom of God and the human historical situation—was accessible to any one at any time through *metanoia*.

Christianity's most striking innovation was its valorization of time. Time itself is ontologized, through God's revelation in the person of Jesus Christ. This uniqueness is not simply the "hierophanizing" of time, familiar in all religions, but the complete concealing of the divine *in* history. Christianity strives to save history by seeing its trans-historicity. History is filled with trans-historical meaning (*Images and Symbols*, 169–71).

With ever increasing innovations in religious activities and experiences, resulting from continued multiplicity and diversity in temporal reality, a more heightened experience of the *coincidentia oppositorum* becomes possible with the passage of time. Although it may often be more difficult to "see" the unity amidst the multiplicity and diversity, nonetheless, when the *coincidentia oppositorum* is experienced, it is experienced as having been "raised" to a newer and more "complete" level.

Christianity too provides a promise of freedom. It allows for the possibility of a sanctified future historical condition through faith.

> Faith ... means absolute emancipation from any kind of natural "law" and hence the highest freedom that man can imagine: freedom to intervene even in the ontological constitution of the universe. It is, consequently, a pre-eminently creative freedom. In other words, it constitutes a new formula for man's collaboration with the creation. (*The Eternal Return*, 160–61)

Eliade senses that the study of the history of religions can play a significant role in realizing a heightened *coincidentia oppositorum*. A new humanism on a world-wide scale could develop based on this deeper knowledge, and Judaeo-Christianity has shown "in what sense history might become glorious and even absolute" (*Images and Symbols*, 66; see also *Quest*, 3). Here Eliade emphasizes again the positive role of history.

Unfortunately, he is not able to accept the full implications of these significant changes and potentials brought by Christianity. Sharing in the eternal *nunc* of the reign of God implies for him that history ceases as totally as it does for those of archaic cultures. Judaeo-Christianity continues to retain "certain traces of the ancient doctrine of periodic regeneration of history" (*The Eternal Return*, 129–30). Christianity brought no real innovation; it also implies a paradoxical return *in illud tempus,* "a leap backwards" (*Images and Symbols*, 168–72).

Here Eliade's paradoxical understanding again becomes clear. The Christ event which has redeemed history has, in fact, ultimately abolished it. When humankind experiences the "favorable moment" in time and history, time is paradoxically transformed into eternity. Concretely the valorization of time is its abolition, and the abolishing of history is its fulfillment. Here in a heightened way Eliade emphasizes the *coincidentia oppositorum,* the coinciding of time and eternity, but in a manner which tends to highlight a negative rather than a positive acceptance of history.

(d) Continuity and Innovation

In spite of Christianity's more positive emphasis on history, Eliade's ambivalence indicates his often uncomfortable feelings with history. While history provides the possibility for further and fuller revelations of the sacred, and the coinciding of opposites in time and history, he sees further historical unfolding as a threat to the struggle for a sanctified mode of being.

For the modern person the sacred has become lost or meaningless. We are all too often "swallowed up" by the multiplicity and diversity of human unfolding in time and history. Eliade is afraid that we have become lost in history, that we see only fragmentation and not the trans-historical meaning in historical events. The terrors of history become overwhelming. But, Eliade should have no such fear. Although it is quite possible to become epistemologically lost in the multiplicity and diversity of history, this should ultimately be of little concern. Those of faith can experience the *coincidentia oppositorum* at any time. How this occurs is mysterious; what is important is that it *can* occur.

We come to discover Eliade's reluctance to develop fully the positive aspect of history. After the publication of *Cosmos and History* and *Images and Symbols* we hear him saying that "my essential preoccupation is precisely the means of escaping history, of saving myself through symbol, myth, rites, and archetypes."[7] The influence of Indian spirituality on Eliade's own Eastern Orthodox tradition appears to cause a certain tension in his thought that is not completely resolved.

Eliade's last book, *A History of Religious Ideas*, sheds certain light on this ambivalent view of history, and provides a partial explanation of his intent. Cain points out that Eliade "sees the human spirit responding to crises and catastrophes with new religio-cultural creations—specific responses to the environmental condition" ("Attitudes towards History," 16). This is in fact the book's central message; that "crises in depth," and creations resulting from them, enable religious traditions to renew themselves. Eliade's stress here is on continuity *and* innovation: "continuous reading reveals above all the *fundamental unity* of all religious phenomena and at the same time the inexorable *newness* of their expressions" (*History of Religious Ideas*, I, xiv).

Changes in human history have resulted in new and creative religious patterns. But, particular patterns cannot explain the whole. Neither positive nor negative attitudes towards history can be used to explain the nature of reality in its entirety. To account for the various attitudes necessitates the examination of the person as a religious being with a central intentionality towards sacred reality. In terms of Eliade's investigations an ambivalent attitude emerges because, from his own framework, this is what the historical pattern of humankind's intentionality towards the sacred has demonstrated. Eliade's writings have been invaluable in presenting overwhelming evidence that the basic role of the religious dimension is constant and universal, in spite of the idiosyncrasies of cultures and diversities of religions. He has helped advance our understanding of the spiritual as an integral dimension of human existence. He struggles heroically to demonstrate that the sacred is the ground of the natural, that it does not abolish the natural, and that it is not ontologically separate from the natural. This forms the basis of his worldview, and is demonstrated in his use of the concept of the *coincidentia oppositorum* as a means of explaining the paradoxical coming together of the sacred and profane.

It is an evident advance in the discussion to speak of profane in terms of an unfulfilled natural existence. Nonetheless, it raises the question whether the fulfilling of the natural, and its grounding in the sacred, must go by way of the *invalidation* of the natural. Even as Eliade maintains that the sacred, is necessary to make sense of the natural, the result is an overshadowing of the natural.

Though Eliade is emphatically clear that profane reality is not negated when the sacred is manifested, a clear contrast is always maintained between the two, with a tendency to regard the natural state as lacking in its entirety. This view hides within it the supposition that the natural, *qua* natural, is anti-sacred, or at best neutral. At this point it is necessary to question the very nature of Eliade's notion of the paradox and the *coincidentia oppositorum* as a way of shedding light on it.

Eliade's use of the paradox implies that the manifestation of the sacred is never complete. Human history prevents full apprehension of the sacred; it will always appear limited and relative. Although he speaks of the future possibility of a "new humanism" in which the sacred will be apprehended on "newer" and "higher" levels, this new existence will always be faced with the same paradoxical, and hence limited, revelation of the sacred. The paradox implies that the sacred is never fully revealed, nor is the profane ever completely transformed into the sacred: the profane never *becomes* the sacred.

Eliade's use of the paradox leads him to seek authentic existence in the transcendent at the expense, though not necessarily the negation, of the historical, natural mode. One could ask, as an arguable alternative, whether the sacred mode of being is not that of living out an authentic creaturely existence, and not one of diminishing this very historical mode of existence.

It is debatable whether Eliade's appropriation of the paradox and *coincidentia oppositorum* adequately accounts for human creaturely existence. The profane does not refer to a category of natural or material things, nor does the sacred merely refer to spiritual things. Rather, the profane refers more to brokenness of life: evil is the profane tendency. The sacred tendency, on the other hand, is the restored creatureliness; the redemption we feel in our lives.

Nonetheless, for studies in the phenomenology of religion, Eliade certainly has given us evidence of the commonality of the human search for the sacred. Though we may question his description of the dynamics of the spiritual mode of human existence, he has clearly pointed to the fact that religion is an integral dimension of human existence in a reality that bespeaks the absolute and the transcendent.

Notes

1. Review of Mircea Eliade, *A History of Religious Ideas*, *New York Times*, April 15, 1979, 15.
2. According to Eliade archaic humankind did not make a separation between the "spiritual" and the "material." These "two planes are complementary," *Images and Symbols*, 177. See also *Quest*, i, and *Sacred and Profane*, 165.
3. Seymour Cain points out that in Eliade's usage the "transhistorical" or sacred mode "does not refer simply to a supermundane realm, but also to human nature as distinguished from human history." "Mircea Eliade: Attitudes Towards History," 15.
4. For Ricketts the relationship is "more paradoxical than dialectic." See Ricketts, "Mircea Eliade and the Death of God," 45.
5. Robert Avens, "Mircea Eliade's Conception of the Polarity 'Sacred-Profane' in Archaic Religions and in Christianity" (PhD thesis, Fordham University, 1971), 52, 70.
6. See also the discussions on the symbolism of ascension in *Myths, Dreams and Mysteries*, 99ff.
7. Dudley, *Religion on Trial*, 29. From a letter dated June 1954.

Myths

20

MYTHOLOGY AND THE HISTORY OF RELIGIONS

Mircea Eliade

Editor's Introduction

Eliade's analysis of mythology might be seen as equal in importance to his under-standing of religion as his analysis of religious symbolism, including the *coincidentia oppositorum*, since he considers mythology and religion to be co-extensive—where there is myth there is religion and vice versa (see *Reconstructing Eliade*, 219). Originally published in *Diogenes* 9 (1955): 105–13. All rights reserved. Copyright © 1973 by D. Reidel Publishing Company, Dordrecht, Holland. Reprinted by permission of Sage Publications, Ltd.

ℰ ℭ

The *opus maximus* of Professor Martin P. Nilsson, his great *Geschichte der griechischen Religion* in two volumes, has already been presented to the readers of *Diogenes* (see Olof Gigon's review in No. 3, July, 1953, 128–31). But the activity of the Nestor of the history of religion is prodigious: while composing his *Geschichte*, the eminent Swedish scholar has published a large number of studies, among which—besides his *Religion populaire dans la Grèce antique*—we must note the second edition (increased by about a hundred pages) of *The Minoan-Mycenaean Religion* (Lund, 1950), the second edition of *The History of Greek Religion* (Oxford, 1949), the two volumes of the *Opuscula Selecta* (Lund, 1951, 1952) and a volume of hitherto unpublished studies,

Cults, Myths, Oracles and Politics in Ancient Greece (Lund, 1951). The little book which has just been translated into French is a work of popularization in the best sense of the term: Professor Nilsson outlines briefly the results of the long and difficult research carried out by a whole generation of scholars on religious life in the rural districts of ancient Greece. He thus shows us aspects of religiosity which classical mythology or the works of the scholars of antiquity generally overlooked. The description of rural beliefs and superstitions makes extremely profitable reading, especially the clear, condensed accounts of seasonal festivities (feasts of the dead, May days, etc.) which still survive in the Christianized folklore of modern Greece. Interesting, too, is the excellent introduction to the study of the mysteries of Eleusis (69ff.), "the finest and most perfect flowering of popular Greek religion." Most aptly, the author recalls that "the silence imposed on the mysteries was well kept" and that "concerning the essential rites attached to the grade of *epopteia*, we have only general notions" (70; see also 75). All that is known is that the Eleusinian mysteries were linked with the Thesmophoria, which proves that both ritual scenarios "were agrarian rites intended to foster the fertility of the grain planted in the earth" (81). As for the myths of Demeter, Kore, Pluto, and their relations with the mysteries of Eleusis, the author resumes the interpretations which he had already proposed in the first volume of his *Geschichte*: Demeter, the wheat mother, and Kore, the grain maiden, symbolize the old and the new harvest (84ff.). In a few fine pages he analyzes "the moral and social consequences of agriculture" (95ff.)—consequences which are illustrated by the opposition between the ideal of Homer's warrior knights and the ideal of the peasants expressed in the work of Hesiod. "I might even speak of an Eleusinian piety founded on the idea that agriculture engendered a civilized and peaceful life worthy of human beings" (96).

All this is true and excellently said. The genetic relations and the relations of morphological structure between agriculture and the mysteries of Eleusis have been known and exploited by the majority of scholars. But since Professor Nilsson has already reminded us (75) that we know nothing precise about "the essential rites attached to the grade of *epopteia*," we hesitate to follow him when he states that at Eleusis "there was no doctrine, but only a few simple, fundamental ideas concerning life and death—represented by the new harvest coming from the old" (105). We know now that such "simple, fundamental ideas concerning life and death" may have great spiritual fecundity: the initiation rites of the primitives are an example. The fact that these ideas may have been, as Professor Nilsson believes, linked with "the new harvest coming from the old" does not in any way diminish their significance as great theoretical syntheses. The agricultural peoples, the *Urpflänzer*, as German ethnologists call them, worked out an admirable system of metaphysics on the basis of the connection which they discovered between food, death and sexuality. (See, in Ad. E. Jensen's *Das religiöse Weltbild einer frühen Kultur*, Stuttgart, 1948, 66ff., the discussion of the mysteries of Eleusis apropos of C. G. Jung and Karl Kerenyi's *Das göttliche*

Mädchen, Amsterdam: Pantheon, 1941.) We must note that what is meant is really a system of metaphysics and not a simple *Weltanschauung*, for among the *Urpflänzer* the link between the primordial murder of a divinity, the appearance of edible plants, and the necessity of sexual reproduction to assure the continuance of the human species which is menaced by death constitutes the explanation of ultimate reality as well as the justification of the present condition of life; the myth fulfils at the same time a cosmological, an ontological and a moral function. Professor Nilsson doubts whether there was a doctrine at Eleusis, and he is probably right if he is thinking of a doctrine in the sense in which the term may be applied to the teachings of the Orphic theologians or the pre-Socratic cosmologists—that is, a systematic explanation of the ultimate realities. But a doctrine may also be found, though in an implicit form, in myths and symbols. Professor Nilsson remains faithful to the rationalistic method and language of his generation, and this is no reproach; but it obliges us to qualify his analyses by translating them into less dogmatic terms. On the other hand, certain statements seem to us difficult to defend: for example, his assertion that "the offering of the first fruits is pre-deistic, earlier than the cult of the gods" (*Cults, Myths, Oracles and Politics*, 46). Now, among the primitives, a very large number of offerings of first fruits are consecrated to the gods. Some ethnologists even think that this type of offering is the oldest sacrifice of which we have any knowledge. The validity of this general explanation may be disputed; but the existence of offerings of first fruits destined for the gods can no longer be denied.

Of primary importance is the methodological lesson to be drawn from Professor Nilsson's work. He wanted to give us a brief but complete description of certain little-known aspects of Greek religiosity, and he has acquitted himself brilliantly of the task. His position in regard to the two sources of Greek religion is also significant: he tries to strike an even balance between the partisans of the primacy of the Mediterranean elements and their adversaries. In the first edition of *The Minoan-Mycenaean Religion and its Survival in Greek Religion* (which dates from 1927), he rather strongly emphasized the importance of the Mediterranean elements, but rectified this position in the first volume of his *Geschichte* (481ff.), and critics of the pro-Mediterranean school promptly made themselves heard (see, for example, Giovanni Patroni in the *Athenaeum*, N.S., XX, 1942, 127–38; Umberto Pestalozza, *Religione mediterranea*, Milan, 1951, 191ff., and *passim*). It should be noted in this connection that the importance of the *Nordic* elements (which Sir Arthur Evans's momentous discoveries had thrown into the background) has again been emphasized by the authors of certain recent works (cf., for example, Rhys Carpenter, *Folk-Tale, Fiction and Saga in the Homeric Epics*, Berkeley and Los Angeles, 1946; Karl Meuli, *Griechische Opferbräuche*, in *Phyllobolia für Peter von der Mühll*, Basel, 1946, 183–288; E. R. Dodds, *The Greeks and the Irrational*, Berkeley and Los Angeles, 1951).

M. Gabriel Germain's rich and absorbing work is addressed as much to the Hellenist as to the historian of religions and the literary critic. The author devotes the first part of his *Genèse de l'Odyssée* (Paris: P.U.F., 1954) to the "prehistory of some Odyssean themes" (11–390): archaic rituals (a royal ritual of the steppes: the bow of royalty and the "marriages by competition"; a pastoral ritual: the Cyclops and the cult of the Ram; an agrarian ritual: Circe's swine); metallurgical techniques and beliefs (the bronze dwellings, Aeolus and the bellows); magic and Yoga (the cattle of the sun and the magic of the huntsmen, beds and magic, magic plants, the food of forgetfulness and sacred poisons, the marvels of Yoga); certain supernatural beings (Circe, the peoples who eat no salt, the subjects of King "Strength-of-Mind," clairvoyant animals); archaic speculations (the journey to the land of the dead, the Sirens and the temptation of knowledge).

These examples show the breadth and the interest of the comparative research undertaken by M. Gabriel Germain in connection with "the prehistory of Odyssean themes." The author puts together series of facts which it would take too long to discuss properly within the limits of a review, but we may summarize some of his results.

In Book XXI of the *Odyssey,* Penelope "promises to marry whichever one of the suitors triumphs in an archery competition. The contestants will have to draw Ulysses' bow—a hero's weapon which it take superhuman strength to use—then send an arrow with one shot through twelve axes placed in line. A queen and a kingdom will be the prize for this exploit" (ii). Now—and this fact seems to have escaped modern Hellenists—a similar episode is recounted in the two Hindu epics. On the occasion of the *svayamvara* (marriage by personal choice) of Draupadi, the contestants must draw a bow (so stiff that none, save Arjuna, can use it) and hit a target placed on the summit of a scaffolding. Similarly, in the *Rāmāyana,* Rāma succeeds in bending a giant bow and breaking it in the middle. Finally, in the *Lalita-Vistara,* the Bodhisattva wins a similar victory: he draws a bow which no one could pick up, and the arrow pierces five shields, then seven trees and an iron figure in the form of a boar. "We are far from Ulysses bow," wrote Philippe-Edouard Foucaux when he compared Rāma's exploits with those of Buddha. But M. Germain's analysis points out clearly the elements which are common to all these stories: the hero wins his wife (or, in the *Odyssey,* wins her back), by winning an archery contest which includes the piercing of several successive targets (*Genèse de l'Odyssée,* 24). The author also furnishes parallels to show that archery is part of the inaugural ceremonies of royalty (45). In conclusion, he thinks he can discern the following stages in the diffusion of the theme:

1. The nomads of central Asia (Turco-Mongols or Iranians) invent the reflex bow before 3000. By this date the weapon is known in Mesopotamia. It probably reaches a part of the Indo-Europeans, future Hellenes or Aryans (in the precise sense of the term) before they are dispersed by the great migrations of the end of the third millennium. The story of the

sovereign who wins his wife and his kingdom through his skill as an archer—which also comes from the steppes and is linked with known practices in the Indo-Iranian world—enters the aristocratic traditions of the future inhabitants of India and Greece. 2. It appears in literature for the first time, with the *Odyssey*, in the Greek world; later it appears with the epics and hagiographic stories of India. 3. One version penetrates Russia with the Mongols or Turcs and survives orally to the middle of the 19th century, when it is picked up. (53)

One may wonder if specialists in the various historical disciplines would accept such a hypothesis. For our part, we wish to note only one important fact: in the *Rig Veda* there is a myth centered around the drawing of a bow. With his bow Indra looses an arrow which flies across a mountain and kills the boar which, on the other side of the mountain, is guarding the "treasure": a bowl of rice. Now, as F. B. Kuiper has recently shown, this myth is East Asiatic in origin even though it was assimilated by the Indo-Aryans as early as the Vedic period. Even the vocabulary is East Asiatic: the words for bow (drumbhūli), arrow (bunda), a bowl of rice (*odanà*), the name of the boar (*Emusa*) are of Munda origin. The historico-cultural perspective in which the episodes of the Hindu epic and of the *Lalita-Vistara* must be seen is consequently modified. As for the meaning of the contest, there seems no doubt about its role as an initiatory test: a "treasure," a wife, or a kingdom, rewards the hero. The fact that, in myths as well as in tales, such initiatory tests are linked with a *svayamvara* seems to indicate, as a historico-cultural context, the passage from a dying matriarchy to a society dominated by the ideology of the *Männerbunde*.

Apropos of the role of the Cyclops (55–129) M. Germain opportunely recalls the role of ogres in initiations: the terrible voice of Polyphemus is not lacking in resemblance to the great uproar that is produced in the initiatory hut (82); the flight under the ram's skin might represent the departure of the initiate after he had symbolically become a ram in a cult dedicated to that animal (86). After having reviewed the ram cults in the Mediterranean world (86ff.) and in North Africa (103ff.), the author concludes that "a relationship between Greek and Lybian facts, in the religious realm, does not seem *a priori* impossible" (114). Though it has fallen into the domain of legends, "the episode of the Cyclops describes the initiation into a ram cult, of a very archaic character" (128).

Circe's swine appear in the schema characteristic of an old agrarian ritual; the relations between the wild or domesticated pig and the forces of vegetation are abundantly shown (130–50). The author comes back to this question when studying the figure of Circe (249–75). Amidst her tamed beasts, Circe resembles Artemis, the Mediterranean and Asiatic *Potnia theron*; the isle of Circe recalls the Semitic sanctuaries surrounded by a sacred barrier, a paradise in the etymological sense of the word (262). However, Circe does not seem to be, as

M. Hiquily claims, "a goddess of mysteries": "the theme of the swine shows characteristics which are more folkloric than mystical" (73). But even without accepting M. Hiquily's hypothesis one may observe that, among numerous *Urpflänzer* populations, swine are related to initiation ceremonies (cf. Jensen's *Das religiöse Weltbild*, mentioned above).

The two chapters devoted to metallurgical techniques and beliefs (159–91) are rich in new suggestions. "Bronze dwellings" often appear in tales of the supernatural, and they seem to be the dwellings of divine or extraordinary beings. The author goes on to say that the day iron came into current usage, bronze received the ritual value of stone (173). As for Aeolus, he would seem to be the archetype of the blacksmith king. The story of the bellows and the winds is derived from metallurgical techniques; as he works his bellows, the smith draws the air into a bladder at will and expels it. The indication that the king's six sons married their six sisters bears an Egyptian imprint (191). Apropos of the cattle of the Sun (the hides that move, the meat that moos while it is on the spit), M. Germain recalls a certain magic belief of hunting peoples according to which the animal is reborn from its own bones (196ff.). Among the "marvels of Yoga" he classes Proteus, whom he considers comparable to "sarcastic *gurus*," Milarepa, for instance (232ff.). "The spiritual master reveals himself only to the one who seems to him capable of supporting the weight of knowledge" (236). It would have been still more exact to say that all these tests have an initiatory character. The author compares the "winged sandals" to certain results of Indo-Tibetan Yoga (238ff.), and the pilotless ships remind him of the chariot Puśpaka which, in the Rāmāyana, went wherever its master directed his desire (243ff.). Comparing the adventure of Ulysses to the well-known Egyptian account of the shipwrecked sailor (299ff.), he finds many points in common, but "it must not necessarily be concluded that our episode has its origin in the version of the shipwrecked sailor which has come down to us" (305). The ritual interpretation of the whole episode proposed by M. Mireaux (an agrarian fecundity rite celebrated at the beginning of spring) does not seem to him convincing (314).

A rather long chapter is devoted to the *Nekya* (329–81), to which the nearest Oriental parallel is Gilgamesh's journey to meet Utnapishtim. The author thinks he can see the influence of Asiatic pessimism (351). However, "one cannot escape the final impression that the poet felt the grandeur of his subject but that he did not develop it either in an entirely epic or an entirely religious way" (370). This is one of the general conclusions of the work: the *Odyssey* abounds in Oriental and archaic elements, but the poet seems to have neglected or ignored their religious significance. The raft of Ulysses has an Egyptian form (403ff.) and Hornell has shown that Egyptian shipbuilding is related to that of the Indian Ocean, not to that of the Mediterranean. Like Hesiod, Homer seems to owe a great debt to earlier—and thus Oriental—cosmogonic ideas, which were also common to Orphism (522). Between the *Odyssey* and the epic of Gilgamesh there exists "a succession of episodes which certain characteristics bring together" (422), but there also exist differences: Ulysses, in the *Nekya,* is hunting for practical information, not the secret of life (423). "The difficult thing is not to find a mystic significance behind an Odyssean episode. Almost all have their sources in traditions whose origins go back to practices or speculations of a religious nature. The difficulty begins when one feels the need of organizing them into a whole animated by the same spirit and tending to show a coherent sense" (630). The problem could not have been better expressed. But is the coherence of myths and traditional stories of a rational nature? The author continues: "In these real tales that are formed by the episodes of the Lotus Eaters, the Cyclops, Aeolus, Circe, the island of the Sun, one cannot find the slightest indication that the poet ever considered them otherwise than as good stories. In the revelation of Achilles, the temptation of the Sirens, we believe we caught the reflection of higher thoughts, which go back much further than our author and are foreign to the traditions of his people. But it seemed to us that he did not himself perceive all their value" (ibid.). Here M. Germain raises the very delicate problem of the interpretation of literary works: to judge the value of a literary work, must one limit oneself to what the author consciously wanted to say or thought he was saying? It is not certain that this is M. Germain's thought: quite aptly, he speaks (511ff.) of the Odyssean "world of the imagination," which must not be opposed only to the geographic world in the narrow sense of the term, but also to every "profane" world—that is, every world which draws its significance only from the conscious level. One wonders, then, whether the episodes of the Cyclops and Circe can have been considered by the poet merely as "good stories." After two centuries of rationalism, a modern critic finds it difficult to consider them as such; it is hard to see why Homer would have been more rationalistic than our contemporaries. M. Germain speaks of a "progressive fall, from transmission to transmission, from the rite to the tale, from the sacred to the supernatural" (634), and that is true. But one must also remember that the "supernatural" prolongs and disguises myths, even in a society which, like ours, has lost its sense of the sacred.

Studying the "world of the imagination," M. Germain has written some fine pages against the "intrepid localizers"; he has also shown the non-historical structure of mythical time, the importance of conventional numbers (cf. also his complementary thesis, *Homère et la Mystique des nombres*, Paris, 1954). One regrets, however, that he did not treat the problem of the genesis of the epic, the passage of myth and legend to oral literature. "Preliminary work would have to be done around many other epics in order for us to know what weight must be given to these parallels and whether, in this way, some truth of a general and permanent nature might be reached" (677). But this work has already been done by H. Munro Chadwick and N. Kershaw Chadwick in the three enormous volumes of their *Growth of Literature* (Cambridge, 1932–1940). It would have been interesting to know what M. Germain thinks of the general hypothesis of the two British scholars on the origin of the epic. Similarly, one would have liked to know what he thinks of the Italian pro-Mediterranean school, of the work of Patroni, Pestallozza, Momolina Marconi on Circe, Calypso, etc., and especially of the *Commenti mediterranei all'Odissea di Omero* (Milan, 1986), the voluminous, prolix but brilliant work of Giovanni Patroni. Though M. Germain's information seems rather rich, one has the impression that for his comparative research he used chiefly manuals and works of synthesis (which is always dangerous for the student of comparative religions or literatures who is preoccupied with some special problem). Specialized reviews, even those in the field of Hellenism, are rather parsimoniously cited. The author warns us in his preface: "The difficulties of documentation in a country which is very unevenly equipped in these fields, like Morocco, where we planned and carried out our work; the isolation into which the war plunged it even more completely than it did Europe; the difficulty of communications in the years which followed the end of hostilities—all this delayed and complicated the final elaboration. Some of the gaps in our work have no other cause" (5–6). In these few lines it seems to us that we read the threat of a very great danger: on the one hand, except for a few cultural centers, students run the risk of having only outdated information at their disposal; on the other hand, if one does not appeal to the collaboration of scholars working in various fields, all comparative research, however laborious, runs the risk of being incomplete and even distorted. The whole future of the history of religions depends on rapid circulation of exact information and broad cooperation among the specialists in numerous fields, from prehistory and archaeology to ethnology and folklore.

21

SURVIVALS AND CAMOUFLAGES OF MYTHS

Mircea Eliade

Editor's Introduction

As mentioned above (this volume, 57) in the editor's introduction to Eliade's "The Sacred in the Secular World," it is characteristic of Eliade's understanding that the sacred is not lost to the secular world, but is more profoundly concealed and more subtly revealed. In this selection on "Survivals and Camouflages of Myths," Eliade explains his understanding of the "modern" (i.e. secular) retention of mythic themes and thus of a fundamentally religious orientation. This position has, of course, been much criticized. See, for example, Robert Segal's opposition to this claim, "Are there Modern Myths?" in *Changing Religious Worlds: The Meaning and End of Mircea Eliade*, edited by Bryan Rennie, 25–32 (Albany, NY: State University of New York Press, 2001). The following selection is taken from *Myth and Reality* by Mircea Eliade, 162–93 (New York: Harper and Row, 1963). All rights reserved. Copyright © 1963 by Harper and Row. Reprinted by permission of HarperCollins Publishers.

೮೦ ೧೪

"The Myths of the Modern World"

S ome forms of "mythical behavior" still survive in our day. This does not mean that they represent "survivals" of an archaic mentality. But certain aspects and functions of mythical thought are constituents of the human being. We have discussed some "myths of the modern world" elsewhere (*Myths, Dreams and Mysteries*, 23–38 [below, 204–14]). The problem is complex and absorbing; we cannot hope to exhaust in a few pages what would furnish the material for a large volume. We will confine ourselves to briefly discussing some aspects of "modern mythologies."

We have seen the importance of the "return to the origins" in archaic societies, a return that can be effected in a number of ways. Now, this prestige of the "origin" has also survived in the societies of Europe. When an innovation was to be made, it was conceived, or presented, as a return to the origin. The Reformation began the return to the Bible and dreamed of recovering the experience of the primitive Church, or even of the earliest Christian communities. The French Revolution had its paradigmatic models in the Romans and the Spartans. The inspirers and leaders of the first successful radical revolution in Europe, which marked not merely the end of a regime but the end of a historical cycle, thought of themselves as restoring the ancient virtues praised by Livy and Plutarch.

At the dawn of the modern World the "origin" enjoyed an almost magical prestige. To have a well-established "origin" meant, when all was said and done, to have the advantage of a noble origin. "We find our origin in Rome!" the Romanian intellectuals of the eighteenth and nineteenth centuries proudly repeated. In their case consciousness of Latin descent was accompanied by a kind of mystical participation in the greatness of Rome. Similarly the Hungarian intelligentsia found a justification for the antiquity, nobility, and historical mission of the Magyars in the origin myth of Hunor and Magor and in the heroic saga of Arpad. All through Central and South-eastern Europe at the beginning of the nineteenth century the mirage of "noble origin" aroused nothing short of a passion for national history, especially for its earliest phases. "A people without history" (read: without "historical documents" or without historiography) "is as if it did not exist!" This anxiety is perceptible in all the national historians of Central and Eastern Europe. Such a passion for national historiography was, to be sure, a consequence of the awakening of nationalities in this part of Europe. Then too, it was soon transformed into an instrument of propaganda and political warfare. But the desire to prove the "noble origin" and "antiquity" of one's people dominates South-eastern Europe to such an extent that, with few exceptions, all of the respective historians confined themselves to national history and finally wound up in cultural provincialism.

The passion for "noble origin" also explains the racist myth of "Aryanism" which periodically gains currency in the West, especially in Germany. The sociopolitical contexts of this myth are too well known to require discussion. What is of concern for our study is the fact that the "Aryan" represented at once the "primordial" Ancestor and the noble "hero," the latter laden with all the virtues that still haunted those who had not managed to reconcile themselves to the ideal of the societies that emerged from the revolutions of 1789 and 1848. The "Aryan" was the exemplary model that must be imitated in order to recover racial "purity," physical strength, nobility, the heroic "ethics" of the glorious and creative "beginnings."

As for Marxist Communism, its eschatological and millennialist structures have been duly noted. We remarked not long ago that Marx had taken over one of the great eschatological myths of the Asianico-Mediterranean world: the redeeming role of the just Man (in our day, the proletariat), whose sufferings are destined to change the ontological status of the World.

> In fact, Marx's classless society, and the consequent disappearance of all historical tensions, find their most exact precedent in the myth of the Golden Age which, according to a number of traditions, lies at the beginning and the end of History. Marx has enriched this venerable myth with a truly messianic Judaeo-Christian ideology; on the one hand, by the prophetic and soteriological function he ascribes to the proletariat; and, on the other, by the final struggle between Good and Evil, which may well be compared with the apocalyptic conflict between Christ and Antichrist, ending in the decisive victory of the former. It is indeed significant that Marx turns to his own account the Judaeo-Christian eschatological hope of *an absolute* [*end to*] *History*; in that he parts company from the other historical philosophers (Croce, for instance, and Ortega y Gasset), for whom the tensions of history are implicit in the human condition, and therefore can never be completely abolished (*Myths, Dreams and Mysteries*, 25–26 [below, 206]).

Myths and Mass Media

Recent studies have brought out the mythical structures of the images and behavior patterns imposed on collectivities by mass media. This phenomenon is found especially in the United States.[1] The characters of the comic strips present the modern version of mythological or folklore Heroes. They incarnate the ideal of a large part of society, to such a degree that any change in their typical conduct or, still worse, their death, will bring on veritable crises among their readers; the latter react violently, and protest by sending thousands of telegrams to the authors of the comic strips or the editors of the newspapers in which they appear. A fantastic character, Superman, has become extremely popular, especially because of his double identity; although coming from a planet destroyed by a catastrophe, and possessing prodigious powers, Superman lives on Earth in the modest guise of a journalist, Clark Kent; he is timid, unassertive, dominated by his colleague Lois Lane. This humiliating camouflage of a Hero whose powers are literally unlimited revives a well-known mythical theme. In the last analysis, the myth of Superman satisfies the secret longings of modern man who, though he knows that he is a fallen, limited creature, dreams of one day proving himself an "exceptional person," a "Hero."

Much the same could be said of the detective novel. On the one hand, the reader witnesses the exemplary struggle between Good and Evil, between the Hero (= the Detective) and the criminal (the modern incarnation of the Demon). On the other, through an unconscious process of projection and iden-tification, he takes part in the mystery and the drama and has the feeling that he is personally involved in a paradigmatic—that is, a dangerous, "heroic"—action.

The mythicization of public figures through the mass media, the transfor-mation of a personality into an exemplary image, has also been analyzed.

> Lloyd Warner tells us of the creation of such a public figure in the first section of his *The Living and the Dead.* Biggy Muldoon, a Yankee City politician who became a national figure because of his colorful opposition to the Hill Street Aristocracy, had a demagogic public image built up by the press and radio. He was presented as a crusading man of the people attacking entrenched wealth. Then, when the public tired of this image, the mass media obligingly turned Biggy into a villain, a corrupt politician seeking personal profit out of the public necessity. Warner points out that the real Biggy was considerably different from either image but actually was forced to modify his style of action to conform to one image and fight the other (Greeley, "Myths, Symbols, and Rituals," 19).

Mythical behavior can be recognized in the obsession with "success" that is so characteristic of modern society and that expresses an obscure wish to transcend the limits of the human condition; in the exodus to Suburbia, in which we can detect the nostalgia for "primordial perfection"; in the paraphernalia and emotional intensity that characterize what has been called the "cult of the sacred automobile." As Andrew Greeley remarks,

> one need merely visit the annual automobile show to realize that it is a highly ritualized religious performance. The colors, the lights, the music, the awe of the worshippers, the presence of the temple priestesses (fashion models), the pomp and splendor, the lavish waste of money, the thronging crowds—all these would represent in any other culture a clearly liturgical service. ... The cult of the sacred car has its adepts and initiati. No gnostic more eagerly awaited a revelation from an oracle than does an automobile worshipper await the first rumors about the new models. It is at this time of the annual seasonal cycle that the high priests of the cult—the auto dealers—take on a new importance as an anxious public eagerly expects the coming of a new form of salvation (Greeley, 24).

Myths of the Elite

Less attention has been paid to what could be called the myths of the elite, especially those crystallized around artistic creation and its cultural and social repercussions. These myths, be it said, have succeeded in imposing themselves far beyond the closed corporation of the initiate, principally because of the inferiority complex that now afflicts both the public and official art circles. The aggressive incomprehension of the public, of critics, and of the official representatives of art toward a Rimbaud or a Van Gogh, the disastrous consequences—especially for collectors and museums—produced by indifference toward innovating movements, from impressionism to cubism and surrealism, have been hard lessons for the critics and the public as well as for art dealers, museum directors, and collectors. Today their only fear is not to be advanced enough and hence not to be in time to recognize genius in a work that is at first sight unintelligible. Perhaps never before in history has the artist been so certain that the more daring, iconoclastic, absurd, and inaccessible he is, the more he will be recognized, praised, spoiled, idolatrized. In some countries the result has even been an academicism in reverse, the academicism of the "avantgarde"—to such a point that any artistic experience that makes no concessions to this new conformism is in danger of being stifled or ignored.

The myth of the damned artist, which obsessed the nineteenth century, is outmoded today. Especially in the United States, but also in Western Europe, audacity and defiance have long since ceased to be harmful to an artist. On the contrary, he is asked to conform to his mythical image, that is, to be strange, irreducible, and to "produce something new." It is the absolute triumph of the permanent revolution in art. "Anything goes" is no longer an adequate formulation: now every novelty is considered a stroke of genius beforehand and put on the same plane as the innovations of a Van Gogh or a Picasso, even if the artist only mutilates a poster or signs a sardine tin.

The significance of this cultural phenomenon is the greater because, perhaps for the first time in the history of art, there is no longer any tension between artists, critics, collectors, and the public. They are all in agreement always, and long before a new work is created or an unknown artist discovered. The one thing that matters is not to have to say later that one did not understand the importance of a new artistic experience.

We cannot, of course, here analyze the mythology of the modern elites in all its manifestations. We shall confine ourselves to a few remarks. First of all, we may note the redeeming function of "difficulty," especially as found in works of modern art. If the elite revel in *Finnegans Wake,* or in atonal music, or in *tachisme,* it is also because such works represent closed worlds, hermetic universes that cannot be entered except by overcoming immense difficulties, like the initiatory ordeals of the archaic and traditional societies. On the one hand, one has the experience of an "initiation," an experience that has almost vanished from the modern World; on the other hand, one proclaims to the "others" (i.e., the "mass") that one belongs to a select minority—not, as once, to an aristocracy (for modern elites lean toward the left), but to a gnosis that has the advantage of being at once spiritual and secular in that it opposes both official values and the traditional churches. Through their cult of extravagant originality, of difficulty, of incomprehensibility, the elites advertise their escape from the banal universe of their parents while at the same time revolting against certain contemporary philosophies of despair.

Basically, being fascinated by the difficulty, not to say the incomprehensibility, of works of art expresses the desire to discover a new, secret, hitherto unknown meaning for the World and human life. One dreams of being "initiated" and thereby made able to understand the occult meaning of all these destructions of artistic languages, these "original" experiences that, at first sight, no longer seem to have anything in common with art. The torn posters, the empty, scorched, slashed canvases, the "art objects" that explode on opening day, the improvised plays in which the actors' speeches are drawn by lot—*all this must have a meaning*, just as certain incomprehensible words in *Finnegans Wake* come to be fraught with many meanings and values and with a strange beauty for the initiate when he discovers that they are derived from modern Greek or Swahili words disfigured by aberrant consonants, and enriched by secret allusions to possible puns when they are spoken aloud and very fast.

To be sure, all the genuine revolutionary experiences of modern art reflect certain aspects of the contemporary spiritual crisis or at least of the crisis in artistic knowledge and creation. But what concerns our investigation is the fact that the "elites" find in the extravagance and unintelligibility of modern works the opportunity for an initiatory gnosis. It is a "new World" being built up from ruins and enigmas, an almost private World, which one would like to keep for oneself and a very few initiates. But the prestige of difficulty and incomprehensibility is such that, very soon, the "public" too is conquered and proclaims its total acceptance of the elite's discoveries.

The destruction of artistic languages was accomplished by cubism, dadaism, and surrealism, by atonality and "musique concrète," by James Joyce, Becket, and Ionesco. Only the epigones are left furiously demolishing what has already been demolished. For, as we pointed out in an earlier chapter, the genuine creators are not willing to take their stand on ruins. Everything leads us to believe that the reduction of "artistic Universes" to the primordial state of *materia prima* is only a phase in a more complex process; just as in the cyclic conceptions of the archaic and traditional societies, "Chaos," the regression of all forms to the indistinction of the *materia prima*, is followed by a new Creation, which can be homologized with a cosmogony.

We cannot here develop and refine these few observations, for the crisis in the modern arts is only of subsidiary concern to our study. Yet we must dwell for a moment on the situation and the role of literature, especially of epic literature, for it is not unrelated to mythology and mythical behavior. We do not intend to discuss the "origins" of epic literature; it is well known that, like the other literary genres, the epic and the novel continue mythological narrative, though on a different plane and in pursuit of different ends. In both cases it is a question of telling a significant story, of relating a series of dramatic events that took place in a more or less fabulous past. There is no need to go over the long and complex process that transformed some particular "mythological material" into the "subject" of an epic. What we consider important is the fact that in modern societies the prose narrative, especially the novel, has taken the place of the recitation of myths in traditional and popular societies. More than this—it is possible to dissect out the "mythical" structure of certain modern novels, in other words, to show the literary survival of great mythological themes and characters. (This is true especially in regard to the initiatory theme, the theme of the ordeals of the Hero-Redeemer and his battles with monsters, the mythologies of Woman and of Wealth.) From this point of view we could say, then, that the modern passion for the novel expresses the desire to hear the greatest possible number of "mythological stories" desacralized or simply camouflaged under "profane" forms.

No less significant is the fact that people feel the need to read "histories" and narratives that could be called paradigmatic, since they proceed in accordance with a traditional model. Whatever the gravity of the present crisis of the novel, it is none the less true that the need to find one's way into "foreign" Universes and to follow the complications of a "story" seems to be consubstantial with the human condition and hence irreducible. It is a difficult need to define, being at once desire to communicate with "others," with "strangers," and share in their dramas and hopes, and at the same time the need to know what *can have taken place*. It is hard to conceive of a human being who is not fascinated by "narrative," that is, by a recounting of significant events, by what has happened to men endowed with the "twofold reality" of literary characters (for, on the one hand, they reflect the historical and psychological reality of members of a modern society and, on the other, they possess all the magical power of an imaginary creation).

But it is especially the "escape from Time" brought about by reading—most effectively by novel reading—that connects the function of literature with that of mythologies. To be sure, the time that one "lives" when reading a novel is not the time that a member of a traditional society recovers when he listens to a myth. But in both cases alike, one "escapes" from historical and personal time and is submerged in a time that is fabulous and trans-historical. The reader is confronted with a strange, imaginary time, whose rhythms vary indefinitely, for each narrative has its own time that is peculiar to it and to it alone. The novel does not have access to the primordial time of myths, but in so far as he tells a credible story, the novelist employs a time that is *seemingly historical* yet is condensed or prolonged, a time, then, that has at its command all the freedoms of imaginary worlds.

More strongly than any of the other arts, we feel in literature a revolt against historical time, the desire to attain to other temporal rhythms than that in which we are condemned to live and work. One wonders whether the day will come when this desire to transcend one's own time—personal, historical time—and be submerged in a "strange" time, whether ecstatic or imaginary, will be completely rooted out. As long as it persists, we can say that modern man preserves at least some residues of "mythological behavior." Traces of such a mythological behavior can also be deciphered in the desire to rediscover the intensity with which one experienced or knew something *for the first time*; and also in the desire to recover the distant past, the blissful period of the "beginnings." Here too, as we might expect, there is always the struggle against Time, the hope to be freed from the weight of "dead Time," of the Time that crushes and kills.

Note

1. Cf., for example, Coulton Waugh, *The Comics* (New York, 1947); Stephen Becker, *Comic Art in America* (New York, 1960); Umberto Eco, "Il Mito di Superman," in *Demitizzazione e Imagine,* ed. Enrico Castelli (Padua, 1962), 131–48.

22

The Myths of the Modern World

Mircea Eliade

Editor's Introduction

From *Myths, Dreams and Mysteries* by Mircea Eliade, 23–38 (London: Harvill Press, 1960). All rights reserved. English translation copyright © 1960 by Harvill Press. Reprinted by permission of the Random House Group Ltd.

ဢ ၚ

What exactly is a myth? In the language current during the nineteenth century, a "myth" meant anything that was opposed to "reality": the creation of Adam, or the invisible man, no less than the history of the world as described by the Zulus, or the Theogony of Hesiod—these were all "myths." Like many another cliché of the Enlightenment and of Positivism, this, too, was of Christian origin and structure; for, according to primitive Christianity, everything which could not be justified by reference to one or the other of the two Testaments was untrue; it was a "fable." But the researches of the ethnologists have obliged us to go behind this semantic inheritance from the Christian polemics against the pagan world. We are at last beginning to know and understand the value of the myth, as it has been elaborated in "primitive" and archaic societies—that is, among those groups of mankind where the myth happens to be the very foundation of social life and culture. Now, one fact strikes us immediately: in such societies the myth is thought to express the absolute truth, because it narrates a sacred history; that is, a transhuman revelation which took place at the dawn of the Great Time, in the holy time of the beginnings (*in illo tempore*). Being real and sacred, the myth becomes exemplary, and consequently repeatable, for it serves as a model, and by the same token as a justification, for all human actions. In other words, a myth is a true history of what came to pass at the beginning of Time, and one which provides the pattern for human behavior. In imitating the exemplary acts of a god or of a mythic hero, or simply by recounting their adventures, the man of an archaic society detaches himself from profane time and magically re-enters the Great Time, the sacred time.

Clearly, what we are dealing with here is a complete reversal of values; whilst current language confuses the myth with "fables," a man of the traditional societies sees it as the only valid revelation of reality. Little time was lost before conclusions were drawn from this discovery. Little by little, one ceased to insist upon the fact that the myth narrates impossibilities or improbabilities: one was content to say that it constituted a way of thinking different from ours, but that in any case we ought not to treat it *a priori* as an aberration. One went still further; one tried to integrate the myth into the general history of thought, by regarding it as the most important form of collective thinking. And, since "collective thinking" is never completely abolished in any society, whatever its degree of evolution, one did not fail to observe that the modern world still preserves some mythical behavior: for example, the participation of an entire society in certain symbols has been interpreted as a survival of "collective thinking." It was not difficult to show that the function of a national flag, with all the affective experiences that go with it, was in no way different from the "participation" in any of the symbols of the archaic societies. This was as much as to say that, upon the plane of social living, there was no break in the continuity between the archaic world and the modern world. The one great difference was that of the presence, in the majority of the individuals who constitute modern societies, of a personal thinking that was absent, or almost so, among the members of traditional societies.

This is not the place to begin a discussion of the general considerations raised by this "collective thinking." Ours is a more modest problem: if the myth is not just an infantile or aberrant creation of "primitive" humanity, but is the expression of a mode of being in the world, what has become of myths in the modern world? Or, more precisely, what has taken the essential place occupied by the myth in traditional societies? For, if certain "participations" in myths and collective symbols still survive in the modern world, they are far from filling the central part played by the myth in traditional societies; in comparison with these, our modern world seems destitute of myths. It has even been held that the diseases and crises of modern societies are rightly attributable to the absence of a mythology appropriate to them. When Jung entitled one of his books *Modern Man in Search of a Soul*, he implied that the modern world—in crisis ever since its profound break with Christianity—is in quest of a new myth, which alone could enable it to draw upon fresh spiritual resources and renew its creative powers.[1]

It is true that, at least apparently, the modern world is not rich in myths. It was said, for instance, of the General Strike, that this was one of the rare myths created by the modern world. But that was a misunderstanding: it was supposed that an idea, accessible to a considerable number of individuals and therefore "popular," could become a myth for the simple reason that its realization was projected into a more or less remote future. But that is not the way myths are "created." The general strike might be an instrument of political combat, but it has no mythical precedents, and that alone is enough to exclude it from mythical status.

Very different is the case of Marxian communism. Let us leave aside all question of the philosophic validity of Marxism and of its historic destiny, and consider only the mythological pattern of communism and the eschatological meaning of its popular success. For whatever we may think of the scientific claims of Marx, it is clear that the author of the Communist Manifesto takes up and carries on one of the great eschatological myths of the Middle Eastern and Mediterranean world, namely: the redemptive part to be played by the just (the "elect," the "anointed," the "innocent," the "missioners," in our own days by the proletariat), whose sufferings are invoked to change the ontological status of the world. In fact, Marx's classless society, and the consequent disappearance of all historical tensions, find their most exact precedent in the myth of the Golden Age which, according to a number of traditions, lies at the beginning and the end of history. Marx has enriched this venerable myth with a truly messianic Judaeo-Christian ideology; on the one hand, by the prophetic and soteriological function he ascribes to the proletariat; and, on the other, by the final struggle between Good and Evil, which may well be compared with the apocalyptic conflict between Christ and Antichrist, ending in the decisive victory of the former. It is indeed significant that Marx turns to his own account the Judaeo-Christian eschatological hope of an *absolute goal of History*; in that he parts company from the other historical philosophers (Croce, for instance, and Ortega y Gasset) for whom the tensions of history are implicit in the human condition, and therefore can never be completely abolished.

In comparison with the grandeur and the vigorous optimism of the communist myth, the mythology propagated by the National Socialists seems peculiarly inept; and this not only because of the limitations of the racial myth (how could one imagine that the rest of Europe would voluntarily accept submission to a master-race?), but above all because of the fundamental pessimism of the Germanic mythology. In its effort to abolish Christian values and rediscover the spiritual sources of "the race"—that is, of Nordic paganism—Nazism was obliged to try to reanimate the Germanic mythology. But from the point of view of the depth-psychologists, such an effort was, in effect, an invitation to collective suicide; for the *eschaton* prophesied and expected by the ancient Germans was the *ragnarök*—that is, a catastrophic end of the world. This included a gigantic combat between the gods and the demons, ending in the death of all the gods and all the heroes and a final regression of the world into chaos. It is true that, after the *ragnarök*, the world was to be reborn, regenerated (for the ancient Germans, too, knew the doctrine of the cosmic cycles, the myth of recurrent creations and destructions of the world); nevertheless, to substitute Nordic mythology for Christianity was to replace an eschatology rich in promises and consolations (for to the Christian, the "end of the world" completes and at the same time regenerates History) by an *eschaton* that was frankly pessimistic. Translated into political terms, this substitution almost amounted to saying: Give up your old Judaeo-Christian stories, and re-kindle, in the depths of your souls, the beliefs of your ancestors the Germans; then prepare yourselves for the last grand battle between our gods and the demonic forces: in that apocalyptic battle our gods and our heroes and we ourselves with them will all perish; that will be the *ragnarök*; but another world will be born later on. The wonder is, how such a pessimistic vision of the end of history could ever have fired the imagination of even a portion of the German people; and the fact that it did so has not yet ceased to raise problems for the psychologists.

Apart from these two political myths, modern societies do not seem to have entertained any others of comparable range. We are thinking of the myth as a type of human behavior and, at the same time, as an element of civilization— that is, of the myth as one finds it in traditional societies. For at the level of individual experience it has never completely disappeared: it makes itself felt in the dreams, the fantasies, and the longings of the modern man; and an abundant psychological literature has now accustomed us to rediscoveries of both the big and the little mythologies in the unconscious and half-conscious activity of every individual. But what now interests us above all is to find out what it is, in the modern world, that fills the central position occupied by the myth in traditional societies. In other words, while recognizing that the great mythical themes continue to repeat themselves in the obscure depths of the psyche, we still wonder whether the myth, as an exemplary pattern of human behavior, may not also survive among our contemporaries in more or less degraded forms. It seems that a myth itself, as well as the symbols it brings into play, never quite disappears from the present world of the psyche; it only changes its aspect and disguises its operations. Would it not be instructive to prolong the enquiry and unmask the operation of myths upon the *social plane*?

Here is one example. It is clearly the case that certain festivals observed in the modern world, though apparently secular, still preserve a mythical structure and function: the rejoicings over the New Year, or the festivities following the birth of a child, or the building of a house, or even the removal into a new flat show the obscurely-felt need for an *entirely new beginning*, of an *incipit vita nova*—that is, of a complete regeneration. Remote as these profane rejoicings may be from their mythic archetype—the periodic repetition of the creation (*The Eternal Return*, 83ff.)—it is nonetheless evident that modern man still feels the need for periodic re-enactments of such scenarios, however secularized they have become. There are no means of estimating how far modern man is still aware of any mythological implications of his festivities; what matters to us is that such celebrations still have a resonance, obscure but profound throughout his being.

That is but one example; it may enlighten us, however, with regard to what appears to be a general situation: that certain mythical themes still survive in modern societies, but are not readily recognizable since they have undergone a long process of laicization. This has long been known: indeed, modern societies might be simply defined as those which have pushed the secularization of life and of the Cosmos far enough: the novelty of the modern world consists in its revaluation, at the secular level, of the ancient sacred values.[2] What we want to know, however, is whether anything else of the "mythical" survives in the model world, besides what presents itself merely in the form of procedures and values re-interpreted to fit the secular plane. If all the phenomena were of that description, we should have to agree that the modern world was radically opposed to all the historic forms that had preceded it. But the very presence of Christianity excludes such a hypothesis. Christianity admits none of the secularized views of the Cosmos or of life which are characteristic of all "modern" culture.

The question this raises is not a simple one; but since the Western world, or a great part of it, still claims to be Christian, it cannot be evaded. I shall not insist upon what are at present called the "mythical elements" in Christianity. Whatever may be said about these "mythical elements" it is a long time since they were Christianized, and, in any case, the importance of Christianity must be judged in another perspective. But, from time to time, voices are raised asserting that the modern world is no longer, or is not yet, Christian. For our present purpose we need not concern ourselves with those who put their hopes in *Entmythologisierung*, who believe it is necessary to "de-mythologize" Christianity to recover its essential truth. Some think just the opposite. Jung, for instance, believes that the crisis of the modern world is in great part due to the fact that the Christian symbols and "myths" are no longer lived by the whole human being; that they have been reduced to words and gestures deprived of life, fossilized, externalized and therefore no longer of any use for the deeper life of the psyche.

To us the question presents itself differently: to what extent is Christianity maintaining, in modern secularized and laicized society, a spiritual horizon comparable to that of archaic societies, where the myth predominates? Let us say at once that Christianity has nothing to fear from such a comparison: its specificity is assured, it is guaranteed by *faith* as the category *sui generis* of religious experience, and by its valorization in *history*. With the exception of

Judaism, no other pre-Christian religion has set a value on history as a direct and irreversible manifestation of God in the world, nor on faith—in the sense inaugurated by Abraham—as a unique means of salvation. Consequently the Christian polemic against the religious world of paganism is, historically speaking, obsolete: Christianity is no longer in danger of being confused with any other religion or gnosis whatsoever. This having been said, and in view of the discovery, which was quite recent, that the myth represents a certain mode of being the world, it is no less true that Christianity, *by the very fact that it is a religion*, has had to preserve at least one mythic attitude—the attitude towards liturgical time; that is, the rejection of profane time and the periodical recovery of the Great Time, *illud tempus* of "the beginnings."

For the Christian, Jesus Christ is not a mythical personage: on the contrary, he is a historical personage; his greatness itself is founded upon that absolute historicity. For the Christ not only made himself man, "man in general," but accepted the historic condition of the people in whose midst he chose to be born; and he had recourse to no miracle to escape from that historicity— although he worked plenty of miracles in order to modify the "historical situations" of others—by curing the paralytic, raising Lazarus, etc. Nevertheless, the religious experience of the Christian is based upon an imitation of the Christ as exemplary pattern upon the liturgical repetition of the life, death and resurrection of the Lord and upon the *contemporaneity* of the Christian with *illud tempus* which begins with the Nativity at Bethlehem and ends, provisionally, with the Ascension. Now, we know that the initiation of a transhuman model, the repetition of an exemplary scenario and the breakaway from profane time through a moment which opens out into the Great Time, are the essential marks of "mythical behavior"—that is, the behavior of the man of the archaic societies, who finds the very source of his existence the myth. One is always *contemporary with a myth*, during the time when one repeats it or imitates the gestures of the mythic personages. Kierkegaard's requirement of the true Christian was that he should be a contemporary of the Christ. But even one who is a "true Christian" in Kierkegaard's sense still is, and cannot *not* be, a contemporary of Christ; for the liturgical time in which the Christian lives during the divine service is no longer profane duration but is essentially sacred time, the time in which the Word is made flesh, the *illud tempus* of the Gospels. A Christian is not taking part in a commemoration of the Passion of Christ, as he might be joining in the annual celebration of the Fourth of July or the Eleventh of November, for example. He is not commemorating an event but reactualizing a mystery. For the Christian, Jesus dies and resurrects before him *hic et nunc*. Through the mystery of the Passion or of the Resurrection, the Christian dispels profane time and is integrated into time primordial and holy.

It is needless to insist upon the radical differences that divide Christianity from the archaic world: they are too obvious to give rise to misunderstandings. But there remains the identity of behavior that we have just recalled. To the

Christian, as to the man of the archaic societies, time is not homogeneous: it is subject to periodical ruptures which divide it into "secular duration" and a "sacred time," the latter being indefinitely reversible, in the sense that it repeats itself to infinity without ceasing to be the same time. It is said that Christianity, unlike the archaic religions, proclaims and awaits the end of Time; which is true of the "profane duration" of History, but not of the liturgical time inaugurated by the Incarnation. The Christological *illud tempus* will not be done away with at the end of History.

These few cursory observations have shown us in what sense Christianity is prolonging a "mythical" conduct of life into the modern world. If we take account of the true nature and function of the myth, Christianity does not appear to have surpassed the mode of being of archaic man; but then it could not. *Homo naturaliter Christianus.* It remains, however, to enquire what has taken the place of the myth among those of the moderns who have preserved nothing of Christianity but the dead letter.

It seems unlikely that any society could completely dispense with myths, for, of what is essential in mythical behavior—the exemplary pattern, the repetition, the break with profane duration and integration into primordial time—the first two at least are consubstantial with every human condition. Thus, it is not so difficult to recognize, in all that modern people call instruction, education and didactic culture, the function that is fulfilled by the myth in archaic societies. This is so not only because myths represent both the sum of ancestral traditions and the norms it is important not to transgress, and because their transmission— generally secret, initiatory—is equivalent to the more or less official "education" of a modern society. The homology of the respective functions of the myth and of our public instruction is verified above all when we consider the origins of the exemplary models upheld by European education. In antiquity there was no hiatus between mythology and history: historical personages endeavored to imitate their archetypes, the gods and mythical heroes.[3]

And the lives and deeds of those personages, in their turn, became paradigms for posterity. Livy had already assembled a rich array of models for young Romans to emulate, when Plutarch wrote his *Lives of Famous Men*, a veritable mine of examples for the centuries to come. The moral and civic virtues of these illustrious personages continued to provide the supreme criteria for European pedagogy, especially after the Renaissance. Right to the end of the nineteenth century European education for citizenship was still following the archetypes of classical antiquity, those models which had been made manifest *in illo tempore*, in that privileged interval of time which educated Europeans regarded as the highest point of the Greco-Latin culture.

But they did not think of assimilating the functions of mythology to the process of instruction, because they overlooked one of the chief characteristics of the myth, which is the creation of exemplary models for a whole society. In this, moreover, we recognize a very general human tendency; namely, to hold up one life-history as a paradigm and turn a historical personage into an archetype. This tendency survives even among the most eminent representatives of the modern mentality. As Gide has rightly observed, Goethe was highly conscious of a mission to lead a life that would be exemplary for the rest of humanity. In all that he did he was trying to create an example. In his own life he, in his turn, was imitating, if not the lives of the gods and mythical heroes, at least their behavior. As Paul Valéry wrote in 1932: "He represents for us, *gentlemen of the human race*, one of our best attempts to render ourselves like gods."

But this imitation of model lives is promoted not only by means of school education. Concurrently with official pedagogy, and long after this has ceased to exert its authority, modern man is subjected to the influence of a potent if diffuse mythology that offers him a number of patterns for imitation. Heroes, real and imaginary, play an important part in the formation of European adolescents: the characters in tales of adventure, heroes of war, screen favorites, etc. This mythology is continually enriched with the growing years; we meet, one after another, the exemplary figures thrown up by changes of fashion, and we try to become like them. Critical writers have often pointed out modern versions of, for example, Don Juan, the political or the military hero, the hapless lover; of the cynic, the nihilist, the melancholy poet, and so forth: all these models are carrying on mythological traditions which their topical forms reveal in mythical behavior. The copying of these archetypes betrays a certain discontent with one's own personal history; an obscure striving to transcend one's own local, provincial history and to recover some "Great Time" or other—though it be only the mythic Time of the first surrealist or existentialist manifesto.

But an adequate analysis of the diffuse mythologies of the modern world would run into volumes: for myths and mythological images are to be found everywhere, laicized, degraded or disguised; one only needs to be able to recognize them. We have referred to the mythological basis of New Year celebrations, and of the festivities that mark any "new beginning"; in which we can discern anew the nostalgia for a *renewal*, the yearning for the world to be renovated; that one might enter upon a new History, in a world reborn; that is, *created afresh*. It would be easy to multiply instances. The myth of the lost paradise still survives in the images of a paradisiac island or a land of innocence; a privilege land where laws are abolished and Time stands still. For it is important to underline this fact—that it is, above all, *by analyzing the attitude of the modern man towards Time that we can penetrate the disguises of his mythological behavior*. We must never forget that one of the essential functions of the myth is its provision of opening into the Great Time, a periodic re-entry into Time primordial. This is shown by a tendency to a neglect of the present time, of what is called the "historic moment."

The Polynesians, when setting out upon a grandiose maritime adventure, are careful to deny its "novelty," its unprecedentedness, its spontaneity; for them, it is only a case of repeating the voyage that was made by some mythical hero *in illo tempore,* to "show men the way," to set an example. But thus to embark on a present adventure as the reiteration of a mythic saga is as much as to put the present time out of mind. Such disinclination to face historic time, together with an obscure desire to share in some glorious, primordial, total Time, is betrayed, in the case of modern people, by a sometimes desperate effort to break through the homogeneity of time, to "get beyond" duration and re-enter a time qualitatively different from that which creates, in its course, their own history. It is with this in mind that we can render the best account of what has become of myths in the world of today. For modern man, too, by means that are multiple, but homologous, is endeavoring to liberate himself from his history and to live in a qualitatively different temporal rhythm. And in doing he is returning, without being aware of it, to the mythic style of life.

One can understand this better if one looks more closely at the two principal ways of "escape" in use by modern people—visual entertainment, and reading. We need not go into all the mythical precedents for our public spectacles; it is enough to recall the ritual origins of bull-fighting, racing and athletic contests; they all have this point in common, that they take place in a "concentrated time," time of a heightened intensity; a residuum of, or substitute for, magico-religious time. This "concentrated time" is also the specific dimension of the theater and the cinema. Even if we take no account of the ritual origins and mythological structure of the drama or the film, there is still the important fact that these are two kinds of spectacle that make us live in time of a quality quite other than that of "secular duration," in a temporal rhythm, at once concentrated and articulated, which, apart from all aesthetic implications, evokes a profound echo in the spectator.

When we turn to reading, the question is of greater subtlety. It is concerned, on the one hand, with the forms and the mythical origins of literature and, on the other, with the mythological function that reading performs in the mind that feeds upon it. The successive stages of myth, legend, epic and modern literature have often been pointed out and need not detain us here. Let us merely recall the fact that the mythical archetypes survive to some degree in the great modern novels. The difficulties and trials that the novelist's hero has to pass through are prefigured in the adventures of the mythic Heroes. It has been possible also to show how the mythic themes of the primordial waters, of the isles of Paradise, of the quest of the Holy Grail, of heroic and mystical initiation, etc., still dominate modern European literature. Quite recently we have seen, in surrealism, a prodigious outburst of mythical themes and primordial symbols. As for the literature of the bookstalls, its mythological character is obvious. Every popular novel has to present the exemplary struggle between Good and Evil, the hero and the villain (modern incarnation of the Demon), and repeat one of those universal motives of folklore, the persecuted young woman, salvation by love, the unknown protector, etc. Even detective novels, as Roger Caillois has so well demonstrated, are full of mythological themes.

Need we recall how much lyric poetry renews and continues the myths? All poetry is an effort to *recreate* the language; in other words, to abolish current language, that of every day, and to invent a new, private and personal speech, in the last analysis *secret*. But poetic creation, like linguistic creation, implies the abolition of time—of the history concentrated in language—and tends towards the recovery of the paradisiac, primordial situation; of the days when one could *create spontaneously*, when the *past* did not exist because there was no consciousness of time, no memory of temporal duration. It is said, moreover, in our own days, that for a great poet the past does not exist: the poet discovers the world as though he were present at the cosmogonic moment, contemporaneous with the first day of the Creation. From a certain point of view, we may say that every great poet is *re-making* the world, for he is trying to see it as if there were no Time, no History. In this his attitude is strangely like that of the "primitive," of the man in traditional society.

But we are interested chiefly in the mythological function reading in itself; for here we are dealing with a specific phenomenon of the modern world, unknown in earlier civilizations. Reading replaces not only the oral folk traditions, such as still survive in rural communities of Europe, but also the recital of the myths in the archaic societies. Now, reading, perhaps even more than visual entertainment, gives one a break in duration, and the same time an "escape from time." Whether we are "killing time" with a detective story, or entering into another temporal universe as we do in reading any kind of novel, we are taken out of our own duration to move in other rhythms, to live in a different history. In this sense reading offers us an "easy way," it provides a modification of experience at little cost: for the modern man it is the supreme "distraction," yielding him the illusion of a *mastery of Time* which, we may well suspect, gratifies a secret desire to withdraw from the implacable becoming that leads towards death.

The defense against Time which is revealed to us in every kind of mythological attitude, but which is, in fact, inseparable from the human condition, reappears variously disguised in the modern world, but above all in its distractions, its amusements. It is here that one sees what a radical difference there is between modern cultures and other civilizations. In all traditional societies, every responsible action reproduced its mythical, transhuman model, and consequently took place in sacred time. Labor, handicrafts, war and love were all sacraments. The re-living of that which the Gods and Heroes had lived *in illo tempore* imparted a sacramental aspect to human existence, which was complemented by the sacramental nature ascribed to life and to the Cosmos. By thus opening out into the Great Time, this sacramental existence, poor as it might often be, was nevertheless rich in significance; at all events it was not under the tyranny of Time. The true "fall into Time" begins with the secularization of work. It is only in modern societies that man feels himself to be the prisoner of his daily work, in which he can never escape from Time. And since

213

he can no longer "kill" time during his working hours—that is, while he is expressing his real social identity—he strives to get away from Time in his hours of leisure: hence the bewildering number of distractions invented by modern civilization. In other terms, it is just as though the order of things were reversed from what it is in traditional societies, for there, "distractions" hardly exist; every responsible occupation is itself an "escape from Time." It is for this reason that, as we have just seen, in the great majority of individuals who do not participate in any authentic religious experience, the mythical attitude can be discerned in their distractions, as well as in their unconscious psychic activity (dreams, fantasies, nostalgias, etc.). And this means that the "fall into Time" becomes confused with the secularization of work and the consequent mechanization of existence—that it brings about a scarcely disguisable loss of freedom; and the only escape that remains possible upon the collective plane is distraction.

These few observations will suffice. We cannot say that the modern world has completely eliminated mythical behavior; but only that its field of action is changed: the myth is no longer dominant in the essential sectors of life: it has been repressed, partly into the obscurer levels of the psyche, partly into the secondary or even irresponsible activities of society. It is true that mythical behavior persists, though disguised, in the part that is played by education, but this is almost exclusively in what concerns the very young; and, what is more, the exemplary function of education is on the way to disappearance: modern pedagogy encourages spontaneity. Except in authentically religious life, the myth functions, as we have seen, chiefly in distractions. But it will never disappear; in the collective life it sometime reasserts itself with considerable force, in the form of a political myth.

It is no less safe to predict that the understanding of the myth will one day be counted among the most useful discoveries of the twentieth century. Western man is no longer the master of the world; he is no longer managing "natives" but talking with other men. It is as well that he should learn how to open the conversation. It is necessary for him to realize that there is no longer any break in the continuity between the "primitive" or "backward" world and that of the modern West. It is not enough, as it was half a century ago, to discover and admire the art of Negroes or Pacific islanders: we have now to rediscover the spiritual sources of these arts in ourselves; we must become aware of what it is, in a modern existence, that is still "mythical" and survives as such simply because this, too, is part and parcel of the human condition, in that it expresses the anxiety of man living in Time.

Notes

1. By the "modern world," we mean contemporary Western society; but also a certain state of mind which has been formed by successive deposits ever since the Renaissance and the Reformation. The active classes of the urban societies are in this sense "modern"—that is, the mass of mankind which has been more or less directly shaped by education and official culture. The rest of the population, especially in central and south-eastern Europe, still maintains its attachment to a traditional and half-Christian spiritual universe. The agricultural societies are, as a rule, passive towards History; most of the time they merely undergo it, and when directly involved in the great historical turmoils (for instance, the barbarian invasions of late antiquity), their reaction is that of passive resistance.

2. This process is very well exemplified by the transformation of the values ascribed to Nature. We have not abolished the relationship of sympathy between man and Nature nor was that possible. But this relationship has changed in value and in its orientation for the magico-religious sympathy we have substituted emotion, either aesthetic or simply sentimental; sporting and hygienic appreciation, etc.; while contemplation of Nature has been ousted by observation, experiment and calculation. It could not be said of a physicist of the Renaissance, or of a naturalist of our own days, that he did not "love Nature"; but in this "love" one could no longer find anything of the spiritual attitude of the man in the archaic societies—such as that which is still maintained in European agricultural societies.

3. Upon this point, one may refer to the researches of Georges Dumézil. Cf. also my *The Myth of the Eternal Return*, 37ff.

Illud Tempus

23

SACRED TIME AND MYTHS

Mircea Eliade

Editor's Introduction

Although I have suggested that Eliade's understanding of "the sacred," his idea of hierophany, his analyses of myth and symbol, particularly the *coincidentia oppositorum*, may be the key characteristics of his thought on religion, it is for his analysis of *illud tempus*—sacred time—that he is more often singled out. From one of his most widely-read volumes, *The Sacred and the Profane*, this selection on sacred time is one of the clearest statements of Eliade's concept. Excerpts from *The Sacred and the Profane: The Nature of Religion* by Mircea Eliade, 68–83 (London: Harcourt Brace Jovanovich, 1959). All rights reservd. Copyright © 1957 Rowohlt Taschenbuch Verlag GmbH. English translation copyright © 1959 and renewed 1987 by Harcourt, Inc. Reprinted by permission of Harcourt, Inc.

ℰↃ ଦ୫

Profane Duration and Sacred Time

For religious man time too, like space, is neither homogeneous nor continuous. On the one hand there are the intervals of a sacred time, the time of festivals (by far the greater part of which are periodical); on the other there is profane time, ordinary temporal duration, in which acts without religious meaning have their setting. Between these two kinds of time there is, of course, solution of continuity; but by means of rites religious man can pass without danger from ordinary temporal duration to sacred time.

One essential difference between these two qualities of time strikes us immediately: *by its very nature sacred time is reversible* in the sense that, properly speaking, it is *a primordial mythical time made present*. Every religious festival, any liturgical time, represents the reactualization of a sacred event that took place in a mythical past, "in the beginning." Religious participation in a festival implies emerging from ordinary temporal duration and reintegration of the mythical time reactualized by the festival itself. Hence sacred time is indefinitely recoverable, indefinitely repeatable. From one point of view it could be said that it does not "pass," that it does not constitute an irreversible duration. It is an ontological, Parmenidean time; it always remains equal to itself, it neither changes nor is exhausted. With each periodical festival, the participants find the same sacred time—the same that had been manifested in the festival of the previous year or in the festival of a century earlier; it is the time that was created and sanctified by the gods at the period of their *gesta*, of which the festival is precisely a reactualization. In other words the participants in the festival meet in it *the first appearance of sacred time*, as it appeared *ab origine, in illo tempore*. For the sacred time in which the festival runs its course did not exist before the divine *gesta* that the festival commemorates. By creating the various realities that today constitute the world, the gods *also founded sacred time*, for the time contemporary with a creation was necessarily sanctified by the presence and activity of the gods.

Hence religious man lives in two kinds of time, of which the more important, sacred time, appears under the paradoxical aspect of a circular time, reversible and recoverable, a sort of eternal mythical present that is periodically reintegrated by means of rites. This attitude in regard to time suffices to distinguish religious from nonreligious man; the former refuses to live solely in what, in modern terms, is called the historical present; he attempts to regain a sacred time that, from one point of view, can be homologized to eternity.

What time is for the nonreligious man of modern societies would be more difficult to put into a few words. We do not intend to discuss the modern philosophies of time nor the concepts that modern science uses in its own investigations. Our aim is to compare not systems or philosophies but existential attitudes and behaviors. Now, what it is possible to observe in respect to a nonreligious man is that he too experiences a certain discontinuity and heterogeneity of time. For him too there is the comparatively monotonous time of his work, and the time of celebrations and spectacles—in short, "festal time." He too lives in varying temporal rhythms and is aware of times of different intensities; when he is listening to the kind of music that he likes or, being in love, waits for or meets his sweetheart, he obviously experiences a different temporal rhythm from that which he experiences when he is working or bored.

But, in comparison with religious man, there is an essential difference. The latter experiences intervals of time that are "sacred," that have no part in the temporal duration that precedes and follows them, that have a wholly different structure and origin, for they are of a primordial time, sanctified by the gods and capable of being made present by the festival. This transhuman quality of liturgical time is inaccessible to a nonreligious man. This is as much as to say that, for him, time can present neither break nor mystery; for him, time constitutes man's deepest existential dimension; it is linked to his own life, hence it has a beginning and an end, which is death, the annihilation of his life. However many the temporal rhythms that he experiences, however great their differences in intensity, nonreligious man knows that they always represent a human experience, in which there is no room for any divine presence.

For religious man, on the contrary, profane temporal duration can be periodically arrested; for certain rituals have the power to interrupt it by periods of a sacred time that is nonhistorical (in the sense that it does not belong to the historical present). Just as a church constitutes a break in plane in the profane space of a modern city, the service celebrated inside it marks a break in profane temporal duration. It is no longer today's historical time that is present—the time that is experienced, for example, in the adjacent streets—but the time in which the historical existence of Jesus Christ occurred, the time sanctified by his preaching, by his passion, death, and resurrection. But we must add that this example does not reveal all the difference between sacred and profane time; Christianity radically changed the experience and the concept of liturgical time, and this is due to the fact that Christianity affirms the historicity of the person of Christ. The Christian liturgy unfolds in *a historical time sanctified by the incarnation of the Son of God.* The sacred time periodically reactualized in pre-Christian religions (especially in the archaic religions) is a *mythical time*, that is, a primordial time, not to be found in the historical past, an *original time*, in the sense that it came into existence all at once, that it was not preceded by another time, because no time could exist *before the appearance of the reality narrated in the myth.*

It is this archaic conception of mythical time that is of chief concern to us. We shall later see how it differs from the conceptions held by Judaism and Christianity.

Templum-Tempus

We shall begin our investigation by presenting certain facts that have the advantage of immediately revealing religious man's behavior in respect to time. First of all, an observation that is not without importance: in a number of North American Indian languages the term world (= Cosmos) is also used in the sense of year. The Yokuts say "the world has passed," meaning "a year has gone by."

For the Yuki, the year is expressed by the words for earth or world. Like the Yokuts, they say "the world has passed" when a year has passed. This vocabulary reveals the intimate religious connection between the world and cosmic time. The cosmos is conceived as a living unity that is born, develops, and dies on the last day of the year, to be reborn on New Year's Day. We shall see that this *rebirth is a birth*, that the cosmos is reborn each year because, at every New Year, time begins *ab initio*.

The intimate connection between the cosmos and time is religious in nature: the cosmos is homologizable to cosmic time (= the Year) because they are both sacred realities, divine creations. Among some North American peoples this cosmic-temporal connection is revealed even in the structure of sacred buildings. Since the temple represents the image of the world, it can also comprise a temporal symbolism. We find this, for example, among the Algonquins and the Sioux. As we saw, their sacred lodge represents the universe; but at the same time it symbolizes the year. For the year is conceived as a journey through the four cardinal directions, signified by the four doors and four windows of the lodge. The Dakotas say: "The Year is a circle around the world"—that is, around their sacred lodge, which is an *imago mundi*.[1]

A still clearer example is found in India. We saw that the erection of an altar is equivalent to a repetition of the cosmogony. The texts add that "the fire altar is the year" and explain its temporal system as follows: the 360 bricks of the enclosure correspond to the 360 nights of the year, and the 360 *yajusmati* bricks to the 360 days (*Shatapatha Brāhmana*, X, 5, 4, 10; etc.). This is as much as to say that, with the building of each fire altar, not only is the world remade but the year is built too; in other words, *time is regenerated by being created anew*. But then, too, the year is assimilated to Prajāpati, the cosmic god; consequently, with each new altar Prajāpati is reanimated—that is, the sanctity of the world is strengthened. It is not a matter of profane time, of mere temporal duration, but of the sanctification of cosmic time. What is sought by the erection of the fire altar is to sanctify the world, hence to place it in a sacred time.

We find a similar temporal symbolism as part of the cosmological symbolism of the Temple at Jerusalem. According to Flavius Josephus (*Ant. Jud.*, III, 7, 7), the twelve loaves of bread on the table signified the twelve months of the year and the candelabrum with seventy branches represented the decans (the zodiacal division of the seven planets into tens). The Temple was an *imago mundi*; being at the Centre of the World, at Jerusalem, it sanctified not only the entire cosmos but also cosmic life—that is, time.

Hermann Usener has the distinction of having been the first to explain the etymological kinship between *templum* and *tempus* by interpreting the two terms through the concept of "intersection" (*Schneidung, Kreuzung*).[2] Later studies have refined the discovery: "*templum* designates the spatial, *tempus* the temporal aspect of the motion of the horizon in space and time."[3]

The underlying meaning of all these facts seems to be the following: for religious man of the archaic cultures, *the world is renewed annually*; in other words, *with each new year it recovers* its original sanctity, the sanctity that it possessed when it came from the Creator's hands. This symbolism is clearly indicated in the architectonic structure of sanctuaries. Since the temple is at once the holy place par excellence and the image of the world, it sanctifies the entire cosmos and also sanctifies cosmic life. This cosmic life was imagined in the form of a circular course; it was identified with the year. The year was a closed circle; it had a beginning and an end, but it also had the peculiarity that it could be reborn in the form of a *new* year. With each New Year, a time that was "new," "pure," "holy"—because not yet worn—came into existence.

But time was reborn, began again, because with each New Year the world was created anew. In the preceding chapter we noted the considerable importance of the cosmogonic myth as paradigmatic model for every kind of creation and construction. We will now add that the cosmogony equally implies the creation of time. Nor is this all. For just as the cosmogony is the archetype of all creation, cosmic time, which the cosmogony brings forth, is the paradigmatic model for all other times—that is, for the times specifically belonging to the various categories of existing things. To explain this further: for religious man of the archaic cultures, every creation, every existence begins in time; *before a thing exists, its particular time could not exist*. Before the cosmos came into existence, there was no cosmic time. Before a particular vegetable species was created, the time that now causes it to grow, bear fruit, and die did not exist. It is for this reason that every creation is imagined as having taken place *at the beginning of time, in principio*. Time gushes forth with the first appearance of a new category of existents. This is why myth plays such an important role; as we shall show later, the way in which a reality came into existence is revealed by its myth.

Annual Repetition of the Creation

It is the cosmogonic myth that tells how the cosmos came into existence. At Babylon during the course of the *akitu* ceremony, which was performed during the last days of the year that was ending and the first days of the New Year, the *Poem of Creation*, the *Enuma elish*, was solemnly recited. This ritual recitation reactualized the combat between Marduk and the marine monster Tiamat, a combat that took place *ab origine* and put an end to chaos by the final victory of the god. Marduk created the cosmos from Tiamat's dismembered body and created man from the blood of the demon Kingu, Tiamat's chief ally. That this commemoration of the Creation was in fact a *reactualization* of the cosmogonic act is shown both by the rituals and in the formulas recited during the ceremony.

The combat between Tiamat and Marduk, that is, was mimed by a battle between two groups of actors, a ceremonial that we find again among the Hittites (again in the frame of the dramatic scenario of the New Year), among the Egyptians, and at Ras Shamra. The battle between two groups of actors *repeated the passage from chaos to cosmos*, actualized the cosmogony. The mythical event became *present* once again. "May he continue to conquer Tiamat and shorten his days!" the priest cried. The combat, the victory, and the Creation took place *at that instant, hic et nunc*.

Since the New Year is a reactualization of the cosmogony, it implies *starting time over again at its beginning*, that is, restoration of the primordial time, the "pure" time, that existed at the moment of Creation. This is why the New Year is the occasion for "purifications," for the expulsion of sins, of demons, or merely of a scapegoat. For it is not a matter merely of a certain temporal interval coming to its end and the beginning of another (as a modern man, for example, thinks); it is also a matter of abolishing the past year and past time. Indeed, this is the meaning of ritual purifications; there is more than a mere "purification"; the sins and faults of the individual and of the community as a whole are annulled, *consumed as by fire*.

The Nawrōz—the Persian New Year—commemorates the day that witnessed the creation of the world and man. It was on the day of Nawrōz that the "renewal of the Creation" was accomplished, as the Arabic historian al-Biruni expressed it. The king proclaimed: "Here is a new day of a new month of a new year; what time has worn must be renewed." Time had worn the human being, society, the cosmos—and this destructive time was profane time, duration strictly speaking; it had to be abolished in order to reintegrate the mythical moment in which the world had come into existence, bathed in a "pure," "strong," and sacred time. The abolition of profane past time was accomplished by rituals that signified a sort of "end of the world." The extinction of fires, the return of the souls of the dead, social confusion of the type exemplified by the Saturnalia, erotic license, orgies, and so on, symbolized the retrogression of the cosmos into chaos. On the last day of the year the universe was dissolved in the primordial waters. The marine monster Tiamat—symbol of darkness, of the formless, the non-manifested—revived and once again threatened. The world that had existed for a whole year *really* disappeared. Since Tiamat was again present, the cosmos was annulled; and Marduk was obliged to create it once again, after having once again conquered Tiamat.[4]

The meaning of this periodical retrogression of the world into a chaotic modality was this: all the "sins" of the year, everything that time had soiled and worn, was annihilated in the physical sense of the word. By symbolically participating in the annihilation and recreation of the world, man too was created anew; he was reborn, for he began a new life. With each New Year, man felt freer and purer, for he was delivered from the burden of his sins and failings. He had reintegrated the fabulous time of Creation, hence a sacred and strong time—sacred because transfigured by the presence of the gods, strong because it was the time that belonged, and belonged only, to the most gigantic creation ever accomplished, that of the universe. Symbolically, man became contemporary with the cosmogony, he was present at the creation of the world. In the ancient Near East, he even participated actively in its creation (cf. the two opposed groups, representing the god and the marine monster).

It is easy to understand why the memory of that marvelous time haunted religious man, why he periodically sought to return to it. *In illo tempore* the gods had displayed their greatest powers. *The cosmogony is the supreme divine manifestation*, the paradigmatic act of strength, superabundance, and creativity. Religious man thirsts for the real. By every means at his disposal, he seeks to reside at the very source of primordial reality, when the world was *in statu nascendi*.

Regeneration through Return to the Time of Origins

All this would warrant detailed study, but for the moment only two features will occupy our attention: (1) through annual repetition of the cosmogony, time was regenerated, that is, it began again as sacred time, for it coincided with the *illud tempus* in which the world had first come into existence; (2) by participating ritually in the end of the world and in its recreation, any man became contemporary with the *illud tempus*; hence he was born anew, he began life over again with his reserve of vital forces *intact,* as it was at the moment of his birth.

These facts are important; they reveal the secret of religious man's attitude and behavior in respect to time. Since the sacred and strong time is the *time of origins,* the stupendous instant in which a reality was created was for the first time fully manifested; man will seek periodically to return to that original time. This ritual reactualizing of the *illud tempus* in which the first epiphany of a reality occurred is the basis for all sacred calendars; the festival is not merely the commemoration of a mythical (and hence religious) event; it *reactualizes* the event.

The paramount *time of origins* is the time of the cosmogony, the instant that saw the appearance of the most immense of realities, the world. This, as we saw in the preceding chapter, is the reason the cosmogony serves as the paradigmatic model for every creation, for every kind of doing. It is for this same reason that *cosmogonic time* serves as the model for all *sacred times*; for if sacred time is that in which the gods manifested themselves and created, obviously the most complete divine manifestation and the most gigantic creation is the creation of the world.

Consequently, religious man reactualizes the cosmogony not only each time he creates something (his "own world"—the inhabited territory—or a city, a house, etc.), but also when he wants to ensure a fortunate reign for a new sovereign, or to save threatened crops, or in the case of a war, a sea voyage, and so on. But, above all, the ritual recitation of the cosmogonic myth plays an important role in healing, when what is sought is the *regeneration* of the human being. In Fiji, the ceremony for installing a new ruler is called creation of the world, and the same ceremony is repeated to save threatened crops. But it is perhaps Polynesia that exhibits the widest application of the cosmogonic myth. The words that Io spoke *in illo tempore* to create the world have become ritual formulas. Men repeat them on many occasions to fecundate a sterile womb, to heal (mental as well as physical ailments), to prepare for war, but also on the occasion of a death or to stimulate poetic inspiration.[5]

Thus the cosmogonic myth serves the Polynesians as the archetypal model for all creations, on whatever plane—biological, psychological, spiritual. But since ritual recitation of the cosmogonic myth implies reactualization of that primordial event, it follows that he for whom it is recited is magically projected *in illo tempore,* into the "beginning of the World"; he becomes contemporary with the cosmogony. What is involved is, in short, a return to the original time, the therapeutic purpose of which is to begin life once again, a symbolic rebirth. The conception underlying these curative rituals seems to be the following: life cannot be repaired, it can only be recreated through symbolic repetition of the cosmogony, for, as we have said, the cosmogony is the paradigmatic model for all creation.

The regenerative function of the return to the time of origins becomes still more clear if we make a detailed examination of an archaic therapy, such, for example, as that of the Na-khi, a Tibeto-Burmese people living in Southwest China (Yün-nan Province). The therapeutic ritual proper consists in the solemn recitation of the myth of the creation of the world, followed by myths of the origin of maladies from the wrath of the snakes and the appearance of the first Shaman-Healer who brought humanity the necessary medicines. Almost all the rituals invoke the mythical *beginning*, the mythical *illud tempus*, when the world was not yet made: "In the beginning, at the time when the heavens, sun, moon, stars, planets and the land had not yet appeared, when nothing had yet come forth," etc. Then comes the cosmogony and the appearance of the snakes: "At the time when heaven came forth, the sun, moon, stars and planets, and the earth was spread out; when the mountains, valleys, trees and rocks came forth … at that time there came forth the Nāgas and dragons," etc. The birth of the First Healer and the appearance of medicines is then narrated. After this it is said: "Unless its origin is related one should not speak about it."[6]

Notes

1. Werner Miller, *Die blaue Hütte* (Wiesbaden, 1954), 133.
2. H. Usener, *Götternamen*, 2nd ed. (Bonn, 1920), 191ff.
3. Werner Miller, *Kreis and Kreuz* (Berlin, 1938, 39); cf. also 33ff.
4. For New Year rituals, cf. *Myth of the Eternal Return*, 55ff.
5. Cf. the bibliographical reference in *Myth of the Eternal Return*, 82ff. and in *Patterns*, 410.
6. J. F. Rock, *The Na-khi Naga Cult and Related Ceremonies* (Rome, 1952), vol. II, 279ff.

24

ILLUD TEMPUS—TIME BY ANY OTHER NAME

Bryan Rennie

Editor's Introduction

From *Reconstructing Eliade: Making Sense of Religion* by Bryan Rennie, 77–87 (Albany, NY: State University of New York Press, 1996). All rights reserved. Copyright © 1996 by the State University of New York Press. Reprinted by permission of the State University of New York Press.

80 03

Eliade's characteristic use of the Latin *illud tempus* indicates an idiosyncratic application of the concept of time and it is, I believe, the tension between this idiosyncrasy and the deeply ingrained common applications of the reader which generates many of the difficulties of comprehension of this aspect of Eliade's thought. As anyone who has tangled with Heidegger's *Sein und Zeit* knows only too well, it is the common and fundamental terms of our conceptual vocabulary which generate the most crucial and labyrinthine problems, time no less than being. Heidegger's influence on Eliade is worthy of consideration (see *The Eternal Return*, 150, 152; *Occultism, Witchcraft and Cultural Fashions*, 45–46). Its exact manifestations in his work remain to be explored, however.

The notions of time and history as they are applied by Eliade himself, as they are manifest in the documents of the study of religion, and as they are commonly applied in the West today, are of fundamental importance to this study in every respect. As Eliade applies them they condition the meaning of his entire oeuvre; as they are manifest in the documents of the study of religion (as Eliade conceived it) they represent an expression of the existential situation of humanity other than our own; and as they are commonly applied in the West today they represent the realities of our own existential situation as it differs from but is conditioned by our cultural precedents. As sacred or sacralizable, as hierophanies, the documents of religious studies are by definition expressions of that which was apprehended as the real. Thus the attitude to time expressed in the sacred traditions of humanity past and present represent the actual apprehensions of those alternative modes of (human) being. Eliade's interpretations of time and history simultaneously condition and are the products of his implicit system and its concomitant methodology.

The Archaic and the Modern Conceptions of Time

As we have seen the attitudes to time and to history of modern and of religious humanity in their continuity and diversity are major factors in their discrimination. Although Eliade admits the difficulty of describing concisely the nature of time for modern humanity (*Sacred and the Profane*, 70), he characterizes clearly the conception of time which he has abstracted from religious documents. For humanity in its religious aspect,

> profane temporal duration can be periodically arrested; for certain rituals have the power to interrupt it by periods of a sacred time that is nonhistorical (in the sense that it does not belong to the historical present). (71–72)

Thus,

> religious man lives in two kinds of time, of which the most important, sacred time, appears under the paradoxical aspect of a circular time, reversible and recoverable, a sort of eternal mythical present that is periodically regenerated by means of rites. (70)

This was Eliade's main means of distinguishing religious, archaic humanity from modern, nonreligious humanity, and finally reflects the thesis of *The Myth of the Eternal Return*. This is no doubt influenced by Bergson's analysis of time and it is helpful to bear this in mind. Eliade felt that *The Myth of the Eternal Return* was "the most significant of my books; and when I am asked in what order they should be read, I always recommend beginning with the present work" (*The Eternal Return*, xv). First published as *Le Mythe de l'éternel retour: archétypes et répétition* by Gallimard in 1949, this work was translated into English as *Cosmos and History* (Princeton, 1954) and reprinted as *The Myth of the Eternal Return* or *Cosmos and History* from 1965 onwards. It contains the most detailed exposition of Eliade's interpretation of time and history. However, before I attempt to clarify Eliade's position by close reference to that work, let me immediately emphasize one point which he makes in *The Sacred and the Profane*. Sacred time "is a *mythical time*, that is a primordial time, *not to be found in the historical past*" (*Sacred and the Profane*, 72, emphasis added; above, 220). Obviously this "primordial time" is not located in any long-gone historical era of our known world, but is notional, conceptual, or imaginary. Eliade is certain that

> the nostalgia for the lost paradise excludes any desire to restore the "paradise of animality." Everything that we know about the mythic memories of "paradise" confronts us, on the contrary, with the image of an ideal humanity enjoying a beatitude and spiritual plenitude forever unrealizable in the present state of "fallen man." (*The Eternal Return*, 91)

That is to say, the nostalgia is not for a chronological past, an actual or historical condition; rather it is for an imaginary ideal which none the less functions as an exemplar. Thus the ontological status of Eliade's analysis should not be assumed. In the very opening words to *The Myth of the Eternal Return* he states that "this book undertakes to study certain aspects of archaic ontology— more precisely, the *conceptions* of being and reality that can be read off from the behavior of the man of premodern societies" (3, emphasis added). Thus it can be seen that he is not discussing archaic ontology; how things *were* in premodern societies, but rather archaic *conceptions* of ontology; how things were *thought to be*, or, to be more factually accurate, how things were *said* to be.

Eliade's thesis is that the "archaic" mentality, seen as typically representative of humanity in its religious mode, apprehended sacred time (as "a primordial mythical time made present," *Sacred and the Profane*, 68) as the locus of real significance, of the sacred, of the real. Thus it was felt that

> neither the objects of the external world nor human acts, properly speaking, have any autonomous intrinsic value. Objects or acts acquire a value, and in so doing become real, because they participate, after one fashion or another, in a reality that transcends them. (*The Eternal Return*, 3–4)

Time is one of the primary categories of knowledge or of humanity's knowledge of the world which is subject to the sociologization of knowledge. Bergson said that

> we may … surmise that time, conceived under the form of a homogenous medium, is some spurious concept, due to the trespassing of the idea of space upon the field of pure consciousness … nothing but a ghost of space haunting the reflective consciousness. (*Time and Free Will*, 98)

Lévy-Bruhl, in his *Primitive Mentality*, pointed out that the linear and unrepeatable nature of time was a feature of the modern, "civilized" time-consciousness.

Despite the fact that he was forced to retract his postulate of a "primitive mentality" Lévy-Bruhl's recognition of the recent nature of the specific apprehension of time as "dimensional" is still borne out by an overwhelming number of sources and theories. All known religious traditions posit a realm or mode of being which is infinitely more significant than the world of everyday personal experience. Other writers agree,

> Eliade's formulation of the sacred as existing outside of time … is a fair characterization of much that is claimed within the religious discourses of most, if not all, the world religions. Thus, in Hinduism, Buddhism, and Catholicism, it can be argued that what is most sacred, that which is concerned with salvation, is that which is outside time. (R. L. Stirrat, "Sacred Models," 202)

The religious person can gain access to this alternative time through performance of ritual, narration of myth, and in "archaic" and "primitive" societies, by the performance of sacralized human functions, such as hunting, fishing, construction, and the more obvious sacraments (to the modern Westerner) of birth, marriage, and death. Eliade suggests that what all of these observances have in common is that they constitute, and are sacralized by, repetitions of a sacred model. This includes, but is not exhausted by, the *imitatio dei* familiar to the Christian West. The implications of the concept that *imitation* can confer ontic substance upon the activities of humanity implies a certain understanding of time:

> insofar as an act (or an object) acquires a certain reality through the repetition of certain paradigmatic gestures, and acquires it through that alone, there is an implicit abolition of profane time, of duration, of "history"; and he who reproduces the exemplary gesture thus finds himself transported into the mythical epoch in which its revelation took place. (*The Eternal Return*, 35)

The concept of the specific imitation or repetition of divine mythical models is not the only indicator of this alternative attitude to time, "the traditional societies (that is, all societies down to those which make up the modern world) knew and applied still other methods to bring about the regeneration of time" (76). Nor is this attitude utterly foreign to contemporary humanity. It can be most easily recognized in New Year scenarios which feature a return to primordial chaos and a repetition of the creation and in

> the Christian liturgical year [which] is based upon a periodic and real repetition of the Nativity, Passion, death, and Resurrection of Jesus, … that is, personal and cosmic regeneration through reactualization *in concreto* of the birth, death, and resurrection of the Savior. (130)

This is of no small significance and emphasizes Eliade's frequent insistence that there is no "solution of continuity" between archaic and modern. However, the present point is that "for traditional man, the imitation of an archetypal model is a reactualization of the mythical moment when the archetype was revealed for the first time" (76). These sacred models Eliade refers to as "archetypal" and as "archetypes," although he expresses regret at this choice of words, which has led to a common equation of his thought with that of C. G. Jung.[1] As we have seen, the sacred models do not belong to the profane, historical realm, no more do they belong to the un- or sub-conscious mind. They issue from the alternative realm, considered to be the locus of the real and the true and the significant. This realm is *illud tempus*, the continuum of a different, sacred time, which is repeated and reactualized by repetition of the sacred model, be it an act, bodily function, or narrative structure.[2] Hence this alternative time is repeatable as well as intensely real.

As has already been mentioned, the concomitant of this attitude to *illud tempus* was an inability to perceive ordinary events and objects as inherently possessed of any real value. Since the objects and events of much of one's everyday experience do not have mythical models, do not reactualize the continuum of real time, they are not in and of themselves of any significance. Since they are not specifically orientated in an extended matrix of familiar, interconnected structures and events of predetermined value, they themselves lack value, they lack a determined response, and hence they lack meaning.

Eliade's Evaluation of Archaic and Modern Conceptions of Time

Although Eliade has been criticized for being a "champion" of the archaic attitude and he is certainly ready to recognize the values of this alternative to the modern view of time, he is not totally uncritical of it.

> The need these [archaic] societies also feel for a periodic regeneration is a proof that they too cannot perpetually maintain their position in what we have just called the paradise of archetypes, and that their memory is capable (though doubtless far less intensely than that of a modern man) of revealing the irreversibility of events, that is, of recording history. (*The Eternal Return*, 75)

This stands against the contention that Eliade valorized the archaic over the modern, *a priori*. Both visions ultimately fail to "maintain their position" independently of some concept of regeneration. Furthermore,

> in the last analysis, modern man, who accepts history or claims to accept it, can reproach archaic man, imprisoned within the mythical horizon of

archetypes and repetition, with his creative impotence, or, what amounts to the same thing, his inability to accept the risks entailed by every creative act. (155–56 and see below, 205–13)

It is true, however, that in the final "dialogue between archaic man and modern man" (155–59) Eliade gives more credence and more space to the archaic point of view. It could credibly be argued that he was simply supporting the underdog, however, since he does finally indicate strengths and weaknesses in both points of view and seems ultimately to support a synthesis.

> All that is needed is a modern man with a sensibility less closed to the miracle of life; and the experience of renewal would revive for him when he built a house or entered it for the first time (just as, in the modern world, the New Year still preserves the prestige of the end of a past and the fresh beginning of a new life). (77)

One thing that Eliade is certain of is that

> the life of archaic man (a life reduced to the repetition of archetypal acts, that is, to categories and not to events, to the unceasing rehearsal of the same primordial myths), although it takes place in time, does not bear the burden of time, does not record time's irreversibility; in other words, completely ignores what is especially characteristic and decisive in a consciousness of time. Like the mystic, like the religious man in general, the primitive lives in a continual present. (86)

This in itself constitutes a cushion between such a mindset and the impact of brute historical event. This superiority in enabling a toleration of history is perceived as the major virtue of the archaic attitude. The major vice of the modern is perceived to be its self-deceptive nature. "Modern man's boasted freedom to make history is illusory for nearly the whole of the human race" (156). This is because it is in truth a small minority of people drawn from a small minority of nations who have any real effect in the "making of history," that is to say, a very small effect on the creation of those events which predate and condition the present. However, on the events which are anyone else's experience, on history as Eliade uses the word, every one of us has an effect. Since we cannot live in isolation we all do have a contribution to make to the history whose conception underlies the whole of Eliade's theoretical edifice. It is Eliade's innate elitism, his refusal to recognize the contribution of the masses to the creation of history which conditions this flaw in his thinking. If history is taken on this personal, experiential level, which I believe it clearly must be in order to render the main body of Eliade's thought coherent, then humanity is unavoidably free to make history since we are all intimately (albeit not totally, deliberately, or in a fully controlled manner) responsible for the personal experiences of others.

The Linearity of the Modern Conception of Time

In an article of 1985, "*Homo Faber* and *Homo Religiosus*" (in this volume, 110–21), Eliade once again makes important reference to time in his analysis of the religious aspect of human life. He reiterates and emphasizes the point he first made in *The Forge and the Crucible* that the labor of *homo faber* "replaces the work of time." For *homo faber,* who in the contemporary Western world has become "modern man," the identification with historical time has become complete and humanity takes the place of time. Not only is humanity the product solely of history, created and determined purely in historical time, but humanity is now seen as the final judge and arbiter of our destiny; (racial) death or (technological) glory. This identification with historical time, which alone is real and thus sacred, is from this perspective a religious act or awareness. Once again "modern man" is not the antithesis of religious man but a very specific (and possibly rather aberrant) example.

In the same edition in which "*Homo Faber*" appeared, Paul Ricoeur described how Steven Toulmin and June Goodfield in *The Discovery of Time* "tell the story of [the] progressive expansion of a uniform timescale from human history to geology, to thermodynamics, and finally to the gigantic changes among galaxies." Ricoeur concludes that "cyclical time appears paradoxically as a particular case of, and not an alternative term for linear time" ("The History of Religions and the Phenomenology of Time Consciousness," 14). However, he had already pointed out that linear time seems to have begun from the Judaeo-Christian notion of time as a 6,000-year period which was then extended to make room for the large-scale phenomena that together constitute the history of humankind, of the earth, of the universe, and even of matter itself (14).

Although teleologically a straight-line progression from Creation to Eschaton, this 6,000-year period was a manifestation of *cyclical* time since it proceeded from and returned to the eternal *illud tempus.* We are all familiar with the phenomena whereby an arc of a circle, if sufficiently small relative to its radius, is perceived to be a straight line. Rather than cyclical time being a particular case of linear time the converse would appear to be more credible. Linear time is a particular case of cyclical time viewed from the limited perspective of human history. Not only does the narrow localism of the original Judaeo-Christian viewpoint explain the perception of (microcosmic) time as linear, but the speculations of astrophysics concerning a "big bang" leading, via the expansion and contraction of the universe, to a "big crunch," re-establishes the view of (macrocosmic) time as cyclical. Thus "repetition of some pattern" is not merely "a complexity superimposed on the linear character of chronological time" (15); linearity is rather a perceptual phenomenon, generated by the scale of embodied human existence, which is then expanded into the abstract notion of linear time as Ricoeur describes it.

Once again the perception of modern man as a specific example of the pan-human *homo religiosus* is justified by such a consideration of time-conscious-ness. It is only the intensely focused self-consciousness (which is admirably utilitarian in certain ways) of modern humanity which has contracted the scale of time consciousness to make our historical time appear linear. Even Eliade's distinction of modern from religious humanity through their alternative percep-tions of time begins to blur.

The Development of Conceptions of Time

Eliade does not simply assume this archaic or religious attitude to time and support it with examples; he also attempts a detailed explanation of its develop-ment from the universal existential situation of humanity in the world. For example, "if the moon in fact serves to 'measure' time, if the moon's phases—long before the solar year and far more concretely—reveal a unit of time (the month), the moon at the same time reveals the 'eternal return' " (*The Eternal Return*, 86). As this "eternal return" is experienced in human life it is evidently cyclical as opposed to circular. That is to say it is nowhere claimed that every actual physical being recommences with the new moon. Obviously, each individual still ages and the solar year still progresses. To think otherwise is to equate personal experience with time, an identification which Eliade does not make, and which he claims that archaic humanity rejected. An analysis of his thought in this area reveals that this identification is part of the characteristic matrix of "modern" thought. For archaic man, on the other hand, the assimi-lation of temporal duration and human life to the lunar cycle

> is important not only because it shows us the "lunar" structure of uni-versal becoming but also because of its optimistic consequences: for, just as the disappearance of the moon is never final, since it is necessarily fol-lowed by a new moon, the disappearance of man is not final either; in particular the disappearance of an entire humanity (deluge, flood, submer-sion of a continent, and so on) is never total, for a new humanity is born from a pair of survivors. (87)

Being cyclical, time is not irreversible. Everything begins over again at its com-mencement every instant (89). Yet the insignificance and the arbitrary nature of much of personal experience cannot be annulled.

The process or development which Eliade seems to envision leading to the modern "historical" view of time is that archaic, cyclically repeated time gives way to a single time cycle from Creation to Apocalypse, from *illud tempus* to *illud tempus*, in which every event is seen as of hierophanic value since it is under the direct control of the one true God. This conception is permitted by the novel religious attitude of *faith*, which emphasizes that "for God everything is possible" (160; see 108–110 on the novelty of faith).

> For the first time, the prophets placed a value on history, succeeded in transcending the traditional vision of the cycle (the conception that ensures all things will be repeated forever), and discovered a one-way time. ... for the first time we find affirmed, and increasingly accepted, the idea that historical events have a value in themselves, insofar as they are determined by the will of God. ... Historical facts thus become "situations" of man in respect to God, and as such they acquire a religious value that nothing had previously been able to confer on them. ... the Hebrews were the first to discover the meaning of history as the epiphany of God. (104)

Thus the Judaeo-Christian tradition, for Eliade, provides a bridge between the two types of, or attitudes to, time.

> Christianity radically changed the experience and the concept of liturgical time, and this is due to the fact that Christianity affirms the historicity of the person of Christ. The Christian liturgy unfolds in *a historical time sanctified by the incarnation of the son of God.* (*Sacred and the Profane* 72; above, 220)

This valorization of time continues the trend which Eliade argues to have begun "among the Hebrews" for whom, "every new historical calamity was regarded as a punishment from Yahweh." In this way there first occurred "History regarded as Theophany" (*The Eternal Return*, 102), and this eventually leads to the situation of modern man who insists that he is "constituted only by human history" (*Sacred and the Profane*, 100), and in that very insistence is distinguished from traditional *homo religiosus*.

George Weckman has pointed out that other scholars do not agree with Eliade's restriction of the source of this valorization of the historical to the Jewish tradition. For example, Helmer Ringgren "does not want to get caught in asserting that Israel was unique in regarding historical events as acts of God" ("Mircea Eliade and the Role of History in Religion," 13). Also Ninian Smart has remarked that "historical events were considered important by the Chinese" (Review of *The History of Religious Ideas*, 70). However, as Weckman continues, "it remains distinctive and consequential that ancient Israel first developed a style of religion on the basis of a special comprehension of historical events" (13). While Weckman's unease is perfectly understandable at this point—Eliade does make strong claims for the priority of the Hebrew valorization of history—it should be pointed out that Eliade does accept a broader base than the purely Jewish for its source. "Those with whom history, properly speaking, begins," he writes, "—that is the Babylonians, Egyptians, Hebrews, Iranians" (*The Eternal Return*, 74). Eliade's recognition of the *phenomena* of the sacralization of the previously profane in the valorization of historical time is undoubtedly valid whatever its source.

This valorization of the historical event has several implications. Firstly it leads to the concomitant *de*-valorization of the traditionally valorized, religious real, "emptied of every religious value or meaning nature could become the 'object' *par excellence* of scientific investigation" (*Symbolism, the Sacred, and the Arts*, 83). Although this is not an explicit doctrine Eliade takes it to be an unavoidable implication of the structure of the Hebrew revelation:

> we may even ask ourselves if monotheism, based on the direct and personal revelation of the divinity, does not necessarily entail the "salvation" of time, its value within the frame of history. Doubtless the idea of revelation is found ... in all religions ... but these revelations occurred in *mythical* time. ... The situation is altogether different in the case of the monotheistic revelation. This takes place in time, in historical duration. (*The Eternal Return*, 104–105)

The implications of this are borne out by the development of the secular, "post-Christian" West. The concept of "general revelation" implied by the valorization of historical time eventually comes to confront that of the "special revelation" of the Biblical text (eg. Copernicus and Biblical criticism).

Secondly, "history as the epiphany of God" leads to a linear notion of time as once-and-for-all. This crystallizes in Christianity with the belief in the Incarnation as the ultimate hierophany—*hapax, ephapax* (Hebrews 9:12; Eliade also refers to 1 Peter 3:18). Not only is the singular unrepeatable notion of historical event emphasized, it is sacralized, and with it the whole of historical time is "redeemed." Also the teleological linearity of time leads irresistibly to the notion of evolution whose "mythical" aspect—that of continual *improvement*—proves more tenacious than its scientific aspect of the chance viability of random mutations (see Midgeley, *Evolution as a Religion*). Time is increasingly perceived as a linear progression, a *direction*, a single continuum outside of eternity (*illud tempus*), rather than an oscillation *in* eternity. With the concomitant increasing devalorization of the traditional concepts of the sacred this time was even extended *ad infinitum*. Rather than a closed cycle returning to *illud tempus* the cosmos was for a while seen as infinite in extent and duration. However, this extension has itself fallen prey to the hierophanization of the manifest. *Observation* has indicated that the universe is not infinite either in time or space. The consensus of scientific opinion is that our universe had a temporal commencement, it is finite, and it may well have a temporal end. This scientific return to a theory of temporal cycles was not lost on Eliade.

> In connection with this rehabilitation of cyclical conceptions, Sorokin rightly observes that present theories concerning the death of the universe do not exclude the hypothesis of the creation of a new universe, somewhat

after the fashion of the Great Year in Greco-Oriental speculation or of the yuga cycle in the thought of India. (*The Eternal Return*, 146)

The Big Bang/Big Crunch concept of time as a closed cycle has certainly gained in scientific support since Sorokin published his observations in 1928;[3] however, the possibility of a recreation is still an open question.

Weckman concludes that "because Eliade thinks of history as contemporary event he has ignored the important role of history as stories about the human past which can function like myth" ("Mircea Eliade and the Role of History," 17). But this fails to grasp the point. History which "functions like myth" is, by that very definition, sacred history. Eliade's contention is that it is by virtue of a spiritual development of the most far-reaching implications that modern humanity has been able to see historical events as themselves exemplary, revelatory, possessed of real meaning. It is in any event *historiography* and not actual history which so functions, and so is not actually a temporal reality. Eliade recognizes the survival of mythology "more than anywhere else" in historiography (*Myth and Reality*, 113). This is the specific characteristic by which Eliade distinguishes "modern" humanity. We have "sacralized" *history*; that is, that we have specifically assumed that the real-time, historical actualities which constitute human experience *can* function as exemplary, that is sacred, history, and in so doing have "camouflaged" the sacred or "confused" it with the profane.

Notes

1. These are *not* Jungian archetypes; see 1958 preface to *Cosmos and History*; *Ordeal by Labyrinth, conversations with Claude-Henri Rocquet*, 122; Mac Ricketts, "The Nature and Extent of Eliade's 'Jungianism'," *Union Seminary Quarterly Review* 25/2 (1970): 211–34. The question of the relationship of Eliade's thought to that of C. G. Jung is a complex one requiring further consideration.
2. *Illud tempus* simply means "that time." It occurs in Jerome's *Vulgate* where it indicates the *heilsgeschichte* in which God's actions were seen as decisive for humanity. *In illo tempore* is simply the locative case, *in* that time. It is a narrative device comparable with "once upon a time," although indicative of greater sacrality.
3. Sorokin, *Contemporary Sociological Theories* (New York, 1928). For a modern conception of the closed cycle of time see Stephen Hawking, *A Brief History of Time* (Boston, MA: G. K. Hall, 1989), 138.

Part III

ELIADE'S METHODOLOGY

Eliade

25

METHODOLOGICAL REMARKS ON THE STUDY OF RELIGIOUS SYMBOLISM

Mircea Eliade

Editor's Introduction

This selection continues from the earlier excerpt from Eliade's *The Two and the One* ("What the Symbols Reveal"). Like the earlier excerpt this one concerns both symbolism and methodology. However, where the first concentrated on establishing the nature of symbol, the present article focuses more on a discussion of methodology and thus makes a fitting introduction to this section on method. The article makes a series of clear statements on Eliade's understanding of methodology:

> In the broad sense of the term, the science of religions embraces both religious phenomenology and the philosophy of religion. … The supreme merit of any historian of religions is precisely his endeavor to discover in a "fact" duly conditioned by the historical moment and the cultural style of the age the existential situation which caused it. … A man is a historian of religions not by virtue of mastering a certain number of philologies, but because he is capable of ordering religious facts in a general perspective.

෨ ෬

Mircea Eliade

The Vogue for Symbolism

As we have frequently insisted, we have for some time been witnessing a vogue for symbolism (*Images and Symbols*, 27ff.). Several factors have combined to give the study of symbolism the privileged position which it enjoys today. On the one hand there have been the discoveries of depth psychology, in the first place the fact that the activity of the unconscious can be detected by the interpretation of figures, images, scenarios, which cannot be taken at their nominal value, but are like the "ciphers" of situations and persons that the conscious mind will not or cannot acknowledge.[1]

There was also, at the beginning of the century, the growth of modern art and, after the First World War, the poetical experiments of surrealism, which familiarized the educated public with non-figurative dream worlds, only capable of presenting a meaning in so far as one managed to decipher their structures, which were "symbolic." A third factor also aroused interest in the study of symbolism: the ethnologists' researches into primitive societies and, especially, the hypotheses of Lucien Lévy-Bruhl concerning the structure and functions of "the primitive mentality." Lévy-Bruhl considered that the "primitive mentality" was pre-logical, since it appeared to be dominated by what he called "participation mystique." At the end of his life Lévy-Bruhl abandoned the hypothesis of a primitive mentality pre-logical and radically different from the modern mentality, and actually argued against it.[2] In fact, his hypothesis had not attracted the widespread adherence of ethnologists and sociologists. Nevertheless, the hypothesis of a "primitive mentality" had been useful in so far as it aroused discussions among philosophers, sociologists and psychologists. In particular it had drawn the attention of the finest intellects to the behavior of "primitive man," his psycho-mental life and cultural creations. The present-day interest of philosophers, particularly in Europe, in myths and symbols is in great part due to Lévy-Bruhl's books and to the controversies which they aroused.

In fact, this vogue we are discussing owes more than can possibly be said to certain philosophers, epistemologists and linguists who set out to show the symbolic character not only of language, but of all other activities of the human mind, from rite and myth to art and science.[3] Since man possesses a symbol-forming power, all that he produces is symbolic.[4]

In recalling the principal factors that have contributed to the growth of interest in symbolism we have at the same time noticed the realms in which the study of symbolism has been undertaken. These are the realms of depth psychology, of the plastic arts and poetry, of ethnology, semantics, epistemology and philosophy. The historian of religions can only rejoice at these researches, undertaken from different points of view, into a subject so important to his own field of work. Since the human sciences are closely interlinked, any important discovery made in one sector has its repercussions on the neighboring disciplines. Anything that psychology or semantics may teach us about the functions of the symbol is bound to affect the science of religions. Is it not fundamentally all one subject? Its purpose also is to understand man and his place in the world. Indeed the relationship between these disciplines and the science of religions would be a fruitful subject for study.

Even so, it is no less true that the field of religious science must not be confused with those of the other disciplines. The attitude proper to a historian of religions is far from identical with that of a psychologist, linguist or sociologist. The religious historian's researches differ from those of the linguist, psychologist and sociologist in that he is preoccupied only with religious symbols, of those belonging to a religious experience or religious conception of the world.

The attitude of the historian of religions also differs from a theologian's. All theology implies systematic reflection on the content of religious experience, with a view to penetrating and elucidating the relationship between God the Creator and the creature man. The religious historian's ways of approach are, on the other hand, empirical. He is dealing with historico-religious facts which he tries to understand and make intelligible to others. His attention is engaged at once by the significance of a religious fact and by its history; he takes pains not to sacrifice either. Of course, the religious historian is also tempted to systematize the results of his researches and reflect on the structure of religious phenomena. But then he is completing his task as historian by a task of phenomenology or religious philosophy. In the broad sense of the term, the science of religions embraces both religious phenomenology and the philosophy of religion. But the historian of religions in the strictest sense can never renounce his concern with the historically concrete. He attempts to decipher, in the temporal sphere of historical actuality, the fate of experiences arising from an inflexible human desire to transcend the temporal and historic.

All authentic religious experience implies a desperate effort to penetrate to the root of things, the ultimate reality. But every expression or conceptual formulation of a given religious experience lies in a historical context. Expressions and formulations consequently become "historical documents" comparable to any other cultural "facts": artistic creation, social or economic phenomena, etc. The supreme merit of any historian of religions is precisely his endeavor to discover in a "fact" duly conditioned by the historical moment and the cultural style of the age the existential situation which caused it.

Another element must also be taken into account: theology is essentially preoccupied with historical and revealed religions—the Jewish, Christian and Muslim monotheisms—and only secondarily with the ancient religions of the Near East and the early Mediterranean. A theological study of religious symbolism will necessarily take account of documents chosen from the great monotheistic religions rather than of "primitive" material.[5] Now the ambition of the historian of religion is to acquaint himself with the greatest possible number of religions, especially with archaic and primitive ones, in which there is a chance of meeting certain religious institutions at a still elementary stage.

In short, though it is advisable to take into account researches undertaken by specialists in other disciplines on the symbol in general and religious symbolism in particular, the historian of religions is ultimately obliged to approach the subject with his own means of investigation and in his own proper perspective. There exists no better perspective in which to view historico-religious facts than that of the general science of religions. It is only out of timidity that religious historians have sometimes accepted an integration proposed by the sociologists or anthropologists. In so far as general considerations can be formulated on the religious behavior of man, no one can make a better formulation than the religious historian. In order to do so, he must of course master and integrate the results of all investigations in all the important sectors of his discipline.

The Inhibitions of the Specialist

Unfortunately this general mastery has become increasingly rare (*Images and Symbols*, 27ff.). Few historians make the effort to follow researches in domains distant from their own field of specialization. Though a historian of the Greek religion may sometimes interest himself in recent studies on Iranian or Indian religions, he is less inclined to follow the results of his specialist colleagues in, let us say, the Altaic, Bantu or Indonesian religions. Should he wish to make a comparison or propose a more general explanation of the Greek of Mediterranean facts, he will turn to a manual, or skim Frazer, or resort to some fashionable theory on the religion of the "primitives." In other words, he will dodge the very work expected of him as a historian of religions: that of keeping himself informed of the researches of his specialist colleagues in other fields, of assimilating and comparing their results, and of finally integrating them in order to improve his understanding of his Greek documents.

This timidity is seemingly explicable by two prejudices. The first might be formulated like this: the history of religions is a limitless field[6] that no single person can master; therefore it is better to know one sector well than to wander as a dilettante through several. The second prejudice, rather implicit than avowed, is that for a "general theory" of religions it is wiser to go to the sociologist, anthropologist, philosopher or theologian. Much could be said about comparison and integration. For the moment it is important to correct an erroneous opinion held about the work of integration. The historian of religions does not have to take the place of the various specialists or master their respective philologies. Not only is such a substitution virtually impossible, it would be of no use. The historian of religions whose field of research is, let us say, Vedic India or classical Greece, does not have to know Chinese, Indonesian or Bantu in order to use in his researches Taoist religious documents or the myths of the aborigines of Ceram or the rites of the Tongans. What he must do is to keep abreast of progress made by specialists in all these fields. A man is a historian of religions not by virtue of mastering a certain number of philologies, but because he is capable of ordering religious facts in a general perspective. The historian of religions does not act as a philologist but as an expounder and interpreter. Mastery of his own specialty has taught him to find his way through a maze of facts, and where to turn for the most important sources, the most reliable translations, the studies that will guide him best in his researches. As a historian of religions, he labors to understand the material put at his disposal by philologists and historians. A few weeks' work are enough for a linguist to discover the structure of an unfamiliar language. The historian of religions should be capable of arriving at similar results when working on religious facts foreign to his own field of study. For he need not make the philological effort required by specialist research, any more than a historian of the French novel needs to repeat work already done on Balzac's or Flaubert's manuscripts, or to make a new stylistic analysis of Stendhal, or reinvestigate the sources of Victor Hugo or Gérard de Nerval. His duty is to keep abreast of all this work, to use its results and to integrate them.

The methods of a historian of religions can also be compared to those of a biologist. When the biologist studies, let us say, the behavior of a certain kind of insect, he does not take the place of the entomologist. He extends, compares and integrates the entomologist's researches. Of course the biologist too is a "specialist" in one of the branches of zoology, that is to say he has a long experience of one or another of the animal species. But his method differs from the zoologist's: he is concerned with the *structures of animal life*, not only with the morphology and "history" of a particular species.

The second prejudice of certain historians of religions, that you must turn to another "specialist" for a world-wide and systematic interpretation, of religious facts, is probably to be explained by the philosophical timidity of a great number of scholars. Two factors in particular have helped to impose and cultivate this timidity: on the one hand the very structure of the disciplines that serve as a kind of introduction to or preparation for the science of religions (it is well known that the majority of historians of religions are recruited from the philologists, archaeologists, historians, orientalists and ethnologists); on the other hand, an inhibition created by the lamentable failure of the great improvisations of the end of the nineteenth and the beginning of the twentieth century (mythology considered as a "disease of language," astral and nature mythologies, pan-Babylonianism, animism and pre-animism, etc.). Be this as it may, the historian of religions considers it safer to leave the risk of syntheses and general theories to the other disciplines—sociology, psychology, anthropology.[7] But this amounts to saying that the historian of religions hesitates to complete his preparatory work as philologist and historian by an act of comprehension, which of course requires an effort of thought.

Questions of Method

We have no intention of developing these few observations concerning the field and methods of the science of religions. Our purpose is more modest; we wish to show that it is possible to envisage the study of religious symbolism in the conspectus of the science of religions, and what the results of this study might be. But in discussing this precise case we shall be brought up against some methodological difficulties inherent in all researches into the history of religions. In other words, we shall have to discuss certain aspects of our method, not in the abstract but as they occur during the actual course of the research.

The first difficulty which confronts a historian of religions is the enormous mass of documents; in our case the vast number of religious symbols. One question occurs at the start: even if we can succeed in mastering this mass (which is not always certain) have we the right to use them indiscriminately, that is to say by grouping them, comparing them, in fact examining them according to the convenience of the author undertaking the researches? These religious documents are at the same time historical documents; they form an integral part of various cultural contexts. In fact, each document has a particular significance, relative to the culture and the historical moment from which it has been detached.

The difficulty is a real one, and we will try later to show how it can be overcome. Let us say for the present that the historian of religions is bound to meet a similar difficulty in everything he undertakes. For, on the one hand, he wants to know all the historical examples of a certain religious behavior and, on the other, he is obliged to isolate the structure of this behavior, as it can be learnt from a number of examples. To take an example: there are countless variants of the symbolism of the Cosmic Tree. A certain number of these variants can be considered as deriving from centers of diffusion. The possibility may even be admitted that all the variants of the Cosmic Tree derive from a single center of diffusion. In this case, it may be hoped that one day the history of the symbolism of the Cosmic Tree may be plotted; the center of origin having been ascertained, the channels of diffusion and the different values which this symbolism took on in course of its wanderings may all be traced.

If practicable, a historical monograph of this kind would be of great service to the history of religions. But the problem of the symbolism of the Cosmic Tree would not be solved all the same. Quite another work would remain to be done: to establish the meaning of this symbol, what it reveals, what it shows in its quality as a religious symbol. Each type or variety reveals with a particular intensity or brilliance certain aspects of the symbolism of the Cosmic Tree, while leaving other aspects in shadow. In certain cases the Cosmic Tree is revealed as primarily an imago mundi, and in others it appears as an axis mundi, as a trunk that supports the sky, connects the three cosmic zones (Heaven, Earth and Hell) and affords a means of communication between Earth and Sky. Finally, other variants principally stress its part in the periodical regeneration of the Universe, or the role of the Cosmic Tree as Center of the World, or its creative powers, etc. I have studied the symbolism of the Cosmic Tree in several of my previous works,[8] and it would serve no purpose to resume the problem in its entirety. It suffices to say that it is impossible to understand the significance of the Cosmic Tree without considering one or several of its variants. The nature of the symbolism can only be completely deciphered when a considerable number of examples have been examined. One cannot understand the significance even of a given type of Cosmic Tree until one has studied the most important types and variants. It is only after elucidating the significance of the Cosmic Tree in Mesopotamia and in India that one can understand the symbolism of Yggdrasil or of the Cosmic Trees of Central Asia and Siberia. In the science of religions, as elsewhere, comparison is used both to relate and to distinguish.

But this is not all: it is only when an inventory of all the variants has been made that their differences in meaning stand out in full relief. It is the degree of its difference from the Altaic symbol of the Cosmic Tree that throws up the great importance of the Indonesian symbol for the history of religions. The question then arises: is there in one case or the other an innovation or obfuscation of meaning, or a loss of the original significance? Knowing the significance of the Cosmic Tree in Mesopotamia or India or Siberia, one wonders what historico-religious circumstances, or what internal reasons, have caused the same symbol to possess a different significance in Indonesia. Diffusion does not solve the problem. For even if it could be proved that the symbol spread from a single center one would still not have answered the question: *why have such-and-such cultures preserved certain primary significances, while others have forgotten, rejected, modified or enriched them*? Now, the understanding of this process of enrichment only becomes possible when the nature of the symbol has been isolated. It is because the Cosmic Tree symbolizes the mystery of a World in perpetual regeneration that it can symbolize—simultaneously or successively—the pillar of the Universe and the cradle of humankind, the cosmic *renovatio* and the lunar rhythms, the Center of the World and the path by which man goes from Earth to Heaven, etc. Each of these new connotations is made possible because the symbolism of the Cosmic Tree was revealed from the beginning as a "cipher" of the World understood as a living, sacred and inexhaustible reality. The historian of religions will have to elucidate the reasons why a certain culture has kept, developed, or forgotten an aspect of the symbolism of the Cosmic Tree—and, in doing so, he will come to penetrate more deeply into the soul of that culture and learn to differentiate it from the rest.

In certain respects one could compare the situation of the historian of religions with that of the depth psychologist. Both have to preserve contact with the given facts; the methods of both are empirical; their aim is to understand "situations": individual situations in the case of the psychologist, historical situations in the case of the historian of religions. But the psychologist knows that he will only succeed in understanding an individual situation, and be able to help his patient to recover to the extent that he succeeds in uncovering the structure underlying a particular combination of symptoms, to the extent that he recognizes in the peculiarities of an individual story the broad lines of the history of the psyche. Therefore the psychologist improves his means of research and rectifies his theoretical conclusions by taking into account during his work of analysis all discoveries that have been made. As we have just seen, the historian of religions is acting in just the same way when studying, for instance, the symbolism of the World Tree. Whether he feels bound to confine himself, let us say, to Central Asia or Indonesia, or on the other hand attempts to cover this symbolism in its entirety, he can only fulfill his task by taking into consideration all the important variants of the Cosmic Tree.

Man being *homo symbolicus*, and all his activities implying symbolism, every religious fact has necessarily a symbolic character. No assumption could be more certain than that every religious act and every cult object has a meta-empirical purpose. The tree that becomes a cult object is not worshipped as a tree, but as a hierophany, a manifestation of the sacred.[9] And every religious act, from the moment that it becomes religious, is charged with a significance which is, in the final instance, "symbolic," since it refers to supernatural values or forms.

One would therefore be justified in saying that any research undertaken on a religious subject implies the study of religious symbolism. But in the current language of the science of religions, the convention is to confine the term symbol to religious facts of which the symbolism is manifest and explicit. One speaks for example of the wheel as a solar symbol, of the cosmogonic egg as a symbol of the undifferentiated totality, of the serpent as a chthonian, sexual or funerary symbol, etc.[10]

It is current practice also to approach a given religious institution—initiation, for example—or religious behavior the *orientatio*, let us say—solely from the symbolic angle. The aim of this kind of investigation is to put on one side the socio-religious contexts of the institution or behavior in question in order to concentrate on the symbolism they imply. Initiation is a complex phenomenon, comprising many kinds of rites, divergent mythologies, different social contexts and disparate aims (*Rites and Symbols*). It is well known that in the final analysis all this is "symbolic." But the study of the symbolism of initiation has a further purpose: to decipher the symbolism underlying such-and-such an initiatory rite or myth (*regresses ad uterem*, ritual death and resurrection, etc.), to study each of these symbols morphologically and historically, to lay bare the existential situation which determined their formation.

The same applies to such religious behavior as the *orientatio*. There exist innumerable rites of orientation and myths justifying them, all certainly deriving from the experience of the sacred ground. To attack this problem in its entirety presupposes the study of ritual orientation, geomancy, the rites of founding a village or constructing a temple or house, the symbolism of tents, huts and houses, etc. But as at the basis of all this lies an experience of the sacred ground and a cosmological idea, one can limit the study of the *orientatio* to the symbolism of the sacred ground. This does not mean that one fails to know or neglects the historical and social contexts of all the forms of *orientatio* that one has been at pains to examine.

One could easily multiply examples of such researches on a particular symbolism: the "magic flight" and ascension, Night and the symbolism of darkness, lunar, solar, telluric, vegetable and animal symbolisms, the symbolism of the quest for immortality, the symbol of the Hero, etc. In each of these cases the approach is essentially the same: one tries to reconstitute the symbolic significance of religious facts apparently heterogeneous but structurally related, which may take the form of ritual rites or behavior, or of myths, legends, supernatural figures and images. Such a procedure does not imply the reduction of all these significances to a common denominator. One cannot sufficiently insist on this point: that the examination of symbolic structures is a work not of reduction but of integration. One compares and contrasts two expressions of a symbol not in order to reduce them to a single, pre-existent expression, but in order to discover the process by which a structure is capable of enriching its meanings. In studying the symbolism of flight and ascension, we have given some examples of this process of enrichment; the reader anxious to verify the results of such a methodological process is referred to *Myths, Dreams and Mysteries*.

Notes

1. A clear exposition of the theories of Freud and Jung about the symbol is to be found in Jolande Jacobi's *Komplex, Archetypus, Symbol in der Psychologie C. G. Jung* (Zurich, 1957), 86ff.
2. See Lucien Lévy-Bruhl, *Les Carnets*, ed. Maurice Leenhardt (Paris, 1946).
3. See Max Schlesinger, *Geschichte des Symbols* (Berlin, 1912); A. N. Whitehead, *Symbolism, its Meaning and Effect* (New York, 1927); W. M. Urban, *Language and Reality: The Philosophy of Language and the Principles of Symbolism* (London and New York, 1939); *Religious Symbolism*, ed. F. Ernest Johnson (New York, 1955); *Symbols and Values: An Initial Study* (XIIIth Symposium of the Conference on Science, Philosophy and Religion) (New York, 1954); *Symbols and Society* (XIVth Symposium of the Conference on Science, Philosophy and Religion) (New York, 1955). See also *Symbolon. Jahrbuch fur Symbol-forschung*, vol. 1 (Basle, 1960).
4. It is enough to recall the works of Ernst Cassirer, *Philosophie der symbolischen Formen*, 3 vols. (Berlin, 1923–29); and *An Essay on Man* (Yale, 1944); and Susanne K. Langer, *Philosophy of Reason, Rite and Art* (Harvard, 1942).
5. Clearly, a theology of the History of Religions will have to take into account all these archaic and primitive religious experiences. But such a theology presupposes the existence of a History of Religions and depends on its findings.
6. This is true of all historical disciplines. More than fifty years ago Anatole France observed that it would take several lives to read all the documents on the French Revolution alone.

7. In fact all the "general theories" which have dominated the History of Religion from its beginnings have been the work of linguists, anthropologists, sociologists and philosophers. See *Images and Symbols*, 30ff.

8. See *Patterns*, 265ff.; *Shamanism*, 269ff; *Images and Symbols*, 39ff, 16ff.

9. On the subject of hierophanies, see *Patterns*, 7ff. [and above, 86–95].

10. It is also conventional to reserve the term "symbolism" for a structurally coherent ensemble; we speak for example of water symbolism, the structure of which can only be understood by studying a great number of religious facts apparently heterogeneous: baptismal rites and lustration, aquatic cosmogonies, myths about floods and disasters at sea, myths whose principal feature is fecundity by contact with water, etc. … (*Patterns*, 188ff.; *Images and Symbols*, 125ff. and 151ff.). Clearly, the current use of the terms "symbol" and "symbolism" lacks precision, but one must adapt oneself to this state of things. In many cases the context sufficiently reveals the meaning.

26

Pettazzoni as Exemplary Historian of Religion

Mircea Eliade

Editor's Introduction

The original context of this excerpt was a review essay of several of Raffaele Pettazzoni's works and also books by Martin P. Nilsson and Gabriel Germain. It proposes both Pettazzoni and Nilsson as an exemplary, if imperfect, figures in the History of Religions and serves sharply to outline Eliade's understanding of a commendable methodology in the field. Especially worthy of note is the claim about "the general intention of his work [the Historian of Religions]: to obtain the largest possible audience for the productions of this oral sacred literature of the primitives." Apparently Eliade did not conceive his History of Religions as a recondite specialist discipline meant to increase the understanding of religion, but as a popularizing cultural endeavor meant to promote the awareness of and familiarity with existing specialist understanding. This is further borne out by his claims, in the Foreword to *Shamanism*, which immediately follows this selection, that "[w]e believe that such a study can be of interest not only to the specialist but also to the cultivated man, and it is to the latter that this book is primarily addressed," and "our aim is not a series of monographs on the various shamanisms, but a general study addressed to nonspecialist readers." Originally published in *Diogenes* 9 (1955): 96–105.

80 03

Professor Raffaele Pettazzoni is one of the most illustrious historians of religion of our time. He belongs to a type of scholar which is unfortunately becoming rare and is perhaps headed for extinction: those who have taken as their specialty the universal history of religion. At first sight such an ambition might seem to pose an impossible task; the historico-cultural field has become so wide that no single mind could pretend to assimilate and master a quantity of documents that is increasing every day. Let us therefore avoid misunderstanding on this point: there is no question of the historian of religions attempting to replace the Americanist, the Sinologist, the Africanist, or to master their knowledge of philology in order to study and interpret the Chinese, Aztec and Bantu religions: it suffices for him to record the results of research carried out by the specialists and to classify and evaluate these results in a perspective which is exclusively his own: that of the general history of religion.

Unfortunately, this is a program which is rarely realized. If he specializes in one single broad sector, the ancient Near East, China, or Greece, for instance, the historian of religion no longer has the time nor the energy to follow and integrate the results obtained by his colleagues in other fields. Instead of studying problems as they emerge from all these special realms of research, the historian of religion usually adopts one of the currently fashionable hypotheses and orients his own studies with relation to it. For a whole generation, historians of religion sought—and found—"agricultural demons" almost everywhere; for another generation they applied themselves to seeking out the *mana* in innumerable religious structures. It is significant that the most striking hypotheses proposed within the past seventy-five years to explain the essence and the origin of religion have been the work of eminent scholars whose specialty was not the history of religion. It was Max Müller, an Indianist of genius, who founded naturistic mythology, and for twenty-five years the historians of religion taught that the Indo-European gods and their mythologies were nothing more than meteorological epiphanies. E. B. Tylor, an anthropologist, identified animism as the first form of religion; Sir James Frazer, an ethnologist as well as a classicist and folklorist, started two great fashions in the history of religions: the agricultural demons (borrowed, incidentally, from Mannhardt) and totemism. Finally, the most recent hypotheses on the origin and the first form of religion— the *mana* and pre-animism, mystic participation and the pre-logical mentality, the Oedipus complex or the archetypes of the collective unconscious—were proposed by sociologists, philosophers, and psychologists. Even the most important reaction against such abusive hypotheses—we are thinking especially of religious phenomenology—was only the application of a well-known philosophic method.

This situation need not, however, be emphasized here. It should be recalled, nevertheless, that for many reasons the history of religions as an autonomous field has yet to find its methodology, while ethnology, sociology, and folklore already have theirs. Historians of religions are dependent for the most part on the methodological progress made in some neighboring field, especially in eth-nology. One even suspects a tacit tendency to leave it to the ethnologists and the sociologists to construct a universal history of religions, which is under-standable to a degree but not devoid of risk.

It is difficult, for example, to imagine a history of initiation, of secret societies and mysteries, or a history of Gnosis constructed with the means used by eth-nology or sociology or in their perspective. For, while tribal initiations and secret societies are well known to the ethnologist, these religious phenomena are prolonged and considerably amplified in the great historical religions; and alongside the Australian puberty rites or the Melanesian *men's societies*, there are Eleusis, the Greco-Oriental mysteries, the Indo-European or Japanese *Männerbünde,* Gnosticism, Hermetism and Tantrism, and so on. Often the study of these evolved forms gives a better understanding of the structure, the intention and the essence of an elementary initiation rite. This task of integra-tion can only be the work of a historian of religion; he alone is able to bring together the results obtained by ethnology and Orientalism, by classicists and folklorists. (In the case of the men's societies, for example, folklore contributes materials of unequaled value.)

For the past half-century ethnology has tended more and more to become a historic discipline. This orientation has already been most useful to the history of religions. Distinction is rarely made between the primitives—the *Naturvölker* without a history—on the one hand, and the historical religions, beginning with that of ancient Egypt and ending with Islam, on the other. Whether or not they accept the theory of cultural cycles worked out by Graebner and Schmidt, ethnologists agree that every primitive people has a history and that this his-tory is sometimes very complex. Hence the historian of religion no longer faces two radically separate universes: the historyless universe of the primitives and the historic universe of the great cultures; whatever be the form of religion under study, there is always a fragment of universal history involved The pro-gress of ethnology has abolished the solution which depends on a continuity between the primitive world and ours: both are historical worlds.

But even after he has assimilated and evaluated this discovery of the ethnolo-gists, the historian of religions has not yet solved his own problem. His task is not over when he realizes that every religious form has a history and that it is an integral part of a well-defined cultural complex; he must still understand and clarify the meaning, the intention, and the message of his religious form. To go back to the example used above, even if one has reconstituted the history of initiations from the Australians to the Greco Oriental mysteries or Tantrism, and has clarified their social and cultural implications, their spread, their trans-formations and degraded forms, one has not yet elucidated the deep sense of these ceremonies. A spiritual attitude of man is inherent in all these initiation rites. No one is better prepared to grasp, interpret and present it than the his-torian of religions, for no one else has the materials and perspective which he commands. In other words, the historian of religion is obliged by his own scientific discipline to deal with the timeless constants of religious experience and the structures which result from it, and which cannot be reduced to historic terms. He must decide whether the history of religion will keep its autonomy, or end by being integrated into ethnology or sociology, abandoning to the psychologists and philosophers, as a monopoly, the study of the structures and constants of religious life.

This long parenthesis has not led us so far from our subject as it might seem. The work of Professor Pettazzoni provides an excellent illustration of what the autonomy of the history of religion means. We said earlier that he had made the study of all religions his specialty. Indeed, after having begun as an archaeologist and a classicist, he has never ceased to broaden his field of research. Though his first vocation led to the writing of some excellent books (*La Religion primitiva in Sardegna*, Plaisance, 1912; *La Religions nella Grecia antica*, Bologna, 1921; *I Misteri*, Bologna, 1924), the greater part of his work is that of a non-specialist, that is to say, of a historian of religion who uses and integrates the results obtained by specialists in other fields. Although he is not an Iranologist, his *Religion di Zarathustra nella Storia religiosa dell'Iran* (Bologna, 1920) remained for a long time one of the best general works on Iranian religions. Assimilating the enormous mass of ethnological literature, Professor Pettazzoni published in 1922 the first volume of his *Dio. Formazione e Sviluppo del Monoteismo nella Storia della religioni (L'Essere celeste nelle Credenze dei Popoli primitivi)*, in 1930 the *Confessione dei Peccati* (this first volume was largely devoted to the primitives), and in 1948 the first volume of his *Mitti e Leggende* (Africa-Australia). Two other volumes of the great monograph on the confession of sins continue the survey to Oriental and Mediterranean religions; a *Mitologia giapponese secondo il I libro il Kojiki* appeared in 1929; finally, he has collected certain more specialized studies in two recent volumes (*Saggi di Storia delle Relgioni e di Mitologia*, Rome, 1946; *Essays on the History of Religion*, Leyden, 1954) and has published in *Italia religiosa* (Bari, 1952) some synthetic studies on the Italian and Roman religions. He also founded, and has directed for thirty years, the review entitled *Studi e Materiali di Storia delle Religioni*, which in 1929 inaugurated a popular collection of texts on archaic religions, *Testi e Documenti per la Storia delle Relgioni*, and has recently become director of the *Classici della Religione* series published by Sansoni of Florence. (The first volume contains a complete Italian translation of the *Edda*, by C. A. Mastrelli. The *Avesta*, the Taoist texts, and the Koran are in preparation.)

Professor Pettazzoni has carried on his scientific work side by side with his activity as an organizer and promoter of studies on the history of religions; it is chiefly due to his efforts that there is such a lively interest in the history of religions in Italy today. As for his theoretical position, it is, first of all, that of a historian who has deeply considered, and partially adopted, Croce's interpretation of history. In an article which recently appeared in *Numen* (Vol. I, Part 1,

January, 1954), he wrote that "the only way to escape the dangers" of a phenomenological interpretation of religion "consists of constantly referring to history." We shall not discuss here the tension between what the Italian scholar includes under the name of phenomenology, and history. Professor Pettazzoni's work seems to us more instructive than his theoretical position, and it proposes a sort of exemplary goal to every historian of religion who is conscious of the dangers which threaten his science (the dangers of specialization, first of all).

He addresses himself to the broad cultivated public in the magnificent series of *Myths and Legends* of which the first volume has just appeared. The texts were chosen and translated according to the best ethnological sources, and most of them are annotated, though always with care not to detract from the reader's pleasure. For the author never for an instant loses sight of the general intention of his work: to obtain the largest possible audience for the productions of this oral sacred literature of the primitives. Each ethnic group is presented in a short introduction, which constitutes almost a résumé of the present state of knowledge on the questions involved, and is completed by an essential bibliography. In the case of Africa (Vol. I) the groups presented go from the Boshimans to the Berbers and Pygmies and include the Hottentots, the Damas, the various Bantu groups, etc. In the case of North America the groups include the Eskimos, the Californians and the Pueblos, Pimas and Papagos. The first volume also includes a selection of Australian myths and legends (460–80).

27

Shamanism: Foreword

Mircea Eliade

Editor's Introduction

One of Eliade's clearest methodological statements is the "Foreword" from *Shamanism*, which remains one of his most significant works, still found in many bookstores. It demonstrates his thesis that the historian of religions can most usefully be employed in such works of integration. Eliade here makes a reference to the "Graebner-Schmidt-Koppers method of cultural cycles." It is worth pointing out for contemporary students who may be unfamiliar with this that Father Wilhelm Schmidt (1868–1954) was author of the twelve-volume *Der Ursprung der Gottesidee*, which argued for a primal monotheism. Along with another clergyman, Wilhelm Koppers (1886–1961), he led a Vienna School of Anthropology, largely built on the works of Fritz Graebner. Their central concept was that of *Kulturkreis* (more accurately the culture-circle) and their approach is thus referred to as *Kulturkreislehre*, which held that the primeval culture-circle could be reconstructed through its contemporary remnants. Secondary culture-circles came about through migrations and the combination of primary culture-circles. The present excerpt is from *Shamanism: Archaic Techniques of Ecstasy* by Mircea Eliade, xi–xix (London: Routledge and Kegan Paul, 1964). All rights reserved. Copyright © 1964 by Bollingen; 1992 renewed Princeton University Press; 1972 paperback edition; 2004 2nd paperback edition with new foreword. Reprinted by permission of Princeton University Press.

෨ ଓ

Today the student has at his disposition a considerable quantity of documents for the various shamanisms—Siberian, North American, South American, Indonesian, Oceanian, and so on. Then too, a number of works, important in their several ways, have broken ground for the ethnological, sociological, and psychological study of shamanism (or rather, of a particular type of shamanism). But with a few notable exceptions—we refer especially to the studies of Altaic shamanism by Holmberg (Harva)—the immense shamanic bibliography has neglected to interpret this extremely complex phenomenon in the framework of the history of religions. It is as a historian of religions that we, in our turn, have attempted to approach, understand, and present shamanism. Far be it from us to think of belittling the admirable studies undertaken from the viewpoints of psychology, sociology, or ethnology; we consider them indispensable to understanding the various aspects of shamanism. But we believe that there is room for another approach—that which we have sought to implement in the following pages.

The writer who approaches shamanism as a psychologist will be led to regard it as primarily the manifestation of a psyche in crisis or even in retrogression; he will not fail to compare it with certain aberrant psychic behavior patterns or to class it among mental diseases of the hysteroid or epileptoid type.

We shall explain why we consider it unacceptable to assimilate shamanism to any kind of mental disease. But one point remains (and it is an important one), to which the psychologist will always be justified in drawing attention: like any other religious vocation, the shamanic vocation is manifested by a crisis, a temporary derangement of the future shaman's spiritual equilibrium. All the observations and analyses that have been made on this point are particularly valuable. They show us, in actual process as it were, the repercussions, within the psyche, of what we have called the "dialectic of hierophanies"—the radical separation between profane and sacred and the resultant splitting of the world. To say this is to indicate all the importance that we attribute to such studies in religious psychology.

The sociologist, for his part, is concerned with the social function of the shaman, the priest, the magician. He will study prestige originating from magical powers, its role in the structure of society, the relations between religious and political leaders, and so on. A sociological analysis of the myths of the First Shaman will elicit revealing indications concerning the exceptional position of the earliest shamans in certain archaic societies. The sociology of shamanism remains to be written, and it will be among the most important chapters in a general sociology of religion. The historian of religions must take all these studies and their conclusions into account. Added to the psychological conditions brought out by the psychologist, the social conditions, in the broadest sense of the term, reinforce the element of human and historical concreteness in the documents that he is called upon to handle.

This concreteness will be accentuated by the studies of the ethnologist. It will be the task of ethnological monographs to situate the shaman in his cultural milieu. There is danger of misunderstanding the true personality of a Chukchee shaman, for example, if one reads of his exploits without knowing anything about the life and traditions of the Chukchee. Again, it will be for the ethnologist to make exhaustive studies of the shaman's costume and drum, to describe the séances, to record texts and melodies, and so on. By undertaking to establish the "history" of one or another constituent element of shamanism (the drum, for example, or the use of narcotics during séances), the ethnologist—joined when circumstances demand it, by a comparativist and a historian—will succeed in showing the circulation of the particular motif in time and space; so far as possible, he will define its center of expansion and the stages and the chronology of its dissemination. In short, the ethnologist will also become a "historian," whether or not he adopts the Graebner-Schmidt-Koppers method of cultural cycles. In any case, in addition to an admirable purely descriptive ethnographical literature, there are now available numerous works of historical ethnology: in the overwhelming "gray mass" of cultural data stemming from the so-called "ahistorical" peoples, we now begin to see certain lines of force appearing; we begin to distinguish "history" where we were in the habit of finding only "Naturvölker," "primitives," or "savages."

It is unnecessary to dwell here on the great services that historical ethnology has already rendered to the history of religions. But we do not believe that it can take the place of the history of religions. The latter's mission is to integrate the results of ethnology, psychology, and sociology. Yet in doing so, it will not renounce its own method of investigation or the viewpoint that specifically defines it. Cultural ethnology may have demonstrated the relation of shamanism to certain cultural cycles, for example, or the dissemination of one or another shamanic complex; yet its object is not to reveal the deeper meaning of all these religious phenomena, to illuminate their symbolism, and to place them in the general history of religions. In the last analysis, it is for the historian of religions to synthesize all the studies of particular aspects of shamanism and to present a comprehensive view which shall be at once a morphology and a history of this complex religious phenomenon.

But an understanding must be reached concerning the importance to be accorded to "history" in this type of investigation. As we have said more than once elsewhere, and as we shall have occasion to show more fully in [*A History of Religious Ideas*], although the historical conditions are extremely important in a religious phenomenon (for every human datum is in the last analysis a historical datum), they do not wholly exhaust it. We will cite only one example here. The Altaic shaman ritually climbs a birch tree in which a certain number of steps have been cut; the birch symbolizes the World Tree, the steps representing the various heavens through which the shaman must pass on his ecstatic journey to the highest heaven; and it is extremely probable that the cosmological schema implied in this ritual is of Oriental origin. Religious ideas of the ancient Near East penetrated far into Central and North Asia and contributed considerably to giving Central Asian and Siberian shamanism their present features. This is a good example of what "history" can teach us concerning the dissemination of religious ideologies and techniques. But, as we said above, the *history* of a religious phenomenon cannot reveal *all* that this phenomenon, by the mere fact of its manifestation, seeks to show us. Nothing warrants the supposition that influences from Oriental cosmology and religion *created* the ideology and ritual of the ascent to the sky among the Altaians; similar ideologies and rituals appear all over the world and in regions where ancient Oriental influences are excluded a priori. More probably, the Oriental ideas merely *modified* the ritual formula and cosmological implications of the celestial ascent; the latter appears to be a primordial phenomenon, that is, it belongs to man as such, not to man as a historical being; witness the dreams, hallucinations, and images of ascent found everywhere in the world, apart from any historical or other "conditions." All these dreams, myths, and nostalgias with a central theme of ascent or flight cannot be exhausted by a psychological explanation; there is always a kernel that remains refractory to explanation, and this indefinable, irreducible element perhaps reveals the real situation of man in the cosmos, a situation that, we shall never tire of repeating, is not solely "historical."

Thus the historian of religions, while taking historico-religious facts into account, does his utmost to organize his documents in the historical perspective—the only perspective that ensures their concreteness. But he must not forget that, when all is said and done, the phenomena with which he is concerned reveal boundary-line situations of mankind, and that these situations demand to be understood and made understandable. This work of deciphering the deep meaning of religious phenomena rightfully falls to the historian of religions. Certainly, the psychologist, the sociologist, the ethnologist, and even the philosopher or the theologian will have their comment to make, each from the viewpoint and in the perspective that are properly his. But it is the historian of religions who will make the greatest number of valid statements on a religious phenomenon *as a religious phenomenon*—and not as a psychological, social, ethnic, philosophical, or even theological phenomenon. On this particular point the historian of religions also differs from the phenomenologist. For the latter, in principle, rejects any work of comparison; confronted with one religious phenomenon or another, he confines himself to "approaching" it and divining its meaning. Whereas the historian of religions does not reach a comprehension of a phenomenon until after he has compared it with thousands of similar or dissimilar phenomena, until he has situated it among them; and these thousands of phenomena are separated not only in time but also in space. For a like reason, the historian of religions will not confine himself merely to a typology or morphology of religious data; he knows that "history" does not exhaust the content of a religious phenomenon, but neither does he forget that it is always in History—in the broadest sense of the term—that a religious datum develops all its aspects and reveals all its meanings. In other words, the historian of religions makes use of all the *historical* manifestations of a religious phenomenon in order to discover what such a phenomenon "has to say"; on the one hand, he holds to the historically concrete, but on the other, he attempts to decipher whatever transhistorical content a religious datum reveals through history.

We need not dwell here on these few methodological considerations; to set them forth adequately would require far more space than a foreword affords. Let us say, however, that the word "history" sometimes leads to confusion, for it can equally well mean historiography (the act of *writing* the history of something) and simply "what has happened" in the world. This second meaning of the word itself comprises several special meanings: history in the sense of what happened within certain spatial or temporal boundaries (history of a particular people, of a particular period), that is, the history of a continuity or of a structure; but then again, history in the general sense, as in the expressions "the historical existence of man," "historical situation," "historical moment," or even in the existentialist use of the term: man is "in situation," that is, *in* history.

The *history* of religions is not always necessarily the *historiography* of religions. For in writing the history of one or another religion or of a given religious phenomenon (sacrifice among the Semites, the myth of Herakles, and so on), we are not always able to show everything "that happened" in a chronological perspective; we can do so, of course, if the documents permit, but we are not obliged to practice *historiography* in order to claim that we are writing the history of religions. The polyvalence of the term "history" has made it easy for scholars to misunderstand one another here; actually, it is the philosophical and general meaning of "history" that best suits our particular discipline. To practice that discipline is to study religious facts as such, that is, on their specific plane of manifestation. This specific plane of manifestation is always *historical*, concrete, existential, even if the religious facts manifested are not always wholly reducible to history. From the most elementary hierophanies—the manifestation of the sacred in some stone or tree, for example—to the most complex (the "vision" of a new "divine form" by a prophet or the founder of a religion), everything is manifested in the historically concrete and everything is in some sort conditioned by history. Yet in the humblest hierophany there is an "eternal new beginning," an eternal return to an atemporal moment, a desire to abolish history, to blot out the past, to recreate the world. All this is "shown" in religious facts; it is not an invention of the historian of religions. Obviously, a historian bent on being only a historian has the right to ignore the specific and transhistorical meanings of a religious fact; an ethnologist, a sociologist, a psychologist may do likewise. A historian of religions cannot ignore them. Familiar with a considerable number of hierophanies, his eye will have learned to decipher the properly religious meaning of one or another fact. And to return to the very point from which we set out, this book strictly deserves to be called a study in the history of religions even if it does not follow the chronological course of historiography.

Then too, this chronological perspective, however interesting to certain historians, is far from having the importance commonly attributed to it. For, as we have attempted to show in *Patterns in Comparative Religion,* the very dialectic of the sacred tends indefinitely to repeat a series of archetypes, so that a hierophany realized at a certain "historical moment" is structurally equivalent to a hierophany a thousand years earlier or later. This tendency on the part of the hierophanic process to repeat the same paradoxical sacralization of reality ad infinitum is what, after all, enables us to understand something of a religious phenomenon and to write its "history." In other words, it is precisely because hierophanies repeat themselves that we can distinguish religious facts and succeed in understanding them. But hierophanies have the peculiarity of seeking to reveal the sacred in its totality, even if the human beings in whose consciousness the sacred "shows itself" fasten upon only one aspect or one small part of it. In the most elementary hierophany *everything is declared.* The manifestation of the sacred in a stone or a tree is neither less mysterious nor less noble than its manifestation in a "god." The process of sacralizing reality is the same; the *forms* taken by the process in man's religious consciousness differ.

This is not without its bearing on the conception of a chronological perspective of religion. Though a *history* of religion exists, it is not, like all other kinds of history, irreversible. A monotheistic religious consciousness is not necessarily monotheistic throughout its span of existence for the reason that it forms part of a monotheistic "history," and that, as we know, within that history one cannot revert to polytheism or paganism after having known and practiced monotheism. On the contrary, one can perfectly well be a polytheist or indulge in the religious practices of a totemist while thinking and maintaining that one is a monotheist. The dialectic of the sacred permits all reversibilities; no "form" is exempt from degradation and decomposition, no "history" is final. Not only can a community—consciously or unconsciously—practice many religions, but the same individual can have an infinite variety of religious experiences, from the "highest" to the most undeveloped and aberrant. This is equally true from the opposite point of view: any cultural moment whatever can provide the fullest revelation of the sacred to which the human condition is capable of acceding. Despite the immense historical differences involved, the experiences of the monotheistic prophets can be repeated in the most "backward" of primitive tribes; the only requirement is "realization" of the hierophany of a celestial god, a god attested nearly everywhere in the world even though he may be absent from the current practice of religion. No religious form, however vitiated, is incapable of producing a perfectly pure and coherent mysticism. If exceptions of this kind are not numerous enough to impress observers, this is due not to the dialectic of the sacred but to human behavior in respect to that dialectic. And the study of human behavior lies beyond the field of the historian of religions; it is the concern of the sociologist, the psychologist, the moralist, the philosopher. In our role of historian of religions, it suffices us to observe that the dialectic of the sacred makes possible the spontaneous reversal of any religious position. The very fact of this reversibility is important, for it is not to be found elsewhere. This is why we tend to remain uninfluenced by certain results attained by historico-cultural ethnology. The various types of civilization are, of course, organically connected with certain religious forms; but this in no sense excludes the spontaneity and, in the last analysis, the ahistoricity of religious life. For all history is in some measure a fall of the sacred, a limitation and diminution. But the sacred does not cease to manifest itself, and with each new manifestation it resumes its original tendency to reveal itself wholly. It is true, of course, that the countless new manifestations of the sacred in the religious consciousness of one or another society repeat the countless manifestations of the sacred that those societies knew in the course of their past, of their "history." But it is equally true that this history does not paralyze the spontaneity of hierophanies; at every moment a fuller revelation of the sacred remains possible.

It happens—and this brings us back to our discussion of chronology in the history of religions—that the reversibility of religious positions is even more striking in the case of the mystical experiences of archaic societies. As we shall frequently show, particularly coherent mystical experiences are possible at any and every degree of civilization and of religious situation. This is as much as to say that, for certain religious consciousnesses in crisis, there is always the possibility of a historical leap that enables them to attain otherwise inaccessible spiritual positions. Certainly, "history"—the religious tradition of the tribe in question—finally intervenes to subject the ecstatic experiences of certain privileged persons to its own canons. But it is no less true that these experiences often have the same precision and nobility as the experiences of the great mystics of East and West.

Critiques of Eliade

28

DISTINGUISHING RELIGIOUS PHENOMENA

Douglas Allen

Editor's Introduction

To complement Eliade's own understanding of his methodology this analysis is taken from Douglas Allen's *Structure and Creativity in Religion: Hermeneutics in Mircea Eliade's Phenomenology and New Directions*, 105–113; 129–30; 144–48; 155–57 (The Hague: Mouton, 1978). All rights reserved. Copyright © 1978 by Mouton de Gruyter. Reprinted by permission of Mouton de Gruyter.

ॐ ও

Introduction

It seems possible to make the distinction between providing the criteria for separating religious from nonreligious phenomena and providing the criteria for interpreting the meaning of a religious phenomenon. This is analogous to the distinction between formulating the criteria for distinguishing a work of art and supplying the criteria for understanding the meaning of the work of art.

In terms of this distinction, it is our thesis that there are two key notions in Mircea Eliade's methodology: the dialectic of the sacred and the profane[1] and the central position of symbolism or symbolic structures. Eliade's interpretation of the dialectic of the sacred allows him to distinguish religious phenomena; his interpretation of symbolism provides the theoretical framework in terms of which he is able to understand the meaning of most of these sacred manifestations. Eliade's general view of symbolism establishes the phenomenological grounds for his structural hermeneutics; the dialectic of the sacred, when combined with Eliade's analysis of symbolism, conveys the irreducibly religious "sense" evidenced throughout his approach.

In this chapter, we shall focus on the first of these key notions: Eliade's attempt to provide criteria for distinguishing religious phenomena. For the sake of analysis, we shall abstract several principles from his methodology. Such an approach might suggest a temporal order in Eliade's hermeneutics: first Eliade insists on the irreducibility of the sacred, which involves the phenomenological *epoché* and the sympathetic effort to participate in the experience of *homo religiosus*; next he attempts to recreate imaginatively the conditions of the sacred manifestation and captures the intentionality of the sacred manifestation in terms of the dialectic of the sacred; then he attempts to understand the meaning of the sacred manifestation in terms of a structural hermeneutics grounded in his interpretation of religious symbolism.

It is imperative that we clearly recognize that such an interpretation, suggesting this temporal sequence in Mircea Eliade's methodology, will not do. For example, we shall describe Eliade's methodological insistence on suspending one's own interpretation and seeing just what one's data reveal. But surely even the most conscientious phenomenologist cannot simply "perform" or "invoke" the *epoché*. The phenomenological *epoché* must involve some explicit method of self-criticism, intersubjective check, factual (as well as "free") variations. Consequently, we could not possibly understand the nature of Eliade's phenomenological *epoché* until we had elucidated the additional methodological principles and hermeneutical framework in terms of which one can suspend his or her own normative judgments, grasp the meaning of the experiences of *homo religiosus*, etc.

In short, we cannot overemphasize that the following hermeneutical principles, along with the structuralistic principles not elucidated in this chapter, must be viewed as functioning together in Mircea Eliade's methodology. Any illusion of temporal order is an unfortunate consequence of the need for an analytic exposition.

Before proceeding with our systematic treatment of Mircea Eliade's phenomenological approach, we may acknowledge that our analysis is in contrast with most of Eliade's interpreters, who seem to feel that Eliade has never developed a systematic methodology. For example, Thomas J. J. Altizer repeatedly describes Eliade's phenomenological method as "mystical" and "romantic"; such a method is completely divorced from any approach which is "rational" and "scientific."[2] Indeed, the proponent of this mystically grounded approach is identified with such roles as "prophet, seer, and shaman."[3]

We must acknowledge that Mircea Eliade himself lends considerable credence to the view that he has never really dealt with the crucial phenomenological issues and consequently lacks a critical systematic methodology. When asked how he arrived at his frequently unexpected and bewildering interpretations, this scholar is apt to reply that he simply looked at his religious documents and this was what they revealed.[4] It is little wonder that such a seemingly uncritical approach is often viewed as either incredibly naïve or charlatanical or at best the brilliant intuitions of a true mystic. In any case, this approach would have little value for the methodological concerns of the rigorous phenomenologist.

Now it is our thesis that Mircea Eliade does in fact have an impressive phenomenological method. We would submit that this is precisely why Eliade is a methodological improvement over the other phenomenologists of religion we have examined. As one studies a major classic in the field, say, Gerardus van der Leeuw's *Religion in Essence and Manifestation*, she or he cannot help but be impressed by the vast amount of data which have been collected and classified. What invariably disturbs the philosophical phenomenologist is that van der Leeuw and his colleagues never appear to have formulated a critical methodology. On what basis do they make their comparisons and generalizations, guard against subjectivity in their interpretations, defend their specific classifications and typologies? What we shall attempt to show is that underlying Eliade's approach is a certain methodological framework which allows him to deal with many of the central phenomenological concerns.

Mircea Eliade as Phenomenologist

Throughout this study, we have referred to Mircea Eliade as a "phenomenologist" and to his approach as "phenomenological" without really justifying the identification of his History of Religions with these terms. It must be stated that such an identification is controversial. Neither Eliade nor his interpreters usually identify his approach with phenomenology. We are aware of no interpreter who has shown a relationship between Eliade's methodology and philosophical phenomenology.

Chapter 5 is intended to lay the hermeneutical framework for Eliade's phenomenological method, and Chapter 6 attempts to relate Eliade's approach to specific notions and concerns of philosophical phenomenology. For now, we may begin to present some evidence to substantiate our controversial claim that Mircea Eliade is a phenomenologist.

Recall that we have discussed the present nature *of Religionswissenschaft* as disclosing a certain methodological tension between approaches tending toward either specialization or synthesis and generality. Phenomenological approaches were viewed as one of the tendencies toward generality.

In previous chapters, we have clearly established that Mircea Eliade is a *generalist*. One of Eliade's consistent themes has been the need for contemporary Historians of Religions to go beyond the self-imposed limitations of specialization and to attempt creative generalizations and syntheses. In fact, Eliade frequently identifies being a Historian of Religions with being a generalist: "It is not a question, for the historian of religions [Historian of Religions], of substituting himself for the various specialists, that is to say, of mastering their respective philologies. ... One is a historian of religions [Historian of Religions] not by virtue of mastering a certain number of philologies, but because one is able to integrate religious data into a general perspective."[5]

In describing Eliade's generalist approach as phenomenological, we should note a distinction which was made in Chapter 2 in our introduction to phenomenological approaches. "The term phenomenology of religion can be used in a double sense": "It means both a scientific method and an independent science, creating monographs and more or less extensive handbooks."[6] Eliade's *Patterns in Comparative Religion* illustrates this second sense of phenomenology of religion.

Our paramount concern is with Eliade's methodology, and we shall not present a comprehensive exposition of his categorization of religious phenomena. Thus, we shall not formulate Eliade's analysis of sacred space, sacred time, myth, ritual, and other major categories for organizing and analyzing religious phenomena. If there is any resemblance between philosophical phenomenology and the phenomenology of religion as a branch of the History of Religions, this is because of the adoption of *a phenomenological method*.

Not only do Mircea Eliade's interpreters usually fail to associate his History of Religions with phenomenology, but they sometimes even distinguish his approach from the phenomenology of religion. For example, in the discussion of a paper given by Ugo Bianchi, Professor Bolgiani remarks that he has the impression that

> Bianchi used such expressions as "typology" and "phenomenology" rather indiscriminately, when it seems to me that in the current state of "religious sciences" we cannot purely and simply equate them. To set the bounds of the problem correctly it strikes me that we ought to distinguish between "typology," "morphology" and even "phenomenology" of religions. To reduce religious phenomenology simply to a "typology" of religions does not seem to me to be entirely right...

Professor Bianchi replies that "some historians of religions [Historians of Religions] have a certain tendency to use such terms as 'typology,' 'phenomenology' and 'morphology' with a promiscuous meaning." "When we mention phenomenology we especially think of scholars such as Wach, Van der Leeuw and Bleeker; when we mention morphology then our mind goes especially to Eliade."[7]

Our position is that although morphology may be distinguished from phenomenology and most morphologists are not phenomenologists, in the case of Professor Eliade, morphology is an integral part of his phenomenological method. In Chapter 5, we shall see that a morphological analysis provides the foundation for Eliade's phenomenological method, primarily by allowing him to reintegrate the particular manifestation within its structural system of symbolic associations. At the same time, we would submit that most interpreters who identify Eliade as a morphologist have simply taken his morphology at face value; as if by some mysterious process, the data simply revealed those essential structures. In Chapter 6, we shall analyze how Eliade proceeds, and we shall elucidate some of the phenomenological principles that allow for his morphological analysis.

At one point, Mircea Eliade specifically dissociates himself from phenomenology:

> [the phenomenologist], in principle, rejects any work of comparison; confronted with one religious phenomenon or another, he confines himself to "approaching" it and divining its meaning. Whereas the historian of religions [Historian of Religions] does not reach a comprehension of a phenomenon until after he has compared it with thousands of similar or dissimilar phenomena, until he has situated it among them.[8]

It seems that this rejection of phenomenology is based on a popular interpretation of Husserl's phenomenological reduction and eidetic intuition.[9] On the basis of one example and through reflection, reductions, and imaginative variation, one may gain insight into the structure and meaning of a phenomenon. The phenomenologist may arrive at this pure vision without the collection of historical examples and factual comparisons. We should note that contemporary phenomenologists (and apparently Husserl himself in some of his last works) reject this view of phenomenology.

In terms of the historical-phenomenological "tension," which Eliade and other scholars often formulate as defining the nature of the History of Religions today, Eliade invariably emphasizes the phenomenological "side." Professor Eliade may state that the Historian of Religions "is attracted to both the *meaning* of a religious phenomenon and to its *history*; he tries to do justice to both and not to sacrifice either one of them."[10] Yet in most of his writings, Eliade seems to indicate that he will not attempt a detailed examination of historical differences, variations, disseminations, etc.; instead he will aim at a phenomenological analysis of the meaning of his data.[11] Eliade's position seems to be that the Historian of Religions only completes his or her task *as a phenomenologist*: "Ultimately, what we desire to know is the meaning of the various historical modifications..."[12]

In "The Sacred in the Secular World," Eliade begins by describing himself "as a historian and phenomenologist of religion" and claims that the Historian of Religions "is also a phenomenologist because of his concern with meaning." This meaning "is given in the intentionality of the structure."

So at some point the historian of religion [Historian of Religion] must become a phenomenologist of religion, because he tries to find meaning. Without hermeneutics, the history of religion [History of Religion] is just another history—bare facts, special classifications, and so on. With the problem of hermeneutics—meaning—we see that every manifestation of the sacred—symbol, myth, ritual—tells of something which is absolutely real, something which is meaningful for that culture, tribe, or religion in which the manifestation takes place. Once the historian of religion [Historian of Religion] takes on the search for meaning, he can, following the phenomenological principle of suspension of judgment, assume the structure of synchronicity, and, therefore, as I have said before, bring together the meanings evident in many different cultures and eras.[13]

The extent to which we can show that Mircea Eliade is a phenomenologist, that his approach can be related to the concerns and notions of philosophical phenomenology, will finally rest on an analysis of what he has done. In short, we must determine whether Eliade approaches the central task of hermeneutics, whether he interprets the meaning of the religious manifestations, on the basis of some phenomenological method.

Before elucidating Eliade's key methodological notions, let us recall from Chapter 3 that religion presupposes religious experience. Investigators begin with religious expressions and attempt to interpret the nature of the experiences expressed in their data. "The greatest claim to merit of the history of religions [History of Religions] is precisely its effort to decipher in a 'fact,' conditioned as it is by the historical moment and the cultural style of the epoch, the existential situation that made it possible."[14]

Over and over again, Eliade argues that the paramount concern of the Historian of Religions is hermeneutics. "For the ultimate goal of the historian of religions [Historian of Religions] is not to point out, that there exist a certain number of types of patterns of religious behavior, with their specific symbologies and theologies, but rather to *understand their meanings*... Ultimately, the historian of religions [Historian of Religions] cannot renounce hermeneutics."[15]

As we have seen on several occasions, Eliade believes that the History of Religions has tended to be cautious and inhibited; the task of interpretation has been left to the various "reductionist" approaches. Yet the "hermeneutical work ought to be done by the historian of religions [Historian of Religions] himself, for only he is prepared to understand and appreciate the semantic complexity of his documents."[16]

According to Eliade, the Historian of Religions "uses an empirical method of approach" and begins by collecting religious documents which need to be interpreted. Unlike Müller, Tylor, Frazer, and other early investigators, the modern scholar realizes that she or he works "exclusively with historical documents."[17] Consequently, Eliade's point of departure is the historical data which express the religious experiences of humanity. Through his phenomenological approach, Eliade attempts to decipher these data, to describe the religious phenomena which constitute the *Lebenswelt* of *homo religiosus* and to interpret their religious meaning.

We have asserted that Mircea Eliade collects *religious* documents which need to be interpreted, attempts to describe the *religious* phenomena, etc. But how does one know which documents to collect, which phenomena to describe and interpret? To answer these and similar questions, we need to introduce several methodological principles in terms of which Eliade can distinguish the religious manifestations.

... At this point, a brief digression may be useful in clarifying one of the main sources of misconceptions in interpreting Eliade's phenomenology: most interpreters do not endeavor to understand Mircea Eliade on his own grounds. We may cite an example from our above discussion: *homo religiosus* evaluates his or her natural existence as a "fall."

Many interpreters have seized upon Eliade's personal doctrine of a "fall" as being a pivotal notion in his thought. It is only because of Eliade's "theological assumptions" that he considers modern secularization to be a "fall."[18] Eliade is a "romantic" who believes that history is a "fall" and who "insists upon the reality of man's prefallen state."[19]

The problem with these interpretations is that Altizer and Hamilton do not take Eliade seriously enough on his own grounds. They are theologians and criticize Eliade's theological position on a "fall." But Eliade at least purports to be a Historian of Religions; his claim is not that Mircea Eliade is committed to these diverse themes of a "fall" but that *homo religiosus* has entertained such beliefs.

To give but one illustration, Eliade finds that "the paradisiac myths" all speak of a "paradisiac epoch" in which primordial beings enjoyed freedom, immortality, easy communication with the gods, etc. Unfortunately, they lost all of this because of "the fall"—the primordial event which caused the "rupture" of the sacred and the profane. These myths help *homo religiosus* to understand his or her present "fallen" existence and express a "nostalgia" for that "prefallen" Paradise.[20] If history is a "fall" for *homo religiosus*, it is because historical existence is seen as separated from and inferior to the "transhistorical" (absolute, eternal, transcendent) realm of the sacred.

...

We recall that Mircea Eliade's phenomenological *epochē* is directed against all forms of reductionism. By suspending all of his interpretations about what is "real," the phenomenologist attempts sympathetically to reenact the experiences of *homo religiosus* and to describe the meaning of the religious phenomena.

270

Such a "bracketing" by itself does not suffice to provide Eliade with insight into the fundamental structures and meanings of religious experience.[21] We saw that Franz Boas and other "specialists" insisted on cultural pluralism and relativity and were reluctant to allow for "common structures." Thus, a respect for the irreducibility of our data and an attempt to reenact the experience of the other might very well lead to the conclusion that there is an unlimited plurality of religious "life-worlds," each having structures highly individualized and varying according to time and place.

If we are to understand how Mircea Eliade attempts to gain insight into the essential meanings of religious experience, we must now elucidate the structuralistic nature of his phenomenological approach. We may begin by summarizing David Rasmussen's interpretation.

Rasmussen submits that Eliade makes "two claims" which allow the "transition" from "perceiving" the appearance of the sacred to understanding its meaning. First, Eliade "suggests that phenomena of sacred manifestation will tend toward archetype," and by "archetype" he means "the initial structure of the sacred" and not the "Jungian definition of archetype as the collective unconscious." Second, Eliade "suggests that phenomena of a given type or structure will tend toward system." The "initial structure tends toward a larger context of structural associations."[22]

It does not seem that Rasmussen is justified in this interpretation of "archetype" as "initial structure of the sacred." As we shall analyze in Chapter 7, Eliade is somewhat ambiguous, and there are two primary meanings of archetype found in his writings. In the "Preface" to *Cosmos and History*, Eliade defines "archetype" as "exemplary model" or "paradigm" and explicitly distinguishes this from the Jungian meaning. This is Eliade's main sense of archetype. However, in a few of his works, he uses the term in a manner quite similar to Jung's concept. As we shall see, this ambiguity is most significant, because each meaning of archetype has radically different methodological consequences for Eliade's phenomenology.[23]

Morphological analysis is Eliade's "hermeneutic alternative" to replace the "historical-evolutionary hypothesis" we have previously considered. Through morphological analysis and classification, he attempts "to separate those phenomena which have structural similarities from those which do not." Rasmussen turns to structural linguistics and cites the diachronic-synchronic distinction found in Ferdinand de Saussure's *Course in General Linguistics* as providing the "analogy which clarifies best a hermeneutic grounded in structuralism." He submits that "Eliade has asked the structural question regarding the place of a religious phenomenon within a total synchronic system. This leads to the basic judgment that religious phenomena tend toward system. This tendency is the intentional mode of every particular sacred manifestation. On this assumption morphological analysis is held to be necessary; its consequence is the transition from appearance to understanding."

Rasmussen concludes that Mircea Eliade has a distinctive "phenomenological procedure" which is grounded in structuralism: "Understanding does not occur by the reconstruction of a particular phenomenon, but rather by the reintegration of that phenomenon within its system of associations through the use of morphology and structuralism."[24]

Professor Rasmussen's interpretation of Eliade's methodology is basically correct, although initially it may not seem very convincing to some of Eliade's interpreters. What needs to be added and developed is the thesis that such a phenomenological approach has considerable support because of the very nature of religious phenomena, especially *religious symbolism*; such a procedure is not arbitrarily superimposed on the data but is largely derived from the nature of structural systems of religious symbols.

If Eliade finds this tendency toward system, toward systems of associations, this is primarily because of "the function of symbols": the "function of unification" of different zones and levels of experience, of enabling "isolated fragments" to "become part of a whole system." His morphological analysis reveals that "the various meanings of a symbol are linked together, interconnected in a system, as it were," and Eliade reserves the term "symbolism" for such a "structurally coherent ensemble."[25] What Eliade finds is that

> we are faced with, respectively, a sky symbolism, or a symbolism of earth, of vegetation, of sun, of space, of time, and so on. We have good cause to look upon these various symbolisms as autonomous "systems" in that they manifest more clearly, more fully, and with greater coherence what the hierophanies manifest in an individual, local and successive fashion. And I have tried, whenever the evidence in question allowed of it, to interpret a given hierophany in the light of its proper symbolism so as to discover its deepest significance.[26]

If understanding occurs when the phenomenon is "reintegrated" into "its systems of associations," this is possible because Mircea Eliade's hermeneutics is grounded in "autonomous," "coherent," "universal" systems of symbolic associations.

Various interpreters, such as Edmund Leach, have criticized Eliade for emphasizing the individual symbol and not the structural relations between symbols.[27] Eliade is certainly inconsistent on this matter. However, if one considers all of Eliade's writings, it becomes clear that what is most important in his phenomenological approach is not the particular symbol but the structure of the whole symbolism; that the phenomenologist cannot grasp the meaning of the specific symbol unless he or she sees the particular as one of many possible "valorizations" of the structural system.[28]

According to Eliade, the symbol arises as a "creation of the psyche," is constituted "as the result of existential tensions," and must be regarded as an "autonomous mode of cognition." "The phenomena of nature are freely transformed by the psyche" in "an autonomous act of creation" into symbols of the power and holiness they reveal to the beholder.[29]

Eliade's primary concern is with determining how religious symbols function and what they reveal. In this regard he makes the following crucial assertions: symbolic thought is an autonomous mode of cognition which has its own structure; symbols have their own "logic" and "fit together" to make up coherent structural systems; every coherent symbolism is universal; the symbolic system will preserve its structure regardless of whether it is understood by the person who uses it.[30]

...

It seems that Eliade has assembled a variety of religious manifestations dealing with snakes or serpents and has attempted to gain insight into the "invariant core" which constitutes their essential meaning. His approach, we would submit, is not unlike the phenomenological method of "free variation."[31] As we saw in Chapter 4, Eliade clearly rejects the phenomenological approach of the "early" Husserl, where one may speak of an "imaginative variation" and pure vision of the essential structure and meaning of a phenomenon, without the collection of historical examples and factual comparisons. Eliade is much closer to Merleau-Ponty and other existential phenomenologists, who in preparing for their eidetic reflection, seem to substitute for an imaginative variation an *actual variation* in the *historical data*.

Morphological analysis reveals that phenomena expressing snake or serpent symbolism in some contexts have structural similarities with phenomena expressing water symbolism, in some contexts with phenomena expressing phallic or erotic symbolism, in some contexts with phenomena expressing vegetation symbolism. There are various other types of religious phenomena which do not seem to share structural similarities with snake symbols and with which phenomena expressing snake symbolism are rarely associated.

Eliade now searches for the *invariant core*, the essential meaning which allows snake symbols to be related to and systematized with other religious symbols. In some cases, snake symbols have a phallic structure, but many other examples do not share this structure, and hence the essential structure of snake symbolism cannot be phallic. Through morphological analysis and variation of data, Eliade deciphers the essential meaning of snake symbolism as revealing inexhaustible life repeating itself rhythmically. And it is the moon as a sacred manifestation which is most able to reveal this profound religious meaning.

Thus, the invariant revealed by the diverse contexts of snake symbolism is seen in terms of a "web" of lunar associations. The religious intuition of the moon and its rhythms is at the "centre" of such a web and has "woven" a sort of system of interdependent lunar relations.

In some contexts, phenomenological understanding occurs when a particular snake phenomenon is reintegrated within its aquatic system or erotic system of symbolic associations. But for the most comprehensive and profound understanding, which involves the reintegration of the particular phenomenon expressing snake symbolism within its *total system* of symbolic associations, Eliade usually grounds his hermeneutics in the framework of a coherent, universal system of lunar symbols. It is in terms of such a structural totality that Eliade attempts to understand the various relationships among snake, water, vegetation, and fertility symbols and what such structural relationships reveal about the meaning of religious phenomena.

We do not intend to evaluate Eliade's specific analysis, since our aim has simply been to convey some general sense of Eliade's phenomenological approach as grounded in coherent systems of symbolic associations. To realize how intricate and complex this hermeneutical foundation is, consider the fact that we have formulated only a partial analysis of only one symbolic valorization—and not one of the major lunar valorizations, at that—of the total lunar symbolism.

The reader may now have some initial sense of Eliade's structuralist approach and may grasp the essential (lunar) structure, but he or she probably finds the snake-lunar relationship rather "forced." Indeed, the "modern" reader might find the interpretation more plausible if the lunar were analyzed as a "secondary center" of a more comprehensive erotic symbolism.[32] Witness the persistent sexual symbolism in recent literature, as seen in the frequent theme of the search for the "perfect" sexual orgasm as a self-transcending and liberating experience. Desacralized human beings seem much less likely to relate consciously to lunar or some other cosmic symbolism.

In all fairness to Eliade's specific analysis, we must recall his methodological principle: one must use a religious scale in order to interpret the meaning of religious phenomena. We know of the paramount importance cosmic phenomena have had in revealing the sacred to *homo religiosus*. It may be that on the plane of reference of the religious, and in terms of the dialectic of the sacred and other criteria we shall elucidate, that we shall be able to realize why a lunar symbolic structure would be much more relevant to the existential situation of *homo religiosus* than to the present situation of the nonreligious person.

In conveying some sense of Eliade's approach, we have suggested several methodological criteria, such as comprehensiveness and eidetic variation, which might serve to evaluate particular interpretations. In the next chapter, we shall analyze the phenomenological method for gaining insight into essential structures, free variation and induction, criteria for determining the essential structure or "center" of a symbolic system, and other methodological topics relevant to the above analysis.

Notes

1. We shall use "the dialectic of the sacred," "the dialectic of the sacred and the profane," and "the dialectic of hierophanies" interchangeably.
2. Thomas J. J. Altizer, *Mircea Eliade and the Dialectic of the Sacred*, 30, 36, 41, 84, and *passim*; and Altizer, "The Religious Meaning of Myth and Symbol," in *Truth, Myth and Symbol*, 97 and *passim*.
3. Altizer, *Mircea Eliade and the Dialectic of the Sacred*, 17. See "Myths for Moderns," *The Times Literary Supplement*, 3, 337 (February 10, 1966): 102.
4. In conversation, Eliade presented an interesting autobiographical explanation for his avoidance of a comprehensive methodological analysis. While in India, he began reading the literature in the History of Religions and was struck by a pervasive dilettantism. In order to avoid superficial, premature conclusions, he would pour himself into all the religious documents and not get involved in methodology. Nevertheless, such an explanation will not do. Methodology is not the kind of thing that one can postpone. Pouring oneself into the documents necessarily entails the adoption of some type of methodology. One of our primary tasks is to render explicit the methodological assumptions and principles which are often implicit in Eliade's phenomenology.
5. "Methodological Remarks in the Study of Religious Symbolism," 90, 91. Cited hereafter as "Methodological Remarks." In this volume, Chapter 25.
6. C. J. Bleeker, "The Future Task of the History of Religions," *Numen* 7, fasc. 3 (1960): 228. See Bleeker, "The Contribution of the Phenomenology of Religion," 39–40.
7. Ugo Bianchi, "The Definition of Religion," 26–29. A good illustration of this lack of identification of Eliade with the phenomenology of religion may be seen in *Religion, Culture and Methodology*, ed. T. P. van Baaren and H. J. W. Drijvers. Although these "Papers of the Groningen Working-group" repeatedly express their dissatisfaction with the phenomenology of religion, and a phenomenologist such as van der Leeuw is repeatedly cited for criticism, Eliade is not even listed in the index. See especially the articles by T. P. van Baaren (35–56), L. Leertouwer (79–98) and the Epilogue by H. J. W. Drijvers and L. Leertouwer (159–68).
8. Mircea Eliade, *Shamanism: Archaic Techniques of Ecstasy*, xv. Cited hereafter as *Shamanism*.
9. This is often classified as the position of the "early" Husserl. In "Phenomenologies and Psychologies," *Review of Existential Psychology and Psychiatry* 5/1 (1965): 80–105, Stephan Strasser points out that there are several types of phenomenology. Eliade's rejection of phenomenology is directed primarily at what Strasser labels "transcendental phenomenology."
10. "Methodological Remarks," 88. See Eliade, "Historical Events and Structural Meaning in Tension," 29–31 [below, 321–24].
11. For example, see *The Myth of the Eternal Return*, 73–74. In most of his books, Eliade refers us to more specialized works which treat these historical questions in greater detail. These historical approaches are meant to substantiate and complement his more phenomenological analysis.
12. "On Understanding Primitive Religions," 501. This is a crucial methodological contention in such articles as "History of Religions and a New Humanism," and "Crisis and Renewal in History of Religions," and in the methodological sections of most of Eliade's books.
13. Mircea Eliade, "The Sacred in the Secular World," 101, 103, 106–107 [above, 57–67].
14. "Methodological Remarks," 89. *The Sacred and the Profane*, 162: "The ultimate aim of the historian of religions [Historian of Religions] is to understand, and to make understandable to others, religious man's behavior and mental universe." [Cf. in this volume, 242–49.]

15. "Australian Religions, Part V," 267–68.

16. "Crisis and Renewal in the History of Religions," 9. On this same page, Eliade writes that "we do not doubt that the 'creative hermeneutics' will finally be recognized as the royal road of the History of Religions."

17. "Methodological Remarks," 88; "The Quest for the "Origins" of Religion," 169. See *The Myth of the Eternal Return*, 5–6; and *Patterns*, xiv-xvi; 2–3.

18. See Kenneth Hamilton, "*Homo Religiosus* and Historical Faith," *Journal of Bible and Religion* 33/3 (1965): 212, 214–16. The following discussion would also apply to Eliade's point that "from the Christian point of view" it could be said that modern nonreligion is equivalent to a new or second "fall." See *The Sacred and the Profane*, 213; "Archaic Myth and Historical Man," 35–36.

19. See Altizer, *Mircea Eliade and the Dialectic of the Sacred*, 84, 86, 88, 161; and Altizer, "Mircea Eliade and the Recovery of the Sacred." See Eliade, *Images and Symbols*, 173; *The Myth of the Eternal Return*, 162.

20. *Myths, Dreams and Mysteries*, 59ff.

21. Of course, in chapter 4, we did uncover certain essential religious structures. However, we must remember that Eliade could not possibly have arrived at those results if his methodology were based solely upon the hermeneutic principles previously elucidated. All of those methodological conclusions, including the very possibility of some sort of phenomenological *epochē*, only make sense when seen as functioning together with the additional hermeneutical principles and framework which we are about to formulate.

22. Rasmussen, "Mircea Eliade: Structural Hermeneutics and Philosophy," 141–42.

23. *Cosmos and History*, viii–ix. *Cosmos and History* is the same as *The Myth of the Eternal Return*, except for the addition of the "Preface to the Torchbook Edition." Interesting interpretations of Eliade's concept of archetypes include the previously cited "The Nature and Extent of Eliade's 'Jungianism,'" by Ricketts; Wilson M. Hudson, "Eliade's Contribution to the Study of Myth," in *Tire Shrinker to Dragster*, 237; Ira Progoff, "The Man Who Transforms Consciousness," *Eranos-Jahrbuch* 1966, Band 35 (1967): 126–30, 133. Progoff not only distinguishes Eliade's conception of archetypes from Jung's but also shows the similarity between Eliade's conception and Tillich's "Method of Correlation."

24. Rasmussen, "Mircea Eliade: Structural Hermeneutics and Philosophy," 143. Cf. the section entitled "synchronicity" (104–106) in Eliade's "The Sacred in the Secular World" [above, 57–67].

25. *Patterns*, 451–53; *Images and Symbols*, 163; "Methodological Remarks," 96.

26. *Patterns*, 449–50.

27. See Edmund Leach, "Sermons by a Man on a Ladder," *New York Review of Books*, October 20, 1966, 30–31. [In this volume, 278–86.]

28. Cf. *Images and Symbols*, 163–64: "But it is not by 'placing' a symbol in its own history that we can resolve the essential problem—namely, to know what is revealed to us, not by any 'particular version' of a symbol but by the *whole* of a symbolism." Eliade goes on to claim that the contradictions between particular versions of a symbol are usually "resolved as soon as we consider the symbolism as a whole and discern its structure."

29. *Images and Symbols*, 9, 177; "Methodological Remarks," 105; Luyster, "The Story of Myth: Two Approaches," 235.

30. For example, see *Patterns*, 450; *Images and Symbols*, 168.

31. The following methodological points will be discussed in greater detail in chapter 6.

32. Eliade would never maintain that all erotic symbolism constitutes a "secondary center" of a more comprehensive "web" of lunar symbolism. Erotic symbolism is itself extremely complex, and, as a revelation of sacred meaning, it is far more comprehensive than its nonreligious (physiological, etc.) domain of meaning would seem to suggest. Eliade's point, if we interpret him correctly, is that the particular erotic symbolic structure, as

illustrated by certain snake phenomena, constitutes a "secondary center" of a more inclusive lunar "web" of symbolic associations. Once again, this should indicate the complexity of Eliade's hermeneutical framework: not only has he formulated extremely complex (lunar, solar, aquatic) systems of symbolic structures, but he has found that these symbolic systems themselves interact and interpenetrate in numerous intricate ways.

29

SERMONS FROM A MAN ON A LADDER

Edmund Leach

Editor's Introduction

One of the earliest and the bitterest of the increasingly hostile criticisms of Eliade, Edmund Leach's review of Eliade's *The Two and the One*, also takes into account many other of Eliade's works so it cannot be accused of the partial reading that often hampers critics. There do, nonetheless, seem to be some fundamental misconceptions in Leach's critique. For example, his insistence" (*pace* Eliade) that there is no radical discontinuity between 'archaic' philosophy and that of modern man" comes despite the fact that Eliade insists precisely on the continuity of "archaic" and "modern" thought. In "Hierophany" (above, 89) Eliade states that "[r]ich and diverse as it is, the religious history of human life evidences no essential discontinuity." In *Myth and Reality* (above, 205), he says, "there was no break in the continuity between the archaic world and the modern world." Still, the most interesting feature of Leach's critique might be its representation of another apparent discontinuity—between the academic analysis of religion with its insistent lack of sympathy towards the perceived credulousness of a more sympathetic and therefore more apparently "theological" analysis. Leach's article appeared in the *New York Review of Books*, vol. VII (Oct. 20, 1966): 28–31. All rights reserved. Copyright © by the New York Review of Books. Reprinted by permission of the New York Review of Books.

෨ ෬

Merlin and his magic forest must be cut down to size before we can see the shape of the trees, but first let us examine the undergrowth. After graduating from the University of Bucharest in 1928 Mircea Eliade spent three years in Calcutta studying classical texts of Indian mysticism. His special concern was with the ascetic and ecstatic techniques whereby the would-be saint, having achieved a state of psychological dissociation, can persuade himself that he has access to the powers of the other world, being himself neither alive nor dead, neither on earth nor in heaven. All of Eliade's subsequent writings have been concerned with this central theme, the symbolic modes through which communication is established between the sacred and the profane. His attitude is that of a Jesuit: he is scholar and believer at the same time. Eliade left Romania at the end of the war and later settled in Paris; for the past ten years he has been Professor of the History of Religion in the University of Chicago. The "history" which he pursues is not concerned with chronological sequences or the analysis of the causes and consequences of particular events, but rather with the development of human thought over vast regions of time and space. But this evolution is a very simple two-stage affair: for Eliade modern man stands to archaic man as Christianity to pre-Christianity. The cosmological ideas which characterize archaic religion are everywhere the same and may be exemplified, in Frazerian fashion, by any snippets of exotic ethnography which conveniently come to hand. Modern man is unique because the religious mythology of Judeo-Christianity is set in a matrix of chronological time. Christian time is ongoing, it had a beginning and will have an end but it is non-repetitive, it is "historical." In all other religions, time is a cyclical process. Instead of advancing boldly towards the discovery of a New Jerusalem, archaic man is content to engage in recurrent but imperfect imitation of divinely ordained archetypes fashioned by the ancestral deities in the first beginning.

Eliade's diagnosis may be challenged on many different grounds: bad history—there has never been a radical discordance between Christian cosmology and cyclical notions of time; bad ethnography—it is not true that the cosmologies of "archaic" man always incorporate notions of cyclical time; bad method—comparative ethnography, in the style which Eliade employs, can only illustrate by example, it can never properly be used as a basis for generalization; bad psychology—Eliade takes for granted the Lévy-Bruhl fashions of his youth which assumed that ethnographic evidence reflects a pre-logical archaic mentality radically different from that of rational thought (Lévy-Bruhl himself abandoned this theory in his later years); confusion of terms—the most interesting parts of Eliade's writings become fogged by his failure to distinguish clearly between the content of a set of symbols and its structure. It is only fair to add that in the last chapter of his latest book, *Mephistopheles and the Androgyne*, Eliade shows himself sensitive to most of these criticisms and seems dimly aware that he may have been maintaining indefensible positions, but he makes no retraction, and so he must be judged.

Whatever may be the faults of method, it is easy to see why the thesis as such should appeal strongly to several kinds of anti-positivist. I observe that the translation of Eliade's larger works was sponsored by the Bollingen Foundation, always a stalwart patron of Jungian psychology; several others were originally prepared for the Jungian *Eranos* circle at Ascona; three books carry the imprint of the Catholic publishers Sheed and Ward; the laudatory comments quoted on the dust covers are consistently of Jungian or Catholic origin. One may suspect that harsh objectivity is not one of Eliade's outstanding virtues.

A difficulty of another kind is bibliographic and linguistic. Down to about 1938 most of Eliade's writings were published either in Romanian or bad French. They included studies of Asian alchemy (1935), Yoga (1938), and Babylonian cosmology (1937). Most of his current volumes appear to be revamped versions of these early works. Thus *The Forge and the Crucible*, English edition 1962, is essentially the same as the 1935 and 1937 Romanian items and although the author claims that "a number of chapters have been added and the whole work rewritten to bring it into line with the most recent view on the subject" it is still entirely naïve. Every methodological error of which Sir James Frazer and his contemporaries have ever been accused is here exhibited in its purest form. The translation factor introduces additional problems, sometimes of labyrinthine complexity: *Yoga*, published in New York and London in 1958, appeared in French in Paris in 1954; the latter version was a combination of two earlier French publications dated 1948 and 1936, this last being a translation from the Romanian of a work originally composed in English! All the books now available in English were originally composed in some other language and in quite a different order but even here the facts are preposterously difficult to disentangle. The Foreword to *Birth and Rebirth* says that it was published in 1958 and that it is a rewrite of lectures delivered in Chicago in 1956 which were first written out in French, but page 17 of *Mephistopheles* (1966) tells us that *Birth and Rebirth* was first published in 1961 and that it is a rehandling of *Naissances Mystiques* (Paris, 1959). As a final complication several extra titles have been thrown in just to improve the sales. *Cosmos and History* (1959) is the same book as *The Myth of the Eternal Return* (1954); *Rites and Symbols of Initiation* (1965) is the same as *Birth and Rebirth* (1958); *Mephistopheles and the Androgyne* (1966) appeared in England as *The Two and the One* (1965). The gentle art of selling the same pup twice is well established among academics, but is seldom manifested on quite this scale or in quite so glaring a fashion.

Since Eliade professes to be an expert on archaic modes of thought he necessarily relies very heavily on anthropological sources and his formidable bibliographies convey the impression of enormous erudition. But here again the proliferation of titles arouses a certain skepticism. A man who publishes a dozen books within fifteen years and appends over a thousand references to at least three of them is probably learned in only a rather superficial sense, but Eliade's long book lists at least indicate what he has *not* read and, in some cases this test is quite shattering. Eliade's basic thesis depends on the recognition that the metaphysical polarity represented by our words *sacred* and *profane* is tied up with an awareness of temporal alternation. Any secular (profane) period A1 can only be distinguished from its successor A2 if there is an intervening "sacred" period B. Likewise any transition of secular status (e.g., that from maiden to married woman) must be marked by an interval of sacred time in which the initiate (the bride) has no secular status at all. Or again, if there are territories which are distinguished there must be an intervening boundary zone which belongs to neither category. Through this polarization of time and space a certain homology is perceived between such oppositions as Summer and Winter, Life and Death, Child and Adult, Man and Nature, Earth and Heaven, and so on, and the transitions between one side and the other are constantly a matter of religious concern. Now this theme has received great attention from professional anthropologists for many years but all modern work is heavily indebted to three classic sources: Mauss (1906),[1] Hertz (1907),[2] Van Gennep (1909),[3] any one of which is far more illuminating than the whole corpus of Eliade's writings put together. But the odd thing is that Eliade ignores them. There are references to Van Gennep's work in the footnotes (but not in the text) of several works published since 1958; the other two items are not mentioned at all. Whatever may be the explanation for this silence it can do Eliade no credit. I am not suggesting that his erudition is wholly fake but that his knowledge of the history of anthropology must be abysmal. This is not a subject which can be understood by reading predigested textbooks and scrabbling through an index to find an appropriate reference. The latest theoretical doctrine of which Eliade shows any understanding is that of the Vienna school of diffusionist culture-history which flourished between 1905 and 1935; functionalism has passed him by and there is no indication that he has ever heard of Lévi-Strauss, who has often concerned himself closely with the kinds of fact which Eliade makes central to his analysis. The musty smell of antiquity is further exaggerated by the translation time-lag. His latest book (1966) has a chapter on Melanesian Cargo Cults but cites no evidence later than 1955. This topic is currently the focus of much lively discussion but Eliade's comments contribute nothing because all earlier work in this field has been made out of date by the glut of new material published during the past decade.

But perhaps this doesn't really matter. "In all Melanesian Cargo Cults," says Eliade, "the expectation of the catastrophe which will precede the Golden Age is marked by a series of actions expressing absolute detachment from ordinary values and behavior." Note the word "all." A writer who is prepared to generalize in this grandiose way is not going to be put out by a mere discordance of evidence or the lack of it. Eliade is a library scholar. What matters for him is that everything he says should be based on what someone else has put in a book. The printed word is authority enough and since there are enough oddities around to write almost everything, it is always quite easy to find "authoritative support" for one's own opinions. This again was Frazer's procedure. If Eliade writes:

> Recent researches have clearly brought out the "shamanic" elements in the religion of the Paleolithic hunters. Horst Kirchner has interpreted the celebrated relief at Lascaux as a representation of a shamanic trance [*Shamanism*, 503],

most readers will believe him simply because it fits the argument. They will be quite unimpressed by the pedant's comment that there are in fact no "reliefs" at Lascaux and that no one has the slightest idea why the paintings were made. Again, when Eliade tells us that:

> Heine Geldern has established a connection between the human sacrifices and skull hunts that are abundantly attested in Assam and Burma and a matriarchal ideology [*Yoga*, 300],

it suffices that he can cite a reference dated 1917. It is futile to point out that Heine Geldern himself had no evidence at all. The technique of citing authorities for everything has the advantage that Eliade is personally committed to no fixed opinion and on some topics he changes his position from book to book without ever saying so. For example in *Images and Symbols*, 23, he says of Robertson-Smith's totemic-communion theory of sacrifice (dated 1885) that it "no longer enjoys any credit among competent ethnologists and historians of religion," but in *The Sacred and the Profane*, 101–102, we meet the following:

> According to the myths of the earliest cultivators man became what he is today—mortal, sexualized and condemned to work—in consequence of a primordial murder....
>
> It is at this stage of Culture that we encounter ritual cannibalism. The cannibal's chief concern would seem to be essentially metaphysical, he must not forget what happened *in illo tempore*. Volhardt and Jensen have shown this very clearly; the killing and devouring of sows at festivals, eating the first fruits when tubers are harvested, are an eating of the divine body exactly as it is eaten at cannibal feasts.

No mention here of course of incompetent ethnologists or the un-creditworthy Robertson-Smith, nor even of the Christian Mass. Eliade's personal mysticism seems to give him a confidence hardly justified by his evidence. He proclaims the truth as an enlightened prophet speaking from a great height. Shamans do not need to be consistent.

But his exposition by citation greatly simplifies my problem—how to find a path through the dark forest. The weight of Eliade's "scholarship" is probably sufficient to overcome the uncertainty of all but the most obstinate Doubting Thomas, but much of it is just blarney. If we hack all this fat away the residue of hard argument is by no means bulky. What does it amount to?

Independently of George Dumezil and Ananda Coomaraswamy, two authors whom he now greatly admires, Eliade's firsthand exploration of Indian mysticism led him to appreciate the importance of notions of polarity. Sin and merit, ascetic inaction and ecstatic violence, this world and the otherworld, now and not-now, life and death, are not isolated categories which can be discussed and analyzed each by itself, but binary interdependent concepts like the *yin* and the *yang* of Chinese cosmogony. The paradox of religious thought and behavior everywhere is that the devotee, having first laboriously sorted out for himself the qualities which distinguish the time and space of things sacred from the time and space of things profane finds himself impelled to sew the two parts of the dichotomy together again. Man puts his heaven in the sky above, but then imagines a rope ladder linking earth and sky and tries to climb the ladder. The Yogin or the Shaman, as the case may be, is a specialist at such ladder climbing; he is the mediator between the powers of the other world and ordinary impotent men.

Eliade makes it all sound terribly complicated and splashes his pages with Sanskrit and theological Latin, but once the anthropological reader sees that the *coincidentia oppositorum* means no more than the synthesis of opposites, he is on familiar ground. As Lévi-Strauss and others have lately shown,[4] the "Hegelian" use of categories is extremely widespread among "primitive" peoples and is one of our principal justifications for insisting (*pace* Eliade) that there is no radical discontinuity between "archaic" philosophy and that of modern man.[5] The cosmological schema in question is not nearly so universal nor homogeneously consistent as Eliade makes out but the ethnographic illustrations which he has assembled are apt enough.

But the trouble with Eliade is that although he stresses his concern with the history of symbols, as distinct from the structure of symbolism, he does not really distinguish one from the other. As part of his Christian-Jungian faith he believes that particular symbols have archetypal and universal significance, so he gives us long essays on *the* meaning of The Cosmic Tree, of Mystical Light, of the symbolism of knots, and so on. Now it is quite true that the same symbols frequently crop up in entirely different religious contexts and that there is then an "historical" problem as to why this should be so. Does the similarity indicate diffusion from a common source, the recurrence of a universal archetype deeply buried in the human psyche, or just a common human aptitude for resorting to analogy? The answers in most cases are just any man's guess. On the other hand, because Eliade has recognized that religious symbols occur not singly but as binary pairs, he is really committed to an analysis of *structure*—not the history of particular symbols but the relations between them. But here he gets into a muddle. At the level of structural analysis his "archaic" system is fairly convincing. The basic religious distinction is between the here-now and the other. The other is the sacred. The here-now is the center of the universe and man constructs it in imitation of a prototype already existing in the other.

Man enters the here-now from the other at birth and returns to the other at death. Time is thus a cycle, an eternal return. For Eliade this "denial of history" is the essential characteristic of archaic thought. The time of secular experience (profane time) is cut up into periods by intervals of religious activity (sacred time) which typically take the form of initiations—dramatic performances which imitate the cyclical transition from life to death and death to life. The shaman is the expert who can control the events of secular time because he has one foot in each camp.

Many anthropologists would agree that this general pattern fits a great many sets of ethnographic data but it is the pattern as a whole, the structure, that fits. The symbols in themselves are of only passing interest. Thus, to take an elementary case: If the other world is distinguished from this world, then it must be in another place. The two worlds are separated by the sky, the sea, a river, a range of mountains—but they can then be joined by a ladder, a tall tree, a boat, a bridge, and so on. In this kind of analysis we attach importance to structural relations rather than to symbols as such; the ladder, the tree, the boat, the bridge are all "the same" because they do the same thing, they link the two worlds. But in Eliade's Jungian scheme it is the symbol *per se* that matters, so he tells us about trees and ladders as means of reaching the other world but never gets around to boats or bridges, or tunnels, or rocky cliffs, or heavenly fishing nets, or magic beanstalks, all of which things, and many others besides, can serve the same function in mythical syntax.

All in all, a comprehensive study of Eliade quickly reaches the limits of marginal utility. *The Myth of the Eternal Return* was the book that established his reputation for Anglo-American readers and it still seems the most worthwhile. Of the others, several are tidied-up essay collections which simply reiterate the same argument with variations in the ethnographic data. *Yoga* is a substantial and professional work but it is packed with technical Sanskrit jargon; *Shamanism* and *Patterns in Comparative Religion* are anthropologically out of date but, like their Frazerian prototypes, full of curious information. Blarney or no, the bibliographies and the footnotes may have their uses. But one theme recurs throughout:

> Archaic man acknowledges no act which has not been previously posited
> ... by someone else. What he does has been done before. His life is the
> ceaseless repetition of gestures initiated by others. [*The Myth of the
> Eternal Return*, 5]

It is a portrait of Eliade himself! Archaic indeed!

Notes

1. M. Mauss, "Les variations saisonnières des sociétés eskimos: Étude de morphologie sociale," *Année Sociologique*, IX (1906): 38–132.
2. R. Hertz, "Contribution à une étude sur la représentation collective de la mort," *Année Sociologique*, X (1907): 48–137.
3. A. Van Gennep, *Les Rites de passage* (Paris, 1909).
4. C. Lévi-Strauss, *La Pensée Sauvage* (Paris: Plon, 1962).
5. G. E. R. Lloyd, *Polarity and Analogy: Two Types of Argumentation in Early Greek Thought* (Cambridge, 1966).

30

ELIADE ON BUDDHISM

Richard Gombrich

Editor's Introduction

Although it concentrates on a single volume (Eliade's *Yoga: Immortality and Freedom*), Richard Gombrich's more studied and cautious criticisms of Eliade's textual and linguistic knowledge appears much more well-founded and less ideologically motivated than the preceding criticism by Edmund Leach. Gombrich reveals some significant failings in Eliade's expertise and in the bases of his analyses. To what extent this undermines the broader foundations and utility of Eliade's understanding of religious phenomena is not immediately conclusive. Published in *Religious Studies* 10 (1974): 225–31. All rights reserved. Copyright © 1974 by Cambridge University Press. Reprinted by permission of Cambridge University Press and the author.

☙ ❧

Mircea Eliade's book *Yoga: Immortality and Freedom* has deservedly become a classic, and has reached, as he intended, a far wider audience than the narrow circle of Indologists. The book's popularity may justify the following remarks. It was originally published in French in 1936, then in an enlarged French version in 1954, and in English translation in 1958. There has thus been ample opportunity for revision, and indeed in the second English edition (1969),[1] which we are taking as our text, Eliade notes (xi) that he has made "numerous minor corrections." However, the accuracy of his observations on early Buddhism still leaves much to be desired. Let us try to set the record straight.

We are principally concerned with chapter V, *Yoga Techniques in Buddhism*, and with three points in chapter VIII. Let us take the latter first. All of them concern the Buddha's alleged connections with shamanistic traditions. On p. 326 we read of the Buddha, "he is no sooner born than he takes seven steps and touches the summit of the world." Reference is given to *Majjhima-nikāya*, III, 123. But that text mentions only the seven steps; nothing about touching the summit of the world. Moreover, Lamotte has assembled[2] all fifteen classical versions of this legendary episode, and in none of them does the (future) Buddha touch the summit of the world. Actually this is unsurprising, because Buddhists do not believe the world to have a summit. Maybe the confusion arose through the word *aggo*: the Pali passage cited has the new-born Buddha say, "*Aggo 'ham asmi lokassa, seṭṭho 'ham asmi lokassa, jeṭṭho 'ham asmi lokassa…*" Lamotte's translation is of course correct: "Je suis le premier du monde, je suis le meilleur du monde, je suis l'aîné du monde;…" This correction makes it more than doubtful that the passage alludes to "the conception of the seven heavens," as Eliade claims lower on the same page; it certainly vitiates his statement that "the Buddha transcends the cosmos by symbolically traversing the seven heavens" (327), and disqualifies the passage from being later adduced as an example of "the symbolism of ascent" (335).

On p. 321 we read, "When the Buddha, after his Illumination, paid his first visit to his native city, Kapilavastu, he exhibited a number of miraculous 'attainments' … he rose into the air, cut his body to pieces, let his limbs and his head fall to the ground, then joined them together again before the spectators' wondering eyes. Even Aśvaghoṣa describes this miracle …" At this point there is a reference, the only one for the passage, to the *Buddhacarita*. "Even" should imply that other authors besides Aśvaghoṣa report the miracle. In his review of the 1958 French edition[3] Lamotte pointed out that neither Aśvaghoṣa nor any other text has the Buddha dismember himself; that was in 1956, but the mistake survives. The point is of some importance, because it is the only classical Indian reference given for the rope trick; if indeed there are no others, it affects the whole section on "Yoga and Shamanism" (318–26).

On p. 331 we read, "The *Majjhima-nikāya* (I, 244) speaks of the 'heat' obtained by holding the breath, and other Buddhist texts say that the Buddha is 'burning.' " This sentence implies that early Buddhist meditation, as typified by the Buddha, produced a sensation of heat. The reference to the *Majjhima-nikāya* is correct so far as it goes, but the passage is part of the Buddha's description of the *wrong* way in which he meditated before his Enlightenment; it is part of the mortification of the flesh which he rejects at the beginning of the First Sermon. For the "burning" Buddha, Eliade gives one reference: *Dhammapada* 387. This is an isolated verse, and reads:

Divā tapati ādicco; rattiṃ ābhāti candimā;
Sannaddho khattiyo tapati; jhāyi tapati brāhmaṇo;
Atha sabbam ahorattam Buddho tapati tejasā.

We accept Buddhadatta's translation:[4] "The sun glows by day; the moon shines by night. In war-array glows the warrior. In meditation glows the Brahman. By day and night glows the Buddha in His splendor." The verse does not seem to provide evidence that the Buddha exudes "magical heat" (the title of this section of the chapter) or that he can be associated with the "practices of 'magical sweating' and of creation through autothermy" as Eliade associates him in the next sentence.

The sum effect of our three objections is to remove all early (say, BC) references to anything which would associate the Buddha or early Buddhists with the shamanistic practices which Eliade is discussing in this chapter. (There remains the association with *iddhi*, super-normal powers, discussed in chapter V—on which see below.) In particular it removes all association between Buddhism and the rope trick, of which Eliade writes (323), "In this 'miracle' we can distinguish two separate shamanic elements: (1) the dismemberment (initiatory rite) and (2) the ascent to heaven." It appears that the Buddhist examples adduced for *both* these phenomena are invalid. We may further note that in his review[5] of the 1954 French edition the Tibetologist David Snellgrove denies any "immediate connection between the Indian rope trick and the Tibetan practice of *gcod*" (323–24), and questions Eliade's interpretation of Tibetan data on p. 325 and his statement that "Magical flight ascending to heaven by the help of a ladder or a rope are also frequent motifs, in Tibet" (329). If both Snellgrove and we are right, very little of this part of the chapter remains viable.

Chapter V contains some spelling mistakes (to begin with the least important points) which are surprising. The Pali word for "monk," *bhikkhu*, is misspelled eleven times in the chapter, *jhāyin* ("meditator") four times and *pīti* ('rapture') three. There are serious mistakes in the Pali which cannot be ascribed to misprinting or even to the shoddy editorial work which pervades much of the book; it is not mere pedantry to be upset when on p. 197 Eliade writes of "meditation 'without an object' (*nirmitta*)," because by confusing the word for a meditation object, *nimitta*, and the privative prefix *nir*, he has reversed the sense. As the linguistic mistakes cited, and others, have survived since the original (1936) version, one hopes that the proofs of the next edition will be read by someone who knows Sanskrit and Pali.

We come now to a series of points concerning the use of the *Sāmañña-phala-sutta* and related texts. The *Sāmañña-phala-sutta*, which Eliade himself quotes and refers to more than once, is the *locus classicus* for an extended account of the Buddhist's progress to Enlightenment via the four yogic meditational states called *jhāna*. Passages from it occur in many other texts,[6] sometimes with small verbal changes or additions to fit the context.

The descriptions of the four *jhāna* quoted from the *Poṭṭhapāda-sutta* on pp. 170–71 occur also, with the exception of a few essentially repetitious phrases, in the *Sāmañña-phala*, so there seems to be no reason to consider it "highly probable" that it was "in the *Poṭṭhapāda-sutta* (10ff.) that the technique of Buddhist meditation was formulated … for the first time" (169–70). Eliade's original reason for citing the *Poṭṭhapāda-sutta* may have been that it goes on to give some extra meditational stages beyond the four *jhāna* (another reason for thinking the text later than the *Sāmañña-phala*) which he proceeds to quote; but here too there is a small muddle, for at the top of page 173 he refers to "the ninth and last *samāpatti* [meditational attainment]" although in the text he has quoted there are only eight stages. It is other texts (see Pali Text Society dictionary s.vv. *samāpatti* and *vimokkha*) which have nine, by inserting as a penultimate stage the mental state of "neither consciousness nor unconsciousness"; these texts also slightly change the definition of the last (highest) *samāpatti*.

In the *Sāmañña-phala-sutta* the stages immediately following the fourth *jhāna* are: meditation on the constitution of one's physical body; the creation of a body "made of mind" (*manomaya*); and the acquisition of a set of supernormal powers (*iddhi*) of which the first is "having been one he becomes many" and vice versa, the next is the power of invisibility, and the rest are all locomotional—flying, etc. The sequence seems logical and important. These are followed by progressively more spiritual attainments, culminating in Enlightenment.

On p. 178 Eliade quotes the *iddhi* and some of the further powers from the *Sāmañña-phala*, and continues, "The same list of powers occurs in the *Akaṅkheya-sutta*; for each *iddhi*, a particular *jhāna* must be practiced" [*sic*]. He then quotes some *iddhi*. Two points here. Firstly, the list is indeed identical, but this fact is obscured by the use of a different translation. Secondly, the *Akaṅkheyya-sutta* (as it is known to its friends) nowhere indicates that different *jhāna* produce different powers, nor is this the case, for the texts show that all four *jhāna* are prerequisite for any of the powers. Thus this whole paragraph (178–79) becomes redundant.

On p. 165 Eliade quotes the passage about creating a body made of mind. (Again, it occurs in the *Sāmañña-phala,* but he cites another text.) His translation says that it has "transcendental faculties [*abhinindriyam*]" though this is only a dubious variant reading for *ahīnindriam*, "lacking no organ of perception" (see the P.T.S. dictionary s.v. *abhinindriyam*). Be that as it may, Eliade is assimilating this mind-made body to initiation symbolism, and Buddhist Enlightenment to mystical death and resurrection. At the bottom of the same page he writes, without reference or substantiation, "The importance of the guru as initiatory master is no less great in Buddhism than in any other Indian soteriology." So far as concerns pre-Tantric Buddhism, we emphatically disagree; early Buddhism was unusually exoteric, and in most strains of the Theravādin tradition to this day the importance of the guru has been radically de-emphasized, compared with other Indian traditions. Moreover, we have shown above that in the texts this mind-made body is created several stages before the meditator achieves Enlightenment, and in fact immediately precedes the acquisition of supernormal powers which seem to flow directly from it. One creates a mind-made body, and the very next thing one multiplies oneself. Now Eliade himself in a later passage, the long paragraph running from p. 179 to p. 180, very well shows that the Buddha devalued and even strongly disparaged the exercise of these *iddhi*. Again, we are all free to choose our own metaphors, but Buddhist symbolism regards the Enlightened person as "dead in life" rather than as reborn to a new life; Professor Zaehner tells us that the very title of the Buddha, Tathāgata, means "dead" in the *Mahābhārata*. Thus it becomes highly unlikely that this mind-made body is considered to have any soteriological value. At the beginning of the next section (167) Eliade compounds the muddle: "To obtain the state of the unconditioned—in other words to die completely to this profane, painful, illusory life and to be reborn (in another 'body'!) to the mystical life that will make it possible to attain *nirvāṇa*—the Buddha employs the traditional yogic techniques..." This at, least puts a gap between the mind-made body and Enlightenment; but "to attain the state of the unconditioned" *is* "to attain *nirvāṇa*"; it is not just an intermediate state which "makes it possible." In fact the Buddhist who attains *nirvāṇa* does so in his own body; he may on the way acquire the ability to create a double of himself, but both the texts and the living tradition make it clear that this is irrelevant to his salvation.

By quoting passages from the *Sāmañña-phala-sutta* out of sequence, mostly under other names, Eliade has performed a variant of the rope trick: plucking the dismembered pieces of the text out of the air, he has "before the spectators' wondering eyes" reconstituted them into something rich but strange.

A still more important point, germane to Eliade's whole thesis about yoga as a means to escape from time, concerns pp. 182–85. Eliade writes (183) that the Buddha "set a very high value on the ability to remember previous lives. This mystical ability made it possible to reach 'the beginning of time'—which, as we shall see in a moment, implied 'emerging from time.'" This last statement, on which depends the argument in the following two pages, is completely wrong: although the Buddha discouraged cosmological speculation, Buddhists certainly do not believe that time has a beginning. That their philosophy precludes such a possibility is well stated by von Glasenapp:[7] "Buddhism knows neither a first cause of the world, nor an all-embracing spiritual substance giving rise to all that is. It is rather that something comes into being in dependence on and conditioned by something else. A first beginning is as impossible as a definite end."

Eliade seems to arrive at his conclusion through failing to take seriously his own comment on the *Brahma-jāla-sutta*, that "The Buddha's refusal to discourse on the metaphysical consequences that might be drawn from one or another supra-normal experience is a part of his teaching" (181–82). In the same paragraph he goes on to talk of "the 'reality' whose beginning had been beyond the karmic cycle." In an attempt to prove that this is indeed how Buddhists conceived the matter, Eliade on p. 183 both misquotes and misinterprets the *Brahma-jāla-sutta*:

> Thus, for a beginning, let us recall that the Buddha attached great importance to *memory* as such; the gods lose their divine condition and fall from their heavens when "their memory is troubled." Even more: inability to remember *all* of one's former existences is equivalent to metaphysical ignorance ... [some of the gods alluded to] become able to remember their former existences, but not *all* of them, in other words, they do not remember the *beginning* of their series of lives.

Three points are subtly misquoted. Firstly, the word translated "memory," *sati*, can indeed have that meaning, but in the Pali canon usually refers to the present and means "self-awareness"; in the passage cited Rhys Davids translates it as "self-possession" and "self-control," which in the context seems correct. It is in this sense that the Buddha attached importance to *sati*. Secondly, the passage describes not "the gods" but a certain group of gods. Thirdly, what they come to remember is "their previous existence, but no further back." Individually these inaccuracies appear trivial, till we focus on the interpretation of the passage, given "in other words": the text carries absolutely no implication about the finitude, or even the length, of the series of lives. This particular passage merely says that some who say they had only one former life are being ridiculous; and the *sutta* as a whole says the same of all sorts of metaphysical views.

The series of one's former lives is infinite. Eliade quotes a Sanskrit scholastic text which says that "the Buddhas remember an unlimited number of *kalpas* [eons]" (184), and in the Pali tradition Buddhaghosa[8] says the same; but on the next page Eliade has the Buddha "declare that he alone had recognized all his former existences," which is not at all the same thing. Thus Eliade has given no evidence valid for Buddhism that "One arrives at the beginning of time and finds nontime" (185).

The last point to be made about Chapter V is comparatively minor, a question of emphasis. On p. 191 Eliade mentions the beginnings of *bhakti* (devotion) in Buddhism, and quotes a text: " 'All who have but faith in me and love for me, have heaven as their destiny.' " Taken out of context this statement may mislead. It is the last in a list of statements in which the Buddha pronounces on the soteriological value of certain attitudes and practices by saying what will happen to those who hold to them. All the other groups are said to be destined to attain *nirvāṇa*. In the context one should probably translate: "All who have nothing but faith in me ..." Buddhists regard all existence in heaven as temporary, and would probably deny that rebirth there had "soteriological value."

Taken singly, the above criticisms of chapter V may not appear momentous, taken together; however, they may cast doubt on the chapter's value as a contribution to our understanding of early Buddhism.

To conclude, let us venture a criticism which is necessarily more subjective but may also be of wider interest. Near the beginning of his chapter on Tantrism, Eliade hypothesises (201–202) that Tantrism represents "the spiritual counter-offensive of the original inhabitants" against Hinduism. The most important theme to emerge in the last part of chapter VIII and in chapter IX, "Conclusions," is a somewhat similar historical view of yoga as a whole. There is a certain fluctuation about the formulation of this more general thesis which makes it difficult to discuss it briefly without running the risk of misrepresenting Eliade's views. But the argument for the aboriginal origin of Tantrism seems unsatisfactory. Tantrism, we are told, first developed in certain northern border regions of India; possibly then also in the south—though the arguments here are tenuous. In any case it was in origin geographically marginal. Aboriginal inhabitants, on the other hand, we know to have been found in every major region of India. (Ethnographic precision is irrelevant at this level of the argument.) Moreover, Eliade himself shows in constructing his more general thesis that other aboriginal features of Indian religion, such as tree worship, and possibly including yogic meditation itself,[9] had appeared in Indian religion well back in the first millennium BC; he even adduces Kuiper's thesis about Austro-asiatic elements in the vocabulary and mythology of the Ṛg-veda. But if all this aboriginal religion has got into the earliest Indo-Aryan documents, why does the whole constellation of Tantrism leave no trace in those documents for two thousand years? We would deduce that Tantrism must have been born from the meeting of (known) Indian traditions with a foreign influence. Eliade writes (202): "We must also reckon with possible Gnostic influences, which could have reached India by way of Iran over the Northwest frontier." But in the previous sentence he has reminded us that "the 'tantric country' par excellence is Kāmarūpa, Assam." Does this not suggest that the seminal influence must have come from China and/or Tibet?[10]

We may speak of languages; we may speak of geographical areas. But we must be wary of speaking of "aboriginal," or for that matter of "Indo-Aryan" religion or spirituality. True, the Indian social system is predominantly endogamous in theory; but how many can have been the speakers of Indo-Aryan who reached the Punjab in the second millennium BC? And it is most unlikely that the discoverer of the Aryan eightfold path can be numbered among their genetic descendants.

Notes

1. Published by Routledge and Kegan Paul, London. The American publishers are the Bollingen Foundation, New York. The pagination of the main text is the same as in the first edition, and is very close to that of the 1954 French edition.
2. *Le Traité de la Grande Vertu de Sagesse de Nāgārjuna*, vol. I (Louvain, 1949), nn. 3–6. Eliade refers to this volume several times.
3. *Le Muséon*, LXIX, 1956, 218–21.
4. *Dhammapadaṃ*, ed. and trans. A. P. Buddhadatta Mahāthera (Colombo, n.d.), 104.
5. *Journal of the Royal Asiatic Society*, 1956, 252–54.
6. See especially T. W. Rhys Davids in the *Introduction* to his translation of the *Sāmañña-phala-sutta*, *Dialogues of the Buddha, Part I* (*Sacred Books of the Buddhists*, vol. II) (London, 1899), 59.
7. H. von Glasenapp, *Buddhism: A Non-theistic Religion*. English trans. (London, 1970), 50.
8. *Visuddhimagga*, XIII, 16.
9. But *vide contra* the review by Jean Filliozat, *Journal Asiatique* CCXLIII (1955): 368–70.
10. The probable influence of Taoism on Tantric yoga (and perhaps vice versa) has since been demonstrated by Jean Filliozat, "Taoisme et Yoga," *Journal Asiatique* CCLVII (1969): 41–87.

31

IN NOSTRO TEMPORE: ON MIRCEA ELIADE

R. J. Zwi Werblowsky

Editor's Introduction

Following from the critique of Richard Gombrich, R. J. Zwi Werblowsky also points out Eliade's lack of detailed philological expertise. Werblowski's claim that "Eliade is no philosopher and does not mean to be one," may show a reciprocal lack of expertise in Eliade's biography. *Religion* 19 (1989): 129–36. All rights reserved. Copyright © 1989 by Elsevier Ltd. Reprinted by permission of Elsevier Ltd.

80 03

The Editor of this volume[1] has expressed the wish that contributors would not produce a "Jubilee Volume" of the usual type, i.e. a collection of learned research papers. What he had in mind was a collection of essays dealing with the personality and work of Mircea Eliade rather than presenting the results of original scholarship. One could not help thinking of the French term for "Jubilee Volume"—*hommages à*. Clearly a homage to Eliade can do justice to its subject only by subjecting his work to critical reflection rather than starry-eyed admiration and hymns of praise. Such critical reflection is a special necessity for all those who (like the writer of these lines) feel bound to Eliade by ties of profound friendship but nevertheless have their problems with certain aspects of this method and "phenomenology." I hasten to add that the technical terms phenomenology and phenomenological do not occur with any frequency in the Eliadean corpus. Moreover, the present writer denies the existence and possibility of a "phenomenology of religion" *stricto sensu*. Nevertheless Eliade's method may be described as phenomenological (in a rather broad, imprecise and almost metaphorical sense), not least because of its explicit and programmatic anti-reductionism and—not unrelated to the latter—its commitment to the distinction between "explaining" and *Verstehen*. It need hardly be pointed out that the quest of "signification" or "sense" is anything but a monopoly of the phenomenological schools or of those tracing their pedigree to Dilthey or Simmel (although some self-appointed disciples of Eliade do not seem to be aware of this fact). Even a structuralist inspired by linguistics and very definitely hostile to any kind of *Geistewissenschaft* and phenomenology like Claude Lévi-Strauss could write *"l'analyse formelle pose immédiatement la question: sens."* Perhaps the whole problem can be expressed in the words that served as the title of a once very celebrated and widely read book on semantics: *The Meaning of Meaning*.

Eliade is a cultural phenomenon *in nostro tempore*, for the influence of his immense and massive work—massive not only in terms of its overwhelming quantitative power but also in its density, i.e. in the sense in which van der Leeuw used this epithet in connection with "myth"—extends beyond the confines of Religious Studies. You do not have to be a Marxist to know that quantity can, at a certain point, become quality. Some critics have said that when you have read two of Eliade's works you have read them all. But this is undoubtedly a half-truth, since it is precisely Eliade's astonishing productivity, comparable only to the equally astonishing breadth of his knowledge and reading, that accounts for the aforementioned massive power of this work. To this we should add another consideration. Eliade explicitly conceives of the study of religion as a decisive contribution to the contemporary cultural process *in nostro tempore*, its struggle with the modern-scientistic impoverishment of human existence and its efforts to regain an adequate spirituality. In other words, the study of religions should be a contribution towards a new humanism, as Eliade himself put it in the lead-essay to the first number of the journal *History of Religions* (1961) of which he was one of the founders. This desire of a "repristination" of dimensions of human existence that have been repressed by modernity and have sunk back, as it were, into the transpersonal unconscious (the similarities to the thinking of C. G. Jung and the Eranos circle, which extend to the concept of "archetype," much used in Eliade's earlier work but found by him independently of Jung, are obvious in spite of basic and important differences) render Eliade's work not only "tendentious" (in the best sense of the word) but also very problematic. At any rate, there is no doubt that Eliade's starting point is the historical situation of modern, western man *in nostro tempore*, i.e. the historicity of human existence. This renders Eliade's essentially non-historical or ahistorical method extremely paradoxical. The paradox is unwittingly illustrated by the use of the term History of Religion, and it is no accident that Eliade's *Traité d'Histoire des Religions* (cf. also his *The Quest: History and Meaning in Religion*, 1969) appeared in English under the more adequate title *Patterns in Comparative Religion*.

Needless to say, a History of Religions which starts from the historicity of human existence and yet is essentially ahistorical has its substantive as well as methodological problems. How "historical" is Eliade's concept of history? Here, Eliade's spiritual and religious background (including, in particular, Romanian Christianity) probably plays a significant, though as yet insufficiently explored, role. It is only this background which, it seems to me, can throw some light on his influential work on "The Myth of the Eternal Return," his ambiguous attitude towards history, as well as his yearning for eternity. Perhaps an analysis of this book could yield much for a better understanding of Eliade's *oeuvre* in general. Eliade is no philosopher and does not mean to be one. Yet he constantly moves at the margins of philosophy, sometimes to the detriment of his *religionswissenschaftliche* intentions. Hegel and other philosophers are amply quoted, but the important contributions of Oscar Cullmann (theology) and Karl Löwith (philosophy) regarding time-and-history are not even mentioned. Eliade's immense erudition which arouses in his readers a *sensus numinis* renders the lacunae, which are perhaps the symptoms of unconscious selectivity, even more striking. Thus, Eliade, like some others, makes much ado about cyclical renewal (including death and resurrection) as it was allegedly enacted on a mythological basis in the Babylonian New Year rites (the *akitu*). Eliade completely ignores the fact that the text VAT 9555, inadequately translated by Zimmern in 1918, and serving as a basis for all this theorizing, hardly permits this interpretation (as has been shown, e.g. by von Soden in *Zeitschrift für Assyriologie*, N.F. xvii, 1955). He also ignores the fact that the hypotheses regarding a ritual New Year's drama (including ritual fight, etc.) in the Temple of Jerusalem are, to put it mildly, more than dubious. But far more important than these finicky details (although scholars would do well to take to heart the dictum of Aby Warburg "it is in the details that God dwells") is the underlying general assumption. Many decades ago Jane Harrison had described every cultic act as being "pre-done" and "re-done" at the same time, i.e. not unique but corresponding to a timeless pattern, though she did not speak of archetypes or atemporal structures. If Jane Harrison is right, we should perhaps consider the possibility of the one, great foundational act *in illo tempore* being a secondary mythological reduction of precisely such a timeless pattern. Incidentally, this objection against Eliade was advanced long ago by Theodore H. Gaster.

More important and more weighty, however, in my opinion, are certain objections to Eliade's view of the cyclical rhythm of the "archaic" experience of the world as an attempt to escape the "terrors of history," whereas the linear concept of time allegedly faces them bravely. Perhaps the truth is the other way round: the linear conception of time is a pathetic attempt to mitigate the terror of history by viewing time as a sequence of meaningful and goal-directed events (with or without divine providence). The cyclical pattern can be something in which you are safely and securely held. But it can also be experienced as a total absence of meaning, a deadly and suffocating vicious circle of

> birth, copulation and death,
> birth, copulation and death,
> I'd be bored
> You'd be bored
> Birth, copulation and death
> (T. S. Eliot)

which you either encounter with a heroism bordering on nihilism (as Nietzsche well realized) or from which you are "saved" by the irruption of goal-directed, historical time. I do not wish to be misunderstood here as arguing in favor of the opposition linear-cyclical. I am leaving this question open. My sole purpose was to show how some of Eliade's theses that have become almost axiomatic commonplaces in much contemporary discourse are in reality highly questionable.

Eliade's humanism, i.e. his program of a recovery of buried levels of spirituality, of a broadening of our horizons to fit our present historical situation, and of transcending our cultural provincialism (meaning our western mentality), requires attention, or even a return, to the primordial depths of the "archaic" on the one hand and to the exotically alien (e.g. the high religions of Asia) on the other. This juxtaposition, too, is extremely dubious, as is illustrated by Eliade's masterly but nonetheless unsatisfactory attempt to combine yoga and shamanism. (Cf. the critical remarks of David Snellgrove in the *Journal of the Asiatic Society*, 1966, and Richard Gombrich in *Religious Studies*, 1975.) Eliade does not hesitate to juxtapose the spirituality of "Asia and the archaic world" or the experience of the "paleolithic hunter and the Buddhist monk," the *tertium comparationis* evidently being their presumed non-western, non-modern existential experience. One is reminded here of Gerardus van der Leeuw's preoccupation with, and his use of, the "primitive religions." Van der Leeuw chose this term not because of any occidental arrogance, but quite simply because he took his material from Lévy-Bruhl and from the accounts given of tribal religions by the ethnologists and anthropologists. (Chronologically van der Leeuw's anthropology ended with Malinowski.) Van der Leeuw never asserted that the structures described by Lévy-Bruhl subsequently vanished and disappeared; on the contrary they were permanent structures though they play a different role in the so-called higher cultures. Fortunately, van der Leeuw was not bothered in the least by the mischievous and supercilious criticism directed at Lévy-Bruhl by younger anthropologists who in fact were saying essentially the same (as Evans-Pritchard pointed out as early as 1934) only in a more modern and pretentious jargon. As C. G. Jung once put it to me, referring to the well-known "revocation" in the *Carnets*: "Lévy-Bruhl allowed himself to be terrorized by the violence of the criticisms leveled at him."

Eliade prefers "archaic" to "primitive," which means that in addition to ethnological and anthropological data he also resorts to prehistoric material viz. to the extremely dubious hypotheses and speculations emitted with regard to prehistoric religions. If van der Leeuw's use of "primitive religions" raised many questions, not least because of its implicit assumptions regarding developmental psychology, Eliade's invocation of the "archaic" experience, mentality and spirituality does so to an even greater degree. We are skating here on the very thin ice of pure speculation, especially as most contemporary scholars would reject as mistaken and illegitimate all comparisons between prehistoric cultures and contemporary societies "without writing" (the current favorite term replacing "primitive societies"). Hence also the name of the "International Association for Ethnological and Prehistoric Religions" provokes more amusement than puzzlement. We are probably safe in assuming that the reference is to religions that are mainly studied by ethnologists and anthropologists. You are then left free to ask whether scriptural religions, studied mainly on the basis of their sacred texts and theological literature, should be called "philological religions."

The use of the category of the "archaic" and its application to a variety of religious forms and symbols (*axis mundi*, cosmic trees, shamanist and rebirth symbols, and other Eliadean archetypes) has provoked much sharp and even vicious criticism. Whilst the sharp and nasty criticism (e.g. E. Leach) easily catches more attention and even panders to academic sensationalism—and, needless to say, almost automatically calls forth apologetic rejoinders from faithful disciples—the quiet and solid criticism of the kind exemplified by Gombrich's aforementioned article is far weightier. (Eliade himself, incidentally, never engages in polemics, and never allows adverse criticism and attacks to divert him from his creative work which he considers as his vocation.) To the general criticism should be added the *Ideologiekritik* to which every author is exposed who seeks the archaic, non-apollonian, primordial roots. One is reminded here of Thomas Mann's reaction to Bachofen: "nocturnal enthusiasm, a Joseph-Görres-complex of earth, people, nation, the past and death. ... a revolutionary obscurantism." Moreover, every liberal and "enlightened" type of rationalism, as well as every leftist or "progressive" ideology, dismisses authors of this kind as fascists or crypto-fascists, in addition to counting them among the propagandists of an irrational occultism and/or decadent mysticism. The case of C. G. Jung is a classic example. (I have dealt elsewhere with the question of C. G. Jung's antisemitism and his attitude to the Third Reich.) Eliade too has not been spared this kind of attack. His attitude to occultism can be easily studied by reading the relevant chapters in his *Occultism, Witchcraft and Cultural Fashions*, 1976. More troublesome are the accusations (without, it should be added, conclusive evidence) concerning his membership in the Iron Guard—the same Iron Guard that also plays such a significant background role in his novel *The Forbidden Forest*. But the lacunae in Eliade's deliberately fragmentary diary *Fragments d'un Journal* remain disconcerting. Especially students interested in Eliade's early activity in the circle of the literary and intellectual elite in the Bucharest of the thirties will be grievously disappointed, for everything bearing on the subject has been omitted.

Several years ago an M.A. thesis submitted to the University of Siena (*Ideologia e falsa coscienza in M. Eliade*) "proved," to the satisfaction of its Marxist author and *con estremo rigore filologico*, the *temi nazo-fascisti di Eliade*. Without taking up here the various biographical and ideological accusations, it should nevertheless be said that a personality of Eliade's stature, whose work possesses such cultural radiation, influence and weight, certainly deserves a serious intellectual biography which would also investigate his ideological, political and literary-publicistic development in the Bucharest of the thirties. This would require a study not only of Eliade's essays in various journals and magazines, but also the writings of the literary and political circles with which Eliade was engaged in the exchange of views, discussions and polemics.[2] These essays and articles are glaringly absent from Eliade-bibliographies, including *Mircea Eliade: A Bibliography* published on the occasion of an Eliade-Symposium held in 1979 by the Department of Religious Studies at the University of California at Santa Barbara. In view of the fact that there are students in the United States who are learning Romanian with the sole aim of doing research on Eliade, it is doubly puzzling that his early essays are nowhere mentioned. I know only very few of these articles since they cannot be found in Western libraries and it is extremely difficult to obtain photocopies from Romania. Nevertheless, the short bibliography which I have compiled and the few articles which I have read (most of them published in *Vremea* 1934) are extremely instructive in several respects. They certainly prove that Eliade was never anti-semitic. On the contrary, when it came to the Jews he did not hesitate publicly to oppose his revered master and guru, the arch-fascist ideologue Nae Ionescu, and to argue that the Jews could not possibly be a people cursed and damned by God. Of even greater interest is the fact that the Eliade of the early thirties still completely identifies with eastern (Byzantine) orthodoxy. Eliade's arguments are neither liberal nor humanist but theological. He argues (against Nae Ionescu and the popular tradition of Eastern Orthodoxy) that according to the teaching and theology of the Fathers—if properly understood—the Jews cannot simply be cursed indiscriminately, since such a doctrine would set a priori dogmatic limits to the unlimited freedom of divine Grace (sic!).

Mention has already been made of the fact that Eliade's work has become the subject of innumerable studies and dissertations, of rejection as well as of enthusiastic praise and admiration. Over twenty years ago Thomas J. Altizer published his *Mircea Eliade and the Dialectic of the Sacred* (1963), and the last years alone have seen a plethora of books (e.g. Ioan P. Culianu, *Mircea Eliade*, 1977; Gilford Dudley III, *Religion on Trial: Mircea Eliade and his Critics*, 1977; Adrian Marino, *L'Hermeneutique de Mircea Eliade*, 1980). Many of these publications help to illuminate another of the difficulties of doing justice to Eliade's work.

Eliade has many enthusiastic admirers but no "disciples" in the strict sense. This may be due to his introvert personality and to his moving humility which, considering the inexhaustible productivity of the man and the scope of this influence, appear incomprehensible. Unlike his predecessor in the History of Religions chair in Chicago, Joachim Wach, whose influence was due not so much to his writings as to his charisma as a teacher (Rainer Flasche has shown in his excellent monograph *Die Religionswissenschaft Joachim Wachs*, 1978, that Wach remained influenced, throughout his life, by his experiences as a youth in the circle of Stefan George with the high value that it attached to the master-disciple relationship), Eliade's influence is due to his literary output. But the critical evaluation of Eliade's work suffers, *in nostro tempore*, from an unavoidable weakness. I am referring here to the immense hiatus between Eliade's rich, almost highbred and overdeveloped central European origins and the abysmal ignorance and primitiveness of many of his disciples. I am emphasizing Eliade's central European origins because they impart a very special cachet to his cultural scope. The Romanian element perhaps deserves special emphasis: a "romance" culture surrounded by Slav and Balkan cultures, and, moreover, connected to the German and Austrian cultural heritage through its Habsburg history. Add to this the special relationship of Romania to French culture and we get a slight idea of the complexity of Eliade's background. If one of the aforementioned dissertations on Eliade is entitled *Religion on Trial* this can only mean that the well-meaning author, carried away by enthusiasm for the master, could not even distinguish between religion and the Eliadean type of study of religion. It is, after all, the latter and not "religion" that is being taken to court by Eliade's critics. In one publication about Eliade (who is responsible for the popularity of the expression *in illo tempore*) mention is made several times of *illus tempus* (sic), which invites depressing conclusions regarding the knowledge of Latin: not only among Eliade's students but also among the proofreaders of some university presses. One author quotes twice (first as a motto of his book, and then again by way of conclusion) the observation of "the philosopher Lakatos" to the effect that the owl of Athena was flying out at dusk only. Lakatos probably took it for granted that every student would know the origin of this aphorism, and hence did not bother to mention Hegel. Even in his worst nightmares Lakatos probably never envisaged a generation of PhDs that would ascribe this aphorism to him. *Sic in nostro tempore!* I may seem to be making much ado about nothing and wasting time on trifles, but these details, ridiculous as they are, are also symptomatic of the wide gulf separating Eliade's culture from that of a new generation of authors who not only claim to be Eliade's disciples and successors but who, as academic teachers, also arrogate to themselves the role of administrators of Eliade's legacy.

Having said this, we can perhaps put our finger on the central dilemma raised by Eliade's *oeuvre*. His critics may be right in details and even points of principle. But all this is more than counterbalanced by the value of the total work and by the wealth of perspectives which it opens. But precisely because only an Eliade can indulge with relative impunity in Eliadean *Religionswissenschaft*, those who try to do so without being Eliade are embarking on an undertaking that is doomed to failure. Fortunately, Eliade is an Eliade, and that is why he more than deserves the gratitude of all students of religion. The deep affection in which he and Christinel are held by all their friends should be mentioned here, for the good order as it were, but shall not be enlarged upon in a context in which emotional exhibitionism would be out of place.

Notes

1. The present essay originally appeared in German, in a jubilee volume dedicated to Mircea Eliade under the title *Die Mitte der Welt*, edited by Hans-Peter Duerr and published by Suhrkamp-Verlag in 1984. The English version should have been rewritten and edited so as to comply with the conventions of a scholarly journal. The author has nevertheless preferred not to tamper with the text and to preserve its original character of a contribution to a *Festschrift*.
2. Possibly the best available recent work is that of Florin Turcanu, although Ricketts' *Romanian Roots* is still very helpful in this respect. [ed.]

32

MIRCEA ELIADE: SOME THEORETICAL PROBLEMS

Ivan Strenski

Editor's Introduction

Ivan Strenski was one of the earliest critics in the English-speaking world to call Eliade's political background into question and to ponder Eliade's silence concerning his political activities in the inter-war period. However, in the current selection from 1973, it is Strenski's questioning of Eliade's attitude towards history that is most significant. Once again, Strenski was earliest to raise the criticism that Eliade operated independently of appropriate historical criteria. This is a criticism that can only be met with a complete and detailed analysis of Eliade's attitude to and understanding of history and so this selection ends Part III of this volume on Eliade's methodology. Part IV concentrates on more specific problems and themes of Eliade's thought, beginning with this specific problem of history. Strenski's article appeared in *The Theory of Myth: Six Studies*, edited by Adrian Cunningham (London: Sheed and Ward, 1973), 40–52. All rights reserved. Copyright © 1973 by Sheed and Ward. Reprinted by permission of Continuum International Publishers.

80 03

I. Introduction

The purpose of this paper is to analyze critically the notion of "myth" as it occurs in the thought of Mircea Eliade. Because the study of myth is subsumed in Professor Eliade's study of religions, it will be necessary first to explain how the general methodology of Eliade's peculiar approach to the study of religions hangs together, before we can fully appreciate the character of his concept of myth.

There is a curious lack of interest among philosophers of religion who count themselves broadly within the tradition of recent Anglo-American philosophy in the methodological problems of the study of religion and mythology. With the recent burst of popularity which the work of Claude Lévi-Strauss has enjoyed—especially since the publication of the third and final volume of his *Mythologiques: L'Origine des manières de table*, the lack of critical study and interest in the methodology of the study of myths is unlikely to continue for long. Indeed, it is part of this paper's task to do such a job on Eliade's theory of myth. It is less likely, however, that the methodological problems of the study of religions will begin to attract serious critical attention by Anglo-American philosophers of religion. Why should this be so?

Part of the explanation certainly is to be found in a kind of cultural parochialism among philosophers of religion too long insulated from the wider sweep of religious issues that arise when one begins to break down the equations between Christianity or monotheism and religion. When one begins to see religion within a world perspective, one sees not so much religion any more, but religions. This suggests the further insight that religion must be seen as a cultural phenomenon composed of various factors—"dimensions" as Ninian Smart calls them (*The Yogi and the Devotee*, London, 1968, ch. 2), which also in turn may be considered as subjects of philosophic investigation. Thus philosophers of religion might examine religious myth, ritual, experience and so on, as well as the issues arising in the comparison of religions or dimensions of different religions. In all this, the philosopher of religion will need to rely on the history, phenomenology and comparative study of religion—of whose various methodological presuppositions he will want to become aware.

If, as we argue, part of the reason why the methodological issues of the study of religions remain neglected is the cultural narrowness of Anglo-American philosophers of religion, the other half of the blame lies with the failure of the historians of religion to advocate theories with firm analytic backing. Unlike the study of myths, which can claim a Lévi-Strauss, the study of religion, since Rudolf Otto anyway, can claim no one of comparable stature—although Eliade is often referred to as such. It is perhaps symptomatic of the intellectual malaise of the study of religions that Eliade is so highly regarded, for, as we want to show, his methodological prescriptions are disastrous for the study of religion. As perhaps the chief—and certainly the most popular—theoretical spokesman for the study of religion, Eliade is disappointing and evasive. In practice, his work is often useful and interesting; *Yoga: Immortality and Freedom*, for instance, is regarded as a definitive work on Indian Yogic methods by Smart (*Doctrine and Argument in Indian Philosophy*, 243) and Zaehner (*Hinduism*, 197), but Eliade's general methodological views on the study of religion and myth leave much to be desired, vitiated as they are by loose thinking and an anti-scientific approach. Thus though the philosopher of religion may want to know about Eliade's theoretical views, it may only be in order to be aware of their corrosive effect upon the materials Eliade presents—in order to separate facts from Eliade's fictions.

Within the past few years, Professor Eliade has made urgent calls (e.g. in "Methodological Remarks on Religious Symbolism," "The History of Religions and a New Humanism," "Crisis and Renewal in the History of Religions," for the adoption of his particular way of studying religion as a "meta-psychoanalysis" (*Images and Symbols*, 35ff.) and a "creative hermeneutic" ("Crisis and Renewal," 27). Along with our main aim of analyzing Professor Eliade's notions of myth and the study of religion, we want indirectly also to reject Eliade's appeal to take up his style of doing history of religions. We want to show, by our critique of Eliade's understanding of myth and the study of religion, why Eliade's history of religions does not deserve the respect which religious scholars have accorded it. In doing so we want to indicate that, contrary to Professor Eliade's gloomy predictions, the study of religions has a bright and hopeful future largely because it will have set aside Professor Eliade's wayward prescriptions.

II. Eliade and the Study of Religion: Against History

First, then, let us try to understand the nature of Professor Eliade's history of religions, followed by an account of his notion of myth. In outline, his history of religions has the following pattern. Though the conclusions apply to historical situations, for both theoretical and practical reasons historical accounts of religious phenomena are acutely unsatisfactory. What is more, empirical falsification of the claims of the history of religions is ruled out. Religious phenomena transcend historical explanation because they are constituted by certain mysterious non-temporal determinants. Although support for his view may be found by considering the often amazing originality, influence and universal similarity of religious experience and its products, Eliade permits no similar evidence to count against his assertions. For Eliade, the supposedly self-authenticating and incorrigible intuitions of the depth-psychologist confirm him in his disdain for the empirical-historical method of investigating religion. Depth-psychology lays bare the determinants of religious experience: both ontologically timeless and constitutive of religious experiences and phenomena, and chronologically prior in their existence to all religious experiences and phenomena. By proclaiming these determinants of religious phenomena, which are also necessary religious truths, to modern man, Eliade believes that the history of religions will be instrumental in reviving modern religious life.

"History of religions," the title Professor Eliade gives to his brand of religious studies, would lead us to suppose that discipline to have a necessary connection with history and the cultural sciences—to the explanatory narrative account of human thought and action. Eliade's avowals of the empirical character of his program and the masses of documents he cites in his studies would also lead us to believe that the history of religions will be measured by the principles and standards of accuracy normal in empirical studies. Eliade says that "the historian of religions in the strictest sense can never renounce his concern with the historically concrete" (*The Two and the One*, 191) and "religious documents are at the same time *historical* documents; they form an integral part of various cultural contexts. In fact each document has a particular significance, relative to the culture and historical moment from which it has been detached" (196).

But, though Eliade does pledge his work's allegiance to history, it is often to a history whose reputation has been slurred: a "history" deprived of plenary explanatory power, either because it is merely an account which is "near chronicle" or apparently because it excludes the intentional aspect of human existence. When Professor Eliade reduces the historian's task to one which "is merely to piece together an event or a series of events" (*Patterns*, 5) he reduces history to something like a chronicle, to a sense perception, and thus bases part of his subsequent assault on the value of history to the history of religions upon an uninteresting sense of "history." If anything, history proper does not begin until the chronicle stage is superseded by an attempt to knit together these elements. Secondly, history proper does not exclude some vital feature from its account, such as human intentions, and therefore "history" proper is not disqualified from explanation because it allegedly neglects some constituent "interior" dimension of human existence as Eliade implies that it does (*Images and Symbols*, 32ff.). Despite Eliade's objections, historical explanations are not therefore disqualified from giving an explanation of, a meaning to, any given human phenomenon. History is not all positivist history any more than history is all chronicle. Thus the dichotomy implied in Eliade's claim that the history of religions "is attracted to both the *meaning* of a religious phenomenon and its *history*" ("Methodological Remarks," 88) is a false one. It is Eliade's practice of using and criticizing "history" in these impoverished senses that thus far gives his support for the historical aspect of the history of religions such a dubious character.

But Professor Eliade also seems to recognize a plenary, explanatory, or meaning-giving sense of history, which the history of religions will accept in order to get at (in a mysterious way) some "higher" trans-historical meanings and explanations. Implying an understanding of history as a limited source of meanings for religious matters—as an explanation-giving discipline of very limited value—Eliade says:

> I am not denying the importance of history ... for the estimate of the true value of this or that symbol *as it was understood and lived in a specific culture...* But it is not by "placing" a symbol in its own history that we can resolve the essential problem—namely, to know what is revealed to us, not by any "particular version" of a symbol, but by the *whole* of a symbolism. (*Images and Symbols*, 163)

Moreover these higher meanings seem to "condition" or "make possible" logically, chronologically and somehow ontologically (*The Eternal Return*, 34–35) the meanings of symbols or myths which history proper gives us. Eliade brings this out by using a favorite example—the Cosmic Tree and its supposed higher meaning, "the perpetual regeneration of the world":

> It is *because* [ontological and/or logical] the Cosmic Tree symbolizes the mystery of a World in perpetual regeneration that it can symbolize— simultaneously or successively—the pillar of the Universe and the cradle of humankind ... Each of these *new* connotations is made *possible because* the symbolism of the Cosmic Tree was revealed *from the beginning* [logical, chronological, and ontological] as a "cipher" of the World under-stood as a living, sacred and inexhaustible reality. (*The Two and the One*, 198; Strenski's emphasis and bracketed annotations.)

Therefore the history of religions cannot remain satisfied with the history of its religious object as a (1) chronicle, (2) positivist history, or (unhappily) (3) a plenary history. The historian of religions is interested in matters of "secret messages" ("The History of Religions and a New Humanism," 5), "higher" (*The Two and the One*, 210), "deeper" (*Shamanism*, xiii), "trans-historical" (*Shamanism*, xvi), "primary" (*The Two and the One*, 198), "original" (*ibid.*, 197) and, finally, necessary or constitutive meanings of the meanings given by plenary history. A chronicle may relate an historical origin of an historical "*x*"; it tells us precious little about the meaning of that "*x*" in the society. A positivist history may give a meaning of our "*x*," but its meaning is impoverished. A plenary history gives meanings both "internal" and "external" but falls short of the higher, transcendent, "prehistoric" meanings which condition the lower or historical meanings.

But it is not only because Eliade believes that the history of religions is a kind of super-"science" and, therefore, because of logical reasons seeks the necessary laws of religious constitution, that he seems to reject history. After all, some kinds of scientific history strive to uncover necessary laws of history. It is Eliade's *belief* that religion is not a phenomenon which is susceptible to historical explanation. Any valid explanation of religion requires, to Eliade's mind, the assumption of the reality of the activity of the sacred (and therefore, for Eliade, the non-temporal or eternal) in the midst of the historically explainable sphere of existence. The historical-empirical explanations of religion are deficient because they do not assume the truth of religion by assuming the existence of its object.

> What distinguishes the historian of religion from the historian … is that he is dealing with facts which, although historical, reveal a behavior that goes far beyond the historical involvement of the human being. Although it is true that man is always found "in situation," his situation is not, for all that, always a historical one in the sense of being conditioned solely by the contemporaneous historical moment. (*Images and Symbols*, 32–33)

Eliade makes these points with respect to the symbol of the Cosmic Tree:

> it may be hoped that one day the history of the symbolism of the Cosmic Tree may be plotted, the center of origin having been ascertained, the channels of diffusion and the different values which this symbolism took on in course of its wanderings may all be traced.
>
> If practicable, a historical monograph of this kind would be of great service to the history of religions. But the problem of the symbolism of the Cosmic Tree would not be solved all the same. Quite another work would remain to be done: to establish the meaning of this symbol, what it *reveals*, what it shows in its quality as a religious symbol. (*The Two and the One*, 196–97)

Added to the notion that the "higher" meanings sought by the historian of religions are not historical truths and therefore that history is, in principle, irrelevant to their discovery, Eliade subverts an historical approach to "higher" religious truths sought by an historian of religion by denying that there are *in principle* historical truths; in practice the historical documents are so fragmentary and corrupt that none but the most tentative conjectures about the nature of religion could be made (*Patterns*, 5). Eliade thinks that practical obstacles to an empirical approach to a study of religion are so insuperable that the only alternative seems to be a kind of nonscientific study of religion. Ironically, the practical drawbacks that have tempered the speculations of generations of religious scholars now prove an encouragement to Eliade's projects.

We may be dismayed by Eliade's maneuverings, by his interpreting these problems of method in such artificial ways. We would be well advised, however, to prepare for more of the same. Not to be out-done by the denigration of an historical approach to the study of religion on theoretical and practical grounds, Eliade deals the historical and inductive part of the history of religions the fatal blow: the history of religions not only seeks explanations which are logically *a priori* to historical ones, it seeks those which somehow can be given chronologically priority as well.

the religious historian faces a bolder task than the historian, whose job is merely to piece together an event or a series of events with the aid of the few bits of evidence that are preserved to him; the religious historian must trace not only the *history* of a given hierophany, but must first of all understand and explain the modality of the sacred that that hierophany discloses. (*Patterns*, 5)

Making mild apologies for the confusions of the past regarding the apparently substantial and prior relation of history to the history of religions, Eliade says:

In short, we have neglected this essential fact: that in the title of the "history of religions" the accent ought not to be on the word *history* but upon the word *religions*. For although there are numerous ways of practicing *history* ... there is only one way of approaching *religion*— namely, to deal with religious facts. Before making the *history* of anything, one must have a proper understanding of what it is, in and for itself. (*Images and Symbols*, 29)

It is not only *as if* the history of religions merely believes that it discovers the necessary laws of religion, but that these laws can be arrived at before the appropriate research is begun. It is as if the historian of religions has "privileged access" to the general truths of religion in a way similar to the way in which one may be said to have privileged access to one's own mind. It is as if, once possessed, this introspectively-detected information allowed one to make assertions about religion with the same force that one makes certain statements about one's own mind. Since the datum of religion is open to our intellectual gaze in the way in which our minds are, and since religion is also a matter with which others are involved, we may be said, in a sense, to know what certain contents of the minds of others are, in advance of our meetings with these "other minds." Because Eliade believes his account of the general truths of religion are necessary ones about the way men look at the world, all that we need to know is that someone is a man in order to know what his general view of the world is and *must* be. If there were in our possession some necessary laws of human perception we should be able to know *a priori* (prior in time to our meeting "all" men) that all men see the world as these necessary laws dictate. Similarly, the history of religions, if it claims to yield such necessary laws of religious perception, would enable us to make certain particular judgments about the religious perception of other individuals which could be made prior in time to our meeting or study of these others. If one discovers a necessary truth of religion and if religion exists in some particular time and place with which one has had no acquaintance—certainly not close acquaintance— one should be able to dispense with empirical investigation of that time and place. Such a rationalistic faith is evidenced in Eliade's saying: "if this dialogue with non-European spiritual traditions leads us to rediscover certain neglected sources of our own spiritual heritage, what is the point of going so far afield and interrogating Indians, Africans, and Oceanians?" (*Myths, Dreams and Mysteries*, 245).

Here Eliade realizes that he can discover the necessary truths of religious meaning without recourse to the social and historical sciences—in this case, ethnology. He implies that he can come by the same truths in either way, with or without ethnology: a fantastic discovery if it be so! His only reason for withdrawal from a full admission of this "fact" is a theoretically irrelevant one: "our own historic moment obliges us to understand the non-European cultures and engage in conversation with their authentic representatives" (*Myths, Dreams and Mysteries*, 245). His only reason for not admitting the theoretical consequences of the independence of the history of religions from the social and historical sciences seems to be the desire to avoid the chorus of criticism such an admission would rain down on his theory. As it is, he avoids the admission only to preserve a certain appearance of humility. Usually, however, the ordinary scientist is nowhere so sure that the laws which he advances are absolutes. The scientist is always willing to revise his theory against empirical evidence, by which it was first supported. But Eliade has cut off his theory from the possibility of revision. His necessary truths of religion are incorrigible because he believes the means of acquiring them are, as we shall see, infallible sources of knowledge.

Therefore those statements giving the impression that the history of religions is an inductive study, which grounds its conclusions on historical fact, are rendered nugatory. This history of religions is either inconsistent on this matter or it stands in *a priori* relation to historical religious texts both logically and chronologically. We do not come to know what religion is, what myths or symbols mean, through history. We invert the process because we know *a priori* what religion is and what myths and symbols mean. Rather than mediating *a posteriori* with the social scientists and historians, the history of religions may dictate to each of these what religion is and what the various aspects of religion, myths, symbols, etc., most profoundly mean.

We may detect in this phase of Professor Eliade's own methodological argument that he is reaching for a method to study religion which does justice to the alleged "autonomy" of religion and the history of religions. In this there is Eliade's endeavor to ensure the highest logical necessity and priority for the truths produced by the history of religions, along with the view that these are truths involving true, original and creative experiences.

We do not dispute the laudability of these aims. We do, however, take exception to Eliade's interpretation of them, for that interpretation, in turn, determines the nature of his solutions, and must be criticized unfavorably. (1) The "autonomies" of religion and the study of religion are interpreted in a way which makes religion not only irreducible to any other feature of culture, and the study of religion the province of no other discipline, but makes religion *independent* of culture and its study independent of cultural and historical disciplines. (2) The *a priori* truths which the history of religions hopes to produce are not only said to have a logical priority to the corresponding historical truths which they ground; they are given a chronological priority as well. It is not as if we discover these truths—explanations, for instance, of the meanings of certain myths or symbols—by inductive means, beginning with statistical generalizations which become more and more refined until we perceive that they are necessary truths of our subject; it is that somehow we can be said to be able to produce these truths before the research has begun. Afterwards we may notice their confirmation from time to time in historical materials, but falsification from those materials seems ruled out. (3) Eliade interprets the originality and influence of religious experience and its products as evidence of their truth and non-historical ontological status.

Part IV

PROBLEMS AND THEMES IN ELIADE'S THOUGHT

History and Historicism

33

THE TERROR OF HISTORY

Mircea Eliade

Editor's Introduction

Eliade's attitude to history is one of the most crucial components of his thought and much has been written about it. Restrictions of length preclude reprinting all of the excellent commentaries that have been written, and I refer the reader particularly to Seymour Cain's "Mircea Eliade: Attitudes Towards History," and to Douglas Allen's "Eliade and History."

The "Terror of History" is one of Eliade's signal phrases. It includes all personal tragedy as well as dreadful current events on the world stage. Eliade would have been quick to point out the urge, apparently irresistible to some, to ascribe such events to divine judgments. How one's understanding of cosmic realities allows one to tolerate such misfortune is one of Eliade's primary criteria of the assessment of religion. From *Cosmos and History: The Myth of the Eternal Return* by Mircea Eliade, 141–51 (Princeton: Princeton University Press, 1954). All rights reserved. Copyright © 1954 by Bollingen. Reprinted by permission of Princeton University Press.

ℵ ℶ

Survival of the Myth of Eternal Return

It would be necessary to confront "historical man" (modern man), who consciously and voluntarily creates history, with the man of the traditional civilizations, who had a negative attitude toward history. Whether he abolishes it periodically, whether he devaluates it by perpetually finding transhistorical models and archetypes for it, whether, finally, he gives it a metahistorical meaning (cyclical theory, eschatological significations, and so on), the man of the traditional civilizations accorded the historical event no value in itself; in other words, he did not regard it as a specific category of his own mode of existence. Now, to compare these two types of humanity implies an analysis of all the modern "historicisms," and such an analysis, to be really useful, would carry us too far from the principal theme of this study. We are nevertheless forced to touch upon the problem of man as consciously and voluntarily historical, because the modern world is, at the present moment, not entirely converted to historicism; we are even witnessing a conflict between the two views: the archaic conception, which we should designate as archetypal and anhistorical; and the modern, post-Hegelian conception, which seeks to be historical. We shall confine ourselves to examining only one aspect of the problem, but an important aspect: the solutions offered by the historicistic view to enable modern man to tolerate the increasingly powerful pressure of contemporary history.

The foregoing chapters have abundantly illustrated the way in which men of the traditional civilizations tolerated history. The reader will remember that they defended themselves against it, either by periodically abolishing it through repetition of the cosmogony and a periodic regeneration of time or by giving historical events a metahistorical meaning, a meaning that was not only consoling but was above all coherent, that is, capable of being fitted into a well-consolidated system in which the cosmos and man's existence had each its *raison d'être*. We must add that this traditional conception of a defense against history, this way of tolerating historical events, continued to prevail in the world down to a time very close to our own; and that it still continues to console the agricultural (= traditional) societies of Europe, which obstinately adhere to an anhistorical position and are, by that fact, exposed to the violent attacks of all revolutionary ideologies. The Christianity of the popular European strata never succeeded in abolishing either the theory of the archetype (which transformed a historical personage into an exemplary hero and a historical event into a mythical category) or the cyclical and astral theories (according to which history was justified, and the sufferings provoked by it assumed an eschatological meaning). Thus—to give only a few examples—the barbarian invaders of the High Middle Ages were assimilated to the Biblical archetype Gog and Magog and thus received an ontological status and an eschatological function. A few centuries later, Christians were to regard Genghis Khan as a new David, destined to accomplish the prophecies of Ezekiel. Thus interpreted, the sufferings and catastrophes provoked by the appearance of the barbarians on the medieval historical horizon were "tolerated" by the same process that, some thousands of years earlier, had made it possible to tolerate the terrors of history in the ancient East. It is such justifications of historical catastrophes that today still make life possible for tens of millions of men, who continue to recognize, in the unremitting pressure of events, signs of the divine will or of an astral fatality.

If we turn to the other traditional conception—that of cyclical time and the periodic regeneration of history, whether or not it involves the myth of eternal repetition—we find that, although the earliest Christian writers began by violently opposing it, it nevertheless in the end made its way into Christian philosophy. We must remind ourselves that, for Christianity, time is real because it has a meaning—the Redemption.

> A straight line traces the course of humanity from initial Fall to final Redemption. And the meaning of this history is unique, because the Incarnation is a unique fact. Indeed, as Chapter 9 of the Epistle to the Hebrews and 1 Peter 3:18 emphasize, Christ died for our sins once only, once for all (*hapax, ephapax, semel*); it is not an event subject to repetition, which can be reproduced several times (*pollakis*). The development of history is thus governed and oriented by a unique fact, a fact that stands entirely alone. Consequently the destiny of all mankind, together with the individual destiny of each one of us,—are both likewise played out once, once for all, in a concrete and irreplaceable time which is that of history and life.[1]

It is this linear conception of time and history, which, already outlined in the second century by St. Irenaeus of Lyon, will be taken up again by St. Basil and St. Gregory and be finally elaborated by St. Augustine.

But despite the reaction of the orthodox Fathers, the theories of cycles and of astral influences on human destiny and historical events were accepted, at least in part, by other Fathers and ecclesiastical writers, such as Clement of Alexandria, Minucius Felix, Arnobius, and Theodoret. The conflict between these two fundamental conceptions of time and history continued into the seventeenth century. We cannot even consider recapitulating the admirable analyses made by Pierre Duhem and Lynn Thorndike, and resumed and completed by Pitirim Sorokin.[2] We must remind the reader that, at the height of the Middle Ages, cyclical and astral theories begin to dominate historiological and eschatological speculation. Already popular in the twelfth century,[3] they undergo systematic elaboration in the next, especially after the appearance of translations from Arabic writers.[4] Increasingly precise correlations are attempted between the cosmic and the geographical factors involved and the respective periodicities (in the direction already indicated by Ptolemy, in the second century of our era, in his *Tetrabiblos*). An Albertus Magnus, a St. Thomas, a Roger Bacon, a Dante (*Convivio*, II, Ch. 14), and many others believe that the cycles and periodicities of the world's history are governed by the influence of the stars, whether this influence obeys the will of God and is his instrument in history or whether—a hypothesis that gains increasing adherence—it is regarded as a force immanent in the cosmos.[5] In short, to adopt Sorokin's formulation, the Middle Ages are dominated by the eschatological conception (in its two essential moments: the creation and the end of the world), complemented by the theory of cyclic undulation that explains the periodic return of events. This twofold dogma dominates speculation down to the seventeenth century, although, at the same time, a theory of the linear progress of history begins to assert itself. In the Middle Ages, the germs of this theory can be recognized in the writings of Albertus Magnus and St. Thomas; but it is with the *Eternal Gospel* of Joachim of Floris that it appears in all its coherence, as an integral element of a magnificent eschatology of history, the most significant contribution of Christianity in this field since St. Augustine's. Joachim of Floris divides the history of the world into three great epochs, successively inspired and dominated by a different person of the Trinity: Father, Son, Holy Ghost. In the Calabrian abbot's vision, each of these epochs reveals, in history, a new dimension of the divinity and, by this fact, allows humanity to perfect itself progressively until finally, in the last phase—inspired by the Holy Ghost—it arrives at absolute spiritual freedom.[6]

But, as we said, the tendency which gains increasing adherence is that of an immanentization of the cyclical theory. Side by side with voluminous astrological treatises, the considerations of scientific astronomy assert themselves. So it is that in the theories of Tycho Brahe, Kepler, Cardano, Giordano Bruno, or Campanella, the cyclical ideology survives beside the new conception of linear progress professed, for example, by a Francis Bacon or a Pascal. From the seventeenth century on, Leninism and the progressivistic conception of history assert themselves more and more, inaugurating faith in an infinite progress, a faith already proclaimed by Leibniz, predominant in the century of "enlightenment," and popularized in the nineteenth century by the triumph of the ideas of the evolutionists. We must wait until our own century to see the beginnings of certain new reactions against this historical linearism and a certain revival of interest in the theory of cycles;[7] so it is that, in political economy, we are witnessing the rehabilitation of the notions of cycle, fluctuation, periodic oscillation; that in philosophy the myth of eternal return is revivified by Nietzsche; or that, in the philosophy of history, a Spengler or a Toynbee concern themselves with the problem of periodicity.[8]

In connection with this rehabilitation of cyclical conceptions, Sorokin rightly observes[9] that present theories concerning the death of the universe do not exclude the hypothesis of the creation of a new universe, somewhat after the fashion of the Great Year in Greco-Oriental speculation or of the yuga cycle in the thought of India. Basically, it may be said that it is only in the cyclical theories of modern times that the meaning of the archaic myth of eternal repetition realizes its full implications. For the medieval cyclical theories confined themselves to justifying the periodicity of events by giving them an integral place in the rhythms of the cosmos and the fatalities of the stars. They thereby also implicitly affirmed the cyclical repetition of the events of history, even when this repetition was not regarded as continuing *ad infinitum*. Even more: by the fact that historical events depended upon cycles and astral situations, they became intelligible and even foreseeable, since they thus acquired a transcendent *model*; the wars, famines, and wretchedness provoked by contemporary history were at most only the repetition of an archetype, itself determined by the stars and by celestial norms from which the divine will was not always absent. As at the close of antiquity, these new expressions of the myth of eternal return were above all appreciated among the intellectual elites and especially consoled those who directly suffered the pressure of history. The peasant masses, in antiquity as in modern times, took less interest in cyclical and astral formulas; indeed, they found their consolation and support in the concept of archetypes and repetition, a concept that they "lived" less on the plane of the cosmos and the stars than on the mythico-historical level (transforming, for example, historical personages into exemplary heroes, historical events into mythical categories, and so on, in accordance with the dialectic [of the Sacred and the Profane, above 46–47, 89, 96–102].

The Difficulties of Historicism

The reappearance of cyclical theories in contemporary thought is pregnant with meaning. Incompetent as we are to pass judgment upon their validity, we shall confine ourselves to observing that the formulation, in modern terms, of an archaic myth betrays at least the desire to find a meaning and a transhistorical justification for historical events. Thus we find ourselves once again in the pre-Hegelian position, the validity of the "historicistic" solutions, from Hegel to Marx, being implicitly called into question. From Hegel on, every effort is directed toward saving and conferring value on the historical event as such, the event in itself and for itself. In his study of the German Constitution, Hegel wrote that if we recognize that things are necessarily as they are, that is, that they are not arbitrary and not the result of chance, we shall at the same time recognize that they *must* be as they are. A century later, the concept of historical necessity will enjoy a more and more triumphant practical application: in fact, all the cruelties, aberrations, and tragedies of history have been, and still are, justified by the necessities of the "historical moment." Probably Hegel did not intend to go so far. But since he had resolved to reconcile himself with his own historical moment, he was obliged to see in every event the will of the Universal Spirit. This is why he considered "reading the morning papers a sort of realistic benediction of the morning." For him, only daily contact with events could orient man's conduct in his relations with the world and with God.

How could Hegel know what was *necessary* in history, what, consequently, must occur exactly as it had occurred? Hegel believed that he knew what the Universal Spirit wanted. We shall not insist upon the audacity of this thesis, which, after all, abolishes precisely what Hegel wanted to save in history—human freedom. But there is an aspect of Hegel's philosophy of history that interests us because it still preserves something of the Judaeo-Christian conception: for Hegel, the historical event was the manifestation of the Universal Spirit. Now, it is possible to discern a parallel between Hegel's philosophy of history and the theology of history of the Hebrew prophets: for the latter, as for Hegel, an event is irreversible and valid in itself inasmuch as it is a new manifestation of the will of God—a proposition really revolutionary, we should remind ourselves, from the viewpoint of traditional societies dominated by the eternal repetition of archetypes. Thus, in Hegel's view, the destiny of a people still preserved a transhistorical significance, because all history revealed a new and more perfect manifestation of the Universal Spirit. But with Marx, history cast off all transcendental significance; it was no longer anything more than the epiphany of the class struggle. To what extent could such a theory justify historical sufferings? For the answer, we have but to turn to the pathetic resistance of a Belinsky or a Dostoevski, for example, who asked themselves how, from the viewpoint of the Hegelian and Marxian dialectic, it was possible to redeem all the dramas of oppression, the collective sufferings, deportations, humiliations, and massacres that fill universal history.

Yet Marxism preserves a meaning to history. For Marxism, events are not a succession of arbitrary accidents; they exhibit a coherent structure and, above all, they lead to a definite end—final elimination of the terror of history, "salvation." Thus, at the end of the Marxist philosophy of history, lies the age of gold of the archaic eschatologies. In this sense it is correct to say not only that Marx "brought Hegel's philosophy back to earth" but also that he reconfirmed, upon an exclusively human level, the value of the primitive myth of the age of gold, with the difference that he puts the age of gold only at the end of history, instead of putting it at the beginning too. Here, for the militant Marxist, lies the secret of the remedy for the terror of history: just as the contemporaries of a "dark age" consoled themselves for their increasing sufferings by the thought that the aggravation of evil hastens final deliverance, so the militant Marxist of our day reads, in the drama provoked by the pressure of history, a necessary evil, the premonitory symptom of the approaching victory that will put an end forever to all historical "evil."

The terror of history becomes more and more intolerable from the viewpoints afforded by the various historicistic philosophies. For in them, of course, every historical event finds its full and only meaning in its realization alone. We need not here enter into the theoretical difficulties of historicism, which already troubled Rickert, Troeltsch, Dilthey, and Simmel, and which the recent efforts of Croce, of Karl Mannheim, or of Ortega y Gasset have but partially overcome.[10] This essay does not require us to discuss either the philosophical value of historicism as such or the possibility of establishing a "philosophy of history" that should definitely transcend relativism. Dilthey himself, at the age of seventy, recognized that "the relativity of all human concepts is the last word of the historical vision of the world." In vain did he proclaim an *allgemeine Lebenserfahrung* as the final means of transcending this relativity. In vain did Meinecke invoke "examination of conscience" as a transsubjective experience capable of transcending the relativity of historical life. Heidegger had gone to the trouble of showing that the historicity of human existence forbids all hope of transcending time and history.

For our purpose, only one question concerns us: How can the "terror of history" be tolerated from the viewpoint of historicism? Justification of a historical event by the simple fact that it is a historical event, in other words, by the simple fact that it "happened that way," will not go far toward freeing humanity from the terror that the event inspires. Be it understood that we are not here concerned with the problem of evil, which, from whatever angle it be viewed, remains a philosophical and religious problem; we are concerned with the problem of history as history, of the "evil" that is bound up not with man's condition but with his behavior toward others. We should wish to know, for example, how it would be possible to tolerate, and to justify, the sufferings and annihilation of so many peoples who suffer and are annihilated for the simple reason that their geographical situation sets them in the pathway of history; that they are neighbors of empires in a state of permanent expansion. How to justify, for example, the fact that south-eastern Europe had to suffer for centuries—and hence to renounce any impulse toward a higher historical existence, toward spiritual creation on the universal plane—for the sole reason that it happened to be on the road of the Asiatic invaders and later the neighbor of the Ottoman Empire? And in our day, when historical pressure no longer allows any escape, how can man tolerate the catastrophes and horrors of history—from collective deportations and massacres to atomic bombings—if beyond them he can glimpse no sign, no transhistorical meaning; if they are only the blind play of economic, social, or political forces, or, even worse, only the result of the "liberties" that a minority takes and exercises directly on the stage of universal history?

We know how, in the past, humanity has been able to endure the sufferings we have enumerated: they were regarded as a punishment inflicted by God, the syndrome of the decline of the "age," and so on. And it was possible to accept them precisely because they had a metahistorical meaning, because, for the greater part of mankind, still clinging to the traditional viewpoint, history did not have, and could not have, value in itself.

Notes

1. Henri-Charles Puech, "Gnosis and Time," in *Man and Time*, ed. Henri Corbin (Princeton, NJ: Princeton University Press, 1957), 48ff. Cf. also the same author's "Temps, histoire et mythes dans le christianisme des premiers siècles," *Proceedings of the VIIth Congress for the History of Religion*, 33–52.

2. Pierre Duhem, *Le Système du monde* (Paris: A. Hermann, 1913–59); Lynn Thorndike, *A History of Magic and Experimental Science* (New York: Macmillan, 1923–58); Pitirim A. Sorokin, *Social and Cultural Dynamics, II* (New York: American Book Co., 1937–).

3. Thorndike, 1, 455ff.; Sorokin, 371.

4. Duhem, V, 223ff.

5. Duhem, 225ff.; Thorndike, II, 267ff., 416ff., etc.; Sorokin, 371.

6. It was a real tragedy for the Western world that Joachim of Floris' prophetico-eschatological speculations, though they inspired and fertilized the thought of a St. Francis of Assisi, of a Dante, and of a Savonarola, so quickly sank into oblivion, the Calabrian monk surviving only as a name to which could be attaches a multitude of apocryphal writings. The immanence of spiritual freedom, not only in respect to dogma but also in respect to society (a freedom that Joachim conceives as a necessity of both divine and historical dialectics), was again professed, at a later period, by the ideologies of the Reformation and the Renaissance, but in entirely different terms and in accordance with different spiritual views.

7. Sorokin, 379ff.

8. Cf. A. Rey, *Le Retour éternel et la philosophie de la physique* (Paris, 1927); Pitirim A. Sorokin, *Contemporary Sociological Theories* (New York, 1928), 728–41; Arnold J. Toynbee, *A Study of History* III (London, 1934); Ellsworth Huntington, *Mainsprings of Civilization* (New York, 1945), especially 453ff.; Jean Claude Antoine, "L'Éternel Retour de l'histoire deviendra-t-il objet de science?", *Critique* (Paris), XXVII (Aug., 1948), 723ff.

9. Sorokin, 383 n. 80.

10. Let us say, first of all, that the terms "historism" or "historicism" cover many different and antagonistic philosophical currents and orientations. It is enough to recall Dilthey's vitalistic relativism, Croce's *storicismo*, Gentile's *attualismo*, and Ortega's "historical reason" to realize the multiplicity of philosophical valuations accorded to history during the first half of the twentieth century. For Croce's present position, see his *La storia come pensiero e come azione* (Bari, 1938; 7th rev. ed., 1965). Also J. Ortega y Gasset, *Historia como sistema* (Madrid, 1941); Karl Mannheim, *Ideology and Utopia,* trans. Louis Wirth and Edward Shils (New York, 1936). On the problem of history, see also Pedro Lain Entralgo, *Medicina e historia* (Madrid, 1941); and Karl Lowith, *Meaning in History* (Chicago, 1949).

34

HISTORICAL EVENTS AND STRUCTURAL MEANING IN TENSION

Mircea Eliade

Editor's Introduction

This important short excerpt give some flavor of Eliade's understanding of the role of the historian of religions vis-à-vis other specialists in the field and vis-à-vis historians in general. Particularly noteworthy is his conclusion that "1) *All* the phases of the human past are, fundamentally, inaccessible to a *total* and *certain* understanding. 2) On the other hand, there is not a single expression of a human life which is absolutely sealed to our understanding." From Mircea Eliade, "Historical Events and Structural Meaning in Tension," *Criterion* (a publication of the University of Chicago Divinity School) 6/1 (winter 1967): 29–31. All rights reserved. Copyright © 1967. Reprinted by permission of *Criterion*.

ॐ ૱

So far as I know, no historian of religions has attempted to write ... a monograph [on "Primitive religions"]. All of our books on primitive religions, from Tylor to Lowie, Radin and Adolph E. Jensen, are products of anthropologists and ethnologists. It has been taken for granted that the study and understanding of primitive religions is exclusively a job for specialists in the field.

But in writing on *all* the forms of "primitive" religions, the anthropologist is bound to transgress his discipline and to accept or propose a general theory on the "origin, function, and meaning" of religion. Now, I think that only a historian of religions can face such problems with some chance of success. I do not see how one can speak of the "origin, function, and meaning" of rituals, myths, or High Gods without being familiar—besides the "primitive" documents—with, let us say, the *Brahmanas*, the *Enuma elish* and the pantheons of the Ancient Near East, India, and Greece. In some cases, the "meaning" of a religious structure is more correctly grasped in a higher religion than in a rather elementary (or regressive) "primitive" culture. Moreover, I am inclined to think that a historian of religions is better equipped than an anthropologist to understand the religious creations of preliterate cultures.

Of course, these endeavors raise a number of methodological problems—and perhaps their great interest resides in this fact. For some time already, but even more so in the last decade, the discipline of history of religions has found itself in a crisis. Many contributing factors have helped precipitate and prolong this crisis; I do not intend to discuss them now (cf. "Crisis and Renewal" in *The Quest*, ch. 4). One problem is of a methodological order: Is history of religions an autonomous discipline, or ought it be considered as one among the other "maid-servants" of historiography as, for instance, numismatics, archeology, philology, epigraphy, etc.? In other words, do religions constitute a specific type of historical reality, or are they to be understood as a "projection" of psychological, socio-economic or political factors? Is the historian of religions entitled to search for *structures*—or is he condemned to study exclusively *historical events*?

One can recognize in these methodological confrontations the opposition between "historicists" and "phenomenologists" or "structuralists." Linguists, of course, found an answer when Ferdinand de Saussure convinced them that language must be studied *both* synchronically and diachronically, i.e., both as structure and as historical phenomenon. But for the historian of religion the problem is more complex—first of all because not all scholars recognize the autonomy of the religious experience. The psychologist approaches religion as a psychological reality, the sociologist regards it as a social fact and the anthropologist considers it to be one among other cultural creations of a human group. Though he does not question all these "conditionings," the historian of religion does not consider them final; he thinks that there is also an irreducible reality, the experience of the sacred, recognizable under the psychological, social, and cultural expressions. But historians of religions do not agree among themselves even apropos of the nature of this experience. For some of them, the "sacred" as such is a historical phenomenon, i.e., it is the result of specific human experiences in specific historical situations. Others, on the contrary, leave open the question of "origins"; for them the experience of the sacred is *irreducible*, in the sense that, through such an experience, man becomes aware of his specific mode of being in the world and consequently assumes responsibilities which cannot be explained in psychological or socio-economic terms.

I have no intention of pursuing these remarks on the present crisis in history of religions here. I have discussed this as well as some related problems in a series of articles which I hope to bring together in a forthcoming book [*The Quest*]. But I do not believe in the efficacy of purely methodological debates. I think that a method must be judged from its practical results. Let us take, for example, the problem of *data*. In studying the "high religions" the historian disposes of a considerable number of written documents. But there are also purely archeological data, religious documents brought to life primarily by excavations of the past hundred years. (And in some instances these archeological documents reveal a religious life which could not have been suspected from the religious documents—as, for example, the Greek fertility cults and cult of the dead, completely ignored by Homer and innumerable other authors presenting the Olympian ereligion.) Finally there is another vast category of religious data: oral traditions, popular rituals and beliefs, and all the immense material known as "folklore." How far, and under what conditions, is the historian of religions entitled to use the archeological and the oral or folkloric documents? A purely theoretical discussion might go on forever. Only a certain number of "experiments in method" will permit us to judge whether or not the enterprise is valid and its results are significant.

This is one of the reasons why I have chosen to study a religious tradition for which we have very few texts, some archeological remains, and an extremely rich religious "folklore." I refer namely to the religious life of the Dacians, the Daco-Romans, and their descendants the Romanians. I have of course chosen this particular subject because, as a native of that part of Europe, I know its languages and I understand the religious horizon of its people. But I think that such "experiments in method" can be undertaken in other areas: for instance, in Tibet, in China, in Southeast Asia, etc.—that is to say in any area where we have few texts, some archeological remains and a rather rich popular religion. (I am speaking of course of the *beginnings* and the protohistory of religions in Tibet, China, and Southeast Asia, not of the later, historical stages.) I have already written and published a few chapters of this book, which I have entitled *From Zalmoxis to Ghengis Khan,* and I am fascinated by the experiment, notwithstanding all its frustrations.

In the last analysis, the main problem is the same as in the study of prehistoric and archaic religions. Granted that absolutely every creation of the human mind is *by its very nature* comprehensible to another mind (and especially after Freud it is difficult to refute such a premise), what hermeneutical tools have we to use in order to decipher a religious universe whose values and meanings are not only camouflaged in unfamiliar images and symbols, but are accessible only in a fragmentary or mutilated form? Presented in these terms, the question seems almost hopeless. But we must keep two things in mind. 1) *All* the phases of the human past are, fundamentally, inaccessible to a *total* and *certain* understanding. 2) On the other hand, there is not a single expression of a human life which is absolutely sealed to our understanding (not even the language or the designs of a mentally disturbed person, the gestures of a child, or the tools and etchings of a paleolithic man). This is not only an epistemological truth; it is a fact of the human condition as such—it is part of human destiny. Man is *bound* to understand other men—though he knows that even in those nearest to him something remains impenetrable. The more difficult, strange, and "irrecognizable" a human life or human mind may be, the more strongly the urge to decipher it is felt— though there are times when even the most familiar milieu seems, to each of us, enigmatic and incomprehensible.

A historian of religion must work bearing this paradoxical situation constantly in mind. But such is also the situation of the artist and, as a matter of fact, of the student of any aspect of human life and human activity.

35

HOW HISTORICAL IS THE HISTORY OF RELIGIONS?

Robert Segal

Editor's Introduction

Segal's identification of the confusion between the meaning and the significance of religious phenomena in Eliade's thought is instructive, and, I believe, accurate. The question is, to what extent does it invalidate or undermine that thought. It may, in the end, support the claim that Eliadean history of religions is something quite other than history as it is commonly conceived. It is something other than the attempt at an accurate reclamation and reconstruction of past events and their present entailments. However, such a claim is entirely consistent with Eliade's own insistence that the History of Religions is a cultural and transformative discipline (*Quest*, 62), and it is also harmonious with recent re-evaluations of historiography as itself value-laden (see Rennie, "History after History"). Robert Segal's "How Historical is the History of Religions?" appeared in *Method and Theory in the Study of Religion* 1/1 (1989): 2–17. All rights reserved. Copyright © Brill Academic Publishers. Reprinted by permission of Brill Academic Publishers and the author.

ༀ ༀ

Quentin Skinner, Professor of Political Science at Cambridge University, is one of a group of scholars in various fields intent on restoring *history* to the history of their fields.[1] Others include J. G. A. Pocock and John Dunn in political theory, George Stocking in anthropology, Robert Alun Jones in sociology, Thomas Kuhn in science, E. H. Gombrich in art, and Alasdair MacIntyre in ethics. Earlier influences are Herbert Butterfield in history and R. G. Collingwood in philosophy. All oppose the ahistorical practices of persons professing to be historians of their disciplines.

How historical the history of religions is has long been debated. I propose applying Skinner's criteria to the writings on religious thought and, even more, religious expression of the figure commonly lauded by fellow "religionists" as their premier historian: Mircea Eliade.

Skinner's Approach to the History of Political Thought

Skinner distinguishes three kinds of historical questions that can be asked of the works of political thinkers: (1) what meaning did the author intend to convey,[2] (2) what caused the author both to espouse that meaning and to want to convey it, and (3) what subsequent significance did the work have? In Skinner's terms, to describe, or "understand," a work is to answer the first question. To "explain" a work is to answer the second. Skinner supplies no term for answers to the third.[3] He uses "interpret" not, like many others, as a synonym for "understanding" but as an overall term for all three approaches to texts. I myself will use "interpret" synonymously with "understand."

Skinner argues that all three questions are proper, just distinct. He objects only to those who confuse either question 2 or question 3 with question 1, with which he himself is concerned. Skinner charges his opponents not with vainly trying to reduce question 1 either to question 2 or to question 3 but with blindly mistaking either 2 or 3 for 1. For Skinner, all three questions are not only proper but also historical.[4] What is ahistorical is the equation of 1 with either 2 or 3.

Because questions 1 and 2 link the work to the author and the author's times, they are closer to each other than either is to question 3, which links the work to other works in other times. For this reason Skinner considers the conflation of question 3 with question 1 far more egregious than the conflation of question 2 with question 1. Where 2, taken properly, supplements 1, 3 properly runs askew to it.

Those who collapse 1 into 3 Skinner labels "textualists."[5] For they invariably treat works as sheer texts, in isolation from both their authors and the world in which those authors lived. Textualists do so for two seemingly opposed reasons: on the one hand because the meaning they seek does not go beyond what the author has stated in the work; on the other hand because that meaning is not limited to the times in which the author lived. Yet the reasons are in fact compatible. Textualists assume both that the work itself reveals its author's meaning and also that that meaning concerns perennial issues.[6]

Because textualists assume that the subject matter of their texts is always the same, they need no biographical or sociological information to determine it. They already know it. Biographical or sociological information helps elucidate only the particular view of each author on these eternal issues—issues like the relationship between the individual and society. Many textualists assume that they can glean an author's view, or doctrine, from the text itself and therefore need no external information to ascertain even it.

Because the issues and doctrines purportedly evinced by texts are in fact ones that, far from perennial, often developed only long after their authors lived, Skinner faults many textualists with conspicuous anachronism. Even issues and doctrines that are not anachronistic are still out of place when, notes Skinner, they get attributed to authors who chronologically might have espoused them but in actuality never did. Here authors are credited with the prophetic capacity to "anticipate" their ideological successors.

Textualists reify issues and doctrines and then seek the manifestations of them in the works they study. Authors who are wise enough to consider these subjects get praised, and ones who fail to do so fully get damned. Ideas become autonomous entities which insightful authors recognize and obtuse ones miss. Perhaps it is not going too far to say that for textualists ideas become what they are for Wilhelm Dilthey and other idealists: entities which use persons to evince and develop themselves.[7]

Skinner objects to textualists not because they seek to answer question 3 but only because they confuse that question with question 1: they mistake significance for intent. Skinner thus objects to the claim that the later influence of the author's work was what an author had intended, or meant. Skinner's fundamental argument is "that no agent can eventually be said to have meant or done something which he could never be brought to accept as a correct description of what he had meant or done." (Skinner, "Meaning and Understanding," 28) Skinner does not, however, require that the intent be conscious: "This special authority of an agent over his intentions does not exclude, of course, the possibility that an observer might be in a position to give a fuller or more convincing account of the agent's behavior than he could give himself. (Psychoanalysis is indeed founded on this possibility)" (Skinner, "Meaning and Understanding," 28).[8] Skinner even allows that "the writer himself may have been self-deceiving" (Skinner, "Motives," 405). But he still demands that a description be acceptable to the agent once it is pointed out to him.[9]

Because Skinner's objection to textualists is that they downplay the context of works, at first glance he might seem no different from the other group of interpreters he lambastes—the "contextualists."[10] As he himself says: "A knowledge of the social context of a given text seems at least to offer considerable help in avoiding the anachronistic mythologies I have tried to anatomize" (Skinner, "Meaning and Understanding," 40).

327

But Skinner in fact differs sharply from contextualists, exemplars of whom include Marxists and behaviorists. Where contextualists consider the biographical and especially social context *sufficient* to understand a work, Skinner considers it at most only *helpful*.[11] For Skinner, to "understand" a work is to determine not what spurred the author to write it but what the author meant by it. However useful, knowledge of the context can never alone answer that question.

Furthermore, the context for *contextualists* is nonintellectual: it is composed of psychological, political, and economic conditions. The context for Skinner is intellectual as well as nonintellectual: it consists of the author's ideology as well as circumstances. For Skinner, an ideology may reflect an author's circumstances, but it is too intellectual and too precise to be reducible to inevitably nonintellectual and crude circumstances like childhood and class.[12] For Skinner, an ideology doubtless *arises* in response to circumstances, but it becomes an independent cause of behavior and not, as for extreme Marxists, a mere rationalization for circumstances.[13] Even if an ideology were reducible to circumstances, those circumstances would still be only the indirect cause of an author's writing. The author's ideology would remain the direct one—the one the author had in mind while writing. It would be equivalent to intent.

On the one hand, then, Skinner objects to contextualists' reduction of intellectual, or intentional, causes to nonintellectual, or unintentional, ones. But on the other hand he objects to contextualists' reduction of meanings to causes, intentional and unintentional alike. Skinner sharply distinguishes between intent as a cause, which it can alternatively be, and intent as a meaning—between intent as the reason an author held and conveyed a view and intent as the view itself. He distinguishes between an author's intent *to* write a work and an author's intent *in* writing it.[14] An author might intend *to* write a work that stirs support for a movement of some kind. The intent to write explains why the author wrote the work. The intent to write can certainly be intellectual as well as nonintellectual: it can be one's belief in the movement as well as one's upbringing. Indeed, it is hard to see how intent can be *other* than intellectual, or mental. Against textualists, Skinner argues that knowledge of the author's intent to write often helps elucidate the meaning of the work. Against contextualists, Skinner argues that the intent to write is not the same as the meaning of the work.

Just as an author might intend *to* write a work that garners support for a cause, so an author might intend to garner that support by writing fiction rather than nonfiction or tragedy rather than comedy. The intent here *categorizes* the work produced as tragedy rather than *explains why* the author produced it. Strictly, Skinner distinguishes even this kind of intent from the meaning, which would be the theme of the tragedy. The distinction between intent to write and intent in writing is not, then, quite the same as the distinction between cause and meaning. Still, this second kind of intent, which Skinner, following J. L. Austin, calls the illocutionary force of a work, is different from a cause and is much closer to the meaning than the first kind. Skinner considers this second kind of intent indispensable to determining the meaning, not merely, like the first kind, possibly useful: "First, this further question about what a given agent may be *doing* in uttering his utterance is not a question about meaning at all, but about a force co-ordinate with the meaning of the utterance itself, *and yet* essential to grasp in order to understand it" (Skinner, "Meaning and Understanding," 46). At times Skinner goes much further: "a knowledge of the writer's intentions in writing … is not merely relevant to, but is actually *equivalent* to, a knowledge of the meaning of what he writes" (Skinner, "Motives," 404). I will, then, use "intent in writing" interchangeably with "meaning."

Against contextualists, Skinner argues that the intent in writing is not inferable from the context—not even from the intellectual context. Against textualists, Skinner argues that the intent in writing is not inferable from the text itself either.[15] From where, then, does it come? It comes either from statements by the author outside the work[16] or, more generally, from familiarity with the "linguistic conventions" of the times: the vocabulary, the genres, the traditions, and the topics.

In sum, against textualists, Skinner asserts that the intent of the author *in* writing both is central to the meaning of the author's work and is not inferable from the work itself. Against contextualists, Skinner asserts both that the intent of the author *to* write is not identical with the author's intent *in* writing and that the intent *in* writing is not inferable from even an exclusively intellectual, let alone wholly nonintellectual, intent *to* write.

Skinner's Approach Applied to the History of Religions

Skinner's approach to the history of political thought applies tellingly to the history of religions, as represented by Eliade. Eliade not only calls himself a *historian* of religions but even contrasts the historian both to the theologian and to the phenomenologist. Where the theologian is concerned with, in Eliade's usage, the "meaning" of religious phenomena, the historian is concerned with their "history" as well:

> The procedure of the historian of religions is just as different from that of the theologian. All theology implies a systematic reflection on the content of religious experience, aiming at a deeper and clearer understanding of the relationships between God-Creator and man-creature. But the historian of religions uses an empirical method of approach. He is concerned with religio-*historical* [italics added] facts which he seeks to understand and to make intelligible to others. He is attracted to both the *meaning* of a religious phenomenon and to its *history*; he tries to do justice to both and not to sacrifice either one of them. ("Methodological Remarks," 88)

Where the phenomenologist is concerned with classes of religious phenomena, the historian is concerned with individual members of those classes. As a comparativist, the phenomenologist somehow naturally ignores the historical context of phenomena. As a particularist, the historian somehow automatically does not:

> Of course, the historian of religions also is led to systematize the results of his findings and to reflect on the structure of the religious phenomena. But then he completes his historical work as phenomenologist. ... But the historian of religions *sensu stricto* can never ignore that which is historically concrete. ("Methodological Remarks," 88)[17]

In the light of Eliade's emphasis on the place of history in deciphering religious phenomena—"all expression or conceptual formulation of ... religious experience is imbedded in a historical context" ("Methodological Remarks," 89)—the application of Skinner's strictures exposes Eliade as an egregious textualist. He mistakes significance for intent: Skinner's question 3 for question 1.

To be sure, Eliade says continually that he is merely *presenting* religion from the believer's point of view, in which case he, like Skinner, would not be venturing beyond question 1. He would be seeking only the intended meaning of the rituals as well as the texts of believers. While the creators of those artifacts are invariably unknown, Eliade would be seeking the meaning of them for those who use them. His relentless deference to the believer suggests strongly that he is seeking merely to capture the believer's point of view:

> A sacred stone remains a stone; apparently (or, more precisely, from the profane point of view), nothing distinguishes it from all other stones. *But for those to whom a stone reveals itself as sacred*, its immediate reality is transmuted into a supernatural reality. In other words, *for those who have a religious experience* all nature is capable of revealing itself as cosmic sacrality. (*Sacred and the Profane*, 12 [italics added])

Certainly most commentators on Eliade assume that capturing the believer's point of view is his aim.[18]

Prior to reading Skinner, I myself had argued that Eliade confuses two of Skinner's three questions, but I had assumed that he confuses *capturing*, or *understanding*, or *interpreting*, the believer's point of view—question 1—with *explaining* it—question 2. Where contextualists collapse interpreting into explaining—question 1 into question 2—Eliade, I had heretofore charged,[19] collapses explaining into interpreting—question 2 into question 1. For his sole argument against those who seek to *explain* religion in psychological, political, economic, or other secular, not necessarily nonintellectual, terms is that they thereby ignore the irreducibly religious *meaning* of religion for believers themselves. Eliade even contends that secular reductionists seek to explain the irreducibly religious meaning of religion nonreligiously *because* they ignore that meaning itself. Eliade assumes that a nonreligious *explanation* of the origin and function of religion presupposes a nonreligious *interpretation* of the meaning of religion:

> a religious phenomenon will only be recognized as such if it is grasped at its own level, that is to say, if it is studied *as* something religious. To try to grasp the essence of such a phenomenon by means of physiology, psychology, sociology, economics, linguistics, art or any other study is false; it misses the one unique and irreducible element in it—the element of the sacred. (*Patterns*, xiii)

I had previously argued that Eliade's reductionistic nemeses scarcely deny that the meaning of religion for believers is irreducibly religious. Rather, they merely account for that meaning nonreligiously. In opposing their explanations of religion, Eliade must be offering his own and so must be giving more than an interpretation of religion. Eliade, I had concluded, thereby confuses interpretation with explanation—not because his explanation is, like his interpretation, irreducibly religious but because his sole justification for it is its accordance with his interpretation. The true explanation of religion, I had acknowledged, may turn out to be irreducibly religious, but it is not irreducibly religious simply because it tallies with an irreducibly religious interpretation of religion.

In the wake of Skinner I now realize that I am doubly wrong. First, Eliade is right to assume a symmetry between explanation and interpretation: a Freudian explanation of the *cause* of religion does presuppose a Freudian interpretation of the *meaning* of it. While Skinner allows for nonintellectual as well as intellectual causes of political theories, his insistence on intellectual ones recognizes the necessary fit between meaning and cause that I had missed. At the same time Skinner's allowance for a Freudian meaning assumes that the meaning need not be the actor's conscious one, which in the case of a believer is presumably an irreducibly religious one. Eliade errs not, as I had supposed, in confusing meaning with cause, question 1 with question 2, but in dogmatically pronouncing the meaning and therefore the cause the believer's conscious one.[20]

Second and more important, I now realize that rather than collapsing question 2 into question 1—the reverse of contextualism—Eliade really collapses question 1 into question 3—textualism itself. As the prior quotation attests, Eliade is really appealing not to the meaning of religion for believers but to the meaning—better, significance—of religion itself. Religion for him is like political thought for Skinner's textualists: a set of eternal ideas which humans harbor. Believers are less the creators and users than the discoverers and carriers of those ideas, the way humans are the discoverers and carriers of culture for Dilthey and of archetypes for Carl Jung. Eliade is a textualist because he effaces the distinction between the significance of religion itself and the meaning of religion for believers themselves. He would be effacing the distinction even if the meaning and the significance coincided.

The meaning of religion for believers themselves need not be limited to their proffered views, so that the distinction between meaning and significance does not depend on the restriction of meaning to the believer's conscious view. Not only are Skinner's authors dead and therefore unavailable for interrogation, but, as noted, they need not for him have been fully conscious of their reconstructed views. Skinner's sole stipulation is, as quoted, "that no agent can eventually be said to have meant or done something which he could never be brought to accept as a correct description of what he had meant or done" (Skinner, "Meaning and Understanding," 28).

It is this prerequisite for meaning, or intent, which Eliade spurns, and spurns *despite* his seeming identification of meaning with the believer's *conscious* point of view. Eliade spurns the prerequisite not by in fact going *beyond* the believer's conscious viewpoint—itself permissible—but by in fact going *against* it. He claims more than that the "message" of religious phenomena is not "confined to the meaning of which a certain number of individuals are fully conscious" ("Methodological Remarks," 106). *Contrary* to most believers, he claims that all gods are agents of an impersonal sacred realm; that all worship is an attempt to return to the pristine point of contact with those agents; and that the sacred objects of individual religions are mere instances of universal categories—specific trees, for example, being sheer instances of the Cosmic Tree. Far more boldly, Eliade claims that "even the most avowedly nonreligious man still, in his deeper being, shares in a religiously oriented behavior" (*Sacred and the Profane,* 211).[21] Here above all Eliade outright contradicts, not merely enriches, the actor's conscious point of view. Eliade is a textualist because he deems the meaning of the believer's and especially the nonbeliever's behavior one which they would never grant.

Since, however, Skinner allows for a psychoanalytic meaning, he himself surely allows for an unconscious, or latent, meaning wholly at odds with the conscious, or manifest, one. How, then, is the latent religiosity that Eliade detects in manifest atheists any different?

To begin with, it is not clear that Skinner, who insists that a description be ultimately acceptable to the author, recognizes the severity of the divide in psychoanalysis between the manifest and the latent levels. For the latent level often reverses, not complements, the manifest one. Admittedly, the psychoanalytic ideal is the patient's acceptance of the latent meaning, but that acceptance is indispensable for therapy, not for the truth of the meaning. Freud's case study of, notably, Dora demonstrates that the cogency of an interpretation does not require the patient's concurrence.[22]

Yet even if Skinner were to permit a latent meaning that clashed with the manifest one, there would still remain an acute difference between Eliade's invocation of a latent meaning and Freud's. The latent level for Freud interprets behavior uninterpretable manifestly—for example, a strong emotional reaction to a seemingly humdrum event. The latent level supplies a meaning which the manifest level lacks. The inability of the manifest level to interpret itself is Freud's *justification* for going beyond and even against it.

By contrast, the latent level for Eliade interprets behavior interpretable entirely manifestly. The latent level offers a meaning which the manifest level in no way invites. Eliade therefore provides no justification for transcending the manifest level. For example, according to Eliade, escapism by moderns expresses not merely a manifest desire for ephemeral diversion—a seemingly sufficient impetus—but a latent yearning for permanent escape from an empty life, empty because secular rather than religious:

> [T]hrough reading, the modern man succeeds in obtaining an "escape from time" comparable to the "emergence from time" effected by myths. Whether modern man "kills" time with a detective story or enters such a foreign temporal universe as is represented by any novel, reading projects him out of his personal duration and incorporates him into other [i.e., religious] rhythms, makes him live in another "history" (*Sacred and the Profane*, 205).

> More strongly than any of the other arts, we feel in literature a revolt against historical [i.e., secular] time, the desire to attain to other temporal rhythms than that in which we are condemned to live and work. One wonders whether the day will come when this desire to transcend one's own time—personal, historical time—and be submerged in a "strange" time, whether ecstatic or imaginary, will be completely rooted out. As long as it persists, we can say that modern man preserves at least some residues of "mythological behavior" (*Myth and Reality*, 192).

Because the latent meaning for Eliade fills no manifest gap, it is far less tightly tied to the manifest level than the latent meaning is for Freud. Applying Skinner, I now realize that the connection is looser not because Eliade fails to justify his latent, irreducibly religious interpretation of the meaning of secular behavior for above all avowed atheists but because he is interested only secondarily in the conscious or even unconscious meaning of their behavior for them themselves. Primarily, he is interested in the *significance* of their behavior for *religion* itself. He *is* interested in showing that atheists behave religiously despite themselves— not, however, because they are unaware that their behavior evinces a religious impulse in them but because their behavior bespeaks the presence of religion itself, regardless of what impels it. Eliade is a textualist not because he leaps beyond meaning to significance but because he blurs the line between the one and the other: actors need not know even unconsciously the meaning of their own behavior, in which case that "meaning" is really significance.

Eliade's concern with religion rather than believers is clearest in his *Patterns in Comparative Religion*. On the one hand he says, as usual, that "every mani-festation of the sacred takes place in some historical situation. Even the most personal and transcendant [sic] mystical experiences are affected by the age in which they occur" (*Patterns*, 2). In stressing the distinctive meaning of each sacred entity, Eliade is undeniably stressing the meaning of it for each group of believers themselves. On the other hand he says that the meaning of a sacred entity is universal: "The fact that a hierophany is always a historical event (that is to say, always occurs in some definite situation) does not lessen its universal quality" (*Patterns*, 3). A specific tree symbolizes the Cosmic Tree.

Again, on the one hand Eliade says that even the universal meaning of a sacred object is its meaning for believers—here all believers—themselves: "The Indians, for instance, venerate a certain tree called *asvattha* ... But note that the *asvattha* ... is venerated, in fact, because [for them] it embodies, is part of, or symbolizes the universe as represented by all the Cosmic Trees in all mythologies" (*Patterns*, 3).

On the other hand Eliade says that the universal meaning of a sacred object is the meaning—better, significance—of the object itself, not just its meaning for believers:

> We shall see in this way that every hierophany in fact supposes such a system; a popular [local] custom bearing a certain relation to "bringing home the May" implies the same sacred meaning of plants expressed in the ideogram of the Cosmic Tree; some hierophanies are not at all clear, are indeed almost cryptic, in that they only reveal the sacred meaning embodied or symbolized in plant life in part, or, as it were, in code, while others (more truly *manifestations*) display the sacred in all its modalities as a whole. (*Patterns*, 8)

Every sacred object, according to Eliade, seeks on its own to shed its particularistic, historical significance and move as close as possible to the pure category, or "archetype," of which it is a case:

> there *is* no religious form [i.e., phenomenon] that does not try to get as close as possible to its true archetype, in other words, to rid itself of "historical" accretions and deposits. Every goddess tends to become a Great Goddess, taking to herself all the attributes and functions that belong to the archetypal Great Goddess. (*Patterns*, 462)

Most of all, Eliade says that the universal significance of a sacred entity remains universal even when the believer whose entity it is is blind to that significance:

> For a symbolism does not depend upon being understood; it remains consistent in spite of every corruption and preserves its structure even when it has been long forgotten, as witness those prehistoric symbols whose meaning was lost for thousands of years to be "rediscovered" later. (*Patterns*, 450)

Eliade is not here merely saying that the meaning of a sacred entity for a believer remains even when the believer no longer *consciously* recognizes it. He is not here distinguishing tamely between a believer's manifestly forgetting the meaning and a believer's latently remembering it. He is saying that a sacred entity retains its meaning—again, significance—even when nobody knows it even unconsciously.[23] Insofar as Eliade is *not* claiming that the meaning of religion for believers *is* its significance, he is no textualist. But insofar as he separates religion from believers, he is no historian either. For by the significance of religion he does not, as Skinner likely does,[24] mean its meaning to *later* believers. He means its significance independent of *any* believers.

In his *History of Religious Ideas*, which is virtually a foil to *Patterns*, Eliade focuses on individual religions rather than on religion per se. He thereby necessarily concentrates on the meaning of each religion for adherents themselves. Whether his *History* is more typical of his writings than *Patterns* is, however, the question. Is it merely coincidental that Eliade is able to say far more about religion in *Patterns*, than in his *History*, which is much more factual than analytical? When Eliade *analyzes* religion, he invariably analyzes its import for more than believers themselves.[25]

Notes

1. See Skinner (esp. 1966, 1969, 1972a, 1972b, 1974, 1975).
2. More precisely, Skinner means the author's intent *in* writing the work rather than the author's intent *to* write, which is the concern of the *second* question. The distinction gets spelled out below.
3. See Skinner (1966: 214; 1969: 46).
4. On the legitimacy and historicity of even the third question see Skinner (1969: 22; 1972a: 404–405).
5. On textualists see Skinner (above all 1969: 4–39; 1966; 1972a).
6. But there is a contradiction between textualists who claim that the work itself reveals its author's meaning, in which case biographical and sociological information is superfluous, and textualists—the same textualists?—who claim that the work, once completed, stands independent of its author's meaning, in which case biographical and sociological information is irrelevant: see Skinner (1972a: 397–410). Skinner usually (for example, 1969) considers only textualists of the former kind and therefore finds nothing contradictory.
7. See, similarly, the contrast drawn by Talcott Parsons (esp. 81–82, 473–87, 584–85, 683, 715, 732) between the idealism of Dilthey and the "voluntarism" of Max Weber, for whom ideas are human creations used by their possessors to achieve their own ends.
8. See also Skinner (1972a: 405).
9. See Skinner (1969: 28–29).
10. On contextualists see Skinner (1969: 39–48).
11. See Skinner (1969: 40, 43).
12. For a similar objection to nonintellectual explanations of scientific beliefs see Laudan (1977: 217–19).

13. In the jargon of the history of science, Skinner, while granting a place to external factors, opposes sheer externalism. He is therefore like Kuhn and would oppose the Edinburgh School of Barry Barnes, David Bloor, and Steven Shapin.
14. See Skinner (1969: 45–47; 1972a: 401–404; 1972b: esp. 143–45).
15. See Skinner (1969: 46–47).
16. See Skinner (1972a: 405).
17. On the relationship between the history and the phenomenology of religions see also Eliade (*Quest*: 8–9, 34–36) and Pettazzoni.
18. As Mac Linscott Ricketts, who is sworn to correcting misconstruals of Eliade's views, says: "Eliade has misled some readers by his definition of the sacred as the 'real.' Some have thought that this means that Eliade himself regards the sacred as Reality. ... All he means here is that *for the believer*, that which is sacred *for him* is the Real, the True, the meaningful in an ultimate sense" ("In Defense of Eliade," 28, original italics).
19. See Segal, "In Defense of Reductionism," esp. 97–103.
20. The fact that Eliade himself veers from the conscious meaning of religion for believers—the issue discussed next—compounds, not dissolves, the problem.
21. As Eliade puts it again: "The majority of the 'irreligious' still behave religiously, even though they are not aware of the fact ... [T]he modern man who feels and claims that he is nonreligious still retains a large stock of camouflaged myths and degenerated rituals ... Strictly speaking, the great majority of the irreligious are not liberated from religious behavior, from theologies and mythologies" (Eliade, *The Sacred and the Profane*, 204–206). On the religiosity of the nonreligious see also Eliade (*The Sacred and the Profane*, 24, 70–72, 186, 201–213; *Myth and Reality*, 181–93; *Myths, Dreams and Mysteries*, ch. 2; *Myth of the Eternal Return*, 147–62; *The Quest*, ch. 7; *Occultism, Witchcraft and Cultural Fashions*, chs. 1–4).
22. On this issue see Adolf Grünbaum, *The Foundations of Psychoanalysis* (Berkeley: University of California Press, 1984), 21–41.
23. Eliade never says what, if not believers, does determine the significance of sacred entities.
24. I am indebted to Ivan Strenski for this point.
25. For their most helpful comments on earlier drafts of this paper, I want to thank Ivan Strenski and Terry Foreman.

36

MIRCEA ELIADE AS THE "ANTI-HISTORIAN" OF RELIGIONS

Guilford Dudley III

Editor's Introduction

This article picks up the criticism that rapidly developed and soon became entrenched that Eliade was in fact an "Anti-Historian." Perhaps Dudley goes too far in insisting that Eliadean History of Religions can only be true to itself "by relinquishing ... empirical verification" and must "surrender the pretence that phenomenological description and the raw data of history are compatible"? If the Eliadean "transconscious" is determined by the encounter with the actual, empirical world, then any specific representations of reality must refer to the empirical and can only be checked against human experience. Dudley provided a great service in recognizing Eliade's affinity with continental thinkers such as Foucault; however, he may have been misled by a lack of awareness of Eliade's roots in Romanian *trăirism* and his concomitant emphasis on empirical experience (on *trăirism* see "The Life and Work of Mircea Eliade" in this volume, 5–6). Dudley's article illustrates clearly the fact that a review of Eliade serves in many ways as a review of the main issues facing the History of Religions in the second half of the 20th century. This article appeared in the *Journal of the American Academy of Religion* 44/2 (1976): 345–59. All rights reserved. Copyright © 1976. Reprinted by permission of Oxford University Press.

ℰ ℛ

For some time now historians of religion have tried to come to grips with a fundamental ambiguity in their field, and one that threatens the very foundations of *Religionswissenschaft* as an autonomous discipline. The ambiguity arises from an unresolved conflict between methodological standards: a "scientific," data-bound methodology—or an intuitive method that uses some maverick version of Husserl's eidetic vision to perceive the all-important "essences" of religious phenomena and behavior. Sometimes the conflict is formulated in the crude terms of an objective method as opposed to a subjective one. In the early days of its development *Religionswissenschaft* justified itself with the argument that the field of religious studies needed a value-free, theologically and philosophically *neutral* description of religious phenomena. At first the phenomenological method seemed tailor-made for this enterprise. But within the past two decades that method has come under increasing fire from those who suspect as least an unbridled virtuosity and at most a covert theology at work. Critics of the phenomenological method want to impose controls in the form of a procedure derived from the natural sciences: namely, moving cautiously from empirical data to hypothesis and then subjecting the hypothesis to an intersubjective testing or verification with reference to the data and in this way ensure a scientific or objective methodology.

At the end of the 1950s, Jerald Brauer introduced a collection of essays on methodology in the history of religions with the warning that unless the field can "exhibit a method adequate to its own content, problems and materials," it will die the death of fragmentation, lapsing back into sub-disciplines within the social sciences and humanities (vii–x). Brauer pointed to Mircea Eliade as a scholar with special promise for leading the history of religions out of its dilemma (x). In the two decades following, Eliade indeed emerged as the leading spokesman for the would-be discipline, and on the general acceptability of his methodology, the future of the history of religions increasingly depended. Eliade's writings either convinced many historians of religion or led them to hope that a hard-and-fast choice between an intuitive or a more objective approach is not necessary. On the one hand, Eliade claims explicitly that the historian of religions is committed to an empirical approach (*Quest*, 7ff., 29, 35–36; *Cosmos and History*, 3); on the other hand, the empirical data themselves seem to yield him insights and understanding that are usually restricted to the domain of metaphysics or theology. For example, he claims that data yield him knowledge of an "archaic ontology" and an existential meaning of religious myth and ritual (*Cosmos and History*, passim; "Methodological Remarks," 98–103; *The Sacred and the Profane*, 95ff.; *Myth and Reality*, passim). Thus it seems that Eliade has shown the historian of religions how to have it both ways: a vision of "essences," and even of ontology, with an empirical approach.

But although Eliade still holds a position of unparalleled eminence in the field, challenges to his credentials as an empiricist have intensified. The British anthropologist, Edmund Leach, has accused Eliade of substituting for an empirical method a "personal mysticism," which "seems to give him a confidence hardly justified by his evidence" (30 [above, 282]). The American anthropologist, Anthony Wallace, also accuses Eliade of adopting a methodology that is mystical, for it takes "speculations about inner meaning as facts to be explained by still further historical and comparative speculations, with no more evidence available than a rich miscellany of illustrations ..." (*Religion*, 252). It has become increasingly evident that Eliade's interpretations of religious phenomena are not subject to disconfirmation on the basis of empirical data. One of the most striking cases in point is his reliance on the "transconscious" or unconscious meaning of the symbol for his postulate of the transconsciousness obviates the necessity of verifying that meaning at a conscious level (*Images and Symbols*, 119–20; *Patterns*, 450). Eliade uses his notion of the transconsciousness to insulate his interpretation of hierophanies, symbols, and archetypes against empirical testing, and his method falls into the category of speculation for it is a hypothesis advanced in such a way that it is not subject to revision or rejection on empirical grounds. As the historian of religions Robert Baird put it,

> [Eliade's methodology] is not historically falsifiable. Since it is an ahistorical approach, however legitimate that might be in itself, when it enters into historical deliberation it becomes a barrier to the attainment of authentic religio-historical understanding (*Category Formation*, 153).

At first sight it would appear that these attacks undermine Eliade's position of leadership and the promise invested in his methodology. But it is the argument of this paper that Eliade can survive this entire line of attack and still remain the most significant figure in the field, albeit on grounds that are fundamentally different than the grounds on which he has been defended. His real contribution lies not in his ability to quiet the turbulent waters of conflicting methodologies, but in his ability to stir them up. That is to say, his real contribution is not that of an elder statesman, but of a young radical. A corollary to this argument is the contention that the waters need stirring up, at least in a different way than they have been stirred up thus far.

Thus far, the waters have been stirred by empiricist-minded historians of religion such as Evaline Lot-Falck, Henri Clavier, and Baird, who reject deductive reasoning, the use of intuition to fill the gaps in empirical data, premature syntheses, and perceptions of essences and trans-historical meanings that go beyond the available data. On the other side are those who have maintained all along that the "understanding" sought by historians of religion cannot be limited to what empirical data can provide. One of the most recent advocates of this position is Frederick J. Streng who stresses that knowledge of religious phenomena points us finally to knowledge of "Ultimate Truth," which is a special kind of "transforming truth" (*Emptiness*, 18) that cannot be apprehended by a scholar who approaches the data "from the outside" (25). Streng insists that

" 'to know' means to have conditioning (and conditioned) apparatus for interiorizing existence" (17–18). Cognizant of the intangible nature of "ultimate" and "transforming" truth and the need for special "patterns of sensitivity" on the part of the knower, Streng describes his approach as one that

> will seek to expose a deep, underlying organizing force within religious meaning: the structure by which the knower apprehends "transforming truth" or ultimate reality—since truth and reality are complementary elements of the sacred. (18)

This particular way of formulating the debate—the "authentic religiohistorical understanding" stripped of all speculations about trans-historical structures (Baird) or understanding those elusive structures by which ultimate and transforming Truth is grasped (Streng)—is provincializing for the field of history of religions and generally misleading. It is provincializing because it focuses too narrowly on the uniqueness of religion and religious phenomena, implying that the conflict is basically an intramural one, cloistered within the walls of *Religionswissenschaft*. The formulation of the debate in terms of "historical vs. trans-historical" interpretation is also misleading, because it obscures the breadth of the epistemological issues. The waters need to be stirred in a way that will bring out precisely those issues that will carry the debate to an interdisciplinary level.

To see the conflict in terms of a historical or trans-historical interpretation of religious phenomena is to do little more than retread the old arguments about whether the scholar-observer can or should share (*Einfühlen*) the religious subject's vision of Ultimate Truth or the Sacred. Along this axis of debate, we have different degrees of skepticism and advocacy regarding the perception of normative theological and metaphysical truth within the framework of a "scientific" or descriptive enterprise. The contributions to this debate by Gerardus van der Leeuw, Joachim Wach, and Raffaele Pettazzoni along with the more recent writings of Baird, Streng, and Ninian Smart are well-known in the history of religions field. Smart's solution of "bracketed realism," i.e., a description that conveys the reality of the "focus" of a particular religious tradition, yet brackets it out of the observer's evaluation as Truth, is symptomatic of a growing need that historians of religion feel for staking out a middle ground between the extremes (*Science of Religion and the Sociology of Knowledge*, 61). As long as the methodological task is seen as staking out a new position along the spectrum of objective description and perception of normative Truth, the debate remains insular and the broader epistemological issues obscure. An issue that needs to be brought out is whether knowledge of religious phenomena, like knowledge of *all* human phenomena, proceeds through inductive, data-bound studies or through a deductive, paradigm-bound approach. Formulated in this fashion, the debate does not stop at the specifically religious level but crosses disciplinary lines into the human sciences. Here the issues do not pivot around the question of the religiosity or special sensitivity of the observer but root themselves in much more general epistemological ground.

The contribution of Eliade's own approach can be to force these issues into the open, but this potential will not be realized until three concessions are made by Eliade and his supporters. First, it must be conceded that Eliade's methodology is hopelessly vulnerable to attack by the empiricists and therefore incapable of reconciling the two approaches or standing as a middle ground between them. In the second place, it must even be conceded that Eliade, although renowned as a "historian of religions," is not a historian by conventional standards for the reasons that Baird points out. Eliade's program is to uncover the structures of the transconsciousness, which are indeed those very trans-historical structures to which Baird objects, and there is no way that those structures can be verified empirically. In the third place, it must be conceded that Eliade's method is not simply deficient as a historical study but is radically anti-historical. The third concession can be viewed not so much as a concession as a counter-attack against the empiricists on grounds that are far more radical and suggestive than the insular plea that there is more to religion than historical studies can show.

Eliade is already committed methodologically and metaphysically to an anti-historicist stance however he might choose to explain himself to be a so-called "historian" of religions. The dependence of interpretation on historical context and the subjection of theories about *homo religiosus* to empirical testing represent to Eliade the tyranny of historicism. That tyranny, according to Eliade, threatens to rob events of their trans-historical meaning. As he puts it,

> ... the historian of religions who does not accept the empiricism or the relativism of some fashionable sociological and historicistic school feels rather frustrated. He knows that he is condemned to work exclusively with historical documents, but at the same time he feels that these documents tell him more than the simple fact that they reveal important truths about man and man's relation to the sacred. But how to grasp these truths?
> ... As so often in the past, a correct question may infuse new life into a worn-out science. (*Quest*, 53)

It is not simply empiricism in methodology but the consciousness of history as a reality determining man's existence against which Eliade's position is so metaphysically entrenched. In *Cosmos and History*, which Eliade regards as his most significant book (*The Eternal Return*, x), he speaks of the consciousness of history as a surrender to what is ultimately the sheer terror that historical existence generates (150–51). Ever since Hegel, according to Eliade, modern man has tried to valorize history as purposeful and historical truth as meaningful, but this valorization of history and its supposedly transparent events has only incarcerated man in a terror-ridden existence leading irremediably to death (139ff.). Eliade writes:

For our purpose, only one question concerns us: How can the "terror of history" be tolerated from the viewpoint of historicism? Justification of historical event by the simple fact that it is a historical event, in other words, by the simple fact that it "happened that way," will not go far toward freeing humanity from the terror that the event inspires … And in our day, when historical pressure no longer allows any escape, how can man tolerate the catastrophes and horrors of history—from collective deportations and massacres to atomic bombings—if beyond them he can glimpse no sign, no trans-historical meaning; if they are only the blind play of economic, social, or political forces, or, even worse, only the result of the "liberties" that a minority takes and exercises directly on the stage of universal history? (150–51)

For a historian to offer a mere objective description of events, as though an accurate rendering of events in some casual nexus were sufficient, would be to simply increase the sense of futility and hopelessness that has already infused the consciousness of modern, historicized man. Our ancestors, Eliade points out, were not so straitjacketed by a consciousness of history. They escaped the meaninglessness of history by an eternal return to mythic time, the fabulous time before the creation of the world and before man's tragic "fall" into history. They escaped through immersing their thought and language in myth and through ritually enacting the archetypes and patterns of that myth. Salvation came to our ancestors as a consciousness of cyclical time, geared to the changing seasons, the stars, and all the rhythms of nature. The New Year, for example, was celebrated not as a milestone in a linear progression of time but as a return to chaos (sometimes experienced in a ritual orgy) and a fresh, new creation—in short, a cyclical return to beginnings without any sense of the inevitable march of historical time into another year, located on a linear continuum.

The soteriological thrust of Eliade's analysis of archaic man's thirst for a world of myth and ritual repetition of beginnings echoes in Eliade's personal life. As late as 1954, when he had written the most substantial part of his mature works on the history of religions, Eliade wrote in his diary that his understanding of *illud tempus* (mythic time) had for him an intensely soteriological meaning. "My essential preoccupation," he wrote, "is precisely the means of escaping History, of saving myself through symbol, myth, rites, archetypes."[1] This impulse is also embodied in the hero of his best-known novel, Stefan in *Forbidden Forest*. Stefan is the symbol of modern man who lives in two realms: historical time, the time that kills, and mythic time, the time that reinstates, recovers, and redeems (*The Sacred and the Profane*, 68–72; *Myths, Dreams and Mysteries*, 14–20; *The Eternal Return*, 3–6, 51ff.; *Images and Symbols*, 14–16, 24–25; *Myth and Reality*, 5–20).

The novel defines historical time as Death-Time, against which Heidegger warns us (*Forbidden Forest*, 56). Near the end of the novel Biris, who serves as a foil for Stefan, says, trying to grasp Stefan's concept of time, "Your longing to go out of Time and to ignore History was probably a desperate effort to recover the bliss of childhood, to reintegrate a lost Paradise" (432).[2] Biris's comment is a succinct statement of Stefan's and Eliade's soteriological yearning to escape Death-Time and return to mythic time, *illud tempus*.

As one literary critic has put it, Eliade in his notion of mythic time is much closer to Faulkner and Dostoevsky than to Proust. Eliade's heroes do not seek a lost time in the Proustian sense, but rather they seek to annihilate time altogether as a psychological, personal and social reality. As for the heroes in the work of Dostoevsky and Faulkner, a metaphysical effort is required to enter this mythic time. Eliade himself confirms the validity of the comparison with Dostoevsky in his diary:

> March 4, 1953: I had forgotten this detail of *The Idiot:* Muichkine had understood the decisive importance of time for historical man, "fallen man." Here is what he says: "At this moment ... I have glimpsed the meaning of the singular expression: time will be no more" (Apocalypse 10:6). This "moment" is the last conscious flash before the attack of epilepsy. It is interesting that Dostoevsky has understood the *metaphysical* value (and not only the *ecstatic* value) of this atemporal "moment," of this *nunc stans* which signifies eternity.[3]

The French literary critic, Dominique Aury, has pointed out the comparison between Eliade and Faulkner, specifically the parallel attitudes toward time in Eliade's *Forêt Interdite* and Faulkner's *Go Down, Moses*. Both show a compulsion to return to beginnings in order to suppress time (See Ierunca, "Literary Work," 351). Faulkner chooses the form of the historical novel to stress the curse that history carries relentlessly with it and to express the hope that had resided in the mythic time before the Snopes and the carpetbaggers had dragged the South away from its mythical moorings. Eliade's vision has the same epic dimension, for he sees the Romanian people wrenched out of their culture, undermined at the base of their existence and plunged into the dark night of war and occupations by foreign powers. But unlike Faulkner's heroes, who are driven by a fate beyond their control or their deciphering, Eliade's characters suffer precisely from "the lucidity with which (they) assume their condition of being tortured by Time, which is to say, by History" (ibid.). It is not a particular fate from which they suffer, but time itself, that is, historical time. The Romanian philosopher, Lucien Blaga, has said that the Romanian people have endured only by "sabotaging history" (ibid.). They have sabotaged it by escaping into the "prohibited forest" *(Forbidden Forest)* which is the collective myth of Romania's history. (The forest is the place where the Romanians literally saved themselves during the invasions of the barbarians). In Romanian folklore and mythology the forest is a kind of archetypal symbol of timelessness, a

Paradise that men can enter to escape the ravaging stream of time threatening to engulf all in its wake.

Vintila Horia has noted that the Romanian people, like Stefan, "live a double drama: on the traditional plane they are forced to remain outside history in order to evade the consequences of historical time, a technique that they have followed since they formed themselves as a people ..." (in Ierunca, *Literary Work*, 390). Horia explains that one part of the Romanian people has remained loyal to the traditional concept of mythic time, and these are the peasants. The other part, the bourgeoisie and workers, became entangled in history and were destroyed by it. This observation helps to explain Eliade's sympathy for folk religion and the values it has preserved. Eliade reminds us, for example, that "the Christianity of the popular (folk) European strata never succeeded in abolishing either the theory of the archetype ... or the cyclical and astral theories ..." (*The Eternal Return*, 142). Instead, he explains in another book, the peasants held fast to the mythic world of archetypes inherited from archaic times (*The Sacred and the Profane*, 164). Thus Eliade uses the Romanian model to interpret Christianity as divided between two groups: on the one hand, urban Christians who are entangled in history and possessed of a historical consciousness and, on the other hand, rural Christians who have adapted Christianity to the world of myth and archetypes inherited from antiquity. He insists that

> we must recognize that their [the peasants' or rural Christians'] religion is not confined to the historical forms of Christianity, that it still retains a cosmic structure that has been almost entirely lost in the experience of urban Christians. We may speak of a primordial, ahistorical Christianity; becoming Christians, the European cultivators incorporated into their new faith the cosmic religion that they had preserved from prehistoric times. (164)

One "sabotages" time, to use Blaga's phrase as well as Eliade's, by adopting a psychic and philosophical attitude that ensures the remoteness of historical time and reinforces that remoteness by an act of contempt for history. This contempt is expressed in the novel by Biris who recites the Hindu myth of Narada and Vishnu in which Vishnu shows Narada that all of his life and loves are an illusion, a dream, since they occurred in a time that is unreal. Then, after hearing three gongs struck by a clock, Biris remarks,

> It's a beetle. The Death Clock, some call it. And it truly is a clock of death. Its ticking alone reveals to me the Death-Time, the time in which we live, we mortals—at least when we say that we are living, that we are alive. Any other beat—of watches or clocks, or the striking of chimes—seems to me a camouflage. We are deceived. They tell us that a half hour has passed or that it's six o'clock, as though this had some importance. What matters is the fact that our time, the Time that we call our Life, is a Time of Death. (*Forbidden Forest*, 56)

The same contempt, this act of "sabotage," is expressed by Eliade directly in an essay he wrote in 1934:

> Learn then to ignore Time, not to fear its implications. Suppress every trace of sentimental memory, suppress evanescent contemplations, memories of infancy, autumns, pressed flowers, nostalgias.[4]

And again in *Cosmos and History* Eliade writes with the same poignancy about the utter futility and sham behind all attempts to valorize historical time by a doctrine of historicism. Then in a footnote he adds:

> We take the liberty of emphasizing that "historicism" was created and professed above all by thinkers belonging to nations for which history has never been a continuous terror. These thinkers would perhaps have adopted another viewpoint had they belonged to nations marked by the "fatality of history" (152 n. 11)

These quotations from Eliade's creative writing, his journal, his early essays, and his more current works as a historian of religion show the direction and intensity of his ideas about *illud tempus* and its polar antithesis, historical time. In this respect he interprets Christianity as the "religion of 'fallen man' " (162), since it is obsessed with historical consciousness, and "Fall" in this case means to him a fall from the paradise of archetypes and repetition in which archaic man lived. For the Christian as well as for any man whom we could call *homo religiosus* the forest is salvation. Just as the forest literally casts up its vegetal and animal forms in an endless repetition of the life-and-death cycle, the forest symbolically is the spatial coordinate of *tempus*; its life is cyclical and totally unifying.

It would be consistent with Eliade's metaphysical and methodological commitment to an anti-historicist stance for him to surrender not only his claim to empirical justification for his interpretations of religious phenomena but also his claim to being a historian according to the conventions to which Baird and other critics appeal. Eliade and his supporters would do far better to call themselves anti-historians of religions and sail under that banner, throwing overboard all the cumbersome rigging that needs to be hauled out to make the Eliade vessel sail more conventionally. Unencumbered of all those conventions, the Eliade enterprise can be recast in a much more radical and provocative light as an "anti-historical" history of religions. In this light Eliade's colors are decidedly French, specifically the French tradition of deductive, systemic thought that derives all actions and ideas from fundamental structures of the human mind. As a recent study of this tradition has characterized it,

> the emergence of mind coincides with that of language; together they constitute an intellectual and qualitative mutation in time and, even more important, represent *a priori* and generic givens from which all further historical events and human creations may be deduced.[5]

One of the most eminent exponents of this tradition is the French scholar, Michael Foucault, who has been dubbed by Hayden White as the "anti-historical historian" of our time.[6] A comparison between Eliade and Foucault can be highly instructive for locating Eliade in this tradition and for bringing out the potential contribution that Eliade can make from this stance even though the obvious differences between the two men necessitates keeping the comparison loose.

Eliade and Foucault

Foucault is a philosopher-historian who writes history in order to stand it on its head, to show its discontinuities instead of its linearity, its ruptures instead of its connectedness, its reversals instead of its progressive unfolding. He regards the claim that history is science, with irrefutable methods of verification by reference to empirical data, as false and misleading. The "human sciences" and especially history are nothing more than language games played with the particular linguistic protocols in which these so-called scientific methods and concepts have been formulated. Furthermore, Foucault wants to show that the historical consciousness which emerged so dominantly in the nineteenth century is rooted in a myth and is in fact a mythic response to the linearity of historical existence. As the historian Hayden White explains Foucault on this point,

> he [Foucault] regards "history" less as a "method" or a "mode of thought" than as a symptom of a peculiarly nineteenth-century malaise which originated in the discovery of the temporality of all things. The vaunted "historical consciousness" of the nineteenth century (and *a fortiori* of our time) is nothing but a formalization of a myth, itself a reaction-formation against the discovery of the *seriality* of existence. Foucault thus regards the works of professional historians with much the same attitude of contempt with which Artaud regarded the works of all modern dramatists or as Robbe-Grillet regards the work of all novelists. He is an anti-historical historian, as Artaud was the anti-dramatistic dramatist and as Robbe-Grillet is the anti-novelistic novelist. (White, "Foucault Decoded," 26)

Foucault's discussion of the mythic nature of modern man's historical consciousness parallels Eliade's discussion of modern man's mythical "fall" into history. Eliade uses the metaphor of the "Fall" in the Genesis myth to depict the regression of Western consciousness since the Enlightenment and especially since the appearance of historicism in the nineteenth century. As Eliade sees this regressive step, it is a retreat from the plethora of archetypes, repetitive gestures and rituals with which alone archaic man was able to exorcise the terror of history. His use of the metaphor of the Fall is not arbitrary, for he explains that

Christianity incontestably proves to be the religion of 'fallen man': and this to the extent to which modern man is irremediably identified with history and progress, and to which history and progress are a fall, both implying the final abandonment of the paradise of archetypes and repetition (*The Eternal Return*, 162).

Like Foucault, Eliade also attacks the other human sciences, in addition to history. Anthropology, sociology, and psychology all advance explanations based on a network of causality that both Foucault and Eliade reject. Foucault sees all the human sciences engaging in language games, just as he finds among historians. Each human science represents nothing more than another wager that language can be transparent to the truth about man. In *Les Mots et les Choses*, Foucault argues that each human science is simply another mode of representation claiming to be the exclusive configuration of language and concepts by which "words" and "things" can be related. Each science claims to be the single universe of discourse which enables the actual "order of things" to be rendered fully accessible through language. These claims are all flawed by the refusal to acknowledge that language is "opaque" rather than transparent and simply cannot give us a final, definitive grasp of the things it seeks to describe or explain. For this reason Foucault rejects all attempts to finally explain man's nature, behavior, or history by reductive techniques, i.e., rendering a definitive account of them in terms of a particular universe of discourse. Another way of putting it is that each of the human sciences, self-constituted as the one universe of discourse that is transparent to the object being explained, is really a "warped and twisted form of reflection" for precisely the reason that each human science "anthropologizes" reality, places man at the centre of the universe. Foucault writes:

> To all those who still wish to talk about man, about his reign or his libera-
> tion, to all those who still ask themselves questions about what man is in his
> essence, to all those who wish to take him as their starting-point in their
> attempts to reach the truth, to all those who refuse to formalize without
> anthropologizing, who refuse to mythologize without demystifying, who
> refuse to think without immediately thinking that it is man who is think-
> ing, to all those warped and twisted forms of reflection we can only answer
> with a philosophical laugh—which means, to a certain extent, a silent one.[7]

To put the matter more precisely, Foucault understands knowledge for modern man to exist in three dimensions: the deductive sciences (mathematics and physics); the empirical sciences such as those of language, life and the production and distribution of wealth; and those of philosophical reflection. The human sciences do not fit into any of these planes or dimensions but rather into the interstices between them. The human sciences engage in mathematical formalization, use models borrowed from biology, and they address themselves

347

to man's finite mode of being as philosophy conceives it. It is because of this "cloudy distribution" among the branches of knowledge that the human sciences are precarious in their own right and pose a threat of empirialism to all knowledge. Foucault speaks of the danger of "thought tumbling over into the domain occupied by the human sciences: hence the danger of 'psychologism,' of 'sociologism,'—of what we might term, in a word, 'anthropologism.' " The real danger to which all other expressions of the threat point is that knowledge will be radically "anthropologized" so that man in his finitude, man limited to the empirical parameters of reality, occupies the centre of knowledge. "Anthropologization is the great internal threat to knowledge in our day," writes Foucault (Foucault, *The Order of Things*, 348).

Eliade shares Foucault's deep suspicion of thought tumbling over into the categories of the sciences, thereby undergoing a process of demystification, empiricization, and reduction to "anthropologism." He calls this the "fallacy of demystification." One of his greatest fears for historians of religions is that "we shall continue to submit to the audacious and irrelevant interpretations of religious realities made by psychologists, sociologists, or devotees of various reductionist ideologies (e.g., historicists)" (*Quest*, 70). Both Foucault and Eliade are deeply disturbed by the effort on the part of historians, social scientists and psychologists to demystify reality, to treat things as objects to be interrogated in the language of man's finitude, a language that enthrones empiricism and discounts all that is outside the "episteme" of man's finite reality. For Eliade what is most tragically excluded by the demystification and reductionism performed by the human sciences is the realm of the sacred; for Foucault it is the autonomy of language. But in both cases there is an anti-reductionist, anti-empirical, as well as specifically anti-historical polemic against "anthropologism."

Foucault envisions a return to the "unity of language," by which he means the power of language to confer unity on what modern man experiences as the disparateness and unconnectedness of thought given his propensity to atomistically objectify all that he sees and experiences. Foucault envisions a return to the unifying and the generative role of language in such a radical sense that it suggests the ascendancy of mythic language over discursive, analytic language; indeed the ascendancy of mythic over historical and scientific accounts of the world. To be sure, what is important for Foucault is not the religious content of myth—not the sacred as such, as it is for Eliade—but the poetic language of myth, which speaks through the unifying and generative power of symbol and metaphor. As the historian Hayden White has felicitously put it, Foucault envisions an epiphany not of the Word made Flesh, but of the "Flesh made Word," for he follows Mallarmé's dictum that "things exist in order to live in books" (White, "Foucault Decoded," 53).

Eliade also understands the power of myth not only in ontological terms, but in terms of the power of its language. He writes that the symbol expresses a "modality of the real inaccessible to human experience" (*Two and the One*, 201 [above, 133]). For Eliade it is the world "speaking" through the medium of symbolic language, not man speaking about the world through one of his many subservient inventions, language (*The Eternal Return*, 154–59). Eliade is very explicit on this point. He writes:

> The first observation that he [the historian of religions] is forced to make is that the World "speaks" in symbols, "reveals" itself through them. It is not a question of a utilitarian and objective language. A symbol is not a replica of objective reality. It reveals something deeper and more funda-mental. (*Two and the One*, 201 [above, 133])

Eliade also understands the symbolic language of myth to be uniquely "capable of revealing a perspective in which diverse realities can be fitted together or even integrated into a 'system' " (203 [above, 134]). In other words it is of the very essence of this symbolic language to unify, integrate and sys-temize what would appear to be disparate realities if left to modern man's discursive language of finite analysis. He cites the example of lunar symbolism, which rescues the world from appearing to be only "an arbitrary assemblage of heterogeneous and divergent realities" (204 [above, 134]). For,

> the various cosmic levels are mutually related, they are, in a sense, "bound together" by the same lunar rhythm, just as human life is "woven" by the moon and predestined by the Spinning Goddesses. (204 [above, 134])

The moon provides a unity through symbolic language, giving a degree of autonomy to nature and language that is utterly foreign to the modern *Zeitgeist*. As Eliade explains his illustration from lunar symbolism, it is proper to speak of the autonomy of the mythic symbol to cast up a unifying system that draws on lunar motifs and images; it is not proper to speak of man telling us about the moon through the utility of words. Not only do mythic symbols form a "system," as Eliade puts it, that unifies and integrates a universe that appears to modern man as fragmented; mythic language can also reconcile diametrically opposed motifs through the *coincidentia oppositorum* (*Patterns*, 419ff.). Here again, it is not man who reconciles opposites through the use of mythic language; it is mythic language that reconciles what for man is irrecon-cilable. Mythic language, for example, can present us with a God who is simul-taneously gentle and terrible in a way that defies rational explanation (419). It is not due to man's paradoxical thought that mythic language represents God paradoxically; rather, it is because mythic language possesses the autonomous power of *coincidentia oppositorum* that a unity of opposites can be attained, according to Eliade (419ff.).

The return of the autonomy of language is not only a vision shared by Foucault and Eliade, it is also an important key to their respective methodolo-gies. Ontological vision and methodological praxis are intricately related to

349

both men. Both cite the ontological significance of the return of language to the autonomous role that it has in myth (Eliade) and in *poesis* (Foucault), but in addition to these similar ontologies both men infuse their own methodologies with their ontological convictions. White's comment on Foucault brings out this point especially well:

> It (hermeneutics) means, as Foucault has suggested as the key to the understanding of his method, "transcription" in such a way as to reveal the inner dynamics of the thought processes by which a given representation of the world in words is grounded in *poesis*. To transform prose into poetry is Foucault's purpose, and thus he is especially interested in showing how all systems of thought in the human sciences can be seen as little more than terminological formalizations of poetic closures with the world of words, rather than with the "things" they purport to represent and explain. (White, "Foucault Decoded," 54)

Foucault writes "anti-history" in order to show the bankruptcy of our rational explanations in the arbitrary way that historians have supplied causal links where none exist. Historians delude themselves, Foucault argues, by thinking they can write in such a way as to convey the meaning of historical events through their discursive analytical prose. Instead, all that one can do, he says, is to show the poetic closures with the world of words. These closures have occurred as men have sought to represent the world in language and have at different times resisted or deferred to the autonomy of language in the creation of meaning.

> In our time, [Foucault writes]—and Nietzsche the philologist testifies to it—they (the possibility and necessity of criticism) are linked to the fact that language exists and that, in the innumerable words spoken by men—whether they are reasonable or senseless, demonstrative or poetic—a meaning has taken shape that hangs over us, leading us forward in our blindness, but awaiting in the darkness for us to attain awareness before emerging into the light of day and speaking. (Foucault, *The Birth of the Clinic*, xv–xvi)

To say that man's language constitutes history rather than the speakers or the content of their speech is a revolutionary method of writing history. And that is precisely what Foucault says. For him man's language constitutes the bobbins of history.

Eliade has given us an "anti-history" of religions. He does not give us a causal nexus to understand the progression of religious thought and behavior. Instead, he gives us a paradigmatic relationship between archetypes, symbols, and hierophanies; symbolic paradigms or systems that become reconstituted in the multivalence of individual symbols; and a "morphology of the sacred," e.g., the *coincidentia oppositorum* reflected in all myths and rituals. His analysis is also radically synchronic. History of religions is an ahistorical study of religious language: primarily the language that is textualized in myth and repeated indefinitely through ritual enactments of those myths. Instead of understanding religious symbols through the prism of historical context, Eliade actually decontextualizes the symbol in order to bring out the paradigm of meanings that it reflects *at any time and place.* In addition to the system of meanings that coalesces about a particular symbol, he also brings out the structure, for example, the divine polarity, the sacred androgyne, and the *axis mundi.* These structures of meaning are operative in what Eliade calls the "transconsciousness" of all men, and the presence of these structures and paradigms is not limited by time or culture. In short, Eliade refers us to something like Jung's postulate of the "collective unconscious." In a very real sense, then, the history of religions for Eliade is patterned after invariable structures and paradigms resident in the human mind.

It could be said of Eliade, as well as of Foucault, that he points us to an epiphany of "the flesh made word." In Eliade's case this epithet owes its justification to the mythicization of history which is both his vision and his method. Historical flux, the novelty and uniqueness of events, the appearance in human flesh and in historical tissue of the new and the unprecedented all are profoundly unreal for Eliade. What is real is the paradigmatic, the model, and the infinite ritual repetitions through which these mythic paradigms and models pass. Eliade's program stands in ironic juxtaposition to that proposed by the Christian theologian, Rudolph Bultmann. Instead of demythologizing the text into history and then into existential encounter, Eliade wants to remythologize history into mythic texts and then to the existential encounter defined by the myth. Historical existence for Eliade is unintelligible and empty apart from the paradigm or model that structures it, thereby "validating" that existence in accordance with the mythic text. Whatever is new in history must be absorbed back into the mythic pattern, for there *in the text* it finds authenticity, reality, and being. To make this point Eliade often cites the example of the Osage Indians, who have a ritual of reciting the creation myth at the event of a new-born child and in this way "to validate the new existence by announcing that it conforms with the mythic paradigms." According to Eliade, "each new birth represents a symbolic recapitulation of the cosmogony and of the tribe's mythical history" (*Myth and Reality*, 33). Thus flesh becomes Word, history becomes mythic text, new existence becomes archaic paradigm.

* * *

Eliade's methodology, presently foundering on the very horns of the dilemma that characterizes the whole field of *Religionswissenschaft*, can be made to sail again only by relinquishing one of the horns: empirical verification. Indeed his methodology can sail with aplomb if it can surrender the pretence that phenomenological description and the raw data of history are compatible and instead take a radically anti-historical tack.

The prescription following from this analysis calls for Eliade's methodology to represent not a synthesis of divergent currents of thought but a radical departure from both. Eliade's historical and ethnographic references, which number in the hundreds, indeed are not meant to constitute the kind of evidence on which a conventional ethnographer or historian (Baird) might rest his case. Instead, these citations are assembled to bring out and exemplify a pre-envisioned system or paradigm. But on the other hand, the system is not simply a particular theology or ontology for explaining Ultimate Truth in a given religious tradition (Streng); it is the author's own systemic, radically synchronic way of "knowing" everything. In other words, it is an epistemological system derived from the author himself, not simply from a particular ontology discovered in a given religious tradition. It is a system ascribed generically to the transconsciousness of the human mind, to *homo religiosus,* rather than a system built from an inductive chain of objectively discovered data. The empiricist historians of religion, such as Baird and Clavier, may want to declare such a radical departure to be outside the parameters set for the field by the Marburg platform drafted at the International Association for the History of Religions (IAHR) meeting of 1960, which defines *Religionswissenschaft* as an "anthropological discipline" (see Scholte, "Epistemic Paradigms," pp. 180ff.). But although the term "anthropological" connotes a social, scientific, data-oriented methodology to the empiricists, it is important to bear in mind that in the field of anthropology there is an alternative to an inductive, data-bound methodology. In fact, it is precisely along the line that separates these two alternatives in anthropology that the real battle in *Religionswissenschaft* will eventually have to be fought. These alternatives can be summarized as (1) the Anglo-American tradition of inductive empiricism that begins with the raw data and returns to those data for final verification, a method derived from the natural sciences; and (2) the French tradition of beginning with a model or paradigm and progressing through deductive reasoning to the data with intelligibility within the original paradigm as the final criterion for verification. The inductive approach assigns priority to observable behavior, while the deductive approach assigns priority to the fundamental categories and structures of the mind and language. The inductive approach limits itself to evidence of man's conscious life and thought; the deductive approach refers us to structures of the mind that are unconscious and generic, universal and invariable. The inductive approach formulates its questions and answers them in terms of diachronic-causal explanations; the deductive approach formulates and answers its questions in terms of a synchronic analysis of data which is derived from a paradigm. A data-bound "religio-historical" approach or an "anti-historical," radically synchronic treatment of religious phenomena—these are the alternatives whose juxtaposition holds the most promise for the debate among historians of religion. By formulating the dilemma in this way the debate can emerge from a certain parochialism that inhabits the dichotomy, between the dialogical/intuitive approach and the methods derived from the natural sciences. What the field needs is not more distinctness or isolation from the other disciplines that study religious phenomena but an identifiable alignment in a debate that cuts across all these disciplines. *Religionswissenschaft* is, by general agreement from all sides, fundamentally interdisciplinary in nature. For that reason alone a lively and informed entry into a debate of interdisciplinary proportions would vastly improve the acceptance of *Religionswissenschaft* as a field by the intellectual community where the debate is taking place. If Eliade can be appreciated as raising the kind of challenges to many of the reigning assumptions in *Religionswissenschaft* that Foucault and the structuralists are raising within the human and social sciences, he will have spurred historians of religion into precisely the kind of discussions that scholars in these other fields find at least unavoidable and at most utterly crucial in our time. Eliade does indeed offer a way out of the dilemma facing *Religionswissenschaft* but on terms that are far more provocative and promising than the terms on which he has hitherto been judged.

To paint Eliade in these radical colors is not to label him a structuralist. He gives far too much attention to the existential meaning of symbols and myths to qualify as a structuralist. But it is to say that he works with an epistemology derived from the French tradition of paradigms and deductive reasoning from which structuralism is also derived. And thus the force of the *detente* with the empirical method has much in common with the opposition of structuralism to empiricism. There are important differences not only between Eliade and Foucault but between Eliade, Lévi-Strauss, Edmund Leach and other structuralist anthropologists. But epistemologically they can be ranged on the same side of a classical divide between the French and Anglo-American traditions of studying man, including the phenomena of his religious experiences.

Notes

1. *Caete de Dor*, 8 (June, 1954): 27, quoted by Virgil Ierunca, "The Literary Work of Mircea Eliade," in *Myths and Symbols*, ed. Joseph M. Kitagawa and Charles H. Long (Chicago: University of Chicago Press, 1969), 351.
2. See also Ierunca, "Literary Work," 349–50.
3. *Caete de Dor*, 9 (December, 1955): 27, quoted and translated by Ierunca, "Literary Work," 350.
4. *Oceanografie*, 191, quoted by Ierunca, "Literary Work," 350.
5. Bob Scholte, "Epistemic Paradigms: Some Problems in Cross-Cultural Research on Social Anthropological History and Theory," in *The Anthropologist as Hero*, ed. E. Nelson Hayes and Tanya Hayes (Cambridge: MIT Press, 1970), 110.
6. Hayden White, "Foucault Decoded: Notes from the Underground," *History and Theory* 12/1 (1973): 26.
7. Michel Foucault, *The Order of Things* (New York: Vintage Books, 1973), 342–43.

Eliade and Postmodernism

37

Mircea Eliade and Postmodernism

Bryan Rennie

Editor's Introduction

The term "postmodernism" and the cluster of ideas associated with it are both confused and criticized. A glance at Jean-Paul Sartre's widely reprinted article of 1946, "Existentialism as a Humanism," shows that precisely the same accusations currently leveled at postmodernism were once leveled at existentialism. These accusations, in both cases, arise more from superficial misunderstandings, "straw man" fallacies, and enthusiasm of epigones who have failed to grasp the full implications of their precursors. There is much of value to be made of the postmodern turn and I suggested, in *Reconstructing Eliade*, that Eliade might be a "precursor of postmodernism" (232). This suggestion elicited a vigorous rejection from Carl Olson ("Mircea Eliade, Postmodernism, and the Problematic Nature of Representational Thinking"). The following selection is my response to Olson and is the clearest statement of my argument.

The emergence and coalescence of postmodernism as an increasingly coherent if somewhat polymorphous and protean matrix of interlinked understandings might serve to explain the difficulties of Douglas Allen, Guilford Dudley *et al.* as we all struggled to grasp a developing phenomenon for which scholars as yet lack a formed vocabulary and taxonomy. Eliade's attitude to history was, I have maintained (although others have disagreed), particularly characteristic of this postmodern turn. It would be foolish simply to say that Eliade "is" postmodern, especially since his quest for universal homologies in religion is almost quintessentially modern. Nonetheless, his position can be characterized in terms of the vocabulary developed in discussions of postmodernism. There is much to the claim that postmodernism developed as a response of the underlying strand of Western Romantic thought, rehabilitated by contact with Eastern philosophies. Of course, the influence of Eastern thought, the extent of which remains debatable in the cases of Heidegger and Derrida, is quite undeniable in the case of Eliade. The following essay is adapted from *Method and Theory in the Study of Religion* 12/3 (2000): 422–25. All rights reserved. Copyright © 2000 by Brill Academic Publishers. Reprinted by permission of Brill Academic Publishers.

ℬ ℭ

In "Archaic, Modern, Postmodern," the penultimate chapter of *Reconstructing Eliade*, I argue that

> careful inspection of Eliade's writings ... reveals his "anti-historical" tendency to be counter-modern and remarkably close to later thought which has been labeled "postmodern." It is, I believe, a more accurate appreciation of Eliade to see him as at least a precursor of postmodernism than it is to reject him as either a sentimental champion of archaic traditions or as simply anti-historical. (232)

I continue to argue that Eliade's thought can be seen to have "marked affinities with that of certain later scholars who have been connected with postmodernism" (232). First with *The Philosophical Discourse of Modernity*, "Habermas's Postmodern Adventure," according to one critic,[1] (233), next with David Ray Griffin, series editor of the SUNY series on "constructive post-modern thought." Then with Brian McHale (*Postmodernist Fiction*), Derrida and Foucault. I further argue that (my interpretation of) Eliade's analysis of creative imagination is closely parallel to the category of "immanences" described by Ihab Hassan. (My interpretation of)[2] Eliade's epistemology and philosophy of history can be seen to agree with Anthony Giddens' description of postmodern thought. I argue that Eliade has specific affinities with certain scholars described in Edgar McKnight's *Postmodern Biblical Criticism*, and, finally, that

> [a]ccording to McHale,[3] in the "postmodern" text the "parallax of subjectivities" gives way to a "parallax of discourses" (McHale, 6) which no longer affords the reader any confidence as to the external existence of an objective world, "no stable landmarks 'out there'" (6). Although we do "persuade ourselves" that we are able to "read through" the screen of style to the "real" events, ... it seems that different readers are differently persuaded about what those "real" events might be (7). Similarly, in Eliade's analysis of archaic and modern ontology, we might persuade ourselves that we can read through to the "real" behind the traditions but all we find is

our own "reality." In *Images and Symbols* (28), discussing the alienation of scholars of religion from "the cultured public," Eliade recognizes "objectivity," like "reality," is subject to fashioning and personal persuasion. ... Eliade's alternative and subjective hierophanies reveal assorted sacred spaces and times, different ontologies to different people. His juxtaposition of "archaic ontology" and modern ontology is well known (*Myth of the Eternal Return*, 34–48). What is less well recognized is the implication that there is no one *general* archaic ontology but a whole series of *specific* archaic ontologies which share the common feature of being founded upon mythical rather than historical models. "Ontological perspectivism, the parallax of discourses, and the worlds they encode, is not a characteristic structure of modernist poetics; but it is characteristic of postmodernism." ... [and I conclude that] [t]his is more than enough to indicate some real affinities between Eliade and postmodernism. (*Reconstructing Eliade*, 237–38, quoting from McHale, *Postmodernist Fiction*, 12)

"Archaic, Modern, Postmodern" is, in many ways, the conclusion of the book's argument. If refuted, as Olson claimed in his article, the entire book is seriously weakened. However, Olson's argument had grave shortcomings. He responded vigorously to this one chapter, but neglected the foregoing chapters, which are its premises. For example, he called the recognition that history is not an empirical category but requires socially constructed models to give it meaning a "minor agreement" between Eliade and Foucault ("Eliade, Postmodernism," 360). For Eliade, historical existence is meaningless until some artifice of human culture be employed to render it meaningful. Olson, however, claims that "the history passed down to us is not a body of facts like Eliade thinks" (360). Yet the whole of my Chapter 9 argues that in Eliade we find a complex understanding of history as something other than a "body of facts." Failing to consider the complexity of history for Eliade, Olson has already refused that which is postmodern about him. Accepting this complexity, the similarities between Eliade's and Foucault's attitudes to history (even as described by Olson—360–64) is immediately apparent.

Olson similarly neglected my analysis of Eliade's equation of the sacred and the real (*Reconstructing Eliade*, ch. 2). He recognizes that "Eliade is convinced that when a religious object comes into being it also becomes real" ("Mircea Eliade, Postmodernism, and the Problematic Nature of Representational Thinking," 363). However, he ignores the dialectic of the sacred and the profane in which religious objects do not "come into being" *ex nihilo*, but by the transformation of the apprehension of the perceiver. Again, to argue that Eliade continues "to hold out the possibility of finding absolutes because all knowledge is not as relative as Foucault claims" (363), is to ignore completely my analysis of Eliade and relativism (ch. 11). Olson's case consistently fails to consider arguments elsewhere in my book. He never quotes from anywhere *other* than chapter 17, although I made comments about Eliade's affinities with post-modernism elsewhere.

Ignoring my analysis of Eliade it was easy to say that he is "in sharp contrast to Foucault" (364). *Considering* my analysis, Eliade can be seen to *agree* with Foucault that there is a plurality of real and meaningful worlds. *Ignoring* my analysis it is easy to write that "[w]hen Eliade writes about Being he presupposes its presence, … whereas Derrida … calls into question the presence of Being" (367). *Considering* my analysis it can be seen that the *apprehension* of Being (=the sacred/real) is relative to the cultural conditioning of the perceiver (*Reconstructing Eliade*, 19, 210). It requires argument, then, to substantiate Olson's unsupported claim that "the radical relativity of Being for Derrida is anathema to Eliade" (368). Olson realizes that "Being … is related to reality in [Eliade's] works" but assumes that this implies that "Being is not a human construct for Eliade" (368). This ignores the Kantian identification of reality as a category of the understanding, which I take to be fundamental to Eliade's work. "Reality" is a human construct insofar as the attribution of reality can be made or withheld relative to cultural conditioning (*Reconstructing Eliade*, 22). This does not mean that I make Eliade into a skeptic as Olson insists (373), but that I make him into a species of relativist as I explicitly state: "Eliade manifests the primary characteristics of the relativist in seeing alternative worldviews as each true" (*Reconstructing Eliade*, 127).

Olson sees Derrida as convinced of "the total relativity of meaning" but insists that Eliade cannot share this conviction "because he cannot imagine how it is possible for human beings to function without an assurance that there is something irreducibly real and meaningful" (364, quoting Eliade, *Ordeal by Labyrinth*, 153). Again Olson ignores my interpretation of Eliade as arguing that human beings fabricate out of their own cultural conditioning the factors that determine what we perceive to be real. In fact, Eliade can be compared to Derrida in many particulars.[4] Where Derrida identifies a longing for a center, Eliade has his symbolism of the center, the desire to live in close proximity to the sacred. Where this leads Derrida to his critique of binary opposition, Eliade analyses the *coincidentia oppositorum*. Derrida considers the longing for the center to spawn a "centering" or privileging of one of the binary pair and to give rise to the play of binary opposites. Eliade has the dialectic of the sacred and the profane (in which one of a pair is—always already—revealed to be "above" the other). In Eliade's thought this elevation is dependent upon the preparation of the subject and could, therefore, always be different (*Reconstructing Eliade*, ch. 1 and esp. 19). Where Eliade concludes that religion is a human universal, Derrida states that "for me there is no religion."[5] The homology is that both thinkers destabilize the binary opposition between religious/non-religious and the unthinking privileging of either one. I do not mean to imply the indebtedness of either author. They were both products of the same philosophical genealogy through Hegel, Nietzsche, Heidegger, and Saussure, both products of similarly marginalized cultures (Algeria and Romania), both influenced by Romantic forebears. It would not be in the least astonishing if they came to similar conclusions.

None of this is to say that Eliade "is" "a postmodernist." Although Olson characterizes me as claiming that Eliade "shared enough affinities with post-modern thinkers to be called postmodern himself" (*Reconstructing Eliade*, 357), I nowhere say that Eliade himself "can be called postmodern," nor do I ever "label" him "a postmodernist." I consistently *separate* Eliade from postmoderns with phrases such as, "[f]or Eliade, and for those who embrace postmodern thought" (*Reconstructing Eliade*, 241), and by stating that, in Eliade's work, "despite the unquestionable emphasis on the archaic, the modern is there, as is the postmodern" (*Reconstructing Eliade*, 238). My point was that

> a consideration of certain "postmodern" characteristics in the thought of Mircea Eliade occasions a substantial improvement in the understanding of both Eliade and of the recent postmodern phenomenon [and that] careful inspection of Eliade's writings … reveals his "anti-historical" tendency to be counter-modern and remarkably close to later thought which has been labeled "postmodern." (*Reconstructing Eliade*, 231, 232)

"Even if it is true that Eliade anticipated some themes associated with post-modernism, this does not necessarily make him a precursor of it or a representa-tive of postmodernism," Olson protests (358). I grant that anticipating the themes of a later mode does not make one a *representative* of that mode. But I did not claim that it did. On the other hand, how can an author anticipate the themes of a later mode of thought *without* being a precursor of it?

Olson is similarly confused about the relation of the Enlightenment, Roman-ticism, and Postmodernism. He writes, "Eliade is not reacting against the Romantic movement and the Enlightenment, whereas postmodernism is a defi-nitive, negative, and critical reaction to the intellectual projects of the Romantic and Enlightenment modes of thinking" (373–74). This treats postmodernism as a monolithic orthodoxy, and it treats Romanticism and the Enlightenment as somehow allies instead of opponents. The Romantic movement was itself a reaction against Enlightenment rationalism, and postmodernism is in many ways a *continuation* of that Romantic project. Reaction against the Enlighten-ment *was* a product of the Enlightenment. Only if it is assumed that Eliade *agreed* with the philosophy of the Enlightenment, whereas "undisputedly recog-nized postmodern thinkers" (Olson, 358) did not, does this separate Eliade from postmodern thinkers. Olson assumes that he does, as is shown (but not sup-ported) by his repeated statement that Eliade is "a product of Enlightenment philosophy" (358, 374, 383). Well, I would argue, so is Derrida.

Nor is this the final confusion in Olson's argument. He interprets Eliade as "captive to a representational mode of thinking" and defines this as assuming "a correspondence between appearance and reality." He goes on to claim that

360

"the phenomenological aspect of Eliade's method ... suggests a metaphysical position and a coherence theory of truth" (374) and finally concludes that Eliade's "coherence theory of truth [is] diametrically opposed to the post-modern position" (382). To begin with an assumption of representational think-ing presupposing a *correspondence* between appearance and reality, and then criticize a *coherence* theory of truth smacks of an astounding philosophical naiveté. I cannot determine whether Olson finally takes Eliade to embrace a correspondence or a coherence theory of truth. My analysis is that he is closer to a *pragmatic* "theory of truth"—a theory of the factors required for a sub-jective attribution of truth, which is, in the final analysis, what *works* to fulfil the existential need of humanity. The practical outcome of belief is a matter of the highest concern for Eliade. For example, his distinction between "modern" and "religious" humanity in *The Myth of the Eternal Return* is based upon the practical ability to tolerate the terror of history.

It is notable that Olson discusses "Eliade's reaction to the postmodern posi-tion on meaning" (378) and tells us that "Eliade cannot accept the postmodern notion of the simulacra" (381). In point of fact, Eliade never mentions post-modernism. Olson presents himself as knowing what Eliade "thinks" (364) and does not think (363), "believes" (363), "assumes" (376), and with whom Eliade "would agree" (362), "would find himself comfortable" (381), and with whom he "shares convictions" (364). This is typical of the unwarranted certainty of the modern as opposed to the warranted uncertainty of the postmodern. The point of the demonstration in *Reconstructing Eliade* of the failings of previous critical scholarship on Eliade (see chs. 14 and 15) was to reveal that there has been a consistent, specifically modernist, misreading of Eliade. Olson continues this misreading. Although he displays a broad knowledge of postmodernist authors he has no sympathy for their position. His interpretation of Eliade is irreducibly modern. His (real) Eliade searches for the one true reality of the singular sacred—whereas mine is irreducibly postmodern—there are a potentially infi-nite number of sacred worlds, limited only by the imagination. My interpreta-tion of Eliade's writings was made assuming the self-coherence of their author and attempted to confer as high a degree of coherence upon them as possible. I conclude that Eliade relativizes the human perception of the real. As such he was a precursor of postmodernism. My interpretation relies upon internal consistency and coherence with the printed word to which I have access, not upon some imagined access to intentional states.

My reading of Eliade is an unusual one, but it is supported throughout *Recon-structing Eliade* more thoroughly than can be appreciated by a reading of one chapter. Nor am I alone in this interpretation. In *Changing Religious Worlds: The Meaning and End of Mircea Eliade* are a number of references to Eliade's links to the postmodern. Rachela Permenter traces the connection between Romanticism and Postmodernism and assesses the presence of "Romantic Postmodernism" in Eliade's fiction. She suggests that Eliade's "work offers a dependable bridge from Romantic to postmodern thought" (97). William Paden argues that Eliade has "two voices." The second voice is "post-foundationalist and to some extent postmodern" (250). Norman Girardot insists that Eliade "stands on the cusp between the modern ... and the postmodern." Girardot states unequivocally that "Eliade's approach was ... (to employ an appropriately clumsy term) proto-postmodern. Eliade is ... a partial anticipation of what we have come to call, rather apocalyptically now, postmodernism" (161–62).[6] Douglas Allen argues that "[i]t is also possible to interpret Eliade's negative judgments about modernity as sharing characteristics with antimodern postmodernist approaches." To be fair, Allen also states that "[a]lthough Eliade sounds like this postmodernism when arguing against modern forms of reductionism, in many fundamental respects he clearly rejects such a postmodernist orientation" (223–24). However, that does not lessen my point, which is not, and never has been, to claim that Eliade "is" postmodern. Rather "I am consciously attempting to clarify Eliade's thought by means of postmodernism and postmodernism by means of his thought in the understanding that both are to some extent imaginary constructs" (*Reconstructing Eliade*, 232).

In the final analysis, Olson's critique of my correlation of Eliade and postmodern thought cannot be considered a serious challenge since it does not consider the whole of my argument. In fact, along with its other serious shortcomings, it merely continues the modernist misreading of Eliade. However, the whole question requires considerable further consideration.

Notes

1. George A. Trey, "The Philosophical Discourse of Modernity: Habermas's Postmodern Adventure," *Diacritics* 19/2 (1989): 67–79.
2. To save us all from boring repetition, please assume that I always already assume that my "knowledge" of Eliade's thought never comes any closer to his actual thought than my own interpretation of his written texts. I do not know what he thought, or felt, or whether my interpretation is "correct." I only know it fits coherently with my own acquaintance with the sum of Eliade's writings.
3. Brian McHale, "Constructing (Post)Modernism: The Case of *Ulysses*," *Style* 24/1 (1990): 1–21. McHale is also the author of *Postmodernist Fiction* (New York: Methuen, 1987).
4. This is adapted from *Changing Religious Worlds: The Meaning and End of Mircea Eliade*, ed. Bryan Rennie (Albany: NY, SUNY Press, 2000), xiv. Even there the treatment is all too brief. Much remains to be done and I have but made some suggestive comments.
5. *Deconstruction in a Nutshell*, ed. John D. Caputo (New York: Fordham University Press, 1997), 21—yet Derrida observes that religious thought, though lost, returns, for example, in the structure of Saussure's linguistics.
6. I attempt to trace more specifically the implications of Eliade's position on this cusp in "Mircea Eliade: A Secular Mystic in the History of Religions," *Origini. Journal of Cultural Studies* 3/4 (2003): 42–54.

Eliade's Literature

38

ON READING ELIADE'S STORIES AS MYTHS FOR MODERNS

Mac Linscott Ricketts

Editor's Introduction

This article, by Mac Linscott Ricketts, is a previously unpublished paper, which was presented at Midwest Modern Language Association Twenty-Fourth Annual Meeting, Cincinnati, Ohio, November, 1982. It is an insightful analysis of Eliade's literature by possibly the only Anglophone historian of religion who thoroughly learned Romanian in order to investigate Eliade's early life and work in real detail and who thus gained the additional benefit of access to Eliade's untranslated fiction.

On the significance of Eliade's literature see the sections in Rennie, *Changing Religious Worlds* and *The International Eliade*, and the books of Eugen Simion. The following article is copyright © 2005 Equinox Publishing. All rights reserved.

ക രു

Mircea Eliade, having made for himself since 1947 a worldwide reputation as an historian of religions, is becoming more known for his literary writings. He was seriously considered for the Nobel Prize in Literature in 1979. His published fiction, which he wrote always in his native Romanian language, consists of some ten novels, all but one written prior to his leaving Romania definitively in 1940; twenty-five novellas and short-stories, many in the genre of the fantastic, the majority written since 1945; and two complete plays, both of which have been staged in Romania.[1] Many of these works of "fiction" have been translated and published in French, German, and other languages, though only a small number have appeared so far in English.

How does Eliade see himself: as a Romanian novelist who happens to make his living teaching and writing books in the field of the history of religions?—or as a scholar of world religions who, for a hobby, indulges himself in the fantasy world of fiction writing? Statements from his published journal excerpts and from elsewhere can be brought forward to support both of these views. Reminiscing about the events that prevented him from becoming an "Indian" as he had sought to do during his youthful sojourn in India in 1928–31, Eliade says that these events were providential:

> Neither the life of an "adopted Bengalese" nor that of an Himalayan hermit would have allowed me to fulfill the possibilities with which I came into the world … I could not have been creative except by remaining in my world—which in the first place was the world of Romanian language and culture. And I had no right to renounce it until I had done my duty to it: that is, until I had exhausted my creative potential.[2]

Eliade seems to be thinking of himself here as a novelist first of all, because it is to his literary creativity that he is referring—seemingly ignoring the teaching, research, and writing he did in the field of the history of religions during the thirties in Bucharest. This latter work could have been—and later was—carried on in another language, of course. Eliade identifies himself here as a Romanian literary personality.

Similarly, in October 1946, having been freshly reminded of his homeland (he was then an exile in Paris), he suddenly is made aware of his "alienation from my true vocation, that of a *Romanian* writer." He laments the fact that he has been "diverted from the course predestined for me" and has lost six years during which he might have been writing.[3] In an entry for 17 July 1963 Eliade likens himself to Georges Bernanos, the Spanish author who renounced writing novels during the Spanish Civil War as a witness against the Christian world. "I realize," Eliade says, "that for nearly ten years I too sacrificed 'literature'; I gave up writing novels (the only literary genre for which I have sufficient talent). I did it to bring about the acceptance of a new understanding of *homo religiosus*. In a certain sense I too 'bore witness' in a religious war which I knew in advance was a lost cause."[4]

But in the preface he wrote for the English edition of his great post-war novel, *Noaptea de Sânziene* (*The Forbidden Forest*), he speaks as though literary writing has been for him primarily a release or safety valve from the pressures of scholarly labor, or a "temptation" to which he yields from time to time. In India, after a lengthy period of intense study, he suddenly set aside his Sanskrit texts and abandoned himself to writing a novel. "I needed *freedom*—that freedom which the writer knows only in the act of literary creation." Similarly, *The Forbidden Forest* was begun when Eliade was under compulsion to write his study on *Shamanism*. He concluded from these and other similar instances that his "spiritual equilibrium—the condition indispensable to any creativity, is assured by this oscillation between research of a scientific nature and literary imagination."[5]

Yet in spite of these statements in which he seems to say he is primarily a writer or *primarily* a scholar, it is plain that Eliade regards himself as both, and he feels that he has a mission to fulfill through both his scholarly and literary activities. Very revealing are his journal notes for 21 February 1955, recording the thoughts that passed through his mind when he awoke in the night aware of a suppurating mole on his armpit, and he imagined it might be a cancer and that he would die. He thought: "How unready I am to pass beyond! A feeling of guilt: almost nothing of what I must do have I done. 'Messages' which only now am I prepared to transmit: my religious and philosophical books, perhaps also my literary works."[6]

We wonder what "messages" he is thinking of here and whether or not he has by now transmitted them. What this passage makes plain, in any event, is that Eliade thinks of himself in some sense as a "messenger" through what he writes. He confesses in his "Autobiographical Fragment" that: "I have never felt myself capable of composing a 'purely scientific' work of ethnography or folklore."[7] Hence his scholarly works should be considered, he says, as "philosophical" rather than "scientific." Hence also his insistence on "hermeneutics," the use of a method of interpretation that will disclose the *meaning* of the documents studied.

He would, in fact, involve the whole discipline of the history of religions in this quest for meaning. These ideas are set forth vigorously in two essays of signal importance, "The History of Religions and a New Humanism" (1961) and "Crisis and Renewal in History of Religions" (1965), both republished in *The Quest* (1969). In the former he argues that the proper study of the history of religions (non-reductive, seeking understanding, employing results obtained through all sciences) can and will produce a new humanism, a second Renaissance. "By attempting to understand the existential situations expressed by the documents he is studying, the historian of religions will inevitably attain a deeper knowledge of man. It is on the basis of such a knowledge that a new humanism on a worldwide scale could develop" (3). In this essay Eliade draws a comparison between the work of the literary critic and the historian of religions, both of whom study a document from within, examining it "as an autonomous universe with its own laws and structures" (5), utilizing and integrating the work of linguists, historians, sociologists, etc. But then he adds, in the case of the literary critic, that when his work is done: "There is always a secret message in the work of great writers, and it is on the plane of philosophy that it is most likely to be grasped" (5). The task of the historian of religions, parallel with that of the critic, is to prepare the ground for an ultimate *philosophical* explanation of a religion's "message," to "open the way to a philosophical anthropology" (9).

In "Crisis and Renewal" Eliade laments the failure of historians of religion to make of their discipline a *"total hermeneutics"* capable of producing a change in both themselves and their readers, and ultimately producing a cultural awakening (58, 62). "Creative hermeneutics *changes* man; it is more than instruction, it is also a spiritual technique susceptible of modifying the quality of existence itself …. A good history of religions book ought to produce in the reader an action of *awakening* (62f.). Addressing his fellow professionals, he chides them for their timidity and lack of imagination, in that they have shrunk back from creating *"oeuvres"* and have written only monographs (61). They have operated according to models drawn from the natural sciences rather than from the humanities (67); they have avoided "taking seriously the spiritual worlds they study" (62). Consequently, he says, the history of religions has not fulfilled its mission to "open new perspectives to Western thought, to philosophy properly speaking as well as to artistic creation" (63).

I believe we are justified in reading between the lines of these essays Eliade's conception of his own mission as an historian of religions, and perhaps also as a writer of literary works. In a word, it is to "awaken" the world, particularly the West, to its all but forgotten religious heritage. This point is brought out most clearly in those places where Eliade contrasts the man of traditional societies with "modern man." While this contrast is a familiar one to readers of Eliade's basic works, an interesting fact emerges when we examine closely what Eliade has said: "modern man" is really not so different from his predecessor, religious man, as at first he seemed!

When one begins to read Eliade's classic, *The Sacred and the Profane* (1957), he is presented with two diametrically opposed types of humanity: *homo religiosus*, the man of traditional or archaic societies, and modern man, "who lives without religious feeling, …who lives, or wishes to live, in a desacralized world" (13). We are told that between the "modes of existence" in the world chosen by these two types there is an "abyss" (14). Later we read: "Modern non-religious man assumes a new existential situation; he regards himself solely as the subject and agent of history, and he refuses all appeal to transcendence. In other words, he accepts no model for humanity outside the human condition as it can be seen in various historical situations" (203).

Yet, having made this dramatic point, Eliade seems to blunt it in the pages which follow and in other books (*Birth and Rebirth*, *Myth and Reality*, etc.) in which he speaks of the hidden, buried, unconscious, and crypto religious behavior of the modern man who is unable to abolish his past—that is, his religious heritage. People still persevere in the ancient rituals—now divested of religious meaning; they still listen to or read or watch "stories"; and they still dream. And in these activities and others they "escape from time" just as *homo religiosus* did by means of his religion. Such activities are of only limited benefit to the modern individual since they are not integrated into a religious vision of the world. They fail to "open him to the universe," to give him "access to the world of spirit"; they do not transform a private situation into a paradigmatic one; they do not reveal "structures of the real" (*Sacred and the Profane*, 210–12).

Modern nonreligious man, then, is considerably more "religious" than he realizes. Indeed, Eliade admits, "Nonreligious man *in the pure state* is a comparatively rare phenomenon," because he can't help behaving in religious ways (*Sacred and the Profane*, 201). What, in fact, is the difference between the two? Modern man has experienced a "second fall," an event that has placed him at an even greater remove from God (to speak in Christian terms) and has driven his religious sensibilities into the unconscious. (Here Eliade accepts a little help from Jung.) But "in his deepest being he still retains a memory of it [religion]," though consciously it has been "forgotten" (213).

The difference, then, between religious and nonreligious man reduces to one of *consciousness* or *unconsciousness* of religious realities. The modern man has "forgotten" or suppressed into the unconscious that which the man of traditional societies knew and celebrated consciously. In the light of this understanding of modern man's "problem," Eliade's statements about the consequences of creative hermeneutics quoted above—that it *changes* man, that it ought to produce an *awakening*—take on new meaning. I note here in passing that Eliade has devoted a special study to "Mythologies of Memory and Forgetting"[8] which deals principally with myths from India, themes from ancient Greece, and certain forms of Gnosticism. Moreover, amnesia and *anamnesis* are prominent themes in a number of Eliade's short stories, as we shall see.

One of the activities in which Eliade says modern man unconsciously behaves "religiously" and one which has greatly interested Eliade is the reading of novels. For modern man, novels play a role analogous to myths in archaic societies. As Eliade has defined myth, some of its essential characteristics are found in novels and in all literature that tells a story.

The key words in Eliade's definition of myth (as given in many places) are "exemplary story." Myths are, of course, about supernatural beings; they take place in the time of beginnings, *in illo tempore* as Eliade is fond of saying; and they have to do with creations, with the origins of things. In these respects, modern novels are not like myths. But what Eliade always stresses about myth are its *narrative* character and its *exemplary* function.

Without trying to account for it, Eliade posits a universal human need to listen to (or read, or watch dramatized) *stories*.

> It is a difficult need to define, being at once desire to communicate with "others," with "strangers," and share in their dramas and hopes, and at the same time the need to know what *can have taken place*. It is hard to conceive of a human being who is not fascinated by "narrative," by a

recounting of significant events, by what has happened to men endowed with the "twofold reality" of literary characters (for on the one hand they reflect the historical and psychological reality of members of a modern society and, on the other, they possess all the power of an imaginary creation (*Myth and Reality*, 192–93).

He was delighted when he discovered "proof" of this thesis in experiments dealing with REM (rapid eye movement in sleep), which indicated the apparent necessity for dreaming.[9]

But years *before* he wrote the above or discovered "proof" of the theory, Eliade was convinced of man's need to be nourished by narratives. On January 5, 1952, at a time when he was struggling with the first part of what became his most important novel, *The Forbidden Forest*, Eliade wrote in his journal: "Must write a long article which could be entitled, 'On the Necessity for the *Roman-roman* (narrative-novel).' To show the autonomous, glorious, irreducible dimension of *narration*, the formula of myth and mythology readapted to the modern consciousness. To show that modern man, like the man of archaic societies, cannot exist without myths, more precisely, without exemplary stories."[10] Thus Eliade has opposed himself to all theories of the novel which would *minimize* or eliminate *plot*. He interprets the contemporary breakdown of the traditional narrative-novel form as another indication of a widely prevalent desire to return to chaos, to destroy the past and create anew (*Myth and Reality*, 190).

As to the paradigmatic value of myth, myths provide models or patterns for human behavior, thus sanctifying it. Although I can't recall Eliade's ever having put it in just these terms, I believe he would agree that the hearers and readers of stories *identify with* characters in myths or literature and vicariously undergo the trials and successes of the fictional figures. This is true particularly of narratives having an initiatory structure—a type of special interest to Eliade. He has commented in several places that "the process of initiation seems to be co-extensive with any and every human condition" (*Birth and Rebirth*, 128; cf. *Myth and Reality*, 202, etc.). Ancient myths, more recent fairy tales, present-day fiction, and dreams frequently follow an initiatory schema, and to varying degrees all such "stories" help man to cope with life and endure the trials of historical existence.[11] But the modern man receives less help than does religious man, because he does not regard the "models" in the stories as having transcendent paradigmatic value.

Another function of myth in societies where it is a living force is that of taking its hearers "out of time," of introducing them into another time, the time of origins. Ritual, of course, has the same function, and the very telling of a myth can be a ritual experience for those who come under its spell. Further, by seeking to imitate the exemplary behavior of mythic people, religious man transposes his life from "history" into the timeless time of myth. Thus did the man of traditional societies escape from the meaninglessness and "terror" of history, which, as Eliade sees it, man has always sought to do (cf. *Cosmos and History*, 11). And today, through novels, the theater, motion pictures, and television modern man still seeks to "kill time," to escape from his historical existence into another temporal dimension (though not the time of origins).

Perhaps the most profound function of myth—which is the function of religion itself—is to "reveal other worlds." "The principal function of religion," Eliade has written, "is that of maintaining an 'opening' toward a world which is superhuman, the world of axiomatic spiritual values.... The function of religion is to awaken and sustain the consciousness of another world, whether it be a divine world or the world of mythical ancestors" ("Structures and Changes in the History of Religion," 366). This latter sentence practically duplicates what Eliade says about myths in *Myth and Reality*: "Myths are the most general and effective means of awakening and maintaining consciousness of another world, a beyond, whether it be a divine world or the world of the Ancestors" (139). Thus Eliade invests myth with a role of supreme importance in religion, above that of ritual, doctrine, or any sociological factor. And if myth can play this role in traditional societies, literature can take its place in the contemporary world!

In his important essay, "Literary Imagination and Religious Structure" (*Criterion*, Summer, 1978, 30–31, incorporating part of the Preface to *The Forbidden Forest*) Eliade draws certain parallels between myth and modern fiction. Both the writer of fiction and the historian of religions dealing with myths are "confronted with different structures of sacred and mythical space, different qualities of time, and more specifically by a considerable number of strange, unfamiliar and enigmatic worlds of meaning" (33).

Like the gods in the myths, the fiction writer creates a "new world." The all-important difference, Eliade says, is that "myth has an exemplary value in traditional societies, and this is no longer true for literary works" ("Literary Imagination and Religious Structure"). Yet even this distinction is not an absolute one, since "a literary creation can likewise reveal forgotten meanings even to a contemporary, sophisticated reader" (*ibid.*). In fact, Eliade continues, a literary work can become what any religious phenomenon is, a *hierophany*. As such it participates in the paradox of all hierophanies: though they are "profane" in themselves, they become bearers of sacred meaning. Eliade calls this here "a dialectical process that transforms a profane object into something that is sacred, i.e., significant, precious and paradigmatic .... Likewise, in the case of literary works, meaningful and exemplary human values are disguised in concrete, historical and thus fragmentary characters and episodes" (*ibid.*). To find these meanings is equivalent to discovering the hidden meaning of religious phenomena.

Eliade has stated on numerous occasions that the "unrecognizability of miracle," i.e., the paradox of the hierophany as explained above, is the theme that pervades all his works. In the passage just quoted we see how Eliade applies the concept to literature. Any work of literature *can* conceal a message, and therefore it would seem that an historian of religions ought to make a keen literary critic! But, curiously, Eliade inverts this and says that "a writer or literary critic is usually better prepared to understand the documents investigated by the historian of religions than is, say, a sociologist or an anthropologist" (*ibid.*). In any event, Eliade sees the literary critic as requiring a training and methodology similar to that of an interpreter of religious phenomena, especially myth. Eliade himself, with his "double vocation," would be especially well equipped to engage in both literary criticism and religious hermeneutics.

Given Eliade's diagnosis of "modern man" and modern society—namely, that they are cut off from spiritual sources that once enriched human life by affording it added temporal dimensions and meaning; given his ability to write fiction and his possession of a rich store of knowledge derived from a lifetime of study of religions; and given, finally, his sense of having a "mission" or "message to transmit" to the world, both as a writer and as a scholar, one might anticipate that he would attempt to create literary works embodying religious themes and messages which would reach the minds and hearts of modern men and women. That is we might anticipate that Mircea Eliade would attempt to produce "myths for moderns."[12] (And this, in fact, seems to be the case—provided, however, that we do not locate Eliade's *primary* motivation or inspiration for writing in some prophetic urge.)

In 1953, speaking of his literary activity *up to that time*, Eliade denied that he had written any work of literature in order to "demonstrate" some philosophical thesis. Rather, he says, "I wrote literature for the pleasure (or the need) of *writing freely*, of inventing, of dreaming—of thinking, even, but without the stringency of systematic thought" (Girardot and Ricketts, *Imagination and Meaning*, 125). He goes on to say here, and he repeats it in his Preface to *The Forbidden Forest*, that his understanding of certain religious structures was enhanced by the activity of his imagination in the production of some of his works of fiction. He does not deny that "the literary imagination utilized materials or meanings I had studied as an historian of religions," but he denies there was a *conscious* influence (*Forbidden Forest*, vi; "Literary Imagination...," 31–32). In one of the interviews he gave to Claude-Henri Rocquet for *L'Épreuve du labyrinthe*, Eliade explained more precisely how he writes:

When one is possessed by a plot, the inner vision is undoubtedly nourished by all one carries within himself, but that vision has no relation to the intellectual knowledge of myths, rites, and symbols. In writing, one forgets all that one knows. When I reread *Pe strada Mântuleasa* (*The Old Man and the Bureaucrats*) I saw that some episodes correspond to certain archetypes. I did not think of them while writing (198).

371

In other words, Eliade denies *consciously* or *deliberately* including myth themes or symbols in his literary works. Yet, when one finds—as is often the case—specific and detailed references to the Upaniṣads, Gnosticism, or Fideli d'Amore, or to Hegel or Heidegger and their philosophies, it is obvious that the scholar has been giving assistance to the writer! Şarpele, the novel of 1937 which was created in fourteen nights of inspired, frantic writing (see *Autobiography*, I, 321–22 and cf. *Ordeal by Labyrinth*, 172–73), may well have been a "pure product of the imagination," but it is hard to accept that *all* Eliade's fiction is equally pure imagination. Nor do I think he means to claim this. What he means is that he does not compose plots deliberately to illustrate this or that thesis or symbolism from the history of religions; and if his novellas are "modern myths," this is because they, like ancient myths, are the products of the imagination.

As we have seen, Eliade regards an "epic" literary work—one that tells a story—as equivalent to a myth and hence capable of revealing a message, capable of being a hierophany. One of his most extensive expositions of this idea is found in his journal entries for the 5th and 10th of March, 1968, where he comments on reviews of *La Ţigănci*[13] that had appeared in Romania. He says here that those who have sought for "symbols" or allegories in the story have missed the point. Rather, one should take the story as a whole, as the

> presentation of a new Universe, heretofore unknown, with its own laws— and this presentation constitutes an *act of creation*, not only in the aesthetic sense of the expression. In penetrating this Universe, learning to know it, to savor it—something is revealed to you. The problem posed for the critic is not how to decipher the "symbolism" of the story. But, allowing that the story has "enchanted" me, has *convinced* me, how to interpret the *message* which is hidden in its reality ...[14]

In the entry for 10 March, immediately following, he elaborates the point to which I alluded earlier, citing from a later article, that inasmuch as a literary work creates a new world, it is a continuation or extension of myth and has the function of myth—i.e., it "reveals unsuspected meanings, gives a meaning to 'everyday' life."

I am convinced that what Eliade says here about one of his novellas applies equally to all his literary creations. They are not allegories nor are they "symbolic" in the sense that Tolkien's or C. S. Lewis' works are, for example. Of course, symbols and symbolic figures can be found quite frequently, just as they are in myths, but that is another matter. The story mentioned above, "With the Gypsy Girls" in its English translation, abounds in symbols drawn from mythology and the history of religions—such as the labyrinth, the carriage driver as Charon, etc.—but deciphering them does not exhaust the meaning Eliade wishes the reader to derive from the story. The "revelation" as Eliade calls it comes from the total impact of the story, conveyed not *rationally*, but *intuitively* ... just as myths make their impact on believers. Eliade would make us "believe" in the world he creates in his stories and, entering into them, be "awakened" and enlightened.[15]

Many, though not all, of Eliade's recent literary works can be classified in the genre of fantastic literature. This is true, for example, of "With the Gypsy Girls," although Eliade does not mention this fact in his journal comments cited above. The story, like all of Eliade's fiction, is set in an *apparently* realistic world, in this case the Bucharest of the 1930s. The hero, Gavrilescu, enters a kind of bordello operated by Gypsies and stays, he thinks, a few hours. When he emerges, some twelve years have elapsed. The passage from one time rhythm or zone to another is a favorite device, of course, of writers of fantasy, and Eliade has used it a number of times. But Eliade states in his *Journal*, that even the "real world" of the first and last parts of "Gypsy Girls" is to be taken as a "mythical geography"—which would mean that the reader enters into a "fantasy world" as soon as he begins to read, a world in which the hero's fantastic adventure is not "unreal."

Eliade's technique is, obviously, decidedly different from that of a writer who creates a "fairy world" utterly alien to our own, such as Tolkien and his "Middle Earth." Eliade's "worlds" are readily recognizable to people of Romania, since almost all are set in that country.[16] In those writings we would call fantastic, Eliade has introduced into a realistic world certain non-realistic elements: a reversal of the aging process, translation into other dimensions of space and time, mystical and oneiric experiences that are treated as real happenings, etc. Matei Calinescu and Walter Strauss have classified Eliade's style as "magic realism," though this is not to imply that Eliade has been influenced by any contemporary writers in this genre. It is a style he has developed by himself, which owes something to the Romanian folktale and something to his vast reading in mythology and literature—but which is finally the product of his own creative genius.

While he was in the midst of writing "In curte la Dionis"—one of his most enigmatic stories, though probably not truly fantastic—he wrote in his journal some thoughts concerning the future of "fantastic literature" (*Journal II*, 278–79). He says he believes that the vogue of the *nouvelle vague* cannot last long, since it and other types of avant-garde literature appear to have no potential for changing or improving the reader's vision of the world or for helping him to "grow" or "open himself" to the world. In place of such literature, Eliade sees the growth of a new type of fantastic, which he says will constitute a "*new mythology*," answering especially to the longings of the younger generations. Concerning this literature Eliade makes the following points: (1) it will be related to "all the past fifty years have revealed to us"—through various fields of study: Eliade names psychoanalysis, ethnology, and the history of religions, but the list could be extended; (2) it will not be like the fantastic genres of the nineteenth century, romantic, symbolistic, or "decadent"; (3) it will not be "escapist," but will be tied to the history of this half-century; (4) it will be readable, in story form; and (5) the myths, symbols, and rituals of past civilizations will be contained in it, but *camouflaged*. Literature of this sort will be, Eliade asserts, a "window onto meaning" for those who are now youths, who are imprisoned in a void.

I consider this passage extremely important for interpreting what Eliade himself is trying to do through his writing. The above points, it seems to me, constitute a kind of program Eliade has been following, at least for the years since he wrote them. Since 1966 he has written some ten pieces of prose, all but two of which contain fantastic or "mystical" elements. The exceptions are the enigmatic "In curte la Dionis," already mentioned, and "Pelerina" ("The Cape"), which I would classify as a mystery, although Eliade himself calls it "fantastic" (*Fragments*, II, 248).

Without attempting to illustrate each of the above points by specific examples drawn from the stories, I content myself with making a few observations. With regard to the first point, Eliade does not hesitate to introduce technical data from all kinds of sources. One recent story, for instance, "Dayan," revolves around mathematics and theories of Einstein, Heisenberg, and Gödel. Data from the history of religions, mythology, ethnology, and philosophy are abundant. While Eliade mentions the "paranormal experiences of hallucinogenic drugs" as another source for the "new mythology," it is perhaps significant that no drug experiences as such appear in any of Eliade's novellas. As for point two, to my knowledge Eliade's fantastic cannot be compared closely with anything from the nineteenth century. Above all, there is nothing "horrible" in it.[17] Gavrilescu ("Gypsy Girls") experiences fright in his labyrinthine journey through death's realm (?), but there is none of the atmosphere of Poe, for example, about the experience (and this is all the more remarkable, given Eliade's acquaintance with mythologies of death, such as the Tibetan *Bardo Thödol* and shamanistic initiations). The supernatural in Eliade's "new mythology" is almost entirely *fascinans* (contra Rudolf Otto!).

Eliade's fantastic is not "escapist" (although Rosemary Jackson would probably say it was).[18] As previously stated, Eliade does not create alien or unrealistic worlds; he cares nothing for science-fiction or the moral-allegorical fairy tale.[19] Since the sacred is always camouflaged in the profane, the supernatural in Eliade's fiction always emerges out of the "real" world. With regard to the fourth point, Eliade's plots, though sometimes obscure, enigmatic, and hard to follow on first reading, are, in my opinion, engrossing stories that compel the reader's attention. I consider, further, that his plots show an exceptional degree of novelty and ingenuity. Finally, Eliade does indeed incorporate (unconsciously, he says) myths, symbols, and rituals in his stories. The myth of Orpheus and Eurydice underlies "Dionis," "Les Trois Grâces," and "Nouăsprezece trandafiri" (Nineteen Roses). This last story includes also something of the Gnostic myth of Sophia who "sought to know the Father." The mythico-ritual scenario

374

of initiation, closely related to the shamanistic journey to the spirit world and to the fairy-tale hero's adventures, is a frequent theme. Themes from certain Romanian folktales and folk ballads recur in Eliade's fiction. These mythic and folk elements, however, are not always "camouflaged," but sometimes are quite explicit.

Another general observation that might be made about Eliade's literary works is that his stories lack any truly *evil* characters. (This is true, certainly, of his postwar writings, though arguable in the case of some of the realistic novels of the thirties.) Neither are there in these latter-day works any of the moral depravity that marks much of the literature of the day, nor any appeal to prurient interests. While Eliade in his history of religions studies shows little interest in religious ethics, nor does he preach any ethical or moralistic message in his literature, still his writings have a wholesome atmosphere about them that John Gardner[20] surely would approve. Perhaps this is because, as Gardner contends, good literature is always "moral" (as he defines the word). Perhaps this quality reflects a basically optimistic view of human nature on Eliade's part—a view whose ultimate roots may be in Eastern Orthodox theology.

In view of Eliade's unconcealed opposition to Communism, both as a philosophy and as a form of government imposed upon Romania and other nations, the critique of Communism in his literature is surprisingly muted and subtle. It is most evident in *The Forbidden Forest*, but in the novellas of the past fifteen or twenty years it is handled with great delicacy. For example, the figure of the "Inspector" or interrogator who appears in a number of novellas (the same Albini in three recent ones) is rather sympathetically developed. The probable reason for this fact is not hard to guess: Eliade is a *Romanian* writer and he wants his post-war writings to be published and read in Romania—and indeed, nearly all of them have been, in an edition of 1981.[21] Significantly, two novellas with obvious anti-Communist sentiment, "Pelerina' and "Nouăsprezece trandafiri," are missing from the collection of sixteen post-war stories. "Pe strada Mântuleasa" rather surprisingly is included; it deals with an earlier Communist regime which the present regime is willing to admit was too harsh. To date, Eliade's major novel, *The Forbidden Forest*, remains unpublished in Romania, though efforts have been made to have it approved; but it contains scenes at which the government censors might well take offence. Eliade seems to want to write a literature which is nonpolitical, but which yet conceals a message about a political kind of freedom capable of delivering modern man of *all* societies from their spiritual bondage (see below). Such a message, he appears to hope, would be missed by the Communist censor who, like the interrogator in Eliade's recent tales, is incapable of grasping spiritual meanings.

The new mythology of which Eliade wrote in 1966 has one other feature: "it will be like a window onto meaning for all the young people enclosed today in their void." In the light of this statement and in view of others cited earlier in the paper, it is indisputable that Eliade wants to be more than a scholar and an entertainer; he wants to leave the world a message. Norman Girardot has spoken of this purpose and has identified the message in a general way in his excellent introductory study in *Imagination and Meaning*. He says: "In the absence of a living mythic tradition Eliade feels he must tell both scholarly and literary stories ...." (9); and "The story that Eliade tells us by means of his scholarly remembrance of past myths and his literary creation of new fables is that religion is the most profound and meaningful way of interpreting the story of human existence" (8).

I concur with Matei Calinescu also in his appraisal of Eliade's work as "aesthetic"—in the special sense he gives the term in his brilliant study, "Imagination and Meaning: Aesthetic Attitudes and Ideas in Mircea Eliade's Thought."[22] By "aesthetic" he means an approach to life that sees it as multiple, diverse, and incapable of being reduced to a single meaning; hence an approach favoring ambiguous and polysemic interpretations of reality. He cites a passage from Eliade's *Journal* (28 Dec. 1963) that admirably illustrates the point he wishes to make:

> In the novella I'm in the process of writing "Podul," (The Bridge), I am obsessed with getting across its secret meaning: the camouflage of mysteries in the events of immediate reality. Consequently, I want to bring out the ambivalence of every event in the sense that an apparently banal happening can reveal a whole universe of transcendent meanings .... (cg. *Journal II*, 205)

Calinescu comments: "For both writer and thinker, the question is not so much to go beyond the camouflage in order to grasp the one 'hidden' truth or 'principle,' as to become *aware* of the richness which participates in the nature of the miraculous and whose existence would be impossible without the plurality of meaning brought about by the very action of camouflage" (5).

Thus it proves to be the case that when we examine Eliade's recent short stories individually and ask what the message is, we get no single answer, except in the general sense that transcendent truth is available to those who know how to "read the signs," how to recognize the miracle, how to identify hierophanies.

The majority of recent stories seem addressed to the question of the survival of society and culture in view of the threat of nuclear catastrophe. "Dionis" speaks of a Savior-Poet who is to come—apparently the hero of the story, Adrian, who unfortunately has forgotten who he is—who will tame bestial humanity through poetry and song, like Orpheus. "Dayan" proposes a savior who is a combination of a mathematical genius and a poet or mystic. In "Tinerețe fără tinerețe" ("Youth without Youth"), the hope is held out (along with others) that perhaps the nuclear holocaust will produce a fortunate mutation in the survivors, as the lightning bolt has done to the story's hero, Dominic Matei.

But if, instead of universal destruction, the earth should enter upon an era of universal totalitarianism (as the only alternative to destruction), some of Eliade's stories offer a means of "salvation" within such a system. It is presented in explicit didactic passages placed on the lips of a character to whom Eliade evidently feels a close affinity: Ieronim Thanase, director of an experimental theater in three recent stories ("Uniforms de général," "Incognito la Buchenwald," and "Nouăsprezece trandafiri"). Ieronim, like Eliade, is a man with a message: it was given him in secret by his aunt on her death bed (in "Uniforms") who made him swear to reveal it to no one but his son, if he should have one (but he remains unmarried). When pressed to disclose it to another elderly relative, Luchian, he replies:

> But Luchian,... ever since that night when Generaleasa called me to her bedside, I have done nothing else except talk about those things she confided in me! But because I swore, I cannot speak of them in the way they were told me by the tongue of the dying—yet I reveal them in parables, in anecdotes, and images. Ever since Generaleasa died, I have done nothing else—I can do nothing else—except speak, but obscurely, as in an old mirror ... in images and parables about the secret which has been entrusted to me.

The message, one presumes, has to do with a means of salvation through "dramatic performance" about which Ieronim speaks in many passages in the three stories in which he appears. Essentially, his view is that man can find freedom in society only by turning history—life—into a play in which we, the actors, determine the meaning and thereby creatively modify it. In his avant-garde performances, Ieronim and his troupe attempt to show forth this idea, but for the reader of the stories, Ieronim and his disciples are allowed to speak quite explicitly: "My dear friend, in our day drama is the only chance we have to know *absolute freedom*, and this will be even truer in the near future" ("Nouăsprezece trandafiri"). "We, this little band, came to the conclusion long ago that only by means of theater ... could we succeed in *showing* that although hemmed in on all sides, we ... are not like mice caught in a trap" ("Incogntio la Buchenwald").

> Our descendents, if they don't know how to discover techniques of escape and how to utilize the *absolute freedom* which is given us in the very structure of our condition—as beings that are free although incarnate—our descendents will discover themselves truly captives, living in a prison without doors and windows ... and eventually they will die. Because man cannot survive without belief in the possibility of freedom... ("Nouăsprezece trandafiri")

"Absolute freedom," as readers of Eliade's works in the history of religions know, is the supreme goal of religious striving, in Eliade's view. To escape the human condition, to attain immortality and god-like freedom: this is mankind's great "nostalgia," he says. And like the yogins and certain others of whom he writes in his scholarly monographs, a few personages in his stories attain freedom and escape "fantastically" from the restraints of time and space (as do, for instance, Pandele, Serdaru, and Niculina in "Nouăsprezece trandafiri").

As we have seen, Eliade, like the Buddha, Plato, Gnostics, and others, regards man's problem as one of *amnesia*. Modern man has "forgotten" the revelations vouchsafed to humanity in earlier times. Not surprisingly, then, the theme of forgetting and remembering plays a major role in at least half of Eliade's most recent literary works, though the theme is developed in a variety of ways. In some cases, a character has forgotten something decisive that happened to him in early life, with the result that his life has been a failure. In the case of Dominic ("Youth without Youth"), who had become forgetful with old age, a bolt of lightning restores to him not only his own memory, but seemingly the "collective memory" of mankind. And in "Les Trois Graces" the thesis is proposed that cancer is a result of an "amnesia" on the part of the biological organism, traceable to the Fall of Man in the Garden of Eden.

While Eliade is pessimistic about the short-range future of man (totalitarianism, nuclear catastrophe), he remains basically optimistic about the long run view. It seems fitting to conclude this section on Eliade's "message" with this quotation from his *Journal*:

> Although I see man crushed, asphyxiated, diminished by industrial civilization, I can't believe he will degenerate, decline morally, and finally perish, completely sterile. I have a limitless confidence in the creative power of the mind. It seems to me that man will succeed—if he wishes—in remaining free and creative, in any circumstance, cosmic or historical. But how can the miracle be brought about? How can the sacramental dimension of existence be rediscovered?... All the things that have existed we have not definitively lost; we find them again in our dreams and our longings. And the poets have kept them .... There must be a way out. (*Journal II*, 80)

It has been possible in this paper to sketch only in broadest outline some of the themes of Eliade's fiction. It was my purpose to provide some background against which to read the remarkable and growing corpus of literary works of Mircea Eliade which I believe deserves to become better known. I have quoted liberally from Eliade's own words to allow him, wherever possible, to speak for himself. It is my thesis that the scholarly and literary activities of Eliade are of one piece, and that in both these endeavors he seeks to convey a message to contemporary man.

Notes

1. There are also a number of "juvenile" works published in Romanian reviews prior to 1930—which have been commented on by Ion Balu in "Les debuts littéraires," in *Mircea Eliade, Cahiers l'Herne* 33 (1978): 381–89.
2. *Autobiography*, I, 199–200. Cf. Eliade's *Journal* for 1 May 1963 (*Journal II*, 188–89).
3. *Journal*, 12 October 1916, from the Romanian typescript. Cf. *Fragments d'un Journal* (Paris: Gallimard, 1973), 12.
4. From the Romanian text. Cf. *Journal II*, 194.
5. *Autobiography*, I, v–vi. Cf. *Journal*, 20 June, 1963 (*Journal II*, 190).
6. From Romanian typescript. Cf. also *Journal II*, 80–81.
7. English translation in Norman J. Girardot and Mac Linscott Ricketts, eds., *Imagination and Meaning: The Scholarly and Literary Worlds of Mircea Eliade*, 114. Published in Romanian in 1953.
8. In *Myth and Reality*, chapter VII; cf. *History of Religious Ideas*, II, paragraphs 183 and 230.
9. See *Journal II*, 279–80; cf. Preface to *The Forbidden Forest*, vii.
10. From the Romanian text in *Caiete de Dor 9* (1955); cf. *Fragments d'un Journal*, 168.
11. *Journal II*, 86. In another Journal note he says, "the literary imagination is the continuation of mythological creativity and oneiric experience," *Journal III*, 284.
12. Borrowing the title of a *London Times* review of *The Two and the One*, Feb. 10, 1966, 102.
13. Translated as "With the Gypsy Girls," by William Ames Coates, in Mircea Eliade, *Tales of the Sacred and the Supernatural* (Philadelphia: Westminster Press, 1981).
14. Translated from the Romanian typescript; cf. *No Souvenirs*, 307–308.
15. Coates stresses that Eliade makes his fantastic worlds believable. See his essay in Tacou, *Mircea Eliade*, 376.
16. Cf. Mircea Handoca, "Nostalgia patriei în opera lui Mircea Eliade," in *Mircea Eliade. Contribuţii biobiblografice* (Bucureşti, 1980), 15–29.
17. "Eliade's fantastic is at the opposite extreme from the Anglo-Saxon horrible." (Eugen Simion, *Scriitori Români de azi II* [Bucureşti, 1976], 335; see also Simion, *Mircea Eliade: A Spirit of Amplitude*, ch. 8.)
18. Rosemary Jackson, *Fantasy, the Literature of Subversion* (London: Methuen, 1981).
19. Cf. Eliade, *L'Épreuve du labyrinthe* (Chicago: Chicago University Press, 1982), 203–204.
20. John Gardner, *On Moral Fiction* (New York: Basic Books, 1978).
21. Eliade, *În curte la Dionis*, ed. Eugen Simion (Bucureşti, 1981).
22. In *Journal of Religion* 57 (1977): 1–15. Cf. Sergiu Al-George, *Arhaic şi universal* (Bucureşti: Editura Eminescu, 1981), 203ff.

39

THE DISGUISES OF MIRACLE: NOTES ON MIRCEA ELIADE'S FICTION

Matei Calinescu

Editor's Introduction

৪৩ ৫৪

The publication in English of Mircea Eliade's major novel *Noaptea de Sânziene* (*The Forbidden Forest*, trans. Mac Linscott Ricketts and Mary Park Stevenson) coincided almost perfectly with the appearance in France of the issue devoted to him by the prestigious *Cahiers de l'Herne* and of the translation of one of his prewar novels, originally published in 1936, *Mademoiselle Christina*, coming only months after the French version of perhaps his best novella, *Le vieil homme et l'officier*, originally published by a small Romanian émigré press as *Pe Strada Mântuleasa*.[1] In Germany too a growing interest in Eliade's fiction has manifested itself recently, shown, among other things, by the three editions of *Auf der Mantuleasa Straße*, 1972) and by the good reception of his novella *Die Pelerine*, which made his German publisher undertake a collection of his tales of the fantastic, *Phantastische Geschichten* and *Die drei Grazien*.

The belated and so far only incipient success of Eliade as a writer does not seem to be a consequence of his world fame as a scholar of myth and religion—actually, this might even have hampered it, the general prejudice being that a scholar's literary activities are just a hobby or a *violon d'Ingres*. What might have played a role in stimulating the curiosity for Eliade's fiction is, I think, his journal, published in French in 1973: this journal not only displays great literary qualities (it reads like a good autobiographical novel), but is full of references to literature and writers, including sometimes lengthy and always exciting discussions of his own literary projects.[2]

When, as a young man, Eliade embarked upon his double career, he took it for granted—encouraged in this by a certain romantic ideal of the polymath, still alive in his native Romania—that there were no incompatibilities between highly specialized scientific-scholarly research and artistic activity.

> At the time [he writes in the preface to *Journal II*, *ix-x*, introducing a quote from the scientist Jacob Bronowski] I was unaware of any structural analogy between the scientific and the literary imagination. One can thus appreciate the enthusiasm with which I read, many years later, statements by renowned scientists, such as the following: "The step by which a new axiom is adduced cannot itself be mechanized. It is a free play of the mind, an invention outside the logical processes. This is the central act of imagination in science and it is in all respects like any similar act in literature."

Not unpredictably, Eliade the writer is confronted essentially by the same problems (sacred/profane qualities of time and space, the "camouflage of myth" and the "unrecognizability of miracle," etc.) that, from a different perspective and working with different materials, the historian of religions has repeatedly encountered over the years. By saying this, I in no way want to imply that Eliade the writer "treats" or "illustrates" motifs, rituals and symbols, ideas and beliefs that Eliade the phenomenologist of religion has previously studied in their historical and transhistorical connections. Actually, the opposite seems to be true in his case. In his career there have been instances in which the writer clearly preceded the scholar, in the sense that the former's *free* imagination made discoveries and arrived at insights whose validity was later confirmed by the hermeneut.

Eliade himself makes this important point in a autobiographical text published in the Romanian émigré magazine *Caete de dor* in 1953.[3] Referring to his 1937 novella *Şarpele* (The Snake), a work in which some of the most original features of his postwar fiction, including *The Forbidden Forest*, are clearly anticipated, Eliade writes:

> Concerning the symbolism of the snake I had at my disposal a considerable amount of folkloric and ethnographic material, but I ignored it. Maybe if I had taken the trouble to consult it, the symbolism of my *Snake* would

have been more coherent—but then, in all likelihood, the literary invention would have been hampered. I don't know. What seems to me worthwhile pointing out is this: although I had "attacked" a subject so dear to the historian of religions that I was, the writer in me refused to *collaborate* with the scholar and the interpreter of symbols; the writer in me wanted to stay *free*, at any cost, and to be able to choose whatever he liked as well as to reject the symbols and the interpretations that he was offered, ready-made, by the erudite and the philosopher.

And he goes on to say quite emphatically:

The experience of *The Snake* has convinced me of two things: 1) that one's theoretical activity cannot influence consciously and deliberately one's literary activity; 2) that the free act of literary creation, on the contrary, can lead to theoretical discoveries. The fact of the matter is that only after having reread *The Snake* as a published book did I realize that in it I had resolved unwittingly a problem which had preoccupied me for a long time (ever since my *Soliloquii*, 1929–32) and which I managed to expound more systematically only in my *Traité*. That is the problem of the *unrecognizability of miracle*, deriving from the fact that the intervention of the *sacred* in the world is always camouflaged in a series of "historical" forms, manifestations that *apparently* are in no way different from millions of other cosmic or historic manifestations (*a sacred* stone is not distinguished, on the plane of appearances, from any other stone, etc.)[4]

A few general observations about the development of Eliade as a writer will help us situate *The Forbidden Forest* within the larger "geography" of his fictional work. Although he had published quite extensively in various periodicals, Eliade made his real debut in 1931 with *Isabel și apele diavolului* (Isabel and the Devil Waters), a novel clearly marked by his Indian discoveries and experiences. It is interesting to note that most of Eliade's fiction inspired by India was written and published while he was still in that country or during the first years after his return to Romania, that is, between 1930 and 1935. Significantly, his early Indian novels are all strongly autobiographical. To take the example of the most successful one, the vibrantly poetic love story *Maitreyi* (1933), which the French philosopher Gaston Bachelard once described to its author in terms of a "mythology of voluptuousness,"[5] the reader cannot avoid the feeling that he is confronted with the fictionalized account of an unmistakably personal affair. *Maitreyi* is Eliade's *Werther*, a modernist version of young Goethe's sentimental novel. As in Goethe's case, it is difficult—and ultimately irrelevant—to distinguish with any degree of precision, on the basis of available external information, what in the book is fact and what fiction. This is all the more so in the case of *Maitreyi* given that within the context of modernism, in which the novel clearly belongs, the grounds for the distinction between fact and fiction become blurred.[6]

The autobiographical bent of Eliade's early Indian inspired literary work is even more perceptible in *Şantier* ("Work in Progress," 1935). This book, which the author labels an "indirect novel," consists of a series of undisguised and in all likelihood real diary entries. In the preface to *Şantier* Eliade readily admits that the work is a journal, but goes on to argue that its being a journal in no way contradicts its fictional character. To understand this paradox one must be aware of two things: first, at that time Eliade thought of himself as primarily a novelist: and second, he was one of the outstanding representatives of the Romanian school of "authenticity," a sort of early modernist "existentialist" group whose members were committed to a literature of passionate self-inquiry and self-expression and who made communication of personal experience the major goal of writing. Thus in the preface to *Şantier* the author could state without being afraid of any possible misunderstanding: "A novelist, even when he writes for himself, will write a novel whenever he speaks of men and events, and not of theories or his own reveries ... I can't help it, everything I relate becomes a page in a novel."[7]

The group of early fictional-personal works about India, in which the author appears caught up in an insoluble conflict between asceticism and the "mythology of voluptuousness," presents certain remarkable differences from the later novellas with Indian subject matter, namely, "The Secret of Dr. Honigberger" and "Nights at Serampore" (originally published in 1940). The two latter works display a more impersonal and objective fantasy (and a richer one, for that matter); their deep themes are more philosophical (they deal with the major problem of the fully mature Eliade, that of the ambiguities of the sacred and the profane in their dialectical relationship); and, most noticeably, they are, unlike the rather loosely structured early works, good stories, efficiently and artfully conducted narratives. Between *Isabel* and "Nights at Serampore," from 1930 to 1940, the author has gone all the way from the modernist obsession with self and from a certain experimentalist temptation (with the exception of *Maitreyi*, Eliade's early fiction is deliberately "not constructed," to convey as directly as possible the immediacy of lived "experience" to the timeless art of storytelling. By 1940, we may say, Eliade has discovered the "ontological" signification of narration.

A similar trend is observed in Eliade's fiction on Romanian themes: such massive and rather loosely constructed novels as *Intoarcerea din Rai* ("The Return from Paradise," 1934), or *Huliganii* ("The Hooligans," 1935) are, like their Indian-inspired counterparts, illustrations of the young author's quest for "authenticity," even though the personal-autobiographical element is harder to trace, Eliade's attempt being now to portray not his own estranged self (projected against the background of an exotic culture) but the "collective self" of his generation of "angry young men," questioning and rejecting their society and cultural milieu with a nihilistic fury equaled only by their deep sense of metaphysical alienation. During the second half of the 1930s a noticeable change occurs, announced by the "tale of terror" *Mademoiselle Christina* (1936), a Romanian adaptation of the "gothic" genre, with ghosts, vampires, scenes of demonic possession and a combination of eroticism and cruelty (is not Sadism the correspondent of gothic imagination in the realm of sexuality?). But *Mademoiselle Christina* remains, I think, an exception in the universe of Eliade's fiction, an exercise in storytelling for its own sake, important especially because it represents the first encounter of the writer with the fantastic, in the form of a dramatic, powerful clash between two radically heterogeneous worlds. *Mademoiselle Christina's* subject matter is largely conventional; what is remarkable about it is the ability of the author to use, often with unexpected effectiveness, the set conventions of a literary genre whose traditions go back to the late 18th-century interest in the esthetics of terror.

The real change in Eliade's fiction, a change which might be described in terms of a *coupure epistémologique* (with major consequences in the other fields of Eliade's activity as well), is marked by *The Snake* (1937). What is this novella about? The best way I can describe it is to say that it is about the contrast *and* the contact between "reality" and "miracle," the profane and the sacred, banality and myth. The interest of Eliade's approach lies in his stressing the notion of contact, to the extent that he implies the contrast between the world of reality and that of miracle would become meaningless and even cease to exist were it not for their close contact, a contact which accounts, among other things, for the possibility of mistaking one for the other.

The sacred, as Eliade has often said, takes on the appearances of everyday banality; it disguises itself and makes itself unrecognizable. Seen from this vantage point, *The Snake* is fundamentally a praise of sexuality as a manifestation of the sacred, a sort of epithalamium in prose which reminds one of certain powerful pages in D. H. Lawrence, a hymn to Eros whose mythical and symbolic embodiments are discovered behind the tritest of middle-class social and moral conventions. Another attractive feature of *The Snake* as a literary work is that its central theme (miracle making itself unrecognizable) is paralleled on the level of literary structures and devices: here is a poem about timeless sacred erotic drives which masquerades as a novella of Romanian middle-class manners in the 1930s.[8]

The problem of miracle and the disguises through which it renders itself unrecognizable is central in Eliade's next novel *Nuntă în cer* ("Marriage in Heaven," 1938), in which the transitional period in the author's creative biography may be said to have come to an end. Unlike *The Snake*, "Marriage in Heaven" does not contain any externally "fantastic" elements; also, the apparent lack of a definite story line in the earlier novella is in sharp contrast to the carefully (almost "geometrically") worked-out plot of the novel. "Marriage in Heaven" presents the reader with two love stories as recounted by two men, Mavrodin and Hasnaş, who have met by chance at a hunting party and share reminiscences to fill the emptiness of a long, sleepless night in the hunting cabin. Mavrodin is an artist, a writer, a successful novelist, and what he narrates during the night coincides with the theme of his autobiographical book, based on his unique love affair with a mysterious woman, Ileana. This book, also entitled "Marriage in Heaven," had been written in the hope of persuading Ileana to return to her abandoned lover. Why had she disappeared from his life without leaving the faintest trace? Why, given that the relation between the two of them had been all along both passionate and happy? Mavrodin knows the answer perfectly well. The breakup had been provoked by Ileana's desire to have a child and by his reluctance to become a father. A true artist, Mavrodin thought, could have only spiritual offspring. For him marriage was, as he put it, "an institution I had only veneration for, but from which I excluded artists and thinkers ... I liked ... to think of the fate of the artist as comparable to the calling of a monk."[9] After Ileana's disappearance, Mavrodin would encounter her only once more, but even then only as a "character" in the story of Hasnaş's love affair with Lena (in Romanian both Ileana and Lena are familiar derivations from Elena or "Helen").

Hasnaş represents a type opposite to that of the artist—he is a "bourgeois" whose life, devoid of any transcendental purpose, becomes meaningless if he does not have to raise a family—the only means of counteracting the irreversible passage of time. So, in his marriage with Lena, Hasnaş is increasingly obsessed with the thought that he must have a child. He is happy with his wife, but this happiness by itself seems to him gratuitous and almost unreal, and he fears that one day it may be lost, as everything is lost in the merciless world of Chronos. But Lena refuses to give him a child and vanishes from his life. The two men have loved the same woman, Ileana/Lena, and have both been "punished" for their failure to recognize the miracle that had come their way under different disguises. In the case of Mavrodin, what is censored is the artist's tendency to downgrade and reject the "normal" time order and his subsequent blindness to the humble, everyday forms through which miracle can choose to manifest itself. In the case of Hasnaş, the opposite blindness—to the *real* timeless quality of happiness—forms the object of the "punishment."

Among the prewar works of Eliade, "Marriage in Heaven" is the one which anticipates most, in both theme and tone, his great postwar novel *The Forbidden Forest,* while *The Snake* and the 1940 tales of the fantastic set in India are in many ways close anticipations of the rich production of novellas and short stories. *The Forbidden Forest* itself is certainly an exception within the framework of Eliade's more recent fiction. It may be seen as a culmination of his passion for the novel and, more than that, as a summa of his whole literary activity. Thus, beyond "Marriage in Heaven," *The Forbidden Forest* is linked to Eliade's early novels, and particularly to "The Return from Paradise" and "The Hooligans," with which it shares a deep concern for contemporary historical reality. But in the early novels the narrator was "existentially" committed to a generational point of view (speaking on behalf of the young generation in rebellion against the old), while the writer of *The Forbidden Forest* has become much more detached and attempts to make sense of the "nightmare of history" (World War II) from the broad perspective of the later Eliade's dialectic of the sacred and the profane, of fundamental Time versus historical time, as expounded in *The Myth of the Eternal Return* (1949) and in *Patterns in Comparative Religion* (1949). On the other hand, the use of mythical patterns and symbols, as well as the sense of a "fantastic presence" which pervades certain key sections of the book, relates *The Forbidden Forest* to the fantastic stories written by Eliade after *The Snake,* and more particularly in the postwar years.

"Great novels are above all great fairy tales," Vladimir Nabokov used to say. This was certainly meant as a paradox, since the fairy-tale nature of the works Nabokov had in mind (Flaubert's *Madame Bovary,* Tolstoy's *Anna Karenina* or Proust's *À la recherche du temps perdu,* among others) is by no means easy to grasp; indeed, to become aware of it, one must first realize that, according to another typically Nabokovian dictum, "Life is the least realistic of fictions." Most serious novelists would be surprised and a little annoyed to hear someone state, no matter how admiringly, that all they do is recount fairy tales. Not so Mircea Eliade. Actually, his most carefully constructed and most ambitious novel, *The Forbidden Forest*, achieves some of its most powerful effects by showing how many unobserved elements of the marvelous enter into what we call reality and, conversely, how real certain aspects of the marvelous are.

A novel and a fairy tale, *The Forbidden Forest* is, through the story of Stefan's initiatory quest, an attempt to rediscover "lost time," not so much the personal time of which Proust speaks as the larger time of myth: a time in which stories, all sorts of stories, are told and happen, and in which happenings themselves are made of the stuff that tales are made of epiphanies. The book is important for any student of Eliade's philosophy of myth, but it should also interest any serious student of the postwar development of the novel. From the latter point of view, *The Forbidden Forest* (written roughly between 1949 and 1954 and published in French translation in 1955 and in the original Romanian in 1971 by the émigré publisher Ion Cuşa) is one of the first novels in which one can identify the signs of what has been called "magic realism," a phenomenon that has been widely discussed in connection with recent Latin American literature but whose independent variant as it emerged in Romania, the only Latin culture in Eastern Europe, has received but little attention. Eliade's project—namely, writing a vast narrative on the theme of Time, including the numerous and dangerous paradoxes brought about by the specific time consciousness imposed upon us by modernity—has led him to the discovery of certain techniques that are very close to those used by the representatives of magic realism: the point of departure is "realistic" (recognizable events in chronological succession, everyday atmosphere, verisimilitude, characters with more or less predictable psychological reactions), but soon certain strange discontinuities or gaps appear in the "normal," true-to-life texture of the narrative. The author sets out to explore these gaps. There are countless images floating there, some of them archetypal, some purely idiosyncratic, which combine and separate according to the laws of the logic of myth (or dream), a logic that somehow compels the writer to take it at least as seriously as he takes the ordinary one. The traditional unity of character is disrupted; there are sudden passages from one plane of vision to another, shifts of identity and bizarre multiplications or dispersions of the self.

The main difference between Eliade and the magic realists is the latter's experimentalist bent, often combined with a polemicism which is both esthetic and social (usually leftist radical), as opposed to Eliade's more serenely meditative outlook. Both the magic realists and Eliade share a deep interest in mythical thought and in "primitive" religious experience, but Eliade's "modernism"—his literary work being undoubtedly an offshoot of the large movement of artistic modernism—does not imply a blunt rejection of the recent past but, on the contrary, an effort to understand it, even though this understanding means relativizing it and assigning it the rather modest place that belongs to it within a greater and fundamentally plural tradition. For Eliade there are always several traditions that must be taken into account at the same time, because only by using them all, in spite of their often heterogeneous or even mutually contradictory aspects, can a writer hope to attain some kind of "totality." This totality, whose possibility, in Eliade's eyes, is granted by the immanent symbolic power with which everything in the world is endowed, has an *epiphanic* quality, which can be seized only when reality is observed with what I would call an *inspired attention*—an attention so great that it becomes visionary.

How to look at things, the most common things of everyday life, in order to see—that is what Stefan sets out to learn. His is an initiatory quest. But from the point of view of the reader, even this quest is hidden, its major stages being almost indistinguishable from among the more or less ordinary events of the life of a Romanian intellectual in a period of extraordinary historical crises (the rise of fascism, the rebellion of the Iron Guards in 1940, the military dictatorship of Antonescu who in 1941 joined Hitler in the attack on the Soviet Union, the Russian occupation and, after the war, the imposition on the country of brutal Stalinist rule) and of natural catastrophes such as the 1940 earthquake that hit Bucharest or the 1946 drought in Moldavia, as a result of which thousands died from starvation. Such upheavals certainly affect Stefan's life. He suffers cruel losses—his wife and son die in the bombing of Bucharest in the spring of 1944; his best friend Biriş, a teacher of philosophy, dies under torture by the Communist secret police in 1947, while Stefan has become a refugee in the West. But the hero's quest takes place on another plane. What he does and says while pursuing his initiatory quest, himself not altogether conscious of it, *seems* to the other characters vaguely, and sometimes plainly, irresponsible. What Eliade appears to suggest is that even the search for the sacred, in our desacralized world, masquerades as absentminded dreaminess, as comic

387

inadequacy, as childish behavior in an adult—a behavior which is not without a certain charm, but whose real significance modern man is unable to understand.

For Stefan, going beyond the "terror of history" is the same thing as achieving a paradisiacal condition. But Stefan does not say that to do this one must simply turn one's back on history. In fact, if history were not what it is, a nightmare, if the tragic did not exist, paradise would lose its significance. Modernity, with its acute awareness of history and historicity, must be assumed before being transcended. If in the past there were other ways to paradise, today this is the only one: passing through history is unavoidable. In an important discussion with Anisie, a "saint" of sorts who fascinates Stefan because of his ability to harmonize his existence with the great rhythms of cosmic time (but at the price of completely ignoring history by leading the life of a recluse on his farm at the foot of the Carpathian Alps), Stefan clearly realizes that the hermit's solution is not the right one: "Human existence," he tells Anisie, "would seem vain to me if it were solely reduced to mythical categories. Even that ahistoric paradise would be hard for me to endure if it didn't have the hell of history accompanying it. I believe—I even hope—that an exit from time is possible even in our historical world. The Kingdom of God is realizable at any time on earth, *hic et nunc* ..." (*The Forbidden Forest*, 314). But paradise, one must keep in mind, is only a possibility, and the hero gets lost in his initiatory pursuit.

What causes Stefan's failure? Is it his love for Ileana—his fascination with the unattainable? Does he stray from the right way due to his cult of the impossible, embodied in Ileana, a cult that is indistinguishable from the idea of romantic love (in the sense defined in *L'amour et l'Occident*, the famous essay by Denis de Rougemont)? As the narrative unfolds, the two women in Stefan's life, Ioana and Ileana, both of whom he strives to love with a love that is more than love (another facet of his cult of impossibility), acquire a symbolic significance. Ioana represents Stefan's "life instinct," Ileana his secret penchant toward self-destruction, the temptation of Thanatos, his "death instinct." Interestingly, while working on the novel, Eliade himself was largely unaware of the symbolism of his two major female characters, Ileana in particular. Only when he came to the very last scene, which describes the meeting between Stefan and Ileana in the wood of Royaumont and the car accident in which the two of them perish on the night of St. John in 1948, exactly twelve years, or a Cosmic Year, after their first meeting in another forest, near Bucharest, did the author realize that Ileana was, and had been all along, "an angel of Death."[10]

And so Eliade's "great fairy tale" ends, unusually as far as normal fairy tales go, with the death of the hero and his love. Actually, the novel ends—quite befittingly, I think, for a work so rich in literary, mythological and philosophical suggestions—by raising a series of questions. Stefan, we are told in the closing sentence, "had known that this last moment, this moment without end, would suffice." Is this the paradisiacal instant of infinite bliss he had longed for all through his initiatory quest? Or is it, on the contrary, a final and truly irreparable act of self-deception? Such questions, when they arise in the mind of the reader, are nothing but a thinly disguised temptation to reread.

Notes

1. The Eliade issue of *l'Herne*, which contains an entire section on his literary oeuvre (315–90), is discussed extremely favorably in an article by Claude Mauriac, "Mircea Eliade et son 'ailleurs' secret," in *Le Monde* of 31 March 1978, 1, 18. For further discussion of Eliade's literary works, see the third section of *Myths and Symbols: Studies in Honor of Mircea Eliade*, ed. Joseph M. Kitagawa and Charles H. Long, 327–414, especially the essay by Virgil Ierunca, "The Literary Work of Mircea Eliade," 543–604. The most helpful recent studies of Eliade's literary work in Romanian are: Sorin Alexandrescu, "Dialectica fantasticului," the introduction to Mircea Eliade, *La ţiganci şi alte povestiri*; Ion Negoitescu, "Mircea Eliade sau de la fantastic la oniric," *Viaţa româneasca* 23 (February 1970): 71–77; Sanda Stolojan, "Mircea Eliade şi Noaptea de sânziene," *Ethos* (Paris), 1 (1973): 232–37; Eugen Simion, "Mircea Eliade," in his *Soriitori romani de azi*, vol. II (Bucharest: Cartea Românească, 1976), 319–36; N. Steinhardt, "Fantasticul lui Mircea Eliade," *Steaua* 28/4 (1977): 18–20.

2. *Fragments d'un journal* (Paris: Gallimard, 1973). An English translation of about two-thirds of this volume was published as *No Souvenirs: Journal II 1957–1969*. There is also a German translation: *Im Mittelpunkt: Bruchstücke eines Tagebuchs* (Vienna: Europa, 1977). About the significance of the journal, see my review "Mircea Eliade's Journals," *Denver Quarterly* 12/1 (Spring 1977): 313–15. For a broader discussion of the importance of the esthetic component in Eliade's thought, see my article "Imagination and Meaning: Aesthetic Attitudes and Ideas in Mircea Eliade's Thought."

3. "Fragment autobiografic," *Caete de dor* (Paris), 7 (July 1953). Since the magazine has been unavailable to me, I have used a typescript of the text, which Eliade has kindly put at my disposal.

4. "Fragment autobiografic" (typescript), 9–10.

5. Ibid., 11. Bachelard had read A. Guillermou's translation of the novel, entitled *La nuit Bengali* (Paris: Gallimard, 1950).

6. We may note, however, that unlike Goethe's Lotte, Eliade's heroine has found it necessary to publish her own version of the story. See Maitreyi Devi, *It Does Not Die*. This is a translation, by the author herself, of the original Bengali *Na Hanyate*, published in 1974. The young Eliade appears under the name Mircea Euclid (an allusion to the *esprit de géométrie* represented by the West?). The book will certainly interest a future biographer of Eliade (among other things, it reproduces—how faithfully?—three letters sent by Eliade from the Svarga Ashram in Risikesh, in November and December of 1930, 250–54).

7. *Şantier* (Bucharest: Cugetarea, 1935), 7.

8. The following passage about *The Snake* (the entry of 24 June 1963, *Journal II*, 191) is an important statement of Eliade's conception of the fantastic: "A young student of social thought, Botinovici, came to see me. He had read *The Snake* in the German translation and had been enthusiastic. He would like to read more of my 'literary' works, but I didn't encourage him. Nevertheless, we spoke about my conception of the fantastic in literature. I reminded him that this conception has its roots in my theory of 'the incognizability of miracles'—or in my theory that, after the Incarnation, the transcendent is camouflaged in the world or in history and thus becomes 'incognizable.' In *The Snake* a banal atmosphere and mediocre characters are gradually transfigured. But what came from 'beyond,' as well

as all the paradisiac images of the end of the story, were already there from the beginning, but camouflaged by the banality of everyday life and, as such, unrecognizable." Eliade's student had read Günther Spaltmann's version of the novella: *Andronic und die Schlange* (Munich: Nymphenburger, 1949).

9. *Nunta in cer* (Bucharest: Pentru Literatura, 1969), 208.
10. *Fragments d'un journal*, 219–20.

Eliade's Religion

40

THE SECRET NOSTALGIA OF MIRCEA ELIADE FOR PARADISE: OBSERVATIONS ON THE METHOD OF THE "HISTORY OF RELIGIONS"

Ansgar Paus

Editor's Introduction

Mircea Eliade's analyses of the history of religions uses a complex methodology that he calls "creative hermeneutics." This methodology has benefited from the suggestions of numerous authors (including Rudolf Otto, Carl Gustav Jung, Surendranath Dasgupta) and from theoretical elements in various disciplines. The fundamental principles of interpretation behind Eliade's history of religions methodology, however, has remained hidden. The following article by Ansgar Paus suggests that this methodology is linked with a special theological interpretation of the Byzantine theory of icons. Ansgar Paus, from *Religion* 19 (1989): 137–50. All rights reserved. Copyright © 1989 by Elsevier Ltd. Reprinted by permission of Elsevier Ltd.

৪০ ୧୪

"He made a more enduring impact on the western, especially German, cultivated public than on historians of religions proper or theologians." In these words Mircea Eliade characterized the influence of the religious thought and the structural descriptions of religious phenomena offered by Rudolph Otto (*Quest*, 23). To a certain degree this observation can be applied to Eliade himself. The fascination of Eliade's books in the field of the "history of religions" has guaranteed them, like those of Otto, considerable vogue among non-specialists.

Both authors have exercised an immense influence upon members of totally diverse intellectual and cultural spheres. On the other hand, their works have been received among scholars of religion, and in professional circles, with remarkable reserve manifesting itself sometimes in violent criticism. Yet, even here their influence has not been inconsiderable.[1]

A recognition of the relationship between these two scholars of religion is not unwarranted. The thought of both revolves around the experience of the sacred. The search for access to the numinous mystery is united for both in the experience of an awful yet, at the same time, fascinating power. The esteem that Eliade manifests for Rudolph Otto does not, however, allow us to overlook the difficulty of comprehending Otto's theoretical religious or philosophical program. Probably Eliade's interest in this program was limited, for his endeavor was directed to the comparative interpretation of manifestations of the sacred as found in the relevant documents, monuments and events of the whole history of mankind. For this purpose Eliade took over certain theoretical systems of thought as well as terminological stock in trade. This was particularly the case with Otto's book *The Idea of the Holy* (*Das Heilige*). Beyond that he allowed himself to be influenced by, among others, Emile Durkheim and Roger Caillois.

For Eliade the sacred is absolute (*The Two and the One*, 189–211, above 132–40). As the "sacred" emerges from its absolute transcendent sphere, and so to speak "alienates itself," the universally valid binary structure of the sacred and the profane is realized in the mental world of those who receive such manifestations of the sacred. The semantic value of the sacred and the profane carries, in accord with Eliade's basic conception of religion, strong ontological characteristics. Whilst for Eliade the "sacred" is, in the final reckoning, a transcendent reality, for Rudolph Otto the "holy" represents a transcendental psychological fact. Otto names this, as is well known, "the religious a priori." Only on the basis of transcendental idealism can it be presumed to be accessible to human understanding. However, Eliade displays scant interest in these assumptions and their relation to the "sacred." For him the sacred bears the character of a metacosmic ontic ultimate ground. This is merged with the self as the innermost of man. Yet it can appear in every cosmic manifestation and in perceptive knowledge or religious experience, on every historical level, without becoming identical with that with which it coalesces. The manifestations at various levels of the cosmos and history named "hierophanies" reveal themselves as historically limited emanations, manifestations, or "modalities" of the "sacred." The holy, as a sacred power, makes its energy or its "life" flow into the forms and shapes of nature and culture. Such manifestations of the "sacred" are encountered, for example, in symbols, rites, myths, divine forms, sacred and venerated objects, cosmologies, consecrated men, animals, plants, sacred places, etc. The "sacred" itself, or in itself, remains invisible and unknowable. It is for the human understanding the ultimate darkness, the "wholly other." Its emanating force or energy, manifest or visible in an individual, is not without reservations identical with itself, but is, nevertheless, a valid and effective manifestation of its essence.

Philosophically, the "sacred" can be defined as the universal being. It over-arches all particular being, penetrates it and unites it to a universe of religious manifestations. Basically the sacred inheres in the particular being. A very special process of human perception through mystical ecstasy, shamanistic trance or some other unusual type of knowledge is needed in order for it to be grasped. These few examples allow the differences between the theoretical religious approach of Eliade and Rudolph Otto to appear clearly. It may be that in the phenomenologically orientated religious history of Eliade basic ideas from the philosophy of Husserl, Dilthey and Heidegger can be discovered. It would also be possible, from a particular viewpoint, with the philosophy of religion of Otto. But one can say with certainty that, at least with regard to Otto, despite all superficial appearances, there is a marked methodological difference between Eliade and Otto, based upon divergent principles.[2]

Eliade adopts numerous theoretical religious and philosophical ideas from what is for him an extraneous context. He endows them with a new meaning according to his religious integrative methodological consciousness. The methodological conditions implied by this eclectic practice lead the reader into not inconsiderable difficulties in comprehending the author's intentions. Thus, after using the term "archetype," Eliade feels himself bound to declare that any apparent affinity between his theory of religious history with the depth psychological theory of archetypes by C. G. Jung is without foundation (*Myth of the Eternal Return, viii*f.).

Using every methodological resource that appeared to him to be capable of service Eliade endeavored, with his "creative hermeneutics," to offer an interpretation and explanation of the meaning of the religious data in the history of religions. Sociological, psychological or natural science principles are not decisive for his interpretation of myths, symbols and rites of human cultures. At first glance it is hard to grasp the special features of "creative hermeneutics."

Very gifted from a literary point of view, Eliade had an instinct for taking up questions of interest for the history of religions from a variety of disciplines such as philology, philosophy, anthropology and psychology, as well as phenomenology and sociology, to name but some, along with methods, parts of methods and other aspects that stimulated him. His eclectically focused gifts for synthesis, together with his enormous knowledge of the history of religions, led to a complex individual method which is difficult to grasp.[3] Superficially observed one can discover possible primary sources for his methodological consciousness in the religious theory of Rudolph Otto and C. G. Jung's work on archetypes.

During his three years of residence in India, Eliade studied in depth certain schools of Indian metaphysics. These he discussed in detail with the famous historian of Indian philosophy, Surendranath Dasgupta.[4] The philosophical explanation and foundation of methodological design fed from these mines of information confronts the scholar with not inconsiderable difficulties. For a deeper understanding, therefore, a rational foundation must be sought and found. Upon it all the apparently incoherent methodological fragments can be built. As such it constitutes the integrating nucleus of all Eliade's hermeneutical initiatives. It can be demonstrated that Eliade took his interpretive principle of all religious phenomena neither from the science of religion nor from any of the philosophical disciplines. He was, in fact, indebted for it to his own specific theology.

In any event the reader should note carefully that the emphatic impulse of Eliade's thought is directed towards reopening for his "profane" fellow citizens, particularly those of Western civilization, the lost entry to the archaic periods in the history of mankind. There, in his opinion, the interface of man with the sacred was not yet severed and was, theoretically, unspoiled. Persons, things, symbols and rites bore immediate revelatory and inspirational qualities. Thereby they "belong in some way to a different order of being, and therefore any contact with them will produce an upheaval at the ontological level" (*Patterns*, 17).

In principle, Eliade holds that experience of the sacred is possible in every epoch of human history. Although burdened with excessively powerful rational discursive pressures man can, in an age of technology such as ours, realize this experience. However, the condition for the realization of this experience of the reality of the sacred is, for Eliade, the readiness to adopt, on the part of man seeking the sacred, a less theoretical and much more practical approach. Through this, via the "sacraments," he unites in enthusiasm and ecstasy with being or the sacred. His own personal religious practice thus also enables the historian of religions best of all to discover the sacred in all the appropriate data of the cosmos and history.

The exercise of "creative hermeneutics" implies not so much rational, discursive analysis but much more a practical realization of the religious experience, in association with rites and symbols, myths and forms. The religious practice of the scholar implies some aesthetic, religious and intuitive vision of the character of "creation." Therein the reasons for the being of all that exists will be revealed, in particular their relation to the ultimate being on "God." In this way the scholar of religion himself exhibits a cosmic religiosity. He achieves the capacity to recognize this in all the obtainable facts of the history of religions, and thus to understand them.

The key to the understanding of the methodological complex of Eliade's works in the history of religions cannot be found in philosophy, as has already been pointed out. The fractured relationship of Eliade with transcendental idealistic phenomenology was commented on long ago. Indeed the religious phenomena that appear in the "Life world" of the *"homo religiosus"* need interpretation. But even philosophical phenomenology cannot offer such an interpretation.[5] No special significance can be attached to concepts which Eliade borrowed for his creative hermeneutics from anthropology or a certain school of psychology whereby the interpretation of religious phenomena in the light of psychoanalysis might be expected to yield meaning. Eliade's often-repeated claim that a specific "archaic" ontology underlies every theoretical and action-orientated religious system therefore astonishes the reader not a little. The answer to the question as to the nature of this ontology with its reference to Plato, remains inadequate.[6] The perplexity of the search for the appropriate key to the interpretation of Eliade's method has, in fact, led to the use of the attributes "mystic" or "romantic,"[7] terms which are intended to describe his scientific procedure. One can, however, demonstrate that the key to the understanding of the whole of Eliade's religious, historical material, seen from his perspective of judgment lies in a theology,[8] or to put it more precisely, in Byzantine Icontheology. Alongside modern concepts, drawn from the most varied disciplines and accompanied by their contemporary context, Eliade presents aggregates of thought of the religious or mystical experience of Orthodox Byzantine Christianity in relation to the icons. These theological ideas form for Eliade integrating principles of research in the comparison of the historically most varied religious fields. Thus he tries to establish hermeneutically the logical structure of the symbols and "to discover the function of symbolism in general" (*The Two and the One*, 201 [above, 132]). The influence of the Byzantine theology of images on the conception of the hierophanies in the works of Eliade cannot be ignored. The proof of this hypothesis can be drawn from Eliade's biography and from specific iconological viewpoints.

First, it should not be forgotten that two scholars in Bucharest exercised a lasting influence on the young Eliade above all others, Nae Ionescu (1890–1940) whose student Eliade was,[9] and even more so Nichifor Crainic (1889–1972). The latter held the chair of Mystical and Ascetical Theology in the faculty of theology at the University of Bucharest. During Eliade's student days both professors were rated as "the undisputed spiritual authorities of religious orthodoxy in Romania." They were convinced that "Orthodoxy was the most important characteristic of the Romanian spirit" and that "an imposed 'Westernization' of Romanians by the political leaders would be a mortal sin."[10] For both, Orthodox Byzantine Christianity was the determining spiritual mother-earth of Romanian culture. It seems certain that in his youth Eliade identified himself with a clerical Eastern Orthodoxy and that theological impulses of thought exercised a lasting influence upon him.[11] Certainly, these religious components formed one thread in the rich tapestry of Eliade's whole cultural personality in which Romanian culture was united with that of Germany and Austria. But the stamp which he received from Romania's Orthodox Christianity was lasting.

When Eliade's affiliation to the Byzantine cultural circle is borne in mind and evaluated, a new light is cast upon the methodological components of his history of religions. The vital intellectual concept of this culture was always a "theological" one. Philosophy was only practiced in an eclectic manner. No philosophical system was ever taken over as a whole or had a continuous principle for the explication and interpretation of theological content worked out from it. One selected, rather, elements of the thought of this or that Platonic, Neoplatonic or Aristotelian writer. In much the same way Eliade's method also displays some eclectic characteristics. These may be seen in the use of this or that philosophical or scientific "system" for his interpretive procedure with myths and symbols. He himself called his method "integrative." However, this means basically eclectic. What is relevant for Byzantium can be applied precisely to Eliade. "For a priori one would not expect a unified and fully worked out theological method in Byzantium. Even reflection about method seldom progresses beyond rhetorically fine sounding formulae."[12] Such a method understandably creates an impression of dilettantism.

Eliade's concept of the science of religion displays a perplexing affinity with the concept of theology or theological teaching in bygone Byzantium. The theology in question here was not understood as a discipline carefully separated from other scientific subjects. On the contrary it saw the security of its very existence only in relation to the entire scientific universe.

> Necessarily, it languished in isolation. Furthermore, it needed its link to its milieu in the broadest sense of the word. The continual interchange and lasting interplay of ideas, whether provocative or simply fruitful, enriches every school of thought. What is valid for science as such, is also valid for its nexus with the totality of cultural and everyday life into which it is inserted or should be. This is indeed relevant for theology in a special degree, because and as far as it proposes itself as the interpretation of a doctrine of salvation, and as long as it wants to be that. (Beck, 167)

Eliade's spiritual formation through Byzantine "theology" in general finds its clear, scientific methodological expression in his integrative procedure. This includes all possible scientific domains that could be in any way connected with the phenomenon of religion. The scholar of religion has, according to Eliade, to occupy himself with these "sectors" and ponder over the results of research in them. He must accept with equanimity the accusation of "dilettantism" and, if the occasion arises, plead the use of a "total hermeneutics" (*The Two and the One*, 193–94).

Thereby Eliade realized *de facto* the "scientific concept" of Byzantine theology as it flourished in his home surroundings in Romania.[13] There he recognized that "cosmic Christianity" had been realized in "the beliefs of the rural populations of southeast Europe and of the Mediterranean" (*No Souvenirs*, 261, 267, 281). In general, he knew the mystical writings of Eastern theologians.

From them he drew his preference for a negative theology, with its distrust of the more rational efforts of Western theologians to elucidate spiritual realities. The theology of the Byzantine spiritual world displayed a marked resemblance to myth, particularly to pictorial representations. A continuity of Byzantine civilization with the Greco-Roman past is confirmed with the testing of Byzantine spirituality in the cult of images. The force of popular tradition was so strong in its own time that it eliminated Stoic or Neoplatonic objections to the image cult by intellectual or rationally inclined critics.[14] This was demonstrated again in the lyrical writings of Nichifor Crainic who is "stamped by the spirit of a mystical, nationalistic Orthodox authenticity."[15] Eliade not only lived upon the iconotheological world of Byzantium but he also took from it the matrix or basic interpretative framework for his scientific, religious "total hermeneutics."

Certainly Eliade did not intend to offer any specifically Christian theological interpretation of the innumerable images and symbols which the history of religions represents. On the contrary, his research intentions can be gauged by the following aim which he set for the historian of religions. "In the perspective I have chosen, one thing alone is important." Every new evaluation "has always been conditioned by the actual structure of the Image, so much so that we can say of an Image that it is awaiting the fulfillment of its meaning" (*Images and Symbols*, 159–60). Thereby Eliade implicitly clarified his basic accord with the distinctive "Eastern" doctrine of images. This never limits an image merely to a functional representation "of the being with a substantial participation (μετοχη) in the object ... thus ειχών does not imply a weakening or a feeble copy of something. It implies the illumination of its inner core and essence."[16] The Orthodox teaching on images, based on Platonic and Neoplatonic foundations, determined to an important degree the course of Byzantine theology. It was, as is well known, the main cause of serious dogmatic and political conflict in the eighth and ninth centuries.[17]

Eliade drew upon this formal iconic theology whose unmistakable content can still be recognized in the most recent phase of the spiritual and cultural history of Orthodox Christianity. From it Eliade borrowed the decisive interpretive framework for his integrative comprehension of myths and images, or his "creative hermeneutics."

Let us sketch rapidly the fundamental formal elements of the image cult, constructed on the basis of the pagan Greco-Roman image worship in the Byzantine Christian area.[18] Its analogous translation into the methodological construction of the "creative hermeneutics" of Eliade is obvious.[19]

(1) An image or an ειχών ("hierophany") is not in itself God in his essence ("sacrum"), but its expression. The figure visible in the picture to the onlooker comes close to the form of the invisible "Archetype"[20] of this figure. The relation between the image and its archetype or prototype is thought of as cosmic and timeless. Just as the moon receives its light from the sun, so the image corresponds to the prototype. Yet between the image and the archetype, despite the similarity of the one to the other, no identity of essence exists.

(2) The outlines of divinity represented in the image can be engraved dimly on the mind and held in the memory. Images are therefore a suitable pragmatic means for the illustration of theological content which is incapable of being circumscribed. (The profound disputes and theological discussions in the Byzantine world, and the political polemic of Iconoclasm, erupted around this pragmatic view. The West was scarcely touched by this controversy.)

(3) An image, a statue or an icon is a material, terrestrial or cosmic receptacle for divine power, energy or life. In the middle of empirical space and in empirical time these material things create places or topoi for the breakthrough of a spiritual power, which itself transcends our world. Nevertheless, it is present at the actual moment in the material ("miraculous portrait"). Images are therefore, without detriment to their material form, endued with a divine power. They are revelations of transcendence, which alone is venerated and taken from the images. The Orthodox icon bears the character of a theophany and finds in that its justification. It leads the beholder through itself and, by its presence, to community or union (*communio*) with transcendent reality, and thus away from empirically experienced space-time (theognosy). Icons share the structure of a "sacrament," that is to say, they function as efficacious tokens of a real presence. Their function lies in the amanuensis of the divine. This is to set in the present time that which took place "*illo tempore*" and now finds its expression in the image. As a result, they are "sacred" and not "profane" images.[21]

(4) The ultimate theological reason for the justification of the veneration of images in Byzantine Christianity, as also of pictorial representations of divine realities in general, lies in the fact that God became man. The absolute unearthly sacred person conjoins to the corporeal bodily form of an earthly human being. In this manner a unique basis for his continuous, lasting earthly presence in the likeness is created. God and Man in one person, this "*coincidentia oppositorum*" represents the Christological foundation of the theology of icons. Its analogous application to Man and the Cosmos leads to the discernment that there is no single created object that must be excluded from being the image of the invisible God, without thereby needing to take on the character of an idol, or more precisely a graven image.

These iconological elements, taken together, form the framework upon which Eliade, as a historian of religions, constructs his "creative hermeneutics." He practices, so to say, an "Iconosophy" of the religions. For Eliade this represents a standard of interpretation from which there are no exceptions. In the light of the Byzantine theology of icons all images and symbols, rites and myths in religious and cultural areas outside Byzantium were then interpreted. At the same time it was suggested that the Byzantine doctrine of icons, in its fusion with the outlook on life of the Romanian husbandman, reflected the state of consciousness of archaic man. Thereby Eliade bestows on his methodological approach to the history of religions not only a strong theological accent but also reconstructs a special "Theology." Eliade poses a question "whether one had understood the hidden message of the book, 'the theology' that is implied in the history of religions, as I myself understand and interpret it" (n. 13 above). Image, symbols and myths are for Eliade "something of a theological order ... outside Time and History." They are "forces that may project the historically conditioned human being into a spiritual world that is infinitely richer than the closed world of his own 'historic moment.' " According to Eliade's conception, it would be of the greatest importance "to rediscover a whole mythology, if not a theology, still concealed in the most ordinary everyday life of contemporary man" (*Images and Symbols*, 12, 13, 18).

Thus, it becomes clear once more that the science of religion, or history of religions in the form of "creative hermeneutics," is developed under the control of a special theological a priori. This is not in the sense that Eliade allows himself to accept the "concept of religion," or the logical structure of a symbol, without relation to any concrete realization in form, purely from the human reason. On the contrary, he takes over the "universal concept" or the "structure" of the religious symbol, myth, rite and image from the Byzantine Icon theology. Through precise observation of the manifold iconic materials and through personal religious acquaintance with holy icons (cf. *Journal I*, 29), Eliade discovered his universally valid historically neutral principle of interpretation. He was also aided towards this discovery through abstractions of the invariable from an ample abundance of examples and comparison of typical types of icons. Thus he sought this pictorial, theological "universal concept" without exception in all the historically and culturally diverse image and symbolic fields. With such a methodological focus Eliade obviously deserts the territory of an empirically directed religious science. This, as a principle, must have a connection with theological explanatory models.[22]

Without going into the individual methodological problems that Eliade's work poses for the science of religion, one can sum up at this point. For Mircea Eliade the dealings with images and symbols, rites and myths on the part of "western" civilization bear the stamp of an empty nominalism. This is on account of its rationalistic enlightenment pathos and its unvarnished utilitarian thought in connection with pedagogic-didactic aims. Eliade recognized the same "logical structure" as operative in all the elements of the history of religions, without regard to their historical and constitutional differences. This "structure" makes it possible that through the material condition of the individual earthly thing (rite, myth, etc.) the immaterial prototype (archetype) becomes present in a platonically or neoplatonically interpreted mode of existence. Without doubt Eliade's understanding of symbols is the enduring manifestation of an attitude to the image, having its rationale in the Byzantine world of the Eastern Orthodox Church. For this, Western theology and science has, during the course of history, been unable to display any comprehensive understanding. Although Eliade, with his concept of the "history of religions" and "creative hermeneutics" stands "on the ground of a typical Byzantine, watered down, minimal tradition,"[23] he endeavors in the realization of his own existence to blend the acquired "western" cultural knowledge with Christian religiosity nurtured by Orthodoxy. Thereby he was able to gain access to experiences of existence other than Christian, as, for example, Hinduism.[24] His intellectual personality thus reflects a lived *"coincidentia oppositorum."* In it East and West meet, in so far as Eliade filtered the orthodox popular piety of a Romanian peasant through the scientific, theoretical, rational sieve of western culture. His own religious quest, on which he was mainly silent and only rarely revealed with due caution (cf. *Journal I*, 205–206 and *Journal II*, 16–25) marks him as a seeker of an encounter with God by means of images and signs. Without doing violence to the facts, Eliade can therefore be classified as a secularized mystic of Byzantine Christianity. His philosophical thought moves on a general platonic-like plane of ontology. If one imagines Eliade engaged in the Byzantine dispute about images, one might depict the difficulties he would fall into with his pantheistical, neo-platonic clothing of the relationship between God and man. Eliade's literary and scientific works on religion emanate from personal religious experience. This constitutes the gauge for his evaluation of texts and documents in religious history. Eliade's longing for a life of fulfillment penetrated by the sacred dominates each of his works. In them his nostalgia for a lost paradise is manifest. His decisive reservations concerning Jewish and Christian religion, particularly as regards rational Western theology, do not prevent Mircea Eliade from being regarded also as a historical witness in the present tense world situation, to the effort to mediate between Western and Eastern Christianity.

Notes

1. The sources for the study of Eliade have multiplied to such an extent that it is scarcely possible to take all of them into account. Cf. D. Allen and D. Doeing, *Mircea Eliade: An Annotated Bibliography* (New York, 1980). The following recent studies deserve special mention in this context: Hans Peter Duerr, ed., *Sehnsucht nach den Ursprung, Zu Mircea Eliade* (Frankfurt, 1983); idem, ed., *Alcheringa oder die beginnende Zeit. Studien zu Mythologie, Schamanismus and Religion* (Frankfurt, 1983); idem, ed., *Die Mitte der Welt. Aufsätze zu Mircea Eliade* (Frankfurt, 1984). Eliade's activity as a novelist remained shrouded in obscurity for a long period, as few readers were able to cope with the Romanian language, but his novels deserve serious attention in any general assessment of his work. It is Eliade himself who stresses this important condition of interpretation of his ideas of religious theory; cf. Eliade, "Notes for a Dialogue," in J. B. Cobb, ed., *The Theology of Altizer: Critique and Response* (Philadelphia, 1970), col. 235–36.
2. An appropriate discussion of the methodological implications of Eliade's "creative hermeneutics" for the history of religions has not yet been produced. The following treatments are unfortunately inadequate: Antonio Barbosa da Silva, *The Phenomenology of Religion as a Philosophical Problem: An Analysis of the Theoretical Background of the Phenomenology of Religion, in General, and of M. Eliade's Phenomenological Approach, in Particular* (Uppsala, 1982). Cf. also Guilford Dudley III, *Religion on Trial: Mircea Eliade and his Critics*, 33, 64, 85, 130, 140. Kurt Rudolph, "Eliade and die 'Religionsgeschichte,'" in

H. P. Duerr, ed., *Die Mitte der Welt* (Frankfurt, 1984), 49–78, 60–61, was able, however, to elucidate important problematical methodological perspectives in Eliade's work. C. Colpe, *Theologie, Ideologie, Religionswissenschaft. Demonstralionen ihrer Unterscheidung* (Munich, 1980), 293 (cf. 49), is exceptional in his detection of the sharp contrast between Eliade and Otto, in stressing that Eliade's route "leads out of the Kantianism via Rudolf Otto's interpretation of the Philosophy of Religion based on Kant and Fries towards the conservative ontology of the sacred."

3. Explicitly Eliade hardly ever developed the method openly and confirmed it. Implicitly, however, it determines the course of the analyses and of the hermenutical processes of Eliade's "history of religions." Cf. Charles H. Long, "A Look at the Chicago Tradition in the History of Religions: 'Retrospects and Future,' " in J. M. Kitagawa, ed., *The History of Religions* (New York, 1985), 87–104, 93.

4. Cf. Eliade, Introduction to Allen, *Structure and Creativity in Religion*, vii-ix. The conglomeration of methods and ideas has always been recognized and has been responsible for a good deal of confusion in research. Cf. on this point, e.g. Olof Pettersson, "The Dilemma of the Phenomenology of Religion: Some Methodological Notes to a Great Problem," in O. Pettersson and H. Akerberg, *Interpreting Religious Phenomena* (Stockholm, 1981), V12. 41–45.

5. Allen, *Structure and Creativity in Religion*, 108–109, justly observes that the classification of Eliade with the group of philosophical phenomenologists is inadmissible. One may even pose the question whether his mode of interpretation of the religious phenomena can be defined as "phenomenological": cf. particularly 190ff. [This may be a little misleading. Allen does say, "we may begin to present some evidence to substantiate our controversial claim that Mircea Eliade is a phenomenologist." So he *does* regard him as such, but not *just*, nor *simply* as such. Ed.]

6. Cf., for example, Eliade, *Cosmos and History*, 34: "Hence it could be said that this 'primitive' ontology has a Platonic structure; and in that case Plato could be regarded as the outstanding philosopher of 'primitive mentality,' that is, as the thinker who succeeded in giving philosophic currency and validity to the modes of life and behavior of archaic humanity."

7. This is the opinion of Thomas J. J. Altizer, *Mircea Eliade and the Dialectic of the Sacred*, 84, 30; on this point cf. Allen, *op. cit.*, 129.

8. The considerable affinity of Eliade to the theology of the Orthodox Church has been observed and stressed; cf. Altizer, *op. cit.*, 37: "First, we must take account of Eliade's roots in Eastern Christendom; although it is never stated explicitly, one can sense in Eliade the Eastern Christian's hostility to the rational spirit of Western 'theology.' "

9. Cf. for this Ioan Petru Culianu, "Mircea Eliade and die blinde Schildkröte," in *Die Mitte der Welt* (cf. n. 2), 224: "The first scholarly works of Eliade are dominated by three ideas, which also form the fundamental ideas of Ionescu's metaphysics: the state of redemption, which represents the highest freedom from every historical limitation and a paradoxical experience of death, whilst the human subject is still biologically alive; the function of the religious symbol, and, finally, the problem of alchemy ... The problem of religious symbolism, which occupied pride of place in Ionescu's metaphysics, was equally one of the most recurring research themes for Eliade—both as essayist and historian of religions."

10. Culianu, *op. cit.*, 225. Among the works of Crainic one finds such typical titles as "Orthodoxy and Ethnocracy" and "Nostalgia for Paradise," to mention only two; cf. such a title as Eliade's "The Quest for the Origin."

11. Cf. R. J. Zwi Werblowsky, "In nostro tempore" [in this volume, 294]. Eliade remained faithful to his commitment to the church even later on. He was unwilling to dispense with the church's blessing on his marriage. The wedding ceremony took place in a Paris drawing-room on 9 January 1950, as Eliade noted in his diary *Journal I*, 101, "because the Romanian, Orthodox church is still closed."

12. H. G. Beck, *Das byzantinische Jahrtausend* (Munich, 1978), 166.

13. Eliade noted in his diary on 8 November 1959: "Today when I was leafing through my *Patterns in Comparative Religion*, I lingered especially over the long chapter on the sky gods; I wonder if the secret message of the book has been understood, the 'theology' implied in the history of religions as I decipher and interpret it" (*Journal II*, 74). Cf. also Altizer, *op. cit.*, 37 and *passim*, who never tires of underlining Eliade's dependence on the Byzantine spiritual universe.

14. Cf. L. W. Barnard, *The Graeco-Roman and Oriental Background of the Iconoclastic Controversy* (Leiden, 1974), 81.

15. Nichifor Crainic, in *Brockhaus Enzyklopädie*, vol. IV (1968), 193.

16. Hermann Kleinknecht, "The Greek use of εικου" in C. Kittel and G. Friedrich, eds., *Theological Dictionary of New Testament*, vol. II (1965), 388–89—cf. on this point Walter Elliger, *Die Stellung der alien Christen zu den Bildern in den ersten vier Jahrhundertn* (Leipzig, 1930), and Hans Willms, ΕΙΚΩΝ; *Eine begriffsgeschlchtliche Untersuchung zum Platonismtus* (Münster, 1935).

17. Cf. Hans-Georg Beck, *Kirche and theologische Literatur im byzantinischen Reich*, 2nd ed. (Munich, 1977), 279–368, 296–306. Further from the same author, *Von der Fragwürdigkeit der Ikone*, Sitzungsberichte der Bayerischen Akademie der Wissenschaften, Philos.-Hist.Klasse, part 7 (Munich, 1975).

18. Cf. Barnard, *op. cit.*, 85 and 101–102—cf., on this subject Klaus Wessel, "Bild," in *Reallexikon zur Byzantinischen Kunst*, vol. I (1966), cols. 616–62, and J. Kolhwitz, "Bind III (christlich)," in *Reallexikon für Antike and Christentum*, vol. II (1954), cols. 318–41. One may also consult: Hilde Zaloscer, *Vom Mumienbild zur Ikone* (Wiesbaden, 1969), 31–46, and Leonid Ouspensky, *Theology of the Icon* (New York, 1978).

19. After his *Patterns* Eliade added to his philosophic-theological privileged method scarcely new elements. Therefore the following works are sufficient as means of argument for our hypothesis: (1) *Patterns in Comparative Religion*, ch. 1, 13; (2) "Observations on Religious Symbolism" (cf. n. 3), particularly 201–208; (3) *Images and Symbols*.

20. The semantic value of this expression is basically different from its use in modern research.

21. It is certainly not lacking in significance that this distinction between "sacred" and "profane" was already established by the Acts of the Council of Nicaea, II (787), to cite but a single witness. Cf. Mansi, *Sacrorum Conciliorum nova et amplissima Colleclio*, vol. 13, 728, where those are condemned who "neque inter sacrum et profanum ullum discrimen posuerunt." This conciliar text formed the standard for the theology of images which the Orthodox Churches were to follow in all the later centuries. Cf. for the whole question Pierre Miquel, "II. Théologie de l'Icône," in *Dictionnaire de Spiritualité*, vol. VII (Paris, 1971), cols. 1229–39. The assumption that Eliade was indebted to his own basic religious instinct for this binary principle of the distinction of "sacred and "profane" as iconologically self-evident is not in contradiction to the view that in reading Emile Durkheim's *The Elementary Forms of the Religious Life* (*Die elementaren Formen des religiosen Lebens*, German translation [Frankfurt, 1981], cf. 61–62), he came across this, in many ways, standard "definition" of religion for a scientific investigation based on these two concepts.

22. Cf. K. Rudolph, "Die Problematik der Religionswissenchaft als akademisches Lehrfach," in *Kairos* IX (1967): 22–42 and X (1968): 290–91.

23. H. G. Beck, *Von der Fragwürdigkeit der Ikone*, 30.

24. The difficult problems involved in this interpretation of alien religious symbols have been indicated by Dietrich Seckel, *Jenseits des Bildes. Anikonische Symbolik in der buddhistischen Kunst* (Heidelberg, 1976). The complications inherent in the use of Eliade's method on non-Christian symbolic complexes have been partially demonstrated by Agehananda Bharati, "Eliade: Privilegierte Information und anthropologische Aporien," in *Sehnsucht nach dem Ursprung* (cf. n. 1), 32–58.

41

ORTHODOX MYSTICAL TRADITION AND THE COMPARATIVE STUDY OF RELIGION: AN EXPERIMENTAL SYNTHESIS

Alexander F. C. Webster

Editor's Introduction

Even before Ansgar Paus's connection of Eliade's methodology to Eastern Orthodox iconography, A. F. C. Webster had suggested a strong connection between Eliade's understanding of religion and the Orthodox tradition. The real extent of this connection and the possible roots of Eliade's understanding of religion in Orthodox theology remains to be fully explored. From the *Journal of Ecumenical Studies* 23 (1986): 621–49. All rights reserved. Copyright © by the *Journal of Ecumenical Studies*. Reprinted by permission of the *Journal of Ecumenical Studies*.

ॐ ଔ

The Phenomenological Dualism of Mircea Eliade

The late Mircea Eliade, the most prolific historian of religions in the world, was surely more of a phenomenologist of religion than Rudolf Otto, but some striking points of comparison still obtain. Although he never posited his metaphysical views as clearly and assertively as Otto did he used his basic category—the "sacred"—in a way that suggests to his readers that this broadly-conceived and widespread, even universal, phenomenon always points beyond itself to a sort of meta-reality. Religious symbols always point to something real, Eliade argued frequently, because in the symbolic world of the *homo religiosus* ("religious man," particularly in so-called primitive cultures) the real is equivalent to the sacred, regardless of whether or not that "real" is tangible or empirically evident to an outside observer. Eliade thus seems to have employed a metaphysical agnosticism in his writings, but the logical structure of the sacred as he elucidated it leaves room for someone with more metaphysical certitude to objectify the "real" as the "numen" or "God."

Similarly, in the major work to be considered here, *The Sacred and the Profane*, Eliade employed a "negative" methodology that may be likened to the apophatic ways of Orthodoxy and Otto (*Sacred and the Profane*, 10). In his analysis of the fundamental dichotomy that characterizes the consciousness of the religious person—namely, sacred versus profane—Eliade necessarily posited the sacred reality "experienced" by the religious person, for that, after all, is the essential phenomenon that Eliade the phenomenologist had to study and explain. However, his presentation of his explanation reverses these priorities in order to conform to the dictates of logic: the profane or nonsacred world is that which is immediately evident to the mind and senses, and so it must be shown by means of negation to be comparatively insignificant, illusory, or false in order to arrive at the true value of the sacred as conceived or perceived by the religious person. To be sure, Eliade showed less concern for the nature of that sacred reality than for the attitudes and the behavior of the people who believe in it, and yet Eliade's phenomenological method was by no means comprehensive. In the process of procuring examples for his major phenomenological types of the sacred in terms of space, time, nature, and the human life-cycle, Eliade appears to have wrenched the items from their own historico-cultural contexts. Thus, while paying due homage to the morphological component of a phenomenology of religion in *The Sacred and the Profane*, he virtually scorned the diachronic dimension of the various phenomena, which cannot be totally isolated or unrooted without a corresponding loss of understanding of the particular phenomena. In fairness it must be said that Eliade virtually admitted as much when he declared as his "primary concern" the need "to present the specific dimensions of religious experience," which experience, he nevertheless concluded on the basis of ethnographic research and historical study, is universal in its salient features.[1]

In balance, however, Eliade's interest in the specific manifestations of the sacred in the ordinary daily lives of religious persons in community provides a counterweight to Otto's sharp focus on the psychological-spiritual effects of the extraordinary numinous experience on individual men and women of faith. This counterweight should prove useful to a fuller understanding of the *liturgical* dimension of the Orthodox mystical heritage, as epitomized in the "holy mystery" (sacrament) of the eucharist, which, in the eloquent phrases of Nicholas

Arseniev, "has a central, living, mystic meaning, but for the whole community." In the eucharist, where "the divine mingles with the human, the terrestrial praise and sacrifice are offered to the Lord for the world and by the world.[2] Nowhere is this more evident in the Divine Liturgies of St. John Chrysostom and St. Basil the Great than when the priest, having recalled the words of institution by Christ at the Last Supper, elevates the *diskos* (paten) and chalice containing the bread and wine in the process of being changed into the mystical Body and blood of Christ, and exclaims: "Thine own of thine own we offer unto Thee in behalf of all and for all."[3]

Since Orthodox liturgy in the cultic sense, like most religious liturgical experience, entails a panoply of concrete phenomena such as special places, times, instruments, materials, and officials, Eliade's analysis of the spatial, temporal, and natural aspects of the "centeredness" of the religious person in the sacred or supernatural realm and the interrelations of these myths, symbols, and rituals would seem made to order for an Orthodox theologian. Particularly striking is the parallel between the orthodox and Eliadean perspectives on the procedures by which the religious person sets apart certain places, times, etc. from the seemingly profane (or "fallen") world in order to resacralize the world first by finding or rerooting oneself in what he or she intuitively knows is the true ultimate reality and, second, by reinterpreting, reimagining, and reconstituting the world around him or her from this restored vantage point. In Orthodox terms, the religious man or woman is motivated to convert the world in accordance with the eschatological vision of wholeness revealed by Christ, wherein he is "all and in all" (Col. 3:11, RSV). The cosmic dimension of this vision is manifested in particular in the special Orthodox liturgical service of the Blessing of the Waters on the Feast of the Theophany (or Epiphany) of Our Lord on January 6, or 19 according to the Julian or "Old" Calendar. The priest prays before a baptismal or special font filled with ordinary water and invokes the blessing of God that the waters "may be sanctified by the might and operation and descent of the Holy Spirit" and "may be given the grace of redemption and the blessing of the Jordan" (Orthodox *Festal Menaion*, 351). The initial revelation of the Holy Trinity on the occasion of Jesus' baptism in the Jordan River by St. John the Forerunner is believed to have begun the restoration and transfiguration of the natural order of creation that was climaxed, of course, at the Resurrection, when the powers of Satan, sin, and death were vanquished for all time. The mystical transformation of nature that commences at the Theophany, however, is symbolized by the prayers and ritual actions pertaining to water—one of the four essential elements according to the ancient Greeks. The first part of the prayer of blessing found in the Greek Orthodox liturgical books contains the following exultation:

> Today the waters of the Jordan are transformed into healing by the coming of the Lord. Today the whole creation is watered by mystical streams.

Today the transgressions of men are washed away by the streams of the Jordan ... Today the bitter water, as once with Moses and the people of Israel, is changed into sweetness by the coming of the Lord (*Festal Menaion*, 354–55).

So striking, in fact, are the parallels between Orthodox liturgical (and theological) mysticism and Eliade's depiction of the "archaic" religious person that one may wonder whether Eliade truly captured in words the structures of archaic and developed religion or allowed his own Romanian Orthodox upbringing to perform his perceptions to an extent far greater than he would have admitted! Several examples should lay the foundation for consideration of this surprising possibility.

First, Eliade's insightful analysis of the sacredness of nature and cosmic religion includes a highly informed "paradigmatic history of baptism" with surprisingly numerous quotations from various church Fathers. These remarks together point to a cosmic redemption symbolized in the liturgical use of water that I discussed above. Eliade links "these new valorizations of baptismal symbolism" to what he contended is "the universally disseminated aquatic symbolism" in pre-Christian religions—most notably water as the lair of mythical monsters of the abyss, and water as a means of spiritual purification and rebirth. On the one hand, Eliade argued that these values are not mutually exclusive and even cited primary teachers in Orthodox Tradition in support of this claim: "Certain fathers of the primitive Church had seen the value of correspondence between the symbols advanced by Christianity and the symbols that are the common property of mankind" (*Sacred and the Profane*, 136). On the other hand, this syncretistic penchant for harmonizing the insights of archaic and more advanced religions was mitigated (or may I say "redeemed"?) by a tendency that reflects an Orthodox patristic understanding of antitypes and fulfillment. For example, concerning baptism he suggested: "It could even be said that the aquatic symbol *awaited* the fulfillment of its deepest meaning through the new values contributed by Christianity" (137, italics original, cf. 129–37).

Second, I have already cited the emphasis on the sacred as the "norm" by which the profane derives its meaning as an inferior, corruptive anti-reality, but Eliade's vigorous critique of "desacralization" is structurally homologous to the Orthodox critique of "secularism." When modern nonreligious man or woman, Eliade argued forcefully, regards her or "himself solely as the subject and agent of history," he or she "desacralizes [her or] himself and the world." The result, in Eliade's estimation, was unmistakably unfortunate: "The sacred is the prime obstacle to his freedom. He will become himself only when he is totally demysticized. He will not be truly free until he has killed the last god."[4] Moreover, frequent references to "crypto-religious behavior" on the part of "profane man" indicate the presumption of a natural religiousness that has been somehow thwarted (e.g. *Sacred and the Profane*, 24).

Third, the key concept of *hierophany* as the "act of manifestation of the sacred" is broad enough to encompass "elementary" forms of "the manifestation of the sacred in some ordinary object" as well as "the supreme hierophany (which, for a Christian, is the incarnation of God in Jesus Christ)" (*Sacred and the Profane*, 11). In *A History of Religious Ideas*, II, moreover, Eliade went so far as to pronounce the church Fathers correct in defending the dogma of the Incarnation, for it "represents the last and most perfect hierophany" due to its concrete, historical quality without however, suffering from a historicizing reductionism. He added that it could even be said that "the kenosis of Jesus Christ not only constitutes the crowning of all the hierophanies accomplished from the beginning of time but also justifies them, that is, proves their validity" (408). This explicit hierarchy of types of hierophanies also displays strong logical affinities to the *epiphanic* theme in Orthodox dogmatic and liturgical theology. The *apolytikion* (theme-hymn) for the Feast of the Theophany proclaims in no uncertain terms, "When Thou, O Lord, wast baptized in the Jordan, the worship of the Trinity was made manifest" (*Festal Menaion*, 359). Every time the Divine Liturgy of St. Basil is celebrated, the priest-celebrant invokes the Holy Spirit upon the assembly and upon the bread and wine antitypes to "bless them and hallow them, and *show* this bread to be itself the precious Body of our Lord, and God, and Savior, Jesus Christ" and likewise with the cup as the Blood of Christ.[5] This particular form of the eucharistic *epiklēsis*, which is older than the corresponding shortened version in the more frequent Divine Liturgy of St. John Chrysostom, clearly demonstrates the epiphanic quality of the regular liturgical event in the lives of Orthodox Christians.

Fourth, Eliade's discussion of cosmogony, particularly the themes of the cosmos as sacred organism and the "earthly reproduction of a transcendent model," employed concrete examples drawn from ancient Judaism and North American Indian religions among others, but he offered as the crowning example the dome-surmounted square Byzantine church architecture: "As 'copy of the cosmos,' the Byzantine church incarnates and at the same time sanctifies the world" (*Sacred and the Profane*, 58, and especially 61–62).

Fifth, Eliade's emphasis on the religious person's thirst for being and life as opposed to nonbeing and death—above all, his or her desire "to transfigure his existence, to make it like its divine model"—partook, to be sure, of a wide variety of religious traditions. In Orthodoxy, however, this emphasis on ontological wholeness and opposition to death is absolutely fundamental and lends to distance Orthodox theology from its Western Christian counterparts with their stress on the more juridical aspects of sin, guilt, and righteousness. The quintessential expression of this Orthodox concern is the *troparion* hymn for Pascha (Easter), which resounds repeatedly among clergy and laity during the Paschal season: "Christ has risen from the dead, by death trampling upon Death, and has bestowed life to those in the tombs."[6]

To be sure, Eliade's use of familiar Orthodox concepts and his occasional explicit deference to Christianity, though unusual for a phenomenologist of religions, have a reciprocal demand. If Christianity represents a pinnacle of sorts, all that went before must be acknowledged by the religionist and Orthodox theologian alike as having some value, even validity: "it is to recognize that the countless pre-Christian generations were not victims of an illusion when they proclaimed the presence of the sacred, that is, of the divine, in the objects and rhythms of the cosmos" (*History of Religious Ideas*, II, 408–409). Again this emphasis on continuity rather than discontinuity between archaic and more advanced religions fits rather well into the self-understanding of Orthodoxy as the "end" of religions and the fullness of revelation. Irrespective of his Romanian Orthodox roots, Eliade probably would have hesitated to affirm the neatness of this fit, but the way he elucidated the sacred-versus-profane dichotomy is nevertheless conducive to the craft of Orthodox theologians.

One Orthodox liturgical theologian whose work obviously was informed by Eliade's phenomenological dualism is the late Fr. Alexander Schmemann. In his most influential work, *For the Life of the World*, Schmemann recognized the popularity of dichotomies in the modern world, including spiritual versus material, supernatural versus natural, and sacred versus profane. However, he considered these destructive of the primordial harmony in the divinely created cosmos that Orthodoxy seeks to restore, albeit in an improved version in the aftermath of the Incarnation. In language redolent of Eliade's portrayal of archaic *homo religiosus*, Schmemann offered an Orthodox description of *homo adorans*, whose worship of God ideally is no mere isolated cultic act but rather a way of life:

> The first basic definition of man is that he is *the priest*. He stands in the center of the world and unifies it in his act of blessing God, of both receiving the world from God and offering it to God—and by filling the world with this eucharist, he transforms his life, the one that he receives from the world, into life in God, into communion with Him. The world was created as the "matter," the material of one all-embracing eucharist, and man was created as the priest of this cosmic sacrament.[7]

This passage more than any other in the book represents a synthesis of Eliade's insights and Orthodox liturgical mysticism.

Similar instances abound. For example, Schmemann discussed the Orthodox sacralization of time by distinguishing "*natural* time," which "was fulfilled in the mystery of time as *history*" (for example the Exodus), which in turn "was transformed into the mystery of eschatological time" (that is, "movement toward fulfillment of the Kingdom" inaugurated by Christ). Pascha, the "Feast of Feasts," does not so much commemorate a historical event as signify "the fulfillment of time itself" (Schmemann, *For the Life of the World*, 56–57). Eliade himself noted that "Christianity radically changed the experience and the concept of liturgical time" insofar as it "affirms the historicity of the person of

Christ." This *historical time* differs somewhat from the *mystical time* "periodically reactualized in pre-Christian religions" (*Sacred and Profane*, 72). However, the continuity in Eliade's view—and, one suspects, in Schmemann's too—is more pronounced than the radical nature of the change from pre-Christian (and pre-Israelite as well) to Christian perspectives on the fundamental sacredness of reality.

I could multiply the examples of Eliade's influence on Schmemann, particularly the latter's virtual validation of the phenomenologist's detection of the natural aquatic symbolism underlying Christian baptismal practice (*Sacred and Profane*, 137, quoted above). Suffice it to state that Schmemann's liturgical theology, so imbued as it was with the spirit and method of Eliade's phenomenological dualism as both a heuristic device and a means of supporting the classic Orthodox perspective on "religion," has already proved the usefulness of Eliade's theory of religion to Orthodox theologians. One need only allow for the primarily historical instead of mythical basis of Orthodox liturgical mysticism before adopting Eliade's approach to religion in its entirety!

Notes

1. *Sacred and the Profane*, 17. Also, in the second volume of his *magnum opus*, Eliade applied his phenomenology (*religionsgeschichtliche*) method to the early historical development of the Christian church. See *A History of Religious Ideas*, II, especially 332–409.
2. Nicholas Arseniev, *Mysticism and the Eastern Church*, trans. Arthur Chambers (Crestwood, NY: St. Vladimir's Seminary Press, 1979), 58.
3. The Koine Greek original is "*Ta sa ek tōn sōn, soi prospheromen, kata panta kai dia panta.*"
4. *Sacred and Profane*, 203. Incidentally, this is the only reference, oblique or otherwise, to mysticism *per se.*
5. Italics added. The Koine Greek original for "show" in the infinitive is *anadeixai.*
6. *Megale Ebdomas Pascha*, comp. George L. Papadeas (Daytona Beach, FL: n.p., 1977), 450–51.
7. Alexander Schmemann, *For the Life of the World: Sacraments and Orthodoxy* (Crestwood, NY: St. Vladimir's Seminary Press, 1973), 15.

Eliade's Politics

42

Blind Pilots

Mircea Eliade

Editor's Introduction

This article by Eliade bears the unmistakable stamp of his philosophical mentor, Nae Ionescu. In 1932, Ionescu wrote:

> My whole effort at understanding and interpreting political events is based on a precise method. … This method proceeds with the identification of *structures* and it appeals, therefore, primarily to intuition, to the *ability to see*. This is not so very easy. (*Roza vânturilor*, 300, quoted in Ricketts, *Romanian Roots*, I, 105)

The trope of blindness and sight seems to derive from Ionescu, as does much of the political content. This in no way is meant to exonerate Eliade or to justify his words. The only defense of Eliade is that this is the worst of his "anti-Semitic" and nationalistic articles. Together with the following "Meditation on the Burning of Cathedrals," it has been frequently quoted by the most vocal of Eliade's critics (Adriana Berger, Daniel Dubuisson, Steven Wasserstrom, and Alexandra Laignel-Lavastine). As an extremely prolific journalist, and as a member of the Department of Press and Propaganda in the wartime Romanian Legation in both London and Lisbon, Eliade had more than sufficient rope to hang himself. That these were the most extreme expressions that have ever been ascribed to his hand appears itself to be evidence of his *lack* of anti-Semitism. For a more complete defense of Eliade, see Fransisc Ion Dworshack, *Defending Mircea Eliade* (Norcross, GA: Criterion Publishing, 2004). The following article was originally published as "Piloţii orbi," in *Vremea*, 19 September 1937, 3, trans. Mac Linscott Ricketts. Published by permission of the translator and the Eliade Literary Estate. All rights reserved. Copyright © 2005 Equinox Publishing.

ഗ ൠ

The immorality of the class of Romanian leaders which has held political power since 1918 is not its most serious crime. That it has stolen shamelessly, that it has destroyed the national bourgeoisie to the benefit of allogenous elements, that it has oppressed the peasantry, that it has introduced petty politics into administration and education, that it has denationalized the free professions—all these crimes against the security of the State and all these attacks against the very being of our nation could—after the great final victory—be forgiven. The memory of future generations will preserve, as is fitting, the efforts and heroism of those terrible years 1916–18, allowing forgetfulness to be spread over the dark epoch which has followed the Union of all Romanians.

But I believe there is a crime which can never be forgotten: these nearly twenty years that have elapsed since the Union. Years which we not only have *wasted* (and when will we ever again have the prospects of such a long, *certain* period of peace?!), but we have used them with satanic delight for the slow undermining of the Romanian State. The governing class which has held the reins of Romanian destiny ever since the Union has been guilty of the gravest betrayal with which a political elite can be branded before its contemporaries and history: loss of the *nationalistic instinct*,[1] total political incapacity. It is not a matter of a simple politicians' petty theft, of a million or a hundred million stolen, of corruption, demagogy, bribery, and blackmail. It is something infinitely more grave, something that can endanger the historical existence of the Romanian nation: the men who have led us, and lead us still, *no longer see!*

In one of the most tragic, stormy, and dangerous eras a sorely-tried Europe has ever known, our ship of state is guided by blind pilots. Now, when the great conflict is in the making, according to which it will be known who deserves to survive and who merits the fate of slave, our elite leadership continues with its little or great affairs, its little or great electoral battles, its little or great dead reforms. No longer does one find words to express his indignation. Criticism, insults, threats—all are in vain. These men are invalids: they don't see, don't hear, don't feel. The principal instinct of the political elite—the *nationalistic instinct*—is dead.

History knows many tragic examples of flourishing, powerful states that have perished in less than a hundred years without anyone's understanding why. The people were just as decent, the soldiers just as brave, the women just as fruitful, the grainfields just as rich. There was no intervening cataclysm. Yet suddenly those states *perished*, disappeared from history. In a few centuries' time, the citizens of those once glorious states lost their language, beliefs, and customs—swallowed up by their neighbors. The ship guided by blind pilots ended up on the rocks. No one knew what happened. The high officials played politics, the merchants attended to their business, the young people attended to love and the peasants to their fields. Time seemed to flow with the same monotony. Summer followed spring, and so forth. Only history knew that it would not be carrying much longer that decaying carcass, that nation which had all the necessary qualities except the main one: the *nationalistic instinct*.

The crime of the elite leaders of Romania consists in the loss of this nationalistic instinct and in their dreadful irresponsibility, their stubborn defense of their "power." There have been Romanian elite who sacrificed themselves willingly, and signed with their own hand their death warrants—only so they would not be found opposing *history*, so they would not get in the way of the destiny of this nation. You will remember how a class of Romanian latifundiaries—not all of whom were tyrants—accepted without a word of protest the agrarian reform that simply removed them from history. The class of political leaders we have now, far from showing this resignation in an hour so tragic for the history of the world, do everything possible to perpetuate their "power." They are thinking of nothing but the millions they can still acquire, the ambitions they can still satisfy, and the orgies they can repeat. And it is not in these billions of lei[2] wasted and the thousands of consciousnesses killed that their great crime consists. Rather, it is in the fact that even *now*, when there is still time, they don't know enough to resign.

Let us recall only a few facts and we shall understand easily where these blind pilots have led us. The first thing the Yugoslavians did after the War was to colonize the Romanian Banat, massing along the frontier the purest Serbian elements. The Yugoslavs, then, as now, were far from having the peace and political cohesion that we have been able to have; the Croatian problem had broken out with violence. In spite of this, knowing that the true border is not that drawn on a map, but the limit to which a people can spread (Nae Ionescu), they have done all in their power to denationalize the Romanian district. And they seem to have succeeded. At any rate, now, at the border of the Banat there is a massive Serbian colonization, whole villages which didn't even exist at the time of the peace conference.

At the plebiscite in 1918–19 *all* the Swabian villages voted for union with Greater Romania. Because of this, an impressive majority was obtained. *No Romanian government*, however, has done anything for these Germanic elements, the only sincere allies we could have had to counterbalance the Magyar elements. On the contrary, from the Union on, the Swabians and Saxons have been continually humiliated—and the Hungarians favored. (What an imbecilic inferiority complex we have shown in being afraid of the Hungarians!)

Hungarians have colonized the border areas since as early as 1920, although today hundreds of thousands of Romanians are found living behind this iron band. We had no need of colonization because all the villages on the frontier were Romanian. On the other hand, we stood with our hands folded and

414

watched as the Jewish elements grew stronger in the cities of Transylvania, as Deva became completely Magyarized, as Ţara Oaşului became overgrown with weeds, as colonies of Jewish farmers were established in Marmureş, as the forests of Marmureş, and Bucovina passed into the hands of Jews and Magyars, etc., etc. The 10,000 Romanian peasants who came from Hungary continue to die of hunger. We have taken villages of Romanians from Banat and have colonized the Quadrilateral, instead of keeping the Banatines where they were and bringing to the Bulgarian frontier the Macedonians, the only men who reply to the knife with the hatchet, and to the insult with the carbine. Today, Banatine Romanians beg in the streets of Balcic.

Among all our minorities, with the exception of the Armenians, the most inoffensive have been the Turks. We have allowed them to leave. Their lands, for the most part, have come under the control of Bulgars. The Bazargic is completely Bulgarized. Furthermore, we have allowed the Bulgars to buy and cultivate the land *all the way to the Danube Delta*! The blind pilots have made themselves the agents of the most frightful crimes against the Romanian State: the advancement of the Slavic element from the lower Danube to the Delta and Bessarabia. There has not been a single Romanian politician who has understood that our last hope, surrounded as we are by an ocean of Slavs, is to resist with all our might the union of the Danubian Slavs with those in Bessarabia. Instead of ruthlessly eradicating the Bulgarian element from the whole of Dobrogea, we have simply colonized the Danube Delta with Bulgarian truck farmers.

At the same time, the blind pilots have opened wide the gates of Bucovina and Bessarabia. From the War on, Jews have invaded the villages of Marmureş and Bucovina, and have obtained the absolute majority in all the cities of Bessarabia. Even worse, the Ruthenians have descended down through Bessarabia, and today they have a very short distance to go before joining hands with the Bulgars who have come up the Danube. Reni is the point of union of these two Slavic peoples—on Romanian soil. Immediately after the War Romanians constituted 68 percent of the population. Today, according to official statistics, they are only 51 percent.

The Romanian political elites, instead of concerning themselves with the problem of the Ukrainians by encouraging separatist agitations—as the Austrian government did up until the War, systematically encouraging the Ruthenians in order to do injury to the Romanians and Poles—have been content to tolerate the spread of the Ukrainians, not only in Bucovina but also in Bessarabia.

In 1848 the Ruthenians from Galicia laid claim to a *part* of Bucovina for their province (Galicia) which was to have become semi-autonomous in the reorganization of Austria on a federal basis (the Palacki Plan). Romanian Bucovinians after that knew how to defend themselves in the Austrian Constituent Assembly at Kremsir. But the Ruthenians, after the Great War, found an unexpected ally in the blind pilots of Romania—who, instead of fighting for the Ukrainian claims *beyond* the Dniester (the creation of a Ukrainian buffer state), have shown friendship for those Slavs, letting them multiply immeasurably in Bucovina and descend farther into Bessarabia. Today, a Ukrainian savant of the University of Warsaw, a political refugee, displays at the Seminar on Geography at Berlin maps of the future Ukrainian state in which both Bucovina and Bessarabia are included. I hope that at the hour when I write this, the friend who called my attention to these maps of the Ukrainian professor (a professor at the university of Warsaw) has succeeded in photographing them all—for proof for both of us, if we ever need it.

It is futile for me to continue. Moreover, I've been possessed by this terrifying feeling of futility all the while I was writing these pages. I know very well they will produce no results.

I know very well that the Jews will scream that I'm an anti-Semite, and the democrats that I'm a hooligan or a Fascist. I know very well that others will say that the "administration" is bad, while others will remind me of the peace treaties and the clauses about minorities. (As if the same treaties have been able to prevent the Kamal Pasha from solving the problem of minorities by butchering 100,000 Greeks in Anatolia. As if the Yugoslavs and the Bulgarians had thought of the treaties when they closed Romanian schools and churches, denationalizing as many as ten villages a year. As if the Hungarians had not permitted themselves to persecute openly, with imprisonment, even *German* villages, to say nothing of other kinds. As if the Czechs had hesitated to paralyze, to the point of strangulation, the German minorities!) I believe we are the only country in the world that respects the treaties concerning minorities, encouraging their every conquest, promoting their culture and helping them create a state within a state. And we do this, not out of goodness or stupidity, but purely and simply because the leadership class no longer knows what is meant by a state; because *it no longer sees.*

I don't get angry when I hear Jews screaming, "Anti-Semitism!" "Fascism!" and "Hitlerism!" These men, who are alive and clear-sighted, are defending their economic and political primacy, which they have obtained with great labor, expending much intelligence and many billions. It would be absurd to expect the Jews to resign themselves to being a minority, with certain rights and a great many obligations, after having tasted the honey of power and having won so many positions of command.

Jews fight with all their might to maintain for the present their positions in anticipation of future offensives—and I, for my part, understand their struggle and I admire their vitality, tenacity, and genius.

My sadness and fear have their sources elsewhere. The *blind pilots*! This governing class, more or less Romanian, petty politicians down to the marrow of their bones, who simply wait for the day to pass, for the night to begin, to hear a new song, play a new game, resolve other maps, make more laws … The same thing, over and over, as if we lived in a joint stock company, as if we had ahead of us a hundred years of peace, as if our neighbors were our brothers and the rest of Europe our uncles and godfathers! And if you tell them that Romanian is no longer heard in the Bucegii, that in Marmureş, Bucovina, and Bessarabia Yiddish is spoken, that Romanian villages are perishing and cities changing their complexion—they consider you to be in the service of the Germans, or they assure you that they have made laws for the protection of national labor.

There are some—good "patriots"—who beat on their chests and remind you that the Romanian has survived over the centuries, that barbarian peoples have passed through the land, etc., etc. These poor men forget that in the Middle Ages Romanians ate wheat and fish, and didn't know pellagra, syphilis, or alcoholism. They forget that the curse began to afflict our people with the introduction of rye at the end of the Middle Ages, which took the place of wheat everywhere. Then came the Phanariots who introduced corn (maize), considerably weakening the resistance of the peasants. After that, the curses followed in succession. Corn brought pellagra, the Jews brought alcoholism (in Moldavia, until the sixteenth century, only beer was drunk), the Austrians in Transylvania and "culture" in the Principalities brought syphilis. The blind pilots had a hand in this too, with their immense political and administrative power.

All Wallachia and lower Moldavia used to feed themselves in the winter on salted fish; the wagons began to cross the Baragan as soon as the corn had been harvested. And those salted and dried fish constituted substantial nourishment. The blind pilots, however, created a fish trust. It's not so bad that in Braila fish cost 60–100 lei per kilogram (instead of five), that whole wagon-loads of fish spoil to keep the price from dropping, that instead of gathering eighty wagon-loads a day from the lakes around Braila, only five are gathered and only one sold (the rest rot). The really bad thing is that the peasant hasn't eaten dried fish for ten years. And now, when the populace on the bank of the Danube is mowed down by malaria, the government spends (it is reported) tens of millions on medicine, forgetting that a people is not regenerated with quinine and aspirin, but with substantial food.

No longer do people talk about those "seven hearts in a breast of bronze," which the Romanian is supposed to have. The poor Romanian struggles to preserve even one tired heart, which beats more and more slowly and faintly. The truth is, the Romanian people no longer have their legendary resistance of several centuries ago. In Moldavia and Bessarabia the people fall at the first conflict with a better-fed ethnic element, one that eats wheat, fish, fruit, and drinks wine rather than ţuică.[3] We haven't yet understood to this day that the Romanian doesn't have the resistance to alcoholic beverages that the Frenchman or Russian has, for example.

We boast that we can "hold our liquor," whereas this glory not only is ridiculous, but it also is false. Alcoholism sterilizes whole regions; it is making us imbeciles at a rate which ought to give us pause.

But the blind pilots stand deaf at the helm, as if nothing were happening. And yet these men, the leaders of a glorious people, are sometimes decent chaps, sometimes men of good faith and good will; but being blind, lacking in the only instinct that counts in the present hour—the nationalistic instinct—they don't see the Slavic torrents streaming from village to village, step by step conquering more and more Romanian land; they don't hear the groans of the classes that are being extinguished, the bourgeoisie and the professions that are disappearing, making way for other peoples; they don't sense that some things have changed in this country which in some places no longer seems Romanian.

Sometimes, when they are in a good humor, they tell you that the number of Jews doesn't matter, because they are industrious and intelligent men, and if they make money, their wealth will remain in the country. If that's how things are, then I don't see why we haven't colonized the country with Englishmen, because they're industrious and intelligent! But a nation in which the governing class thinks this way, which tells you about the good qualities of foreigners, no longer has much time to live. It might change itself into a well-managed federation. But as a *nation*, a *people*, it no longer has the right to compete in history.

If a good idea ever had a deadly result for a nation, then, in the case of Romania, that good idea was democracy. Through democracy began the modern Romanian State—through a democracy which was, at that time, violently nationalistic. The "right" of 1848–80 represented the last resistance of the "foreigners" (Phanariots); the "left" was, in the main, nationalistic, even chauvinistic. Let us recall that in 1870 the representative of the extreme left was Hasdeu, and that he wrote then the most violently anti-Semitic and chauvinistic articles.

Democracy, from the end of the War on, has succeeded in nullifying any effort at national reawakening. Through the blind pilots at the helm of the country, democracy has brought us to where we are today. Democracy has crushed completely our helmsmen's nationalistic instinct. Whether they have or have not made themselves into tools in the hands of foreigners matters little for the time being. The only thing that matters is the fact that not one Romanian politician from 1918 on has known what is meant by a *State*.

And that's enough to make one weep ...

Notes

1. The expression translated "nationalistic instinct" is an approximation of the Romanian *înstinctul statal*, "statist instinct," that is, the sense of knowing what a "state" is.
2. "Lei" are the Romanian units of currency [ed.].
3. The Romanian national spirit, akin to slivovitz [ed.].

43

MEDITATION ON THE BURNING OF CATHEDRALS

Mircea Eliade

Editor's Introduction

This is another article that has often been quoted from as proof of Eliade's political culpability. Together with the preceding one it constitutes the most damning evidence thus far available on Eliade's interwar political position. It reminds us, among other things, that the atrocities of the Holocaust were not known in 1937, and that our contemporary revulsion for Hitler's National Socialism is informed by hindsight. Originally published as "Meditație asupra arderii catedralelor," in *Vremea*, 7 February 1937, 3. Translated by Mac Linscott Ricketts. Published by permission of the translator and the Eliade Literary Estate. All rights reserved. Copyright © 2005 Equinox Publishing.

ℰↃ ℭℛ

At Berlin, whenever I passed the beautiful Synagogue in Charlottenburg, I recalled the sixth of February. I was not reminded of the Bolshevik Revolution in Russia, the hundreds of churches burned, the thousands of priests shot, the millions of "Whites" executed by the fratricidal and demented hysteria of Djerjinski. I didn't want to go back even that far. But I asked myself, how does it happen that under a Fascist dictatorship of a violent anti-Semite like Hitler, a synagogue nevertheless stands, proud and peaceful, in the heart of Berlin—while on the sixth of February, in Paris, the first thing the French Communists attempted to do was to set fire to the cathedrals?

Sine ire et studio ... I don't know if it's possible to write today *sine ire et studio* about certain situations like these. But I am trying to understand this simple thing: why the French Communists, as well as the Russian and the Spanish, attacked the churches first, whereas the anti-Semitic Germans have been content to apply rigorous laws against the Jews, without giving themselves over to acts of barbarity? Whatever people say to me about the Hitlerist terror, I can't forget one thing: that a synagogue stands, solemn and inviolate, in the very center of Berlin—as no church has stood in Russia. Whatever people say to me about the Hitlerist massacres, I cannot get past a simple fact: that even the most anti-Fascist press in the world has never spoken about "thousands" assassinated in Germany—while Soviet journals published a year ago an official figure of the number of counterrevolutionaries executed: one and a half million. That's how many they *admit* having killed ...

Stop now and judge for yourself: an anti-Semitic Fascist revolution which has not violated synagogues and has not executed Jews *en masse*; and a Communist revolution which burns thousands of churches and executes a million and a half people.

Were all those unfortunate persons executed political opponents? No one says so, and it would be difficult to believe it anyway. Far too many priests were stood against the wall, far too many women hanged, far too many children burned alive for it to be a matter of political opponents *only*. The truth is simpler: it is a matter of hysteria, of that bestial insanity produced by the sight of blood. The same thing happened in the French Revolution, and it happened again last summer in Spain, in the first days of the Civil War. Militia and women, at the sight of blood, were overtaken by a collective hysteria which drove them to massacre until they were exhausted. *La Passionaria* is not an unfortunate exception to Hispano-Communist heroism. It is a somewhat more emphatic example of a neurotic ferocity, rather easily explained clinically. From the English newspapers we read at the beginning of the Civil War we learned horrifying details: women who forced the militiamen to kill rather than take prisoners; women who massacred the wounded after the battle, who threatened the soldiers with revolvers because they refused to execute, being weary and disgusted by so much bloodshed.

When it is said about the Civil War in Spain that atrocities are equal on both sides—it is an exaggeration due to an excess of prudence.

Atrocities are more savage on the part of those "armies" in which women participate and the men in general are guards (militiamen in the case of Spain). Regular army soldiers are accustomed to blood; men tire more quickly than women when it comes to massacres (cf. the case of Sarmizegetuza, the case of the Belgian women at Turtucaia). Moreover, if that visitor who arrived recently from Spain should decide someday to tell us how those 20,000 men were executed at Madrid, we would, undoubtedly, learn some very interesting details!

One thing remains a well-established fact: any revolutionary movement with a Communist character is bloody and anti-religious. Honest Communists, if you ask them, always give you the same answer: It has to be bloody, because otherwise it wouldn't be a revolution; and churches have to be burned, because Christianity is bound up with capitalism and the bourgeois regime ... Answers which seem to me completely unfounded.

It is not at all true that revolutions have to be bloody (that is, carried out or followed by massacres *en masse*. We are not speaking of England, the classic land of bloodless revolutions. We are speaking of Romania where, in the space of seventy years, there were at least five major social and national revolutions without the shedding of blood: 1) the emancipation of the peasants, 2) the secularization of the monastic properties, 3) the agrarian reform, 4) the nationalization of the land beneath the surface, and 5) the conversion of debts. If we think about it, that which the Communists tried to obtain in Spain (*before* the Civil War, in the spring of 1936) by the burning of churches and the terrorizing of priests, was obtained in our country half a century ago by the secularization of the properties of the monasteries. The same with the agrarian reform. It is said that the Romanian lacks a consciousness of class (e.g., of a nobility) and that is why he didn't react violently when he was dispossessed. Does this lack of "class consciousness" seem such a serious thing to you? The Romanian phenomenon presents, from any angle it is judged, a character of *unity* which the French or the German, for example, does not possess. It seems very natural to me that class consciousness does not exist in Romania, when I know that the Romanian language does not have dialects and that the Romanian people were formed in the middle of a vast area beginning in the Tatra Mountains and ending in the Balkans, without so-called "cyclonic movements." It seems natural to me also that social revolutions in Romania would be made naturally, "patriotically," somehow "in the family." I don't understand why demands for social justice should be made only through Karl Marx. Do we not have a Nicolae Bălcescu, a Bogdan Petriceicu Hasdeu, an Eminescu, all of whom called for social reforms on "racist" and "patriotic" bases—that is, who made themselves exponents of the autochthonous peasantry against the Phanariots and foreigners (Germans, Russians, Jews, Bulgars)?

Let us return to the second argument of the honest Communist: the Roman Catholic Church is reactionary and has become the tool of capitalism. From the outset let it be said that this would be no argument for the destruction of cathedrals and the execution of priests. Let us remind ourselves that for Hitlerites, Jews are "enemies of humanity," and yet the synagogues have not been burned and the 600,000 Jews in Germany have not been massacred. To that you may respond, "But in Germany there was no revolution!" Let us admit that indeed there was not, but there was a seizing of power. Hitler today has *full power*; he *could* burn synagogues and he *could* massacre the Jews. But he has done neither. Out of prudence? Out of weakness? Out of a spirit of tolerance? Hitler has not given much evidence of such Christian virtues. If he has not burned and if he has not massacred, it is because he did not encourage luciferic hysteria, he did not provoke the human beast by preliminary executions. He contented himself with concentration camps—something less serious, at any rate, than a revolver fired at the back of the head or a hanging. Assassinations Hitlerism has known. But does anyone dare mention Hitler's assassinations alongside those million and a half of Bolshevik Russia?

Those who speak about the "reactionaryism" of the Roman Catholic Church forget rather quickly all that modern Europe owes to this Catholicism. They forget the culture preserved, deepened, and transmitted by the Church. They forget that the "European" would have become an hysterical beast and would have perished in a few centuries—like Attila's Huns—if he had not known Christian *caritas*, Christian ethics, and Christian philosophy. Can the whole Roman Catholic Church be held guilty for a few wrongdoings of certain popes and bishops? Kings, emperors, democrats, republicans, dictators—all have committed wrongs a thousand times more serious and numerous! Is the Church opposed to social demands? But the nineteenth century knew a Christian socialism parallel to secular and Marxist socialism! The work of *social assistance* of the Christian churches in a single year surpasses all the "Red aid" from the beginning until 1936. Is the Church *organically* linked to capitalism? Remember that it has been connected with *all* economic and social forms in the world: it accepted feudalism, monarchy, and the republic. It was in conflict with all these forms of life—and it made peace with all of them. The Roman Catholic Church (we speak of it because Orthodoxy and Protestantism, for different reasons of course, do not interfere much in the affairs of the State) also promotes economic demands and reforms (take, for example, the Social Code). If a social revolution can be made without the Church, it can be made very well also *alongside* it, but not *against* it.

And yet, the first thing the brave French, Spanish, and Russian Communists attack are the churches. Meditate a little on these details which are self-explanatory: the craving for blood, for futile savagery; the passion for burning churches; the refusal of the primacy of the spiritual (any spiritual primacy, be it even secular or Buddhist), the debasing of European values (monogamy, family, *caritas*, Mediterranean beauty, personality). These things do not happen in *every* revolution: Fascism or Hitlerism, good or bad as the case may be, does not know burnings or massacres. Lucifer is at full liberty only in the East…

BIBLIOGRAPHY

Bibliography

Editor's Introduction

Eliade's bibliography is increasingly vast—too vast to contain in chapter-length entry. In this light I list only those foreign-language publications to which actual reference is made in this volume and otherwise concentrate on English-language publications available to the research scholar.

ဆ ର

Eliade, Mircea (Non-Fiction, books)

Alchimia Asiatica ("Asiatic Alchemy"). Bucharest: Editura Cultura Poporului, 1934.

Australian Religion. London: Cornell University Press, 1973.

Briser le Toit de la Maison. Lausanne: Gallimard, 1985.

Comentarii la legenda Mesterului Manole ("Commentaries on the Legend of Master Manole"). Bucharest: Editura Publicom, 1943.

Cosmologie si Alchimie Babiloniana ("Babylonian Cosmology and Alchemy"). Bucharest: Editura Vremea, 1937.

Cosmos and History: The Myth of the Eternal Return. Princeton: Princeton University Press, 1954. Translated from the French by Willard Trask.

Dictionaire des Religions (with Ioan Culianu). Paris: Plon, 1990.

Encyclopedia of Religion, First Edition (Editor in Chief). New York: Macmillan, 1987.

The Forge and the Crucible. London: Rider and Co., 1962 (*Forgerons et Alchimistes*). Translated from the French by Stephen Corrin.

Fragmentarium ("Essays"). Bucharest: Editura Vremea, 1939.

A History of Religious Ideas, vol. I, *From the Stone Age to the Eleusinian Mysteries*. Chicago: University of Chicago Press, 1978 (Paris: Payot, 1976). Translated from the French by Willard Trask. Originally planned as a four-volume work it is worthy of note that Eliade's *History of Religious Ideas* was not finished before his death; however, a German-language anthology seeks to complete the project—see Culianu 1991, 2005.

A History of Religious Ideas, vol. II, *From Gautama Buddha to the Triumph of Christianity*.

Chicago: University of Chicago Press, 1982 (Paris: Payot, 1978). Translated from the French by Willard Trask.

A History of Religious Ideas, vol. III, *From Muhammad to the Age of the Reforms*. Chicago: University of Chicago Press, 1985 (Paris: Payot, 1983). Translated from the French by Alf Hiltebeitel and Diane Apostolos-Cappadona.

Images and Symbols: Studies in Religious Symbolism. London: Harvill Press, 1961. Translated from the French by Philip Mairet.

India. Bucharest: Editura Cugetarea, 1934.

Mitul Reintegrarii ("The Myth of Reintegration"). Bucharest: Editura Vremea, 1942.

Myth and Reality. New York: Harper & Row, 1963 (*Aspects du Mythe*). Translated from the French by Willard Trask.

Myths, Dreams and Mysteries: The Encounter between Contemporary Faiths and Archaic Realities. London: Harvill Press, 1960.

Myths, Rites and Symbols. A Mircea Eliade Reader. Eds. Wendell C. Beane and William G. Doty. New York: Harper & Row, 1975.

Occultism, Witchcraft and Cultural Fashions. Chicago: University of Chicago Press, 1976.

Ordeal by Labyrinth: Conversations with Claude-Henri Rocquet. Chicago: Chicago University Press, 1982. Translated from the French by Derek Coltman.

Patañjali and Yoga. New York: Funk and Wagnalls, 1969. Translated from the French by Charles Lam Markmann.

Patterns in Comparative Religion. London: Sheed and Ward, 1958 (*Traité d'Histoire des Religions*). Translated from the French by Rosemary Sheed.

From Primitives to Zen: A Sourcebook in Comparative Religion. New York: Harper & Row, 1967.

The Quest: History and Meaning in Religion. London: University of Chicago Press, 1969. (Revised as *La Nostalgié des Origins*, Paris: Gallimard, 1970.)

Rites and Symbols of Initiation. London: Harvill Press, 1958 (*Birth and Rebirth*). Translated from the French by Willard Trask.

Roza Vânturilor ("The Compass Rose"). Bucharest: Editura Cultura, Naţională, 1937.

The Sacred and the Profane: The Nature of Religion. London: Harcourt Brace Jovanovich, 1959. Translated from the French by Willard Trask.

Salazar şi revolutia in Portugalia ("Salazar and the Revolution in Portugal"). Bucharest: Editura Gorjan, 1942.

Shamanism: Archaic Techniques of Ecstasy. London: Routledge and Kegan Paul, 1964. Translated from the French by Willard Trask.

Symbolism, the Sacred, and the Arts. Ed. Diane Apostolos-Cappadona. New York: Crossroad, 1986. Translations from the French by Diane Apostolos-Cappadona, Frederica Adel, and Derek Coltman, and from the Romanian by Mac Linscott Ricketts.

The Two and the One. Chicago: University of Chicago Press, 1965 (*Mephistopheles and the Androgyne*). Translated from the French by J. M. Cohen.

—and David Tracy, eds. *What is Religion*. Edinburgh: T. & T. Clark, 1980.

Yoga: Essai sur les origines de la mystique Indienne. Paris: Guethner, 1936.

Yoga: Immortalité et liberté. Paris: Payot, 1954.

Yoga, Immortality and Freedom. London and New York: Routledge and Kegan Paul, 1958. Translated from the French by Willard Trask.

Zalmoxis, the Vanishing God. Chicago: University of Chicago Press, 1972 (*De Zalmoxis à Ghengis Khan*). Translated from the French by Willard Trask.

Eliade, Mircea (Non-Fiction, articles)

"American Paradise." *Art Papers* 10/6 (1986): 11.

"Archaic Myth and Historical Man." *McCormick Quarterly* 18 (Special Supplement, *Myth and Modern Man*, 1965): 23–36. (Reappears as *The Sacred and the Profane*, ch. 4 and *Myth and Reality*, chs. 1 and 2.)

"Australian Religions, Part I: An Introduction." *History of Religions* 6/2 (1966): 108–134. (Reappears as *Australian Religion*, ch. 1.)

"Australian Religions, Part II: An Introduction." *History of Religions* 6/3 (1967): 208–35. (Reappears as *Australian Religion*, ch. 2.)

"Australian Religions, Part V: Death, Eschatology, and Some Conclusions." *History of Religions* 7/3 (1967): 244–68. (Reappears as *Australian Religion*, 5.)

"Briser le toit de la Maison: Symbolisme Architechtonique et Physiologie Subtile." *Studies in Mysticism and Religion*, ed. E. E. Urbach, 131–39. Jerusalem: Magnes Press, 1967. Also in Constantin Tacou, ed., *Mircea Eliade*. Cahiers de l'Herne 33. Paris: Editions de l'Herne, 1978.

"Cargo Cults and Cosmic Regeneration." In *Millenial Dreams in Action*, ed. S. Thrupp. The Hague: Mouton, 1962 (reproduces much material from *The Two and the One*, 125–40).

"Comparative Religion: Its Past and Future." In *Knowledge and the Future of Man*, Walter J. Ong SJ, 245–54. New York: Holt, Rhinehard and Winston, 1968.

"Cosmical Homology and Yoga." *Journal of the Indian Society of Oriental Art* 5 (1937): 188–203.

"Crisis and Renewal in the History of Religions." *History of Religions* 5/1 (1965): 1–17. (Reappears as *The Quest*, ch. 4. and *New Theology No. 4*, ed. Martin E. Marty and D. G. Peerman, New York: Macmillan Company, 1967.)

"The Dragon and the Shaman. Notes on a South American Mythology." In *Man and his Salvation*, ed. Eric J. Sharpe and John R. Hinnells, 99–105. Manchester University Press, 1972.

"Encounters at Ascona." In *Spiritual Disciplines*, Papers from the Eranos Jahrbuch, Bollingen series, vol. 4 (1959): xvii–xxi.

"Folklorul ca instrument de cunoaştere." *Revista Fundaţilor Regale*, IV/4 (April 19, 1937): 137–52.

"Foreword to *The Rise of Modern Mythology, 1600–1800*," by Burton Feldman and Richard D. Richardson. Bloomington, IN: Indiana University Press, 1972.

"*The Forge and the Crucible*: A Postscript." *History of Religions* 8 (1968): 74–88.

"Guiseppe Tucci (1895–1984)." *History of Religions* 24/2 (1984): 157–59.

"Henri Corbin." *History of Religions* 18 (1979): 293–95.

"Historical Events and Structural Meaning in Tension." *Criterion* 6 (1967): 29–31.

"History and the Cyclical View of Time." *Perspectives* 5 (1960): 11–14.

"The History of Religions and a New Humanism." *History of Religions* 1 (1961): 7–8. (Reappears as *The Quest*, ch. 1.)

"History of Religions and 'Popular' Cultures." *History of Religions* 20/1 (1980): 1–26.

Homo Faber and *Homo Religiosus. The History of Religions: Retrospect and Prospect*. Ed. Joseph Kitagawa. New York: Macmillan, 1985.

"In Memoriam: Paul Tillich." *Criterion* 5 (1966): 11–14.

"Indologica I." *History of Religions* 19 (1980): 270–75.

"Initiation Dreams and Visions among the Siberian Shamans." In *The Dream and Human Societies*, ed. G. E. Grunebaum and Roger Callois, 331–40. Berkeley: University of California Press, 1966.

"Interview by Delia O'Hara." *Chicago* 35/6 (June 1986): 147–51, 177–80.

"Interview by Leslie Maitland." *New York Times*, February 4, 1979.

"Literary Imagination and Religious Structure." *Criterion* (Summer 1978): 30–31.

Bibliography

"Marc Chagall et l'amour du Cosmos." *XXieme Siècle* 29 (1967): 137–39.

"Meditaţie asupra arderii catedralelor." *Vremea* (February 7, 1937): 3.

"Mystery and Spiritual Regeneration in Extra-European Religions." In *Man and Transformation: Papers from the Eranos Yearbooks*, vol. V., ed. Joseph Campbell, 3–26. New York: Pantheon, 1964.

"The Myth of Alchemy." *Parabola* 3/3 (1978): 6–23.

"Mythology and the History of Religions." *Diogenes* 9 (1955): 96–113.

"Myths and Mythical Thought." In *The Universal Myths*, ed. Alexander Eliot. New York: New American Library, 1990. (First published as *Myths* by McGraw Hill, 1976.)

"Nostalgia for Paradise: Symbolism of the Center and the Ritual Approach to Immortality." *Parabola* 1/1 (1967): 6–15.

"Notes on the Calusari." *Journal of the Ancient Near Eastern Society of Colombia University* 5 (1973): 115–22.

"Notes for a Dialogue." In *The Theology of T. J. J. Altizer*, ed. J. B. Cobb. Philadelphia: Westminster Press, 1970.

"Notes on the Symbolism of the Arrow." In *Religions in Antiquity*, ed. J. Neusner, 463–75. Leiden: E. J. Brill, 1968.

"The Occult and the Modern World." *Journal of the Philadelphia Association for Psychoanalysis* 1 (1974): 195–213.

"On Prehistoric Religions." *History of Religions* 14 (1974): 140–47.

"On Understanding Primitive Religion." In *Glaube, Geist, Geschichte: Festschrift for Ernst Benz*, eds. G. Muller and W. Zeller. Leiden: E. J. Brill, 1967. (Reappears as "Preface," in *Australian Religion*.)

"Paul Tillich and the History of Religions." In *Paul Tillich: The Future of Religion*, ed. J. C. Brauer. New York: Harper & Row, 1966.

"Piloţii orbi." *Vremea* (September 19, 1937): 3.

"Preface. Gail Kligman." *Calus: Symbolic Transformation in Romanian Ritual*. Chicago: University of Chicago Press, 1981.

"Preface. Thomas N. Munson." *Reflective Theology*. New Haven: Yale University Press, 1968.

"The Quest for the Origins of Religion." *History of Religions* 4 (1964): 154–69. (Reappears as *The Quest*, ch. 3.)

"Recent Works on Shamanism: A Review Article." *History of Religions* 1 (1962): 152–86.

"Les représentations du mort chez les primitifs." *Temoinages. Cahier de la Pierre-qui-vire* 41 (1954): 166–74.

"Review of *Religion in Essence and Manifestation* by G. van der Leeuw." *Review d'Histoire de Religions* 138 (1950): 108–11.

"The Sacred in the Secular World." *Cultural Hermeneutics* 1 (1973): 101–13. (Renamed *Philosophy and Social Criticism* after 1978.)

"Sacred Tradition and Modern Man: A Conversation with Mircea Eliade." *Parabola* 1/3 (1976): 74–80.

"Shamanism in South-East Asia and Oceania." *International Journal for Parapsychology* 6 (1964): 329–61.

"Smiths, Shamans, and Mystagogues." *East and West* 6 (1955): 206–15.

"Some Notes on Theosophia Perennis: Ananda K. Coomaraswamy and Henry Corbin." *History of Religion* 19 (1979): 167–76.

"Some Observations on European Witchcraft." *History of Religions* 14 (1975): 149–72.

"South American High Gods, part I." *History of Religions* 8 (1969): 338–54.

"South American High Gods, part II." *History of Religions* 10 (1971): 234–66.

"The Structure of Religious Symbols." *Proceedings of the IX International Congress for the History of Religions*, Tokyo (1958): 506–512.

"Structures and Changes in the History of Religion." In *City Invincible: A Symposium of Urbanization and Cultural Development in the Ancient Near East*, ed. C. Kraeling and R. Adams. Chicago: University of Chicago Press, 1960.

"Techniques de l'extase et langages secrets." *Confirenze di Istituto Italiano per il Medio ed Estremo Oriente* II (1953): 1–23.

"La terre-mère et les hiérogamies cosmiques." *Eranos Jahrbuch* 22 (1954): 57–95.

"Two Spiritual Traditions in Rumania." *Arena* 11 (1963): 15–25.

"The Yearning for Paradise in Primitive Tradition." *Diogenes* 3 (1953). Reprinted in *Daedalus* 88 (1959): 258, 261–66.

"Yoga and Modern Philosophy." *Journal of General Education* 2 (1963): 124–37.

Eliade, Mircea (Journals)

Journal I, 1945–1955. Chicago: University of Chicago Press, 1989. (1–228 of *Fragments d'un Journal*, Paris: Gallimard, 1973.) Translated from the Romanian by Mac Linscott Ricketts.

Journal II, 1957–1969. Chicago: University of Chicago Press, 1989. (Also published as *No Souvenirs: Journal, 1957–1969.* New York: Harper & Row, 1977.) (229–571 of *Fragments d'un Journal*, with additional preface by Eliade dated 1976.) Translated from the French by Fred H. Johnson, Jr.

Journal III, 1970–1978. Chicago: University of Chicago Press, 1989. (Fragments d'un Journal II, Paris, Gallimard, 1981.) Translated from the French by Teresa Lavender Fagan.

Journal IV, 1979–1985. Chicago: University of Chicago Press, 1989. Translated from the Romanian by Mac Linscott Ricketts.

Autobiography, vol. I. Journey East, Journey West, 1907–1938. San Fransisco: Harper & Row, 1981. Translated from the Romanian by Mac Linscott Ricketts.

Autobiography, vol. II. Exile's Odyssey, 1938–1969. Chicago: University of Chicago Press, 1988. Translated from the Romanian by Mac Linscott Ricketts.

Eliade, Mircea (Fiction)

The Cape. Translated from the Romanian by Mac Linscott Ricketts. In *Three Fantastic Novellas.* London: Forest Books, 1989.

Domnişoara Christina ("Miss Christina"). Bucharest: Editura Cultura Nationala, 1936. *Mademoiselle Christina.* Paris: L'Herne, 1978.

The Endless Column (Coloana nesfârşită). Play, in *Dialectics and Humanism* 10/1 (1983): 44–88. Trans. Mary Park Stevenson.

The Forbidden Forest (Noaptea de Sânziene). Notre Dame: University of Notre Dame Press, 1978. Trans. M. L. Ricketts and Mary Park Stevenson.

A Fourteen Year Old Photograph. The Louisberg College Journal, 8 (1974): 3–15. Trans. Mac L. Ricketts. First published in *Nuvele*, Madrid: Colectia Destin, 1963.

"A Great Man" (*Un Om Mare*). Translated by Eric Tappe. In *Fantastic Tales.* London: Dillon's, 1969.

"With the Gypsy Girls" (La ţiganci). Translated by William Ames Coates. In *Tales of the Sacred and Supernatural.* Philadelphia: Westminster Press, 1981.

Huliganii ("The Hooligans"). 2 vols. Bucharest: Editura Nationala-Ciornei, 1935.

Insula lui Euthanasius ("The Island of Euthanasius"). Bucharest: Editure Fundatia Regala pentru Arta si Literatura, 1943.

Întoarcerea din Rai ("Return from Paradise"). Bucharest: Editura Nationala-Ciornei, 1934.

Intr'o mânastire din Himalaya ("In a Himalayan Monastery"). Bucharest: Editura Cartea Româneasca, 1932.

Iphigenia. Play, first published as *Iphigenia: piesa in trei acte.* Valle Hermosa, Argentina: Editura Cartea Pribegnei, 1951. Also published as *Ifigenia: peisa in trei acte: cinci tablouri.* Bucharest, 1974.

Isabel şi Apele Diavolului ("Isabel and the Devil's Waters"). Bucharest: Editura Nationala-Ciornei, 1930.

Lumina ce se Stinge ("The Light Goes Out"). Bucharest: Editura Cartea Romaneasca, 1934.

Maitreyi. Bucharest: Naţională, 1933. Translated from the Romanian by Alain Guillermou—*La Nuit Bengali*, Lausanne: Gallimard, 1950. Translated from the French by Catherine Spencer—*Bengal Nights*, Chicago: University of Chicago Press, 1994.

"The Man Who Could Read Stones." Trans. M. L. Ricketts. In Rennie, *Changing Religious Worlds.*

"Men and Stones. Play." Trans. M. L. Ricketts. In Rennie, *The International Eliade.*

"Nights at Serampore." Trans. William Ames Coates. In *Two Tales of the Occult*, New York, Herder, 1972 and *Two Strange Tales*, Boston and London: Shambala, 1986.

Nineteen Roses. Trans. Mac Linscott Ricketts. In *Three Fantastic Novellas.* London: Forest Books, 1989.

Nuntă în cer ("Marriage in Heaven"). Bucharest: Editura Cugetarea, 1938.

Nuvele ("Short Stories"). Madrid: Editura Destin, 1963.

Oceanografie ("Oceanography"). Bucharest: Editure Cultura Poporului, 1934.

The Old Man and The Bureaucrats (*Pe Strada Mântuleasa*). Notre Dame and London: University of Notre Dame Press, 1979. Trans. Mary Park Stevenson.

Romanul adolescentului miop. Bucharest: Muzeul Literaturii Române, 1988. *L'adolescent miop.* Paris: Acte Sud, 1992.

Santier ("Work in Progress"). Bucharest: Editura Cugetarea, 1935.

Şarpele ("The Snake"). Bucharest: Editura Nationala-Ciornei, 1937. *Andronic et le Serpente.* Paris: L'Herne, 1979.

"The Secret of Dr. Honigberger." Trans. William Ames Coates. In *Two Tales of the Occult*, New York, Herder, 1972 and *Two Strange Tales*, Boston and London: Shambala, 1986.

Soliloquii ("Soliloquies"). Bucharest: Editura Cartea cu Semne, 1932.

La ţiganci şi alte povestiri. Bucharest: Editura pentru Literatura, 1969.

Les Trois Grâces. Trans. Mac Linscott Ricketts. In *Tales of the Sacred and Supernatural.* Philadelphia: Westminster Press, 1981.

"Twelve Thousand Head of Cattle" (*Douăsprezece mii de capete de Vite*). Translated by Eric Tappe. In *Fantastic Tales.* London: Dillon's, 1969.

Youth Without Youth. Trans. Mac Linscott Ricketts. In *Three Fantastic Novellas.* London: Forest Books, 1989.

Other Authors (Commentaries on Eliade and Works Cited)

Albright, W. F. *From the Stone Age to Christianity.* Baltimore: The Johns Hopkins University Press, 1946.

Al-George, Sergiu. "India in the Cultural Destiny of Mircea Eliade." *The Mankind Quarterly* 25 (1984): 115–35.

Allen, Douglas. "Mircea Eliade's Phenomenological Analysis of Religious Experience." *Journal of Religion* 52/2 (1972): 170–86. (Also appears in *Structure and Creativity*, ch. 4.)

—"A Phenomenological Evaluation of Religious Mysticism." *Darshana International* 12/3 (July 1972): 71–78. (Revised in ch. 7 of *Structure and Creativity*.)

—*Structure and Creativity in Religion: Hermeneutics in Mircea Eliade's Phenomenology and New Directions*. The Hague: Mouton, 1978.

—*Mircea Eliade et le phénomène religieux*. Paris: Payot, 1982.

—"Eliade and History." *Journal of Religion* 68 (1988): 545–65.

—"Recent Defenders of Eliade: A Critical Evaluation." *Religion* 24 (1994): 333–51.

—*Myth and Religion in Mircea Eliade*. New York and London: Garland Publishing, Inc., 1998.

Allen, Douglas, and Denis Doeing. *Mircea Eliade: An Annotated Bibliography*. New York and London: Garland, 1980.

Alles, Gregory D. "Wach, Eliade and the Critique from Totality." *Numen* 35 (1988): 108–38.

Altizer, Thomas J. J. "Mircea Eliade and the Recovery of the Sacred." *The Christian Scholar* 45/4 (1962): 267–89.

—*Mircea Eliade and the Dialectic of the Sacred*. Philadelphia: Westminster Press, 1963.

—"Mircea Eliade and the Death of God." *CrossCurrents* 29/3 (1979): 257–68.

Altizer, Thomas J. J., W. Beardsley, and J. Young, eds. *Truth, Myth and Symbol*. Englewood Cliffs, NJ: Prentice Hall, 1962.

Apostolos-Cappadona, Diane. "To Create a New Universe: Mircea Eliade on Modern Art." *CrossCurrents* 33/4 (1982–83): 408–19.

—, ed. *Symbolism, the Sacred, and the Arts: Mircea Eliade*. New York: Crossroad, 1985.

Arcade, L. M., Ion Manea, and Elena Stamatescu, eds., *Homo Religiosus*. Los Angeles: American-Romanian Academy of Arts and Sciences, 1990. (Selected papers from the 12th congress of the ARA, Université de Paris-Sorbonne, June 24–27, 1987.)

Baird, Robert D. "Normative Elements in Eliade's Phenomenology of Symbolism." *Union Seminary Quarterly Review* 25/4 (1970): 505–516. Included in "Phenomenological Understanding: Mircea Eliade," in *Category Formation and the History of Religion*, 74–91. The Hague: Mouton, 1971.

Barbosa da Silva, Antonio. *Phenomenology as a Philosophical Problem*. Uppsala: G.W.K. Gleerup, 1982.

Beane, Wendell C. "Introduction" and "Conclusion." In *Myths, Rites and Symbols: A Mircea Eliade Reader*, ed. Wendell C. Beane and William G. Doty. New York: Harper & Row, 1975.

Berger, Adriana. "Eliade's Double Approach: A Desire for Unity." *Religious Studies Review* 11 (1985): 9–12.

—"Cultural Hermeneutics: The Concept of Imagination in the Phenomenological Approaches of Henry Corbin and Mircea Eliade." *Journal of Religion* 66/2 (1986): 141–56.

—"Fascism and Religion in Romania." *The Annals of Scholarship* 6/4 (1989): 455–65.

—"Anti-Judaism and Anti-Historicism in Eliade's Writings." Paper presented at the American Academy of Religion Annual Meeting, New Orleans. Published in Hebrew in *Hadoar* 70/25 (1990): 14–17.

—"Mircea Eliade: Romanian Fascism and the History of Religions in the United States." In *Tainted Greatness: Antisemitism and Cultural Heroes*, ed. Nancy A. Harrowitz, 51–73. Philadelphia: Temple University Press, 1994.

Bergson, Henri. *Time and Free Will: An Essay on the Immediate Data of Consciousness*. Trans. F. L. Pogson. Mineola, NY: Dover Publications, 2001. (Macmillan, 1910.)

Bianchi, Ugo. "Mircea Eliade and the Morphology of the Holy: Contrasting Opinions on the 'Holy' and on History." In *The History of Religions*, 184–91. Leiden: E. J. Brill, 1975.

Bleeker, Claas Jouco. *The Sacred Bridge: Researches into the Nature and Structure of Religion*. Leiden: Brill, 1963.

—"The Contribution of the Phenomenology of Religion to the Study of the History of Religions." In *Problems and Methods in the History of Religions: Proceedings of the Study Conference Organized by the Italian Society for the History of Religions on the Occasion of the Tenth*

Bibliography

Anniversary of the Death of Raffaele Pettazzoni, ed. Ugo Bianchi, Claas Bleeker, and Alessandro Bausani, 35–54. Leiden: E. J. Brill, 1972.

Bolle, Kees. "Mircea Eliade: 1907–1986." *Epoché* 15 (1987): 3–5. This edition (105pp.) is a festschrift for Eliade.

Brandon, S. G. F. "Time as the 'Sorrowful Weary Wheel' and as Illusion." In *History, Time and Deity*, Ch. 4, pt. I. Manchester: Manchester University Press, 1965.

Brauer, Jerome C. "Mircea Eliade and the Divinity School." *Criterion* 24 (1985): 23–27.

Breu, G. "Teacher: Shamans? Hippies? They're All Creative to the World's Leading Historian of Religion." *People Weekly* (March 27, 1978), 9, 12.

Brown, Robert F. "Eliade on Archaic Religions: Some Old and New Criticisms." *Sciences Religieuses* 10/4 (1981): 429–49.

Buchanan, James. "The Total Hermeneutics of Mircea Eliade." *Religious Studies Review* 9/1 (1983): 22–24.

Burckhardt, Jacob. *The Civilization of the Renaissance in Italy*. Oxford: Phaidon, 1981.

Cain, Seymour. "Mircea Eliade." *International Encyclopedia of the Social Sciences, Biographical Supplement*, 18: 166–72. New York: Macmillan, 1979.

—"Mircea Eliade: Attitudes Towards History." *Religious Studies Review* 6/1 (1980): 13–16.

—"Mircea Eliade: Creative Exile." *Midstream* 28/6 (1982): 50–58.

—"Mircea Eliade, the Iron Guard, and Romanian Anti-Semitism." *Midstream* 35/8 (1989): 27–31.

Calinescu, Matei. "Imagination and Meaning. Aesthetic Attitudes and Ideas in Mircea Eliade's Thought." *Journal of Religion* 57/1 (1977): 1–15.

—"Mircea Eliade's Journals." *The Denver Quarterly* 12/1 (1977): 313–15.

—"The Disguises of Miracle: Notes on Mircea Eliade's Fiction." *World Literature Today* 52/4 (1978): 558–64.

—"Between History and Paradise: Initiation Trials." *Journal of Religion* 59/2 (1979): 218–23.

—"Creation as Duty." Review article of *Autobiography II, History of Religious Ideas III*, and *Ordeal by Labyrinth*. *Journal of Religion* 65 (1985): 250–57.

—Review of *The History of Religious Ideas*, vol. I. *Journal of Religion* 65 (1985): 250–57.

—"Romania's 1930s Revisited." *Salmagundi* 97 (1993): 133–51.

—"The 1927 Generation in Romania: Friendships and Ideological Choices (Mihail Sebastian, Mircea Eliade, Nae Ionescu, Eugène Ionesco, E. M. Cioran)." *East European Politics and Societies* 15/3 (2001): 649–77.

Carrasco, Davíd, and Jane Marie Law. *Waiting for the Dawn: Mircea Eliade in Perspective*. Boulder and London: Westview Press, 1985.

Cave, John David. *Mircea Eliade's Vision for a New Humanism*. New York: Oxford University Press, 1992.

Christ, Carol P. "Mircea Eliade and the Feminist Paradigm Shift." *Journal of Feminist Studies* 7 (1991): 75–94.

Codrington, Robert H. *The Melanesians: Studies in their Anthropology and Folk-lore*. Oxford: Clarendon Press, 1891.

"A Conversation with Mircea Eliade. Interview." *Encounter* (London), March 1980, 21–27.

Corless, Roger. "Building on Eliade's Magnificent Failure." In Rennie, *Changing Religious Worlds*, 3–9.

Cronin, Edward J. J. "Eliade, Joyce and the 'Nightmare of History.'" *Journal of the American Academy of Religion* 50 (1982): 435–48.

Culianu, Ioan. P. *Mircea Eliade*. Assisi: Cittadella, 1977.

—"Mircea Eliade Aujourd'hui." *Revue d'Études Roumaines et des Traditions Orales Méditerranéennes* 8 (1982): 39–52.

—"Mircea Eliade at the Crossroads of Anthropology." *Neue Zeitschrift für systematische Theologie und Religionsphilosophie* 27/2 (1985): 123–31.

—"Mahaparinirvana." In *Mircea Eliade: dialogues avec le sacré*, ed. Fernand Schwarz. Paris: Editions N.A.D.P., 1986.

—"Mircea Eliade et la tortue borgne." In *Homo Religiosus*, eds. L. M. Arcade, Ion Manea, and Elena Stamatescu. Los Angeles: American–Romanian College of the Arts and Sciences, 1990.

—, ed. *Geschichte der religiösen Ideen, Band IV: Vom Zeitalter der Entdeckungen bis zur Gegenwart*. Freiburg im Breisgau: Verlag Herder, 1991, 2005.

Dasgupta, Surendranath. *A History of Indian Philosophy*. Cambridge: Cambridge University Press, 1922.

Demetrio y Radaza, F. *Symbols in Comparative Religion and the Georgics*. Manila: Loyola House of Studies, 1968.

Devi, Maitreyi. *It Does Not Die: A Romance*. Calcutta: Writers' Workshop Publications, 1976. Reprinted by the University of Chicago Press, 1994.

Dobbs, Betty Jo Teeter. *The Foundations of Newton's Alchemy or the Hunting of the Greene Lyon*. Cambridge: Cambridge University Press, 1975.

Dubuisson, Daniel. *Mythologies du XXᵉ Siècle (Dumézil, Lévi-Strauss, Eliade)*. Villeneuve d'Ascq: Presses Universitaires de Lille, 1993.

Dudley III, Guilford. "Mircea Eliade as 'Anti-historian' of Religion." *Journal of the American Academy of Religion* 44/2 (1976): 345–59.

—*Religion on Trial; Mircea Eliade and his Critics*. Philadelphia: Temple University, 1977.

—"Jung and Eliade: A Difference of Opinion." *Psychological Perspectives* 10 (1979): 38–47.

Duerr, Hans Peter, ed. *Die Mitte Der Welt*. Frankfurt: Suhrkamp, 1984.

Dupré, Wilhelm. *Religion in Primitive Cultures: A Study in Ethnophilosophy*. The Hague: Mouton, 1975.

Durkheim, Emile. *The Elementary Forms of the Religious Life*. Trans. Joseph Ward Swain. New York: Free Press, 1965.

—"Concerning the Definition of Religious Phenomena." In W. S. F. Pickering, ed., *Durkheim on Religion: A Selection of Readings with Bibliographies*, trans. Jacqueline Redding and W. S. F. Pickering, 74–99. London and Boston: Routledge & Kegan Paul, 1975.

Dworschak, Fransisc Ion. *Defending Mircea Eliade*. Norcross, GA: Criterion Publishing, 2004.

Foucault, Michel. *The Birth of the Clinic: An Archaeology of Medical Perception*. Translated from the French by A. M. Sheridan Smith. New York: Pantheon, 1973.

Frazer, James George. *The Golden Bough: A Study in Comparative Religion*. New York and London: Macmillan and Co., 1894.

—*The Worship of Nature*. London: New York and London: Macmillan and Co., 1926.

Frye, Northrop. "World Enough without Time." *The Hudson Review* 12 (1959): 423–31.

Gamwell, Frank I. "Opening Remarks on the Occasion of the Establishment of the Mircea Eliade Chair in the History of Religions." *Criterion* 24/3 (1985): 18–19.

Gilhus, Ingvild S. "The Tree of Life and the Tree of Death: A Study of Gnostic Symbols." *Religion* 17 (1987): 337–53.

Gilkey, Langdon. *Naming the Whirlwind: The Renewal of God-Language*. Indianapolis: Bobbs-Merrill, 1969.

—*Reaping the Whirlwind: A Christian Interpretation of History*. New York: Seabury Press, 1976.

Gill, Sam. *Storytracking: Texts, Stories, and Histories in Central Australia*. New York: Oxford University Press, 1998.

Girardot, Norman. "Smiles and Whispers: Nostalgic Reflections on Mircea Eliade's Significance for the Study of Religion." In Rennie, *Changing Religious Worlds*, 143–63.

—and Mac Linscott Ricketts, eds. *Imagination and Meaning. The Scholarly and Literary Works of Mircea Eliade*. New York: The Seabury Press, 1982.

Gligor, Mihaela and Mac Linscott Ricketts, eds. *Encounters with Mircea Eliade*. Cluj-Napoca: Casa Cărții de Științǎ, 2005.

Gombrich, Richard. "Eliade on Buddhism." *Religious Studies* 10 (1974): 225–31.

Granet, Marcel. *La Pensée Chinoise*. Paris: A. Michel, 1968.

Greeley, Andrew M. "Mass Culture Milieu." *Worship* 33/1 (1958): 19–26.

—"Myths, Symbols and Rituals in the Modern World." *The Critic* 20/3 (1961–62): 18–25.

Hamilton, Kenneth G. "*Homo Religiosus* and Historical Faith." *Journal of Bible and Religion* 33 (1965): 213–22. Reply, D. L. Miller, 34 (1966): 305–15.

Harrison, Jane. *Prolegomena to the Study of Greek Religion*, 3rd ed. Cambridge: Cambridge University Press, 1922.

Hogbin, Herbert Ian. "Mana." *Oceania* 36/4 (1936): 241–74.

Hudson, Wilson M. "Eliade's Contribution to the Study of Myth." In *From Tire Shrinker to Dragster*, ed. W. M. Hudson, 219–41. Austin: Encino Press, 1968.

Hyers, Conrad. "Mircea Eliade: A Retrospective." *Theology Today* 44 (1987): 251–58.

Idinopulos, Thomas A., and Edward Yonan, eds. *Religion and Reductionism: Essays on Eliade, Segal, and the Challenge of the Social Sciences for the Study of Religion*. Leiden: Brill, 1994.

Ierunca, Virgil. "The Literary Work of Mircea Eliade." In Kitagawa and Long, *Myths and Symbols*, 543–64.

Jacobsen, Knut A. "The Anthropological Bias in Eliade's Interpretation of the Sāṃkhya and the Sāṃkhya-Yoga Systems of Religious Thought." *Religion* 25/2 (1995): 213–25.

Johnston, Ilinca Zarifopol. Review of *Autobiography, vol. I*. *Religious Studies Review* 9/1 (1983): 11–13.

Kamani, Ginu. "A Terrible Hurt: The Untold Story behind the Publishing of Maitreyi Devi." *The Toronto Review* (Summer 1996): 29–40.

Kim, Jay J. "Hierophany and History." *Journal of the American Academy of Religion* 40/3 (1972): 334–48.

King, Ursula. *A Hermeneutical Circle of Religious Ideas*. (Review of *The History of Religious Ideas*.) *Religious Studies* 17 (1981): 565–69.

—"Women Scholars and the *Encyclopedia of Religion*." *Method and Theory in the Study of Religion* 2 (1990): 91–97.

Kitagawa, Joseph. "Remarks on the Mircea Eliade Chair." *Criterion* 24/3 (1985): 22.

—"Mircea Eliade and Eliade and Tillich." In *History of Religions: Understanding Human Experience*. Atlanta, Georgia: Scholars Press, 1987.

—and Charles H. Long, eds. *Myths and Symbols: Studies in Honor of Mircea Eliade*. Chicago: University of Chicago Press, 1969.

Laignel-Lavastine, "Alexandra." *Cioran, Eliade, Ionesco: L'oubli du Fascisme*. Paris: Presses Universitaires de France, 2002.

Laudan, Larry. *Progress and its Problems*. Berkeley: University of California Press, 1977.

Leach, Edmund. "Sermons from a Man on a Ladder." *New York Review of Books* 8 (October 20, 1966), 28–31.

Long, Charles H. *Alpha: The Myths of Creation*. New York: G. Braziller, 1963.

—"The Significance for Modern Man of Mircea Eliade's Work." In *Cosmic Piety, Modern Man and the Meaning of the Universe*, ed. C. Derrick. New York: P. J. Kennedy and Sons, 1967.

—"Human Centres: an Essay on Method in the History of Religions." *Soundings* 61 (1978): 400–14.

—and Kees Bolle. "Two Letters: Eliade and Politics." *Epoché* 15 (1987): 92–105.

Lukes, Steven. *Emile Durkheim: His Life and Work*. New York: Harper & Row, 1972.

Luyster, Robert. "The Study of Myth: Two Approaches." *Journal of Bible and Religion* 34/3 (1966): 235–43.

Mairet, Philip. "The Primordial Myths: A Note on the Works of Professor Eliade." *Aryan Path* 34 (1963): 8–12.

Malefijit, Annemarie de Waal. *Religion and Culture*. New York: Macmillan, 1968.

433

Manea, Norman. "Happy Guilt: Mircea Eliade, Fascism and the Unhappy Fate of Romania." *The New Republic* (August 5, 1991): 27–36.

—"The Incompatibilities." *The New Republic* (April 20, 1998): 32–37.

Marino, Adrian. *L'Hermeneutique de Mircea Eliade*. Translated from the Romanian by Jean Gouillard. Paris: Gallimard, 1981.

Marty, Martin. "That Nice Man." [Mircea Eliade Reminiscences.] *The Christian Century* 103/17 (1986): 503.

Mason, John R. *Reading and Responding to Mircea Eliade's* History of Religious Ideas*: The Lure of the Late Eliade*. Lampeter: Edwin Mellen Press, 1993.

Masuzawa, Tomoko. *In Search of Dreamtime: The Quest for the Origin of Religion*. Chicago: University of Chicago Press, 1993.

McCutcheon, Russell T. "The Myth of the Apolitical Scholar." *Queen's Quarterly* 100 (1993): 642–46.

—"Method, Theories, and the Terror of History: Closing the Eliadean Era with Some Dignity." In Rennie, *Changing Religious Worlds*, 11–23.

McGuire, James E., and P. M. Rattansi. "Newton and the 'Pipes of Pan.'" *Notes and Records of the Royal Society* 21 (1966): 108–43.

Meadow, Mary Jo. "Archetypes and Patriarchy: Eliade and Jung." *Journal of Religion and Health* 31 (1992): 187–95.

Midgley, Mary. *Evolution as a Religion: Strange Hopes and Stranger Fears*. London and New York: Methuen, 1985.

Mugerauer, Robert. "Mircea Eliade: Restoring the Possibilities of Place." *The Environmental and Architectural Phenomenology Newsletter* (1993): 10–12.

Munson, Thomas. "Freedom: A Philosophical Reflection on Spirituality." *Philosophy Today* 11 (1967): 47–54.

—*Reflective Theology, Philosophical Orientations in Religion*. New Haven, CT: Yale University Press, 1968.

Nemoianu, Virgil. "Wrestling with Time: Some Tendencies in Nabokov and Eliade's Later Works." *Southeastern Europe* 7/1 (1980): 74–90.

—"Naming the Secret: Fantastic and Political Dimensions of Charles William's and Eliade's Fiction." *Bulletin of the American-Romanian Academy of the Arts and Sciences* 4 (1983): 50–59.

O'Flaherty, Wendy Doniger. "Remembering Eliade: 'He Loved It All.'" *The Christian Century* 103/19 (1986): 540.

—"Time, Sleep, and Death in the Life, Fiction, and Academic Writings of Mircea Eliade." In *Mircea Eliade e le Religione Asiatiche*, ed. Gherardo Gnoli. Rome: Instituto Italiano per il medio ed estremo oriente, 1989.

Olson, Carl. "The Concept of Power in the Works of Eliade and van der Leeuw." *Studia Theologica* 42/1 (1988): 39–54.

—"The Fore-Structure of Eliade's Hermeneutics." *Philosophy Today* 32 1/4 (1988): 43–53.

—"Theology of Nostalgia: Reflections on the Theological Aspects of Eliade's Work." *Numen* 36/1 (1989): 98–112.

—*The Theology and Philosophy of Eliade*. New York: St. Martin's Press, 1992.

—"Mircea Eliade, Postmodernism, and the Problematic Nature of Representational Thinking." *Method and Theory in the Study of Religion* 11/4 (1999): 357–85.

Oxtoby, Willard, "Religionswissenschaft Revisited." In *Religions in Antiquity: Essays in Memory of Erwin Ramsdell Goodenough*, ed. Jacob Neusner. Leiden: E. J. Brill, 1968.

Paden, William. "Before the Sacred Became Theological: Rereading the Durkheimian Legacy." In Idinopulos and Yonan, *Religion and Reductionism*, 198–209.

Pals, Daniel. *Eight Theories of Religion*. 2nd ed. New York: Oxford University Press, 2005.

Parsons, Talcot. "The Structure of Social Actions." Glencoe, IL: Free Press, 1937.

Bibliography

Paus, Ansgar. "The Secret Nostalgia of Mircea Eliade for Paradise: Observations on Method in the Study of Religion." *Religion* 19 (1989): 137–50.

Penner, Hans H. "Bedeutung und Probleme der Religiosen Symbolik bei Tillich und Eliade." *Antaios* 9 (1967): 127–43.

—*Impasse and Resolution: A Critique of the Study of Religion*. New York: Peter Lang Press, 1990.

Pettazzoni, Raffaele. *The All-knowing God: Researches into Early Religion and Culture*. London: Methuen, 1956 and New York: Arno Press, 1978.

Pierre, Jacques. "Epistemologie de l'interpretation: pour un relecture de l'oeuvre de Mircea Eliade." *Sciences Religieuses* 11/3 (1982): 265–84.

—*Mircea Eliade: le jour et le nuit*. Québec: Éditions Hurtubise, 1988.

Progoff, Ira. "Culture and Being: Mircea Eliade's Studies in Religion." *International Journal for Parapsychology* 3 (1961): 47–60.

Quinn, William W. *The Only Tradition*. Albany, NY: State University of New York Press, 1997.

—"Mircea Eliade and Sacred Tradition (a Personal Account)." *Nova Religio* 3/1 (1999): 147–53.

Rasmussen, David. "Mircea Eliade: Structural Hermeneutics and Philosophy." *Philosophy Today* 12 (1968): 138–46. Also in, *Symbol and Interpretation*. The Hague: Martinus Nijhoff, 1974.

Ray, Richard A. "Is Eliade's Metapsychoanalysis an End Run around Bultmann's Demythologization?" In *Myth and the Crisis of Historical Consciousness*, ed. L. W. Gibbs and W. Taylor Stevenson, 57–74. Missoula, MT: Scholars Press, 1975.

Rennie, Bryan. "The Diplomatic Career of Mircea Eliade: A Response to Adriana Berger." *Religion* 22/4 (1992): 375–92.

—"The Religious Creativity of Modern Humanity: Some Observations on Eliade's Unfinished Thought." *Religious Studies* 31/2 (1995): 221–35.

—*Reconstructing Eliade: Making Sense of Religion*. Albany, NY: State University of New York Press, 1996.

—, ed. *Changing Religious Worlds: The Meaning and End of Mircea Eliade*. Albany, NY: State University of New York Press, 2001.

—Review of *Journal, 1935–1944: The Fascist Years*, by Mihail Sebastian, Ivan R. Dee, 2000. *Religion* 32/2 (2002): 172–75.

—"Religion after Religion, History after History: Postmodern Historiography and the Study of Religions." *Method and Theory in the Study of Religion* 15/3 (2003): 68–99.

—"Eliade, Mircea (Further Considerations)." In *Encyclopedia of Religion*, 2nd ed. Macmillan, 2005.

—*The International Eliade*. Albany, NY: State University of New York Press, 2006.

Reno, Stephen J. "Eliade's Progressional View of Hierophanies." *Religious Studies* 8 (1972): 153–60.

Reynolds, Frank E. "A Tribute to Mircea Eliade." *Criterion* 24/3 (1985): 20–21.

Ricketts, Mac Linscott. "Eliade and Altizer: Very Different Outlooks." *Christian Advocate* (October 1967): 11–12.

—"Mircea Eliade and the Death of God." *Religion in Life* 36/1 (1967): 40–52.

—"The Nature and Extent of Eliade's 'Jungianism.'" *Union Seminary Quarterly Review* 25/2 (1970): 211–34.

—"In Defense of Eliade: Bridging the Gap between Anthropology and the History of Religions." *Religion* 1/3 (1973): 13–34.

—"Fate in the *Forbidden Forest*." *Dialogue* 8 (1982): 101–19.

—"On Reading Eliade's Stories as Myths for Moderns." Unpublished paper read at the Midwestern Modern Language Association, Cincinati, Ohio, 1982.

—*Mircea Eliade: The Romanian Roots*. 2 vols. New York: Columbia University Press, 1988.

—*Former Friends and Forgotten Facts*. Norcross, GA: Criterion Publishing, 2003.

Ricoeur, Paul. Review of *The History of Religious Ideas*. *Religious Studies Review* 2/4 (1976): 1–4.

—"The History of Religions and the Phenomenology of Time Consciousness." In *The History of Religions: Retrospect and Prospect*, ed. Joseph Kitagawa, 13–30. New York: Macmillan, 1985.

Robertson Smith, William. *The Religion of the Semites*. New Brunswick, NJ: Transaction Publishers, 2002 (New York: Meridian Books, 1956; first published 1889).

Rudolph, Kurt. "Mircea Eliade and the 'History of Religions.'" *Religion* 19 (1989): 101–28 (trans. Gregory Alles).

Ruyer, Raymond. *La Gnose de Princeton: des savants à la recherche d'une religion*. Paris: le Livre de Poche, 1977.

Sabre, Jeanette M. "The Sacred Wood in Three 20th Century Narratives: *The Forbidden Forest* (Eliade), *Daniel Martin* (John Fowles), and *Heart of Darkness* (Joseph Conrad)." *Christian Scholars' Review* 13/1 (1984): 34–47.

Saiving, Valerie. "Androcentrism in Religious Studies." *Journal of Religion* 56 (1973): 117–97.

Saliba, John A. "Eliade's View of Primitive Man: Some Anthropological Reflections." *Religion* 6 (1976): 150–75.

—"Homo Religiosus *in the Works of Mircea Eliade*." Leiden: E. J. Brill, 1976.

—"Review of *Australian Religion. Horizons* 4 (1977): 148–49.

—"Review of *The History of Religious Ideas. Horizons* 7 (1980): 148–49.

Schebesta, Paul. *Among Congo Pigmies*. Translated from the German by Gerald Griffin. New York: AMS Press, 1977.

Scheler, Max. *On the Eternal in Man*. Trans. Bernard Noble. London and New York: Harper, 1960.

Schlette, Heinz Robert. *Towards a Theology of Religions*. Trans. W. J. O'Hara. New York: Herder and Herder, 1966.

Scholte, Robert. "Epistemic Paradigms: Some Problems in Cross-Cultural Research on Social Anthropological History and Theory." *American Anthropologist* 68/5 (1966): 1192–1201.

Schwarz, Fernand, ed. *Mircea Eliade: dialogues avec le sacré*. Paris: Editions N.A.D.P., 1986.

Segal, Robert A. "Eliade's Theory of Millenarianism." *Religious Studies* 14 (1978): 159–73.

—"In Defense of Reductionism." *Journal of the American Academy of Religion* 51 (1983): 97–124.

—"How Historical is the History of Religions?" *Method and Theory in the Study of Religion* 1/1 (1989): 2–17.

—*Religion and the Social Sciences: Essays on the Confrontation*. Brown Studies in Religion, 3. Atlanta, GA: Scholars Press, 1989.

Sharpe, Eric J. Review of *Zalmoxis, the Vanishing God. Religion* 7 (1977): 105–106.

—"History and 'Belief': A Response to Robert Segal." *Religious Traditions* 11 (1988): 1–20.

—Review of *Encyclopedia of Religion. Journal of Religion* 70/3 (1990): 340–52.

Shiner, Larry E. "Sacred Space, Profane Space, Human Space." *Journal of the American Academy of Religion* 40 (1972): 425–36.

Simion, Eugen. *Mircea Eliade: A Spirit of Amplitude*. New York: Columbia University Press, 2001.

Skinner, Quentin. "The Limits of Historical Explanation." *Philosophy* 41 (1966): 199–215.

—"Meaning and Understanding in the History of Ideas." *History and Theory* 8 (1969): 3–53.

—"Motives, Intentions, and the Interpretations of Texts." *New Literary History* 3 (1972): 393–408.

—"'Social Meaning' and the Interpretation of Social Action." In *Philosophy, Politics, and Society*, ed. Peter Laslett, W. G. Runciman, and Quentin Skinner, 136–57. Oxford: Blackwell.

—"Some Problems in the Analysis of Political Thought and Action." *Political Theory* 2 (1974): 277–303.

—"Hermeneutics and the Role of History." *New Literary History* 7 (1975): 209–32.

—*The Foundations of Modern Political Thought*. Cambridge: Cambridge University Press, 1978.

—*Machiavelli*. Past Masters Series. New York: Hill and Wang, 1981.

—"Introduction: The Return of Grand Theory." In *The Return of Grand Theory in the Human Sciences*, ed. Quentin Skinner, 3–20. Cambridge: Cambridge University Press, 1985.

Smart, Ninian. *Doctrine and Argument in Indian Philosophy*. London: Allen and Unwin, 1964.

—Review of *The Quest*. *Religious Studies* 7 (1971): 77–79.

—*The Science of Religion and the Sociology of Knowledge*. Princeton, NJ: Princeton University Press, 1973.

—"Beyond Eliade: The Future of Theory in Religion." *Numen* 25 (1978): 171–83.

—Review of *The History of Religious Ideas*. *Journal of Religion* 60 (1980): 67–71.

—Review of *Ordeal by Labyrinth*. *Scottish Journal of Religious Studies* 5/2 (1984): 152–54.

Smart, Ninian, and Dewey D. Wallace. 1988. Review of *The Encyclopedia of Religion*. *Religious Studies Review* 14/3: 196–206.

Smith, Jonathan Z. "The Wobbling Pivot." *Journal of Religion* 52/2 (1972): 134–49.

—"Mythos und Geschicte." In *Alcheringa oder der beginnende Zeit*, ed. Hans-Peter Duerr. Frankfurt-am-Main: Suhrkamp, 1983.

Snellgrove, David L. Review of *Le Yoga, immortalité et liberté*. *Journal of the Royal Asiatic Society* (1956): 252–54.

Soderblom, Nathan. *The Living God: Basal Forms of Personal Religion*. London: Oxford University Press, 1933.

Spariosu, Mihail. "Orientalist Fictions in Eliade's *Maitreyi*." In *Fiction and Drama in Southeastern Europe*, ed. Henrik Birnbaun and Thomas Eekman, 349–60. Columbus, OH: Slavica Publishers Inc., 1980.

Stancu, Zaharia. "Chaff from the Carts of the Enemy." Unpublished translation from the Romanian by M. L. Ricketts.

Stewart, Mary Z. "Royal Road Towards the Centre: Fictional Hermeneutics and Hermeneutical Fiction in Eliade's Two Tales of the Occult." *Ohio Journal of Religious Studies* 6 (1978): 29–44.

Stirrat, R. L. "Sacred Models." *Man: the Journal of the Royal Anthropological Institute* 19/2 (1984): 199–215.

Streng, Frederick J. *Emptiness: A Study in Religious Meaning*. Nashville: Abingdon Press, 1967.

—"Beyond Religious Symbols and Insight: Understanding Religious Life as Processes of Valuation." *Religious Traditions* 10 (1987): 77–94.

Strenski, Ivan. "Mircea Eliade: Some Theoretical Problems." In *The Theory of Myth: Six Studies*, ed. Adrian Cunningham. London: Sheed and Ward, 1973.

—"Love and Anarchy in Romania." *Religion* 12/4 (1982): 391–404.

—"Mircea Eliade." In *Four Theories of Myth in Twentieth Century History*. London: Macmillan, 1989.

Studstill, Randall. "Eliade, Phenomenology, and the Sacred." *Religious Studies* 36 (2000): 177–94.

Sullivan, Lawrence E. Review of *The History of Religious Ideas*. *Religious Studies Review* 9/1 (1983): 13–22.

—"Creative Writing and Imitatio Dei: The Book and the Fall." *Revista Asociatiei Culturale Internationale a Etniei Romane* 2 (1984): 21–22.

—Review of *Encyclopedia of Religion*. *Journal of Religion* 70/3 (1990): 315–39.

Tacou, Constantin, ed. *Mircea Eliade*. Cahiers de l'Herne, 33. Paris: Editions de l'Herne, 1978.

Tillich, Paul. "The Significance of the History of Religions for the Systematic Theologian." In *Paul Tillich: The Future of Religion*, ed. J. C. Brauer. New York: Harper & Row, 1966.

Tissot, George. "Camouflages et Méconaissances." *Sciences Religieuses* 10/1 (1981): 45–58.

Toulmin, Stephen Edelston, and June Goodfield. *The Discovery of Time*. New York: Harper & Row, 1965.

Valk, John. "The Concept of the *Coincidentia-Oppositorum* in the Thought of Mircea Eliade." *Religious Studies* 28 (1992): 31–41.

Verene, Donald Phillip. "Eliade's Vichianism: The Regeneration of Time and the Terror of History." *New Vico Studies* 4 (1986): 115–21.

Vernoff, Charles. E. "Mircea Eliade and the Fundamental Structure of Religious Life." *Journal of Dharma* 11/2 (1986): 147–60.

Volovici, Leon. *Nationalist Ideology and Antisemitism: The Case of Romanian Intellectuals in the 30s.* New York: Pergamon, 1991.

Wallace, Anthony F. C. *Religion: An Anthropological View.* New York: Random House, 1967.

Wasserstrom, Steven. *Religion after Religion: Gershom Scholem, Mircea Eliade, and Henri Corbin at Eranos.* Princeton, NJ: Princeton University Press, 1999.

Webster, Alexander F. C. "Orthodox Mystical Tradition and the Comparative Study of Religion: An Experimental Synthesis." *Journal of Ecumenical Studies* 23 (1986): 621–49.

Webster, Hutton. *Taboo: A Sociological Study.* Stanford, CA: Stanford University Press, 1942.

Weckman, George. "Mircea Eliade and the Role of History in Religion." *Journal of Religious Studies (Ohio)* 10/2 (1983): 9–18.

Welbon, George R. "Some Remarks on the Work of Mircea Eliade." *Acta Philosophica et Theologica* 2 (1964): 465–92.

Werblowsky, R. J. Zwi. Review of *The History of Religious Ideas. History of Religions* 23 (1983): 181–87.

—"*In Nostro Tempore*: On Mircea Eliade." *Religion* 19 (1989): 129–36.

Westermarck, Edward. *Pagan Survivals in Mahommedan Civilization.* London: Macmillan, 1933.

Whaling, Frank. Review of *From Primitives to Zen. Religious Studies* 15 (1979): 421–23.

—"Mircea Eliade." In *Contemporary Approaches to the Study of Religion*, 214–20. The Hague: Mouton, 1985.

Widengren, Geo. "Mircea Eliade Sixty Years Old." *Numen* 14 (1967): 165–66.

Zaehner, Robert C. Review of *Some Methodological Remarks. Journal of Theological Studies* 11 (1960): 449–50.

—*Hinduism.* London and New York: Oxford University Press, 1962.

—Review of *From Primitives to Zen. Religious Studies* 3 (1968): 561–62.

Ziolkowski, Eric J. "Between Religion and Literature: Mircea Eliade and Northrop Frye." *Journal of Religion* 71/4 (1991): 498–522.

INDEX OF NAMES

439

INDEX OF SUBJECTS